Fox's Book of Martyrs
Or A History of the Lives, Sufferings, and Triumphant Deaths of the Primitive Protestant Martyrs

John Foxe

Contents

PREFACE.	8
CHAPTER I.	12
CHAPTER II.	17
CHAPTER III.	48
CHAPTER IV.	58
CHAPTER V.	77
CHAPTER VI.	118
CHAPTER VII.	174
CHAPTER VIII.	196
CHAPTER IX.	208
CHAPTER X.	210
CHAPTER XI.	218
CHAPTER XII.	228
CHAPTER XIII.	238
CHAPTER XIV.	350
CHAPTER XV.	370
CHAPTER XVI.	390
CHAPTER XVII.	405
CHAPTER XVIII.	431
CHAPTER XX.	520
CHAPTER XXI.	533
CHAPTER XXII.	542
CHAPTER XXIII.	571

FOX'S BOOK OF MARTYRS
OR A HISTORY OF THE LIVES, SUFFERINGS, AND TRIUMPHANT DEATHS OF THE PRIMITIVE PROTESTANT MARTYRS
BY
John Foxe

FOX'S BOOK OF MARTYRS OR
A HISTORY OF THE
LIVES, SUFFERINGS, AND TRIUMPHANT DEATHS
OF THE
PRIMITIVE PROTESTANT MARTYRS
FROM THE
INTRODUCTION OF CHRISTIANITY
TO THE
LATEST PERIODS OF PAGAN, POPISH, AND INFIDEL
PERSECUTIONS

EMBRACING, TOGETHER WITH THE USUAL SUBJECTS CONTAINED IN
SIMILAR WORKS

The recent persecutions in the cantons of Switzerland; and the persecutions of the Methodist and Baptist Missionaries in the West India Islands; and the narrative of the conversion, capture, long imprisonment, and cruel sufferings of Asaad Shidiak, a native of Palestine.

LIKEWISE
A SKETCH OF THE FRENCH REVOLUTION
AS CONNECTED WITH PERSECUTION

COMPILED FROM FOX'S BOOK OF MARTYRS, AND OTHER AUTHENTIC
SOURCES
THE JOHN C. WINSTON CO.

CHICAGO PHILADELPHIA TORONTO

PREFACE.

This work is strictly what its title page imports, a COMPILATION. Fox's "Book of Martyrs" has been made the basis of this volume. Liberty, however, has been taken to abridge wherever it was thought necessary;--to alter the antiquated form of the phraseology; to introduce additional information; and to correct any inaccuracy respecting matters of fact, which had escaped the author of the original work, or which has been found erroneous by the investigation of modern research.

The object of this work, is to give a brief history of persecution since the first introduction of christianity, till the present time. In doing this, we have commenced with the martyrdom of Stephen, and following the course of events, have brought the History of persecution down to the year 1830. In all ages, we find that a disposition to persecute for opinion's sake, has been manifested by wicked men, whatever may have been their opinions or sentiments on religious subjects. The intolerant jew, and the bigoted pagan, have exhibited no more of a persecuting spirit, than the nominal professor of christianity, and the *infidel* and the avowed *atheist*. Indeed, it seems to be an "inherent vice," in unsanctified nature to endeavour by the pressure of physical force, to restrain obnoxious sentiments, and to propagate favourite opinions. It is only when the heart has been renewed and sanctified by divine grace, that men have rightly understood and practised the true principles of toleration. We do not say that none but real christians have adopted correct views respecting civil and religious liberty;--but we affirm that these views owe their origin entirely to christianity and its genuine disciples.

Though nearly all sects have persecuted their opponents, during a brief season, when men's passions were highly excited, and true religion had mournfully declined, yet no denomination except the papal hierarchy, has adopted as an article of religious belief, and a principle of practical observance, the right to destroy heretics for opinion's sake. The decrees of councils, and the bulls of popes, issued in conformity with those decrees, place this matter beyond a doubt. Persecution, therefore, and popery, are inseparably connected; because claiming infallibility, what she has once done is right for her to do again; yea, must be done under similar circumstances, or the claims of infallibility given up. There is no escaping this conclusion. It is right, therefore, to charge upon popery, all the persecutions and horrid cruelties which have stained the annals of the papal church during her long and bloody career of darkness and crime. Every sigh which has been heaved in the dungeons of the Inquisition--every groan which has been extorted by the racks and instruments of torture, which the malice of her bigoted votaries, stimulated by infernal wisdom, ever invented, has witnessed in the ear of God, against the "Mother of Harlots;" and those kings of the earth, who giving their power to the "Beast" have aided her in the cruel work of desolation and death. The valleys of Piedmont, the mountains of Switzerland, the vine crowned hills of Italy and France--and all parts of Germany and the low countries, have by turns, been lighted by the fires of burning victims, or crimsoned with the blood of those who have suffered death at the hands of the cruel emissaries of popery. England too, has drunken deep of the "wine of the fierceness of her wrath," as the blood of Cobham, and the ashes of the Smithfield martyrs can testify. Ireland and Scotland, likewise, have each been made the theatre of her atrocities. But no where has the system been exhibited in its native unalleviated deformity, as in Spain, Portugal and their South American dependencies. For centuries, such a system of police was established by the *Holy Inquisitors*, that these countries resembled a vast whispering gallery, where the slightest murmur of discontent could be heard and punished. Such has been the effect of superstition and the terror of the Holy Office, upon the mind, as completely to break the pride of the Castillian noble, and make him the unresisting victim of every mendicant friar and "hemp-sandaled monk."

Moreover, the papal system has opposed the march of civilization and liberty throughout the world, by denouncing the circulation of the Bible, and the general diffusion of knowledge. Turn to every land where popery predominates, and you will find an ignorant and debased peasantry, a profligate nobility, and a priesthood, licentious, avaricious, domineering and cruel.

But it may be asked, is popery the same system now as in the days of Cardinal Bonner and the "Bloody Mary." We answer yes. It is the boast of all catholics that their church never varies, either in spirit or in practice. For evidence of this, look at the demonstrations of her spirit in the persecutions in the south of France, for several years after the restoration of the Bourbons, in 1814. All have witnessed with feelings of detestation, the recent efforts of the apostolicals in Spain and Portugal, to crush the friends of civil and religious liberty in those ill-fated countries. The narrative of Asaad Shidiak, clearly indicates that the spirit of popery, has lost none of its ferocity and bloodthirstiness since the Piedmontese war, and the Bartholomew massacre. Where it has power, its victims are still crushed by the same means which filled the dungeons of the inquisition, and fed the fires of the *auto de fe*.

This is the religion, to diffuse which, strenuous efforts are now making in this country. Already the papal church numbers more than half a million of communicants. This number is rapidly augmenting by emigration from catholic countries, and by the conversion of protestant children who are placed in their schools for instruction. The recent events in Europe, will, no doubt, send to our shores hundreds of jesuit priests, with a portion of that immense revenue which the papal church has hitherto enjoyed. Another thing, which will, no doubt, favour their views, is the disposition manifested among some who style themselves *liberalists*, to aid catholics in the erection of mass houses, colleges, convents and theological seminaries. This has been done in numerous instances; and when a note of warning is raised by the true friends of civil and religious liberty, they are treated as bigots by those very men who are contributing of their substance to diffuse and foster the most intolerant system of bigotry, and cruel, unrelenting despotism, the world has ever seen. Other sects have persecuted during some periods of their history; but all now deny the right, and reprobate the practice except catholics. The right to destroy heretics, is a fundamental article in the creed of the papal church. And wherever her power is not cramped, she still exercises that power to the destruction of all who oppose her unrighteous usurpation. All the blood shed by all other christian sects, is no more in comparison to that shed by the papacy, than the short lived flow of a feeble rill, raised by the passing tempest, to the deep overwhelming tide of a mighty river, which receives as tributaries, the waters of a thousand streams.

We trust the present work, therefore, will prove a salutary check to the progress of that system whose practical effects have ever been, and ever must be, licentiousness, cruelty, and blood.

The narratives of Asaad Shidiak, Mrs. Judson, the persecutions in the West Indies, and in Switzerland, have never before been incorporated in any book of Martyrs. They serve to show the hideous nature of persecution, and the benefit of christian missions.

At the close of this volume will be found a sketch of the French revolution of 1789, as connected with persecution. It has long been the practice of infidels to sneer at christianity, because some of its nominal followers have exhibited a persecuting spirit. And although they knew that christianity condemns persecution in the most pointed manner, yet they have never had the generosity to discriminate between the system, and the abuse of the system by wicked men. Infidelity on the other hand, has nothing to redeem it. It imposes no restraint on the violent and lifelong passions of men. Coming to men with the Circean torch of licentiousness in her hand, with fair promises of freedom, she first stupefies the conscience, and brutifies the affections; and then renders her votaries the most abject slaves of guilt and crime. This was exemplified in the French revolution. For centuries, the bible had been taken away, and the key of knowledge wrested from the people. For a little moment, France broke the chains which superstition had flung around her. Not content, however, with this, she attempted to break the yoke of God: she stamped the bible in the dust, and proclaimed the jubilee of licentiousness, unvisited, either by present or future retribution. Mark the consequence. Anarchy broke in like a flood, from whose boiling surge blood spouted up in living streams, and on whose troubled waves floated the headless bodies of the learned, the good, the beautiful and the brave. The most merciless proscription for opinion's sake, followed. A word, a sigh, or a look supposed inimical to the ruling powers, was followed with instant death. The calm which succeeded, was only the less dreaded, because it presented fewer objects of terrific interest, as the shock of the earthquake creates more instant alarm, than the midnight pestilence, when it walks unseen, unknown amidst the habitations of a populous city.

The infidel persecutions in France and Switzerland, afford a solemn lesson to the people of this country. We have men among us now, most of them it is true, vagabond foreigners, who are attempting to propagate the same sentiments which produced such terrible consequences in France. Under various names they are scattering their pestilent doctrines through the country. As in France, they have commenced their attacks upon the bible, the Sabbath, marriage, and all the social and domestic relations of life. With flatteries and lies, they are attempting to sow the seeds of discontent and future rebellion among the people. The ferocity of their attacks upon those who differ from them, even while restrained by public opinion, shews what they would do, provided they could pull down our institutions and introduce disorder and wild misrule. We trust, therefore, that the article on the revolution in France, will be found highly instructive and useful.

BOOK OF MARTYRS

CHAPTER I.

HISTORY OF CHRISTIAN MARTYRS TO THE FIRST GENERAL PERSECUTION UNDER NERO.

The history of the church may almost be said to be a history of the trials and sufferings of its members, as experienced at the hands of wicked men. At one time, persecution, as waged against the friends of Christ, was confined to those without; at another, schisms and divisions have arrayed brethren of the same name against each other, and scenes of cruelty and woe have been exhibited within the sanctuary, rivalling in horror the direst cruelties ever inflicted by pagan or barbarian fanaticism. This, however, instead of implying any defect in the gospel system, which breathes peace and love; only pourtrays in darker colours the deep and universal depravity of the human heart. Pure and unsophisticated morality, especially when attempted to be inculcated on mankind, as essential to their preserving an interest with their Creator, have constantly met with opposition. It was this which produced the premature death of John the Baptist. It was the cutting charge of adultery and incest, which excited the resentment of Herodias, who never ceased to persecute him, until she had accomplished his destruction. The same observation is equally applicable to the Jewish doctors, in their treatment of our blessed Lord and Saviour JESUS CHRIST. In the sudden martyrdom of John the Baptist, and the crucifixion of our Lord, the history of christian martyrdom must be admitted to commence; and from these, as a basis for the subsequent occurrences, we may fairly trace the origin of that hostility, which produced so lavish an effusion of christian blood, and led to so much slaughter in the progressive state of christianity.

As it is not our business to enlarge upon our Saviour's history, either before or after his crucifixion, we shall only find it necessary to remind our readers of the discomfiture of the Jews by his subsequent resurrection. Though one apostle had betrayed him; though another had denied him, under the solemn sanction of an oath; and though the rest had forsaken him, unless we may except "the disciple who was known unto the high-priest;" the history of his resurrection gave a new direction to all their hearts, and, after the mission of the Holy Spirit, imparted new confidence to their minds. The powers with which they were endued emboldened them to proclaim his name, to the confusion of the Jewish rulers, and the astonishment of Gentile proselytes.

I. St. Stephen

ST. STEPHEN suffered the next in order. His death was occasioned by the faithful manner in which he preached the gospel to the betrayers and murderers of Christ. To such a degree of madness were they excited, that they cast him out of the city and stoned him to death. The time when he suffered is generally supposed to have been at the passover which succeeded to that of our Lord's crucifixion, and to the aera of his ascension, in the following spring.

Upon this a great persecution was raised against all who professed their belief in Christ as the Messiah, or as a prophet. We are immediately told by St. Luke, that "there was a great persecution against the church, which was at Jerusalem;" and that "they were all scattered abroad throughout the regions of Judea and Samaria, except the apostles."

About two thousand christians, with Nicanor, one of the seven deacons, suffered martyrdom during the "persecution which arose about Stephen."

II. James the Great.

The next martyr we meet with, according to St. Luke, in the History of the Apostles' Acts, was James the son of Zebedee, the elder brother of John, and a relative of our Lord; for his mother Salome was cousin-german to the Virgin Mary. It was not until ten years after the death of Stephen, that the second martyrdom took place; for no sooner had Herod Agrippa been appointed governor of Judea, than, with a view to ingratiate himself with them, he raised a sharp persecution against the christians, and determined to make an effectual blow, by striking at their leaders. The account given us by an eminent primitive writer, Clemens Alexandrinus, ought not to be overlooked; that, as James was led to the place of martyrdom, his accuser was brought to repent of his conduct by the apostle's extraordinary courage and undauntedness, and fell down at his feet to request his pardon, professing himself a christian, and resolving that James should not receive the crown of martyrdom alone. Hence they were both beheaded at the same time. Thus did the first apostolic martyr cheerfully and resolutely receive that cup, which he had told our Saviour he was ready to drink. Timon and Parmenas suffered martyrdom about the same time; the one at Phillippi, and the other in Macedonia. These events took place A. D. 44.

III. Philip.

Was born at Bethsaida, in Galilee, and was the first called by the name of "Disciple." He laboured diligently in Upper Asia, and suffered martyrdom at Heliopolis, in Phrygia. He was scourged, thrown into prison, and afterwards crucified, A. D. 54.

IV. Matthew,

Whose occupation was that of a toll-gatherer, was born at Nazareth. He wrote his gospel in Hebrew, which was afterwards translated into Greek by James the Less. The scene of his labors was Parthia, and Ethiopia, in which latter country he suffered martyrdom, being slain with a halberd in the city of Nadabah, A. D. 60.

V. James the Less,

Is supposed by some to have been the brother of our Lord, by a former wife of Joseph. This is very doubtful, and accords too much with the catholic superstition, that Mary never had any other children except our Saviour. He was elected to the oversight of the churches of Jerusalem; and was the author of the epistle ascribed to James in the sacred canon. At the age of ninety-four, he was beat and stoned by the Jews; and finally had his brains dashed out with a fuller's club.

VI. Matthias,

Of whom less is known than of most of the other disciples, was elected to fill the vacant place of Judas. He was stoned at Jerusalem and then beheaded.

VII. Andrew,

Was the brother of Peter. He preached the gospel to many Asiatic nations; but on his arrival at Edessa, he was taken and crucified on a cross, the two ends of which were fixed transversely in the ground. Hence the derivation of the term, St. Andrew's Cross.

VIII. St. Mark,

Was born of Jewish parents of the tribe of Levi. He is supposed to have been converted to christianity by Peter, whom he served as an amanuensis, and under whose inspection he wrote his gospel in the Greek language. Mark was dragged to pieces by the people of Alexandria, at the great solemnity of Serapis their idol, ending his life under their merciless hands.

IX. Peter,

Was born at Bethsaida, in Galilee. He was by occupation a fisherman. Christ gave him a name which in Syriac implies a rock. Peter is supposed to have suffered martyrdom at Rome, during the reign of the emperor Nero, being crucified with his head downward, at his own request.

[It is, however, very uncertain, whether Peter ever visited Rome at all. The evidence rather favouring the supposition that he ended his days in some other country.--*Ed.*]

X. Paul,

The great apostle of the Gentiles, was a Jew of the tribe of Benjamin, a native of Tarsus in Cilicia, and before his conversion was called Saul. After suffering various persecutions at Jerusalem, Iconium, Lystra, Phillippi and Thessalonica, he was carried prisoner to Rome, where he continued for two years, and was then released. He afterwards visited the churches of Greece and Rome, and preached the gospel in Spain and France, but returning to Rome, he was apprehended by order of Nero, and beheaded.

XI. *Jude*,

The brother of James, was commonly called Thaddeus. He was crucified at Edessa, A. D. 72.

XII. *Bartholomew*,

Preached in several countries, and having translated the gospel of Matthew into the language of India, he propagated it in that country. He was at length cruelly beaten and then crucified by the impatient idolaters.

XIII. *Thomas*,

Called Didymus, preached the gospel in Parthia and India, where exciting the rage of the pagan priests, he was martyred by being thrust through with a spear.

XIV. *Luke*,

The evangelist, was the author of the gospel which goes under his name. He travelled with Paul through various countries, and is supposed to have been hanged on an olive tree, by the idolatrous priests of Greece.

XV. *Simon*,

Surnamed Zelotes, preached the gospel in Mauritania, Africa, and even in Britain, which latter country he was crucified, A. D. 74.

XVI. *John*,

The "beloved disciple," was brother to James the Great. The churches of Smyrna, Pergamos, Sardis, Philadelphia, Laodicea, and Thyatira, were founded by him. From Ephesus he was ordered to be sent to Rome, where it is affirmed he was cast into a cauldron of boiling oil. He escaped by miracle, without injury. Domitian afterwards banished him to the Isle of Patmos, where he wrote the Book of Revelation. Nerva, the successor of Domitian, recalled him. He was the only apostle who escaped a violent death.

XVII. Barnabas,

Was of Cyprus, but of Jewish descent, his death is supposed to have taken place about A. D. 73.

CHAPTER II.

THE TEN PRIMITIVE PERSECUTIONS.

The First Persecution under Nero, A. D. 67.

The first persecution of the church took place in the year 67, under Nero, the sixth emperor of Rome. This monarch reigned for the space of five years, with tolerable credit to himself, but then gave way to the greatest extravagancy of temper, and to the most atrocious barbarities. Among other diabolical whims, he ordered that the city of Rome should be set on fire, which order was executed by his officers, guards, and servants. While the imperial city was in flames, he went up to the tower of Macaenas, played upon his harp, sung the song of the burning of Troy, and openly declared, "That he wished the ruin of all things before his death." Besides the noble pile, called the circus, many other palaces and houses were consumed; several thousands perished in the flames, were smothered in the smoke, or buried beneath the ruins.

This dreadful conflagration continued nine days; when Nero, finding that his conduct was greatly blamed, and a severe odium cast upon him, determined to lay the whole upon the christians, at once to excuse himself, and have an opportunity of glutting his sight with new cruelties. This was the occasion of the first persecution; and the barbarities exercised on the christians were such as even excited the commisseration of the Romans themselves. Nero even refined upon cruelty, and contrived all manner of punishments for the christians that the most infernal imagination could design. In particular, he had some sewed up in the skins of wild beasts, and then worried by dogs till they expired; and others dressed in shirts made stiff with wax, fixed to axletrees, and set on fire in his gardens, in order to illuminate them. This persecution was general throughout the whole Roman empire; but it rather increased than diminished the spirit of christianity. In the course of it, St. Paul and St. Peter were martyred.

To their names may be added, Erastus, chamberlain of Corinth; Aristarchus, the Macedonian; and Trophimus, an Ephesian, converted by St. Paul, and fellow-labourer with him; Joseph, commonly called Barsabas; and Ananias, bishop of Damascus; each of the seventy.

The Second Persecution, under Domitian, A. D. 81.

The emperor Domitian, who was naturally inclined to cruelty, first slew his brother, and then raised the second persecution against the christians. In his rage he put to death some of the Roman senators, some through malice; and others to confiscate their estates. He then commanded all the lineage of David to be put to death.

Among the numerous martyrs that suffered during this persecution was Simeon, bishop of Jerusalem, who was crucified; and St. John, who was boiled in oil, and afterward banished to Patmos. Flavia, the daughter of a Roman senator, was likewise banished to Pontus; and a law was made, "That no christian, once brought before the tribunal, should be exempted from punishment without renouncing his religion."

A variety of fabricated tales were, during this reign, composed in order to injure the christians. Such was the infatuation of the pagans, that, if famine, pestilence, or earthquakes afflicted any of the Roman provinces, it was laid upon the christians. These persecutions among the christians increased the number of informers and many, for the sake of gain, swore away the lives of the innocent.

Another hardship was, that, when any christians were brought before the magistrates, a test oath was proposed, when, if they refused to take it, death was pronounced against them; and if they confessed themselves christians, the sentence was the same.

The following were the most remarkable among the numerous martyrs who suffered during this persecution.

Dionysius, the Areopagite, was an Athenian by birth, and educated in all the useful and ornamental literature of Greece. He then travelled to Egypt to study astronomy, and made very particular observations on the great and supernatural eclipse, which happened at the time of our Saviour's crucifixion.

The sanctity of his conversation, and the purity of his manners, recommended him so strongly to the christians in general, that he was appointed bishop of Athens.

Nicodemus, a benevolent christian of some distinction, suffered at Rome during the rage of Domitian's persecution.

Protasius and Gervasius were martyred at Milan.

Timothy was the celebrated disciple of St. Paul, and bishop of Ephesus, where he zealously governed the church till A. D. 97. At this period, as the pagans were about to celebrate a feast called Catagogion, Timothy, meeting the procession, severely reproved them for their ridiculous idolatry, which so exasperated the people, that they fell upon him with their clubs, and beat him in so dreadful a manner, that he expired of the bruises two days after.

The Third Persecution, under Trajan, A. D. 108.

Nerva, succeeding Domitian, gave a respite to the sufferings of the christians; but reigning only thirteen months, his successor Trajan, in the tenth year of his reign A. D. 108, began the third persecution against the christians. While the persecution raged, Pliny 2d, a heathen philosopher wrote to the emperor in favor of the Christians; to whose epistle Trajan returned this indecisive answer: "The christians ought not to be sought after, but when brought before the magistracy, they should be punished." Trajan, however, soon after wrote to Jerusalem, and gave orders to his officers to exterminate the stock of David; in consequence of which, all that could be found of that race were put to death.

Symphorosa, a widow, and her seven sons, were commanded by the emperor to sacrifice to the heathen deities. She was carried to the temple of Hercules, scourged, and hung up, for some time, by the hair of her head: then being taken down, a large stone was fastened to her neck, and she was thrown into the river, where she expired. With respect to the sons, they were fastened to seven posts, and being drawn up by pullies, their limbs were dislocated: these tortures, not affecting their resolution, they were martyred by stabbing, except Eugenius, the youngest, who was sawed asunder.

Phocas, bishop of Pontus, refusing to sacrifice to Neptune, was, by the immediate order of Trajan, cast first into a hot lime-kiln, and then thrown into a scalding bath till he expired.

Trajan likewise commanded the martyrdom of Ignatius, bishop of Antioch. This holy man was the person whom, when an infant, Christ took into his arms, and showed to his disciples, as one that would be a pattern of humility and innocence. He received the gospel afterward from St. John the Evangelist, and was exceedingly zealous in his mission. He boldly vindicated the faith of Christ before the emperor, for which he was cast into prison, and tormented in a most cruel manner. After being dreadfully scourged, he was compelled to hold fire in his hands, and, at the same time, papers clipped in oil were put to his sides, and set on fire. His flesh was then torn with red hot pincers, and at last he was despatched by being torn to pieces by wild beasts.

Trajan being succeeded by Adrian, the latter continued this third persecution with as much severity as his predecessor. About this time Alexander, bishop of Rome, with his two deacons, were martyred; as were Quirinus and Hernes, with their families; Zenon, a Roman nobleman, and about ten thousand other christians.

In Mount Ararat many were crucified, crowned with thorns, and spears run into their sides, in imitation of Christ's passion. Eustachius, a brave and successful Roman commander, was by the emperor ordered to join in an idolatrous sacrifice to celebrate some of his own victories; but his faith (being a christian in his heart) was so much greater than his vanity, that he nobly refused it. Enraged at the denial, the ungrateful emperor forgot the service of this skilful commander, and ordered him and his whole family to be martyred.

At the martyrdom of Faustines and Jovita, brothers and citizens of Brescia, their torments were so many, and their patience so great, that Calocerius, a pagan, beholding them, was struck with admiration, and exclaimed in a kind of ecstacy, "Great is the God of the christians!"

for which he was apprehended, and suffered a similar fate.

Many other similar cruelties and rigours were exercised against the christians, until Quadratus, bishop of Athens, made a learned apology in their favour before the emperor, who happened to be there and Aristides, a philosopher of the same city, wrote an elegant epistle, which caused Adrian to relax in his severities, and relent in their favour.

Adrian dying A. D. 138, was succeeded by Antoninus Pius, one of the most amiable monarchs that ever reigned, and who stayed the persecution against the Christians.

The fourth persecution, under Marcus Aurelius Antoninus, A. D. 162.

This commenced A. D. 162, under Marcus Aurelius Antoninus Philosophus, a strong pagan.

The cruelties used in this persecution were such, that many of the spectators shuddered with horror at the sight, and were astonished at the intrepidity of the sufferers. Some of the martyrs were obliged to pass, with their already wounded feet, over thorns, nails, sharp shells, &c. upon their points, others were scourged till their sinews and veins lay bare, and after suffering the most excruciating tortures that could be devised, they were destroyed by the most terrible deaths.

Germanicus, a young man, but a true christian, being delivered to the wild beasts on account of his faith, behaved with such astonishing courage, that several pagans became converts to a faith which inspired such fortitude.

Polycarp, the venerable bishop of Smyrna, hearing that persons were seeking for him, escaped, but was discovered by a child. After feasting the guards who apprehended him, he desired an hour in prayer, which being allowed, he prayed with such fervency, that his guards repented that they had been instrumental in taking him. He was, however, carried before the proconsul, condemned, and burnt in the market-place. Twelve other christians, who had been intimate with Polycarp, were soon after martyred.

The circumstances attending the execution of this venerable old man, as they were of no common nature, so it would be injurious to the credit of our professed history of martyrdom to pass them over in silence. It was observed by the spectators, that, after finishing his prayer at the stake, to which he was only tied, but not nailed as usual, as he assured them he should stand immoveable, the flames, on their kindling the fagots, encircled his body, like an arch, without touching him; and the executioner, on seeing this, was ordered to pierce him with a sword, when so great a quantity of blood flowed out as extinguished the fire. But his body, at the instigation of the enemies of the gospel, especially Jews, was ordered to be consumed in the pile, and the request of his friends, who wished to give it christian burial, rejected. They nevertheless collected his bones and as much of his remains as possible, and caused them to be decently interred.

Metrodorus, a minister, who preached boldly; and Pionius, who made some excellent apologies for the christian faith; were likewise burnt. Carpus and Papilus, two worthy christians, and Agathonica, a pious woman, suffered martyrdom at Pergamopolis, in Asia.

Felicitatis, an illustrious Roman lady, of a considerable family and the most shining virtues, was a devout christian. She had seven sons, whom she had educated with the most exemplary piety.

Januarius, the eldest, was scourged, and pressed to death with weights; Felix and Philip, the two next had their brains dashed out with clubs; Silvanus, the fourth, was murdered by being thrown from a precipice; and the three younger sons, Alexander, Vitalis, and Martial, were beheaded. The mother was beheaded with the same sword as the three latter.

Justin, the celebrated philosopher, fell a martyr in this persecution. He was a native of Neapolis, in Samaria, and was born A. D. 103. Justin was a great lover of truth, and a universal scholar; he investigated the Stoic and Peripatetic philosophy, and attempted the Pythagorean; but the behaviour of one of its professors disgusting him, he applied himself to the Platonic, in which he took great delight. About the year 133, when he was thirty years of age, he became a convert to christianity, and then, for the first time, perceived the real nature of truth.

He wrote an elegant epistle to the Gentiles, and employed his talents in convincing the Jews of the truth of the christian rites; spending a great deal of time in travelling, till he took up his abode in Rome, and fixed his habitation upon the Viminal mount.

He kept a public school, taught many who afterward became great men, and wrote a treatise to confute heresies of all kinds. As the pagans began to treat the christians with great severity, Justin wrote his first apology in their favour. This piece displays great learning and genius, and occasioned the emperor to publish an edict in favor of the christians.

Soon after, he entered into frequent contests with Crescens, a person of a vicious life and conversation, but a celebrated cynic philosopher; and his arguments appeared so powerful, yet disgusting to the cynic, that he resolved on, and in the sequel accomplished, his destruction.

The second apology of Justin, upon certain severities, gave Crescens the cynic an opportunity of prejudicing the emperor against the writer of it; upon which Justin, and six of his companions, were apprehended. Being commanded to sacrifice to the pagan idols, they refused, and were condemned to be scourged, and then beheaded; which sentence was executed with all imaginable severity.

Several were beheaded for refusing to sacrifice to the image of Jupiter; in particular Concordus, a deacon of the city of Spolito.

Some of the restless northern nations having risen in arms against Rome, the emperor marched to encounter them. He was, however, drawn into an ambuscade, and dreaded the loss of his whole army. Enveloped with mountains, surrounded by enemies, and perishing with thirst, the pagan deities were invoked in vain; when the men belonging to the militine, or thundering legion, who were all christians, were commanded to call upon their God for succour. A miraculous deliverance immediately ensued; a prodigious quantity of rain fell, which, being caught by the men, and filling their dykes, afforded a sudden and astonishing relief. It appears, that the storm which miraculously flashed in the faces of the enemy, so intimidated them, that part deserted to the Roman army; the rest were defeated, and the revolted provinces entirely recovered.

This affair occasioned the persecution to subside for some time, at least in those parts immediately under the inspection of the emperor; but we find that it soon after raged in France, particularly at Lyons, where the tortures to which many of the christians were put, almost exceed the powers of description.

The principal of these martyrs were Vetius Agathus, a young man; Blandina, a christian lady, of a weak constitution; Sanctus, a deacon of Vienna; red hot plates of brass were placed upon the tenderest parts of his body; Biblias, a weak woman, once an apostate. Attalus, of Pergamus; and Pothinus, the venerable bishop of Lyons, who was ninety years of age. Blandina, on the day when she and the three other champions were first brought into the amphitheatre, she was suspended on a piece of wood fixed in the ground, and exposed as food for the wild beasts; at which time, by her earnest prayers, she encouraged others. But none of the wild beasts would touch her, so that she was remanded to prison. When she was again produced for the third and last time, she was accompanied by Ponticus, a youth of fifteen and the constancy of their faith so enraged the multitude, that neither the sex of the one nor the youth of the other were respected, being exposed to all manner of punishments and tortures. Being strengthened by Blandina, he persevered unto death; and she, after enduring all the torments heretofore mentioned, was at length slain with the sword.

When the christians, upon these occasions, received martyrdom, they were ornamented, and crowned with garlands of flowers; for which they, in heaven, received eternal crowns of glory.

The torments were various; and, exclusive of those already mentioned, the martyrs of Lyons were compelled to sit in red-hot iron chairs till their flesh broiled. This was inflicted with peculiar severity on Sanctus, already mentioned, and some others. Some were sewed up in nets, and thrown on the horns of wild bulls; and the carcases of those who died in prison, previous to the appointed time of execution, were thrown to dogs. Indeed, so far did the malice of the pagans proceed that they set guards over the bodies while the beasts were devouring them, lest the friends of the deceased should get them away by stealth; and the offals left by the dogs were ordered to be burnt.

The martyrs of Lyons, according to the best accounts we could obtain, who suffered for the gospel, were forty-eight in number, and their executions happened in the year of Christ 177.

Epipodius and Alexander were celebrated for their great friendship, and their christian union with each other. The first was born at Lyons, the latter at Greece. Epipodius, being compassionated by the governor of Lyons, and exhorted to join in their festive pagan worship, replied, "Your pretended tenderness is actually cruelty; and the agreeable life you describe is replete with everlasting death Christ suffered for us, that our pleasures should be immortal, and hath prepared for his followers an eternity of bliss. The frame of man being composed of two parts, body and soul, the first, as mean and perishable, should be rendered subservient to the interests of the last. Your idolatrous feasts may gratify the mortal, but they injure the immortal part; that cannot therefore be enjoying life which destroys the most valuable moiety of your frame. Your pleasures lead to eternal death, and our pains to perpetual happiness." Epipodius was severely beaten, and then put to the rack, upon which being stretched, his flesh was torn with iron hooks. Having borne his torments with incredible patience and unshaken fortitude, he was taken from the rack and beheaded.

Valerian and Marcellus, who were nearly related to each other, were imprisoned at Lyons, in the year 177, for being christians. The father was fixed up to the waist in the ground; in which position, after remaining three days, he expired, A. D. 179. Valerian was beheaded.

Apollonius, a Roman senator, an accomplished gentleman, and a sincere christian, suffered under Commodus, because he would not worship him as Hercules.

Eusebius, Vincentius, Potentianus, Peregrinus, and Julius, a Roman senator, were martyred on the same account.

The Fifth Persecution, commencing with Severus, A. D. 192.

Severus, having been recovered from a severe fit of sickness by a christian, became a great favourer of the christians in general; but the prejudice and fury of the ignorant multitude prevailing, obsolete laws were put in execution against the christians. The progress of christianity alarmed the pagans, and they revived the stale calumny of placing accidental misfortunes to the account of its professors, A. D. 192.

But, though persecuting malice raged, yet the gospel shone with resplendent brightness; and, firm as an impregnable rock, withstood the attacks of its boisterous enemies with success. Turtullian, who lived in this age, informs us, that if the christians had collectively withdrawn themselves from the Roman territories, the empire would have been greatly depopulated.

Victor, bishop of Rome, suffered martyrdom in the first year of the third century, A. D. 201. Leonidus, the father of the celebrated Origen, was beheaded for being a christian. Many of Origen's hearers likewise suffered martyrdom; particularly two brothers, named Plutarchus and Serenus; another Serenus, Heron, and Heraclides, were beheaded. Rhais had boiled pitch poured upon her head, and was then burnt, as was Marcella her mother. Potamiena, the sister of Rhais, was executed in the same manner as Rhais had been; but Basilides, an officer belonging to the army, and ordered to attend her execution, became her convert.

Basilides being, as an officer, required to take a certain oath, refused, saying, that he could not swear by the Roman idols, as he was a christian. Struck with surprise, the people could not, at first, believe what they heard; but he had no sooner confirmed the same, than he was dragged before the judge, committed to prison, and speedily afterward beheaded.

Irenaeus, bishop of Lyons, was born in Greece, and received both a polite and a christian education. It is generally supposed, that the account of the persecutions at Lyons was written by himself. He succeeded the martyr Pothinus as bishop of Lyons, and ruled his diocese with great propriety; he was a zealous opposer of heresies in general, and, about A. D. 187, he wrote a celebrated tract against heresy. Victor, the bishop of Rome, wanting to impose the keeping of Easter there, in preference to other places, it occasioned some disorders among the christians. In particular, Irenaeus wrote him a synodical epistle, in the name of the Gallic churches. This zeal, in favour of christianity, pointed him out as an object of resentment to the emperor; and in A. D. 202, he was beheaded.

The persecutions now extending to Africa, many were martyred in that quarter of the globe; the most particular of whom we shall mention.

Perpetua, a married lady, of about twenty-two years. Those who suffered with her were, Felicitas, a married lady, big with child at the time of her being apprehended; and Revocatus, catechumen of Carthage, and a slave. The names of the other prisoners, destined to suffer upon this occasion, were Saturninus, Secundulus and Satur. On the day appointed for their execution, they were led to the amphitheatre. Satur, Saturninus, and Revocatus, were ordered to run the gauntlet between the hunters, or such as had the care of the wild beasts. The hunters being drawn up in two ranks, they ran between, and were severely lashed as they passed. Felicitas and Perpetua were stripped, in order to be thrown to a mad bull, which made his first attack upon Perpetua, and stunned her; he then darted at Felicitas, and gored her dreadfully; but not killing them, the executioner did that office with a sword. Revocatus and Satur were destroyed by wild beasts; Saturninus was beheaded; and Secundulus died in prison. These executions were in the year 205, on the 8th day of March.

Speratus, and twelve others, were likewise beheaded; as was Andocles in France. Asclepiades, bishop of Antioch, suffered many tortures, but his life was spared.

Cecilia, a young lady of good family in Rome, was married to a gentleman named Valerian. She converted her husband and brother, who were beheaded; and the maximus, or officer, who led them to execution, becoming their convert, suffered the same fate. The lady was placed naked in a scalding bath, and having continued there a considerable time, her head was struck off with a sword, A. D. 222.

Calistus, bishop of Rome, was martyred, A. D. 224; but the manner of his death is not recorded; and Urban, bishop of Rome, met the same fate A. D. 232.

The Sixth Persecution, under Maximinus, A. D. 235.

A. D. 235, was in the time of Maximinus. In Cappadocia, the president, Seremianus, did all he could to exterminate the christians from that province.

The principal persons who perished under this reign were Pontianus, bishop of Rome; Anteros, a Grecian, his successor, who gave offence to the government, by collecting the acts of the martyrs, Pammachius and Quiritus, Roman senators, with all their families, and many other christians; Simplicius, senator; Calepodius, a christian minister, thrown into the Tyber; Martina, a noble and beautiful virgin; and Hippolitus, a christian prelate, tied to a wild horse, and dragged till he expired.

During this persecution, raised by Maximinus, numberless christians were slain without trial, and buried indiscriminately in heaps, sometimes fifty or sixty being cast into a pit together, without the least decency.

The tyrant Maximinus dying, A. D. 238, was succeeded by Gordian, during whose reign, and that of his successor Philip, the church was free from persecution for the space of more than ten years; but A. D. 249, a violent persecution broke out in Alexandria, at the instigation of a pagan priest, without the knowledge of the emperor.

The Seventh Persecution, under Decius A. D. 249.

This was occasioned partly by the hatred he bore to his predecessor Philip, who was deemed a christian, and partly to his jealousy concerning the amazing increase of christianity; for the heathen temples began to be forsaken, and the christian churches thronged.

These reasons stimulated Decius to attempt the very extirpation of the name of christian; and it was unfortunate for the gospel, that many errors had, about this time, crept into the church: the christians were at variance with each other; self-interest divided those whom social love ought to have united; and the virulence of pride occasioned a variety of factions.

The heathens in general were ambitious to enforce the imperial decrees upon this occasion, and looked upon the murder of a christian as a merit to themselves. The martyrs, upon this occasion, were innumerable; but the principal we shall give some account of.

Fabian, the bishop of Rome, was the first person of eminence who felt the severity of this persecution. The deceased emperor, Philip, had, on account of his integrity, committed his treasure to the care of this good man. But Decius, not finding as much as his avarice made him expect, determined to wreak his vengeance on the good prelate. He was accordingly seized; and on the 20th of January, A. D. 250, he suffered decapitation.

Julian, a native of Cilicia, as we are informed by St. Chrysostom, was seized upon for being a christian. He was put into a leather bag, together with a number of serpents and scorpions, and in that condition thrown into the sea.

Peter, a young man, amiable for the superior qualities of his body and mind, was beheaded for refusing to sacrifice to Venus. He said, "I am astonished you should sacrifice to an infamous woman, whose debaucheries even your own historians record, and whose life consisted of such actions as your laws would punish.--No, I shall offer the true God the acceptable sacrifice of praises and prayers." Optimus, the proconsul of Asia, on hearing this, ordered the prisoner to be stretched upon a wheel, by which all his bones were broken, and then he was sent to be beheaded.

Nichomachus, being brought before the proconsul as a christian, was ordered to sacrifice to the pagan idols. Nichomachus replied, "I cannot pay that respect to devils, which is only due to the Almighty." This speech so much enraged the proconsul, that Nichomachus was put to the rack. After enduring the torments for a time, he recanted; but scarcely had he given this proof of his frailty, than he fell into the greatest agonies, dropped down on the ground, and expired immediately.

Denisa, a young woman of only sixteen years of age, who beheld this terrible judgment, suddenly exclaimed, "O unhappy wretch, why would you buy a moment's ease at the expense of a miserable eternity!" Optimus, hearing this, called to her, and Denisa avowing herself to be a christian, she was beheaded, by his order, soon after.

Andrew and Paul, two companions of Nichomachus the martyr, A. D. 251, suffered martyrdom by stoning, and expired, calling on their blessed Redeemer.

Alexander and Epimachus, of Alexandria, were apprehended for being christians: and, confessing the accusation, were beat with staves, torn with hooks, and at length burnt in the fire; and we are informed, in a fragment preserved by Eusebius, that four female martyrs suffered on the same day, and at the same place, but not in the same manner; for these were beheaded.

Lucian and Marcian, two wicked pagans, though skilful magicians, becoming converts to christianity, to make amends for their former errors, lived the lives of hermits, and subsisted upon bread and water only. After some time spent in this manner, they became zealous preachers, and made many converts. The persecution, however, raging at this time, they were seized upon, and carried before Sabinus, the governor of Bithynia. On being asked by what authority they took upon themselves to preach, Lucian answered, "That the laws of charity and humanity obliged all men to endeavour the conversion of their neighbours, and to do every thing in their power to rescue them from the snares of the devil."

Lucian having answered in this manner, Marcian said, that "Then conversion was by the same grace which was given to St. Paul, who, from a zealous persecutor of the church, became a preacher of the gospel."

The proconsul, finding that he could not prevail with them to renounce their faith, condemned them to be burnt alive, which sentence was soon after executed.

Trypho and Respicius, two eminent men, were seized as Christians, and imprisoned at Nice. Their feet were pierced with nails; they were dragged through the streets, scourged, torn with iron hooks, scorched with lighted torches, and at length beheaded, February 1, A. D. 251.

Agatha, a Sicilian lady, was not more remarkable for her personal and acquired endowments, than her piety: her beauty was such, that Quintian, governor of Sicily, became enamoured of her, and made many attempts upon her chastity without success.

In order to gratify his passions with the greater conveniency, he put the virtuous lady into the hands of Aphrodica, a very infamous and licentious woman. This wretch tried every artifice to win her to the desired prostitution; but found all her efforts were vain; for her chastity was impregnable, and she well knew that virtue alone could procure true happiness. Aphrodica acquainted Quintian with the inefficacy of her endeavours, who, enraged to be foiled in his designs, changed his lust into resentment. On her confessing that she was a christian, he determined to gratify his revenge, as he could not his passion. Pursuant to his orders, she was scourged, burnt with red-hot irons, and torn with sharp hooks. Having borne these torments with admirable fortitude, she was next laid naked upon live coals, intermingled with glass, and then being carried back to prison, she there expired on the 5th of Feb. 251.

Cyril, bishop of Gortyna, was seized by order of Lucius, the governor of that place, who, nevertheless, exhorted him to obey the imperial mandate, perform the sacrifices, and save his venerable person from destruction; for he was now eighty-four years of age. The good prelate replied, that as he had long taught others to save their souls, he should only think now of his own salvation. The worthy prelate heard his fiery sentence without emotion, walked cheerfully to the place of execution, and underwent his martyrdom with great fortitude.

The persecution raged in no place more than the Island of Crete; for the governor, being exceedingly active in executing the imperial decrees, that place streamed with pious blood.

Babylas, a christian of a liberal education, became bishop of Antioch, A. D. 237, on the demise of Zebinus. He acted with inimitable zeal, and governed the church with admirable prudence during the most tempestuous times.

The first misfortune that happened to Antioch during his mission, was the siege of it by Sapor, king of Persia; who, having overrun all Syria, took and plundered this city among others, and used the christian inhabitants with greater severity than the rest, but was soon totally defeated by Gordian.

After Gordian's death, in the reign of Decius, that emperor came to Antioch, where, having a desire to visit an assembly of christians, Babylas opposed him, and absolutely refused to let him come in. The emperor dissembled his anger at that time; but soon sending for the bishop, he sharply reproved him for his insolence, and then ordered him to sacrifice to the pagan deities as an expiation for his offence. This being refused, he was committed to prison, loaded with chains, treated with great severities, and then beheaded, together with three young men who had been his pupils. A. D. 251.

Alexander, bishop of Jerusalem, about this time was cast into prison on account of his religion, where he died through the severity of his confinement.

Julianus, an old man, lame with the gout, and Cronion, another christian, were bound on the backs of camels, severely scourged, and then thrown into a fire and consumed. Also forty virgins, at Antioch, after being imprisoned and scourged, were burnt.

In the year of our Lord 251, the emperor Decius having erected a pagan temple at Ephesus, he commanded all who were in that city to sacrifice to the idols. This order was nobly refused by seven of his own soldiers, viz. Maximianus, Martianus, Joannes, Malchus, Dionysius, Seraion, and Constantinus. The emperor wishing to win these soldiers to renounce their faith by his entreaties and lenity, gave them a considerable respite till he returned from an expedition. During the emperor's absence, they escaped, and hid themselves in a cavern; which the emperor being informed of at his return, the mouth of the cave was closed up, and they all perished with hunger.

Theodora, a beautiful young lady of Antioch, on refusing to sacrifice to the Roman idols, was condemned to the stews, that her virtue might be sacrificed to the brutality of lust. Didymus, a christian, disguised himself in the habit of a Roman soldier, went to the house, informed Theodora who he was, and advised her to make her escape in his clothes. This being effected, and a man found in the brothel instead of a beautiful lady, Didymus was taken before the president, to whom confessing the truth, and owning that he was a christian the sentence of death was immediately pronounced against him. Theodora, hearing that her deliverer was likely to suffer, came to the judge, threw herself at his feet, and begged that the sentence might fall on her as the guilty person; but, deaf to the cries of the innocent, and insensible to the calls of justice, the inflexible judge condemned both, when they were executed accordingly, being first beheaded, and their bodies afterward burnt.

Secundianus, having been accused as a christian, was conveyed to prison by some soldiers. On the way, Verianus and Marcellinus said, "Where are you carrying the innocent?" This interrogatory occasioned them to be seized, and all three, after having been tortured, were hanged and decapitated.

Origen, the celebrated presbyter and catechist of Alexandria, at the age of sixty-four, was seized, thrown into a loathsome prison, laden with fetters, his feet placed in the stocks, and his legs extended to the utmost for several successive days. He was threatened with fire, and tormented by every lingering means the most infernal imaginations could suggest. During thus cruel temporizing, the emperor Decius died, and Gallus, who succeeded him, engaging in a war with the Goths, the christians met with a respite. In this interim, Origen obtained his enlargement, and, retiring to Tyre, he there remained till his death, which happened when he was in the sixty-ninth year of his age.

Gallus, the emperor, having concluded his wars, a plague broke out in the empire: sacrifices to the pagan deities were ordered by the emperor, and persecutions spread from the interior to the extreme parts of the empire, and many fell martyrs to the impetuosity of the rabble, as well as the prejudice of the magistrates. Among these were Cornelius, the christian bishop of Rome, and Lucius, his successor, in 253.

Most of the errors which crept into the church at this time, arose from placing human reason in competition with revelation; but the fallacy of such arguments being proved by the most able divines, the opinions they had created vanished away like the stars before the sun.

The Eighth Persecution, under Valerian, A. D. 257,

Began under Valerian, in the month of April, 257, and continued for three years and six months. The martyrs that fell in this persecution were innumerable, and their tortures and deaths as various and painful. The most eminent martyrs were the following, though neither rank, sex, or age were regarded.

Rufina and Secunda, two beautiful and accomplished ladies, daughters of Asterius, a gentleman of eminence in Rome. Rufina, the elder, was designed in marriage for Armentarius, a young nobleman; Secunda, the younger, for Verinus a person of rank and opulence. The suitors, at the

time of the persecution's commencing, were both christians; but when
danger appeared, to save their fortunes, they renounced their faith.
They took great pains to persuade the ladies to do the same, but,
disappointed in their purpose, the lovers were base enough to inform
against the ladies, who, being apprehended as christians, were brought
before Junius Donatus, governor of Rome, where, A. D. 257, they sealed
their martyrdom with their blood.

Stephen, bishop of Rome, was beheaded in the same year, and about that
time Saturnius, the pious orthodox bishop of Thoulouse, refusing to
sacrifice to idols, was treated with all the barbarous indignities
imaginable, and fastened by the feet to the tail of a bull. Upon a
signal given, the enraged animal was driven down the steps of the
temple, by which the worthy martyr's brains were dashed out.

Sextus succeeded Stephen as bishop of Rome. He is supposed to have been
a Greek by birth or by extraction, and had for some time served in the
capacity of a deacon under Stephen. His great fidelity, singular wisdom,
and uncommon courage, distinguished him upon many occasions; and the
happy conclusion of a controversy with some heretics is generally
ascribed to his piety and prudence. In the year 258, Marcianus, who had
the management of the Roman government, procured an order from the
emperor Valerian, to put to death all the christian clergy in Rome, and
hence the bishop with six of his deacons, suffered martyrdom in 258.

Laurentius, generally called St. Laurence, the principal of the deacons,
who taught and preached under Sextus, followed him to the place of
execution; when Sextus predicted, that he should, three days after, meet
him in heaven.

Laurentius, looking upon this as a certain indication of his own
approaching martyrdom, at his return gathered together all the christian
poor, and distributed the treasures of the church, which had been
committed to his care, among them.

This liberality alarmed the persecutors, who commanded him to give an
immediate account to the emperor of the church treasures. This he
promised to do in three days, during which interval, he collected
together a great number of aged, helpless, and impotent poor; he
repaired to the magistrate, and presenting them to him, said, "These are
the true treasures of the church." Incensed at the disappointment, and
fancying the matter meant in ridicule, the governor ordered him to be
immediately scourged. He was then beaten with iron rods, set upon a
wooden horse, and had his limbs dislocated. These tortures he endured

with fortitude and perseverance; when he was ordered to be fastened to a large gridiron, with a slow fire under it, that his death might be the more lingering. His astonishing constancy during these trials, and serenity of countenance while under such excruciating torments, gave the spectators so exalted an idea of the dignity and truth of the christian religion, that many became converts upon the occasion, of whom was Romanus, a soldier.

In Africa the persecution raged with peculiar violence; many thousands received the crown of martyrdom, among whom the following were the most distinguished characters:

Cyprian, bishop of Carthage, an eminent prelate, and a pious ornament of the church. The brightness of his genius was tempered by the solidity of his judgment; and with all the accomplishments of the gentleman, he blended the virtues of a christian. His doctrines were orthodox and pure; his language easy and elegant; and his manners graceful and winning: in fine, he was both the pious and polite preacher. In his youth he was educated in the principles of Gentilism, and having a considerable fortune, he lived in the very extravagance of splendour, and all the dignity of pomp.

About the year 246, Coecilius, a christian minister of Carthage became the happy instrument of Cyprian's conversion: on which account, and for the great love that he always afterward bore for the author of his conversion, he was termed Coecilius Cyprian. Previous to his baptism, he studied the scriptures with care, and being struck with the beauties of the truths they contained, he determined to practise the virtues therein recommended. Subsequent to his baptism, he sold his estate, distributed the money among the poor, dressed himself in plain attire, and commenced a life of austerity. He was soon after made a presbyter; and, being greatly admired for his virtues and works, on the death of Donatus, in A. D. 248, he was almost unanimously elected bishop of Carthage.

Cyprian's care not only extended over Carthage, but to Numidia and Mauritania. In all his transactions he took great care to ask the advice of his clergy, knowing, that unanimity alone could be of service to the church, this being one of his maxims, "That the bishop was in the church, and the church in the bishop; so that unity can only be preserved by a close connexion between the pastor and his flock."

A. D. 250, Cyprian was publicly proscribed by the emperor Decius, under the appellation of Coecilius Cyprian, bishop of the christians; and the universal cry of the pagans was, "Cyprian to the lions, Cyprian to the beasts." The bishop, however, withdrew from the rage of the populace, and his effects were immediately confiscated. During his retirement, he wrote thirty pious and elegant letters to his flock; but several schisms that then crept into the church, gave him great uneasiness. The rigour of the persecution abating, he returned to Carthage, and did every thing in his power to expunge erroneous opinions. A terrible plague breaking out in Carthage, it was as usual, laid to the charge of the christians; and the magistrates began to persecute accordingly, which occasioned an epistle from them to Cyprian, in answer to which he vindicates the cause of christianity. A. D. 257, Cyprian was brought before the proconsul Aspasius Paturnus, who exiled him to a little city on the Lybian sea. On the death of this proconsul, he returned to Carthage, but was soon after seized, and carried before the now governor, who condemned him to be beheaded; which sentence was executed on the 14th of September, A. D. 258.

The disciples of Cyprian, martyred in this persecution, were Lucius, Flavian, Victoricus, Remus, Montanus, Julian, Primelus, and Donatian.

At Utica, a most terrible tragedy was exhibited: 300 christians were, by the orders of the proconsul, placed round a burning limekiln. A pan of coals and incense being prepared, they were commanded either to sacrifice to Jupiter, or to be thrown into the kiln. Unanimously refusing, they bravely jumped into the pit, and were immediately suffocated.

Fructuosus, bishop of Tarragon, in Spain, and his two deacons, Augurius and Eulogius, were burnt for being christians.

Alexander, Malchus, and Priscus, three christians of Palestine, with a woman of the same place, voluntarily accused themselves of being christians; on which account they were sentenced to be devoured by tigers, which sentence was executed accordingly.

Maxima, Donatilla, and Secunda, three virgins of Tuburga, had gall and vinegar given them to drink, were then severely scourged, tormented on a gibbet, rubbed with lime, scorched on a gridiron, worried by wild beasts, and at length beheaded.

It is here proper to take notice of the singular but miserable fate of the emperor Valerian, who had so long and so terribly persecuted the christians.

This tyrant, by a stratagem, was taken prisoner by Sapor, emperor of Persia, who carried him into his own country, and there treated him with the most unexampled indignity, making him kneel down as the meanest slave, and treading upon him as a footstool when he mounted his horse.

After having kept him for the space of seven years in this abject state of slavery, he caused his eyes to be put out, though he was then 83 years of age. This not satiating his desire of revenge, he soon after ordered his body to be flayed alive, and rubbed with salt, under which torments he expired; and thus fell one of the most tyrannical emperors of Rome, and one of the greatest persecutors of the christians.

A. D. 260, Gallienus, the son of Valerian, succeeded him, and during his reign (a few martyrs excepted) the church enjoyed peace for some years.

The Ninth Persecution under Aurelian, A. D. 274.

The principal sufferers were, Felix, bishop of Rome. This prelate was advanced to the Roman see in 274. He was the first martyr to Aurelian's petulancy, being beheaded on the 22d of December, in the same year.

Agapetus, a young gentleman, who sold his estate, and gave the money to the poor, was seized as a christian, tortured, and then beheaded at Praeneste, a city within a day's journey of Rome.

These are the only martyrs left upon record during this reign, as it was soon put a stop to by the emperor's being murdered by his own domestics, at Byzantium.

Aurelian was succeeded by Tacitus, who was followed by Probus, as the latter was by Carus: this emperor being killed by a thunder storm, his sons, Carnious and Numerian, succeeded him, and during all these reigns the church had peace.

Diocletian mounted the imperial throne, A. D. 284; at first he showed great favour to the christians. In the year 286, he associated Maximian with him in the empire; and some christians were put to death before any general persecution broke out. Among these were Felician and Primus, two brothers.

Marcus and Marcellianus were twins, natives of Rome, and of noble descent. Their parents were heathens, but the tutors, to whom the education of the children was intrusted, brought them up as christians.

Their constancy at length subdued those who wished them to become pagans, and their parents and whole family became converts to a faith they had before reprobated. They were martyred by being tied to posts, and having their feet pierced with nails. After remaining in this situation for a day and a night, their sufferings were put an end to by thrusting lances through their bodies.

Zoe, the wife of the jailer, who had the care of the before-mentioned martyrs, was also converted by them, and hung upon a tree, with a fire of straw lighted under her. When her body was taken down, it was thrown into a river, with a large stone tied to it, in order to sink it.

In the year of Christ 286, a most remarkable affair occurred; a legion of soldiers, consisting of 6666 men, contained none but christians. This legion was called the Theban Legion, because the men had been raised in Thebias: they were quartered in the east till the emperor Maximian ordered them to march to Gaul, to assist him against the rebels of Burgundy. They passed the Alps into Gaul, under the command of Mauritius, Candidus, and Exupernis, their worthy commanders, and at length joined the emperor.

Maximian, about this time, ordered a general sacrifice, at which the whole army was to assist; and likewise he commanded, that they should take the oath of allegiance and swear, at the same time, to assist in the extirpation of christianity in Gaul.

Alarmed at these orders, each individual of the Theban Legion absolutely refused either to sacrifice or take the oaths prescribed. This so greatly enraged Maximian, that he ordered the legion to be decimated, that is, every tenth man to be selected from the rest, and put to the sword. This bloody order having been put in execution, those who remained alive were still inflexible, when a second decimation took place, and every tenth man of those living were put to death.

This second severity made no more impression than the first had done; the soldiers preserved their fortitude and their principles, but by the advice of their officers they drew up a loyal remonstrance to the emperor. This, it might have been presumed, would have softened the emperor, but it had a contrary effect: for, enraged at their perseverance and unanimity, he commanded, that the whole legion should be put to death, which was accordingly executed by the other troops, who cut them to pieces with their swords, 22d Sept. 286.

Alban, from whom St. Alban's, in Hertfordshire, received its name, was the first British martyr. Great Britain had received the gospel of Christ from Lucius, the first christian king, but did not suffer from the rage of persecution for many years after. He was originally a pagan, but converted by a christian ecclesiastic, named Amphibalus, whom he sheltered on account of his religion. The enemies of Amphibalus, having intelligence of the place where he was secreted, came to the house of Alban; in order to facilitate his escape, when the soldiers came, he offered himself up as the person they were seeking for. The deceit being detected, the governor ordered him to be scourged, and then he was sentenced to be beheaded, June 22, A. D. 287.

The venerable Bede assures us, that, upon this occasion, the executioner suddenly became a convert to christianity, and entreated permission to die for Alban, or with him. Obtaining the latter request, they were beheaded by a soldier, who voluntarily undertook the task of executioner. This happened on the 22d of June, A. D. 287, at Verulam, now St. Albans, in Hertfordshire, where a magnificent church was erected to his memory about the time of Constantine the Great. This edifice, being destroyed in the Saxon wars, was rebuilt by Offa, king of Mercia, and a monastery erected adjoining to it, some remains of which are still visible, and the church is a noble Gothic structure.

Faith, a christian female, of Acquitain, in France, was ordered to be broiled upon a gridiron, and then beheaded; A. D. 287.

Quintin was a christian, and a native of Rome, but determined to attempt the propagation of the gospel in Gaul, with one Lucian, they preached together in Amiens; after which Lucian went to Beaumaris, where he was martyred. Quintin remained in Picardy, and was very zealous in his ministry.

Being seized upon as a christian, he was stretched with pullies till his joints were dislocated: his body was then torn with wire scourges, and boiling oil and pitch poured on his naked flesh; lighted torches were applied to his sides and armpits; and after he had been thus tortured, he was remanded back to prison, and died of the barbarities he had suffered, October 31, A. D. 287. His body was sunk in the Somme.

The Tenth Persecution under Diocletian, A. D. 303,

Under the Roman Emperors, commonly called the Era of the Martyrs, was occasioned partly by the increasing numbers and luxury of the christians, and the hatred of Galerius, the adopted son of Diocletian, who, being stimulated by his mother, a bigoted pagan, never ceased persuading the emperor to enter upon the persecution, till he had accomplished his purpose.

The fatal day fixed upon to commence the bloody work, was the 23d of February, A. D. 303, that being the day in which the Terminalia were celebrated, and on which, as the cruel pagans boasted, they hoped to put a termination to christianity. On the appointed day, the persecution began in Nicomedia, on the morning of which the prefect of that city repaired, with a great number of officers and assistants, to the church of the christians, where, having forced open the doors, they seized upon all the sacred books, and committed them to the flames.

The whole of this transaction was in the presence of Diocletian and Galerius, who, not contented with burning the books, had the church levelled with the ground. This was followed by a severe edict, commanding the destruction of all other christian churches and books; and an order soon succeeded, to render christians of all denominations outlaws.

The publication of this edict occasioned an immediate martyrdom for a bold christian not only tore it down from the place to which it was affixed, but execrated the name of the emperor for his injustice.

A provocation like this was sufficient to call down pagan vengeance upon his head; he was accordingly seized, severely tortured, and then burned alive.

All the christians were apprehended and imprisoned; and Galerius privately ordered the imperial palace to be set on fire, that the christians might be charged as the incendiaries, and a plausible pretence given for carrying on the persecution with the greatest severities. A general sacrifice was commenced, which occasioned various martyrdoms. No distinction was made of age or sex; the name of Christian was so obnoxious to the pagans, that all indiscriminately fell sacrifices to their opinions. Many houses were set on fire, and whole christian families perished in the flames; and others had stones fastened about their necks, and being tied together were driven into the sea. The persecution became general in all the Roman provinces, but more particularly in the east; and as it lasted ten years, it is impossible to ascertain the numbers martyred, or to enumerate the various modes of martyrdom.

Racks, scourges, swords, daggers, crosses, poison, and famine, were made use of in various parts to despatch the christians; and invention was exhausted to devise tortures against such as had no crime, but thinking differently from the votaries of superstition.

A city of Phrygia, consisting entirely of christians, was burnt, and all the inhabitants perished in the flames.

Tired with slaughter, at length, several governors of provinces represented to the imperial court, the impropriety of such conduct. Hence many were respited from execution, but, though they were not put to death, as much as possible was done to render their lives miserable, many of them having their ears cut off, their noses slit, their right eyes put out, their limbs rendered useless by dreadful dislocations, and their flesh seared in conspicuous places with red-hot irons.

It is necessary now to particularize the most conspicuous persons who laid down their lives in martyrdom in this bloody persecution.

Sebastian, a celebrated martyr, was born at Narbonne, in Gaul, instructed in the principles of christianity at Milan, and afterward became an officer of the emperor's guard at Rome. He remained a true christian in the midst of idolatry; unallured by the splendours of a court, untainted by evil examples, and uncontaminated by the hopes of preferment. Refusing to be a pagan, the emperor ordered him to be taken to a field near the city, termed the Campus Martius, and there to be shot to death with arrows; which sentence was executed accordingly. Some pious christians coming to the place of execution, in order to give his body burial, perceived signs of life in him, and immediately moving him to a place of security, they, in a short time effected his recovery, and prepared him for a second martyrdom; for, as soon as he was able to go out, he placed himself intentionally in the emperor's way as he was going to the temple, and reprehended him for his various cruelties and unreasonable prejudices against christianity. As soon as Diocletian had overcome his surprise, he ordered Sebastian to be seized, and carried to a place near the palace, and beaten to death; and, that the christians should not either use means again to recover or bury his body, he ordered that it should be thrown into the common sewer. Nevertheless, a christian lady, named Lucina, found means to remove it from the sewer, and bury it in the catacombs, or repositories of the dead.

The christians, about this time, upon mature consideration, thought it unlawful to bear arms under a heathen emperor. Maximilian, the son of Fabius Victor, was the first beheaded under this regulation.

Vitus, a Sicilian of considerable family, was brought up a christian; when his virtues increased with his years, his constancy supported him under all afflictions, and his faith was superior to the most dangerous perils. His father, Hylas, who was a pagan, finding that he had been instructed in the principles of christianity by the nurse who brought him up, used all his endeavours to bring him back to paganism and at length sacrificed his son to the idols, June 14, A. D. 303.

Victor was a Christian of a good family at Marseilles, in France; he spent a great part of the night in visiting the afflicted, and confirming the weak; which pious work he could not, consistently with his own safety, perform in the daytime; and his fortune he spent in relieving the distresses of poor christians.

He was at length, however, seized by the emperor's Maximian's decree, who ordered him to be bound, and dragged through the streets. During the execution of this order, he was treated with all manner of cruelties and indignities by the enraged populace. Remaining still inflexible, his courage was deemed obstinacy.

Being by order stretched upon the rack, he turned his eyes towards heaven, and prayed to God to endue him with patience, after which he underwent the tortures with most admirable fortitude. After the executioners were tired with inflicting torments on him, he was conveyed to a dungeon. In his confinement, he converted his jailers, named Alexander, Felician, and Longinus. This affair coming to the ears of the emperor, he ordered them immediately to be put to death, and the jailers were accordingly beheaded. Victor was then again put to the rack, unmercifully beaten with batons, and again sent to prison.

Being a third time examined concerning his religion, he persevered in his principles; a small altar was then brought, and he was commanded to offer incense upon it immediately. Fired with indignation at the request, he boldly stepped forward, and with his foot overthrew both altar and idol. This so enraged the emperor Maximian, who was present, that he ordered the foot with which he had kicked the altar to be immediately cut off; and Victor was thrown into a mill, and crushed to pieces with the stones, A. D. 303.

Maximus, governor of Cilicia, being at Tarsus, three christians were brought before him; their names were Tarachus, an aged man; Probus, and Andronicus. After repeated tortures and exhortations to recant, they, at length, were ordered for execution.

Being brought to the amphitheatre, several beasts were let loose upon them; but none of the animals, though hungry, would touch them. The keeper then brought out a large bear, that had that very day destroyed three men; but this voracious creature and a fierce lioness both refused to touch the prisoners. Finding the design of destroying them by the means of wild beasts ineffectual, Maximus ordered them to be slain by the sword, on the 11th of October, A. D. 303.

Romanus, a native of Palestine, was deacon of the church of Caesarea, at the time of the commencement of Diocletian's persecution. Being condemned for his faith at Antioch, he was scourged, put to the rack, his body torn with hooks, his flesh cut with knives, his face scarified, his teeth beaten from their sockets, and his hair plucked up by the roots. Soon after he was ordered to be strangled, Nov. 17, A. D. 303.

Susanna, the niece of Caius, bishop of Rome, was pressed by the emperor Diocletian to marry a noble pagan, who was nearly related to him. Refusing the honour intended her, she was beheaded by the emperor's order.

Dorotheus, the high chamberlain of the household to Diocletian, was a christian, and took great pains to make converts. In his religious labours, he was joined by Gorgonius, another christian, and one belonging to the palace. They were first tortured and then strangled.

Peter, a eunuch belonging to the emperor, was a christian of singular modesty and humility. He was laid on a gridiron, and broiled over a slow fire till he expired.

Cyprian, known by the title of the magician, to distinguish him from Cyprian, bishop of Carthage, was a native of Antioch. He received a liberal education in his youth, and particularly applied himself to astrology; after which he travelled for improvement through Greece, Egypt, India, &c. In the course of time he became acquainted with Justina, a young lady of Antioch, whose birth, beauty, and accomplishments, rendered her the admiration of all who knew her.

A pagan gentleman applied to Cyprian, to promote his suit with the beautiful Justina; this he undertook, but soon himself became converted, burnt his books of astrology and magic, received baptism, and felt animated with a powerful spirit of grace. The conversion of Cyprian had a great effect on the pagan gentleman who paid his addresses to Justina, and he in a short time embraced christianity. During the persecution of

Diocletian, Cyprian and Justina were seized upon as christians, when the former was torn with pincers, and the later chastised and, after suffering other torments, were beheaded.

Eulalia, a Spanish lady of a christian family, was remarkable in her youth for sweetness of temper, and solidity of understanding seldom found in the capriciousness of juvenile years. Being apprehended as a christian, the magistrate attempted by the mildest means, to bring her over to paganism, but she ridiculed the pagan deities with such asperity, that the judge, incensed at her behaviour, ordered her to be tortured. Her sides were accordingly torn by hooks, and her breasts burnt in the most shocking manner, till she expired by the violence of the flames, Dec. A. D. 303.

In the year 304, when the persecution reached Spain, Dacian, the governor of Terragona ordered Valerius the bishop, and Vincent the deacon, to be seized, loaded with irons, and imprisoned. The prisoners being firm in their resolution, Valerius was banished, and Vincent was racked, and his limbs dislocated, his flesh torn with hooks, and was laid on a gridiron, which had not only a fire placed under it, but spikes at the top, which ran into his flesh. These torments neither destroying him, nor changing his resolutions, he was remanded to prison, and confined in a small, loathsome, dark dungeon, strewed with sharp flints, and pieces of broken glass, where he died, Jan. 22, 304.--His body was thrown into the river.

The persecution of Diocletian began particularly to rage in A. D. 304, when many christians were put to cruel tortures, and the most painful and ignominious deaths; the most eminent and particular of whom we shall enumerate.

Saturninus, a priest of Albitina, a town of Africa, after being tortured, was remanded to prison, and there starved to death. His four children, after being variously tormented, shared the same fate with their father.

Dativas, a noble Roman senator; Thelico, a pious Christian, Victoria, a young lady of considerable family and fortune, with some others of less consideration, all auditors of Saturninus, were tortured in a similar manner, and perished by the same means.

Agrape, Chioma, and Irene, three sisters, were seized upon at Thessalonica, when Diocletian's persecution reached Greece. They were burnt, and received the crown of martyrdom in the flames, March 25, A.

D. 304. The governor, finding that he could make no impression on Irene, ordered her to be exposed naked in the streets, which shameful order having been executed, she was burnt, April 1, A. D. 304, at the same place where her sisters suffered.

Agatho, a man of a pious turn of mind, with Cassice, Phillippa, and Eutychia, were martyred about the same time; but the particulars have not been transmitted to us.

Marcellinus, bishop of Rome, who succeeded Caius in that see, having strongly opposed paying divine honours to Diocletian, suffered martyrdom, by a variety of tortures, in the year 321, comforting his soul till he expired with the prospect of those glorious rewards it would receive by the tortures suffered in the body.

Victorius, Carpophorus, Severus, and Severianus, were brothers, and all four employed in places of great trust and honour in the city of Rome. Having exclaimed against the worship of idols, they were apprehended, and scourged, with the plumbetae, or scourges, to the ends of which were fastened leaden balls. This punishment was exercised with such excess of cruelty, that the pious brothers fell martyrs to its severity.

Timothy, a deacon of Mauritania, and Maura his wife, had not been united together by the bands of wedlock above three weeks, when they were separated from each other by the persecution.--Timothy, being apprehended as a christian, was carried before Arrianus, the governor of Thebais, who, knowing that he had the keeping of the Holy Scriptures, commanded him to deliver them up to be burnt; to which he answered, "Had I children, I would sooner deliver them up to be sacrificed, than part with the word of God." The governor being much incensed at this reply, ordered his eyes to be put out with red-hot irons, saying "The books shall at least be useless to you, for you shall not see to read them." His patience under the operation was so great, that the governor grew more exasperated; he, therefore, in order, if possible, to overcome his fortitude, ordered him to be hung up by the feet, with a weight tied about his neck, and a gag in his mouth. In this state, Maura, his wife, tenderly urged him for her sake to recant; but, when the gag was taken out of his mouth, instead of consenting to his wife's entreaties, he greatly blamed her mistaken love, and declared his resolution of dying for the faith. The consequence was, that Maura resolved to imitate his courage and fidelity and either to accompany or follow him to glory. The governor, after trying in vain to alter her resolution, ordered her to be tortured which was executed with great severity. After this, Timothy and Maura were crucified near each other, A. D. 304.

Sabinus, bishop of Assisium, refusing to sacrifice to Jupiter, and pushing the idol from him, had his hand cut off by the order of the governor of Tuscany. While in prison, he converted the governor and his family, all of whom suffered martyrdom for the faith. Soon after their execution, Sabinus himself was scourged to death. Dec.. A. D. 304.

Tired with the farce of state and public business, the emperor Diocletian resigned the imperial diadem, and was succeeded by Constantius and Galerius; the former a prince of the most mild and humane disposition and the latter equally remarkable for his cruelty and tyranny. These divided the empire into two equal governments, Galerius ruling in the east, and Constantius in the west; and the people in the two governments felt the effects of the dispositions of the two emperors; for those in the west were governed in the mildest manner, but such as resided in the east, felt all then miseries of oppression and lengthened tortures.

Among the many martyred by the order of Galerius, we shall enumerate the most eminent.

Amphianus was a gentleman of eminence in Lucia, and a scholar of Eusebius; Julitta, a Lycaonian of royal descent, but more celebrated for her virtues than noble blood. While on the rack, her child was killed before her face. Julitta, of Cappadocia, was a lady of distinguished capacity, great virtue, and uncommon courage.--To complete the execution, Julitta had boiling pitch poured on her feet, her sides torn with hooks, and received the conclusion of her martyrdom, by being beheaded, April 16, A. D. 305.

Hermolaus, a venerable and pious christian, of a great age, and an intimate acquaintance of Panteleon's, suffered martyrdom for the faith on the same day, and in the same manner as Panteleon.

Eustratius, secretary to the governor of Armina, was thrown into a fiery furnace, for exhorting some christians who had been apprehended, to persevere in their faith.

Nicander and Marcian, two eminent Roman military officers, were apprehended on account of their faith. As they were both men of great abilities in their profession, the utmost means were used to induce them to renounce christianity: but these endeavours being found ineffectual, they were beheaded.

In the kingdom of Naples, several martyrdoms took place, in particular, Januaries, bishop of Beneventum; Sosius, deacon of Misene Proculus, another deacon; Eutyches and Acutius, two laymen: Festus, a deacon; and Desiderius, a reader; were all, on account of being christians, condemned by the governor of Campania, to be devoured by the wild beasts. The savage animals, however, not touching them, they were beheaded.

Quirinus, bishop of Siscia, being carried before Matenius, the governor, was ordered to sacrifice to the pagan deities, agreeably to the edicts of various Roman emperors. The governor, perceiving his constancy, sent him to jail, and ordered him to be heavily ironed; flattering himself, that the hardships of a jail, some occasional tortures and the weight of chains, might overcome his resolution. Being decided in his principles, he was sent to Amantius, the principal governor of Pannonia, now Hungary, who loaded him with chains, and carried him through the principal towns of the Danube, exposing him to ridicule wherever he went. Arriving at length at Sabaria, and finding that Quirinus would not renounce his faith, he ordered him to be cast into a river, with a stone fastened about his neck. This sentence being put into execution, Quirinus floated about for some time, and, exhorting the people in the most pious terms, concluded his admonitions with this prayer: "It is no new thing, O all-powerful Jesus, for thee to stop the course of rivers, or to cause a man to walk upon the water as thou didst thy servant Peter; the people have already seen the proof of thy power in me; grant me now to lay down my life for thy sake, O my God." On pronouncing the last words he immediately sank, and died, June 4, A. D. 308; his body was afterwards taken up, and buried by some pious christians.

Pamphilus, a native of Phoenicia, of a considerable family, was a man of such extensive learning, that he was called a second Origen. He was received into the body of the clergy at Caesarea, where he established a public library and spent his time in the practice of every christian virtue. He copied the greatest part of the works of Origen with his own hand, and, assisted by Eusebius, gave a correct copy of the Old Testament, which had suffered greatly by the ignorance or negligence of firmer transcribers. In the year 307, he was apprehended, and suffered torture and martyrdom.

Marcellus, bishop of Rome, being banished on account of his faith, fell a martyr to the miseries he suffered in exile, 16th Jan. A. D. 310.

Peter, the sixteenth bishop of Alexandria, was martyred Nov. 25, A. D. 311, by order of Maximus Caesar, who reigned in the east.

Agnes, a virgin of only thirteen years of age, was beheaded for being a christian; as was Serene, the empress of Diocletian. Valentine, a priest, suffered the same fate at Rome; and Erasmus, a bishop, was martyred in Campania.

Soon after this the persecution abated in the middle parts of the empire, as well as in the west; and Providence at length began to manifest vengeance on the persecutors. Maximian endeavoured to corrupt his daughter Fausta to murder Constantine her husband; which she discovered, and Constantine forced him to choose his own death, when he preferred the ignominious death of hanging, after being an emperor near twenty years.

Galerius was visited by an incurable and intolerable disease, which began with an ulcer in his secret parts and a fistula in ano, that spread progressively to his inmost bowels, and baffled all the skill of physicians and surgeons. Untried medicines of some daring professors drove the evil through his bones to the very marrow, and worms began to breed in his entrails; and the stench was so preponderant as to be perceived in the city; all the passages separating the passages of the urine, and excrements being corroded and destroyed. The whole mass of his body was turned unto universal rottenness; and, though living creatures, and boiled animals, were applied with the design of drawing out the vermin by the heat, by which a vast hive was opened, a second imposthume discovered a more prodigious swarm, as if his whole body was resolved into worms. By a dropsy also his body was grossly disfigured; for although his upper parts were exhausted, and dried to a skeleton, covered only with dead skin; the lower parts were swelled up like bladders, and the shape of his feet could scarcely be perceived. Torments and pains insupportable, greater than those he had inflicted upon the christians, accompanied these visitations, and he bellowed out like a wounded bull, often endeavouring to kill himself and destroying several physicians for the inefficacy of their medicines. These torments kept him in a languishing state a full year, and his conscience was awakened, at length, so that he was compelled to acknowledge the God of the christians, and to promise, in the intervals of his paroxysms, that he would rebuild the churches, and repair the mischief done to them. An edict in his last agonies, was published in his name, and the joint names of Constantine and Licinius, to permit the christians to have the free use of religion, and to supplicate their God for his health and the good of the empire; on which many prisoners in Nicomedia were liberated, and amongst others Donatus.

At length, Constantine the Great, determined to redress the grievances of the christians, for which purpose he raised an army of 30,000 foot, and 8000 horse, which he marched towards Rome against Maxentius, the emperor; defeated him, and entered the city of Rome in triumph. A law was now published in favour of the christians, in which Licinius was joined by Constantine, and a copy of it was sent to Maximus in the east. Maximus, who was a bigoted pagan, greatly disliked the edict, but being afraid of Constantine, did not openly avow his disapprobation. Maximus at length invaded the territories of Licinius, but, being defeated, put an end to his life by poison. Licinius afterwards persecuting the christians, Constantine the Great marched against him, and defeated him: he was afterwards slain by his own soldiers.

We shall conclude our account of the tenth and last general persecution with the death of St. George, the titular saint and patron of England. St. George was born in Cappadocia, of christian parents; and giving proofs of his courage, was promoted in the army of the emperor Diocletian. During the persecution, St. George threw up his command, went boldly to the senate house, and avowed his being a christian, taking occasion at the same time to remonstrate against paganism, and point out the absurdity of worshipping idols. This freedom so greatly provoked the senate, that St. George was ordered to be tortured, and by the emperor's orders was dragged through the streets, and beheaded the next day.

CHAPTER III.

PERSECUTIONS OF THE CHRISTIANS IN PERSIA.

The gospel having spread itself into Persia, the pagan priests, who worshipped the sun, were greatly alarmed, and dreaded the loss of that influence they had hitherto maintained over the people's minds and properties. Hence they thought it expedient to complain to the emperor, that the christians were enemies to the state, and held a treasonable correspondence with the Romans, the great enemies of Persia.

The emperor Sapores, being naturally averse to christianity, easily believed what was said against the christians, and gave orders to persecute them in all parts of his empire. On account of this mandate, many eminent persons in the church and state fell martyrs to the ignorance and ferocity of the pagans.

Constantine the Great being informed of the persecutions in Persia, wrote a long letter to the Persian monarch, in which he recounts the vengeance that had fallen on persecutors, and the great success that had attended those who had refrained from persecuting the christians. The persecution by this means ended during the life of Sapores; but it was again renewed under the lives of his successors.

Persecutions under the Arian Heretics.

The author of the Arian heresy was Arius, a native of Lybia, and a priest of Alexandria, who, in A. D. 318, began to publish his errors. He was condemned by a council of Lybian and Egyptian bishops, and that sentence was confirmed by the council of Nice, A. D. 325. After the death of Constantine the Great, the Arians found means to ingratiate themselves into the favour of the emperor Constantinus, his son and successor in the east; and hence a persecution was raised against the orthodox bishops and clergy. The celebrated Athanasius, and other bishops, were banished, and their sees filled with Arians.

In Egypt and Lybia, thirty bishops were martyred, and many other christians cruelly tormented; and, A. D. 386, George, the Arian bishop of Alexandria, under the authority of the emperor, began a persecution in that city and its environs, and carried it on with the most infernal severity. He was assisted in his diabolical malice by Catophonius, governor of Egypt; Sebastian, general of the Egyptian forces; Faustinus the treasurer; and Herachus, a Roman officer.

The persecution now raged in such a manner, that the clergy were driven from Alexandria, their churches were shut, and the severities practised by the Arian heretics were as great as those that had been practised by the pagan idolaters. If a man, accused of being a christian, made his escape, then his whole family were massacred, and his effects confiscated.

Persecution under Julian the Apostate.

This emperor was the son of Julius Constantius, and the nephew of

Constantine the Great. He studied the rudiments of grammar under the inspection of Mardomus, a eunuch, and a heathen of Constantinople. His father sent him some time after to Nicomedia, to be instructed in the christian religion, by the bishop of Eusebius, his kinsman, but his principles were corrupted by the pernicious doctrines of Ecebolius the rhetorician, and Maximus the magician.

Constantius dying in the year 361, Julian succeeded him, and had no sooner attained the imperial dignity, than he renounced Christianity and embraced paganism, which had for some years fallen into great disrepute. Though he restored the idolatrous worship, he made no public edicts against christianity. He recalled all banished pagans, allowed the free exercise of religion to every sect, but deprived all christians of offices at court, in the magistracy, or in the army. He was chaste, temperate, vigilant, laborious, and pious; yet he prohibited any christian from keeping a school or public seminary of learning, and deprived all the christian clergy of the privileges granted them by Constantine the Great.

Bishop Basil made himself first famous by his opposition to Arianism, which brought upon him the vengeance of the Arian bishop of Constantinople; he equally opposed paganism. The emperor's agents in vain tampered with Basil by means of promises, threats, and racks, he was firm in the faith, and remained in prison to undergo some other sufferings, when the emperor came accidentally to Ancyra. Julian determined to examine Basil himself, when that holy man being brought before him, the emperor did every thing in his power to dissuade him from persevering in the faith. Basil not only continued as firm as ever, but, with a prophetic spirit foretold the death of the emperor, and that he should be tormented in the other life. Enraged at what he heard, Julian commanded that the body of Basil should be torn every day in seven different parts, till his skin and flesh were entirely mangled. This inhuman sentence was executed with rigour, and the martyr expired under its severities, on the 28th day of June, A. D. 362.

Donatus, bishop of Arezzo, and Hilarinus, a hermit, suffered about the same time; also Gordian, a Roman magistrate. Artemius, commander in chief of the Roman forces in Egypt, being a christian, was deprived of his commission, then of his estate, and lastly of his head.

The persecution raged dreadfully about the latter end of the year 363; but, as many of the particulars have not been handed down to us, it is necessary to remark in general, that in Palestine many were burnt alive, others were dragged by their feet through the streets naked till they expired; some were scalded to death, many stoned, and great numbers had their brains beaten out with clubs. In Alexandria, innumerable were the martyrs who suffered by the sword, burning, crucifixion, and being stoned. In Arethusa, several were ripped open, and corn being put into their bellies, swine were brought to feed therein, which, in devouring the grain, likewise devoured the entrails of the martyrs, and, in Thrace, Emilianus was burnt at a stake; and Domitius murdered in a cave, whither he had fled for refuge.

The emperor, Julian the apostate, died of a wound which he received in his Persian expedition, A. D. 363, and even while expiring, uttered the most horrid blasphemies. He was succeeded by Jovian, who restored peace to the church.

After the decease of Jovian, Valentinian succeeded to the empire, and associated to himself Valens, who had the command in the east, and was an Arian, of an unrelenting and persecuting disposition.

Persecution of the Christians by the Goths and Vandals.

Many Scythian Goths having embraced Christianity about the time of Constantine the Great, the light of the gospel spread itself considerably in Scythia, though the two kings who ruled that country, and the majority of the people continued pagans. Fritegern, king of the West Goths, was an ally to the Romans, but Athanarick, king of the East Goths, was at war with them. The christians, in the dominions of the former, lived unmolested, but the latter, having been defeated by the Romans, wreaked his vengeance on his christian subjects, commencing his pagan injunctions in the year 370.

Eusebius, bishop of Samosata, makes a most distinguished figure in the ecclesiastical history, and was one of the most eminent champions of Christ against the Arian heresy. Eusebius, after being driven from his church, and wandering about through Syria and Palestine, encouraging the orthodox, was restored with other orthodox prelates to his see, which however he did not long enjoy, for an Arian woman threw a tile at him from the top of a house, which fractured his skull, and terminated his life in the year 380.

The Vandals passing from Spain to Africa in the fifth century, under their leader Genseric, committed the most unheard-of cruelties. They persecuted the christians wherever they came, and even laid waste the country as they passed, that the christians left behind, who had escaped them, might not be able to subsist. Sometimes they freighted a vessel with martyrs, let it drift out to sea, or set fire to it, with the sufferers shackled on the decks.

Having seized and plundered the city of Carthage, they put the bishop, and the clergy, into a leaky ship, and committed it to the mercy of the waves, thinking that they must all perish of course; but providentially the vessel arrived safe at Naples. Innumerable orthodox christians were beaten, scourged, and banished to Capsur, where it pleased God to make them the means of converting many of the Moors to christianity; but this coming to the ears of Genseric, he sent orders that they and their new converts should be tied by the feet to chariots, and dragged about until they were dashed to pieces Pampinian, the bishop of Mansuetes, was tortured to death with plates of hot iron; the bishop of Urice was burnt, and the bishop of Habensa was banished, for refusing to deliver up the sacred books which were in his possession.

The Vandalian tyrant Genseric, having made an expedition into Italy, and plundered the city of Rome, returned to Africa, flushed with the success of his arms. The Arians took this occasion to persuade him to persecute the orthodox christians, as they assured him that they were friends to the people of Rome.

After the decease of Huneric, his successor recalled him, and the rest of the orthodox clergy; the Arians, taking the alarm, persuaded him to banish them again, which he complied with, when Eugenius, exiled to Languedoc in France, died there of the hardships he underwent on the 6th of September, A. D. 305.

Persecutions from about the Middle of the Fifth, to the Conclusion of the Seventh Century.

Proterius was made a priest by Cyril, bishop of Alexandria, who was well acquainted with his virtues, before he appointed him to preach. On the death of Cyril, the see of Alexandria was filled by Discorus, an inveterate enemy to the memory and family of his predecessor. Being condemned by the council of Chalcedon for having embraced the errors of Eutyches, he was deposed, and Proterius chosen to fill the vacant see, who was approved of by the emperor. This occasioned a dangerous insurrection, for the city of Alexandria was divided into two factions; the one to espouse the cause of the old, and the other of the new prelate. In one of the commotions, the Eutychians determined to wreak their vengeance on Proterius, who fled to the church for sanctuary: but on Good Friday, A. D. 457, a large body of them rushed into the church, and barbarously murdered the prelate; after which they dragged the body through the streets, insulted it, cut it to pieces, burnt it, and scattered the ashes in the air.

Hermenigildus, a Gothic prince, was the eldest son of Leovigildus, a king of the Goths, in Spain. This prince, who was originally an Arian, became a convert to the orthodox faith, by means of his wife Ingonda. When the king heard that his son had changed his religious sentiments, he stripped him of the command at Seville, where he was governor, and threatened to put him to death unless he renounced the faith he had newly embraced. The prince, in order to prevent the execution of his father's menaces, began to put himself into a posture of defence; and many of the orthodox persuasion in Spain declared for him. The king, exasperated at this act of rebellion, began to punish all the orthodox christians who could be seized by his troops; and thus a very severe persecution commenced: he likewise marched against his son at the head of a very powerful army. The prince took refuge in Seville, from which he fled, and was at length besieged and taken at Asieta. Loaded with chains, he was sent to Seville, and at the feast of Easter refusing to receive the Eucharist from an Arian bishop, the enraged king ordered his guards to cut the prince to pieces, which they punctually performed, April 13, A. D. 586.

Martin, bishop of Rome, was born at Todi, in Italy. He was naturally inclined to virtue, and his parents bestowed on him an admirable education. He opposed the heretics called Monothothelites, who were patronized by the emperor Heraclius. Martin was condemned at Constantinople, where he was exposed in the most public places to the ridicule of the people, divested of all episcopal marks of distinction, and treated with the greatest scorn and severity. After lying some months in prison, Martin was sent to an island at some distance, and there cut to pieces, A. D. 655.

John, bishop of Bergamo, in Lombardy, was a learned man, and a good christian. He did his utmost endeavours to clear the church from the errors of Arianism, and joining in this holy work with John, bishop of Milan, he was very successful against the heretics, on which account he was assassinated on July 11, A. D. 683.

Killien was born in Ireland, and received from his parents a pious and christian education. He obtained the Roman pontiff's license to preach to the pagans in Franconia, in Germany. At Wurtzburg he converted Gozbert, the governor, whose example was followed by the greater part of the people in two years after. Persuading Gozbert that his marriage with his brother's widow was sinful, the latter had him beheaded, A. D. 689.

Persecutions from the early part of the Eighth, to near the Conclusion of the Tenth Century.

Boniface, archbishop of Mentz, and father of the German church, was an Englishmen, and is, in ecclesiastical history, looked upon as one of the brightest ornaments of this nation. Originally, his name was Winfred, or Winfrith, and he was born at Kirton, in Devonshire, then part of the West-Saxon kingdom. When he was only about six years of age, he began to discover a propensity to reflection, and seemed solicitous to gain information on religious subjects. Wolfrad, the abbot, finding that he possessed a bright genius, as well as a strong inclination to study, had him removed to Nutscelle, a seminary of learning in the diocese of Winchester, where he would have a much greater opportunity of attaining improvement than at Exeter.

After due study, the abbot seeing him qualified for the priesthood, obliged him to receive that holy order when he was about thirty years old. From which time he began to preach and labour for the salvation of his fellow-creatures; he was released to attend a synod of bishops in the kingdom of West-Saxons. He afterwards, in 719, went to Rome, where Gregory II. who then sat in Peter's chair, received him with great friendship, and finding him full of all the virtues that compose the character of an apostolic missionary, dismissed him with commission at large to preach the gospel to the pagans wherever he found them. Passing through Lombardy and Bavaria, he came to Thuringia, which country had before received the light of the gospel, he next visited Utrecht, and then proceeded to Saxony, where he converted some thousands to christianity.

During the ministry of this meek prelate, Pepin was declared king of France. It was that prince's ambition to be crowned by the most holy prelate he could find, and Boniface was pitched on to perform that ceremony, which he did at Soissons, in 752. The next year, his great age and many infirmities lay so heavy on him, that, with the consent of the new king, the bishops, &c. of his diocese, he consecrated Lullus, his countryman, and faithful disciple, and placed him in the see of Mentz. When he had thus eased himself of his charge, he recommended the church of Mentz to the care of the new bishop in very strong terms, desired he would finish the church at Fuld, and see him buried in it, for his end was near. Having left these orders, he took boat to the Rhine, and went to Friesland, where he converted and baptized several thousands of barbarous natives, demolished the temples, and raised churches on the ruins of those superstitious structures. A day being appointed for confirming a great number of new converts, he ordered them to assemble in a new open plain, near the river Bourde. Thither he repaired the day before; and, pitching a tent, determined to remain on the spot all night, in order to be ready early in the morning.

Some pagans, who were his inveterate enemies, having intelligence of this, poured down upon him and the companions of his mission in the night, and killed him and fifty-two of his companions and attendants on June 5, A. D. 755. Thus fell the great father of the Germanic church, the honour of England, and the glory of the age in which he lived.

Forty-two persons of Armorian in Upper Phrygia, were martyred in the year 845, by the Saracens, the circumstances of which transaction are as follows:

In the reign of Theophilus, the Saracens ravaged many parts of the eastern empire, gained several considerable advantages over the christians, took the city of Armorian, and numbers suffered martyrdom.

Flora and Mary, two ladies of distinction, suffered martyrdom at the same time.

Perfectus was born at Corduba, in Spain, and brought up in the christian faith. Having a quick genius, he made himself master of all the useful and polite literature of that age; and at the same time was not more celebrated for his abilities than admired for his piety. At length he took priest's orders, and performed the duties of his office with great assiduity and punctuality. Publicly declaring Mahomet an impostor, he was sentenced to be beheaded, and was accordingly executed, A. D. 850; after which his body was honourably interred by the christians.

Adalbert, bishop of Prague, a Bohemian by birth, after being involved in many troubles, began to direct his thoughts to the conversion of the infidels, to which end he repaired to Dantzic, where he converted and baptised many, which so enraged the pagan priests, that they fell upon him, and despatched him with darts, on the 23d of April, A. D. 997.

Persecutions in the Eleventh Century.

Alphage, archbishop of Canterbury, was descended from a considerable family in Gloucestershire, and received an education suitable to his illustrious birth. His parents were worthy christians, and Alphage seemed to inherit their virtues.

The see of Winchester being vacant by the death of Ethelwold, Dunstan, archbishop of Canterbury, as primate of all England, consecrated Alphage to the vacant bishopric, to the general satisfaction of all concerned in the diocese.

Dunstan had an extraordinary veneration for Alphage, and, when at the point of death, made it his ardent request to God, that he might succeed him in the see of Canterbury; which accordingly happened, though not till about eighteen years after Dunstan's death in 1006.

After Alphage had governed the see of Canterbury about four years, with great reputation to himself, and benefit to his people, the Danes made an incursion into England, and laid siege to Canterbury. When the design of attacking this city was known, many of the principal people made a flight from it, and would have persuaded Alphage to follow their example. But he, like a good pastor, would not listen to such a proposal. While he was employed in assisting and encouraging the people, Canterbury was taken by storm; the enemy poured into the town, and destroyed all that came in their way by fire and sword. He had the courage to address the enemy, and offer himself to their swords, as more worthy of their rage than the people: he begged they might be saved, and that they would discharge their whole fury upon him. They accordingly seized him, tied his hands, insulted and abused him in a rude and barbarous manner, and obliged him to remain on the spot until his church was burnt, and the monks massacred. They then decimated all the inhabitants, both ecclesiastics and laymen, leaving only every tenth person alive; so that they put 7236 persons to death, and left only four monks and 800 laymen alive, after which they confined the archbishop in a dungeon, where they kept him close prisoner for several months.

During his confinement they proposed to him to redeem his liberty with the sum of L3000, and to persuade the king to purchase their departure out of the kingdom, with a further sum of L10,000. As Alphage's circumstances would not allow him to satisfy the exorbitant demand, they bound him, and put him to severe torments, to oblige him to discover the treasure of the church; upon which they assured him of his life and liberty, but the prelate piously persisted in refusing to give the pagans any account of it. They remanded him to prison again, confined him six days longer, and then, taking him prisoner with them to Greenwich, brought him to trial there. He still remained inflexible with respect to the church treasure; but exhorted them to forsake their idolatry, and embrace christianity. This so greatly incensed the Danes, that the soldiers dragged him out of the camp, and beat him unmercifully. One of the soldiers, who had been converted by him, knowing that his pains would be lingering, as his death was determined on, actuated by a kind of barbarous compassion, cut off his head, and thus put the finishing stroke to his martyrdom, April 19, A. D. 1012. This transaction happened on the very spot where the church at Greenwich, which is dedicated to him, now stands. After his death his body was thrown into the Thames, but being found the next day, it was buried in the cathedral of St. Paul's by the bishops of London and Lincoln; from whence it was, in 1023, removed to Canterbury by Ethelmoth, the archbishop of that province.

Gerard, a Venitian, devoted himself to the service of God from his tender years: entered into a religious house for some time, and then determined to visit the Holy Land. Going into Hungary, he became acquainted with Stephen, the king of that country, who made him bishop of Chonad.

Ouvo and Peter, successors of Stephen, being deposed, Andrew, son of Ladislaus, cousin-german to Stephen, had then a tender of the crown made him upon condition that he would employ his authority in extirpating the christian religion out of Hungary. The ambitious prince came into the proposal, but Gerard being informed of his impious bargain, thought it his duty to remonstrate against the enormity of Andrew's crime, and persuade him to withdraw his promise. In this view he undertook to go to that prince, attended by three prelates, full of like zeal for religion. The new king was at Alba Regalis, but, as the four bishops were going to cross the Danube, they were stopped by a party of soldiers posted there. They bore an attack of a shower of stones patiently, when the soldiers beat them unmercifully, and at length despatched them with lances. Their martyrdoms happened in the year 1045.

Stanislaus, bishop of Cracow, was descended from an illustrious Polish family. The piety of his parents was equal to their opulence, and the latter they rendered subservient to all the purposes of charity and benevolence. Stanislaus remained for some time undetermined, whether he should embrace a monastic life, or engage among the secular clergy. He was at length persuaded to the latter by Lambert Zula, bishop of Cracow, who gave him holy orders, and made him a canon of his cathedral. Lambert died on November 25, 1071, when all concerned in the choice of a successor declared for Stanislaus, and he succeeded to the prelacy.

Bolislaus, the second king of Poland, had, by nature, many good qualities, but giving away to his passions he ran into many enormities, and at length had the appellation of Cruel bestowed upon him. Stanislaus alone had the courage to tell him of his faults, when, taking a private opportunity, he freely displayed to him the enormities of his crimes. The king, greatly exasperated at his repeated freedoms, at length determined, at any rate, to get the better of a prelate who was so extremely faithful. Hearing one day that the bishop was by himself, in the chapel of St. Michael, at a small distance from the town, he despatched some soldiers to murder him. The soldiers readily undertook the bloody task; but, when they came into the presence of Stanislaus, the venerable aspect of the prelate struck them with such awe, that they could not perform what they had promised. On their return, the king, finding that they had not obeyed his orders, stormed at them violently, snatched a dagger from one of them, and ran furiously to the chapel, where, finding Stanislaus at the altar, he plunged the weapon into his heart. The prelate immediately expired on the 8th of May, A. D. 1079.

CHAPTER IV.

PAPAL PERSECUTIONS.

Thus far our history of persecution has been confined principally to the pagan world. We come now to a period, when persecution under the guise of christianity, committed more enormities than ever disgraced the annals of paganism. Disregarding the maxims and the spirit of the gospel, the papal church, arming herself with the power of the sword, vexed the church of God and wasted it for several centuries, a period most appropriately termed in history, the "dark ages." The kings of the earth, gave their power to the "beast," and submitted to be trodden on by the miserable vermin that often filled the papal chair, as in the case of Henry, emperor of Germany. The storm of papal persecution first burst upon the Waldenses in France.

Persecution of the Waldenses in France.

Popery having brought various innovations into the church, and overspread the christian world with darkness and superstition, some few, who plainly perceived the pernicious tendency of such errors, determined to show the light of the gospel in its real purity, and to disperse those clouds which artful priests had raised about it, in order to blind the people, and obscure its real brightness.

The principal among these was Berengarius, who, about the year 1000, boldly preached gospel truths, according to their primitive purity. Many, from conviction, assented to his doctrine, and were, on that account, called Berengarians. To Berengarius succeeded Peter Bruis, who preached at Thoulouse, under the protection of an earl, named Hildephonsus; and the whole tenets of the reformers, with the reasons of their separation from the church of Rome, were published in a book written by Bruis, under the title of ANTI-CHRIST.

By the year of Christ 1140, the number of the reformed was very great, and the probability of its increasing alarmed the pope, who wrote to several princes to banish them from their dominions, and employed many learned men to write against their doctrines.

A. D. 1147, Henry of Thoulouse, being deemed their most eminent preacher, they were called Henericians; and as they would not admit of any proofs relative to religion, but what could be deduced from the scriptures themselves, the popish party gave them the name of apostolics. At length, Peter Waldo, or Valdo, a native of Lyons, eminent for his piety and learning, became a strenuous opposer of popery; and from him the reformed, at that time, received the appellation of Waldenses or Waldoys.

Pope Alexander III being informed by the bishop of Lyons of these transactions, excommunicated Waldo and his adherents, and commanded the bishop to exterminate them, if possible, from the face of the earth; and hence began the papal persecutions against the Waldenses.

The proceedings of Waldo and the reformed, occasioned the first rise of the inquisitors; for pope Innocent III. authorized certain monks as inquisitors, to inquire for, and deliver over, the reformed to the secular power. The process was short, as an accusation was deemed adequate to guilt, and a candid trial was never granted to the accused.

The pope, finding that these cruel means had not the intended effect, sent several learned monks to preach among the Waldenses, and to endeavour to argue them out of their opinions. Among these monks was one Dominic, who appeared extremely zealous in the cause of popery. This Dominic instituted an order, which, from him, was called the order of Dominican friars; and the members of this order have ever since been the principal inquisitors in the various inquisitions in the world. The power of the inquisitors was unlimited; they proceeded against whom they pleased, without any consideration of age, sex, or rank. Let the accusers be ever so infamous, the accusation was deemed valid; and even anonymous informations, sent by letter, were thought sufficient evidence. To be rich was a crime equal to heresy; therefore many who had money were accused of heresy, or of being favourers of heretics, that they might be obliged to pay for their opinions. The dearest friends or nearest kindred could not, without danger, serve any one who was imprisoned on account of religion. To convey to those who were confined, a little straw, or give them a cup of water, was called favouring of the heretics, and they were prosecuted accordingly. No lawyer dared to plead for his own brother, and their malice even extended beyond the grave; hence the bones of many were dug up and burnt, as examples to the living. If a man on his death-bed was accused of being a follower of Waldo, his estates were confiscated, and the heir to them defrauded of his inheritance; and some were sent to the Holy Land, while the Dominicans took possession of their houses and properties, and, when the owners returned, would often pretend not to know them. These persecutions were continued for several centuries under different popes and other great dignitaries of the catholic church.

Persecutions of the Albigenses.

The Albigenses were a people of the reformed religion, who inhabited the country of Albi. They were condemned on the score of religion, in the council of Lateran, by order of Pope Alexander III. Nevertheless, they increased so prodigiously, that many cities were inhabited by persons only of their persuasion, and several eminent noblemen embraced their doctrines. Among the latter were Raymond earl of Thoulouse, Raymond earl of Foix, the earl of Beziers, &c.

A friar, named Peter, having been murdered in the dominions of the earl of Thoulouse, the pope made the murder a pretence to persecute that nobleman and his subjects. To effect this, he sent persons throughout all Europe, in order to raise forces to act coercively against the Albigenses, and promised paradise to all that would come to this war, which he termed a Holy War, and bear arms for forty days. The same indulgences were likewise held out to all who entered themselves for the purpose as to such as engaged in crusades to the Holy Land. The brave earl defended Thoulouse and other places with the most heroic bravery and various success against the pope's legates and Simon earl of Montfort, a bigoted catholic nobleman. Unable to subdue the earl of Thoulouse openly, the king of France, and queen mother, and three archbishops, raised another formidable army, and had the art to persuade the earl of Thoulouse to come to a conference, when he was treacherously seized upon, made a prisoner, forced to appear bare-footed and bare-headed before his enemies, and compelled to subscribe an abject recantation. This was followed by a severe persecution against the Albigenses; and express orders that the laity should not be permitted to read the sacred scriptures. In the year 1620 also the persecution against the Albigenses was very severe. In 1648 a heavy persecution raged throughout Lithuania and Poland. The cruelty of the Cossacks was so excessive, that the Tartars themselves were ashamed of their barbarities. Among others who suffered, was the Rev. Adrian Chalinski, who was roasted alive by a slow fire, and whose sufferings and mode of death may depict the horrors which the professors of christianity have endured from the enemies of the Redeemer.

The reformation of papistical error very early was projected in France; for in the third century a learned man, named Almericus, and six of his disciples, were ordered to be burnt at Paris, for asserting that God was no otherwise present in the sacramental bread than in any other bread; that it was idolatry to build altars or shrines to saints and that it was ridiculous to offer incense to them.

The martyrdom of Almericus and his pupils did not, however, prevent many from acknowledging the justness of his notions, and seeing the purity of the reformed religion, so that the truth of Christ continually increased, and in time not only spread itself over many parts of France, but diffused the light of the gospel over various other countries.

In the year 1524, at a town in France, called Melden, one John Clark set up a bill on the church door, wherein he called the pope Anti-christ. For this offence he was repeatedly whipped, and then branded on the forehead. Going afterward to Mentz, in Lorraine, he demolished some images, for which he had his right hand and nose cut off, and his arms and breasts torn with pincers. He sustained these cruelties with amazing fortitude, and was even sufficiently cool to sing the 115th psalm, which expressly forbids idolatry; after which he was thrown into the fire, and burnt to ashes.

Many persons of the reformed persuasion were, about this time, beaten, racked, scourged, and burnt to death, in several parts of France but more particularly at Paris, Malda, and Limosin.

A native of Malda was burnt by a slow fire, for saying that mass was a plain denial of the death and passion of Christ. At Limosin, John de Cadurco, a clergyman of the reformed religion, was apprehended, degraded, and ordered to be burnt.

Francis Bribard, secretary to cardinal de Pellay, for speaking in favour of the reformed, had his tongue cut out, and was then burnt, A. D. 1545. James Cobard, a schoolmaster in the city of St. Michael, was burnt, A. D. 1545, for saying "That mass was useless and absurd;" and about the same time, fourteen men were burnt at Malda, their wives being compelled to stand by and behold the execution.

A. D. 1546, Peter Chapot brought a number of bibles in the French tongue to France, and publicly sold them there; for which he was brought to trial, sentenced, and executed a few days afterward. Soon after, a cripple of Meaux, a schoolmaster of Fera, named Stephen Polliot, and a man named John English, were burnt for the faith.

Monsieur Blondel, a rich jeweller, was, A. D. 1548, apprehended at Lyons, and sent to Paris; where he was burnt for the faith, by order of the court, A. D. 1549. Herbert, a youth of nineteen years of age, was committed to the flames at Dijon; as was Florent Venote, in the same year.

In the year 1554, two men of the reformed religion, with the son and daughter of one of them, were apprehended and committed to the castle of Niverne. On examination, they confessed their faith, and were ordered for execution; being smeared with grease, brimstone, and gunpowder, they cried, "Salt on, salt on this sinful and rotten flesh!" Their tongues were then cut out, and they were afterward committed to the flames, which soon consumed them, by means of the combustible matter with which they were besmeared.

The Bartholomew Massacre at Paris, &c.

On the 22d of August, 1572, commenced this diabolical act of sanguinary brutality. It was intended to destroy at one stroke the root of the protestant tree, which had only before partially suffered in its branches. The king of France had artfully proposed a marriage between his sister and the prince of Navarre, the captain and prince of the protestants. This imprudent marriage was publicly celebrated at Paris, August 18, by the cardinal of Bourbon, upon a high stage erected for the purpose. They dined in great pomp with the bishop, and supped with the king at Paris. Four days after this, the prince, as he was coming from the council, was shot in both arms; he then said to Maure, his deceased mother's minister, "O my brother, I do now perceive that I am indeed beloved of my God, since for his most holy sake I am wounded." Although the Vidam advised him to fly, yet he abode in Paris, and was soon after slain by Bemjus; who afterward declared he never saw a man meet death more valiantly than the admiral. The soldiers were appointed at a certain signal to burst out instantly to the slaughter in all parts of the city. When they had killed the admiral, they threw him out at a window into the street, where his head was cut off, and sent to the pope. The savage papists, still raging against him, cut off his arms and private members, and, after dragging him three days through the streets, hung him up by the heels without the city. After him they slew many great and honourable persons who were protestants; as count Rochfoucault, Telinius, the admiral's son-in-law, Antonius, Clarimontus, marquis of Ravely, Lewes Bussius, Bandineus, Pluvialius, Burneius, &c. &c. and falling upon the common people, they continued the slaughter for many days; in the three first, they slew of all ranks and conditions to the number of 10,000. The bodies were thrown into the rivers, and blood ran through the streets with a strong current, and the river appeared presently like a stream of blood. So furious was their hellish rage, that they slew all papists whom they suspected to be not very staunch to their diabolical religion. From Paris the destruction spread to all quarters of the realm.

At Orleans, a thousand were slain of men, women, and children, and 6000 at Rouen.

At Meldith, two hundred were put into prison, and brought out by units, and cruelly murdered.

At Lyons, eight hundred were massacred. Here children hanging about their parents, and parents affectionately embracing their children, were pleasant food for the swords and blood-thirsty minds of those who call themselves the catholic church. Here 300 were slain only in the bishop's house; and the impious monks would suffer none to be buried.

At Augustobona, on the people hearing of the massacre at Paris, they shut their gates that no protestants might escape, and searching diligently for every individual of the reformed church, imprisoned and then barbarously murdered them. The same cruelty they practised at Avaricum, at Troys, at Thoulouse, Rouen and many other places, running from city to city, towns, and villages, through the kingdom.

As a corroboration of this horrid carnage, the following interesting narrative, written by a sensible and learned Roman catholic, appears in this place, with peculiar propriety.

"The nuptials (says he) of the young king of Navarre with the French king's sister, was solemnized with pomp; and all the endearments, all the assurances of friendship, all the oaths sacred among men, were profusely lavished by Catharine, the queen-mother, and by the king; during which, the rest of the court thought of nothing but festivities, plays, and masquerades. At last, at twelve o'clock at night, on the eve of St. Bartholomew, the signal was given. Immediately all the houses of the protestants were forced open at once. Admiral Coligni, alarmed by the uproar jumped out of bed; when a company of assassins rushed in his chamber. They were headed by one Besme, who had been bred up as a domestic in the family of the Guises. This wretch thrust his sword into the admiral's breast, and also cut him in the face. Besme was a German, and being afterwards taken by the protestants, the Rochellers would have bought him, in order to hang and quarter him; but he was killed by one Bretanville. Henry, the young duke of Guise, who afterwards framed the catholic league, and was murdered at Blois, standing at the door till the horrid butchery should be completed, called aloud, 'Besme! is it done?' Immediately after which, the ruffians threw the body out of the window, and Coligni expired at Guise's feet.

"Count de Teligny also fell a sacrifice. He had married, about ten months before, Coligni's daughter. His countenance was so engaging, that the ruffians, when they advanced in order to kill him, were struck with compassion; but others, more barbarous, rushing forward, murdered him.

"In the meantime, all the friends of Coligni were assassinated throughout Paris; men, women, and children, were promiscuously slaughtered; every street was strewed with expiring bodies. Some priests, holding up a crucifix in one hand, and a dagger in the other, ran to the chiefs of the murderers, and strongly exhorted them to spare neither relations nor friends.

"Tavannes, marshal of France, an ignorant, superstitious soldier, who joined the fury of religion to the rage of party, rode on horseback through the streets of Paris, crying to his men, 'Let blood! let blood!

bleeding is as wholesome in August as in May.' In the memoirs of the life of this enthusiastic, written by his son, we are told, that the father, being on his death-bed, and making a general confession of his actions, the priest said to him, with surprise, 'What! no mention of St. Bartholomew's massacre?' to which Tavannes replied, 'I consider it as a meritorious action, that will wash away all my sins.' Such horrid sentiments can a false spirit of religion inspire!

"The king's palace was one of the chief scenes of the butchery: the king of Navarre had his lodgings in the Louvre, and all his domestics were protestants. Many of these were killed in bed with their wives; others, running away naked, were pursued by the soldiers through the several rooms of the palace, even to the king's antichamber. The young wife of Henry of Navarre, awaked by the dreadful uproar, being afraid for her consort, and for her own life, seized with horror, and half dead, flew from her bed, in order to throw herself at the feet of the king her brother. But scarce had she opened her chamber-door, when some of her protestant domestics rushed in for refuge. The soldiers immediately followed, pursued them in sight of the princess, and killed one who had crept under her bed. Two others, being wounded with halberds, fell at the queen's feet, so that she was covered with blood.

"Count de la Rochefoucault, a young nobleman, greatly in the king's favour for his comely air, his politeness, and a certain peculiar happiness in the turn of his conversation, had spent the evening till eleven o'clock with the monarch, in pleasant familiarity; and had given a loose, with the utmost mirth, to the sallies of his imagination. The monarch felt some remorse, and being touched with a kind of compassion, bid him, two or three times, not to go home, but lie in the Louvre. The count said, he must go to his wife; upon which the king pressed him no farther, but said, 'Let him go! I see God has decreed his death.' And in two hours after he was murdered.

"Very few of the protestants escaped the fury of their enthusiastic persecutors. Among these was young La Force (afterwards the famous Marshal de la Force) a child about ten years of age, whose deliverance was exceedingly remarkable. His father, his elder brother, and himself were seized together by the Duke of Anjou's soldiers. These murderers flew at all three, and struck them at random, when they all fell, and lay one upon another. The youngest did not receive a single blow, but appearing as if he was dead, escaped the next day; and his life, thus wonderfully preserved, lasted four score and five years.

"Many of the wretched victims fled to the water-side, and some swam over the Seine to the suburbs of St. Germaine. The king saw them from his window, which looked upon the river, and fired upon them with a carbine that had been loaded for that purpose by one of his pages; while the queen-mother, undisturbed and serene in the midst of slaughter, looking down from a balcony, encouraged the murderers and laughed at the dying groans of the slaughtered. This barbarous queen was fired with a restless ambition, and she perpetually shifted her party in order to satiate it.

"Some days after this horrid transaction, the French court endeavoured to palliate it by forms of law. They pretended to justify the massacre by a calumny, and accused the admiral of a conspiracy, which no one believed. The parliament was commanded to proceed against the memory of Coligni; and his dead body was hung in chains on Montfaucon gallows. The king himself went to view this shocking spectacle; when one of his courtiers advising him to retire, and complaining of the stench of the corpse, he replied, 'A dead enemy smells well.'--The massacres on St. Bartholomew's day are painted in the royal saloon of the Vatican at Rome, with the following inscription: **Pontifex** Coligni *necem probat*, i. e. 'The pope approves of Coligni's death.'

"The young king of Navarre was spared through policy, rather than from the pity of the queen-mother, she keeping him prisoner till the king's death, in order that he might be as a security and pledge for the submission of such protestants as might effect their escape.

"This horrid butchery was not confined merely to the city of Paris. The like orders were issued from court to the governors of all the provinces in France; so that, in a week's time, about one hundred thousand protestants were cut to pieces in different parts of the kingdom! Two or three governors only refused to obey the king's orders. One of these, named Montmorrin, governor of Auvergne, wrote the king the following letter, which deserves to be transmitted to the latest posterity.

"SIRE--I have received an order, under your majesty's seal, to put to death all the protestants in my province. I have too much respect for your majesty, not to believe the letter a forgery; but if (which God forbid) the order should be genuine, I have too much respect for your majesty to obey it."

At Rome the horrid joy was so great, that they appointed a day of high festival, and a jubilee, with great indulgence to all who kept it and showed every expression of gladness they could devise! and the man who first carried the news received 1000 crowns of the cardinal of Lorrain for his ungodly message. The king also commanded the day to be kept with every demonstration of joy, concluding now that the whole race of Huguenots was extinct.

Many who gave great sums of money for their ransom were immediately after slain; and several towns, which were under the king's promise of protection and safety, were cut off as soon as they delivered themselves up, on those promises, to his generals or captains.

At Bordeaux, at the instigation of a villanous monk, who used to urge the papists to slaughter in his sermons, 264 were cruelly murdered; some of them senators. Another of the same pious fraternity produced a similar slaughter at Agendicum, in Maine, where the populace at the holy inquisitors' satanical suggestion, ran upon the protestants, slew them, plundered their houses, and pulled down their church.

The duke of Guise, entering into Bloise, suffered his soldiers to fly upon the spoil, and slay or drown all the protestants they could find. In this they spared neither age nor sex; defiling the women, and then murdering them; from whence he went to Mere, and committed the same outrages for many days together. Here they found a minister named Cassebonius, and threw him into the river.

At Anjou, they slew Albiacus, a minister; and many women were defiled and murdered there; among whom were two sisters, abused before their father, whom the assassins bound to a wall to see them, and then slew them and him.

The president of Turin, after giving a large sum for his life, was cruelly beaten with clubs, stripped of his clothes, and hung feet upwards, with his head and breast in the river: before he was dead, they opened his belly, plucked out his entrails, and threw them into the river; and then carried his heart about the city upon a spear.

At Barre great cruelty was used, even to young children, whom they cut open, pulled out their entrails, which through very rage they knawed with their teeth. Those who had fled to the castle, when they yielded, were almost all hanged. Thus they did at the city of Matiscon; counting it sport to cut off their arms and legs and afterward kill them; and for the entertainment of their visiters, they often threw the protestants from a high bridge into the river, saying, "Did you ever see men leap so well?"

At Penna, after promising them safety, 300 were inhumanly butchered; and five and forty at Albin, on the Lord's day. At Nonne, though it yielded on conditions of safeguard, the most horrid spectacles were exhibited. Persons of both sexes and conditions were indiscriminately murdered; the streets ringing with doleful cries, and flowing with blood; and the houses flaming with fire, which the abandoned soldiers had thrown in. One woman, being dragged from her hiding place with her husband, was first abused by the brutal soldiers, and then with a sword which they commanded her to draw, they forced it while in her hands into the bowels of her husband.

At Samarobridge, they murdered above 100 protestants, after promising them peace; and at Antisidor, 100 were killed, and cast part into a jakes, and part into a river. One hundred put into prison at Orleans, were destroyed by the furious multitude.

The protestants at Rochelle, who were such as had miraculously escaped the rage of hell, and fled there, seeing how ill they fared who submitted to those holy devils, stood for their lives; and some other cities, encouraged thereby, did the like. Against Rochelle, the king sent almost the whole power of France, which besieged it seven months, though, by their assaults, they did very little execution on the inhabitants, yet, by famine, they destroyed eighteen thousand out of two and twenty. The dead being too numerous for the living to bury, became food for vermin and carnivorous birds. Many taking their coffins into the church yard, laid down in them, and breathed their last. Their diet had long been what the minds of those in plenty shudder at; even human flesh entrails, dung, and the most loathsome things, became at last the only food of those champions for that truth and liberty, of which the world was not worthy. At every attack, the besiegers met with such an intrepid reception, that they left 132 captains, with a proportionate number of men, dead in the field. The siege at last was broken up at the request of the duke of Anjou, the king's brother, who was proclaimed king of Poland, and the king, being wearied out, easily complied, whereupon honourable conditions were granted them.

It is a remarkable interference of Providence, that, in all this dreadful massacre, not more than two ministers of the gospel were involved in it.

The tragical sufferings of the protestants are too numerous to detail; but the treatment of Philip de Deux will give an idea of the rest. After the miscreants had slain this martyr in his bed, they went to his wife, who was then attended by the midwife, expecting every moment to be delivered. The midwife entreated them to stay the murder, at least till the child, which was the twentieth, should be born. Notwithstanding this, they thrust a dagger up to the hilt into the poor woman. Anxious to be delivered, she ran into a corn loft; but hither they pursued her, stabbed her in the belly, and then threw her into the street. By the fall, the child came from the dying mother, and being caught up by one of the catholic ruffians, he stabbed the infant, and then threw it into the river.

From the Revocation of the Edict of Nantes, to the French Revolution in 1789.

The persecutions occasioned by the revocation of the edict of Nantes, took place under Louis XIV. This edict was made by Henry the Great of France in 1598, and secured to the protestants an equal right in every respect, whether civil or religious, with the other subjects of the realm. All those privileges Louis the XIII. confirmed to the protestants by another statute, called the edict of Nismes, and kept them inviolably to the end of his reign.

On the accession of Louis XIV. the kingdom was almost ruined by civil wars. At this critical juncture, the protestants, heedless of our Lord's admonition, "They that take the sword, shall perish with the sword," took such an active part in favour of the king, that he was constrained to acknowledge himself indebted to their arms for his establishment on the throne. Instead of cherishing and rewarding that party who had fought for him, he reasoned, that the same power which had protected could overturn him, and, listening to the popish machinations, he began to issue out proscriptions and restrictions, indicative of his final determination. Rochelle was presently fettered with an incredible number of denunciations. Montaban and Millau were sacked by soldiers. Popish commissioners were appointed to preside over the affairs of the protestants, and there was no appeal from their ordinance, except to the king's council. This struck at the root of their civil and religious exercises, and prevented them, being protestants, from suing a catholic in any court of law. This was followed by another injunction, to make an inquiry in all parishes into whatever the protestants had said or done for twenty years past. This filled the prisons with innocent victims, and condemned others to the galleys or banishment. Protestants were expelled from all offices, trades, privileges and employs; thereby depriving them of the means of getting their bread: and they proceeded to such excess in their brutality, that they would not suffer even the midwives to officiate, but compelled their women to submit themselves in that crisis of nature to their enemies, the brutal catholics. Their children were taken from them to be educated by the catholics, and at seven years made to embrace popery. The reformed were prohibited from relieving their own sick or poor, from all private worship, and divine service was to be performed in the presence of a popish priest. To prevent the unfortunate victims from leaving the kingdom, all the passages on the frontiers were strictly guarded; yet, by the good hand of God, about 150,000 escaped their vigilance, and emigrated to different countries to relate the dismal narrative.

All that has been related hitherto were only infringements on their established charter, the edict of Nantes. At length the diabolical revocation of that edict passed on the 18th of October, 1685, and was registered the 22d in the vacation, contrary to all form of law. Instantly the dragoons were quartered upon the protestants throughout the realm, and filled all France with the like news, that the king would no longer suffer any Huguenots in his kingdom, and therefore they must resolve to change their religion. Hereupon the intendants in every parish (which were popish governors and spies set over the protestants) assembled the reformed inhabitants, and told them, they must without delay turn catholics, either freely or by force. The protestants replied, "They were ready to sacrifice their lives and estates to the king, but their consciences being God's, they could not so dispose of them."

Instantly the troops seized the gates and avenues of the cities, and placing guards in all the passages, entered with sword in hand, crying, "Die, or be catholics!" In short, they practised every wickedness and horror they could devise, to force them to change their religion.

They hung both men and women by their hair or their feet, and smoked them with hay till they were nearly dead; and if they still refused to sign a recantation, they hung them up again and repeated their barbarities, till, wearied out with torments without death, they forced many to yield to them.

Others, they plucked off all the hair of their heads and beards with pincers. Others they threw on great fires, and pulled them out again, repeating it till they extorted a promise to recant.

Some they stripped naked, and after offering them the most infamous insults, they stuck them with pins from head to foot, and lanced them with penknives; and sometimes with red-hot pincers they dragged them by the nose till they promised to turn. Sometimes they tied fathers and husbands, while they ravished their wives and daughters before their eyes. Multitudes they imprisoned in the most noisome dungeons, where they practised all sorts of torments in secret. Their wives and children they shut up in monasteries.

Such as endeavoured to escape by flight were pursued in the woods and hunted in the fields, and shot at like wild beasts; nor did any condition or quality screen them from the ferocity of these infernal dragoons: even the members of parliament and military officers, though on actual service, were ordered to quit their posts, and repair directly to their houses to suffer the like storm. Such as complained to the king were sent to the Bastile, where they drank of the same cup. The bishops and the intendants marched at the head of the dragoons, with a troop of missionaries, monks, and other ecclesiastics, to animate the soldiers to an execution so agreeable to their holy church, and so glorious to their demon god and their tyrant king.

In forming the edict to repeal the edict of Nantes, the council were divided; some would have all the ministers detained and forced into popery as well as the laity: others were for banishing them, because their presence would strengthen the protestants in perseverance: and if they were forced to turn, they would ever be secret and powerful enemies in the bosom of the church, by their great knowledge and experience in controversial matters. This reason prevailing, they were sentenced to banishment, and only fifteen days allowed them to depart the kingdom.

The same day the edict for revoking the protestant's charter was published, they demolished their churches, and banished their ministers, whom they allowed but twenty-four hours to leave Paris. The papists would not suffer them to dispose of their effects, and threw every obstacle in their way to delay their escape till the limited time was expired which subjected them to condemnation for life to the galleys. The guards were doubled at the seaports, and the prisons were filled with the victims, who endured torments and wants at which human nature must shudder.

The sufferings of the ministers and others, who were sent to the galleys, seemed to exceed all. Chained to the oar, they were exposed to the open air night and day, at all seasons, and in all weathers; and when through weakness of body they fainted under the oar, instead of a cordial to revive them, or viands to refresh them, they received only the lashes of a scourge, or the blows of a cane or rope's end. For the want of sufficient clothing and necessary cleanliness, they were most grievously tormented with vermin, and cruelly pinched with the cold, which removed by night the executioners who beat and tormented them by day. Instead of a bed, they were allowed, sick or well, only a hard board, eighteen inches broad, to sleep on, without any covering but their wretched apparel; which was a shirt of the coarsest canvass, a little jerkin of red serge, slit up each side up to the arm-holes, with open sleeves that reached not to the elbow; and once in three years they had a coarse frock, and a little cap to cover their heads, which were always kept close shaved as a mark of their infamy. The allowance of provision was as narrow as the sentiments of those who condemned them to such miseries, and their treatment when sick is too shocking to relate, doomed to die upon the boards of a dark hold; covered with vermin, and without the least convenience for the calls of nature. Nor was it among the least of the horrors they endured, that, as ministers of Christ, and honest men, they were chained side by side to felons and the most execrable villains, whose blasphemous tongues were never idle. If they refused to hear mass, they were sentenced to the bastinado, of which dreadful punishment the following is a description. Preparatory to it, the chains are taken off, and the victims delivered into the hands of the Turks that preside at the oars, who strip them quite naked, and stretching them upon a great gun, they are held so that they cannot stir; during which there reigns an awful silence throughout the galley. The Turk who is appointed the executioner, and who thinks the sacrifice acceptable to his prophet Mahomet, most cruelly beats the wretched victim with a rough cudgel, or knotty rope's end, till the skin is flayed off his bones, and he is near the point of expiring; then they apply a most tormenting mixture of vinegar and salt, and consign him to that most intolerable hospital where thousands under their cruelties have expired.

Martyrdom of John Calas.

We pass over many other individual martyrdoms to insert that of John Calas, which took place so lately as 1761, and is an indubitable proof of the bigotry of popery, and shows that neither experience nor improvement can root out the inveterate prejudices of the Roman catholics, or render them less cruel or inexorable to protestants.

John Calas was a merchant of the city of Thoulouse, where he had been settled, and lived in good repute, and had married an English woman of French extraction. Calas and his wife were protestants, and had five sons, whom they educated in the same religion; but Lewis, one of the sons, became a Roman catholic, having been converted by a maid-servant, who had lived in the family about thirty years. The father, however, did not express any resentment or ill-will upon the occasion, but kept the maid in the family and settled an annuity upon the son. In October, 1761, the family consisted of John Calas and his wife, one woman servant, Mark Antony Calas, the eldest son, and Peter Calas, the second son. Mark Antony was bred to the law, but could not be admitted to practise, on account of his being a protestant; hence he grew melancholy, read all the books he could procure relative to suicide, and seemed determined to destroy himself. To this may be added, that he led a dissipated life, was greatly addicted to gaming, and did all which could constitute the character of a libertine; on which account his father frequently reprehended him and sometimes in terms of severity, which considerably added to the doom that seemed to oppress him.

On the 13th of October, 1761, Mr. Gober la Vaisse, a young gentleman about 19 years of age, the son of La Vaisse, a celebrated advocate of Thoulouse, about five o'clock in the evening, was met by John Calas, the father, and the eldest son Mark Antony, who was his friend. Calas, the father, invited him to supper, and the family and their guest sat down in a room up one pair of stairs; the whole company, consisting of Calas the father and his wife, Antony and Peter Calas, the sons, and La Vaisse the guest, no other person being in the house, except the maid-servant who has been already mentioned.

It was now about seven o'clock; the super was not long; but before it was over, Antony left the table, and went into the kitchen, which was on the same floor, as he was accustomed to do. The maid asked him if he was cold? He answered, "Quite the contrary, I burn;" and then left her. In the mean time his friend and family left the room they had supped in, and went into a bed-chamber; the father and La Vaisse sat down together on a sofa; the younger son Peter in an elbow chair; and the mother in another chair; and, without making any inquiry after Antony, continued in conversation together till between nine and ten o'clock, when La Vaisse took his leave, and Peter, who had fallen asleep, was awakened to attend him with a light.

On the ground floor of Calas's house was a shop and a ware-house, the latter of which was divided from the shop by a pair of folding-doors. When Peter Calas and La Vaisse came down stairs into the shop, they were extremely shocked to see Antony hanging in his shirt, from a bar which he had laid across the top of the two folding-doors, having half opened them for that purpose. On discovery of this horrid spectacle, they shrieked out, which brought down Calas the father, the mother being seized with such terror as kept her trembling in the passage above. When the maid discovered what had happened, she continued below, either because she feared to carry an account of it to her mistress, or because she busied herself in doing some good office to her master, who was embracing the body of his son, and bathing it in his tears. The mother, therefore, being thus left alone, went down and mixed in the scene that has been already described, with such emotions as it must naturally produce. In the mean time Peter had been sent for La Moire, a surgeon in the neighbourhood. La Moire was not at home, but his apprentice, Mr. Grosle, came instantly. Upon examination, he found the body quite dead; and by this time a papistical crowd of people were gathered about the house, and, having by some means heard that Antony Calas was suddenly dead, and that the surgeon who had examined the body, declared that he had been strangled, they took it into their heads he had been murdered; and as the family was protestant, they presently supposed that the young man was about to change his religion, and had been put to death for that reason.

The poor father, overwhelmed with grief for the loss of his child, was advised by his friends to send for the officers of justice to prevent his being torn to pieces by the catholic multitude, who supposed he had murdered his son. This was accordingly done, and David, the chief magistrate, or capitoul, took the father, Peter the son, the mother, La Vaisse, and the maid, all into custody, and set a guard over them. He sent for M. de la Tour, a physician, and MM. la Marque and Perronet, surgeons, who examined the body for marks of violence, but found none except the mark of the ligature on the neck; they found also the hair of the deceased done up in the usual manner, perfectly smooth, and without the least disorder; his clothes were also regularly folded up, and laid upon the counter, nor was his shirt either torn or unbuttoned.

Notwithstanding these innocent appearances, the capitoul thought proper to agree with the opinion of the mob, and took it into his head that old Calas had sent for La Vaisse, telling him that he had a son to be hanged; that La Vaisse had come to perform the office of executioner: and that he had received assistance from the father and brother.

As no proof of the supposed fact could be procured, the capitoul had recourse to a monitory, or general information, in which the crime was taken for granted, and persons were required to give such testimony against it as they were able. This recites, that La Vaisse was commissioned by the protestants to be their executioner in ordinary, when any of their children were to be hanged for changing their religion; it recites also, that, when the protestants thus hang their children, they compel them to kneel, and one of the interrogatories was whether any person had seen Antony Calas kneel before his father when he strangled him; it recites likewise, that Antony died a Roman catholic, and requires evidence of his catholicism.

But before this monitory was published, the mob had got a notion that Antony Calas was the next day to have entered into the fraternity of the White Penitents. The capitoul therefore caused his body to be buried in the middle of St. Stephen's church. A few days after the interment of the deceased, the White Penitents performed a solemn service for him in their chapel; the church was hung with white, and a tomb was raised in the middle of it, on the top of which was placed a human skeleton, holding in one hand a paper, on which was written, "Abjuration of heresy," and in the other a palm, the emblem of martyrdom. The next day the Franciscans performed a service of the same kind for him.

The capitoul continued the persecution with unrelenting severity, and, without the least proof coming in, thought fit to condemn the unhappy father, mother, brother, friend, and servant, to the torture, and put them all into irons on the 18th of November.

From these dreadful proceedings the sufferers appealed to the parliament, which immediately took cognizance of the affair, and annulled the sentence of the capitoul as irregular, but they continued the prosecution, and, upon the hangman deposing it was impossible Antony should hang himself as was pretended, the majority of the parliament were of the opinion, that the prisoners were guilty, and therefore ordered them to be tried by the criminal court of Thoulouse. One voted him innocent, but after long debates the majority was for the torture and wheel, and probably condemned the father by way of experiment, whether he was guilty or not, hoping he would, in the agony, confess the crime, and accuse the other prisoners, whose fate therefore, they suspended.

Poor Calas, however, an old man of 68, was condemned to this dreadful punishment alone. He suffered the torture with great constancy, and was led to execution in a frame of mind which excited the admiration of all that saw him, and particularly of the two Dominicans (father Bourges and father Coldagues) who attended him in his last moments, and declared that they thought him not only innocent of the crime laid to his charge, but an exemplary instance of true christian patience, fortitude, and charity. When he saw the executioner prepared to give him the last stroke, he made a fresh declaration to father Bourges, but while the words were still in his mouth, the capitoul, the author of this catastrophe, and who came upon the scaffold merely to gratify his desire of being a witness of his punishment and death, ran up to him, and bawled out, "Wretch, there are the fagots which are to reduce your body to ashes! speak the truth." M. Calas made no reply, but turned his head a little aside, and that moment the executioner did his office.

The popular outcry against this family was so violent in Languedoc, that every body expected to see the children of Calas broke upon the wheel, and the mother burnt alive.

Young Donat Calas was advised to fly into Switzerland: he went, and found a gentleman who, at first, could only pity and relieve him, without daring to judge of the rigour exercised against the father, mother, and brothers. Soon after, one of the brothers, who was only banished, likewise threw himself into the arms of the same person, who, for more than a month, took every possible precaution to be assured of the innocence of the family. Once convinced, he thought himself obliged, in conscience, to employ his friends, his purse, his pen, and his credit, to repair the fatal mistake of the seven judges of Thoulouse, and to have the proceedings revised by the king's council. This revision lasted three years, and it is well known what honour Messrs. de Grosne and Bacquancourt acquired by investigating this memorable cause. Fifty masters of the Court of Requests unanimously declared the whole family of Calas innocent, and recommended them to the benevolent justice of his majesty. The duke de Choiseul, who never let slip an opportunity of signalizing the greatness of his character, not only assisted this unfortunate family with money, but obtained for them a gratuity of 36,000 livres from the king.

On the ninth of March, 1765, the arret was signed which justified the family of Calas, and changed their fate. The ninth of March, 1762, was the very day on which the innocent and virtuous father of that family had been executed. All Paris ran in crowds to see them come out of prison, and clapped their hands for joy while the tears streamed from their eyes.

This dreadful example of bigotry employed the pen of Voltaire in deprecation of the horrors of superstition; and though an infidel himself, his essay on toleration does honour to his pen, and has been a blessed means of abating the rigour of persecution in most European states. Gospel purity will equally shun superstition and cruelty, as the mildness of Christ's tenets teaches only to comfort in this world, and to procure salvation in the next. To persecute for being of a different opinion, is as absurd as to persecute for having a different countenance: if we honour God, keep sacred the pure doctrines of Christ, put a full confidence in the promises contained in the holy scriptures, and obey the political laws of the state in which we reside, we have an undoubted right to protection instead of persecution, and to serve heaven as our consciences, regulated by the gospel rules, may direct.

CHAPTER V.

AN ACCOUNT OF THE INQUISITION.

When the reformed religion began to diffuse the gospel light throughout church. He accordingly instituted a number of inquisitors, or persons who were to make inquiry after, apprehend, and punish, heretics, as the reformed were called by the papists.

At the head of these inquisitors was one Dominic, who had been canonized by the pope, in order to render his authority the more respectable. Dominic, and the other inquisitors, spread themselves into various Roman catholic countries, and treated the protestants with the utmost severity. In process of time, the pope, not finding these roving inquisitors so useful as he had imagined, resolved upon the establishment of fixed and regular courts of inquisition. After the order for these regular courts, the first office of inquisition was established in the city of Thoulouse, and Dominic became the first regular inquisitor, as he had before been the first roving inquisitor.

Courts of inquisition were now erected in several countries; but the Spanish inquisition became the most powerful, and the most dreaded of any. Even the kings of Spain themselves, though arbitrary in all other respects, were taught to dread the power of the lords of the inquisition; and the horrid cruelties they exercised compelled multitudes, who differed in opinion from the Roman catholics, carefully to conceal their sentiments.

The most zealous of all the popish monks, and those who most implicitly obeyed the church of Rome, were the Dominicans and Franciscans: these, therefore, the pope thought proper to invest with an exclusive right of presiding over the different court of inquisition, and gave them the most unlimited powers, as judges delegated by him, and immediately representing his person: they were permitted to excommunicate, or sentence to death whom they thought proper, upon the most slight information of heresy. They were allowed to publish crusades against all whom they deemed heretics, and enter into leagues with sovereign princes, to join their crusades with their forces.

In 1244, their power was farther increased by the emperor Frederic the Second, who declared himself the protector and friend of all the inquisitors, and published the cruel edicts, viz. 1. That all heretics who continued obstinate, should be burnt. 2. That all heretics who repented, should be imprisoned for life.

This zeal in the emperor, for the inquisitors of the Roman catholic persuasion, arose from a report which had been propagated throughout Europe, that he intended to renounce christianity, and turn Mahometan; the emperor therefore, attempted, by the height of bigotry to contradict the report, and to show his attachment to popery by cruelty.

The officers of the inquisition are three inquisitors, or judges, a fiscal proctor, two secretaries, a magistrate, a messenger, a receiver, a jailer, an agent of confiscated possessions; several assessors, counsellors, executioners, physicians, surgeons, door-keepers, familiars, and visiters, who are sworn to secrecy.

The principal accusation against those who are subject to this tribunal is heresy, which comprises all that is spoken, or written, against any of the articles of the creed, or the traditions of the Roman church. The inquisition likewise takes cognizance of such as are accused of being magicians, and of such who read the bible in the common language, the Talmud of the Jews, or the Alcoran of the Mahometans.

Upon all occasions the inquisitors carry on their processes with the utmost severity, and punish those who offend them with the most unparalleled cruelty. A protestant has seldom any mercy shown him, and a Jew, who turns christian, is far from being secure.

A defence in the inquisition is of little use to the prisoner, for a suspicion only is deemed sufficient cause of condemnation, and the greater his wealth the greater his danger. The principal part of the inquisitors' cruelties is owing to their rapacity: they destroy the life to possess the property; and, under the pretence of zeal, plunder each obnoxious individual.

A prisoner in the inquisition is never allowed to see the face of his accuser, or of the witnesses against him, but every method is taken by threats and tortures, to oblige him to accuse himself, and by that means corroborate their evidence. If the jurisdiction of the inquisition is not fully allowed, vengeance is denounced against such as call it in question for if any of its officers are opposed, those who oppose them are almost certain to be sufferers for their temerity; the maxim of the inquisition being to strike terror, and awe those who are the objects of its power into obedience. High birth, distinguished rank, great dignity, or eminent employments, are no protection from its severities; and the lowest officers of the inquisition can make the highest characters tremble.

When the person impeached is condemned, he is either severely whipped, violently tortured, sent to the galleys, or sentenced to death; and in either case the effects are confiscated. After judgment, a procession is performed to the place of execution, which ceremony is called an AUTO DE FE, or act of faith.

The following is an account of an auto de fe, performed at Madrid in the year 1682.

The officers of the inquisition, preceded by trumpets, kettle-drums, and their banner, marched on the 30th of May, in cavalcade, to the palace of the great square, where they declared by proclamation, that, on the 30th of June, the sentence of the prisoners would be put in execution.

Of these prisoners, twenty men and women, with one renegade Mahometan, were ordered to be burned; fifty Jews and Jewesses, having never before been imprisoned, and repenting of their crimes were sentenced to a long confinement, and to wear a yellow cap. The whole court of Spain was present on this occasion. The grand inquisitor's chair was placed in a sort of tribunal far above that of the king.

Among those who were to suffer, was a young Jewess of exquisite beauty, and but seventeen years of age. Being on the same side of the scaffold where the queen was seated, she addressed her, in hopes of obtaining a pardon, in the following pathetic speech: "Great queen, will not your royal presence be of some service to the in my miserable condition! Have regard to my youth; and, oh! consider, that I am about to die for professing a religion imbibed from my earliest infancy!" Her majesty seemed greatly to pity her distress, but turned away her eyes, as she did not dare to speak a word in behalf of a person who had been declared a heretic.

Now mass began, in the midst of which the priest came from the altar, placed himself near the scaffold, and seated himself in a chair prepared for that purpose.

The chief inquisitor then descended from the amphitheatre, dressed in his cope, and having a mitre on his head. After having bowed to the altar, he advanced towards the king's balcony, and went up to it, attended by some of his officers, carrying a cross and the gospels, with a book containing the oath by which the kings of Spain oblige themselves to protect the catholic faith, to extirpate heretics, and to support with all their power and force the prosecutions and decrees of the inquisition: a like oath was administered to the counsellors and whole assembly. The mass was begun about twelve at noon, and did not end till nine in the evening, being protracted by a proclamation of the sentences of the several criminals, which were already separately rehearsed aloud one after the other.

After this, followed the burning of the twenty-one men and women, whose intrepidity in suffering that horrid death was truly astonishing. The king's near situation to the criminals rendered their dying groans very audible to him; he could not, however, be absent from this dreadful scene, as it is esteemed a religious one; and his coronation oath obliges him to give a sanction by his presence to all the acts of the tribunal.

What we have already said may be applied to inquisitions in general, as well as to that of Spain in particular. The inquisition belonging to Portugal is exactly upon a similar plan to that of Spain, having been instituted much about the same time, and put under the same regulations. The inquisitors allow the torture to be used only three times, but during those times it is so severely inflicted, that the prisoner either dies under it, or continues always after a cripple, and suffers the severest pains upon every change of weather. We shall give an ample description of the severe torments occasioned by the torture, from the account of one who suffered it the three respective times, but happily survived the cruelties he underwent.

At the first time of torturing, six executioners entered, stripped him naked to his drawers, and laid him upon his back on a kind of stand, elevated a few feet from the floor. The operation commenced by putting an iron collar round his neck, and a ring to each foot, which fastened him to the stand. His limbs being thus stretched out, they wound two ropes round each thigh; which ropes being passed under the scaffold, through holes made for that purpose, were all drawn tight at the same instant of time, by four of the men, on a given signal.

It is easy to conceive that the pains which immediately succeeded were intolerable; the ropes, which were of a small size, cut through the prisoner's flesh to the bone, making the blood to gush out at eight different places thus bound at a time. As the prisoner persisted in not making any confession of what the inquisitors required, the ropes were drawn in this manner four times successively.

The manner of inflicting the second torture was as follows: they forced his arms backwards so that the palms of his hands were turned outward behind him; when, by means of a rope that fastened them together at the wrists, and which was turned by an engine, they drew them by degrees nearer each other, in such a manner that the back of each hand touched, and stood exactly parallel to each other. In consequence of this violent contortion, both his shoulders became dislocated, and a considerable quantity of blood issued from his mouth. This torture was repeated thrice; after which he was again taken to the dungeon, and the surgeon set the dislocated bones.

Two months after the second torture, the prisoner being a little recovered, was again ordered to the torture-room, and there, for the last time, made to undergo another kind of punishment, which was inflicted twice without any intermission. The executioners fastened a thick iron chain round his body, which crossing at the breast, terminated at the wrists. They then placed him with his back against a thick board, at each extremity whereof was a pulley, through which there ran a rope that caught the end of the chain at his wrists. The executioner then, stretching the end of this rope by means of a roller, placed at a distance behind him, pressed or bruised his stomach in proportion as the ends of the chains were drawn tighter. They tortured him in this manner to such a degree, that his wrists, as well as his shoulders, were quite dislocated. They were, however, soon set by the surgeons; but the barbarians, not yet satisfied with this species of cruelty, made him immediately undergo the like torture a second time, which he sustained (though, if possible, attended with keener pains,) with equal constancy and resolution. After this, he was again remanded to his dungeon, attended by the surgeon to dress his bruises and adjust the part dislocated, and here he continued till their Auto de Fe, or jail delivery, when he was discharged, crippled and diseased for life.

An account of the cruel Handling and Burning of Nicholas Burton, an English Merchant, in Spain.

The fifth day of November, about the year of our Lord 1560, Mr. Nicholas Burton, citizen sometime of London, and merchant, dwelling in the parish of Little St. Bartholomew, peaceably and quietly following his traffic in the trade of merchandize, and being in the city of Cadiz, in the party of Andalusia, in Spain, there came into his lodging a Judas, or, as they term them, a familiar of the fathers of the inquisition; who asking for the said Nicholas Burton, feigned that he had a letter to deliver into his own hands; by which means he spake with him immediately. And having no letter to deliver to him, then the said promoter, or familiar, at the motion of the devil his master, whose messenger he was, invented another lie, and said, that he would take lading for London in such ships as the said Nicholas Burton had freighted to lade, if he would let any; which was partly to know where he loaded his goods, that they might attach them, and chiefly to protract the time until the sergeant of the inquisition might come and apprehend the body of the said Nicholas Burton; which they did incontinently.

He then well perceiving that they were not able to burden or charge him that he had written, spoke, or done any thing there in that country against the ecclesiastical or temporal laws of the same realm, boldly asked them what they had to lay to his charge that they did so arrest him, and bade them to declare the cause, and he would answer them. Notwithstanding they answered nothing, but commanded him with threatening words to hold his peace, and not speak one word to them.

And so they carried him to the filthy common prison of the town of Cadiz, where he remained in irons fourteen days amongst thieves.

All which time he so instructed the poor prisoners in the word of God, according to the good talent which God had given him in that behalf, and also in the Spanish tongue to utter the same, that in that short space he had well reclaimed several of those superstitious and ignorant Spaniards to embrace the word of God, and to reject their popish traditions.

Which being known unto the officers of the inquisition, they conveyed him laden with irons from thence to a city called Seville, into a more cruel and straiter prison called Triana, where the said fathers of the inquisition proceeded against him secretly according to their accustomable cruel tyranny, that never after he could be suffered to write or speak to any of his nation: so that to this day it is unknown who was his accuser.

Afterward, the 20th of December, they brought the said Nicholas Burton,

with a great number of other prisoners, for professing the true
Christian religion, into the city of Seville, to a place where the said
inquisitors sat in judgment which they called Auto, with a canvass coat,
whereupon in divers parts was painted the figure of a huge devil,
tormenting a soul in a flame of fire, and on his head a copping tank of
the same work.

His tongue was forced out of his mouth with a cloven stick fastened upon
it, that he should not utter his conscience and faith to the people, and
so he was set with another Englishman of Southampton, and divers other
condemned men for religion, as well Frenchmen as Spaniards, upon a
scaffold over against the said inquisition, where their sentences and
judgments were read and pronounced against them.

And immediately after the said sentences given, they were carried from
thence to the place of execution without the city, where they most
cruelly burned them, for whose constant faith, God be praised.

This Nicholas Burton by the way, and in the flames of fire, had so
cheerful a countenance, embracing death with all patience and gladness,
that the tormentors and enemies which stood by, said, that the devil had
his soul before he came to the fire; and therefore they said his senses
of feeling were past him.

It happened that after the arrest of Nicholas Burton aforesaid,
immediately all the goods and merchandize which he brought with him into
Spain by the way of traffic, were (according to their common usage)
seized, and taken into the sequester; among which they also rolled up
much that appertained to another English merchant, wherewith he was
credited as factor. Whereof so soon as news was brought to the merchant
as well of the imprisonment of his factor, as of the arrest made upon
his goods, he sent his attorney into Spain, with authority from him to
make claim to his goods, and to demand them; whose name was John
Fronton, citizen of Bristol.

When his attorney was landed at Seville, and had shown all his letters
and writings to the holy house, requiring them that such goods might be
delivered into his possession, answer was made to him that he must sue
by bill, and retain an advocate (but all was doubtless to delay him,)
and they forsooth of courtesy assigned him one to frame his supplication
for him, and other such bills of petition, as he had to exhibit into
their holy court, demanding for each bill eight rials, albeit they stood
him in no more stead than if he had put up none at all. And for the
space of three or four months this fellow missed not twice a day

attending every morning and afternoon at the inquisitors' palace, suing unto them upon his knees for his despatch, but especially to the bishop of Tarracon, who was at that very time chief in the inquisition at Seville, that he of his absolute authority would command restitution to be made thereof; but the booty was so good and great, that it was very hard to come by it again.

At length, after he had spent four whole months in suits and requests, and also to no purpose, he received this answer from them, That he must show better evidence, and bring more sufficient certificates out of England for proof of this matter, than those which he had already presented to the court. Whereupon the party forthwith posted to London, and with all speed returned to Seville again with more ample and large letters testimonial, and certificates, according to their requests, and exhibited them to the court.

Notwithstanding the inquisitors still shifted him off, excusing themselves by lack of leisure, and for that they were occupied in more weighty affairs, and with such answers put him off, four months after.

At last, when the party had well nigh spent all his money, and therefore sued the more earnestly for his despatch, they referred the matter wholly to the bishop. Of whom, when he repaired unto him, he made this answer, That for himself, he knew what he had to do, howbeit he was but one man, and the determination appertained to the other commissioners as well as unto him; and thus by posting and passing it from one to another, the party could obtain no end of his suit. Yet for his importunity's sake, they were resolved to despatch him: it was on this sort: one of the inquisitors, called Gasco, a man very well experienced in these practices, willed the party to resort unto him after dinner.

The fellow being glad to hear this news, and supposing that his goods should be restored unto him, and that he was called in for that purpose to talk with the other that was in prison to confer with him about their accounts, rather through a little misunderstanding, hearing the inquisitors cast out a word, that it should be needful for him to talk with the prisoner, and being thereupon more than half persuaded, that at length they meant good faith, did so, and repaired thither about the evening. Immediately upon his coming, the jailer was forthwith charged with him, to shut him up close in such a prison where they appointed him.

The party, hoping at the first that he had been called for about some other matter, and seeing himself, contrary to his expectation, cast into a dark dungeon, perceived at length that the world went with him far otherwise than he supposed it would have done.

But within two or three days after, he was brought into the court where he began to demand his goods: and because it was a device that well served their turn without any more circumstance, they bid him say his Ave Maria; "Ave Maria gratia plena, Dominus tecum, benedicta tu in mulieribus, et benedictus fructus ventris tui Jesus. Amen."

The same was written word by word as he spake it, and without any more talk of claiming his goods, because it was needless, they commanded him to prison again, and entered an action against him as a heretic, forasmuch as he did not say his Ave Maria after the Romish fashion, but ended it very suspiciously, for he should have added moreover; "Sancta Maria mater Dei, ora pro nobis peccatoribus:" by abbreviating whereof, it was evident enough (said they) that he did not allow the mediation of saints.

Thus they picked a quarrel to detain him in prison a longer season, and afterward brought him forth upon their stage disguised after their manner; where sentence was given, that he should lose all the goods which he sued for, though they were not his own, and besides this, suffer a year's imprisonment.

Mark Brughes, an Englishman, master of an English ship called the Minion, was burnt in a city in Portugal.

William Hoker, a young man about the age of sixteen years, being an Englishman, was stoned to death by certain young men in the city of Seville, for the same righteous cause.

Some private Enormities of the inquisition laid open, by a very singular occurrence.

When the crown of Spain was contested for in the beginning of the present century, by two princes, who equally pretended to the sovereignty, France espoused the cause of one competitor, and England of the other.

The duke of Berwick, a natural son of James II. who abdicated England, commanded the Spanish and French forces, and defeated the English at the celebrated battle of Almanza. The army was then divided into two parts; the one consisting of Spaniards and French, headed by the duke of

Berwick, advanced towards Catalonia; the other body, consisting of French troops only, commanded by the duke of Orleans, proceeded to the conquest of Arragon.

As the troops drew near to the city of Arragon, the magistrates came to offer the keys to the duke of Orleans; but he told them, haughtily, they were rebels, and that he would not accept the keys, for he had orders to enter the city through a breach.

He accordingly made a breach in the walls with his cannon, and then entered the city through it, together with his whole army.--When he had made every necessary regulation here, he departed to subdue other places, leaving a strong garrison at once to overawe and defend, under the command of his lieutenant-general M. de Legal. This gentleman, though brought up a Roman catholic, was totally free from superstition: he united great talents with great bravery: and was, at once, the skilful officer, and accomplished gentleman.

The duke, before his departure, had ordered that heavy contributions should be levied upon the city to the following manner:

1. That the magistrates and principal inhabitants should pay a thousand crowns per month for the duke's table.

2. That every house should pay one pistole, which would monthly amount to 18,000 pistoles.

3. That every convent and monastery should pay a donative, proportionable to its riches and rents.

The two last contributions to be appropriated to the maintenance of the army.

The money levied upon the magistrates and principal inhabitants, and upon every house, was paid as soon as demanded; but when the proper persons applied to the heads of convents and monasteries, they found that the ecclesiastics were not so willing, as other people, to part with their cash.

Of the donatives to be raised by the clergy:

The college of Jesuits to pay	2000 pistoles
Carmelites,	1000
Augustins,	1000
Dominicans	1000

M. de Legal sent to the Jesuits a peremptory order to pay the money immediately. The superior of the Jesuits returned for answer, that for the clergy to pay money for the army was against all ecclesiastical immunities; and that he knew of no argument which could authorize such a procedure. M. de Legal then sent four companies of dragoons to quarter themselves in the college, with this sarcastic message, "To convince you of the necessity of paying the money, I have sent four substantial arguments to your college, drawn from the system of military logic; and, therefore, hope you will not need any further admonition to direct your conduct."

These proceedings greatly perplexed the Jesuits, who despatched an express to court to the king's confessor, who was of their order; but the dragoons were much more expeditious in plundering and doing mischief, than the courier in his journey: so that the Jesuits, seeing every thing going to wreck and ruin, thought proper to adjust the matter amicably, and paid the money before the return of their messenger. The Augustins and Carmelites, taking warning by what had happened to the Jesuits, prudently went and paid the money, and by that means escaped the study of military arguments, and of being taught logic by dragoons.

But the Dominicans, who were all familiars of, or agents dependent on, the inquisition, imagined, that that very circumstance would be their protection; but they were mistaken, for M. de Legal neither feared nor respected the inquisition. The chief of the Dominicans sent word to the military commander that his order was poor, and had not any money whatever to pay the donative; for, says he, the whole wealth of the Dominicans consists only in the silver images of the apostles and saints, as large as life, which are placed in our church, and which it would be sacrilege to remove.

This insinuation was meant to terrify the French commander, whom the inquisitors imagined would not dare to be so profane as to wish for the possession of the precious idols.

He, however, sent word that the silver images would make admirable substitutes for money, and would be more in character in his possession, than in that of the Dominicans themselves, "For, (said he) while you possess them in the manner you do at present, they stand up in niches, useless and motionless, without being of the least benefit to mankind in general, or even to yourselves; but, when they come into my possession, they shall be useful; I will put them in motion; for I intend to have them coined, when they may travel like the apostles, be beneficial in various places, and circulate for the universal service of mankind."

The inquisitors were astonished at this treatment, which they never expected to receive, even from crowned heads; they therefore determined to deliver their precious images in a solemn procession, that they might excite the people to an insurrection. The Dominican friars were accordingly ordered to march to De Legal's house, with the silver apostles and saints, in a mournful manner, having lighted tapers with them, and bitterly crying all the way, heresy, heresy.

M. de Legal, hearing these proceedings, ordered four companies of grenadiers to line the street which led to his house; each grenadier was ordered to have his loaded fuzee in one hand, and a lighted taper in the other; so that the troops might either repel force with force, or do honour to the farcical solemnity.

The friars did all they could to raise the tumult, but the common people were too much afraid of the troops under arms to obey them, the silver images were, therefore, of necessity delivered up to M. de Legal, who sent them to the mint, and ordered them to be coined immediately.

The project of raising an insurrection having failed, the inquisitors determined to excommunicate M. de Legal, unless he would release their precious silver saints from imprisonment in the mint, before they were melted down, or otherwise mutilated. The French commander absolutely refused to release the images, but said they should certainly travel and do good; upon which the inquisitors drew up the form of excommunication, and ordered their secretary to go and read it to M. De Legal.

The secretary punctually performed his commission, and read the excommunication deliberately and distinctly. The French commander heard it with great patience, and politely told the secretary he would answer it the next day.

When the secretary of the inquisition was gone, M. De Legal ordered his own secretary to prepare a form of excommunication, exactly like that sent by the inquisition; but to make this alteration, instead of his name to put in those of the inquisitors.

The next morning he ordered four regiments under arms, and commanded them to accompany his secretary, and act as he directed.

The secretary went to the inquisition, and insisted upon admittance, which, after a great deal of altercation, was granted. As soon as he entered, he read, in an audible voice, the excommunication sent by M. De Legal against the inquisitors. The inquisitors were all present, and heard it with astonishment, never having before met with any individual who dared behave so boldly. They loudly cried out against De Legal, as a heretic; and said, this was a most daring insult against the catholic faith. But, to surprise them still more, the French secretary told them, they must remove from their present lodgings; for the French commander wanted to quarter the troops in the inquisition, as it was the most commodious place in the whole city.

The inquisitors exclaimed loudly upon this occasion, when the secretary put them under a strong guard, and sent them to a place appointed by M. De Legal to receive them. The inquisitors, finding how things went, begged that they might be permitted to take their private property, which was granted, and they immediately set out for Madrid, where they made the most bitter complaints to the king; but the monarch told them, he could not grant them any redress, as the injuries they had received were from his grandfather, the king of France's troops, by whose assistance alone he could be firmly established in his kingdom. "Had it been my own troops, (said he) I would have punished them; but as it is, I cannot pretend to exert any authority."

In the mean time, M. De Legal's secretary set open all the doors of the inquisition, and released the prisoners, who amounted in the whole to 400; and among these were 60 beautiful young women, who appeared to form a seraglio for the three principal inquisitors.

This discovery, which laid the enormity of the inquisitors so open, greatly alarmed the archbishop, who desired M. De Legal to send the women to his palace, and he would take proper care of them; and at the same time he published an ecclesiastical censure against all such as should ridicule, or blame, the holy office of the inquisition.

The French commander sent word to the archbishop, that the prisoners had either run away, or were so securely concealed by their friends, or even by his own officers, that it was impossible for him to send them back again; and, therefore, the inquisition having committed such atrocious actions, must now put up with their exposure.

One of the ladies thus happily delivered from captivity, was afterward married to the very French officer who opened the door of her dungeon, and released her from confinement. The lady related the following circumstances to her husband, and to M. Gavin, (author of the Master Key to Popery) from the latter of whom we have selected the most material particulars.

"I went one day (says the lady) with my mother, to visit the countess Attarass, and I met there Don Francisco Tirregon, her confessor and second inquisitor of the holy office.

After we had drunk chocolate, he asked me my age, my confessor's name, and many intricate questions about religion. The severity of his countenance frightened me, which he perceiving, told the countess to inform me, that he was not so severe as he looked for. He then caressed me in a most obliging manner, presented his hand, which I kissed with great reverence and modesty; and, as he went away, he made use of this remarkable expression. My dear child, I shall remember you till the next time. I did not, at the time, mark the sense of the words; for I was inexperienced in matters of gallantry, being, at that time but fifteen years old. Indeed, he unfortunately did remember me, for the very same night, when our whole family were in bed, we heard a great knocking at the door.

The maid, who laid in the same room with me, went to the window, and inquired who was there. The answer was, THE HOLY INQUISITION. On hearing this I screamed out, Father! father! dear father, I am ruined forever! My father got up, and came to me to know the occasion of my crying out; I told him the inquisitors were at the door. On hearing this, instead of protecting me, he hurried down stairs as fast as possible; and, lest the maid should be too slow, opened the street door himself; under such abject and slavish fears, are bigoted minds! as soon as he knew they came for me, he fetched me with great solemnity, and delivered me to the officers with much submission.

I was hurried into a coach, with no other clothing than a petticoat and a mantle, for they would not let me stay to take any thing else. My fright was so great, I expected to die that very night; but judge my surprise, when I was ushered into an apartment, decorated with all the elegance that taste, united with opulence, could bestow.

Soon after the officers left me, a maid servant appeared with a silver salver, on which were sweetmeats and cinnamon water. She desired me to take some refreshment before I went to bed; I told her I could not, but should be glad if she could inform me whether I was to be put to death that night or not.

"To be put to death! (exclaimed she) you do not come here to be put to death, but to live like a princess, and you shall want for nothing in the world, but the liberty of going out; so pray don't be afraid, but go to bed and sleep easy; for to-morrow you shall see wonders within this house; and as I am chosen to be your waiting-maid, I hope you'll be very kind to me."

I was going to ask some questions, but she told me she must not answer any thing more till the next day, but assured me that nobody would come to disturb me. I am going, she said, about a little business but I will come back presently, for my bed is in the closet next yours, so she left me for about a quarter of an hour, and then returned. She then said, madam, pray let me know when you will be pleased have your chocolate ready in the morning.

This greatly surprised me, so that without replying to her question, I asked her name;--she said, my name is Mary. Mary, then, said I, for heaven's sake, tell me whether I am brought here to die or not?--I have told you already, replied she, that you came here to be one of the happiest ladies in the world.

We went to bed, but the fear of death prevented me from sleeping the whole night; Mary waked; she was surprised to find me up, but she soon rose, and after leaving me for about half an hour, she brought in two cups of chocolate, and some biscuit on a silver plate.

I drank one cup of chocolate, and desired her to drink the other, which she did: when we had done, I said, well, Mary, can you give me any account of the reasons for my being brought here? To which she answered, not yet, madam, you must have patience, and immediately slipped out of the room.

About half an hour after, she brought a great quantity of elegant clothes, suitable to a lady of the highest rank, and told me, I must dress myself. Among several trinkets which accompanied the clothes, I observed, with surprise, a snuff box, in the lid of which was a picture of Don Francisco Tirregon. This unravelled to me the mystery of my confinement, and at the same time roused my imagination to contrive how to evade receiving the present. If I absolutely refused it, I thought immediate death must ensue; and to accept it, was giving him too much encouragement against my honour. At length I hit upon a medium, and said to Mary, pray present my respects to Don Francisco Tirregon, and tell him, that, as I could not bring my clothes along with me last night, modesty permits me to accept of these garments, which are requisite to keep me decent; but since I do not take snuff, I hope his lordship will excuse me in not accepting his box.

Mary went with my answer, and soon returned with Don Francisco's portrait elegantly set in gold, and richly embellished with diamonds. This message accompanied it: "That his lordship had made a mistake, his intent not being to send me a snuffbox, but his portrait." I was at a great loss what to do; when Mary said, pray, madam, take my poor advice; accept of the portrait, and every thing else that his lordship sends you; for if you do not, he can compel you to do what he pleases, and put you to death when he thinks proper, without any body being able to defend you. But if you are obliging to him, continued she, he will be very kind, and you will be as happy as a queen; you will have elegant apartments to live in, beautiful gardens to range in, and agreeable ladies to visit you: therefore, I advise you to send a civil answer, or even not to deny a visit from his lordship, or perhaps you may repent of your disrespect.

O, my God! exclaimed I, must I sacrifice my honour to my fears, and give up my virtue to his despotic power? Alas! what can I do? To resist, is vain. If I oppose his desires, force will obtain what chastity refuses. I now fell into the greatest agonies, and told Mary to return what answer she thought proper.

She said she was glad of my humble submission, and ran to acquaint Don Francisco with it. In a few minutes she returned, with joy in her countenance, telling me his lordship would honour me with his company to supper. "And now give me leave, madam, (said she) to call you mistress, for I am to wait upon you. I have been in a holy office fourteen years, and know all the customs perfectly well; but as silence is imposed upon me, under pain of death, I can only answer such questions as immediately relate to your own person. But I would advise you never to oppose the holy father's will; or if you see any young ladies about, never ask them any questions. You may divert yourself sometimes among them, but must never tell them any thing: three days hence you will dine with them; and at all times you may have music, and other recreations. In fine, you will be so happy, that you will not wish to go abroad; and when your time is expired, the holy fathers will send you out of this country, and marry you to some nobleman." After saying these words she left me, overwhelmed with astonishment, and scarce knowing what to think. As soon as I recovered myself, I began to look about, and finding a closet, I opened it, and perceived that it was filled with books: they ware chiefly upon historical and profane subjects, but not any on religious matter. I chose out a book of history, and so passed the interval with some degree of satisfaction till dinner time.

The dinner was served up with the greatest elegance, and consisted of all that could gratify the most luxurious appetite. When dinner was over, Mary left me, and told me, if I wanted any thing I might ring a bell, which she pointed out to me.

I read a book to amuse myself during the afternoon, and at seven in the evening, Don Francisco came to visit me in his night-gown and cap, not with the gravity of an inquisitor, but with the gayety of a gallant.

He saluted me with great respect, and told me, that he came to see me in order to show the great respect he had for my family, and to inform me that it was my lovers who had procured my confinement, having accused me in matters of religion; and that the informations were taken, and the sentence pronounced against me, to be burnt in a dry pan, with a gradual fire; but that he, out of pity and love to my family, had stopped the execution of it.

These words were like daggers to my heart; I dropped at his feet, and said, "Ah, my lord! have you stopped the execution for ever?" He replied, "that belongs to yourself only," and abruptly wished me good night.

As soon as he was gone I burst into tears, when Mary came and asked me what could make me cry so bitterly. To which I answered, oh, Mary! what is the meaning of the dry pan and gradual fire? for I am to die by them!

Madam, said she, never fear, you shall see, ere long, the dry pan and gradual fire; but they are made for those who oppose the holy father's will, not for you who are so good as to obey it. But pray, says she, was Don Francisco very obliging? I don't know, said I, for he frightened me out of my wits by his discourse; he saluted me with civility, but left me abruptly.

Well, said Mary, you do not yet know his temper, he is extremely obliging to them that are kind to him; but if they are disobedient he is unmerciful as Nero; so, for your own sake, take care to oblige him in all respects: and now, dear madam, pray go to supper, and be easy. I went to supper, indeed, and afterward to bed; but I could neither eat nor sleep, for the thoughts of the dry pan and gradual fire deprived me of appetite, and banished drowsiness.

Early the next morning Mary said, that as nobody was stirring, if I would promise her secrecy, she would show me the dry pan and gradual fire; so taking me down stairs, she brought me to a large room, with a thick iron door, which she opened. Within it was an oven, with fire in it at the time, and a large brass upon it, with a cover of the same, and a lock to it. In the next room there was a great wheel, covered on both sides with thick boards, opening a little window in the centre, Mary desired me to look in with a candle; there I saw all the circumference of the wheel set with sharp razors, which made me shudder.

She then took me to a pit, which was full of venomous animals. On my expressing great horror at the sight, she said, "Now my good mistress, I'll tell you the use of these things. The dry pan is for heretics, and those who oppose the holy father's will and pleasure; they are put alive into the pan, being first stripped naked; and the cover being locked down, the executioner begins to put a small fire into the oven, and by degrees he augments it, till the body is reduced to ashes. The wheel is designed for those who speak against the pope, or the holy fathers of the inquisition; for they are put into the machine through the little wheel, which is locked after them, and then the wheel is turned swiftly, till they are cut to pieces. The pit is for those who contemn the images, and refuse to give proper respect to ecclesiastical persons; for they are thrown into the pit, and so become the food of poisonous animals."

We went back again to my chamber, and Mary said, that another day she would show me the torments designed for other transgressors, but I was in such agonies at what I had seen, that I begged to be terrified with no more such sights. She soon after left me, but not without enjoining my strict obedience to Don Francisco; for if you do not comply with his will, said she, the dry pan and gradual fire will be your fate.

The horrors which the sight of these things, and Mary's expressions, impressed on my mind, almost bereaved me of my senses, and left me in such a state of stupefaction that I seemed to have no manner of will of my own.

The next morning Mary said, now let me dress you as nice as possible, for you must go and wish Don Francisco good-morrow, and breakfast with him. When I was dressed, she conveyed me through a gallery into his apartment, where I found that he was in bed. He ordered Mary to withdraw, and to serve up breakfast in about two hours time. When Mary was gone, he commanded me to undress myself and come to bed to him. The manner in which he spoke, and the dreadful ideas with which my mind was filled, so terribly frightened me, that I pulled off my cloths, without knowing what I did, and stepped into bed, insensible of the indecency I was transacting: so totally had the care of self preservation absorbed all my other thoughts, and so entirely were the ideas of delicacy obliterated by the force of terror!

Thus, to avoid the dry pan, did I entail upon myself perpetual infamy; and to escape the so much dreaded gradual fire, give myself up to the flames of lust. Wretched alternative, where the only choice is an excruciating death, or everlasting pollution!

Mary came at the expiration of two hours, and served us with chocolate in the most submissive manner; for she kneeled down by the bedside to present it. When I was dressed, Mary took me into a very delightful apartment, which I had never yet seen. It was furnished with the most costly elegance; but what gave me the greatest astonishment was, the prospect from its windows, of a beautiful garden, and a fine meandering river. Mary told me, that the young ladies she had mentioned would come to pay their compliments to me before dinner, and begged me to remember her advice in keeping a prudent guard over my tongue.

In a few minutes a great number of very beautiful young ladies, richly dressed, entered my room, and successively embracing me, wished me joy. I was so surprised, that I was unable to answer their compliments: which one of the ladies perceiving, said, "Madam, the solitude of this place will affect you in the beginning, but whenever you begin to feel the pleasures and amusements you may enjoy, you will quit those pensive thoughts. We, at present, beg the honour of you to dine with us to-day, and henceforward three days in a week." I returned them suitable thanks in general terms, and so went to dinner, in which the most exquisite and savoury dishes, of various kinds, were served up with the most delicate and pleasant fruits and sweetmeats. The room was long, with two tables on each side, and a third in the front. I reckoned fifty-two young ladies, the eldest not exceeding twenty-four years of age. There were five maid-servants besides Mary, to wait upon us; but Mary confined her attention to me alone. After dinner we retired to a capacious gallery, where they played on musical instruments, a few diverted themselves with cards, and the rest amused themselves with walking about. Mary, at length, entered the gallery, and said, ladies, this is a day of recreation, and so you may go into whatever rooms you please till eight o'clock in the evening.

They unanimously agreed to adjourn to my apartment. Here we found a most elegant cold collation, of which all the ladies partook, and passed the time in innocent conversation and harmless mirth; but none mentioned a word concerning the inquisition, or the holy fathers, or gave the least distant hint concerning the cause of their confinement.

At eight o'clock Mary rang a bell, which was a signal for all to retire to their respective apartments, and I was conducted to the chamber of Don Francisco, where I slept. The next morning Mary brought me a richer dress than any I had yet had; and as soon as I retired to my apartment, all the ladies came to wish me good-morning, dressed much richer than the preceding day. We passed the time till eight o'clock in the evening, in much the same manner as we had done the day before. At that time the bell rang, the separation took place, and I was conducted to Don Francisco's chamber. The next morning I had a garment richer than the last, and they accosted me in apparel still more sumptuous than before. The transactions of the two former days were repeated on the third, and the evening concluded in a similar manner.

On the fourth morning Mary came into Don Francisco's chamber and told me I must immediately rise, for a lady wanted me in her own chamber. She spoke with a kind of authority which surprised me; but as Don Francisco did not speak a syllable, I got up and obeyed. Mary then conveyed me into a dismal dungeon, not eight feet in length; and said sternly to me, This is your room, and this lady your bed-fellow and companion. At which words she bounced out of the room, and left me in the utmost consternation.

After remaining a considerable time in the most dreadful agonies tears came to my relief, and I exclaimed, "What is this place, dear lady! Is it a scene of enchantment, or is it a hell upon earth! Alas! I have lost my honour and my soul forever!"

The lady took me by the hand, and said in a sympathizing tone of voice, "Dear sister, (for this is the name I shall henceforth give you) forbear to cry and grieve, for you can do nothing by such an extravagant behaviour, but draw upon yourself a cruel death. Your misfortunes, and those of all the ladies you have seen, are exactly of a piece, you suffer nothing but what we have suffered before you; but we dare not show our grief, for fear of greater evils. Pray take courage, and hope in God, for he will surely deliver us from this hellish place; but be sure you discover no uneasiness before Mary, who is the only instrument either of our torments or comfort. Have patience until we go to bed, and then I will venture to tell you more of the matter."

My perplexity and vexation were inexpressible: but my new companion, whose name was Leonora, prevailed on me to disguise my uneasiness from Mary. I dissembled tolerably well when she came to bring our dinners, but could not help remarking, in my own mind, the difference between this repast, and those I had before partook of. This consisted only of plain, common food, and of that a scanty allowance, with one plate, and one knife and fork for us both, which she took away as soon as we had dined.

When we were in bed, Leonora was as good as her word; and upon my solemn promise of secrecy thus began to open her mind to me.

"My dear sister, you think your case very hard, but I assure you all the ladies in the house have gone through the same. In time, you will know all their stories, as they hope to know yours. I suppose Mary has been the chief instrument of your fright, as she has been of ours; and I warrant she has shown you some horrible places, though not all; and that, at the very thought of them you were so terrified, that you chose the same way we have done to redeem yourself from death. By what hath happened to us, we know that Don Francisco hath been your Nero, your tyrant; for the three colours of our clothes are the distinguishing tokens of the three holy fathers. The red silk belongs to Don Francisco, the blue to Don Guerrero, and the green to Don Aliga; and they always give those colours (after the farce of changing garments and the short-lived recreations are over) to those ladies whom they bring here for their respective uses.

"We are strictly commanded to express all the demonstrations of joy, and to be very merry for three days, when a young lady first comes amongst us, as we did with you, and as you must now do with others. But afterward we live like the most wretched prisoners, without seeing any body but Mary, and the other maid-servants, over whom Mary hath a kind of superiority, for she acts as housekeeper. We all dine in the great hall three days in a week; and when any one of the inquisitors hath a mind for one of his slaves, Mary comes about nine o'clock, and leads her to his apartment.

"Some nights Mary leaves the doors of our chambers open, and that is a token that one of the inquisitors hath a mind to come that night; but he comes so silent that we are ignorant whether he is our patron or not. If one of us happens to be with child, she is removed into a better chamber till she is delivered; but during the whole of her pregnancy, she never sees any body but the person appointed to attend her.

"As soon as the child is born it is taken away, and carried we know not whither; for we never hear a syllable mentioned about it afterward. I have been in this house six years, was not fourteen when the officers took me from my father's house, and have had one child. There are, at this present time, fifty-two young ladies in the house; but we annually lose six or eight, though we know not what becomes of them, or whither they are sent. This, however, does not diminish our number, for new ones are always brought in to supply the place of those who are removed from hence; and I remember, at one time, to have seen seventy-three ladies here together. Our continual torment is to reflect that when they are tired of any of the ladies, they certainly put to death those they pretend to send away; for it is natural to think, that they have too much policy to suffer their atrocious and infernal villanies to be discovered, by enlarging them. Hence our situation is miserable indeed, and we have only to pray that the Almighty will pardon those crimes which we are compelled to commit. Therefore, my dear sister, arm yourself with patience, for that is the only palliative to give you comfort, and put a firm confidence in the providence of Almighty God."

This discourse of Leonora greatly affected me; but I found everything to be as she told me, in the course of time, and I took care to appear as cheerful as possible before Mary. In this manner I continued eighteen months, during which time eleven ladies were taken from the house; but in lieu of them we got nineteen new ones, which made our number just sixty, at the time we were so happily relieved by the French officers, and providentially restored to the joys of society, and to the arms of our parents and friends. On that happy day, the door of my dungeon was opened by the gentleman who is now my husband, and who with the utmost expedition, sent both Leonora and me to his father's; and (soon after the campaign was over) when he returned home, he thought proper to make me his wife, in which situation I enjoy a recompense for all the miseries I before suffered.

From the foregoing narrative it is evident, that the inquisitors are a set of libidinous villains, lost to every just idea of religion, and totally destitute of humanity. Those who possess wealth, beauty, or liberal sentiments, are sure to find enemies in them. Avarice, lust, and prejudice, are their ruling passions; and they sacrifice every law, human and divine, to gratify their predominant desire. Their supposed piety is affectation; their pretended compassion hypocrisy; their justice depends on their will: and their equitable punishments are founded on their prejudices. None are secure from them, all ranks fall equally victims to their pride, their power, their avarice, or their aversion.

Some may suggest, that it is strange crowned heads and eminent nobles, have not attempted to crush the power of the inquisition, and reduce the authority of those ecclesiastical tyrants, from whose merciless fangs neither their families nor themselves are secure.

But astonishing as it is, superstition hath, in this case, always overcome common sense, and custom operated against reason. One prince, indeed, intended to abolish the inquisition, but he lost his life before he became king, and consequently before he had the power so to do; for the very intimation of his design procured his destruction.

This was that amiable prince Don Carlos, son of Philip the Second, king of Spain, and grandson of the celebrated emperor Charles V. Don Carlos, possessed all the good qualities of his grandfather without any of the bad ones of his father; and was a prince of great vivacity, admirable learning, and the most amiable disposition.--He had sense enough to see into the errors of popery, and abhorred the very name of the inquisition. He inveighed publicly against the institution, ridiculed the affected piety of the inquisitors, did all he could to expose their atrocious deeds, end even declared, that if he ever came to the crown, he would abolish the inquisition, and exterminate its agents.

These things were sufficient to irritate the inquisitors against the prince: they, accordingly, bent their minds to vengeance, and determined on his destruction.

The inquisitors now employed all their agents and emissaries to spread abroad the most artful insinuations against the prince; and, at length, raised such a spirit of discontent among the people, that the king was under the necessity of removing Don Carlos from court. Not content with this, they pursued even his friends, and obliged the king likewise to banish Don John, duke of Austria, his own brother, and consequently uncle to the prince; together with the prince of Parma, nephew to the king, and cousin to the prince, because they well knew that both the duke of Austria, and the prince of Parma, had a most sincere and inviolable attachment to Don Carlos.

Some few years after, the prince having shown great lenity and favour to the protestants in the Netherlands, the inquisition loudly exclaimed against him, declaring, that as the persons in question were heretics, the prince himself must necessarily be one, since he gave them countenance. In short, they gained so great an ascendency over the mind of the king, who was absolutely a slave to superstition, that, shocking to relate, he sacrificed the feelings of nature to the force of bigotry, and, for fear of incurring the anger of the inquisition, gave up his only son, passing the sentence of death on him himself.

The prince, indeed, had what was termed an indulgence; that is, he was permitted to choose the manner of his death. Roman like, the unfortunate young hero chose bleeding and the hot bath; when the veins of his arms and legs being opened, he expired gradually, falling a martyr to the malice of the inquisitors, and the stupid bigotry of his father.

The Persecution of Dr. AEgidio.

Dr. AEgidio was educated at the university of Alcala, where he took his several degrees, and particularly applied himself to the study of the sacred scriptures and school divinity. The professor of theology dying, he was elected into his place, and acted so much to the satisfaction of every one, that his reputation for learning and piety was circulated throughout Europe.

AEgidio, however, had his enemies, and these laid a complaint against him to the inquisitors, who sent him a citation, and when he appeared to it, cast him into a dungeon.

As the greatest part of those who belonged to the cathedral church at Seville, and many persons belonging to the bishopric of Dortois highly approved of the doctrines of AEgidio, which they thought perfectly consonant with true religion, they petitioned the emperor in his behalf. Though the monarch had been educated a Roman catholic, he had too much sense to be a bigot, and therefore sent an immediate order for his enlargement.

He soon after visited the church of Valladolid, did every thing he could to promote the cause of religion, and returning home he soon after fell sick, and died in an extreme old age.

The inquisitors having been disappointed of gratifying their malice against him while living, determined (as the emperor's whole thoughts were engrossed by a military expedition) to wreak their vengeance on him when dead. Therefore, soon after he was buried, they ordered his remains to be dug out of the grave; and a legal process being carried on, they were condemned to be burnt, which was executed accordingly.

The Persecution of Dr. Constantine.

Dr. Constantine, an intimate acquaintance of the already mentioned Dr. AEgidio, was a man of uncommon natural abilities and profound learning; exclusive of several modern tongues, he was acquainted with the Latin, Greek, and Hebrew languages, and perfectly well knew not only the sciences called abstruse, but those arts which come under the denomination of polite literature.

His eloquence rendered him pleasing, and the soundness of his doctrines a profitable preacher; and he was so popular, that he never preached but to a crowded audience. He had many opportunities of rising in the church, but never would take advantage of them; for if a living of greater value than his own was offered him, he would refuse it, saying, I am content with what I have; and he frequently preached so forcibly against simony, that many of his superiors, who were not so delicate upon the subject, took umbrage at his doctrines upon that head.

Having been fully confirmed in protestantism by Dr. AEgidio, he preached boldly such doctrines only as were agreeable to gospel purity, and uncontaminated by the errors which had at various times crept into the Romish church. For these reasons he had many enemies among the Roman catholics, and some of them were fully determined on his destruction.

A worthy gentleman named Scobaria, having erected a school for divinity lectures, appointed Dr. Constantine to be reader therein. He immediately undertook the task, and read lectures, by portions, on the Proverbs, Ecclesiastes, and Canticles; and was beginning to expound the book of Job, when he was seized by the inquisitors.

Being brought to examination, he answered with such precaution that they could not find any explicit charge against him, but remained doubtful in what manner to proceed, when the following circumstances occurred to determine them.

Dr. Constantine had deposited with a woman named Isabella Martin several books, which to him were very valuable, but which he knew, in the eyes of the inquisition, were exceptionable.

This woman having been informed against as a protestant, was apprehended, and, after a small process, her goods were ordered to be confiscated. Previous, however, to the officers coming to her house, the woman's son had removed away several chests full of the most valuable articles; and among these were Dr. Constantine's books.

A treacherous servant giving intelligence of this to the inquisitors, an officer was despatched to the son to demand the chests. The son, supposing the officer only came for Constantine's books, said, I know what you come for, and I will fetch them to you immediately. He then fetched Dr. Constantine's books and papers, when the officer was greatly surprised to find what he did not look for. He, however, told the young man, that he was glad these books and papers were produced, but nevertheless he must fulfil the end of his commission, which was, to carry him and the goods he had embezzled before the inquisitors, which he did accordingly; for the young man knew it would be in vain to expostulate, or resist, and therefore quietly submitted to his fate.

The inquisitors being thus possessed of Constantine's books and writings, now found matter sufficient to form charges against him. When he was brought to a re-examination, they presented one of his papers, and asked him if he knew the hand writing! Perceiving it was his own, he guessed the whole matter, confessed the writing, and justified the doctrine it contained: saying, "In that, and all my other writings, I have never departed from the truth of the gospel, but have always kept in view the pure precepts of Christ, as he delivered them to mankind."

After being detained upwards of two years in prison, Dr. Constantine was seized with a bloody flux, which put an end to his miseries in this world. The process, however, was carried on against his body, which, at the ensuing auto de fe, was publicly burnt.

The Life of William Gardiner.

William Gardiner was born at Bristol, received a tolerable education, and was, at a proper age, placed under the care of a merchant, named Paget.

At the age of twenty-six years, he was, by his master, sent to Lisbon, to act as factor. Here he applied himself to the study of the Portuguese language, executed his business with assiduity and despatch, and behaved with the most engaging affability to all persons with whom he had the least concern. He conversed privately with a few, whom he knew to be zealous protestants; and, at the same time cautiously avoided giving the least offence to any who were Roman catholics; he had not, however, hitherto gone into any of the popish churches.

A marriage being concluded between the king of Portugal's son, and the Infanta of Spain, upon the wedding-day the bride-groom, bride, and the whole court went to the cathedral church, attended by multitudes of all ranks of people, and among the rest William Gardiner who stayed during the whole ceremony, and was greatly shocked at the superstitions he saw.

The erroneous worship which he had seen ran strongly in his mind, he was miserable to see a whole country sunk into such idolatry, when the truth of the gospel might be so easily obtained. He, therefore, took the inconsiderate, though laudable design, into his head, of making a reform in Portugal, or perishing in the attempt; and determined to sacrifice his prudence to his zeal, though he became a martyr upon the occasion.

To this end, he settled all his worldly affairs, paid his debts, closed his books, and consigned over his merchandize. On the ensuing Sunday he went again to the cathedral church, with a New Testament in his hand, and placed himself near the altar.

The king and the court soon appeared, and a cardinal began mass at that part of the ceremony in which the people adore the wafer, Gardiner could hold out no longer, but springing towards the cardinal, he snatched the host from him, and trampled it under his feet.

This action amazed the whole congregation, and one person drawing a dagger, wounded Gardiner in the shoulder, and would, by repeating the blow, have finished him, had not the king called to him to desist.

Gardiner, being carried before the king, the monarch asked him what countryman he was: to which he replied, I am an Englishman by birth, a protestant by religion, and a merchant by occupation. What I have done is not out of contempt to your royal person, God forbid it should, but out of an honest indignation, to see the ridiculous superstitions and gross idolatries practised here.

The king, thinking that he had been stimulated by some other person to act as he had done, demanded who was his abetter, to which he replied, My own conscience alone. I would not hazard what I have done for any man living, but I owe that and all other services to God.

Gardiner was sent to prison, and a general order issued to apprehend all Englishmen in Lisbon. This order was in a great measure put into execution, (some few escaping) and many innocent persons were tortured to make them confess if they knew any thing of the matter; in particular, a person who resided in the same house with Gardiner, was treated with unparallelled barbarity to make him confess something which might throw a light upon the affair.

Gardiner himself was then tormented in the most excruciating manner; but in the midst of all his torments he gloried in the deed. Being ordered for death, a large fire was kindled near a gibbet, Gardiner was drawn up to the gibbet by pulleys, and then let down near the fire, but not so close as to touch it; for they burnt or rather roasted him by slow degrees. Yet he bore his sufferings patiently and resigned his soul to the Lord cheerfully.

It is observable that some of the sparks were blown from the fire, (which consumed Gardiner) towards the haven, burnt one of the king's ships of war, and did other considerable damage. The Englishmen who were taken up on this occasion were, soon after Gardiner's death, all discharged, except the person who resided in the same house with him, who was detained two years before he could procure his liberty.

An account of the Life and Sufferings of Mr. William Lithgow, a native of Scotland.

This gentleman was descended from a good family, and having a natural propensity for travelling, he rambled, when very young, over the northern and western islands; after which he visited France, Germany, Switzerland and Spain. He set out on his travels in the month of March, 1609, and the first place he went to was Paris, where he stayed for some time. He then prosecuted his travels through Germany and other parts, and at length arrived at Malaga, in Spain, the seat of all his misfortunes.

During his residence here, he contracted with the master of a French ship for his passage to Alexandria, but was prevented from going by the following circumstances. In the evening of the 17th of October, 1620, the English fleet, at that time on a cruise against the Algerine rovers, came to anchor before Malaga, which threw the people of the town into the greatest consternation, as they imagined them to be Turks. The morning, however, discovered the mistake, and the governor of Malaga, perceiving the cross of England in their colours, went on board Sir Robert Mansell's ship, who commanded on that expedition, and after staying some time returned, and silenced the fears of the people.

The next day many persons from on board the fleet came ashore. Among these were several well known by Mr. Lithgow, who, after reciprocal compliments, spent some days together in festivity and the amusements of the town. They then invited Mr. Lithgow to go on board, and pay his respects to the admiral. He accordingly accepted the invitation, was kindly received by him, and detained till the next day when the fleet sailed. The admiral would willingly have taken Mr. Lithgow with him to Algiers; but having contracted for his passage to Alexandria, and his baggage, &c. being in the town, he could not accept the offer.

As soon as Mr. Lithgow got on shore, he proceeded towards his lodgings by a private way, (being to embark the same night for Alexandria) when, in passing through a narrow uninhabited street, he found himself suddenly surrounded by nine sergeants, or officers, who threw a black cloak over him, and forcibly conducted him to the governor's house. After some little time the governor appeared when Mr. Lithgow earnestly begged he might be informed of the cause of such violent treatment. The governor only answered by shaking his head, and gave orders that the prisoner should be strictly watched till he (the governor) returned from his devotions; directing at the same time, that the captain of the town, the alcade major, and town notary, should be summoned to appear at his examination, and that all this should he done with the greatest secrecy, to prevent the knowledge thereof reaching the ears of the English merchants then residing in the town.

These orders were strictly discharged, and on the governor's return, he, with the officers, having seated themselves, Mr. Lithgow was brought before them for examination. The governor began by asking several questions, namely, of what country he was, whither bound, and how long he had been in Spain. The prisoner, after answering these and other questions, was conducted to a closet, where, in a short space of time, he was visited by the town-captain, who inquired whether he had ever been at Seville, or was lately come from thence; and patting his cheeks with an air of friendship conjured him to tell the truth: "For (said he) your very countenance shows there is some hidden matter in your mind, which prudence should direct you to disclose." Finding himself, however, unable to extort anything from the prisoner, he left him, and reported the same to the governor and the other officers; on which Mr. Lithgow was again brought before them, a general accusation was laid against him, and he was compelled to swear that he would give true answers to such questions as should be asked him.

The governor proceeded to inquire the quality of the English commander, and the prisoner's opinion what were the motives that prevented his accepting an invitation from him to come on shore. He demanded, likewise, the names of the English captains in the squadron, and what knowledge he had of the embarkation, or preparation for it before his departure from England. The answers given to the several questions asked were set down in writing by the notary; but the junto seemed surprised at his denying any knowledge of the fitting out of the fleet, particularly the governor, who said he lied that he was a traitor and a spy, and came directly from England to favour and assist the designs that were projected against Spain, and that he had been for that purpose nine months in Seville, in order to procure intelligence of the time the Spanish navy was expected from the Indies. They exclaimed against his familiarity with the officers of the fleet, and many other English gentlemen, between whom, they said, unusual civilities had passed, but all these transactions had been carefully noticed.

Besides, to sum up the whole, and put the truth past all doubt, they said, he came from a council of war, held that morning on board the admiral's ship, in order to put in execution the orders assigned him. They upbraided him with being accessary to the burning of the island of St. Thomas, in the West Indies. "Wherefore, (said they) these Lutherans, and sons of the devil, ought to have no credit given to what they say or swear."

In vain did Mr. Lithgow, endeavour to obviate every accusation laid against him, and to obtain belief from his prejudiced judges. He begged permission to send for his cloak-bag, which contained his papers, and might serve to show his innocence. This request they complied with, thinking it would discover some things of which they were ignorant. The cloak-bag was accordingly brought, and being opened, among other things, was found a license from king James the First, under the sign manuel, setting forth the bearer's intention to travel into Egypt; which was treated by the haughty Spaniards with great contempt. The other papers consisted of passports, testimonials, &c. of persons of quality. All these credentials, however, seemed rather to confirm than abate the suspicions of these prejudiced judges, who, after seizing all the prisoner's papers, ordered him again to withdraw.

In the mean time a consultation was held to fix the place where the prisoner should be confined. The alcade, or chief judge, was for putting him into the town prison; but this was objected to, particularly by the corregidor, who said, in Spanish, "In order to prevent the knowledge of his confinement from reaching his countrymen, I will take the matter on myself, and be answerable for the consequences;" upon which it was agreed, that he should be confined in the governor's house with the greatest secrecy.

This matter being determined, one of the sergeants went to Mr. Lithgow, and begged his money, with liberty to search him. As it was needless to make any resistance, the prisoner quietly complied, when the sergeant (after rifling his pockets of eleven ducatoons) stripped him to his shirt; and searching his breeches he found, enclosed in the waistband, two canvass bags, containing one hundred and thirty-seven pieces of gold. The sergeant immediately took the money to the corregidor, who, after having told it over, ordered him to clothe the prisoner, and shut him up close till after supper.

About midnight, the sergeant and two Turkish slaves released Mr. Lithgow from his then confinement, but it was to introduce him to one much more horrible. They conducted him through several passages, to a chamber in a remote part of the palace, towards the garden, where they loaded him with irons, and extended his legs by means of an iron bar above a yard long, the weight of which was so great that he could neither stand nor sit, but was obliged to lie continually on his back. They left him in this condition for some time, when they returned with a refreshment of food, consisting of a pound of boiled mutton and a loaf, together with a small quantity of wine; which was not only the first, but the best and last of the kind, during his confinement in this place. After delivering these articles, the sergeant locked the door, and left Mr. Lithgow to his own private contemplations.

The next day he received a visit from the governor, who promised him his liberty, with many other advantages, if he would confess being a spy; but on his protesting that he was entirely innocent, the governor left him in a rage, saying, He should see him no more till farther torments constrained him to confess, commanding the keeper, to whose care he was committed, that he should permit no person whatever to have access to, or commune with him; that his sustenance should not exceed three ounces of musty bread, and a pint of water every second day; that he shall be allowed neither bed, pillow, nor coverlid. "Close up (said he) this window in his room with lime and stone, stop up the holes of the door with double mats: let him have nothing that bears any likeness to comfort." These, and several other orders of the like severity, were given to render it impossible for his condition to be known to those of the English nation.

In this wretched and melancholy state did poor Lithgow continue without seeing any person for several days, in which time the governor received an answer to a letter he had written, relative to the prisoner from Madrid; and, pursuant to the instructions given him, began to put in practice the cruelties devised, which they hastened, because Christmas holy-days approached, it being then the forty-seventh day since his imprisonment.

About two o'clock in the morning, he heard the noise of a coach in the street, and some time after heard the opening of the prison doors, not having had any sleep for two nights; hunger, pain, and melancholy reflections having prevented him from taking any repose.

Soon after the prison doors were opened, the nine sergeants, who had first seized him, entered the place where he lay, and without uttering a word, conducted him in his irons through the house into the street, where a coach waited, and into which they laid him at the bottom on his back, not being able to sit. Two of the sergeants rode with him, and the rest walked by the coach side, but all observed the most profound silence. They drove him to a vinepress house, about a league from the town, to which place a rack had been privately conveyed before; and here they shut him up for that night.

At day-break the next morning, arrived the governor and the alcade, into whose presence Mr. Lithgow was immediately brought to undergo another examination. The prisoner desired he might have an interpreter, which was allowed to strangers by the laws of that country, but this was refused, nor would they permit him to appeal to Madrid, the superior court of judicature. After a long examination, which lasted from morning till night, there appeared in all his answers so exact a conformity with what he had before said, that they declared he had learned them by heart, there not being the least prevarication. They, however, pressed him again to make a full discovery; that is, to accuse himself of crimes never committed, the governor adding, "You are still in my power; I can set you free if you comply, if not, I must deliver you to the alcade." Mr. Lithgow still persisting in his innocence, the governor ordered the notary to draw up a warrant for delivering him to the alcade to be tortured.

In consequence of this he was conducted by the sergeants to the end of a stone gallery, where the rack was placed. The encarouador or executioner, immediately struck off his irons, which put him to very great pains, the bolts being so close riveted, that the sledge hammer tore away half an inch of his heel, in forcing off the bolt; the anguish of which, together with his weak condition, (not having the least sustenance for three days) occasioned him to groan bitterly; upon which the merciless alcade said, "Villain, traitor, this is but the earnest of what you shall endure."

When his irons were off he fell on his knees, uttering a short prayer, that God would be pleased to enable him to be steadfast, and undergo courageously the grievous trial he had to encounter. The alcade and notary having placed themselves in chairs, he was stripped naked, and fixed upon the rack, the office of these gentlemen being to be witness of, and set down the confessions and tortures endured by the delinquent.

It is impossible to describe all the various tortures inflicted upon him. Suffice it to say, that he lay on the rack for above five hours, during which time he received above sixty different tortures of the most hellish nature; and had they continued them a few minutes longer, he must have inevitably perished.

These cruel persecutors being satisfied for the present, the prisoner was taken from the rack, and his irons being again put on, he was conducted to his former dungeon, having received no other nourishment than a little warm wine, which was given him rather to prevent his dying, and reserve him for future punishments, than from any principle of charity or compassion.

As a confirmation of this, orders were given for a coach to pass every morning before day by the prison, that the noise made by it might give fresh terrors and alarms to the unhappy prisoner, and deprive him of all possibility of obtaining the least repose.

He continued in this horrid situation, almost starved for want of the common necessaries to preserve his wretched existence, till Christmas day, when he received some relief from Mariane, waiting-woman to the governor's lady. This woman having obtained leave to visit him, carried with her some refreshments, consisting of honey, sugar, raisins, and other articles: and so affected was she at beholding his situation, that she wept bitterly, and at her departure expressed the greatest concern at not being able to give him further assistance.

In this loathsome prison was poor Mr. Lithgow kept till he was almost devoured by vermin. They crawled about his beard, lips, eye-brows, &c. so that he could scarce open his eyes; and his mortification was increased by not having the use of his hands or legs to defend himself, from his being so miserably maimed by the tortures. So cruel was the governor, that he even ordered the vermin to be swept on him twice in every eight days. He, however obtained some little mitigation of this part of his punishment, from the humanity of a Turkish slave that attended him, who, when he could do it with safety, destroyed the vermin, and contributed every refreshment to him that laid in his power.

From this slave Mr. Lithgow at length received information which gave him little hopes of ever being released, but, on the contrary, that he should finish his life under new tortures. The substance of this information was, that an English seminary priest, and a Scotch cooper, had been for some time employed by the governor to translate from the English into the Spanish language, all his books and observations; and that it was commonly said in the governor's house, that he was an arch heretic.

This information greatly alarmed him, and he began, not without reason, to fear that they would soon finish him, more especially as they could neither by torture or any other means, bring him to vary from what he had all along said at his different examinations.

Two days after he had received the above information, the governor, an inquisitor, and a canonical priest, accompanied by two Jesuits, entered his dungeon, and being seated, after several idle questions, the inquisitor asked Mr. Lithgow if he was a Roman catholic, and acknowledged the pope's supremacy? He answered, that he neither was the one or did the other; adding, that he was surprised at being asked such questions, since it was expressly stipulated by the articles of peace between England and Spain, that none of the English subjects should be liable to the inquisition, or any way molested by them on account of diversity in religion, &c. In the bitterness of his soul he made use of some warm expressions not suited to his circumstances: "As you have almost murdered me (said he) for pretended treason, so now you intend to make a martyr of me for my religion." He also expostulated with the governor on the ill return he made to the king of England, (whose subject he was) for the princely humanity exercised towards the Spaniards in 1588, when their armada was shipwrecked on the Scotch coast, and thousands of the Spaniards found relief, who must otherwise have miserably perished.

The governor admitted the truth of what Mr. Lithgow said, but replied with a haughty air, that the king, who then only ruled Scotland, was actuated more by fear than love, and therefore did not deserve any thanks. One of the Jesuits said, there was no faith to be kept with heretics. The inquisitor then rising, addressed himself to Mr Lithgow in the following words: "You have been taken up as a spy, accused of treachery, and tortured, as we acknowledge, innocently: (which appears by the account lately received from Madrid of the intentions of the English) yet it was the divine power that brought those judgments upon you, for presumptuously treating the blessed miracle of Loretto with ridicule, and expressing yourself in your writings irreverently of his holiness, the great agent and Christ's vicar upon earth; therefore you are justly fallen into our hands by their special appointment: thy books and papers are miraculously translated by the assistance of Providence influencing thy own countrymen."

This trumpery being ended, they gave the prisoner eight days to consider and resolve whether he would become a convert to their religion; during which time the inquisitor told him he, with other religious orders, would attend, to give him such assistance thereto as he might want. One of the Jesuits said, (first making the sign of the cross upon his breast) "My son, behold, you deserve to be burnt alive; but by the grace of our lady of Loretto, whom you have blasphemed, we will both save your soul and body."

In the morning, the inquisitor with three other ecclesiastics returned, when the former asked the prisoner what difficulties he had on his conscience that retarded his conversion; to which he answered, "he had not any doubts in his mind, being confident in the promises of Christ, and assuredly believing his revealed will signified in the gospels, as professed in the reformed catholic church, being confirmed by grace, and having infallible assurance thereby of the christian faith." To these words the inquisitor replied, "Thou art no christian, but an absurd heretic, and without conversion a member of perdition." The prisoner then told him, it was not consistent with the nature and essence of religion and charity to convince by opprobrious speeches, racks, and torments, but by arguments deduced from the scriptures; and that all other methods would with him be totally ineffectual.

The inquisitor was so enraged at the replies made by the prisoner, that he struck him on the face, used many abusive speeches, and attempted to stab him, which he had certainly done had he not been prevented by the Jesuits: and from this time he never again visited the prisoner.

The next day the two Jesuits returned, and putting on a very grave supercilious air, the superior asked him, what resolution he had taken? To which Mr. Lithgow replied, that he was already resolved, unless he could show substantial reasons to make him alter his opinion. The superior, after a pedantic display of their seven sacraments, the intercession of saints, transubstantiation, &c. boasted greatly of their church, her antiquity, universality, and uniformity; all which Mr. Lithgow denied: "For (said he) the profession of the faith I hold hath been ever since the first days of the apostles, and Christ had ever his own church (however obscure) in the greatest time of your darkness."

The Jesuits, finding their arguments had not the desired effect, that torments could not shake his constancy, nor even the fear of the cruel sentence he had reason to expect would be pronounced and executed on him, after severe menaces, left him. On the eighth day after being the last of their inquisition, when sentence is pronounced, they returned again, but quite altered both in their words and behaviour after repeating much of the same kind of arguments as before, they with seeming tears in their eyes, pretended they were sorry from their heart he must be obliged to undergo a terrible death, but above all, for the loss of his most precious soul; and falling on their knees, cried out, "Convert, convert, O dear brother, for our blessed lady's sake convert!" To which he answered, "I fear neither death nor fire, being prepared for both."

The first effects Mr. Lithgow felt of the determination of this bloody tribunal was, a sentence to receive that night eleven different tortures, and if he did not die in the execution of them, (which might be reasonably expected from the maimed and disjointed condition he was in) he was, after Easter holy-days, to be carried to Grenada, and there burnt to ashes. The first part of this sentence was executed with great barbarity that night; and it pleased God to give him strength both of body and mind, to stand fast to the truth, and to survive the horrid punishments inflicted on him.

After these barbarians had glutted themselves for the present, with exercising on the unhappy prisoner the most distinguished cruelties, they again put irons on, and conveyed him to his former dungeon. The next morning he received some little comfort from the Turkish slave before mentioned, who secretly brought him, in his shirt sleeve, some raisins and figs, which he licked up in the best manner his strength would permit with his tongue. It was to this slave Mr. Lithgow attributed his surviving so long in such a wretched situation; for he found means to convey some of these fruits to him twice every week. It is very extraordinary, and worthy of note, that this poor slave, bred up from his infancy, according to the maxims of his prophet and parents, in the greatest detestation of christians, should be so affected at the miserable situation of Mr. Lithgow, that he fell ill, and continued so for upwards of forty days. During this period Mr. Lithgow was attended by a negro woman, a slave, who found means to furnish him with refreshments still more amply than the Turk, being conversant in the house and family. She brought him every day some victuals, and with it some wine in a bottle.

The time was now so far elapsed, and the horrid situation so truly loathsome, that Mr. Lithgow waited with anxious expectation for the day, which, by putting an end to his life, would also end his torments. But his melancholy expectations were, by the interposition of Providence, happily rendered abortive, and his deliverance obtained from the following circumstances.

It happened that a Spanish gentleman of quality came from Grenada to Malaga, who being invited to an entertainment by the governor, he informed him of what had befallen Mr. Lithgow from the time of his being apprehended as a spy, and described the various sufferings he had endured. He likewise told him, that after it was known the prisoner was innocent, it gave him great concern. That on this account he would gladly have released him, restored his money and papers, and made some atonement for the injuries he had received but that, upon an inspection into his writings, several were found of a very blasphemous nature, highly reflecting on their religion. That on his refusing to abjure these heretical opinions, he was turned over to the inquisition, by whom he was finally condemned.

While the governor was relating this tragical tale, a Flemish youth (servant to the Spanish gentleman) who waited at the table, was struck with amazement and pity at the sufferings of the stranger described. On his return to his master's lodgings he began to revolve in his mind what he had heard, which made such an impression on him that he could not rest in his bed. In the short slumbers he had, his imagination painted to him the person described, on the rack, and burning in the fire. In this anxiety he passed the night; and when the morning came, without disclosing his intentions to any person whatever, he went into the town, and enquired for an English factor. He was directed to the house of a Mr. Wild, to whom he related the whole of what he had heard pass, the preceding evening, between his master and the governor; but could not tell Mr. Lithgow's name. Mr. Wild, however, conjectured it was him, by the servant's remembering the circumstance of his being a traveller, and his having had some acquaintance with him.

On the departure of the Flemish servant, Mr. Wild immediately sent for the other English factors, to whom he related all the particulars relative to their unfortunate countryman. After a short consultation it was agreed, that an information of the whole affair should be sent, by express, to Sir Walter Aston, the English ambassador to the king of Spain, then at Madrid. This was accordingly done, and the ambassador having presented a memorial to the king and council of Spain, he obtained an order for Mr. Lithgow's enlargement, and his delivery to the English factory. This order was directed to the governor of Malaga; and was received with great dislike and surprise by the whole assembly of the bloody inquisition.

Mr. Lithgow was released from his confinement on the eve of Easter Sunday, when he was carried from his dungeon on the back of the slave who had attended him, to the house of one Mr. Bosbich, where all proper comforts were given him. It fortunately happened, that there was at this time a squadron of English ships in the road, commanded by Sir Richard Hawkins, who being informed of the past sufferings and present situation of Mr. Lithgow, came the next day ashore, with a proper guard, and received him from the merchants. He was instantly carried in blankets on board the Vanguard, and three days after was removed to another ship, by direction of the general Sir Robert Mansel, who ordered that he should have proper care taken of him. The factory presented him with clothes, and all necessary provisions, besides which they gave him 200 reals in silver; and Sir Richard Hawkins sent him two double pistoles.

Before his departure from the Spanish coast, Sir Richard Hawkins demanded the delivery of his papers, money, books, &c. but could not obtain any satisfactory answer on that head.

We cannot help making a pause here to reflect, how manifestly Providence interfered in behalf of this poor man, when he was just on the brink of destruction; for by his sentence, from which there was no appeal, he would have been taken, in a few days, to Grenada, and burnt to ashes: and that a poor ordinary servant, who had not the least knowledge of him, nor was any ways interested in his preservation, should risk the displeasure of his master, and hazard his own life, to disclose a thing of so momentous and perilous a nature, to a strange gentleman, on whose secrecy depended his own existence. By such secondary means does Providence frequently interfere in behalf of the virtuous and oppressed; of which this is a most distinguished example.

After lying twelve days in the road, the ship weighed anchor, and in about two months arrived safe at Deptford. The next morning, Mr. Lithgow was carried on a feather bed to Theobalds, in Hertfordshire, where at that time was the king and royal family. His majesty happened to be that day engaged in hunting, but on his return in the evening, Mr. Lithgow was presented to him, and related the particulars of his sufferings, and his happy delivery. The king was so affected at the narrative, that he expressed the deepest concern, and gave orders that he should be sent to Bath, and his wants properly supplied from his royal munificence. By these means, under God, after some time, Mr. Lithgow was restored, from the most wretched spectacle, to a great share of health and strength; but he lost the use of his left arm, and several of the smaller bones were so crushed and broken, as to be ever after rendered useless.

Notwithstanding every effort was used, Mr. Lithgow could never obtain any part of his money or effects, though his majesty and the ministers of state, interested themselves in his behalf. Gondamore, the Spanish ambassador, indeed, promised that all his effects should be restored, with the addition of L1000 English money, as some atonement for the tortures he had undergone, which last was to be paid him by the governor of Malaga. These engagements, however, were but mere promises; and though the king was a kind of guarantee for the well performance of them, the cunning Spaniard found means to elude the same. He had, indeed, too great a share of influence in the English council during the time of that pacific reign, when England suffered herself to be bullied into slavish compliance by most of the states and kings in Europe.

Croly on the Inquisition.

We shall conclude this chapter with the subjoined extract from the New Interpretation of the Apocalypse by the Rev. George Croly.

In our fortunate country, the power of the Romish church has so long perished, that we find some difficulty in conceiving the nature, and still more in believing the tyranny of its dominion. The influence of the monks and the murders of the inquisition have passed into a nursery tale; and we turn with a generous, yet rash and most unjustifiable scepticism from the history of Romish authority.

Through almost the entire of Italy, through the Flemish dominions of Germany, through a large portion of France, and through the entire of Spain, a great monastic body was established, which, professing a secondary and trivial obedience to the sovereign, gave its first and real obedience to the pope. The name of spiritual homage cloaked the high treason of an oath of allegiance to a foreign monarch; and whoever might be king of France, or Spain, the pope was king of the Dominicans. All the other monastic orders were so many papal outposts. But the great Dominican order, immensely opulent in its pretended poverty; formidably powerful in its hypocritical disdain of earthly influence; and remorselessly ambitious, turbulent, and cruel in its primitive zeal; was an actual lodgment and province of the papacy, an inferior Rome, in the chief European kingdoms.

In the closest imitation of Rome, this spiritual power had fiercely assumed the temporal sword; the inquisition was army, revenues, and throne in one. With the racks and fires of a tribunal worthy of the gulf of darkness and guilt from which it rose, the Dominicans bore popery in triumph through christendom, crushing every vestige of religion under the wheels of its colossal idol. The subjugation of the Albigenses in 1229 had scattered the church; the shock of the great military masses was past; a subtler and more active force was required to destroy the wandering people of God; and the inquisition multiplied itself for the work of death. This terrible tribunal set every principle, and even every form of justice at defiance. Secrecy, that confounds innocence with guilt, was the spirit of its whole proceeding. All its steps were in darkness. The suspected revolter from popery was seized in secret, tried in secret, never suffered to see the face of accuser, witness, advocate, or friend, was kept unacquainted with the charge, was urged to criminate himself; if tardy, was compelled to this self-murder by the rack; if terrified, was only the more speedily murdered for the sport of the multitude. From the hour of his seizure he never saw the face of day, until he was brought out as a public show, a loyal and festal sacrifice, to do honor to the entrance of some travelling viceroy, some new married princess, or, on more fortunate occasions, to the presence of the sovereign. The dungeons were then drained, the human wreck of the torture and scourge were gathered out of darkness, groups of misery and exhaustion with wasted forms and broken limbs, and countenances subdued by pain and famine into idiotism, and despair, and madness; to feed the fires round which the Dominicans were chanting the glories of popery, and exulting in the destruction of the body for the good of the soul!

In the original establishment of the inquisition in 1198, it had raged against the Vaudois and their converts. But the victims were exhausted; or not worth the pursuit of a tribunal which looked to the wealth as keenly as to the faith of the persecuted. Opulence and heresy were at length to be found only to Spain, and there the inquisition turned with a gigantic step. In the early disturbances of the Peninsula, the Jews, by those habits of trade, and mutual communion, which still make them the lords of commerce, had acquired the chief wealth of the country. The close of the Moorish war in the 15th century had left the Spanish monarch at leisure for extortion; and he grasped at the Jewish gains in the spirit of a robber, as he pursued his plunder with the cruelty of a barbarian. The inquisition was the great machine, the comprehensive torturer, ready to squeeze out alike the heart and the gold. In 1481, an edict was issued against the Jews; before the end of the year, in the single diocess of Cadiz, two thousand Jews were burnt alive! The fall of the kingdom of Grenada, in 1492, threw the whole of the Spanish Moors into the hands of the king. They were cast into the same furnace of plunder and torture. Desperate rebellions followed; they were defeated and, in 1609, were finally exiled. "In the space of one hundred and twenty nine years, the inquisition deprived Spain of three millions of inhabitants."

On the death of Leo X. in 1521, Adrian, the inquisitor general was elected pope. He had laid the foundation of his papal celebrity in Spain. "It appears, according to the most moderate calculation, that during the five years of the ministry of Adrian, 24,025 persons were condemned by the inquisition, of whom one thousand six hundred and twenty were burned alive."

It is the constant sophism of those who would cast christianity bound hand and foot at the mercy of her enemies, that the pope desires to exercise no interference in the internal concerns of kingdoms; that, if he had the desire, he has not the power; and that, if he possessed the power, he would be resisted by the whole body of the national clergy. For the exposure of this traitorous delusion, we are to look to the times, when it was the will of popery to put forth its strength; not to the present, when it is its will to lull us into a belief of its consistency with the constitution, in defiance of common sense, common experience, the spirit of British law, and the loud warnings of insulted and hazarded religion.

Of the multitudes who perished by the inquisition throughout the world, no authentic record is now discoverable. But wherever popery had power, there was the tribunal. It had been planted even in the east, and the Portuguese inquisition of Goa was, till within these few years, fed with many an agony. South America was partitioned into provinces of the inquisition; and with a ghastly mimickry of the crimes of the mother state, the arrivals of viceroys, and the other popular celebrations were thought imperfect without an auto de fe. The Netherlands were one scene of slaughter from the time of the decree which planted the inquisition among them. In Spain the calculation is more attainable. Each of the *seventeen* tribunals during a long period burned annually on an average ten miserable beings! We are to recollect that this number was in a country where persecution had for ages abolished all religious differences, and where the difficulty was not to find the stake, but the offering. Yet, even in Spain, thus gleaned of all heresy, the inquisition could still swell its list of murders to thirty-two thousand! The numbers burned in effigy, or condemned to penance, punishments generally equivalent to exile, confiscation, and taint of blood, to all ruin but the mere loss of worthless life amounted to three hundred and nine thousand. But the crowds who perished in dungeons, of the torture, of confinement, and of broken hearts, the millions of dependent lives made utterly helpless, or hurried to the grave by the death of the victims, are beyond all register; or recorded only before HIM, who has sworn that "He who leadeth into captivity, shall go into captivity: and he that killeth with the sword shall be killed by the sword."

Such was the inquisition, declared by the Spirit of God to be at once the offspring and the *image* of the popedom. To feel the force of the parentage, we must look to the time. In the thirteenth century, the popedom was at the summit of mortal dominion; it was independent of all kingdoms; it ruled with a rank of influence never before or since possessed by a human sceptre; it was the acknowledged sovereign of body and soul; to all earthly intents its power was immeasurable for good or evil. It might have spread literature, peace, freedom, and christianity to the ends of Europe, or the world. But its nature was hostile; its fuller triumph only disclosed its fuller evil; and, to the shame of human reason, and the terror and suffering of human virtue, Rome, in the hour of its consummate grandeur, teemed with the monstrous and horrid birth of the INQUISITION!

CHAPTER VI.

AN ACCOUNT OF THE PERSECUTION IN ITALY, UNDER THE PAPACY.

We shall now enter on an account of the persecutions in Italy, a country which has been, and still is,

1. The centre of popery.

2. The seat of the pontiff.

3. The source of the various errors which have spread themselves over

other countries, deluded the minds of thousands, and diffused the clouds of superstition and bigotry over the human understanding.

In pursuing our narrative we shall include the most remarkable persecutions which have happened, and the cruelties which have been practised,

1. By the immediate power of the pope.

2. Through the power of the inquisition.

3. At the instigation of particular orders of the clergy.

4. By the bigotry of the Italian princes.

In the 12th century, the first persecutions under the papacy began in Italy, at the time that Adrian, an Englishman, was pope, being occasioned by the following circumstances:

A learned man, and an excellent orator of Brixia, named Arnold came to Rome, and boldly preached against the corruptions and innovations which had crept into the church. His discourses were so clear, consistent, and breathed forth such a pure spirit of piety, that the senators, and many of the people, highly approved of, and admired his doctrines.

This so greatly enraged Adrian, that he commanded Arnold instantly to leave the city, as a heretic. Arnold, however, did not comply, for the senators, and some of the principal people, took his part, and resisted the authority of the pope.

Adrian now laid the city of Rome under an interdict, which caused the whole body of clergy to interpose; and, at length, persuaded the senators and people to give up the point, and suffer Arnold to be banished. This being agreed to, he received the sentence of exile, and retired to Germany, where he continued to preach against the pope, and to expose the gross errors of the church of Rome.

Adrian, on this account, thirsted for his blood, and made several attempts to get him into his hands; but Arnold, for a long time, avoided every snare laid for him. At length, Frederic Barbarossa arriving at the imperial dignity, requested that the pope would crown him with his own hand. This Adrian complied with, and at the same time asked a favour of the emperor, which was, to put Arnold into his hands. The emperor very readily delivered up the unfortunate preacher, who soon fell a martyr to

Adrian's vengeance, being hanged, and his body burnt to ashes, at Apulia. The same fate attended several of his old friends and companions.

Encenas, a Spaniard, was sent to Rome, to be brought up in the Roman catholic faith; but having conversed with some of the reformed, and read several treatises which they had put into his hands, he became a protestant. This, at length, being known, one of his own relations informed against him, when he was burnt by order of the pope, and a conclave of cardinals. The brother of Encenas had been taken up much about the same time, for having a New Testament, in the Spanish language, in his possession; but before the time appointed for his execution, he found means to escape out of prison, and retired to Germany.

Faninus, a learned layman, by reading controversial books, became of the reformed religion. An information being exhibited against him to the pope, he was apprehended, and cast into prison. His wife, children, relations and friends, visited him in his confinement, and so far wrought upon his mind, that he renounced his faith, and obtained his release. But he was no sooner free from confinement, than his mind felt the heaviest of chains; the weight of a guilty conscience. His horrors were so great, that he found them insupportable, till he had returned from his apostasy, and declared himself fully convinced of the errors of the church of Rome. To make amends for his falling off, he now openly and strenuously did all he could to make converts to protestantism, and was pretty successful in his endeavours. These proceedings occasioned his second imprisonment, but he had his life offered him if he would recant again. This proposal he rejected with disdain, saying, that he scorned life upon such terms. Being asked why he would obstinately persist in his opinions and leave his wife and children in distress, he replied, I shall not leave them in distress; I have recommended them to the care of an excellent trustee. What trustee? said the person who had asked the question, with some surprise: to which Faninus answered, Jesus Christ is the trustee I mean, and I think I could not commit them to the care of a better. On the day of execution he appeared remarkably cheerful, which one observing, said, it is strange you should appear so merry upon such an occasion, when Jesus Christ himself, just before his death, was in such agonies, that he sweated blood and water. To which Faninus replied; Christ sustained all manner of pangs and conflicts, with hell and death, on our accounts; and thus, by his sufferings, freed those who really believe in him from the fear of them. He was then strangled, and his body being burnt to ashes, they were scattered about by the wind.

Dominicus, a learned soldier, having read several controversial writings, became a zealous protestant, and retiring to Placentia, he preached the gospel in its utmost purity, to a very considerable congregation. At the conclusion of his sermon one day, he said, "If the congregation will attend to-morrow, I will give them a description of Anti-christ, and paint him out in his proper colours."

A vast concourse of people attended the next day, but just as Dominicus was beginning his sermon, a civil magistrate went up to the pulpit, and took him into custody. He readily submitted; but as he went along with the magistrate, made use of this expression: I wonder the devil hath let me alone so long. When he was brought to examination, this question was put to him: Will you renounce your doctrines? To which he replied: My doctrines! I maintain no doctrines of my own; what I preach are the doctrines of Christ, and for those I will forfeit my blood, and even think myself happy to suffer for the sake of my Redeemer. Every method was taken to make him recant from his faith, and embrace the errors of the church of Rome; but when persuasions and menaces were found ineffectual, he was sentenced to death, and hanged in the market-place.

Galeacius, a protestant gentleman, who resided near the castle of St. Angelo, was apprehended on account of his faith. Great endeavours being used by his friends he recanted, and subscribed to several of the superstitious doctrines propagated by the church of Rome. Becoming, however, sensible of his error, he publicly renounced his recantation. Being apprehended for this, he was condemned to be burnt, and agreeable to the order, was chained to a stake, where he was left several hours before the fire was put to the faggots, in order that his wife, relations, and friends, who surrounded him, might induce him to give up his opinions. Galeacius, however, retained his constancy of mind, and entreated the executioner to put fire to the wood that was to burn him. This at length he did, and Galeacius was soon consumed in the flames, which burnt with amazing rapidity and deprived him of sensation in a few minutes.

Soon after this gentleman's death, a great number of protestants were put to death in various parts of Italy, on account of their faith, giving a sure proof of their sincerity in their martyrdoms.

An account of the Persecutions of Calabria.

In the 14th century, many of the Waldenses of Pragela and Dauphiny, emigrated to Calabria, and settling some waste lands, by the permission of the nobles of that country, they soon, by the most industrious cultivation, made several wild and barren spots appear with all the beauties of verdure and fertility.

The Calabrian lords were highly pleased with their new subjects and tenants, as they were honest, quiet, and industrious; but the priests of the country exhibited several negative complaints against them; for not being able to accuse them of anything bad which they did do, they founded accusations on what they did not do, and charged them,

With not being Roman catholics.

With not making any of their boys priests.

With not making any of their girls nuns.

With not going to mass.

With not giving wax tapers to their priests as offerings.

With not going on pilgrimages.

With not bowing to images.

The Calabrian lords, however, quieted the priests, by telling them that these people were extremely harmless; that they gave no offence to the Roman catholics, and cheerfully paid the tithes to the priests, whose revenues were considerably increased by their coming into the country, and who, of consequence, ought to be the last persons to complain of them.

Things went on tolerably well after this for a few years, during which the Waldenses formed themselves into two corporate towns, annexing several villages to the jurisdiction of them. At length, they sent to Geneva for two clergymen; one to preach in each town, as they determined to make a public profession of their faith. Intelligence of this affair being carried to the pope, Pius the Fourth, he determined to exterminate them from Calabria.

To this end he sent cardinal Alexandrino, a man of very violent temper and a furious bigot, together with two monks, to Calabria, where they were to act as inquisitors. These authorized persons came to St. Xist, one of the towns built by the Waldenses, and having assembled the people told them, that they should receive no injury or violence, if they would accept of preachers appointed by the pope; but if they would not, they should be deprived both of their properties and lives; and that their intentions might be known, mass should be publicly said that afternoon, at which they were ordered to attend.

The people of St. Xist, instead of attending mass, fled into the woods, with their families, and thus disappointed the cardinal and his coadjutors. The cardinal then proceeded to La Garde, the other town belonging to the Waldenses, where, not to be served as he had been at St. Xist, he ordered the gates to be locked, and all avenues guarded. The same proposals were then made to the inhabitants of La Garde, as had previously been offered to those of St. Xist, but with this additional piece of artifice: the cardinal assured them that the inhabitants of St. Xist had immediately come into his proposals, and agreed that the pope should appoint them preachers. This falsehood succeeded; for the people of La Garde, thinking what the cardinal had told them to be the truth, said they would exactly follow the example of their brethren at St. Xist.

The cardinal having gained his point by deluding the people of one town, sent for troops of soldiers, with a view to murder those of the other. He, accordingly, despatched the soldiers into the woods, to hunt down the inhabitants of St. Xist like wild beasts, and gave them strict orders to spare neither age nor sex, but to kill all they came near. The troops entered the woods, and many fell a prey to their ferocity, before the Waldenses were properly apprised of their design. At length, however, they determined to sell their lives as dear as possible, when several conflicts happened, in which the half-armed Waldenses performed prodigies of valour, and many were slain on both sides. The greatest part of the troops being killed in the different rencontres, the rest were compelled to retreat, which so enraged the cardinal, that he wrote to the viceroy of Naples for reinforcements.

The viceroy immediately ordered a proclamation to be made throughout all the Neapolitan territories, that all outlaws, deserters, and other proscribed persons should be surely pardoned for their respective offences, on condition of making a campaign against the inhabitants of St. Xist, and continuing under arms till those people were exterminated.

Many persons of desperate fortunes, came in upon this proclamation, and being formed into light companies, were sent to scour the woods, and put to death all they could meet with of the reformed religion. The viceroy himself likewise joined the cardinal, at the head of a body of regular forces; and, in conjunction, they did all they could to harass the poor people in the woods. Some they caught and hanged up upon trees, cut down boughs and burnt them, or ripped them open and left their bodies to be devoured by wild beasts, or birds of prey. Many they shot at a distance, but the greatest number they hunted down by way of sport. A few hid themselves in caves, but famine destroyed them in their retreat; and thus all these poor people perished, by various means, to glut the bigoted malice of their merciless persecutors.

The inhabitants of St. Xist were no sooner exterminated, than those of La Garde engaged the attention of the cardinal and viceroy.

It was offered, that if they should embrace the Roman catholic persuasion, themselves and families should not be injured, but their houses and properties should be restored, and none would be permitted to molest them; but, on the contrary, if they refused this mercy, (as it was termed) the utmost extremities would be used, and the most cruel deaths the certain consequence of their non-compliance.

Notwithstanding the promises on one side, and menaces on the other, these worthy people unanimously refused to renounce their religion, or embrace the errors of popery. This exasperated the cardinal and viceroy so much, that 30 of them were ordered to be put immediately to the rack, as a terror to the rest.

Those who were put to the rack were treated with such severity, that several died under the tortures; one Charlin, in particular, was so cruelly used, that his belly burst, his bowels came out, and he expired in the greatest agonies. These barbarities, however, did not answer the purposes for which they were intended; for those who remained alive after the rack, and those who had not felt the rack, remained equally constant in their faith, and boldly declared, that no tortures of body, or terrors of mind, should ever induce them to renounce their God, or worship images.

Several were then, by the cardinal's order, stripped stark naked, and whipped to death with iron rods; and some were hacked to pieces with large knives; others were thrown down from the top of a large tower, and many were covered over with pitch, and burnt alive.

One of the monks who attended the cardinal, being naturally of a savage and cruel disposition, requested of him that he might shed some of the blood of these poor people with his own hands; when his request being granted, the barbarous man took a large sharp knife, and cut the throats of fourscore men, women, and children, with as little remorse as a butcher would have killed so many sheep. Every one of these bodies were then ordered to be quartered, the quarters placed upon stakes, and then fixed in different parts of the country, within a circuit of 30 miles.

The four principal men of La Garde were hanged, and the clergyman was thrown from the top of his church steeple. He was terribly mangled, but not quite killed by the fall; at which time the viceroy passing by, said, is the dog yet living? Take him up, and give him to the hogs, when, brutal as this sentence may appear, it was executed accordingly.

Sixty women were racked so violently, that the cords pierced their arms and legs quite to the bone; when, being remanded to prison, their wounds mortified, and they died in the most miserable manner. Many others were put to death by various cruel means; and if any Roman catholic, more compassionate than the rest, interceded for any of the reformed, he was immediately apprehended, and shared the same fate as a favourer of heretics.

The viceroy being obliged to march back to Naples, on some affairs of moment which required his presence, and the cardinal being recalled to Rome, the marquis of Butane was ordered to put the finishing stroke to what they had begun; which he at length effected, by acting with such barbarous rigour, that there was not a single person of the reformed religion left living in all Calabria.

Thus were a great number of inoffensive and harmless people deprived of their possessions, robbed of their property, driven from their homes, and, at length, murdered by various means, only because they would not sacrifice their consciences to the superstitions of others, embrace idolatrous doctrines which they abhorred, and accept of teachers whom they could not believe. Tyranny is of three kinds, viz., that which enslaves the person, that which seizes the property, and that which prescribes and dictates to the mind. The two first sorts may be termed civil tyranny, and have been practised by arbitrary sovereigns in all ages, who have delighted in tormenting the persons, and stealing the properties of their unhappy subjects. But the third sort, viz. prescribing and dictating to the mind, may be called ecclesiastical tyranny: and this is the worst kind of tyranny, as it includes the other two sorts; for the Romish clergy not only do torture the bodies and seize the effects of those they persecute, but take the lives, torment the minds, and, if possible, would tyrannize over the souls of the unhappy victims.

Account of the Persecutions in the Valleys of Piedmont.

Many of the Waldenses, to avoid the persecutions to which they were continually subjected in France, went and settled in the valleys of Piedmont, where they increased exceedingly, and flourished very much for a considerable time.

Though they were harmless in their behaviour, inoffensive in their conversation, and paid tithes to the Roman clergy, yet the latter could not be contented, but wished to give them some disturbance; they, accordingly, complained to the archbishop of Turin, that the Waldenses of the valleys of Piedmont were heretics, for these reasons:

1. That they did not believe in the doctrines of the church of Rome.

2. That they made no offerings or prayers for the dead.

3. That they did not go to mass.

4. That they did not confess, and receive absolution.

5. That they did not believe in purgatory, or pay money to get the souls of their friends out of it.

Upon these charges the archbishop ordered a persecution to be commenced, and many fell martyrs to the superstitious rage of the priests and monks.

At Turin, one of the reformed had his bowels torn out, and put in a basin before his face, where they remained in his view till he expired. At Revel, Catelin Girard being at the stake, desired the executioner to give him a stone; which he refused, thinking that he meant to throw it at somebody; but Girard assuring him that he had no such design, the executioner complied; when Girard, looking earnestly at the stone, said, When it is in the power of a man to eat and digest this solid stone, the religion for which I am about to suffer shall have an end, and not before. He then threw the stone on the ground, and submitted cheerfully to the flames. A great many more of the reformed were oppressed, or put to death, by various means, till the patience of the Waldenses being tired out, they flew to arms in their own defence, and formed themselves into regular bodies.

Exasperated at this, the bishop of Turin procured a number of troops and sent against them; but in most of the skirmishes and engagements the Waldenses were successful, which partly arose from their being better acquainted with the passes of the valleys of Piedmont than their adversaries, and partly from the desperation with which they fought; for they well knew, if they were taken, they should not be considered as prisoners of war, but tortured to death as heretics.

At length, Philip the seventh, duke of Savoy, and supreme lord of Piedmont, determined to interpose his authority, and stop these bloody wars, which so greatly disturbed his dominions. He was not willing to disoblige the pope, or affront the archbishop of Turin; nevertheless, he sent them both messages, importing, that he could not any longer tamely see his dominions overrun with troops, who were directed by priests instead of officers, and commanded by prelates instead of generals; nor would he suffer his country to be depopulated, while he himself had not been even consulted upon the occasion.

The priests, finding the resolution of the duke, did all they could to prejudice his mind against the Waldenses; but the duke told them, that though he was unacquainted with the religious tenets of these people, yet he had always found them quiet, faithful, and obedient, and therefore he determined they should be no longer persecuted.

The priests now had recourse to the most palpable and absurd falsehoods: they assured the duke that he was mistaken in the Waldenses for they were a wicked set of people, and highly addicted to intemperance, uncleanness, blasphemy, adultery, incest, and many other abominable crimes; and that they were even monsters in nature, for their children were born with black throats, with four rows of teeth, an bodies all over hairy.

The duke was not so devoid of common sense as to give credit to what the priests said, though they affirmed in the most solemn manner the truth of their assertions. He, however, sent twelve very learned and sensible gentlemen into the Piedmontese valleys, to examine into the real characters of the inhabitants.

These gentlemen, after travelling through all their towns and villages, and conversing with people of every rank among the Waldenses returned to the duke, and gave him the most favourable account of those people; affirming, before the faces of the priests who villified them, that they were harmless, inoffensive, loyal, friendly, industrious, and pious: that they abhorred the crimes of which they were accused; and that, should an individual, through his depravity, fall into any of those crimes, he would, by their laws, be punished in the most exemplary manner. With respect to the children, the gentlemen said, the priests had told the most gross and ridiculous falsities, for they were neither born with black throats, teeth in their mouths, nor hair on their bodies, but were as fine children as could be seen. "And to convince your highness of what we have said, (continued one of the gentlemen), we have brought twelve of the principal male inhabitants, who are come to ask pardon in the name of the rest, for having taken up arms without your leave, though even in their own defence, and to preserve their lives from their merciless enemies. And we have likewise brought several women, with children of various ages, that your highness may have an opportunity of personally examining them as much as you please."

The duke, after accepting the apology of the twelve delegates, conversing with the women, and examining the children, graciously dismissed them. He then commanded the priests, who had attempted to mislead him, immediately to leave the court; and gave strict orders, that the persecution should cease throughout his dominions.

The Waldenses had enjoyed peace many years, when Philip, the seventh duke of Savoy, died, and his successor happened to be a very bigoted papist. About the same time, some of the principal Waldenses proposed, that their clergy should preach in public, that every one might know the purity of their doctrines: for hitherto they had preached only in private, and to such congregations as they well knew to consist of none but persons of the reformed religion.

On hearing these proceedings, the new duke was greatly exasperated, and sent a considerable body of troops into the valleys, swearing that if the people would not change their religion, he would have them flayed alive. The commander of the troops soon found the impracticability of conquering them with the number of men he had with him, he, therefore, sent word to the duke, that the idea of subjugating the Waldenses, with so small a force, was ridiculous; that those people were better acquainted with the country than any that were with him; that they had secured all the passes, were well armed, and resolutely determined to defend themselves; and, with respect to flaying them alive, he said, that every skin belonging to those people would cost him the lives of a dozen of his subjects.

Terrified at this information, the duke withdrew the troops, determining to act not by force, but by stratagem. He, therefore, ordered rewards for the taking of any of the Waldenses, who might be found straying from their places of security; and these, when taken, were either flayed alive, or burnt.

The Waldenses had hitherto only had the new Testament and a few books of the Old, in the Waldensian tongue; but they determined now to have the sacred writings complete in their own language. They, therefore, employed a Swiss printer to furnish them with a complete edition of the Old and New Testaments in the Waldensian tongue, which he did for the consideration of fifteen hundred crowns of gold, paid him by those pious people.

Pope Paul the third, a bigoted papist, ascending the pontifical chair, immediately solicited the parliament of Turin to persecute the Waldenses, as the most pernicious of all heretics.

The parliament readily agreed, when several were suddenly apprehended and burnt by their order. Among these was Bartholomew Hector, a bookseller and stationer of Turin, who was brought up a Roman catholic, but having read some treatises written by the reformed clergy, he was fully convinced of the errors of the church of Rome; yet his mind was, for some time, wavering, and he hardly knew what persuasion to embrace.

At length, however, he fully embraced the reformed religion, and was apprehended, as we have already mentioned, and burnt by order of the parliament of Turin.

A consultation was now held by the parliament of Turin, in which it was agreed to send deputies to the valleys of Piedmont, with the following propositions:

1. That if the Waldenses would come to the bosom of the church of Rome, and embrace the Roman catholic religion, they should enjoy their houses, properties and lands, and live with their families, without the least molestation.

2. That to prove their obedience, they should send twelve of their principal persons, with all their ministers and schoolmasters, to Turin, to be dealt with at discretion.

3. That the pope, the king of France, and the duke of Savoy, approved of, and authorized the proceedings of the parliament of Turin, upon this occasion.

4. That if the Waldenses of the valleys of Piedmont, refused to comply with these propositions, persecution should ensue, and certain death be

their portion.

To each of these propositions the Waldenses nobly replied in the following manner, answering them respectively:

1. That no considerations whatever should make them renounce their religion.

2. That they would never consent to commit their best and most respectable friends, to the custody and discretion of their worst and most inveterate enemies.

3. That they valued the approbation of the King of kings, who reigns in heaven, more than any temporal authority.

4. That their souls were more precious than their bodies.

These pointed and spirited replies greatly exasperated the parliament of Turin; they continued, with more avidity than ever, to kidnap such Waldenses as did not act with proper precaution, who were sure to suffer the most cruel deaths. Among these, it unfortunately happened, that they got hold of Jeffery Varnagle, minister of Angrogne, whom they committed to the flames as a heretic.

They then solicited a considerable body of troops of the king of France, in order to exterminate the reformed entirely from the valleys of Piedmont; but just as the troops were going to march, the protestant princes of Germany interposed, and threatened to send troops to assist the Waldenses, if they should be attacked. The king of France, not caring to enter into a war, remanded the troops, and sent word to the parliament of Turin, that he could not spare any troops at present to act in Piedmont. The members of the parliament were greatly vexed at this disappointment, and the persecution gradually ceased, for as they could only put to death such of the reformed as they caught by chance, and as the Waldenses daily grew more cautious, their cruelty was obliged to subside, for want of objects on whom to exercise it.

After the Waldenses had enjoyed a few years tranquility, they were again disturbed by the following means: the pope's nuncio coming to Turin to the duke of Savoy upon business, told that prince, he was astonished he had not yet either rooted out the Waldenses from the valleys of Piedmont entirely, or compelled them to enter into the bosom of the church of Rome. That he could not help looking upon such conduct with a suspicious eye, and that he really thought him a favourer of those heretics, and should report the affair accordingly to his holiness the pope.

Stung by this reflection, and unwilling to be misrepresented to the pope, the duke determined to act with the greatest severity, in order to show his zeal, and to make amends for former neglect by future cruelty. He, accordingly, issued express orders for all the Waldenses to attend mass regularly on pain of death. This they absolutely refused to do, on which he entered the Piedmontese valleys, with a formidable body of troops, and began a most furious persecution, in which great numbers were hanged, drowned, ripped open, tied to trees, and pierced with prongs, thrown from precipices, burnt, stabbed, racked to death, crucified with their heads downwards, worried by dogs, &c.

These who fled had their goods plundered, and their houses burnt to the ground: they were particularly cruel when they caught a minister or a schoolmaster, whom they put to such exquisite tortures, as are almost incredible to conceive. If any whom they took seemed wavering in their faith, they did not put them to death, but sent them to the galleys, to be made converts by dint of hardships.

The most cruel persecutors, upon this occasion, that attended the duke, were three in number, viz. 1. Thomas Incomel, an apostate, for he was brought up in the reformed religion, but renounced his faith, embraced the errors of popery, and turned monk. He was a great libertine, given to unnatural crimes, and sordidly solicitous for plunder of the Waldenses. 2. Corbis, a man of a very ferocious and cruel nature, whose business was to examine the prisoners.--3. The provost of justice, who was very anxious for the execution of the Waldenses, as every execution put money in his pocket.

These three persons were unmerciful to the last degree; and wherever they came, the blood of the innocent was sure to flow. Exclusive of the cruelties exercised by the duke, by these three persons, and the army, in their different marches, many local barbarities were committed. At Pignerol, a town in the valleys, was a monastery, the monks of which, finding they might injure the reformed with impunity, began to plunder the houses and pull down the churches of the Waldenses. Not meeting with any opposition, they seized upon the persons of those unhappy people, murdering the men, confining the women, and putting the children to Roman catholic nurses.

The Roman catholic inhabitants of the valley in St. Martin, likewise, did all they could to torment the neighbouring Waldenses: they destroyed their churches, burnt their houses, seized their properties, stole their cattle, converted their lands to their own use, committed their ministers to the flames, and drove the Waldenses to the woods, where they had nothing to subsist on but wild fruits, roots, the bark of trees, &c.

Some Roman catholic ruffians having seized a minister as he was going to preach, determined to take him to a convenient place, and burn him. His parishioners having intelligence of this affair, the men armed themselves, pursued the ruffians, and seemed determined to rescue their minister; which the ruffians no sooner perceived than they stabbed the poor gentleman, and leaving him weltering in his blood, made a precipitate retreat. The astonished parishioners did all they could to recover him, but in vain; for the weapon had touched the vital parts, and he expired as they were carrying him home.

The monks of Pignerol having a great inclination to get the minister of a town in the valleys, called St. Germain, into their power, hired a band of ruffians for the purpose of apprehending him. These fellows were conducted by a treacherous person, who had formerly been a servant to the clergyman, and who perfectly well knew a secret way to the house, by which he could lead them without alarming the neighbourhood. The guide knocked at the door, and being asked who was there, answered in his own name. The clergyman, not expecting any injury from a person on whom he had heaped favours, immediately opened the door; but perceiving the ruffians, he started back, and fled to a back door; but they rushed in, followed, and seized him. Having murdered all his family, they made him proceed towards Pignerol, goading him all the way with pikes, lances, swords, &c. He was kept a considerable time in prison, and then fastened to the stake to be burnt; when two women of the Waldenses, who had renounced their religion to save their lives, were ordered to carry fagots to the stake to burn him; and as they laid them down, to say, Take these, thou wicked heretic, in recompense for the pernicious doctrines thou hast taught us. These words they both repeated to him to which he calmly replied, I formerly taught you well, but you have since learned ill. The fire was then put to the fagots, and he was speedily consumed, calling upon the name of the Lord as long as his voice permitted.

As the troops of ruffians, belonging to the monks, did great mischief about the town of St. Germain, murdering and plundering many of the inhabitants, the reformed of Lucerne and Angrogne, sent some bands of armed men to the assistance of their brethren of St. Germain. These bodies of armed men frequently attacked the ruffians, and often put them to the rout, which so terrified the monks, that they left the monastery of Pignerol for some time, till they could procure a body of regular troops to guard them.

The duke not thinking himself so successful as he at first imagined he should be, greatly augmented his forces; ordered the bands of ruffians, belonging to the monks, should join him; and commanded, that a general jail-delivery should take place, provided the persons released would bear arms, and form themselves into light companies, to assist in the extermination of the Waldenses.

The Waldenses, being informed of the proceedings, secured as much of their properties as they could, and quitting the valleys, retired to the rocks and caves among the Alps; for it is to be understood, that the valleys of Piedmont are situated at the foot of those prodigious mountains called the Alps, or the Alpine hills.

The army now began to plunder and burn the towns and villages wherever they came; but the troops could not force the passes to the Alps, which were gallantly defended by the Waldenses, who always repulsed their enemies: but if any fell into the hands of the troops, they were sure to be treated with the most barbarous severity.

A soldier having caught one of the Waldenses, bit his right ear off, saying, I will carry this member of that wicked heretic with me into my own country, and preserve it as a rarity. He then stabbed the man and threw him into a ditch.

A party of the troops found a venerable man, upwards of a hundred years of age, together with his grand-daughter, a maiden, of about eighteen, in a cave. They butchered the poor old man in the most inhuman manner, and then attempted to ravish the girl, when she started away and fled from them; but they pursuing her, she threw herself from a precipice and perished.

The Waldenses, in order the more effectually to be able to repel force by force, entered into a league with the protestant powers of Germany, and with the reformed of Dauphiny and Pragela. These were respectively to furnish bodies of troops; and the Waldenses determined, when thus reinforced, to quit the mountains of the Alps, (where they must soon have perished, as the winter was coming on,) and to force the duke's army to evacuate their native valleys.

The duke of Savoy was now tired of the war; it had cost him great fatigue and anxiety of mind, a vast number of men, and very considerable sums of money. It had been much more tedious and bloody than he expected, as well as more expensive than he could at first have imagined, for he thought the plunder would have discharged the expenses of the expedition; but in this he was mistaken, for the pope's nuncio, the bishops, monks, and other ecclesiastics, who attended the army and encouraged the war, sunk the greatest part of the wealth that was taken under various pretences. For these reasons, and the death of his duchess, of which he had just received intelligence, and fearing that the Waldenses, by the treaties they had entered into, would become more powerful than ever, he determined to return to Turin with his army, and to make peace with the Waldenses.

This resolution he executed, though greatly against the will of the ecclesiastics, who were the chief gainers, and the best pleased with revenge. Before the articles of peace could be ratified, the duke himself died, soon after his return to Turin; but on his death-bed he strictly enjoined his son to perform what he intended, and to be as favourable as possible to the Waldenses.

The duke's son, Charles Emmanuel, succeeded to the dominions of Savoy, and gave a full ratification of peace to the Waldenses, according to the last injunctions of his father, though the ecclesiastics did all they could to persuade him to the contrary.

An account of the Persecutions in Venice.

While the state of Venice was free from inquisitors, a great number of protestants fixed their residence there, and many converts were made by the purity of the doctrines they professed, and the inoffensiveness of the conversation they used.

The pope being informed of the great increase of protestantism, in the year 1512 sent inquisitors to Venice to make an inquiry into the matter, and apprehend such as they might deem obnoxious persons. Hence a severe persecution began, and many worthy persons were martyred for serving God with purity, and scorning the trappings of idolatry.

Various were the modes by which the protestants were deprived of life; but one particular method, which was first invented upon this occasion, we shall describe; as soon as sentence was passed, the prisoner had an iron chain which ran through a great stone fastened to his body. He was then laid flat upon a plank, with his face upwards, and rowed between two boats to a certain distance at sea, when the two boats separated, and he was sunk to the bottom by the weight of the stone.

If any denied the jurisdiction of the inquisitors at Venice, they were sent to Rome, where, being committed purposely to damp prisons, and never called to a hearing, their flesh mortified, and they died miserably in jail.

A citizen of Venice, Anthony Ricetti, being apprehended as a protestant, was sentenced to be drowned in the manner we have already described. A few days previous to the time appointed for his execution, his son went to see him, and begged him to recant, that his wife might be saved, and himself not left fatherless. To which the father replied, a good christian is bound to relinquish not only goods and children, but life itself, for the glory of his Redeemer: therefore I am resolved to sacrifice every thing in this transitory world, for the sake of salvation in a world that will last to eternity. The lords of Venice likewise sent him word, that if he would embrace the Roman catholic religion, they would not only give him his life, but redeem a considerable estate which he had mortgaged, and freely present him with it. This, however, he absolutely refused to comply with, sending word to the nobles that he valued his soul beyond all other considerations; and being told that a fellow-prisoner, named Francis Sega, had recanted, he answered, if he has forsaken God, I pity him; but I shall continue steadfast in my duty. Finding all endeavours to persuade him to renounce his faith ineffectual, he was executed according to his sentence, dying cheerfully, and recommending his soul fervently to the Almighty.

What Ricetti had been told concerning the apostacy of Francis Sega, was absolutely false, for he had never offered to recant, but steadfastly persisted in his faith, and was executed, a few days after Ricetti, in the very same manner.

Francis Spinola, a protestant gentleman of very great learning, being apprehended by order of the inquisitors, was carried before their tribunal. A treatise on the Lord's supper was then put into his hands and he was asked if he knew the author of it. To which he replied, I confess myself to be the author of it, and at the same time solemnly affirm, that there is not a line in it but what is authorized by, and consonant to, the holy scriptures. On this confession he was committed close prisoner to a dungeon for several days.

Being brought to a second examination, he charged the pope's legate, and the inquisitors, with being merciless barbarians, and then represented the superstitions and idolatries practised by the church of Rome in so glaring a light, that not being able to refute his arguments, they sent him back to his dungeon, to make him repent of what he had said.

On his third examination, they asked him if he would recant his errors! To which he answered, that the doctrines he maintained were not erroneous, being purely the same as those which Christ and his apostles had taught, and which were handed down to us in the sacred writings. The inquisitors then sentenced him to be drowned, which was executed in the manner already described. He went to meet death with the utmost serenity, seemed to wish for dissolution, and declaring, that the prolongation of his life did but tend to retard that real happiness which could only be expected in the world to come.

An account of several remarkable individuals, who were martyred in different parts of Italy, on account of their religion.

John Mollius was born at Rome, of reputable parents. At twelve years of age they placed him in the monastery of Gray Friars, where he made such a rapid progress in arts, sciences, and languages, that at eighteen years of age he was permitted to take priest's orders.

He was then sent to Ferrara, where, after pursuing his studies six years longer, he was made theological reader in the university of that city. He now, unhappily, exerted his great talents to disguise the gospel truths, and to varnish over the errors of the church of Rome. After some years residence in Ferrara, he removed to the university of Bononia, where he became a professor. Having read some treatises written by ministers of the reformed religion, he grew fully sensible of the errors of popery, and soon became a zealous protestant in his heart.

He now determined to expound, accordingly to the purity of the gospel, St. Paul's epistle to the Romans, in a regular course of sermons. The concourse of people that continually attended his preaching was surprising, but when the priests found the tenor of his doctrines, they despatched an account of the affair to Rome; when the pope sent a monk, named Cornelius, to Bononia, to expound the same epistle, according to the tenets of the church of Rome. The people, however, found such a disparity between the two preachers, that the audience of Mollius increased, and Cornelius was forced to preach to empty benches.

Cornelius wrote an account of his bad success to the pope, who immediately sent an order to apprehend Mollius, who was seized upon accordingly, and kept in close confinement. The bishop of Bononia sent him word that he must recant, or be burnt; but he appealed to Rome, and was removed thither.

At Rome he begged to have a public trial, but that the pope absolutely denied him, and commanded him to give an account of his opinions in writing, which he did under the following heads:

Original sin. Free-will. The infallibility of the church of Rome. The infallibility of the pope. Justification by faith. Purgatory. Transubstantiation. Mass. Auricular confession. Prayers for the dead. The host. Prayers for saints. Going on pilgrimages. Extreme unction. Performing service in an unknown tongue, &c. &c.

All these he confirmed from scripture authority. The pope, upon this occasion, for political reasons, spared him for the present, but soon after had him apprehended, and put to death; he being first hanged, and his body burnt to ashes, A. D. 1553.

The year after, Francis Gamba, a Lombard, of the protestant persuasion, was apprehended, and condemned to death by the senate of Milan. At the place of execution, a monk presented a cross to him, to whom he said, My mind is so full of the real merits and goodness of Christ, that I want not a piece of senseless stick to put me in mind of him. For this expression his tongue was bored through, and he was afterwards burnt.

A. D. 1555, Algerius, a student in the university of Padua, and a man of great learning, having embraced the reformed religion, did all he could to convert others. For these proceedings he was accused of heresy to the pope, and being apprehended, was committed to the prison at Venice.

The pope, being informed of Algerius's great learning, and surprising natural abilities, thought it would be of infinite service to the church of Rome, if he could induce him to forsake the protestant cause. He, therefore, sent for him to Rome, and tried, by the most profane promises, to win him to his purpose. But finding his endeavours ineffectual, he ordered him to be burnt, which sentence was executed accordingly.

A. D. 1559, John Alloysius, being sent from Geneva to preach in Calabria, was there apprehended as a protestant, carried to Rome, and burnt by order of the pope; and James Bovellus, for the same reason, was burnt at Messina.

A. D. 1560, pope Pius the Fourth, ordered all the protestants to be severely persecuted throughout the Italian states, when great numbers of every age, sex, and condition, suffered martyrdom. Concerning the cruelties practised upon this occasion, a learned and humane Roman catholic thus spoke of them, in a letter to a noble lord:

"I cannot, my lord, forbear disclosing my sentiments, with respect to the persecution now carrying on: I think it cruel and unnecessary; I tremble at the manner of putting to death, as it resembles more the slaughter of calves and sheep, than the execution of human beings. I will relate to your lordship a dreadful scene, of which I was myself an eye-witness: seventy protestants were cooped up in one filthy dungeon together; the executioner went in among them, picked out one from among the rest, blindfolded him, led him out to an open place before the prison, and cut his throat with the greatest composure. He then calmly walked into the prison again, bloody as he was, and with the knife in his hand selected another, and despatched him in the same manner; and this, my lord, he repeated till the whole number were put to death. I leave it to your lordship's feelings to judge of my sensations upon this occasion; my tears now wash the paper upon which I give you the recital. Another thing I must mention--the patience with which they met death: they seemed all resignation and piety, fervently praying to God, and cheerfully encountering their fate. I cannot reflect without shuddering, how the executioner held the bloody knife between his teeth; what a dreadful figure he appeared, all covered with blood, and with what unconcern he executed his barbarous office."

A young Englishman who happened to be at Rome, was one day passing by a church, when the procession of the host was just coming out. A bishop carried the host, which the young man perceiving, he snatched it from him, threw it upon the ground, and trampled it under his feet, crying out, Ye wretched idolaters, who neglect the true God, to adore a morsel of bread. This action so provoked the people, that they would have torn him to pieces on the spot; but the priests persuaded them to let him abide by the sentence of the pope.

When the affair was represented to the pope, he was so greatly exasperated that he ordered the prisoner to be burnt immediately; but a cardinal dissuaded him from this hasty sentence, saying, it was better to punish him by slow degrees, and to torture him, that they might find out if he had been instigated by any particular person to commit so atrocious an act.

This being approved, he was tortured with the most exemplary severity, notwithstanding which they could only get these words from him, It was the will of God that I should do as I did.

The pope then passed this sentence upon him.

1. That he should be led by the executioner, naked to the middle, through the streets of Rome.

2. That he should wear the image of the devil upon his head.

3. That his breeches should be painted with the representation of flames.

4. That he should have his right hand cut off.

5. That after having been carried about thus in procession, he should be burnt.

When he heard this sentence pronounced, he implored God to give him strength and fortitude to go through it. As he passed through the streets he was greatly derided by the people, to whom he said some severe things respecting the Romish superstition. But a cardinal, who attended the procession, overhearing him, ordered him to be gagged.

When he came to the church door, where he trampled on the host, the hangman cut off his right hand, and fixed it on a pole. Then two tormentors, with flaming torches, scorched and burnt his flesh all the rest of the way. At the place of execution he kissed the chains that were to bind him to the stake. A monk presenting the figure of a saint to him, he struck it aside, and then being chained to the stake, fire was put to the fagots, and he was soon burnt to ashes.

A little after the last mentioned execution, a venerable old man, who had long been a prisoner in the inquisition, was condemned to be burnt, and brought out for execution. When he was fastened to the stake, a priest held a crucifix to him, on which he said "If you do not take that idol from my sight, you will constrain me to spit upon it." The priest rebuked him for this with great severity; but he bade him remember the first and second commandments, and refrain from idolatry, as God himself had commanded. He was then gagged, that he should not speak any more, and fire being put to the fagots, he suffered martyrdom in the flames.

An Account of the Persecutions in the Marquisate of Saluces.

The Marquisate of Saluces, on the south side of the valleys of Piedmont, was in A. D. 1561, principally inhabited by protestants, when the marquis, who was proprietor of it, began a persecution against them at the instigation of the then pope. He began by banishing the ministers, and if any of them refused to leave their flocks, they were sure to be imprisoned, and severely tortured; however, he did not proceed so far as to put any to death.

Soon after the marquisate fell into the possession of the duke of Savoy, who sent circular letters to all the towns and villages, that he expected the people should all conform to go to mass.

The inhabitants of Saluces, upon receiving this letter, returned a general epistle, in answer.

The duke, after reading the letter, did not interrupt the protestants for some time; but, at length, he sent them word, that they must either conform to the mass, or leave his dominions in fifteen days. The protestants, upon this unexpected edict, sent a deputy to the duke to obtain its revocation, or at least to have it moderated. But their remonstrances were in vain, and they were given to understand that the edict was absolute.

Some were weak enough to go to mass, in order to avoid banishment, and preserve their property; others removed, with all their effects, to different countries; and many neglected the time so long, that they were obliged to abandon all they were worth, and leave the marquisate in haste. Those, who unhappily staid behind, were seized, plundered, and put to death.

An Account of the Persecutions in the Valleys of Piedmont, in the Seventeenth Century.

Pope Clement the eighth, sent missionaries into the valleys of Piedmont, to induce the protestants to renounce their religion; and these missionaries having erected monasteries in several parts of the valleys, became exceedingly troublesome to those of the reformed, where the monasteries appeared, not only as fortresses to curb, but as sanctuaries for all such to fly to, as had any ways injured them.

The protestants petitioned the duke of Savoy against these missionaries, whose insolence and ill-usage were become intolerable; but instead of getting any redress, the interest of the missionaries so far prevailed, that the duke published a decree, in which he declared, that one witness should be sufficient in a court of law against a protestant, and that any witness, who convicted a protestant of any crime whatever, should be entitled to one hundred crowns.

It may be easily imagined, upon the publication of a decree of this nature, that many protestants fell martyrs to perjury and avarice; for several villanous papists would swear any thing against the protestants for the sake of the reward, and then fly to their own priests for absolution from their false oaths. If any Roman catholic, of more conscience than the rest, blamed these fellows for their atrocious crimes, they themselves were in danger of being informed against and punished as favourers of heretics.

The missionaries did all they could to get the books of the protestants into their hands, in order to burn them; when the protestants doing their utmost endeavours to conceal their books, the missionaries wrote to the duke of Savoy, who, for the heinous crime of not surrendering their bibles, prayer-books, and religious treatises, sent a number of troops to be quartered on them. These military gentry did great mischief in the houses of the protestants, and destroyed such quantities of provisions, that many families were thereby ruined.

To encourage, as much as possible, the apostacy of the protestants, the duke of Savoy published a proclamation wherein he said, "To encourage the heretics to turn catholics, it is our will and pleasure, and we do hereby expressly command, that all such as shall embrace the holy Roman catholic faith, shall enjoy an exemption, from all and every tax for the space of five years, commencing from the day of their conversion." The duke of Savoy likewise established a court, called the council for extirpating the heretics. This court was to enter into inquiries concerning the ancient privileges of the protestant churches, and the decrees which had been, from time to time, made in favour of the protestants. But the investigation of these things was carried on with the most manifest partiality; old charters were wrested to a wrong sense, and sophistry was used to pervert the meaning of every thing, which tended to favour the reformed.

As if these severities were not sufficient, the duke, soon after, published another edict, in which he strictly commanded, that no protestant should act as a schoolmaster, or tutor, either in public or private, or dare to teach any art, science, or language, directly or indirectly, to persons of any persuasion whatever.

This edict was immediately followed by another, which decreed, that no protestant should hold any place of profit, trust, or honour; and to wind up the whole, the certain token of an approaching persecution came forth in a final edict, by which it was positively ordered, that all protestants should diligently attend mass.

The publication of an edict, containing such an injunction, may be compared to unfurling the bloody flag; for murder and rapine were sure to follow. One of the first objects that attracted the notice of the papists, was Mr. Sebastian Basan, a zealous protestant, who was seized by the missionaries, confined, tormented for fifteen months, and then burnt.

Previous to the persecution, the missionaries employed kidnappers to steal away the protestants' children, that they might privately be brought up Roman catholics; but now they took away the children by open force, and if they met with any resistance, murdered the parents.

To give greater vigour to the persecution, the duke of Savoy called a general assembly of the Roman catholic nobility and gentry when a solemn edict was published against the reformed, containing many heads, and including several reasons for extirpating the protestants among which were the following:

1. For the preservation of the papal authority.

2. That the church livings may be all under one mode of government.

3. To make a union among all parties.

4. In honour of all the saints, and of the ceremonies of the church of Rome.

This severe edict was followed by a most cruel order, published on January 25, A. D. 1655, under the duke's sanction, by Andrew Gastaldo, doctor of civil laws. This order set forth, "That every head of a family, with the individuals of that family, of the reformed religion, of what rank, degree, or condition soevor, none excepted inhabiting and possessing estates in Lucerne, St. Giovanni, Bibiana, Campiglione, St. Secondo, Lucernetta, La Torre, Fenile, and Bricherassio, should, within three days after the publication thereof, withdraw and depart, and be withdrawn out of the said places, and translated into the places and limits tolerated by his highness during his pleasure; particularly Bobbio, Angrogna, Villaro, Rorata, and the county of Bonetti.

"And all this to be done on pain of death, and confiscation of house and goods, unless within the limited time they turned Roman catholics."

A flight with such speed, in the midst of winter, may be conceived as no agreeable task, especially in a country almost surrounded by mountains. The sudden order affected all, and things, which would have been scarcely noticed at another time, now appeared in the most conspicuous light. Women with child, or women just lain-in, were not objects of pity on this order for sudden removal, for all were included in the command; and it unfortunately happened, that the winter was remarkably severe and rigourous.

The papists, however, drove the people from their habitations at the time appointed, without even suffering them to have sufficient clothes to cover them; and many perished in the mountains through the severity of the weather, or for want of food. Some, however, who remained behind after the decree was published, met with the severest treatment, being murdered by the popish inhabitants, or shot by the troops who were quartered in the valleys. A particular description of these cruelties is given in a letter, written by a protestant, who was upon the spot, and who happily escaped the carnage. "The army (says he) having got footing, became very numerous, by the addition of a multitude of the neighbouring popish inhabitants, who finding we were the destined prey of the plunderers, fell upon us with an impetuous fury. Exclusive of the duke of Savoy's troops, and the popish inhabitants, there were several regiments of French auxiliaries, some companies belonging to the Irish brigades, and several bands formed of outlaws, smugglers, and prisoners, who had been promised pardon and liberty in this world, and absolution in the next, for assisting to exterminate the protestants from Piedmont.

"This armed multitude being encouraged by the Roman catholic bishops and monks, fell upon the protestants in a most furious manner. Nothing now was to be seen but the face of horror and despair, blood stained the floors of the houses, dead bodies bestrewed the streets, groans and cries were heard from all parts. Some armed themselves, and skirmished with the troops; and many, with their families, fled to the mountains. In one village they cruelly tormented 150 women and children after the men were fled, beheading the women, and dashing out the brains of the children. In the towns of Villaro and Bobbio, most of those who refused to go to mass, who were upwards of fifteen years of age, they crucified with their heads downwards; and the greatest number of those who were under that age were strangled."

Sarah Rastignole des Vignes, a woman of 60 years of age, being seized by some soldiers, they ordered her to say a prayer to some saints, which she refusing, they thrust a sickle into her belly, ripped her up, and then cut off her head.

Martha Constantine, a handsome young woman, was treated with great indecency and cruelty by several of the troops, who first ravished, and then killed her, by cutting off her breasts. These they fried, and set before some of their comrades, who ate them without knowing what they were. When they had done eating, the others told them what they had made a meal of, in consequence of which a quarrel ensued, swords were drawn, and a battle took place. Several were killed in the fray, the greater part of whom were those concerned in the horrid massacre of the woman, and who had practised such an inhuman deception on their companions.

Some of the soldiers seized a man of Thrassiniere, and ran the points of their swords through his ears, and through his feet. They then tore off the nails of his fingers and toes with red-hot pincers, tied him to the tail of an ass, and dragged him about the streets; and, finally fastened a cord round his head, which they twisted with a stick in so violent a manner as to wring it from his body.

Peter Symonds, a protestant, of about eighty years of age, was tied neck and heels, and then thrown down a precipice. In the fall the branch of a tree caught hold of the ropes that fastened him, and suspended him in the midway, so that he languished for several days, and at length miserably perished of hunger.

Esay Garcino, refusing to renounce his religion, was cut into small pieces; the soldiers, in ridicule, saying, they had minced him. A woman, named Armand, had every limb separated from each other, and then the respective parts were hung upon a hedge. Two old women were ripped open, and then left in the fields upon the snow where they perished; and a very old woman, who was deformed, had her nose and hands cut off, and was left, to bleed to death in that manner.

A great number of men, women, and children, were flung from the rocks, and dashed to pieces. Magdalen Bertino, a protestant woman of La Torre, was stripped stark naked, her head tied between her legs, and thrown down one of the precipices; and Mary Raymondet, of the same town, had the flesh sliced from her bones till she expired.

Magdalen Pilot, of Villaro, was cut to pieces in the cave of Castolus; Ann Charboniere had one end of a stake thrust up her body; and the other being fixed in the ground, she was left in that manner to perish, and Jacob Perrin the elder, of the church of Villaro, and David, his brother, were flayed alive.

An inhabitant of La Torre, named Giovanni Andrea Michialm, was apprehended, with four of his children, three of them were hacked to pieces before him, the soldiers asking him, at the death of every child, if he would renounce his religion which he constantly refused. One of the soldiers then took up the last and youngest by the legs, and putting the same question to the father he replied as before, when the inhuman brute dashed out the child's brains. The father, however, at the same moment started from them, and fled: the soldiers fired after him, but missed him; and he, by the swiftness of his heels, escaped, and hid himself in the Alps.

Further Persecutions in the Valleys of Piedmont, in the seventeenth Century.

Giovanni Pelanchion, for refusing to turn papist, was tied by one leg to the tail of a mule, and dragged through the streets of Lucerne, amidst the acclamations of an inhuman mob, who kept stoning him, and crying out, He is possessed with the devil, so that, neither stoning, nor dragging him through the streets, will kill him, for the devil keeps him alive. They then took him to the river side, chopped off his head, and left that and his body unburied, upon the bank of the stream.

Magdalen, the daughter of Peter Fontaine, a beautiful child of ten years of age, was ravished and murdered by the soldiers. Another girl of about the same age, they roasted alive at Villa Nova; and a poor woman, hearing the soldiers were coming toward her house, snatched up the cradle in which her infant son was asleep, and fled toward the woods. The soldiers, however, saw and pursued her, when she lightened herself by putting down the cradle and child, which the soldiers no sooner came to, than they murdered the infant, and continuing the pursuit, found the mother in a cave, where they first ravished, and then cut her to pieces.

Jacob Michelino, chief elder of the church of Bobbio, and several other protestants, were hung up by means of hooks fixed in their bellies and left to expire in the most excruciating tortures.

Giovanni Rostagnal, a venerable protestant, upwards of fourscore years of age, had his nose and ears cut off, and slices cut from the fleshy parts of his body, till he bled to death.

Seven persons, viz. Daniel Seleagio and his wife, Giovanni Durant, Lodwich Durant, Bartholomew Durant, Daniel Revel, and Paul Reynaud, had their mouths stuffed with gunpowder, which being set fire to, their heads were blown to pieces.

Jacob Birone, a schoolmaster of Rorata, for refusing to change his religion, was stripped quite naked; and after having been very indecently exposed, had the nails of his toes and fingers torn off with red-hot pincers, and holes bored through his hands with the point of a dagger. He then had a cord tied round his middle, and was led through the streets with a soldier on each side of him. At every turning the soldier on his right hand side cut a gash in his flesh, and the soldier on his left hand side struck him with a bludgeon, both saying, at the same instant, Will you go to mass? will you go to mass? He still replied in the negative to these interrogatories, and being at length taken to the bridge, they cut off his head on the balustrades, and threw both that and his body into the river.

Paul Garnier, a very pious protestant, had his eyes put out, was then flayed alive, and being divided into four parts, his quarters were placed on four of the principal houses of Lucerne. He bore all his sufferings with the most exemplary patience, praised God as long as he could speak, and plainly evinced, what confidence and resignation a good conscience can inspire.

Daniel Cardon, of Rocappiata, being apprehended by some soldiers, they cut his head off, and having fried his brains, ate them. Two poor old blind women, of St. Giovanni, were burnt alive; and a widow of La Torre, with her daughter, were driven into the river, and there stoned to death.

Paul Giles, on attempting to run away from some soldiers, was shot in the neck: they then slit his nose, sliced his chin, stabbed him, and gave his carcase to the dogs.

Some of the Irish troops having taken eleven men of Garcigliana prisoners, they made a furnace red hot, and forced them to push each other in till they came to the last man, whom they pushed in themselves.

Michael Gonet, a man of 90, was burnt to death; Baptista Oudri, another old man, was stabbed; and Bartholomew Frasche had holes made in his heels, through which ropes being put, he was dragged by them to the jail, where his wounds mortified and killed him.

Magdalene de la Piere being pursued by some of the soldiers, and taken, was thrown down a precipice, and dashed to pieces. Margaret Revella, and Mary Pravillerin, two very old women, were burnt alive; and Michael Bellino, with Ann Bochardno, were beheaded.

The son and daughter of a counsellor of Giovanni were rolled down a steep hill together, and suffered to perish in a deep pit at the bottom. A tradesman's family, viz: himself, his wife, and an infant in her arms, were cast from a rock, and dashed to pieces; and Joseph Chairet, and Paul Carniero, were flayed alive.

Cypriania Bustia, being asked if he would renounce his religion and turn Roman catholic, replied, I would rather renounce life, or turn dog; to which a priest answered, For that expression you shall both renounce life, and be given to the dogs. They, accordingly, dragged him to prison, where he continued a considerable time without food, till he was famished; after which they threw his corpse into the street before the prison, and it was devoured by dogs in the most shocking manner.

Margaret Saretta was stoned to death, and then thrown into the river; Antonio Bartina had his head cleft asunder; and Joseph Pont was cut through the middle of his body.

Daniel Maria, and his whole family, being ill of a fever, several papist ruffians broke into his house, telling him they were practical physicians, and would give them all present ease, which they did by knocking the whole family on the head.

Three infant children of a protestant, named Peter Fine, were covered with snow, and stifled; an elderly widow, named Judith, was beheaded, and a beautiful young woman was stripped naked, and had a stake driven through her body, of which she expired.

Lucy, the wife of Peter Besson, a woman far gone in her pregnancy, who lived in one of the villages of the Piedmontese valleys, determined, if possible, to escape from such dreadful scenes as every where surrounded her: she, accordingly took two young children, one in each hand, and set off towards the Alps. But on the third day of the journey she was taken in labour among the mountains, and delivered of an infant, who perished through the extreme inclemency of the weather, as did the two other children; for all three were found dead by her, and herself just expiring, by the person to whom she related the above particulars.

Francis Gros, the son of a clergyman, had his flesh slowly cut from his body into small pieces, and put into a dish before him; two of his children were minced before his sight; and his wife was fastened to a post, that she might behold all these cruelties practised on her husband and offspring. The tormentors, at length, being tired of exercising their cruelties, cut off the heads of both husband and wife, and then gave the flesh of the whole family to the dogs.

The sieur Thomas Margher fled to a cave, when the soldiers shut up the mouth, and he perished with famine. Judith Revelin, with seven children, were barbarously murdered in their beds; and a widow of near fourscore years of age, was hewn to pieces by soldiers.

Jacob Roseno was ordered to pray to the saints, which he absolutely refused to do: some of the soldiers beat him violently with bludgeons to make him comply, but he still refusing, several of them fired at him and lodged a great many balls in his body. As he was almost expiring, they cried to him, Will you call upon the saints? Will you pray to the saints? To which he answered, No! No! No! when one of the soldiers, with a broad sword, clove his head asunder, and put an end to his sufferings in this world; for which undoubtedly, he is gloriously rewarded in the next.

A soldier, attempting to ravish a young woman, named Susanna Gacquin, she made a stout resistance, and in the struggle pushed him over a precipice, when he was dashed to pieces by the fall. His comrades, instead of admiring the virtue of the young woman, and applauding her for so nobly defending her chastity, fell upon her with their swords, and cut her to pieces.

Giovanni Pulhus, a poor peasant of La Torre, being apprehended as a protestant by the soldiers, was ordered, by the marquis of Pianesta, to be executed in a place near the convent. When he came to the gallows, several monks attended, and did all they could to persuade him to renounce his religion. But he told them he never would embrace idolatry, and that he was happy at being thought worthy to suffer for the name of Christ. They then put him in mind of what his wife and children, who depended upon his labour, would suffer after his decease; to which he replied, I would have my wife and children, as well as myself, to consider their souls more than their bodies, and the next world before this; and with respect to the distress I may leave them in, God is merciful, and will provide for them while they are worthy of his protection. Finding the inflexibility of this poor man, the monks cried,--Turn him off, turn him off, which the executioner did almost immediately, and the body being afterward cut down, was flung into the river.

Paul Clement, an elder of the church of Rossana, being apprehended by the monks of a neighbouring monastery, was carried to the market-place of that town, where some protestants having just been executed by the soldiers, he was shown the dead bodies, in order that the sight might intimidate him. On beholding the shocking subjects, he said, calmly, You may kill the body, but you cannot prejudice the soul of a true believer; but with respect to the dreadful spectacles which you have here shown me, you may rest assured, that God's vengeance will overtake the murderers of those poor people, and punish them for the innocent blood they have spilt. The monks were so exasperated at this reply, that they ordered him to be hung up directly; and while he was hanging, the soldiers amused themselves in standing at a distance, and shooting at the body as at a mark.

Daniel Rambaut, of Villaro, the father of a numerous family, was apprehended, and, with several others, committed to prison, in the jail of Paysana. Here he was visited by several priests, who with continual importunities did all they could to persuade him to renounce the protestant religion, and turn papist; but this he peremptorily refused, and the priests finding his resolution, pretended to pity his numerous family, and told him that he might yet have his life, if he would subscribe to the belief of the following articles:

1. The real presence in the host.

2. Transubstantiation.

3. Purgatory.

4. The pope's infallibility.

5. That masses said for the dead will release souls from purgatory.

6. That praying to saints will procure the remission of sins.

M. Rambaut told the priests, that neither his religion, his understanding, nor his conscience, would suffer him to subscribe to any of the articles, for the following reasons:

1. That to believe the real presence in the host, is a shocking union of both blasphemy and idolatry.

2. That to fancy the words of consecration perform what the papists call transubstantiation, by converting the wafer and wine into the real and identical body and blood of Christ, which was crucified, and which afterward ascended into heaven, is too gross an absurdity for even a child to believe, who was come to the least glimmering of reason; and that nothing but the most blind superstition could make the Roman catholics put a confidence in any thing so completely ridiculous.

3. That the doctrine of purgatory was more inconsistent and absurd than a fairy tale.

4. That the pope's being infallible was an impossibility, and the pope arrogantly laid claim to what could belong to God only, as a perfect being.

5. That saying masses for the dead was ridiculous, and only meant to keep up a belief in the fable of purgatory, as the fate of all is finally decided, on the departure of the soul from the body.

6. That praying to saints for the remission of sins, is misplacing adoration; as the saints themselves have occasion for an intercessor in Christ. Therefore, as God only can pardon our errors, we ought to sue to him alone for pardon.

The priests were so highly offended at M. Rambaut's answers to the articles to which they would have had him subscribe, that they determined to shake his resolution by the most cruel method imaginable: they ordered one joint of his finger to be cut off every day, till all his fingers were gone; they then proceeded in the same manner with his toes; afterward they alternately cut off, daily, a hand and a foot; but finding that he bore his sufferings with the most admirable patience, increased both in fortitude and resignation, and maintained his faith with steadfast resolution, and unshaken constancy, they stabbed him to the heart, and then gave his body to be devoured by the dogs.

Peter Gabriola, a protestant gentleman of considerable eminence, being seized by a troop of soldiers, and refusing to renounce his religion, they hung a great number of little bags of gunpowder about his body, and then setting fire to them, blew him up.

Anthony, the son of Samuel Catieris, a poor dumb lad who was extremely inoffensive, was cut to pieces by a party of the troops; and soon after the same ruffians entered the house of Peter Moniriat, and cut off the legs of the whole family, leaving them to bleed to death, as they were unable to assist themselves, or to help each other.

Daniel Benech being apprehended, had his nose slit, his ears cut off, and was then divided into quarters, each quarter being hung upon a tree, and Mary Monino, had her jaw bones broke and was then left to languish till she was famished.

Mary Pelanchion, a handsome widow, belonging to the town of Villaro, was seized by a party of the Irish brigades, who having beat her cruelly, and ravished her, dragged her to a high bridge which crossed the river, and stripped her naked in a most indecent manner, hung her by the legs to the bridge, with her head downwards towards the water, and then going into boats, they fired at her till she expired.

Mary Nigrino, and her daughter who was an idiot, were cut to pieces in the woods, and their bodies left to be devoured by wild beasts: Susanna Bales, a widow of Villaro, was immured till she perished through hunger; and Susanna Calvio running away from some soldiers and hiding herself in a barn, they set fire to the straw and burnt her.

Paul Armand was hacked to pieces; a child named Daniel Bertino was burnt; Daniel Michialino had his tongue plucked out, and was left to perish in that condition; and Andreo Bertino, a very old man, who was lame, was mangled in a most shocking manner, and at length had his belly ripped open, and his bowels carried about on the point of a halbert.

Constantia Bellione, a protestant lady, being apprehended on account of her faith, was asked by a priest if she would renounce the devil and go to mass; to which she replied, "I was brought up in a religion, by which I was always taught to renounce the devil; but should I comply with your desire, and go to mass, I should be sure to meet him there in a variety of shapes." The priest was highly incensed at what she said, and told her to recant, or she should suffer cruelly. The lady, however, boldly answered, that she valued not any sufferings he could inflict, and in spite of all the torments he could invent, she would keep her conscience pure and her faith inviolate. The priest then ordered slices of her flesh to be cut off from several parts of her body, which cruelty she bore with the most singular patience, only saying to the priest, what horrid and lasting torments will you suffer in hell, for the trifling and temporary pains which I now endure. Exasperated at this expression, and willing to stop her tongue, the priest ordered a file of musqueteers to draw up and fire upon her, by which she was soon despatched, and sealed her martyrdom with her blood.

A young woman named Judith Mandon, for refusing to change her religion, and embrace popery, was fastened to a stake, and sticks thrown at her from a distance, in the very same manner as that barbarous custom which was formerly practised on Shrove-Tuesday, of shying at rocks, as it was termed. By this inhuman proceeding, the poor creature's limbs were beat and mangled in a terrible manner, and her brains were at last dashed out by one of the bludgeons.

David Paglia and Paul Genre, attempting to escape to the Alps, with each his son, were pursued and overtaken by the soldiers in a large plain. Here they hunted them for their diversion, goading them with their swords, and making them run about till they dropped down with fatigue. When they found that their spirits were quite exhausted, and that they could not afford them any more barbarous sport by running, the soldiers hacked them to pieces, and left their mangled bodies on the spot.

A young man of Bobbio, named Michael Greve, was apprehended to the town of La Torre, and being led to the bridge, was thrown over into the river. As he could swim very well, he swam down the stream, thinking to escape, but the soldiers and mob followed on both sides the river, and kept stoning him, till receiving a blow on one of his temples, he was stunned, and consequently sunk and was drowned.

David Armand was ordered to lay his head down on a block, when a soldier, with a large hammer, beat out his brains. David Baridona being apprehended at Villaro, was carried to La Torre, where, refusing to renounce his religion, he was tormented by means of brimstone matches being tied between his fingers and toes, and set fire to; and afterward, by having his flesh plucked off with red-hot pincers, till he expired; and Giovanni Barolina, with his wife, were thrown into a pool of stagnant water, and compelled, by means of pitchforks and stones, to duck down their heads till they were suffocated.

A number of soldiers went to the house of Joseph Garniero, and before they entered, fired in at the window, to give notice of their approach. A musket ball entered one of Mrs. Garniero's breasts, as she was suckling an infant with the other. On finding their intentions, she begged hard that they would spare the life of the infant, which they promised to do, and sent it immediately to a Roman catholic nurse. They then took the husband and hanged him at his own door, and having shot the wife through the head, they left her body weltering in its blood, and her husband hanging on the gallows.

Isaiah Mondon, an elderly man, and a pious protestant, fled from the merciless persecutors to a cleft in a rock, where he suffered the most dreadful hardships; for, in the midst of the winter he was forced to lay on the bare stone, without any covering; his food was the roots he could scratch up near his miserable habitation; and the only way by which he could procure drink, was to put snow in his mouth till it melted. Here, however, some of the inhuman soldiers found him, and after having beaten him unmercifully, they drove him towards Lucerne, goading him with the points of their swords.--Being exceedingly weakened by his manner of living, and his spirits exhausted by the blows he had received, he fell down in the road. They again beat him to make him proceed: when on his knees, he implored them to put him out of his misery, by despatching him. This they at last agreed to do; and one of them stepping up to him shot him through the head with a pistol, saying, there, heretic, take thy request.

Mary Revol, a worthy protestant, received a shot in her back, as she was walking along the street. She dropped down with the wound, but recovering sufficient strength, she raised herself upon her knees, and lifting her hands towards heaven, prayed in a most fervent manner to the Almighty, when a number of soldiers, who were near at hand, fired a whole volley of shot at her, many of which took effect, and put an end to her miseries in an instant.

Several men, women, and children secreted themselves in a large cave, where they continued for some weeks in safety. It was the custom for two of the men to go when it was necessary, and by stealth procure provisions. These were, however, one day watched, by which the cave was discovered, and soon after, a troop of Roman catholics appeared before it. The papists that assembled upon this occasion were neighbours and intimate acquaintances of the protestants in the cave; and some of them were even related to each other. The protestants, therefore, came out, and implored them, by the ties of hospitality, by the ties of blood, and as old acquaintances and neighbours, not to murder them. But superstition overcomes every sensation of nature and humanity; so that the papists, blinded by bigotry, told them they could not show any mercy to heretics, and, therefore, bade them prepare to die. Hearing this, and knowing the fatal obstinacy of the Roman catholics, the protestants all fell prostrate, lifted their hands and hearts to heaven, prayed with great sincerity and fervency, and then bowing down, put their faces close to the ground, and patiently waited their fate, which was soon decided, for the papists fell upon them with unremitting fury, and having cut them to pieces, left the mangled bodies and limbs in the cave.

Giovanni Salvagiot, passing by a Roman catholic church, and not taking off his hat, was followed by some of the congregation, who fell upon and murdered him; and Jacob Barrel and his wife, having been taken prisoners by the earl of St. Secondo, one of the duke of Savoy's officers, he delivered them up to the soldiery, who cut off the woman's breasts, and the man's nose, and then shot them both through the head.

Anthony Guigo, a protestant, of a wavering disposition, went to Periero, with an intent to renounce his religion and embrace popery. This design he communicated to some priests, who highly commended it, and a day was fixed upon for his public recantation. In the mean time, Anthony grew fully sensible of his perfidy, and his conscience tormented him so much night and day, that he determined not to recant, but to make his escape. This he effected, but being soon missed and pursued, he was taken. The troops on the way did all they could to bring him back to his design of recantation; but finding their endeavours ineffectual, they beat him violently on the road, when coming near a precipice, he took an opportunity of leaping down it, and was dashed to pieces.

A protestant gentleman, of considerable fortune, at Bobbio, being nightly provoked by the insolence of a priest, retorted with great severity; and among other things, said, that the pope was Antichrist, mass idolatry, purgatory a farce, and absolution a cheat. To be revenged, the priest hired five desperate ruffians, who, the same evening, broke into the gentleman's house, and seized upon him in a violent manner. The gentleman was terribly frightened, fell on his knees, and implored mercy; but the desperate ruffians despatched him without the least hesitation.

A Narrative of the Piedmontese War.

The massacres and murders already mentioned to have been committed in the valleys of Piedmont, nearly depopulated most of the towns and villages. One place only had not been assaulted, and that was owing to the difficulty of approaching it; this was the little commonalty of Roras, which was situated upon a rock.

As the work of blood grew slack in other places, the earl of Christople, one of the duke of Savoy's officers, determined, if possible, to make himself master of it; and, with that view, detached three hundred men to surprise it secretly.

The inhabitants of Roras, however, had intelligence of the approach of these troops, when captain Joshua Gianavel, a brave protestant officer, put himself at the head of a small body of the citizens, and waited in ambush to attack the enemy in a small defile.

When the troops appeared, and had entered the defile, which was the only place by which the town could be approached, the protestants kept up a smart and well-directed fire against them, and still kept themselves concealed behind bushes from the sight of the enemy. A great number of the soldiers were killed, and the remainder receiving a continued fire, and not seeing any to whom they might return it, thought proper to retreat.

The members of this little community then sent a memorial to the marquis of Pianessa, one of the duke's general officers, setting forth, "That they were sorry, upon any occasion, to be under the necessity of taking up arms; but that the secret approach of a body of troops, without any reason assigned, or any previous notice sent of the purpose of their coming, had greatly alarmed them; that as it was their custom never to suffer any of the military to enter their little community, they had repelled force by force, and should do so again; but in all other respects, they professed themselves dutiful, obedient, and loyal subjects to their sovereign, the duke of Savoy."

The marquis of Pianessa, that he might have the better opportunity of deluding and surprising the protestants of Roras, sent them word in answer, "That he was perfectly satisfied with their behaviour, for they had done right, and even rendered a service to their country, as the men who had attempted to pass the defile were not his troops, or sent by him, but a band of desperate robbers, who had, for some time, infested those parts, and been a terror to the neighbouring country." To give a greater colour to his treachery, he then published an ambiguous proclamation seemingly favourable to the inhabitants.

Yet, the very day after this plausible proclamation, and specious conduct, the marquis sent 500 men to possess themselves of Roras, while the people, as he thought, were lulled into perfect security by his specious behaviour.

Captain Gianavel, however, was not to be deceived so easily: he, therefore, laid an ambuscade for this body of troops, as he had for the former, and compelled him to retire with very considerable loss.

Though foiled in these, two attempts, the marquis Pianessa determined on a third, which should be still more formidable; but first he imprudently published another proclamation, disowning any knowledge of the second attempt.

Soon after, 700 chosen men were sent upon the expedition, who, in spite of the fire from the protestants, forced the defile, entered Roras, and began to murder every person they met with, without distinction of age or sex. The protestant captain Gianavel, at the head of a small body, though he had lost the defile, determined to dispute their passage through a fortified pass that led to the richest and best part of the town. Here he was successful, by keeping up a continual fire, and by means of his men being all complete marksmen. The Roman catholic commander was greatly staggered at this opposition, as he imagined that he had surmounted all difficulties. He, however, did his endeavours to force the pass, but being able to bring up only twelve men in front at a time, and the protestants being secured by a breastwork, he found he should be baffled by the handful of men who opposed him.

Enraged at the loss of so many of his troops, and fearful of disgrace if he persisted in attempting what appeared so impracticable, he thought it the wisest thing to retreat. Unwilling, however, to withdraw his men by the defile at which he had entered, on account of the difficulty and danger of the enterprise, he determined to retreat towards Villaro, by another pass called Piampra, which, though hard of access, was easy of descent. But in this he met with a disappointment, for captain Gianavel having posted his little band here, greatly annoyed the troops as they passed, and even pursued their rear till they entered the open country.

The marquis of Pianessa, finding that all his attempts were frustrated, and that every artifice he used was only an alarm-signal to the inhabitants of Roras, determined to act openly, and therefore proclaimed, that ample rewards should be given to any one who would bear arms against the obstinate heretics of Roras, as he called them; and that any officer who would exterminate them should be rewarded in a princely manner.

This engaged captain Mario, a bigoted Roman catholic, and a desperate ruffian, to undertake the enterprise. He, therefore, obtained leave to raise a regiment in the following six towns: Lucerne, Borges, Famolas, Bobbio, Begnal, and Cavos.

Having completed his regiment, which consisted of 1000 men, he laid his plan not to go by the defiles or the passes, but to attempt gaining the summit of a rock, from whence he imagined he could pour his troops into the town without much difficulty or opposition.

The protestants suffered the Roman catholic troops to gain almost the summit of the rock, without giving them any opposition, or ever appearing in their sight: but when they had almost reached the top they made a most furious attack upon them; one party keeping up a well-directed and constant fire, and another party rolling down huge stones.

This stopped the career of the papist troops: many were killed by the musketry, and more by the stones, which beat them down the precipices. Several fell sacrifices to their hurry, for by attempting a precipitate retreat, they fell down, and were dashed to pieces; and captain Mario himself narrowly escaped with his life, for he fell from a craggy place into a river which washed the foot of the rock. He was taken up senseless, but afterwards recovered, though he was ill of the bruises for a long time; and, at length, he fell into a decline at Lucerne, where he died.

Another body of troops was ordered from the camp at Villaro, to make an attempt upon Roras; but these were likewise defeated, by means of the protestants' ambush-fighting, and compelled to retreat again to the camp at Villaro.

After each of these signal victories, captain Gianavel made a suitable discourse to his men, causing them to kneel down, and return thanks to the Almighty for his providential protection; and usually concluded with the eleventh psalm, where the subject is placing confidence in God.

The marquis of Pianessa was greatly enraged at being so much baffled by the few inhabitants of Roras: he, therefore, determined to attempt their expulsion in such a manner as could hardly fail of success.

With this view he ordered all the Roman catholic militia of Piedmont to be raised and disciplined. When these orders were completed, he joined to the militia eight thousand regular troops, and dividing the whole into three distinct bodies, he designed that three formidable attacks should be made at the same time, unless the people of Roras, to whom he sent an account of his great preparations, would comply with the following conditions:

1. To ask pardon for taking up arms. 2. To pay the expenses of all the expeditions sent against them. 3. To acknowledge the infallibility of the pope. 4. To go to mass. 5. To pray to the saints. 6. To wear beards. 7. To deliver up their ministers. 8. To deliver up their schoolmasters. 9. To go to confession. 10. To pay loans for the delivery of souls from purgatory. 11. To give up captain Gianavel at discretion. 12. To give up the elders of their church at discretion.

The inhabitants of Roras, on being acquainted with these conditions, were filled with an honest indignation, and, in answer, sent word to the marquis, that sooner than comply with them they would suffer three things, which, of all others, were the most obnoxious to mankind, viz.

1. Their estates to be seized. 2. Their houses to be burnt. 3. Themselves to be murdered.

Exasperated at this message, the marquis sent them this laconic epistle.

To the obstinate Heretics inhabiting Roras.

You shall have your request, for the troops sent against you have strict injunctions to plunder, burn, and kill.

PIANESSA.

The three armies were then put in motion, and the attacks ordered to be made thus: the first by the rocks of Villaro; the second by the pass of Bagnol; and the third by the defile of Lucerne.

The troops forced their way by the superiority of numbers, and having gained the rocks, pass, and defile, began to make the most horrid depredations, and exercise the greatest cruelties. Men they hanged, burnt, racked to death, or cut to pieces; women they ripped open, crucified, drowned, or threw from the precipices; and children they tossed upon spears, minced, cut their throats, or dashed out their brains. One hundred and twenty-six suffered in this manner, on the first day of their gaining the town.

Agreeable to the marquis of Pianessa's orders, they likewise plundered the estates, and burnt the houses of the people. Several protestants, however, made their escape, under the conduct of Captain Gianavel, whose wife and children were unfortunately made prisoners, and sent under a strong guard to Turin.

The marquis of Pianessa wrote a letter to captain Gianavel, and released a protestant prisoner that he might carry it him. The contents were, that if the captain would embrace the Roman catholic religion, he should be indemnified for all his losses since the commencement of the war; his wife and children should be immediately released, and himself honourably promoted in the duke of Savoy's army; but if he refused to accede to the proposals made him, his wife and children should be to put to death; and so large a reward should be given to take him, dead or alive, that even some of his own confidential friends should be tempted to betray him, from the greatness of the sum.

To this epistle, the brave Gianavel sent the following answer.

My Lord Marquis,

There is no torment so great or death so cruel, but what I would prefer to the abjuration of my religion: so that promises lose their effects, and menaces only strengthen me in my faith.

With respect to my wife and children, my lord, nothing can be more afflicting to me than the thoughts of their confinement, or more dreadful to my imagination, than their suffering a violent and cruel death. I keenly feel all the tender sensations of husband and parent; my heart is replete with every sentiment of humanity; I would suffer any torment to rescue them from danger; I would die to preserve them.

But having said thus much, my lord, I assure you that the purchase of their lives must not be the price of my salvation. You have them in your power it is true; but my consolation is, that your power is only a temporary authority over their bodies: you may destroy the mortal part, but their immortal souls are out of your reach, and will live hereafter to bear testimony against you for your cruelties. I therefore recommend them and myself to God, and pray for a reformation in your heart.

JOSHUA GIANAVEL.

This brave protestant officer, after writing the above letter, retired to the Alps, with his followers; and being joined by a great number of other fugitive protestants, he harassed the enemy by continual skirmishes.

Meeting one day with a body of papist troops near Bibiana, he, though inferior in numbers, attacked them with great fury, and put them to the rout without the loss of a man, though himself was shot through the leg in the engagement, by a soldier who had hid himself behind a tree; but Gianavel perceiving from whence the shot came, pointed his gun to the place, and despatched the person who had wounded him.

Captain Gianavel hearing that a captain Jahier had collected together a considerable body of protestants, wrote him a letter, proposing a junction of their forces. Captain Jahier immediately agreed to the proposal, and marched directly to meet Gianavel.

The junction being formed, it was proposed to attack a town, (inhabited by Roman catholics) called Garcigliana. The assault was given with great spirit, but a reinforcement of horse and foot having lately entered the town, which the protestants knew nothing of, they were repulsed; yet made a masterly retreat, and only lost one man in the action.

The next attempt of the protestant forces was upon St. Secondo, which they attacked with great vigour, but met with a strong resistance from the Roman catholic troops, who had fortified the streets, and planted themselves in the houses, from whence they poured musket balls in prodigious numbers. The protestants, however, advanced, under cover of a great number of planks, which some held over their heads, to secure them from the shots of the enemy from the houses, while others kept up a well directed fire; so that the houses and entrenchments were soon forced, and the town taken.

In the town they found a prodigious quantity of plunder, which had been taken from protestants at various times, and different places, and which were stored up in the warehouses, churches, dwelling houses, &c. This they removed to a place of safety, to be distributed, with as much justice as possible, among the sufferers.

This successful attack was made with such skill and spirit, that it cost very little to the conquering party, the protestants having only 17 killed, and 26 wounded; while the papists suffered a loss of no less than 450 killed and 511 wounded.

Five protestant officers, viz. Gianavel, Jahier, Laurentio, Genolet, and Benet, laid a plan to surprise Biqueras. To this end they marched in five respective bodies, and by agreement were to make the attack at the same time. The captains Jahier and Laurentio passed through two defiles in the woods, and came to the place in safety, under covert; but the other three bodies made their approaches through an open country, and, consequently, were more exposed to an attack.

The Roman catholics taking the alarm, a great number of troops were sent to relieve Biqueras from Cavors, Bibiana, Fenile, Campiglione, and some other neighbouring places. When these were united, they determined to attack the three protestant parties, that were marching through the open country.

The protestant officers perceiving the intent of the enemy, and not being at a great distance from each other, joined their forces with the utmost expedition, and formed themselves in order of battle.

In the mean time, the captains Jahier and Laurentio had assaulted the town of Biqueras, and burnt all the out houses, to make their approaches with the greater ease; but not being supported as they expected by the other three protestant captains, they sent a messenger, on a swift horse, towards the open country, to inquire the reason.

The messenger soon returned and informed them that it was not in the power of the three protestant captains to support their proceedings, as they were themselves attacked by a very superior force in the plain, and could scarce sustain the unequal conflict.

The captains Jahier and Laurentio, on receiving this intelligence, determined to discontinue the assault on Biqueras, and to proceed, with all possible expedition, to the relief of their friends on the plain. This design proved to be of the most essential service, for just as they arrived at the spot where the two armies were engaged, the papist troops began to prevail, and were on the point of flanking the left wing, commanded by captain Gianavel. The arrival of these troops turned the scale in favour of the protestants; and the papist forces, though they fought with the most obstinate intrepidity, were totally defeated. A great number were killed and wounded on both sides, and the baggage, military stores, &c. taken by the protestants were very considerable.

Captain Gianavel, having information that three hundred of the enemy were to convoy a great quantity of stores, provisions, &c. from La Torre to the castle of Mirabac, determined to attack them on the way. He, accordingly, began the assault at Malbec, though with a very inadequate force. The contest was long and bloody, but the protestants, at length, were obliged to yield to the superiority of numbers, and compelled to make a retreat, which they did with great regularity, and but little loss.

Captain Gianavel advanced to an advantageous post, situated near the town of Villaro, and then sent the following information and commands to the inhabitants.

1. That he should attack the town in twenty-four hours.

2. That with respect to the Roman catholics who had borne arms, whether they belonged to the army or not, he should act by the law of retaliation, and put them to death, for the numerous depredations, and many cruel murders, they had committed.

3. That all women and children, whatever their religion might be, should be safe.

4. That he commanded all male protestants to leave the town and join him.

5. That all apostates, who had, through weakness, abjured their religion, should be deemed enemies, unless they renounced their abjuration.

6. That all who returned to their duty to God, and themselves, should be received as friends.

The protestants, in general, immediately left the town, and joined captain Gianavel with great satisfaction, and the few, who through weakness or fear, had abjured their faith, recanted their abjuration, and were received into the bosom of the church. As the marquis of Pianessa had removed the army, and encamped in quite a different part of the country, the Roman catholics of Villaro thought it would be folly to attempt to defend the place with the small force they had. They, therefore, fled with the utmost precipitation, leaving the town and most of their property, to the discretion of the protestants.

The protestant commanders having called a council of war, resolved to make an attempt upon the town of La Torre.

The papists being apprized of the design, detached some troops to defend a defile, through which the protestants must make their approach; but these were defeated, compelled to abandon the pass, and forced to retreat to La Torre.

The protestants proceeded on their march, and the troops of La Torre, on their approach, made a furious sally, were repulsed with great loss, and compelled to seek shelter in the town. The governor now only thought of defending the place, which the protestants began to attack in form; but after many brave attempts, and furious assaults, the commanders determined to abandon the enterprise for several reasons, particularly, because they found the place itself too strong, their own number too weak, and their cannon not adequate to the task of battering down the walls.

This resolution taken, the protestant commanders began a masterly retreat, and conducted it with such regularity, that the enemy did not choose to pursue them, or molest their rear, which they might have done, as they passed the defiles.

The next day they mustered, reviewed the army, and found the whole to amount to four hundred and ninety-five men. They then held a council of war, and planned an easier enterprise: this was to make an attack on the commonalty of Crusol, a place, inhabited by a number of the most bigoted Roman catholics, and who had exercised, during the persecutions, the most unheard-of cruelties on the protestants.

The people of Crusol, hearing of the design against them, fled to a neighbouring fortress, situated on a rock, where the protestants could not come to them, for a very few men could render it inaccessible to a numerous army. Thus they secured their persons, but were in too much hurry to secure their property, the principal part of which, indeed, had been plundered from the protestants, and now luckily fell again to the possession of the right owners. It consisted of many rich and valuable articles, and what, at that time, was of much more consequence, viz. a great quantity of military stores.

The day after the protestants were gone with their booty, eight hundred troops arrived to the assistance of the people of Crusol, having been despatched from Lucerne, Biqueras, Cavors, &c. But finding themselves too late, and that pursuit would be vain, not to return empty handed, they began to plunder the neighbouring villages, though what they took was from their friends. After collecting a tolerable booty, they began to divide it, but disagreeing about the different shares, they fell from words to blows, did a great deal of mischief, and then plundered each other.

On the very same day in which the protestants were so successful at Crusol, some papists marched with a design to plunder and burn the little protestant village of Rocappiatta, but by the way they met with the protestant forces belonging to the captains Jahier and Laurentio, who were posted on the hill of Angrognia. A trivial engagement ensued, for the Roman catholics, on the very first attack, retreated in great confusion, and were pursued with much slaughter. After the pursuit was over, some straggling papist troops meeting with a poor peasant, who was a protestant, tied a cord round his head, and strained it till his skull was quite crushed.

Captain Gianavel and captain Jahier concerted a design together to make an attack upon Lucerne; but captain Jahier not bringing up his forces at the time appointed, captain Gianavel determined to attempt the enterprise himself.

He, therefore, by a forced march, proceeded towards that place during the whole night, and was close to it by break of day. His first care was to cut the pipes that conveyed water into the town, and then to break down the bridge, by which alone provisions from the country could enter.

He then assaulted the places and speedily possessed himself of two of the out posts; but finding he could not make himself master of the place, he prudently retreated with very little loss, blaming, however captain Jahier, for the failure of the enterprise.

The papists being informed that captain Gianavel was at Angrognia with only his own company, determined if possible to surprise him. With this view, a great number of troops were detached from La Torre and other places: one party of these got on top of a mountain, beneath which he was posted; and the other party intended to possess themselves of the gate of St. Bartholomew.

The papists thought themselves sure of taking captain Gianavel and every one of his men, as they consisted but of three hundred, and their own force was two thousand five hundred. Their design, however, was providentially frustrated, for one of the popish soldiers imprudently blowing a trumpet before the signal for attack was given, captain Gianavel took the alarm, and posted his little company so advantageously at the gate of St. Bartholomew, and at the defile by which the enemy must descend from the mountains, that the Roman catholic troops failed in both attacks, and were repulsed with very considerable loss.

Soon after, captain Jahier came to Angrognia, and joined his forces to those of captain Gianavel, giving sufficient reasons to excuse his before-mentioned failure. Captain Jahier now made several secret excursions with great success, always selecting the most active troops, belonging both to Gianavel and himself. One day he had put himself at the head of forty-four men, to proceed upon an expedition, when entering a plain near Ossac, he was suddenly surrounded by a large body of horse. Captain Jahier and his men fought desperately, though oppressed by odds, and killed the commander-in-chief, three captains, and fifty-seven private men, of the enemy. But captain Jahier himself being killed, with thirty-five of his men, the rest surrendered. One of the soldiers cut off captain Jahier's head, and carrying it to Turin, presented it to the duke of Savoy, who rewarded him with six hundred ducatoons.

The death of this gentleman was a signal loss to the protestants, as he was a real friend to, and companion of, the reformed church. He possessed a most undaunted spirit, so that no difficulties could deter him from undertaking an enterprise, or dangers terrify him in its execution. He was pious without affectation, and humane without weakness; bold in a field, meek in a domestic life, of a penetrating genius, active in spirit, and resolute in all his undertakings.

To add to the affliction of the protestants, captain Gianavel was, soon after, wounded in such a manner that he was obliged to keep his bed. They, however, took new courage from misfortunes, and determining not to let their spirits droop, attacked a body of popish troops with great intrepidity; the protestants were much inferior in numbers, but fought with more resolution than the papists, and at length routed them with considerable slaughter. During the action, a sergeant named Michael Bertino was killed; when his son, who was close behind him, leaped into his place, and said, I have lost my father; but courage, fellow soldiers, God is a father to us all.

Several skirmishes likewise happened between the troops of La Torre and Tagliaretto, and the protestant forces, which in general terminated in favour of the latter.

A Protestant gentleman, named Andrion, raised a regiment of horse, and took the command of it himself. The sieur John Leger persuaded a great number of protestants to form themselves into volunteer companies; and an excellent officer, named Michelin, instituted several bands of light troops. These being all joined to the remains of the veteran protestant troops, (for great numbers had been lost in the various battles, skirmishes, sieges, &c.) composed a respectable army, which the officers thought proper to encamp near St. Giovanni.

The Roman catholic commanders, alarmed at the formidable appearance, and increased strength of the protestant forces, determined, if possible, to dislodge them from their encampment. With this view, they collected together a large force, consisting of the principal part of the garrisons of the Roman catholic towns, the draft from the Irish brigades, a great number of regulars sent by the marquis of Pianessa, the auxiliary troops, and the independent companies.

These, having formed a junction, encamped near the protestants, and spent several days in calling councils of war, and disputing on the most proper mode of proceeding. Some were for plundering the country, in order to draw the protestants from their camp; others were for patiently waiting till they were attacked; and a third party were for assaulting the protestant camp, and trying to make themselves masters of every thing in it.

The last of them prevailed, and the morning after the resolution had been taken was appointed to put it into execution. The Roman catholic troops were accordingly separated into four divisions, three of which were to make an attack in different places; and the fourth to remain as a body of reserve to act as occasion might require.

One of the Roman catholic officers, previous to the attack, thus harangued his men:

"Fellow-soldiers, you are now going to enter upon a great action, which will bring you fame and riches. The motives of your acting with spirit are likewise of the most important nature; namely, the honour of showing your loyalty to your sovereign, the pleasure of spilling heretic blood, and the prospect of plundering the protestant camp. So, my brave fellows, fall on, give no quarter, kill all you meet, and take all you come near."

After this inhuman speech the engagement began, and the protestant camp was attacked in three places with inconceivable fury. The fight was maintained with great obstinacy and perseverance on both sides, continuing without intermission for the space of four hours; for the several companies on both sides relieved each other alternately, and by that means kept up a continual fire during the whole action.

During the engagement of the main armies, a detachment was sent from the body of reserve to attack the post of Castelas, which, if the papists had carried, it would have given them the command of the valleys of Perosa, St. Martino, and Lucerne; but they were repulsed with great loss, and compelled to return to the body of reserve, from whence they had been detached.

Soon after the return of this detachment, the Roman catholic troops, being hard pressed in the main battle, sent for the body of reserve to come to their support. These immediately marched to their assistance, and for some time longer held the event doubtful, but at length the valour of the protestants prevailed, and the papists were totally defeated, with the loss of upwards of three hundred men killed, and many more wounded.

When the cyndic of Lucerne, who was indeed a papist, but not a bigoted one, saw the great number of wounded men brought into that city, he exclaimed, ah! I thought the wolves used to devour the heretics, but now I see the heretics eat the wolves. This expression being reported to M. Marolles, the Roman catholic commander in chief at Lucerne, he sent a very severe and threatening letter to the cyndic, who was so terrified, that the fright threw him into a fever, and he died in a few days.

This great battle was fought just before the harvest was got in, when the papists, exasperated at their disgrace, and resolved on any kind of revenge, spread themselves by night in detached parties over the finest corn-fields of the protestants, and set them on fire in sundry places. Some of these straggling parties, however, suffered for their conduct; for the protestants, being alarmed in the night by the blazing of the fire among the corn, pursued the fugitives early in the morning, and overtaking many, put them to death. The protestant captain Bellin, likewise, by way of retaliation, went with a body of light troops, and burnt the suburbs of La Torre, making his retreat afterward with very little loss.

A few days after, captain Bellin, with a much stronger body of troops, attacked the town of La Torre itself, and making a breach in the wall of the convent, his men entered, driving the garrison into the citadel, and burning both town and convent. After having effected this, they made a regular retreat, as they could not reduce the citadel for want of cannon.

An Account of the Persecutions of Michael de Molinos, a Native of Spain.

Michael de Molinos, a Spaniard of a rich and honourable family, entered, when young, into priest's orders, but would not accept of any preferment in the church. He possessed great natural abilities, which he dedicated to the service of his fellow-creatures, without any view of emolument to himself. His course of life was pious and uniform; nor did he exercise those austerities which are common among the religious orders of the church of Rome.

Being of a contemplative turn of mind, he pursued the track of the mystical divines, and having acquired great reputation in Spain, and being desirous of propagating his sublime mode of devotion, he left his own country, and settled at Rome. Here he soon connected himself with some of the most distinguished among the literati, who so approved of his religious maxims, that they concurred in assisting him to propagate them; and, in a short time, he obtained a great number of followers, who, from the sublime mode of their religion, were distinguished by the name of Quietists.

In 1675, Molinos published a book entitled "Il Guida Spirituale," to which were subjoined recommendatory letters from several great personages. One of these was by the archbishop of Reggio; a second by the general of the Franciscans; and a third by father Martin de Esparsa, a Jesuit, who had been divinity-professor both at Salamanca and Rome.

No sooner was the book published, than it was greatly read, and highly esteemed, both in Italy and Spain; and this so raised the reputation of the author, that his acquaintance was coveted by the most respectable characters. Letters were written to him from numbers of people, so that a correspondence was settled between him, and those who approved of his method, in different parts of Europe. Some secular priests, both at Rome and Naples, declared themselves openly for it, and consulted him, as a sort of oracle, on many occasions. But those who attached themselves to him with the greatest sincerity, were some of the fathers of the Oratory; in particular three of the most eminent, namely, Caloredi, Ciceri, and Petrucci. Many of the cardinals also courted his acquaintance, and thought themselves happy in being reckoned among the number of his friends. The most distinguished of them was the cardinal d'Estrees, a man of very great learning, who so highly approved of Molinos' maxims, that he entered into a close connexion with him. They conversed together daily, and notwithstanding the distrust a Spaniard has naturally of a Frenchman, yet Molinos, who was sincere in his principles, opened his mind without reserve to the cardinal; and by this means a correspondence was settled between Molinos and some distinguished characters in France.

Whilst Molinos was thus labouring to propagate his religious mode, father Petrucci wrote several treatises relative to a contemplative life; but he mixed in them so many rules for the devotions of the Romish church, as mitigated that censure he might have otherwise incurred. They were written chiefly for the use of the nuns, and therefore the sense was expressed in the most easy and familiar style.

Molinos had now acquired such reputation, that the Jesuits and Dominicans began to be greatly alarmed, and determined to put a stop to the progress of this method. To do this, it was necessary to decry the author of it; and as heresy is an imputation that makes the strongest impression at Rome, Molinos and his followers were given out to be heretics. Books were also written by some of the Jesuits against Molinos and his method; but they were all answered with spirit by Molinos.

These disputes occasioned such disturbance in Rome, that the whole affair was taken notice of by the inquisition. Molinos and his book, and father Petrucci, with his treatises and letters, were brought under a severe examination; and the Jesuits were considered as the accusers. One of the society had, indeed, approved of Molinos' book but the rest took care he should not be again seen at Rome. In the course of the examination both Molinos and Petrucci acquitted themselves so well, that their books were again approved, and the answers which the Jesuits had written were censured as scandalous.

Petrucci's conduct on this occasion was so highly approved, that it not only raised the credit of the cause, but his own emolument; for he was soon after made bishop of Jesis, which was a new declaration made by the pope in their favour. Their books were now esteemed more than ever, their method was more followed, and the novelty of it, with the new approbation given after so vigorous an accusation by the Jesuits, all contributed to raise the credit, and increase the number of the party.

The behaviour of father Petrucci in his new dignity greatly contributed to increase his reputation, so that his enemies were unwilling to give him any further disturbance; and, indeed, there was less occasion given for censure by his writings than those of Molinos. Some passages in the latter were not so cautiously expressed, but there was room to make exceptions to them; while, on the other hand, Petrucci so fully explained himself, as easily to remove the objections made to some parts of his letter.

The great reputation acquired by Molinos and Petrucci, occasioned a daily increase of the Quietists. All who were thought sincerely devout, or at least affected the reputation of it, were reckoned among the number. If these persons were observed to become more strict in their lives and mental devotions, yet there appeared less zeal in their whole deportment as to the exterior parts of the church ceremonies. They were not so assiduous at mass, nor so earnest to procure masses to be said for their friends; nor were they so frequently either at confession, or in processions.

Though the new approbation given to Molinos' book by the inquisition had checked the proceedings of his enemies; yet they were still inveterate against him in their hearts, and determined if possible to ruin him. They insinuated that he had ill designs, and was, in his heart, an enemy to the Christian religion: that under pretence of raising men to a sublime strain of devotion, he intended to erase from their minds a sense of the mysteries of christianity. And because he was a Spaniard, they gave out that he was descended from a Jewish or Mahometan race, and that he might carry in his blood, or in his first education, some seeds of those religions which he had since cultivated with no less art than zeal. This last calumny gained but little credit at Rome, though it was said an order was sent to examine the registers of the place where Molinos was baptised.

Molinos finding himself attacked with great vigour, and the most unrelenting malice, took every necessary precaution to prevent these imputations being credited. He wrote a treatise, entitled Frequent and Daily Communion, which was likewise approved by some of the most learned of the Romish clergy. This was printed with his Spiritual Guide, in the year 1675; and in the preface to it he declared, that he had not written it with any design to engage himself in matters of controversy, but that it was drawn from him by the earnest solicitations of many pious people.

The Jesuits, failing, in their attempts of crushing Molinos' power in Rome, applied to the court of France, when, in a short time, they so far succeeded, that an order was sent to cardinal d'Estrees, commanding him to prosecute Molinos with all possible rigour. The cardinal, though so strongly attached to Molinos, resolved to sacrifice all that is sacred in friendship to the will of his master. Finding, however, there was not sufficient matter for an accusation against him, he determined to supply that defect himself. He, therefore, went to the inquisitors, and informed them of several particulars, not only relative to Molinos, but also Petrucci, both of whom, together with several of their friends, were put into the inquisition.

When they were brought before the inquisitors, (which was the beginning of the year 1684) Petrucci answered the respective questions put to him with so much judgment and temper, that he was soon dismissed; and though Molinos' examination was much longer, it was generally expected he would have been likewise discharged: but this was not the case. Though the inquisitors had not any just accusation against him, yet they strained every nerve to find him guilty of heresy. They first objected to his holding a correspondence in different parts of Europe; but of this he was acquitted, as the matter of that correspondence could not be made criminal. They then directed their attention to some suspicious papers found in his chamber; but Molinos so clearly explained their meaning, that nothing could be made of them to his prejudice. At length, cardinal d'Estrees, after producing the order sent him by the king of France for prosecuting Molinos, said, he could prove against him more than was necessary to convince them he was guilty of heresy. To do this he perverted the meaning of some passages in Molinos' books and papers, and related many false and aggravating circumstances relative to the prisoner. He acknowledged he had lived with him under the appearance of friendship, but that it was only to discover his principles and intentions: that he had found them to be of a bad nature, and that dangerous consequences were likely to ensue; but in order to make a full discovery, he had assented to several things, which, in his heart, he detested; and that, by these means, he saw into the secrets of Molinos, but determined not to take any notice, till a proper opportunity should offer of crushing him and his followers.

In consequence of d'Estrees' evidence, Molinos was closely confined by the inquisition, where he continued for some time, during which period all was quiet, and his followers prosecuted their mode without interruption. But on a sudden the Jesuits determined to extirpate them, and the storm broke out with the most inveterate vehemence.

The count Vespiniani and his lady, Don Paulo Rocchi, confessor to the prince Borghese, and some of his family, with several others, (in all seventy persons) were put into the inquisition, among whom many were highly esteemed both for their learning and piety. The accusation laid against the clergy was, their neglecting to say the breviary; and the rest were accused of going to the communion without first attending confession. In a word, it was said, they neglected all the exterior parts of religion, and gave themselves up wholly to solitude and inward prayer.

The countess Vespiniani exerted herself in a very particular manner on her examination before the inquisitors. She said, she had never revealed her method of devotion to any mortal but her confessor, and that it was impossible they should know it without his discovering the secret; that, therefore it was time to give over going to confession, if priests made this use of it, to discover the most secret thoughts intrusted to them; and that, for the future, she would only make her confession to God.

From this spirited speech, and the great noise made in consequence of the countess's situation, the inquisitors thought it most prudent to dismiss both her and her husband, lest the people might be incensed, and what she said might lessen the credit of confession. They were, therefore, both discharged, but bound to appear whenever they should be called upon.

Besides those already mentioned, such was the inveteracy of the Jesuits against the Quietists, that within the space of a month upwards of two hundred persons were put into the inquisition; and that method of devotion which had passed in Italy as the most elevated to which mortals could aspire, was deemed heretical, and the chief promoters of it confined in a wretched dungeon.

In order, if possible, to extirpate Quietism, the inquisitors sent a circular letter to cardinal Cibo, as the chief minister, to disperse it through Italy. It was addressed to all prelates, informing them, that whereas many schools and fraternities were established in several parts of Italy, in which some persons, under a pretence of leading people into the ways of the Spirit, and to the prayer of quietness, instilled into them many abominable heresies, therefore a strict charge was given to dissolve all those societies, and to oblige the spiritual guide to tread in the known paths; and, in particular, to take care none of that sort should be suffered to have the direction of the nunneries. Orders were likewise given to proceed, in the way of justice, against those who should be found guilty of these abominable errors.

After this a strict inquiry was made into all the nunneries in Rome; when most of their directors and confessors were discovered to be engaged in this new method. It was found that the Carmelites, the nuns of the Conception, and those of several other convents, were wholly given up to prayer and contemplation, and that, instead of their beads, and the other devotions to saints, or images, they were much alone, and often in the exercise of mental prayer; that when they were asked why they had laid aside the use of their beads, and their ancient forms, their answer was, their directors had advised them so to do. Information of this being given to the inquisition, they sent orders that all books written in the same strain with those of Molinos and Petrucci, should be taken from them, and that they should be compelled to return to their original form of devotion.

The circular letter sent to cardinal Cibo, produced but little effect, for most of the Italian bishops were inclined to Molinos' method. It was intended that this, as well as all other orders from the inquisitors, should be kept secret; but notwithstanding all their care, copies of it were printed, and dispersed in most of the principal towns in Italy. This gave great uneasiness to the inquisitors, who use every method they can to conceal their proceedings from the knowledge of the world. They blamed the cardinal, and accused him of being the cause of it; but he retorted on them, and his secretary laid the fault on both.

During these transactions, Molinos suffered great indignities from the officers of the inquisition; and the only comfort he received was, from being sometimes visited by father Petrucci.

Though he had lived in the highest reputation in Rome for some years, he was now as much despised, as he had been admired, being generally considered as one of the worst of heretics.

The greater part of Molinos' followers, who had been placed in the inquisition, having abjured his mode, were dismissed; but a harder fate awaited Molinos, their leader.

After lying a considerable time in prison, he was at length brought again before the inquisitors to answer to a number of articles exhibited against him from his writings. As soon as he appeared in court, a chain was put round his body, and a wax-light in his hand, when two friars read aloud the articles of accusation. Molinos answered each with great steadiness and resolution; and notwithstanding his arguments totally defeated the force of all, yet he was found guilty of heresy, and condemned to imprisonment for life.

When he left the court he was attended by a priest, who had borne him the greatest respect. On his arrival at the prison he entered the cell allotted for his confinement with great tranquility; and on taking leave of the priest, thus addressed him: Adieu, father, we shall meet again at the day of judgment, and then it will appear on which side the truth is, whether on my side, or on yours.

During his confinement, he was several times tortured in the most cruel manner, till, at length, the severity of the punishments overpowered his strength, and finished his existence.

The death of Molinos struck such an impression on his followers, that the greater part of them soon abjured his mode; and by the assiduity of the Jesuits, Quietism was totally extirpated throughout the country.

CHAPTER VII.

An Account of the Persecutions in Bohemia under the Papacy.

The Roman pontiffs having usurped a power over several churches were particularly severe on the Bohemians, which occasioned them to send two ministers and four lay-brothers to Rome, in the year 977, to obtain redress of the pope. After some delay, their request was granted, and their grievances redressed. Two things in particular they were permitted to do, viz. to have divine service performed in their own language, and to give the cup to the laity in the sacrament.

The disputes, however, soon broke out again, the succeeding popes exerting their whole power to impose on the minds of the Bohemians; and the latter, with great spirit, aiming to preserve their religious liberties.

A. D. 1375, some zealous friends of the gospel applied to Charles, king of Bohemia, to call an economical council, for an inquiry into the abuses that had crept into the church, and to make a full and thorough reformation. The king, not knowing how to proceed, sent to the pope for directions how to act; but the pontiff was so incensed at this affair, that his only reply was, severely punish those rash and profane heretics. The monarch, accordingly banished every one who had been concerned in the application, and, to oblige the pope, laid a great number of additional restraints upon the religious liberties of the people.

The victims of persecution, however, were not so numerous in Bohemia, until after the burning of John Huss and Jerom of Prague. These two eminent reformers were condemned and executed at the instigation of the pope and his emissaries, as the reader will perceive by the following short sketch of their lives.

John Huss.

John Huss was born at Hussenitz, a village in Bohemia, about the year 1380. His parents gave him the best education their circumstances would admit; and having acquired a tolerable knowledge of the classics at a private school, he was removed to the university of Prague, where he soon gave strong proofs of his mental powers, and was remarkable for his diligence and application to study.

In 1398, Huss commenced bachelor of divinity, and was after successively chosen pastor of the church of Bethlehem, in Prague, and dean and rector of the university. In these stations he discharged his duties with great fidelity; and became, at length, so conspicuous for his preaching, which was in conformity with the doctrines of Wickliffe, that it was not likely he could long escape the notice of the pope and his adherents, against whom he inveighed with no small degree of asperity.

The English reformist Wickliffe, had so kindled the light of reformation, that it began to illumine the darkest corners of popery and ignorance. His doctrines spread into Bohemia, and were well received by great numbers of people, but by none so particularly as John Huss, and his zealous friend and fellow-martyr, Jerom of Prague.

The archbishop of Prague, finding the reformists daily increasing, issued a decree to suppress the farther spreading of Wickliffe's writings: but this had an effect quite different to what he expected, for it stimulated the friends of those doctrines to greater zeal, and almost the whole university united to propagate them.

Being strongly attached to the doctrines of Wickliffe, Huss opposed the decree of the archbishop, who, however, at length, obtained a bull from the pope, giving him commission to prevent the publishing of Wickliffe's doctrines in his province. By virtue of this bull, the archbishop condemned the writings of Wickliffe: he also proceeded against four doctors, who had not delivered up the copies of that divine, and prohibited them, notwithstanding their privileges, to preach to any congregation. Dr. Huss, with some other members of the university, protested against these proceedings, and entered an appeal from the sentence of the archbishop.

The affair being made known to the pope, he granted a commission to cardinal Colonna, to cite John Huss to appear personally at the court of

Rome, to answer the accusations laid against him, of preaching both errors and heresies. Dr. Huss desired to be excused from a personal appearance, and was so greatly favoured in Bohemia, that king Winceslaus, the queen, the nobility, and the university, desired the pope to dispense with such an appearance; as also that he would not suffer the kingdom of Bohemia to lie under the accusation of heresy, but permit them to preach the gospel with freedom in their places of worship.

Three proctors appeared for Dr. Huss before cardinal Colonna. They endeavoured to excuse his absence, and said, they were ready to answer in his behalf. But, the cardinal declared Huss contumacious, and excommunicated him accordingly. The proctors appealed to the pope, and appointed four cardinals to examine the process: these commissioners confirmed the former sentence, and extended the excommunication not only to Huss but to all his friends and followers.

From this unjust sentence Huss appealed to a future council, but without success; and, notwithstanding so severe a decree, and an expulsion in consequence from his church in Prague, he retired to Hussenitz, his native place, where he continued to promulgate his new doctrine, both from the pulpit and with the pen.

The letters which he wrote at this time were very numerous; and he compiled a treatise in which he maintained, that reading the book of protestants could not be absolutely forbidden. He wrote in defence of Wickliffe's book on the Trinity; and boldly declared against the vices of the pope, the cardinals, and clergy, of those corrupt times. He wrote also many other books, all of which were penned with a strength of argument that greatly facilitated the spreading of his doctrines.

In the month of November, 1414, a general council was assembled at Constance, in Germany, in order, as was pretended, for the sole purpose of determining a dispute then pending between three persons who contended for the papacy; but the real motive was, to crush the progress of the reformation.

John Huss was summoned to appear at this council; and, to encourage him, the emperor sent him a safe-conduct: the civilities, and even reverence, which Huss met with on his journey, were beyond imagination. The streets, and, sometimes the very roads, were lined with people, whom respect, rather than curiosity, had brought together.

He was ushered into the town with great acclamations and it may be said, that he passed through Germany in a kind of triumph. He could not help expressing his surprise at the treatment he received: "I thought (said he) I had been an outcast. I now see my worst friends are in Bohemia."

As soon as Huss arrived at Constance, he immediately took lodgings in a remote part of the city. A short time after his arrival, came one Stephen Paletz, who was employed by the clergy at Prague to manage the intended prosecution against him. Paletz was afterward joined by Michael de Cassis, on the part of the court of Rome. These two declared themselves his accusers, and drew up a set of articles against him, which they presented to the pope and the prelates of the council.

When it was known that he was in the city, he was immediately arrested, and committed prisoner to a chamber in the palace. This violation of common law and justice, was particularly noticed by one of Huss' friends, who urged the imperial safe-conduct; but the pope replied, he never granted any safe-conduct, nor was he bound by that of the emperor.

While Huss was in confinement, the council acted the part of inquisitors. They condemned the doctrines of Wickliffe, and even ordered his remains to be dug up and burnt to ashes; which orders were strictly complied with. In the mean time, the nobility of Bohemia and Poland strongly interceded for Huss; and so far prevailed as to prevent his being condemned unheard, which had been resolved on by the commissioners appointed to try him.

When he was brought before the council, the articles exhibited against him were read: they were upwards of forty in number, and chiefly extracted from his writings.

After his examination, he was taken from the court, and a resolution was formed by the council to burn him as a heretic if he would not retract. He was then committed to a filthy prison, where, in the daytime, he was so laden with fetters on his legs, that he could hardly move, and every night he was fastened by his hand to a ring against the walls of the prison.

After continuing some days in this situation, many noblemen of Bohemia interceded in his behalf. They drew up a petition for his release, which was presented to the council by several of the most distinguished nobles of Bohemia; a few days after the petition was presented, four bishops and two lords were sent by the emperor to the prison, in order to prevail on Huss to make a recantation. But he called God to witness, with tears in his eyes, that he was not conscious of having preached or written, against the truth of God, or the faith of his orthodox church.

On the 4th of July, Dr. Huss was brought for the last time before the council. After a long examination he was desired to abjure, which he refused without the least hesitation. The bishop of Lodi then preached a sanguinary sermon, concerning the destruction of heretics, the prologue to his intended punishment. After the close of the sermon, his fate was determined, his vindication was disregarded, and judgment pronounced. Huss heard this sentence without the least emotion. At the close of it he knelt down, with his eyes lifted towards heaven, and with all the magnanimity of a primitive martyr, thus exclaimed: "May thy infinite mercy, O my God! pardon this injustice of mine enemies. Thou knowest the injustice of my accusations; how deformed with crimes I have been represented; how I have been oppressed with worthless witnesses, and a false condemnation; yet, O my God! let that mercy of thine, which no tongue can express, prevail with thee not to avenge my wrongs."

These excellent sentences were esteemed as so many expressions of treason, and tended to inflame his adversaries. Accordingly, the bishops appointed by the council stripped him of his priestly garments, degraded him, put a paper mitre on his head, on which was painted devils, with this inscription, "A ringleader of heretics." Our heroic martyr received this mock mitre with an air of unconcern, which seemed to give him dignity rather than disgrace. A serenity, nay, even a joy appeared in his looks, which indicated that his soul had cut off many stages of a tedious journey in her way to the realms of everlasting peace.

After the ceremony of degradation was over, the bishops delivered Dr. Huss to the emperor, who put him into the hands of the duke of Bavaria. His books were burnt at the gates of the church; and on the 6th of July, he was led to the suburbs of Constance, to be burnt alive. On his arrival at the place of execution, he fell on his knees, sung several portions of the Psalms, looked steadfastly towards heaven, and repeated these words: "Into thy hands, O Lord! do I commit my spirit: thou hast redeemed me, O most good and merciful God!"

When the chain was put about him at the stake, he said, with a smiling countenance, "My Lord Jesus Christ was bound with a harder chain than this for my sake, and why then should I be ashamed of this rusty one?"

When the fagots were piled up to his very neck, the duke of Bavaria was so officious as to desire him to abjure. "No, (said Huss;) I never preached any doctrine of an evil tendency; and what I taught with my lips I now seal with my blood." He then said to the executioner, "You are now going to burn a goose, (Huss signifying goose in the Bohemian language;) but in a century you will have a swan whom you can neither roast nor boil." If he were prophetic, he must have meant Martin Luther, who shone about a hundred years after, and who had a swan for his arms.

The flames were now applied to the fagots, when our martyr sung a hymn with so loud and cheerful a voice, that he was heard through all the cracklings of the combustibles, and the noise of the multitude. At length his voice was interrupted by the severity of the flames, which soon closed his existence.

Jerom of Prague.

This reformer, who was the companion of Dr. Huss, and may be said to be a co-martyr with him, was born at Prague, and educated in that university, where he particularly distinguished himself for his great abilities and learning. He likewise visited several other learned seminaries in Europe, particularly the universities of Paris, Heidelburg, Cologn, and Oxford. At the latter place he became acquainted with the works of Wickliffe, and being a person of uncommon application, he translated many of them into his native language, having with great pains, made himself master of the English tongue.

On his return to Prague, he professed himself an open favourer of Wickliffe, and finding that his doctrines had made considerable progress in Bohemia, and that Huss was the principal promoter of them, he became an assistant to him in the great work of reformation.

On the 4th of April, 1415, Jerom arrived at Constance, about three months before the death of Huss. He entered the town privately, and consulting with some of the leaders of his party, whom he found there, was easily convinced he could not be of any service to his friends.

Finding that his arrival in Constance was publicly known, and that the council intended to seize him, he thought it most prudent to retire. Accordingly, the next day he went to Iberling, an imperial town, about a mile from Constance. From this place he wrote to the emperor, and proposed his readiness to appear before the council, if he would give him a safe-conduct; but this was refused. He then applied to the council, but met with an answer no less unfavourable than that from the emperor.

After this, he set out on his return to Bohemia. He had the precaution to take with him a certificate, signed by several of the Bohemian nobility, then at Constance, testifying that he had used all prudent means in his power to procure a hearing.

Jerom, however, did not thus escape. He was seized at Hirsaw, by an officer belonging to the duke of Sultsbach, who, though unauthorized so to act, made little doubt of obtaining thanks from the council for so acceptable a service.

The duke of Sultsbach, having Jerom now in his power, wrote to the council for directions how to proceed. The council, after expressing their obligations to the duke, desired him to send the prisoner immediately to Constance. The elector palatine met him on the way, and conducted him into the city, himself riding on horseback, with a numerous retinue, who led Jerom in fetters by a long chain; and immediately on his arrival he was committed to a loathsome dungeon.

Jerom was treated nearly in the same manner as Huss had been, only that he was much longer confined, and shifted from one prison to another. At length, being brought before the council, he desired that he might plead his own cause, and exculpate himself: which being refused him, he broke out into the following elegant exclamation:

"What barbarity is this! For three hundred and forty days have I been confined in a variety of prisons. There is not a misery, there is not a want, that I have not experienced. To my enemies you have allowed the fullest scope of accusation: to me, you deny, the least opportunity of defence. Not an hour will you now indulge me in preparing for my trial. You have swallowed the blackest calumnies against me. You have represented me as a heretic, without knowing my doctrine; as an enemy to the faith, before you knew what faith I professed; as a persecutor of priests before you could have an opportunity of understanding my sentiments on that head. You are a general council: in you centre all this world can communicate of gravity, wisdom, and sanctity: but still you are men, and men are seducible by appearances. The higher your character is for wisdom, the greater ought your care to be not to deviate into folly. The cause I now plead is not my own cause: it is the cause of men, it is the cause of christians; it is a cause which is to affect the rights of posterity, however the experiment is to be made in my person."

This speech had not the least effect; Jerom was obliged to hear the charge read, which was reduced under the following heads:--1. That he was a derider of the papal dignity;--2. An opposer of the pope;--3. An enemy to the cardinals;--4. A persecutor of the prelates;--and 5. A hater of the christian religion.

The trial of Jerom was brought on the third day after his accusation and witnesses were examined in support of the charge. The prisoner was prepared for his defence, which appears almost incredible, when we consider he had been three hundred and forty days shut up in loathsome prisons, deprived of daylight, and almost starved for want of common necessaries. But his spirit soared above these disadvantages, under which a man less animated would have sunk; nor was he more at a loss for quotations from the fathers and ancient authors than if he had been furnished with the finest library.

The most bigoted of the assembly were unwilling he should be heard, knowing what effect eloquence is apt to have on the minds of the most prejudiced. At length, however, it was carried by the majority, that he should have liberty to proceed in his defence, which he began to such an exalted strain of moving elocution, that the heart of obdurate zeal was seen to melt, and the mind of superstition seemed to admit a ray of conviction. He made an admirable distinction between evidence as resting upon facts, and as supported by malice and calumny. He laid before the assembly the whole tenor of his life and conduct. He observed that the greatest and most holy men had been known to differ in points of speculation, with a view to distinguish truth, not to keep it concealed. He expressed a noble contempt of all his enemies, who would have induced him to retract the cause of virtue and truth. He entered upon a high encomium of Huss; and declared he was ready to follow him in the glorious track of martyrdom. He then touched upon the most defensible doctrines of Wickliffe; and concluded with observing that it was far from his intention to advance any thing against the state of the church of God; that it was only against the abuse of the clergy he complained; and that he could not help saying, it was certainly impious that the patrimony of the church, which was originally intended for the purpose of charity and universal benevolence, should be prostituted to the pride of the eye, in feasts, foppish vestments, and other reproaches to the name and profession of christianity.

The trial being over, Jerom received the same sentence that had been passed upon his martyred countryman. In consequence of this he was, in the usual style of popish affectation, delivered over to the civil power: but as he was a layman, he had not to undergo the ceremony of degradation. They had prepared a cap of paper painted with red devils, which being put upon his head, he said, "Our Lord Jesus Christ, when he suffered death for me a most miserable sinner, did wear a crown of thorns upon his head, and for His sake will I wear this cap."

Two days were allowed him in hopes that he would recant; in which time the cardinal of Florence used his utmost endeavours to bring him over. But they all proved ineffectual. Jerom was resolved to seal the doctrine with his blood; and he suffered death with the most distinguished magnanimity.

In going to the place of execution he sung several hymns, and when he came to the spot, which was the same where Huss had been burnt, he knelt down, and prayed fervently. He embraced the stake with great cheerfulness, and when they went behind him to set fire to the fagots, he said, "Come here, and kindle it before my eyes; for if I had been afraid of it, I had not come to this place." The fire being kindled, he sung a hymn, but was soon interrupted by the flames; and the last words he was heard to say these:--"This soul in flames I offer."

The elegant Pogge, a learned gentleman of Florence, secretary to two popes, and a zealous but liberal catholic, in a letter to Leonard Arotin, bore ample testimony of the extraordinary powers and virtues of Jerom whom he emphatically styles, A prodigious man!

Zisca.

The real name of this zealous servant of Christ was John de Trocznow, that of Zisca is a Bohemian word, signifying one-eyed, as he had lost an eye. He was a native of Bohemia, of a good family and left the court of Winceslaus, to enter into the service of the king of Poland against the Teutonic knights. Having obtained a badge of honour and a purse of ducats for his gallantry, at the close of the war he returned to the court of Winceslaus, to whom he boldly avowed the deep interest he took in the bloody affront offered to his majesty's subjects at Constance in the affair of Huss. Winceslaus lamented it was not in his power to revenge it; and from this moment Zisca is said to have formed the idea of asserting the religious liberties of his country. In the year 1418, the council was dissolved, having done more mischief than good, and in the summer of that year a general meeting was held of the friends of religious reformation, at the castle of Wilgrade, who, conducted by Zisca, repaired to the emperor with arms in their hands, and offered to defend him against his enemies. The king bid them use their arms properly, and this stroke of policy first insured to Zisca the confidence of his party.

Winceslaus was succeeded by Sigismond, his brother, who rendered himself odious to the Reformers; and removed all such as were obnoxious to his government. Zisca and his friends, upon this, immediately flew to arms, declared war against the emperor and the pope, and laid siege to Pilsen with 40,000 men. They soon became masters of the fortress, and in a short time all the south-west part of Bohemia submitted, which greatly increased the army of the reformers. The latter having taken the pass of Muldaw, after a severe conflict of five days and nights, the emperor became alarmed, and withdrew his troops from the confines of Turkey, to march them into Bohemia. At Berne in Moravia, he halted, and sent despatches to treat of peace, as a preliminary to which, Zisca gave up Pilsen and all the fortresses he had taken. Sigismond proceeding in a manner that clearly manifested he acted on the Roman doctrine, that no faith was to be kept with heretics, and treating some of the authors of the late disturbances with severity, the alarm-bell of revolt was sounded from one end of Bohemia to the other. Zisca took the castle of Prague by the power of money, and on the 19th of August, 1420, defeated the small army the emperor had hastily got together to oppose him. He next took Ausea by assault, and destroyed the town with a barbarity that disgraced the cause in which he fought.

Winter approaching, Zisca fortified his camp on a strong hill about forty miles from Prague, which he called Mount Tabor, from whence he surprised a body of horse at midnight, and made a thousand men prisoners. Shortly after, the emperor obtained possession of the strong fortress of Prague, by the same means that Zisca had before done: it was soon blockaded by the latter, and want began to threaten the emperor, who saw the necessity of a retreat.

Determined to make a desperate effort, Sigismond attacked the fortified camp of Zisca on Mount Tabor, and carried it with great slaughter. Many other fortresses also fell, and Zisca withdrew to a craggy hill, which he strongly fortified, and whence he so annoyed the emperor in his approaches against the town of Prague, that he found he must either abandon the siege or defeat his enemy. The marquis of Misnia was deputed to effect this with a large body of troops, but the event was fatal to the imperialists; they were defeated, and the emperor having lost nearly one third of his army, retreated from the siege of Prague, harassed in his rear by the enemy.

In the spring of 1421, Zisca commenced the campaign, as before, by destroying all the monasteries in his way. He laid siege to the castle of Wisgrade, and the emperor coming to relieve it, fell into a snare, was defeated with dreadful slaughter, and this important fortress was taken. Our general had now leisure to attend to the work of reformation, but he was much disgusted with the gross ignorance and superstition of the Bohemian clergy, who rendered themselves contemptible in the eyes of the whole army. When he saw any symptoms of uneasiness in his camp, he would spread alarm in order to divert them, and draw his men into action. In one of these expeditions, he encamped before the town of Rubi, and while pointing out the place for an assault, an arrow shot from the wall struck him in the eye. At Prague it was extracted, but, being barbed, it tore the eye out with it. A fever succeeded, and his life was with difficulty preserved. He was now totally blind, but still desirous of attending the army. The emperor having summoned the states of the empire to assist him, it was resolved, with their assistance, to attack Zisca in the winter, when many of his troops departed till the return of spring.

The confederate princes undertook the siege of Soisin, but at the approach merely of the Bohemian general, they retreated. Sigismond nevertheless advanced with his formidable army, consisting of 15,000 Hungarian horse and 25,000 infantry, well equipped for a winter campaign. This army spread terror through all the east of Bohemia. Wherever Sigismond marched, the magistrates laid their keys at his feet, and were treated with severity or favour, according to their merits in his cause. Zisca, however, with speedy marches, approached, and the emperor resolved to try his fortune once more with that invincible chief. On the 13th of January, 1422, the two armies met on a spacious plain near Kamnitz. Zisca appeared in the centre of his front line, guarded, or rather conducted, by a horseman on each side, armed with a pole-axe. His troops having sung a hymn with a determined coolness drew their swords, and waited for a signal. When his officers had informed him that the ranks were all well closed, he waved his sabre round his head, which was the sign of battle.

This battle is described as a most awful sight. The extent of the plain was one continued scene of disorder. The imperial army fled towards the confines of Moravia, the Taborites, without intermission, galling their rear. The river Igla, then frozen, opposed their flight. The enemy pressing furiously, many of the infantry, and in a manner the whole body of the cavalry attempted the river. The ice gave way and not fewer than 2000 were swalled up in the water. Zisca now returned to Tabor, laden with all the spoils and trophies which the most complete victory could give.

Zisca now began again to pay attention to the reformation; he forbid all the prayers for the dead, images, sacerdotal vestments, fasts, and festivals. Priests were to be preferred according to their merits, and no one to be persecuted for religious opinions. In every thing Zisca consulted the liberal minded, and did nothing without general concurrence. An alarming disagreement now arose at Prague between the magistrates who were Calixtans, or receivers of the sacraments in both kinds, and the Taborites, nine of the chiefs of whom were privately arraigned, and put to death. The populace, enraged, sacrificed the magistrates, and the affair terminated without any particular consequence. The Calixtans having sunk into contempt, Zisca was solicited to assume the crown of Bohemia; but this he nobly refused, and prepared for the next campaign, in which Sigismond resolved to make his last effort. While the marquis of Misnia penetrated into Upper Saxony, the emperor proposed to enter Moravia, on the side of Hungary. Before the marquis had taken the field, Zisca sat down before the strong town of Ausig, situate on the Elbe. The marquis flew to its relief with a superior army, and, after an obstinate engagement, was totally defeated and Ausig capitulated. Zisca then went to the assistance of Procop, a young general whom he had appointed to keep Sigismond in check, and whom he compelled to abandon the siege of Pernitz, after laying eight weeks before it.

Zisca, willing to give his troops some respite from fatigue, now entered Prague, hoping his presence would quell any uneasiness that might remain after the late disturbance: but he was suddenly attacked by the people; and he and his troop having beaten off the citizens effected a retreat to his army, whom he acquainted with the treacherous conduct of the Calixtans. Every effort of address was necessary to appease their vengeful animosity, and at night, in a private interview between Roquesan, an ecclesiastic of great eminence in Prague, and Zisca, the latter became reconciled, and the intended hostilities were done away.

Mutually tired of the war, Sigismond sent to Zisca, requesting him to sheath his sword, and name his conditions. A place of congress being appointed, Zisca, with his chief officers, set out to meet the emperor. Compelled to pass through a part of the country where the plague raged, he was seized with it at the castle of Briscaw and departed this life, October 6, 1424. Like Moses, he died in view of the completion of his labours, and was buried in the great church of Czaslow, in Bohemia, where a monument is erected to his memory, with this inscription on it--"Here lies John Zisca, who, having defended his country against the encroachments of papal tyranny, rests in this hallowed place in despite of the pope."

After the death of Zisca, Procop was defeated, and fell with the liberties of his country.

After the death of Huss and Jerom, the pope, in conjunction with the council of Constance, ordered the Roman clergy every where, to excommunicate such as adopted their opinions, or commisserated their fate.

These orders occasioned great contentions between the papists and reformed Bohemians, which was the cause of a violent persecution against the latter. At Prague, the persecution was extremely severe, till, at length, the reformed being driven to desperation, armed themselves, attacked the senate-house, and threw twelve senators, with the speaker, out of the senate-house windows, whose bodies fell upon spears, which were held up by others of the reformed in the street, to receive them.

Being informed of these proceedings, the pope came to Florence, and publicly excommunicated the reformed Bohemians, exciting the emperor of Germany, and all kings, princes, dukes, &c. to take up arms, in order to extirpate the whole race; and promising, by way of encouragement, full remission of all sins whatever, to the most wicked person, if he did but kill one Bohemian protestant.

This occasioned a bloody war; for several popish princes undertook the extirpation, or at least expulsion, of the proscribed people; and the Bohemians, arming themselves, prepared to repel force by force, in the most vigorous and effectual manner. The popish army prevailing against the protestant forces at the battle of Cuttenburgh, the prisoners of the reformed were taken to three deep mines near that town and several hundreds were cruelly thrown into each, where they miserably perished.

A merchant of Prague, going to Breslaw, in Silesia, happened to lodge in the same inn with several priests. Entering into conversation upon the subject of religious controversy, he passed many encomiums upon the martyred John Huss, and his doctrines. The priests taking umbrage at this, laid an information against him the next morning, and he was committed to prison as a heretic. Many endeavours were used to persuade him to embrace the Roman catholic faith, but he remained steadfast to the pure doctrines of the reformed church. Soon after his imprisonment, a student of the university was committed to the same jail; when, being permitted to converse with the merchant, they mutually comforted each other. On the day appointed for execution, when the jailer began to fasten ropes to their feet, by which they were to be dragged through the streets, the student appeared quite terrified, and offered to abjure his faith, and turn Roman catholic if he might be saved. The offer was accepted, his abjuration was taken by a priest, and he was set at liberty. A priest applying to the merchant to follow the example of the student, he nobly said, "Lose no time in hopes of my recantation, your expectations will be vain; I sincerely pity that poor wretch, who has miserably sacrificed his soul for a few more uncertain years of a troublesome life; and, so far from having the least idea of following his example, I glory in the very thoughts of dying for the sake of Christ." On hearing these words, the priest ordered the executioner to proceed, and the merchant being drawn through the city was brought to the place of execution, and there burnt.

Pichel, a bigoted popish magistrate, apprehended 24 protestants, among whom was his daughter's husband. As they all owned they were of the reformed religion, he indiscriminately condemned them to be drowned in the river Abbis. On the day appointed for the execution, a great concourse of people attended, among whom was Pichel's daughter. This worthy wife threw herself at her father's feet, bedewed them with tears, and in the most pathetic manner, implored him to commisserate her sorrow, and pardon her husband. The obdurate magistrate sternly replied, "Intercede not for him, child, he is a heretic, a vile heretic." To which she nobly answered, "Whatever his faults may be, or however his opinions may differ from yours, he is still my husband, a name which, at a time like this, should alone employ my whole consideration." Pichel flew into a violent passion and said, "You are mad! cannot you, after the death of this, have a much worthier husband?" "No, sir, (replied she) my affections are fixed upon this, and death itself shall not dissolve my marriage vow." Pichel, however, continued inflexible, and ordered the prisoners to be tied with their hands and feet behind them, and in that manner be thrown into the river. As soon as this was put into execution, the young lady watched her opportunity, leaped into the waves, and embracing the body of her husband, both sunk together into one watery grave. An uncommon instance of conjugal love in a wife, and of an inviolable attachment to, and personal affection for, her husband.

The emperor Ferdinand, whose hatred to the Bohemian protestants was without bounds, not thinking he had sufficiently oppressed them, instituted a high court of reformers, upon the plan of the inquisition, with this difference, that the reformers were to remove from place to place, and always to be attended by a body of troops.

These reformers consisted chiefly of Jesuits, and from their decision, there was no appeal, by which it may be easily conjectured, that it was a dreadful tribunal indeed.

This bloody court, attended by a body of troops, made the tour of Bohemia, to which they seldom examined or saw a prisoner, suffering the soldiers to murder the protestants as they pleased, and then to make a report of the matter to them afterward.

The first victim of their cruelty was an aged minister whom they killed as he lay sick in his bed, the next day they robbed, and murdered another, and soon after shot a third, as he was preaching in his pulpit.

A nobleman and clergyman, who resided in a protestant village, hearing of the approach of the high court of reformers and the troops, fled from the place, and secreted themselves. The soldiers, however, on their arrival, seized upon a schoolmaster, asked him where the lord of that place and the minister were concealed, and where they had hid their treasures. The schoolmaster replied, he could not answer either of the questions. They then stripped him naked, bound him with cords, and beat him most unmercifully with cudgels. This cruelty not extorting any confession from him, they scorched him in various parts of his body; when, to gain a respite from his torments, he promised to show them where the treasures were hid. The soldiers gave ear to this with pleasure, and the schoolmaster led them to a ditch full of stones, saying, Beneath these stones are the treasures ye seek for. Eager after money, they went to work, and soon removed those stones, but not finding what they sought after, beat the schoolmaster to death, buried him in the ditch, and covered him with the very stones he had made them remove.

Some of the soldiers ravished the daughters of a worthy protestant before his face, and then tortured him to death. A minister and his wife they tied back to back and burnt. Another minister they hung upon a cross beam, and making a fire under him, broiled him to death. A gentleman they hacked into small pieces, and they filled a young man's mouth with gunpowder, and setting fire to it, blew his head to pieces.

As their principal rage was directed against the clergy, they took a pious protestant minister, and tormented him daily for a month together, in the following manner, making their cruelty regular, systematic, and progressive.

They placed him amidst them, and made him the subject of their derision and mockery, during a whole day's entertainment, trying to exhaust his patience, but in vain, for he bore the whole with true christian fortitude. They spit in his face, pulled his nose, and pinched him in most parts of his body. He was hunted like a wild beast, till ready to expire with fatigue. They made him run the gauntlet between two ranks of them, each striking him with a twig. He was beat with their fists. He was beat with ropes. They scourged him with wires. He was beat with cudgels. They tied him up by the heels with his head downwards, till the blood started out of his nose, mouth, &c. They hung him by the right arm till it was dislocated, and then had it set again. The same was repeated with his left arm. Burning papers dipped in oil, were placed between his fingers and toes. His flesh was torn with red-hot pincers. He was put to the rack. They pulled off the nails of his right hand. The same repeated with his left hand. He was bastinadoed on his feet. A slit was made in his right ear. The same repeated on his left ear. His nose was slit. They whipped him through the town upon an ass. They made several incisions in his flesh. They pulled off the toe nails of his right foot. The same repeated with his left foot. He was tied up by the loins, and suspended for a considerable time. The teeth of his upper jaw were pulled out. The same was repeated with his lower jaw. Boiling lead was poured upon his fingers. The same repeated with his toes. A knotted cord was twisted about his forehead in such a manner as to force out his eyes.

During the whole of these horrid cruelties, particular care was taken that his wounds should not mortify, and not to injure him mortally till the last day, when the forcing out of his eyes proved his death.

Innumerable were the other murders and depredations committed by those unfeeling brutes, and shocking to humanity were the cruelties which they inflicted on the poor Bohemian protestants. The winter being far advanced, however, the high court of reformers, with their infernal band of military ruffians, thought proper to return to Prague; but on their way, meeting with a protestant pastor, they could not resist the temptation of feasting their barbarous eyes with a new kind of cruelty, which had just suggested itself to the diabolical imagination of one of the soldiers. This was to strip the minister naked, and alternately to cover him with ice and burning coals. This novel mode of tormenting a fellow-creature was immediately put into practice, and the unhappy victim expired beneath the torments, which seemed to delight his inhuman persecutors.

A secret order was soon after issued by the emperor, for apprehending all noblemen and gentlemen, who had been principally concerned in supporting the protestant cause, and in nominating Frederic elector Palatine of the Rhine, to be king of Bohemia. These, to the number of fifty, were apprehended in one night, and at one hour, and brought from the places where they were taken, to the castle of Prague, and the estates of those who were absent from the kingdom were confiscated, themselves were made outlaws, and their names fixed upon a gallows, as marks of public ignominy.

The high court of reformers then proceeded to try the fifty, who had been apprehended, and two apostate protestants were appointed to examine them. These examinants asked a great number of unnecessary and impertinent questions, which so exasperated one of the noblemen, who was naturally of a warm temper, that he exclaimed opening his breast at the same time, "Cut here, search my heart, you shall find nothing but the love of religion and liberty; those were the motives for which I drew my sword, and for those I am willing to suffer death."

As none of the prisoners would change their religion, or acknowledge they had been in error, they were all pronounced guilty; but the sentence was referred to the emperor. When that monarch had read their names, and an account of the respective accusations against them, he passed judgment on all, but in a different manner, as his sentences were of four kinds, viz. death, banishment, imprisonment for life, and imprisonment during pleasure.

Twenty being ordered for execution, were informed they might send for Jesuits, monks, or friars, to prepare for the awful change they were to undergo; but that no protestants should be permitted to come near them. This proposal they rejected, and strove all they could to comfort and cheer each other upon the solemn occasion.

On the morning of the day appointed for the execution, a cannon was fired as a signal to bring the prisoners from the castle to the principal market-place, in which scaffolds were erected, and a body of troops were drawn up to attend the tragic scene.

The prisoners left the castle with as much cheerfulness as if they had been going to an agreeable entertainment, instead of a violent death.

Exclusive of soldiers, Jesuits, priests, executioners, attendants, &c. a prodigious concourse of people attended, to see the exit of these devoted martyrs, who were executed in the following order.

Lord Schilik was about fifty years of age, and was possessed of great natural and acquired abilities. When he was told he was to be quartered, and his parts scattered in different places, he smiled with great serenity, saying, The loss of a sepulchre is but a trifling consideration. A gentleman who stood by, crying, courage, my lord; he replied, I have God's favour, which is sufficient to inspire any one with courage: the fear of death does not trouble me; formerly I have faced him in fields of battle to oppose Antichrist; and now dare face him on a scaffold, for the sake of Christ. Having said a short prayer, he told the executioner he was ready, who cut off his right hand and his head, and then quartered him. His hand and head were placed upon the high tower of Prague, and his quarters distributed in different parts of the city.

Lord Viscount Winceslaus, who had attained the age of seventy years, was equally respectable for learning, piety, and hospitality. His temper was so remarkably patient, that when his house was broke open, his property seized, and his estates confiscated, he only said, with great composure, The Lord hath given, and the Lord hath taken away. Being asked why he could engage in so dangerous a cause as that of attempting to support the elector Palatine Frederic against the power of the emperor, he replied, I acted strictly according to the dictates of my conscience, and, to this day, deem him my king. I am now full of years, and wish to lay down life, that I may not be a witness of the farther evils which are to attend my country. You have long thirsted for my blood, take it, for God will be my avenger. Then approaching the block, he stroked his long grey beard, and said, Venerable hairs, the greater honour now attends ye, a crown of martyrdom is your portion. Then laying down his head, it was severed from his body at one stroke, and placed upon a pole in a conspicuous part of the city.

Lord Harant was a man of good sense, great piety, and much experience gained by travel, as he had visited the principal places in Europe, Asia, and Africa. Hence he was free from national prejudices and had collected much knowledge.

The accusations against this nobleman, were, his being a protestant and having taken an oath of allegiance to Frederic, elector Palatine of the Rhine, as king of Bohemia. When he came upon the scaffold he said, "I have travelled through many countries, and traversed various barbarous nations, yet never found so much cruelty as at home. I have escaped innumerable perils both by sea and land, and surmounted inconceivable difficulties, to suffer innocently in my native place. My blood is likewise sought by those for whom I, and my forefathers, have hazarded our estates; but, Almighty God! forgive them, for they know not what they do." He then went to the block, kneeled down, and exclaimed with great energy, into thy hands, O Lord! I commend my spirit; in thee have I always trusted; receive me, therefore, my blessed Redeemer. The fatal stroke was then given, and a period put to the temporary pains of this life.

Lord Frederic de Bile suffered as a protestant, and a promoter of the late war; he met his fate with serenity, and only said, he wished well to the friends whom he left behind, forgave the enemies who caused his death, denied the authority of the emperor in that country, acknowledged Frederic to be the only true king of Bohemia, and hoped for salvation in the merits of his blessed Redeemer.

Lord Henry Otto, when he first came upon the scaffold, seemed greatly confounded, and said, with some asperity, as if addressing himself to the emperor, "Thou tyrant Ferdinand, your throne is established in blood; but if you kill my body, and disperse my members, they shall still rise up in judgment against you." He then was silent, and having walked about for some time, seemed to recover his fortitude, and growing calm, said to a gentleman who stood near, I was, a few minutes since, greatly discomposed, but now I feel my spirits revive; God be praised for affording me such comfort; death no longer appears as the king of terrors, but seems to invite me to participate of some unknown joys. Kneeling before the block, he said, Almighty God! to thee I commend my soul, receive it for the sake of Christ, and admit it to the glory of thy presence. The executioner put this nobleman to considerable pain, by making several strokes before he severed the head from the body.

The earl of Rugenia was distinguished for his superior abilities, and unaffected piety. On the scaffold he said, "We who drew our swords, fought only to preserve the liberties of the people, and to keep our consciences sacred: as we were overcome, I am better pleased at the sentence of death, than if the emperor had given me life; for I find that it pleases God to have his truth defended, not by our swords, but by our blood." He then went boldly to the block, saying, I shall now be speedily with Christ, and received the crown of martyrdom with great courage.

Sir Gaspar Kaplitz was 86 years of age. When he came to the place of execution, he addressed the principal officer thus: "Behold a miserable ancient man, who hath often entreated God to take him out of this wicked world, but could not until now obtain his desire, for God reserved me till these years to be a spectacle to the world and a sacrifice to himself; therefore God's will be done." One of the officers told him, in consideration of his great age, that if he would only ask pardon, he would immediately receive it. "Ask pardon, (exclaimed he) I will ask pardon of God, whom I have frequently offended; but not of the emperor, to whom I never gave any offence should I sue for pardon, it might be justly suspected I had committed some crime for which I deserved this condemnation. No, no, as I die innocent, and with a clear conscience, I would not be separated from this noble company of martyrs:" so saying, he cheerfully resigned his neck to the block.

Procopius Dorzecki on the scaffold said, "We are now under the emperor's judgment; but in time he shall be judged, and we shall appear as witnesses against him." Then taking a gold medal from his neck, which was struck when the elector Frederic was crowned king of Bohemia, he presented it to one of the officers, at the same time uttering these words, "As a dying man, I request, if ever king Frederic is restored to the throne of Bohemia, that you will give him this medal. Tell him, for his sake, I wore it till death, and that now I willingly lay down my life for God and my king." He then cheerfully laid down his head and submitted to the fatal blow.

Dionysius Servius was brought up a Roman catholic, but had embraced the reformed religion for some years. When upon the scaffold the Jesuits used their utmost endeavours to make him recant, and return to his former faith, but he paid not the least attention to their exhortations. Kneeling down he said, they may destroy my body, but cannot injure my soul, that I commend to my Redeemer; and then patiently submitted to martyrdom, being at that time fifty-six years of age.

Valentine Cockan, was a person of considerable fortune and eminence, perfectly pious and honest, but of trifling abilities; yet his imagination seemed to grow bright, and his faculties to improve on death's approach, as if the impending danger refined the understanding. Just before he was beheaded, he expressed himself with such eloquence, energy, and precision, as greatly amazed those who knew his former deficiency in point of capacity.

Tobias Steffick was remarkable for his affability and serenity of temper. He was perfectly resigned to his fate, and a few minutes before his death spoke in this singular manner, "I have received, during the whole course of my life, many favours from God; ought I not therefore cheerfully to take one bitter cup, when he thinks proper to present it? Or rather, ought I not to rejoice, that it is his will I should give up a corrupted life for that of immortality!"

Dr. Jessenius, an able student of physic, was accused of having spoken disrespectful words of the emperor, of treason in swearing allegiance to the elector Frederic, and of heresy in being a protestant: for the first accusation he had his tongue cut out; for the second he was beheaded; and for the third, and last, he was quartered, and the respective parts exposed on poles.

Christopher Chober, as soon as he stepped upon the scaffold said, 'I come in the name of God, to die for his glory; I have fought the good fight, and finished my course; so, executioner, do your office.' The executioner obeyed, and he instantly received the crown of martyrdom.

No person ever lived more respected, or died more lamented, than John Shultis. The only words he spoke, before receiving the fatal stroke, were, "The righteous seem to die in the eyes of fools, but they only go to rest. Lord Jesus! thou hast promised that those who come to thee shall not be cast off. Behold, I am come; look on me, pity me, pardon my sins, and receive my soul."

Maximilian Hostialick was famed for his learning, piety, and humanity. When he first came on the scaffold, he seemed exceedingly terrified at the approach of death. The officer taking notice of his agitation, he said, "Ah! sir, now the sins of my youth crowd upon my mind; but I hope God will enlighten me, lest I sleep the sleep of death, and lest mine enemies say, we have prevailed." Soon after he said, "I hope my repentance is sincere, and will be accepted, in which case the blood of Christ will wash me from my crimes." He then told the officer he should repeat the song of Simeon; at the conclusion of which the executioner might do his duty. He, accordingly, said, Lord! now lettest thou thy servant depart in peace, according to thy word, for mine eyes have seen thy salvation; at which words his head was struck off at one blow.

When John Kutnaur came to the place of execution, a Jesuit said to him, "Embrace the Roman catholic faith, which alone can save and arm you against the terrors of death." To which he replied, "Your superstitious faith I abhor, it leads to perdition, and I wish for no other arms against the terrors of death, than a good conscience." The Jesuit turned away, saying, sarcastically, The protestants are impenetrable rocks. You are mistaken, said Kutnaur, it is Christ that is the rock, and we are firmly fixed upon him.

This person not being born independent, but having acquired a fortune by a mechanical employment, was ordered to be hanged.--Just before he was turned off, he said, "I die, not for having committed any crime, but for following the dictates of my own conscience, and defending my country and religion."

Simeon Sussickey was father-in-law to Kutnaur, and like him, was ordered to be executed on a gallows. He went cheerfully to death and appeared impatient to be executed, saying, "Every moment delays me from entering into the kingdom of Christ."

Nathaniel Wodnianskey was hanged for having supported the protestant cause, and the election of Frederic to the crown of Bohemia. At the gallows, the Jesuits did all in their power to induce him to renounce his faith. Finding their endeavours ineffectual, one of them said, If you will not abjure your heresy, at least repent of your rebellion! To which Wodnianskey replied, "You take away our lives under a pretended charge of rebellion; and, not content with that, seek to destroy our souls; glut yourselves with blood, and be satisfied; but tamper not with our consciences."

Wodnianskey's own son then approached the gallows, and said to his father, "Sir, if life should be offered to you on condition of apostacy, I entreat you to remember Christ, and reject such pernicious overtures." To this the father replied, "It is very acceptable, my son, to be exhorted to constancy by you; but suspect me not; rather endeavour to confirm in their faith your brothers, sisters, and children, and teach them to imitate that constancy of which I shall leave them an example." He had no sooner concluded these words than he was turned off, receiving the crown of martyrdom with great fortitude.

Winceslaus Gisbitzkey, during his whole confinement, had great hopes of life given him, which made his friends fear for the safety of his soul. He, however, continued steadfast in his faith, prayed fervently at the gallows, and met his fate with singular resignation.

Martin Foster was an ancient cripple; the accusations against whom were, being charitable to heretics, and lending money to the elector Frederic. His great wealth, however, seems to have been his principal crime; and that he might be plundered of his treasures, was the occasion of his being ranked in this illustrious list of martyrs.

CHAPTER VIII.

GENERAL PERSECUTIONS IN GERMANY.

The general persecutions in Germany were principally occasioned by the doctrines and ministry of Martin Luther. Indeed, the pope was so terrified at the success of that courageous reformer, that he determined to engage the emperor, Charles the Fifth, at any rate, in the scheme to attempt their extirpation.

To this end;

1. He gave the emperor two hundred thousand crowns in ready money.

2. He promised to maintain twelve thousand foot, and five thousand horse, for the space of six months, or during a campaign.

3. He allowed the emperor to receive one-half the revenues of the clergy of the empire during the war.

4. He permitted the emperor to pledge the abbey lands for five hundred thousand crowns, to assist in carrying on hostilities against the protestants.

Thus prompted and supported, the emperor undertook the extirpation of the protestants, against whom, indeed, he was particularly enraged himself; and, for this purpose, a formidable army was raised in Germany, Spain and Italy.

The protestant princes, in the mean time, formed a powerful confederacy, in order to repel the impending blow. A great army was raised, and the command given to the elector of Saxony, and the landgrave of Hesse. The imperial forces were commanded by the emperor of Germany in person, and the eyes of all Europe were turned on the event of the war.

At length the armies met, and a desperate engagement ensued, in which the protestants were defeated, and the elector of Saxony, and landgrave of Hesse, both taken prisoners. This fatal blow was succeeded by a horrid persecution, the severities of which were such, that exile might be deemed a mild fate, and concealment in a dismal wood pass for happiness. In such times a cave is a palace, a rock a bed of down, and wild roots delicacies.

Those who were taken experienced the most cruel tortures the infernal imaginations could invent; and, by their constancy evinced that a real christian can surmount every difficulty, and despise ever danger to acquire a crown of martyrdom.

Henry Voes and John Esch, being apprehended as protestants, were brought to examination; when Voes, answering for himself and the other, gave the following answers to some questions asked by a priest, who examined them by order of the magistracy.

Priest. Were you not both, some years ago, Augustine friars?

Voes. Yes.

Priest. How came you to quit the bosom of the church of Rome?

Voes. On account of her abominations.

Priest. In what do you believe?

Voes. In the Old and New Testaments.

Priest. Do you believe in the writings of the fathers, and the decrees of the councils?

Voes. Yes, if they agree with Scripture.

Priest. Did not Martin Luther seduce you both?

Voes. He seduced us even in the very same manner as Christ seduced the apostles; that is, he made us sensible of the frailty of our bodies, and the value of our souls.

This examination was sufficient; they were both condemned to the flames, and soon after, suffered with that manly fortitude which becomes christians, when they receive a crown of martyrdom.

Henry Sutphen, an eloquent and pious preacher, was taken out of his bed in the middle of the night, and compelled to walk barefoot a considerable way, so that his feet were terribly cut. He desired a horse, but his conductors said, in derision, A horse for a heretic! no no, heretics may go barefoot. When he arrived at the place of his destination, he was condemned to be burnt; but, during the execution, many indignities were offered him, as those who attended not content with what he suffered in the flames, cut and slashed him in a most terrible manner.

Many were murdered at Halle; Middleburg being taken by storm all the protestants were put to the sword, and great numbers were burned at Vienna.

An officer being sent to put a minister to death, pretended, when he came to the clergyman's house, that his intentions were only to pay him a visit. The minister, not suspecting the intended cruelty, entertained his supposed guest in a very cordial manner. As soon as dinner was over, the officer said to some of his attendants, "Take this clergyman, and hang him." The attendants themselves were so shocked, after the civility they had seen, that they hesitated to perform the commands of their master; and the minister said, "Think what a sting will remain on your conscience, for thus violating the laws of hospitality." The officer, however, insisted upon being obeyed, and the attendants, with reluctance, performed the execrable office of executioners.

Peter Spengler, a pious divine, of the town of Schalet, was thrown into the river, and drowned. Before he was taken to the banks of the stream which was to become his grave, they led him to the market-place, that his crimes might be proclaimed; which were, not going to mass, not making confession, and not believing in transubstantiation. After this ceremony was over, he made a most excellent discourse to the people, and concluded with a kind of hymn, of a very edifying nature.

A protestant gentleman being ordered to lose his head for not renouncing his religion, went cheerfully to the place of execution. A friar came to him, and said these words in a low tone of voice, "As you have a great reluctance publicly to abjure your faith, whisper your confession in my ear, and I will absolve your sins." To this the gentleman loudly replied, "Trouble me not, friar, I have confessed my sins to God, and obtained absolution through the merits of Jesus Christ." Then turning to the executioner, he said, "Let me not be pestered with these men, but perform your duty." On which his head was struck off at a single blow.

Wolfgang Scuch, and John Huglin, two worthy ministers, were burned, as was Leonard Keyser, a student of the university of Wertembergh; and

George Carpenter, a Bavarian, was hanged for refusing to recant protestantism.

The persecutions in Germany having subsided many years, again broke out in 1630, on account of the war between the emperor and the king of Sweden, for the latter was a protestant prince, and consequently the protestants of Germany espoused his cause, which greatly exasperated the emperor against them.

The imperialists having laid siege to the town of Passewalk, (which was defended by the Swedes) took it by storm, and committed the most horrid cruelties on the occasion. They pulled down the churches, burnt the houses, pillaged the properties, massacred the ministers, put the garrison to the sword, hanged the townsmen, ravished the women, smothered the children, &c. &c.

A most bloody tragedy was transacted at Magdeburg, in the year 1631. The generals Tilly and Pappenheim, having taken that protestant city by storm, upwards of 20,000 persons, without distinction of rank, sex, or age, were slain during the carnage, and 6,000 were drowned in attempting to escape over the river Elbe. After this fury had subsided, the remaining inhabitants were stripped naked, severely scourged, had their ears cropped, and being yoked together like oxen were turned adrift.

The town of Hoxter was taken by the popish army, and all the inhabitants as well as the garrison, were put to the sword; when the houses being set on fire, the bodies were consumed in the flames.

At Griphenburg, when the imperial forces prevailed, they shut up the senators in the senate-chamber, and surrounding it by lighted straw suffocated them.

Franhendal surrendered upon articles of capitulation, yet the inhabitants were as cruelly used as at other places, and at Heidelburg, many were shut up in prison and starved.

The cruelties used by the imperial troops, under count Tilly in Saxony, are thus enumerated.

Half strangling, and recovering the persons again repeatedly. Rolling sharp wheels over the fingers and toes. Pinching the thumbs in a vice. Forcing the most filthy things down the throat, by which many were choked. Tying cords round the head so tight that the blood gushed out of the eyes, nose, ears, and mouth. Fastening burning matches to the fingers, toes, ears, arms, legs, and even tongue. Putting powder in the mouth and setting fire to it, by which the head was shattered to pieces. Tying bags of powder to all parts of the body, by which the person was blown up. Drawing cords backwards and forwards through the fleshy parts. Making incisions with bodkins and knives in the skin. Running wires through the nose, ears, lips, &c. Hanging protestants up by the legs, with their heads over a fire, by which they were smoked dried. Hanging up by one arm till it was dislocated. Hanging upon hooks by the ribs. Forcing people to drink till they burst. Baking many in hot ovens. Fixing weights to the feet, and drawing up several with pulleys. Hanging, stifling, roasting, stabbing, frying, racking, ravishing, ripping open, breaking the bones, rasping off the flesh, tearing with wild horses, drowning, strangling, burning, broiling, crucifying, immuring, poisoning, cutting off tongues, nose, ears, &c. sawing off the limbs, hacking to pieces, and drawing by the heels through the streets.

The enormous cruelties will be a perpetual stain on the memory of count Tilly, who not only permitted, but even commanded the troops to put them in practice. Wherever he came, the most horrid barbarities, and cruel depredations ensued: famine and conflagration marked his progress: for he destroyed all the provisions he could not take with him, and burnt all the towns before he left them; so that the full result of his conquests were murder, poverty, and desolation.

An aged and pious divine they stripped naked, tied him on his back upon a table, and fastened a large fierce cat upon his belly. They then pricked and tormented the cat in such a manner, that the creature with rage tore his belly open, and knawed his bowels.

Another minister, and his family, were seized by these inhuman monsters; when they ravished his wife and daughter before his face; stuck his infant son upon the point of a lance, and then surrounding him with his whole library of books, they set fire to them, and he was consumed in the midst of the flames.

In Hesse-Cassel some of the troops entered an hospital, in which were principally mad women, when stripping all the poor wretches naked, they made them run about the streets for their diversion, and then put them all to death.

In Pomerania, some of the imperial troops entering a small town, seized upon all the young women, and girls of upwards of ten years, and then placing their parents in a circle, they ordered them to sing psalms, while they ravished their children, or else they swore they would cut them to pieces afterward. They then took all the married women who had young children, and threatened, if they did not consent to the gratification of their lusts, to burn their children before their faces in a large fire, which they had kindled for that purpose.

A band of count Tilly's soldiers meeting a company of merchants belonging to Basil, who were returning from the great market of Strasburg, they attempted to surround them: all escaped, however, but ten, leaving their properties behind. The ten who were taken begged hard for their lives; but the soldiers murdered them saying, You must die because you are heretics, and have got no money.

The same soldiers met with two countesses, who, together with some young ladies, the daughters of one of them, were taking an airing in a landau. The soldiers spared their lives, but treated them with the greatest indecency, and having stripped them all stark naked, bade the coachman drive on.

By means and mediation of Great Britain, peace was at length restored to Germany, and the protestants remained unmolested for several years, till some new disturbances broke out in the Palatinate which were thus occasioned.

The great church of the Holy Ghost, at Heidelburg, had, for many years, been shared equally by the protestants and Roman catholics in this manner: the protestants performed divine service in the nave or body of the church; and the Roman catholics celebrated mass in the choir. Though this had been the custom time immemorial, the elector Palatinate, at length, took it into his head not to suffer it any longer, declaring, that as Heidelburg was the place of his residence, and the church of the Holy Ghost the cathedral of his principal city, divine service ought to be performed only according to the rites of the church of which he was a member. He then forbade the protestants to enter the church, and put the papists in possession of the whole.

The aggrieved people applied to the protestant powers for redress, which so much exasperated the elector, that he suppressed the Heidelburg catechism. The protestant powers, however, unanimously agreed to demand satisfaction, as the elector, by this conduct, had broke an article of the treaty of Westphalia; and the courts of Great Britain, Prussia, Holland, &c., sent deputies to the elector, to represent the injustice of his proceedings, and to threaten, unless he changed his behaviour to the protestants in the Palatinate, that they would treat their Roman catholic subjects with the greatest severity. Many violent disputes took place between the Protestant powers and those of the elector, and these were greatly augmented by the following incident; the coach of the Dutch minister standing before the door of the resident sent by the prince of Hesse, the host was by chance carrying to a sick person; the coachman took not the least notice, which those who attended the host observing, pulled him from his box, and compelled him to kneel: this violence to the domestic of a public minister, was highly resented by all the protestant deputies; and still more to heighten these differences, the protestants presented to the deputies three additional articles of complaint.

1. That military executions were ordered against all protestant shoemakers who should refuse to contribute to the masses of St. Crispin.

2. That the protestants were forbid to work on popish holydays even in harvest time, under very heavy penalties, which occasioned great inconveniences, and considerably prejudiced public business.

3. That several protestant ministers had been dispossessed of their churches, under pretence of their having been originally founded and built by Roman Catholics.

The protestant deputies, at length became so serious, as to intimate to the elector, that force of arms should compel him to do the justice he denied to their representations. This menace brought him to reason, as he well knew the impossibility of carrying on a war against the powerful states who threatened him. He, therefore, agreed, that the body of the church of the Holy Ghost should be restored to the protestants. He restored the Heidelburg catechism, put the protestant ministers again in possession of the churches of which they had been dispossessed, allowed the protestants to work on popish holydays, and, ordered, that no person should be molested for not kneeling when the host passed by.

These things he did through fear; but to show his resentment to his protestant subjects, in other circumstances where protestant states had no right to interfere, he totally abandoned Heidelburg, removing all the courts of justice to Manheim, which was entirely inhabited by Roman catholics. He likewise built a new palace there, making it his place of residence; and, being followed by the Roman catholics of Heidelburg, Manheim became a flourishing place.

In the mean time the protestants of Heidelburg sunk into poverty and many of them became so distressed, as to quit their native country, and seek an asylum in protestant states. A great number of these coming into

England, in the time of queen Anne, were cordially received there, and met with a most humane assistance, both by public and private donations.

In 1732, above 30,000 protestants were, contrary to the treaty of Westphalia, driven from the archbishopric of Saltzburg. They went away to the depth of winter, with scarce clothes to cover them, and without provisions, not having permission to take any thing with them. The cause of these poor people not being publicly espoused by such states as could obtain them redress, they emigrated to various protestant countries, and settled in places where they could enjoy the free exercise of their religion, without hurting their consciences, and live free from the trammels of popish superstition, and the chains of papal tyranny.

An Account of the Persecutions in the Netherlands.

The light of the gospel having successfully spread over the Netherlands, the pope instigated the emperor to commence a persecution against the protestants; when many thousand fell martyrs to superstitious malice and barbarous bigotry, among whom the most remarkable were the following:

Wendelinuta, a pious protestant widow, was apprehended on account of her religion, when several monks, unsuccessfully, endeavoured to persuade her to recant. As they could not prevail, a Roman catholic lady of her acquaintance desired to be admitted to the dungeon in which she was confined, and promised to exert herself strenuously towards inducing the prisoner to abjure the reformed religion. When she was admitted to the dungeon, she did her utmost to perform the task she had undertaken; but finding her endeavours ineffectual, she said, Dear Wendelinuta, if you will not embrace our faith, at least keep the things which you profess secret within your own bosom, and strive to prolong your life. To which the widow replied, Madam you know not what you say; for with the heart we believe to righteousness, but with the tongue confession is made unto salvation. As she positively refused to recant, her goods were confiscated, and she was condemned to be burnt. At the place of execution a monk held a cross to her, and bade her kiss and worship God. To which she answered, "I worship no wooden god, but the eternal God who is in heaven." She was then executed, but through the before-mentioned Roman catholic lady, the favour was granted, that she should be strangled before fire was put to the fagots.

Two protestant clergymen were burnt at Colen; a tradesman of Antwerp, named Nicholas, was tied up in a sack, thrown into the river, and drowned; and Pistorius, a learned student, was carried to the market of a Dutch village in a fool's coat, and committed to the flames.

Sixteen protestants having received sentence to be beheaded, a protestant minister was ordered to attend the execution. This gentleman performed the function of his office with great propriety, exhorted them to repentance, and gave them comfort in the mercies of their Redeemer. As soon as the sixteen were beheaded, the magistrate cried out to the executioner, "There is another stroke remaining yet; you must behead the minister; he can never die at a better time than with such excellent precepts in his mouth, and such laudable examples before him." He was accordingly beheaded, though even many of the Roman catholics themselves reprobated this piece of treacherous and unnecessary cruelty.

George Scherter, a minister of Saltzburg, was apprehended and committed to prison for instructing his flock in the knowledge of the gospel. While he was in confinement he wrote a confession of his faith; soon after which he was condemned, first to be beheaded, and afterward to be burnt to ashes. In his way to the place of execution he said to the spectators, "That you may know I die a true christian, I will give you a sign." This was indeed verified in a most singular manner; for after his head was cut off, the body lying a short space of time with the belly to the ground, it suddenly turned upon the back, when the right foot crossed over the left, as did also the right arm over the left: and in this manner it remained till it was committed to the flames.

In Louviana, a learned man, named Percinal, was murdered in prison; and Justus Insparg was beheaded, for having Luther's sermons in his possession.

Giles Tilleman, a cutler of Brussels, was a man of great humanity and piety. Among others he was apprehended as a protestant, and many endeavours were made by the monks to persuade him to recant. He had once, by accident, a fair opportunity of escaping from prison and being asked why he did not avail himself of it, he replied, "I would not do the keepers so much injury, as they must have answered for my absence, had I gone away." When he was sentenced to be burnt, he fervently thanked God for granting him an opportunity, by martyrdom, to glorify his name. Perceiving, at the place of execution, a great quantity of fagots, he desired the principal part of them might be given to the poor, saying, a small quantity will suffice to consume me. The executioner offered to strangle him before the fire was lighted, but he would not consent, telling him that he defied the flames and, indeed, he gave up the ghost with such composure amidst them that he hardly seemed sensible of their effects.

In the year 1543 and 1544, the persecution was carried on throughout all Flanders, in a most violent and cruel manner. Some were condemned to perpetual imprisonment, others to perpetual banishment but most were put to death either by hanging, drowning, immuring, burning, the rack, or burying alive.

John de Boscane, a zealous protestant, was apprehended on account of his faith, in the city of Antwerp. On his trial, he steadfastly professed himself to be of the reformed religion, which occasioned his immediate condemnation. The magistrate, however, was afraid to put him to death publicly, as he was popular through his great generosity, and almost universally beloved for his inoffensive life, and exemplary piety. A private execution being determined on, an order was given to drown him in prison. The executioner, accordingly, put him in a large tub; but Boscane struggling, and getting his head above the water, the executioner stabbed him with a dagger in several places, till he expired.

John de Buisons, another protestant, was, about the same time, secretly apprehended, and privately executed at Antwerp. The number of protestants being great in that city, and the prisoner much respected, the magistrates feared an insurrection, and for that reason ordered him to be beheaded in prison.

A. D. 1568, three persons were apprehended in Antwerp, named Scoblant, Hues, and Coomans. During their confinement they behaved with great fortitude and cheerfulness, confessing that the hand of God appeared in what had befallen them, and bowing down before the throne of his providence. In an epistle to some worthy protestants, they express themselves in the following words; Since it is the will of the Almighty that we should suffer for his name, and be persecuted for the sake of his gospel, we patiently submit, and are joyful upon the occasion; though the flesh may rebel against the spirit, and hearken to the council of the old serpent, yet the truths of the gospel shall prevent such advice from being taken, and Christ shall bruise the serpent's head. We are not comfortless to confinement, for we have faith; we fear not affliction, for we have hope; and we forgive our enemies, for we have charity. Be not under apprehensions for us, we are happy in confinement through the promises of God, glory in our bonds, and exult in being thought worthy to suffer for the sake of Christ. We desire not to be released, but to be blessed with fortitude, we ask not liberty, but the power of perseverance; and wish for no change in our condition, but that which places a crown of martyrdom upon our heads.

Scoblant was first brought to his trial; when, persisting in the profession of his faith, he received sentence of death. On his return to prison, he earnestly requested the jailer not to permit any friar to come near him; saying, "They can do me no good, but may greatly disturb me. I hope my salvation is already sealed in heaven, and that the blood of Christ, in which I firmly put my trust, hath washed me from my iniquities. I am now going to throw off this mantle of clay, to be clad in robes of eternal glory, by whose celestial brightness I shall be freed from all errors. I hope I may be the last martyr to papal tyranny, and the blood already spilt found sufficient to quench the thirst of popish cruelty; that the church of Christ may have rest here, as his servants will hereafter." On the day of execution, he took a pathetic leave of his fellow-prisoners. At the stake he fervently said the Lord's Prayer, and sung the fortieth psalm; then commending his soul to God, he was burnt alive.

Hues, soon after, died in prison; upon which occasion Coomans wrote thus to his friends, "I am now deprived of my friends and companions; Scoblant is martyred, and Hues dead, by the visitation of the Lord; yet I am not alone, I have with me the God of Abraham, of Isaac, and of Jacob; he is my comfort, and shall be my reward. Pray unto God to strengthen me to the end, as I expect every hour to be freed from this tenement of clay."

On his trial he freely confessed himself of the reformed religion, answered with a manly fortitude to every charge against him, and proved the scriptural part of his answers from the gospel. The judge told him the only alternatives were, recantation or death; and concluded by saying, "Will you die for the faith you profess?" To which Coomans replied, "I am not only willing to die, but to suffer the most excruciating torments for it; after which my soul shall receive its confirmation from God himself, in the midst of eternal glory." Being condemned, he went cheerfully to the place of execution, and died with the most manly fortitude, and christian resignation.

William Nassau fell a sacrifice to treachery, being assassinated in the fifty-first year of his age, by Beltazar Gerard, a native of Franche Compte, in the province of Burgundy. This murderer, in hopes of a reward here and hereafter, for killing an enemy to the king of Spain and an enemy to the catholic religion, undertook to destroy the prince of Orange. Having procured fire arms, he watched him as he passed through the great hall of his palace to dinner, and demanded a passport. The princess of Orange, observing that the assassin spoke with a hollow and confused voice, asked who he was? saying, she did not like his countenance. The prince answered, it was one that demanded a passport, which he should presently have.

Nothing farther passed before dinner, but on the return of the prince and princess through the same hall, after dinner was over, the assassin, standing concealed as much as possible by one of the pillars, fired at the prince, the balls entering at the left side, and passing through the right, wounding in their passage the stomach and vital parts. On receiving the wounds, the prince only said, Lord, have mercy upon my soul, and upon these poor people, and then expired immediately.

The lamentations throughout the United Provinces were general, on account of the death of the prince of Orange; and the assassin who was immediately taken, received sentence to be put to death in the most exemplary manner, yet such was his enthusiasm, or folly that when his flesh was torn by red-hot pincers, he coolly said, If I was at liberty, I would commit such an action over again.

The prince of Orange's funeral was the grandest ever seen in the Low Countries, and perhaps the sorrow for his death the most sincere, as he left behind him the character he honestly deserved, viz. that of Father of his people.

To conclude, multitudes were murdered in different parts of Flanders; in the city of Valence, in particular, fifty-seven of the principal inhabitants were butchered in one day, for refusing to embrace the Romish superstition; and great numbers were suffered to languish in confinement, till they perished through the inclemency of their dungeons.

CHAPTER IX.

AN ACCOUNT OF THE PERSECUTIONS IN LITHUANIA AND POLAND.

The persecutions in Lithuania began in 1648, and were carried on with great severity by the Cossacks and Tartars. The cruelty of the Cossacks was much, that even the Tartars, at last, grew ashamed of it, and rescued some of the intended victims from their hands.

The barbarities exercised were these: skinning alive, cutting off hands, taking out the bowels, cutting the flesh open, putting out the eyes, beheading, scalping, cutting off feet, boring the shin bones, pouring melted lead into the flesh, hanging, stabbing, and sending to perpetual banishment.

The Russians, taking advantage of the devastations which had been made in the country, and of its incapability of defence, entered it with a considerable army, and, like a flood, bore down all before them. Every thing they met with was an object of destruction; they razed cities, demolished castles, ruined fortresses, sacked towns, burnt villages, and murdered people. The ministers of the gospel were peculiarly marked out as the objects of their displeasure, though every worthy christian was liable to the effects of their cruelty.

As Lithuania recovered itself after one persecution, succeeding enemies again destroyed it. The Swedes, the Prussians, and the Courlanders, carried fire and sword through it, and continual calamities, for some years, attended that unhappy district. It was then attacked by the prince of Transylvania, who had in his army, exclusive of his own Transylvanians, Hungarians, Moldavians, Servians, Walachians, &c. These, as far as they penetrated, wasted the country, destroyed the churches, rifled the nobility, burnt the houses, enslaved the healthy, and murdered the sick.

A clergyman, who wrote an account of the misfortunes of Lithuania, in the seventeenth century, says, "In consideration of these extremities, we cannot but adore the judgment of God poured upon us for our sins, and deplore our sad condition. Let us hope for a deliverance from his mercy, and wish for restitution in his benevolence. Though we are brought low, though we are wasted, troubled, and terrified, yet his compassion is greater than our calamities, and his goodness superior to our afflictions. Our neighbours hate us at present, as much as our more distant enemies did before; they persecute the remnant of us still remaining, deprive us of our few churches left, banish our preachers, abuse our schoolmasters, treat us with contempt, and oppress us in the most opprobrious manner. In all our afflictions the truth of the gospel shone among us, and gave us comfort; and we only wished for the grace of Jesus Christ, (not only to ourselves, but to soften the hearts of our enemies) and the sympathy of our fellow christians."

The protestants of Poland were persecuted in a dreadful manner. The ministers in particular were treated with the most unexampled barbarity; some having their tongues cut out, because they had preached the gospel truths; others being deprived of their sight on account of their having read the bible; and great numbers were cut to pieces for not recanting.

Private persons were put to death by various methods; the most cruel being usually preferred. Women were murdered without the least regard to their sex; and the persecutors even went so far as to cut off the heads of sucking babes, and fasten them to the breasts of the mothers.

Even the solemnity of the grave did not exempt the bodies of protestants from the malice of persecutors; for they sacrilegiously dug up the bodies of many eminent persons, and either cut them to pieces, and exposed them to be devoured by birds and beasts, or hung them up in conspicuous or public places.

The city of Lesna particularly suffered in this persecution; for being besieged and taken, the inhabitants were all put to the sword.

CHAPTER X.

AN ACCOUNT OF THE PERSECUTIONS IN CHINA AND SEVERAL OTHER COUNTRIES.

Christianity was first established in China by three Italian missionaries, called Roger the Neapolitan, Pasis of Bologne, and Matthew Ricci of Mazerata, in the marquisate of Ancona. These entered China about the beginning of the sixteenth century, being well circumstanced to perform their important commission with success, as they had previously studied the Chinese language.

These three missionaries were very assiduous to the discharge of their duty; but Roger and Pasis returning to Europe in a few years, the whole labour fell upon Ricci, who aimed to establish christianity with a degree of zeal that was indefatigable.

Ricci, though much disposed to indulge his converts as far as possible, made great hesitation at their ceremonies, which seemed to amount to idolatry. At length, after eighteen years consideration, he began to soften his opinion, and tolerated all the parts of those customs which were ordered by the laws of the empire, but strictly enjoined his Chinese christians to omit the rest.

This was the condition of christianity in China, when the christian church established there was governed only by Ricci, who, by his moderation, made innumerable converts. In 1630, however, his tranquility was disturbed by the arrival of some new missionaries, these being unacquainted with the Chinese customs, manners, and language, and with the arguments on which Ricci's toleration was founded, were astonished when they saw christian converts prostrate before Confucius and the tables of their ancestors, and condemned the custom accordingly.

A warm controversy now ensued between Ricci, seconded by his converts, and the new missionaries; and the latter wrote an account of the whole affair to the pope, and the society for the propagation of the christian faith. The society soon pronounced, that the ceremonies were idolatrous and intolerable, and the pope confirmed the sentence. In this both the society and the pope were excusable, as the matter had been misrepresented to them; for the enemies of Ricci had affirmed the halls, in which the ceremonies were performed, to be temples, and the ceremonies themselves idolatrous sacrifices.

The sentence above mentioned was sent over to China, but treated with contempt, and matters remained as they were for some time. At length, a true representation of the matter was sent over, setting forth, that the Chinese customs and ceremonies alluded to were entirely free from idolatry, being merely political, and tending only to the peace and welfare of the empire. The pope, finding that he had made himself ridiculous, by confirming an absurd sentence upon a false report, wanted to get rid of the affair, and therefore referred the representation to the inquisition, which reversed the sentence immediately, at the private desire of the pope, as may be naturally supposed.

The christian church, for all these divisions, flourished in China till the death of the first Tartar emperor, whose successor was a minor. During this minority of the young emperor Cang-hi, the regents and nobles conspired to extirpate the christian religion. The execution of this design was begun with expedition, and carried on with severity, so that every christian teacher in China, as well as those who professed the faith, were struck with amazement. John Adam Schall, a German ecclesiastic, and one of the principals of the mission, was thrown into a dungeon in the year 1664, being then in the seventy-fourth year of his age, and narrowly escaped with his life.

The ensuing year, viz. 1665, the ministers of state publicly and unanimously resolved, and made a decree specifying, viz.

1. That the christian doctrines were false.

2. That they were dangerous to the interest of the empire.

3. That they should not be practised under pain of death.

The publication of this decree occasioned a furious general persecution, in which some were put to death, many were ruined, and all were, in some manner, oppressed. This decree was general, and the persecution universal accordingly throughout the empire; for, previous to this, the christians had been partially persecuted at different times, and in different provinces.

Four years after, viz. 1669, the young emperor was declared of age, and took the reins of government upon himself, when the persecution immediately ceased by his order.

An account of the Persecutions in Japan.

Christianity was first introduced into the idolatrous empire of Japan by some Portuguese missionaries in the year of our Lord 1552, and their endeavours in making converts to the light of the gospel met with a degree of success equal to their most sanguine wishes.

This continued till the year 1616, when the missionaries being accused of having concerned themselves in politics, and formed a plan to subvert the government, and dethrone the emperor, great jealousies subsisted till 1622, when the court ordered a dreadful persecution to commence against both foreign and native christians. Such was the rage of this persecution, that, during the first four years, no less than 20,570 christians were massacred. The public profession of christianity was prohibited under pain of death, and the churches were shut up by an express edict.

Many who were informed against, as privately professing christianity, suffered martyrdom with great heroism. The persecution continued many years, when the remnant of the innumerable christians, with which Japan abounded, to the number of 37,000 souls, retired to the town and castle of Siniabara, in the island of Xinio, where they determined to make a

stand, to continue in their faith, and to defend themselves to the very last extremity.

The Japanese army pursued the christians, and laid siege to the place. The christians defended themselves with great bravery, and held out against the besiegers for the space of three months, but were at length compelled to surrender, when men, women and children, were indiscriminately murdered; and christianity, in their martyrdoms, entirely extirpated from Japan.

This event took place on the 12th of April, 1638, since which period no christians but the Dutch are allowed to land in the empire, and even they are obliged to conduct themselves with the greatest precaution, and to carry on their commerce with the utmost circumspection.

An account of the Persecutions against the Christians in Abyssinia, or

Ethiopia.

Towards the conclusion of the fifteenth century, and soon after the discovery of the Cape of Good Hope, some Portuguese missionaries made a voyage to Abyssinia, and were indefatigable in propagating the Roman catholic doctrine among the Abyssinians, who professed christianity before the arrival of the missionaries.

The priests, employed in this mission, gained such an influence at court, that the emperor consented to abolish the established rites of the Ethiopian church, and to admit those of Rome. He soon after consented to receive a patriarch from Rome, and to acknowledge the pope's supremacy.

Many of the most powerful lords, and a majority of the people who professed the primitive christianity, as first established in Abyssinia, opposed these innovations, and took up arms against the emperor.--Thus, by the artifices of the court of Rome, and its emissaries, a most furious civil war was begun, and the whole empire thrown into commotion. This war was carried on through several reigns, its continuance being above 100 years, and the court constantly siding with the Roman catholics, the primitive christians of Abyssinia were severely persecuted, and multitudes perished by the most inhuman means.

An account of the Persecutions against the Christians in Turkey.

Mahomet, (the impostor) in the infancy of his new religion, tolerated christianity through a political motive, as he was sensible, that even in those early times it had several powerful espousers among the princes, who were his cotemporaries. As a proof that this was his sole view, as soon as he found his doctrine was established on a more permanent situation, he altered his forbearance to a system of the most rigid and barbarous persecution; which diabolical plan he has particularly recommended to his misguided followers, in that part of his Alcoran, entitled The Chapter of the Sword; and as proofs of the blind zeal his followers have adopted from his infernal tenets, the many bloody battles of the Turks with the whole of the professors of Christ's gospel, and their cruel massacres of them at various periods, sufficiently evince.

Constantine was, in the year 1453, besieged in Constantinople, by Mahomet the Second, with an army of 300,000 men, when, after a bloody siege of about six week, on the 29th of May, 1453, it fell into the hands of the infidels, after being an imperial christian city for some centuries; and the Turks have, to this day, retained possession of it, as well as of the adjoining suburb of Pera.

On entering Constantinople, the Turks exercised on the wretched christians the most unremitting barbarity, destroying them by every method the most hellish cruelty could invent, or the most unfeeling heart could practise: some they roasted alive on spits, others they flayed alive, and in that horrid manner left to expire with hunger; many were sawed asunder, and others torn to pieces by horses.--For full three days and nights the Turks were striving to exceed each other in the exercise of their shocking carnage, and savage barbarity; murdering, without distinction of age or sex, all they met, and brutishly violating the chastity of women, of every distinction and age.

During the year 1529, Solyman the First retook Buda from the christians, and showed the most horrible persecution of the inhabitants; some had their eyes torn out, others their hands, ears, and noses cut off, and the children their privities, the virgins were deflowered, the matrons had their breasts cut off, and such as were pregnant had their wombs ripped open, and their unborn babes thrown into the flames. Not content with this, he repeated these horrid examples all the way on his march to Vienna, which he ineffectually besieged, during which, this diabolical barbarian, having made a body of christians prisoners, he sent three of them into the city to relate the great strength of his army, and the rest he ordered to be torn limb from limb by wild horses in sight of their christian brethren, who could only lament by their cries and tears their dreadful fate.

In many places the tender children were in sight of their wretched parents torn to pieces by beasts, others dragged at horses' heels, some famished with hunger, and others buried up to their necks in earth, and in that manner left to perish. In short, were we to relate the innumerable massacres and deplorable tragedies acted by the infidels, the particulars would at least make a volume of themselves, and from their horrid similarity be not only shocking, but disgusting to the reader.

Persecutions and Oppressions in Georgia and Mingrelia.

The Georgians, are christians, and being very handsome people, the Turks and Persians persecute them by the most cruel mode of taxation ever invented, namely, in lieu of money, they compel them to deliver up their children for the following purposes.

The females to increase the number of concubines in their seraglios, to serve as maids of honour to sultanas, the ladies of bashaws, &c., and to be sold to merchants of different nations, by whom the price is proportioned to the beauty of the purchased fair one.

The males are used as mutes and eunuchs in the seraglio, as clerks in the offices of state, and as soldiers in the army.

To the west of Georgia is Mingrelia, a country likewise inhabited by christians, who are persecuted and oppressed in the same manner as the Georgians by the Turks and Persians, their children being extorted from them, or they murdered for refusing to consent to the sale.

An Account of the Persecutions in the States of Barbary.

In Algiers the christians are treated with particular severity; as the Algerines are some of the most perfidious, as well as the most cruel of all the inhabitants of Barbary. By paying a most exorbitant fine, some christians are allowed the title of Free christians, and these are permitted to dress in the fashion of their respective countries, but the christian slaves are obliged to wear a coarse gray suit and a seaman's cap.

The punishments among the Algerines are various, viz.

1. If they join any of the natives in open rebellion, they are strangled with a bowstring, or hanged on an iron hook.

2. If they speak against Mahomet, they must either turn Mahometan, or be impaled alive.

3. If they turn christians again, after having changed to the Mahometan persuasion, they are roasted alive, or thrown from the city walls, and caught upon large sharp hooks, where they hang in a miserable manner several days, and expire in the most exquisite tortures.

4. If they kill a Turk, they are burnt.

5. Those christians who attempt to escape from slavery, and are retaken, suffer death in the following manner, which is equally singular and brutal: the criminal is hung naked on a high gallows, by two hooks, the

one fastened quite through the palm of one hand, and the other through the sole of the opposite foot, where he is left till death relieves him from his cruel sufferings.

Other punishments, for trifling crimes committed by the christians, are left to the discretion of the respective judges, who being usually of malicious and vindictive dispositions, decree them in the most inhuman manner.

In Tunis, if a christian slave is caught in attempting to escape, his limbs are all broken, and if he murders his master, he is fastened to the tail of a horse, and dragged about the streets till he expires.

Morocco and Fez conjointly form an empire, and are together the most considerable of the Barbary states. In this empire christian slaves are treated with the greatest cruelty: the rich have exorbitant ransoms fixed upon them; the poor are hard worked, and half starved sometimes murdered by the emperor, or their masters, for mere amusement.

An Account of the Persecutions in Spanish America.

The bloody tenets of the Roman catholic persuasion, and the cruel disposition of the votaries of that church, cannot be more amply displayed or truly depicted, than by giving an authentic and simple narrative of the horrid barbarities exercised by the Spaniards on the innocent and unoffending natives of America. Indeed, the barbarities were such, that they would scarce seen credible from their enormity, and the victims so many, that they would startle belief by their numbers, if the facts were not indisputably ascertained, and the circumstances admitted by their own writers, some of whom have even gloried in their inhumanity, and, as Roman catholics, deemed these atrocious actions meritorious, which would make a protestant shudder to relate.

The West Indies, and the vast continent of America, were discovered by that celebrated navigator, Christopher Columbus, in 1492. This distinguished commander landed first in the large island of St. Domingo, or Hispaniola, which was at that time exceedingly populous, but this population was of very little consequence, the inoffensive inhabitants being murdered by multitudes, as soon as the Spaniards gained a permanent footing on the island. Blind superstition, bloody bigotry, and craving avarice, rendered that, in the course of years, a dismal desert, which, at the arrival of the Spaniards, seemed to appear as an earthly paradise; so that at present there is scarce a remnant of the ancient natives remaining.

The natives of Guatemala, a country of America, were used with great barbarity. They were formerly active and valiant, but from ill usage and oppression, grew slothful, and so dispirited, that they not only trembled at the sight of fire-arms, but even at the very looks of a Spaniard. Some were so plunged into despair, that after returning home from labouring hard for their cruel taskmasters, and receiving only contemptuous language and stripes for their pains, they have sunk down in their cabins, with a full resolution to prefer death to such slavery; and, in the bitterness of their anguish, have refused all sustenance till they perished.

By repeated barbarities, and the most execrable cruelties, the vindictive and merciless Spaniards not only depopulated Hispaniola, Porto-Rico, Cuba, Jamaica, and the Bahama islands, but destroyed above 12,000,000 of souls upon the continent of America, in the space of forty years.

The cruel methods by which they massacred and butchered the poor natives, were innumerable, and of the most diabolical nature.

The Spaniards stripped a large and very populous town of all its inhabitants, whom they drove to the mines, leaving all the children behind them, without the least idea of providing for their subsistence, by which inhuman proceeding six thousand helpless infants perished.

Whenever the people of any town had the reputation of being rich, an order was immediately sent that every person in it should turn Roman catholics: if this was not directly complied with, the town was instantly plundered, and the inhabitants murdered; and if it was complied with, a pretence was soon after made to strip the inhabitants of their wealth.

One of the Spanish governors seized upon a very worthy and amiable Indian prince, and in order to extort from him where his treasures were concealed, caused his feet to be burnt till the marrow dropped from his bones, and he expired through the extremity of the torments he underwent.

In the interval, between the years 1514 and 1522, the governor of Terra Firma put to death, and destroyed, 800,000 of the inhabitants of that country.

Between the years 1523 and 1533, five hundred thousand natives of Nicaragua were transported to Peru, where they all perished by incessant labour in the mines.

In the space of twelve years, from the first landing of Cortez on the continent of America, to the entire reduction of the populous empire of Mexico, the amazing number of 4,000,000 of Mexicans perished, through the unparalleled barbarity of the Spaniards. To come to particulars, the city of Cholula, consisted of 30,000 houses, by which its great population may be imagined. The Spaniards seized on all the inhabitants, who refusing to turn Roman catholics, as they did not know the meaning of the religion they were ordered to embrace, the Spaniards put them all to death, cutting to pieces the lower sort of people, and burning those of distinction.

CHAPTER XI.

AN ACCOUNT OF THE PERSECUTIONS IN GREAT BRITAIN AND IRELAND PRIOR TO THE REIGN OF QUEEN MARY I.

Gildas, the most ancient British writer extant, who lived about the time that the Saxons left the island of Great Britain, has drawn a most shocking instance of the barbarity of those people.

The Saxons, on their arrival, being heathens like the Scots and Picts, destroyed the churches and murdered the clergy wherever they came: but they could not destroy christianity, for those who would not submit to the Saxon yoke, went and resided beyond the Severn. Neither have we the names of those christian sufferers transmitted to us, especially those of the clergy.

The most dreadful instance of barbarity under the Saxon government, was the massacre of the monks of Bangor, A. D. 586. These monks were in all respects different from those men who bear the same name at present.

In the eighth century, the Danes, a roving crew of barbarians, landed in different parts of Britain, both in England and Scotland.

At first they were repulsed, but in A. D. 857, a party of them landed somewhere near Southampton, and not only robbed the people, but burnt down the churches, and murdered the clergy.

In A. D. 868, these barbarians penetrated into the centre of England, and took up their quarters at Nottingham; but the English, under their king Ethelfrid, drove them from their posts, and obliged them to retire to Northumberland.

In 870, another body of these barbarians landed at Norfolk, and engaged in battle with the English at Hertford. Victory declared in favour of the pagans, who took Edmund, king of the East Angles, prisoner, and after treating him with a thousand indignities, transfixed his body with arrows, and then beheaded him.

In Fifeshire, in Scotland, they burnt many of the churches, and among the rest that belonging to the Culdees, at St. Andrews. The piety of these men made them objects of abhorrence to the Danes, who, wherever they went singled out the christian priests for destruction, of whom no less than 200 were massacred in Scotland.

It was much the same in that part of Ireland now called Leinster, there the Danes murdered and burnt the priests alive in their own churches; they carried destruction along with them wherever they went, sparing neither age nor sex, but the clergy were the most obnoxious to them, because they ridiculed their idolatry, and persuaded their people to have nothing to do with them.

In the reign of Edward III. the church of England was extremely corrupted with errors and superstition; and the light of the gospel of Christ was greatly eclipsed and darkened with human inventions, burthensome ceremonies, and gross idolatry.

The followers of Wickliffe, then called Lollards, were become extremely numerous, and the clergy were so vexed to see them increase whatever power or influence they might have to molest them in an underhand manner, they had no authority by law to put them to death. However, the clergy embraced the favourable opportunity, and prevailed upon the king to suffer a bill to be brought into parliament, by which all Lollards who remained obstinate, should be delivered over to the secular power, and burnt as heretics. This act was the first in Britain for the burning of people for their religious sentiments; it passed in the year 1401, and was soon after put into execution.

The first person who suffered in consequence of this cruel act was William Santree, or Sawtree, a priest, who was burnt to death in Smithfield.

Soon after this, lord Cobham, in consequence of his attachment to the doctrines of Wickliffe, was accused of heresy, and being condemned to be hanged and burnt, was accordingly executed in Loncoln's-Inn Fields, A. D. 1419.

The next man who suffered under this bloody statute was Thomas Bradley, a tailor, and a layman; and a letter having been tendered him, which he refused, he was declared an obstinate heretic, and tied to the stake in Smithfield; where he was burnt alive, rejoicing in the Lord his God.

The next person we read of who was tried upon this abominable statute, was William Thorpe, a man of some knowledge, who adhered to all the doctrines taught by Wickliffe. He was brought many times before archbishop Arundel, and at last committed a close prisoner, where he died, but in what manner cannot now be ascertained.

About this time 36 persons, denominated Lollards, suffered death in St. Giles', for no other reason than professing their attachment to the doctrines of Wickliffe. They were hung on gibbets, and fagots being placed under them, as soon as they were suspended, fire was set to them, so that they were burnt while hanging. Only one of their names has been transmitted to us, which is that of Sir Roger Archer whom they distinguished from the rest by stripping him stark naked, and executing him in that indecent manner.

Much about the same time one Richard Turning was burnt alive in Smithfield, and suffered with all that constancy, fortitude, and resignation, which have so much distinguished the primitive christians.

In 1428, Abraham, a monk of Colchester, Milburn White, a priest and John Wade, a priest, were all three apprehended on a charge of heresy.

Soon after, father Abraham suffered at Colchester, and with him John Whaddon; both of whom died in a constant adherence to the truth of the gospel. Milburn White and John Wade suffered also about the same time in London.

In the year 1431, Richard Ilvedon, a wool-comber, and a citizen of London, was brought before the archbishop, and being declared an obstinate heretic, was burnt alive on Tower-hill, for no other reason than that he embraced and professed the doctrines of Wickliffe.

In the year 1431, Thomas Bagley, a priest, who had a living near Malden, in Essex, was brought before the bishop of London, and being declared an obstinate heretic, was condemned and burnt alive in Smithfield.

In the year 1430, Richard Wick, a priest, was burnt alive on Tower-hill, for preaching the doctrines of Wickliffe.

In 1440, some of the greatest persons in the kingdom were condemned to perpetual imprisonment for heresy, as being Lollards;--among whom was the dutchess of Gloucester, who had long been a follower of Wickliffe. It was otherwise, however, with Roger Only, a priest, who being condemned as an obstinate heretic, was burnt alive in Smithfield.

In August, 1473, one Thomas Granter was apprehended to London; he was accused of professing the doctrines of Wickliffe, for which he was condemned as an obstinate heretic. This pious man being brought to the sheriff's house, on the morning of the day appointed for his execution, desired a little refreshment, and having ate some, he said to the people present, "I eat now a very good meal, for I have a strange conflict to engage with before I go to supper;" and having eaten, he returned thanks to God for the bounties of his all-gracious providence, requesting that he might be instantly led to the place of execution, to bear testimony to the truth of those principles which he had professed. Accordingly he was chained to a stake on Tower-hill, where he was burnt alive, professing the truth with his last breath.

April 28th, 1494, Joan Boughton, a lady of considerable rank, was burnt in Smithfield for professing the doctrines of Wickliffe. This lady was a widow, and no less than 80 years of age.

In 1498, the king being then at Canterbury, a priest was brought before him, accused of heresy, who was immediately ordered to be burnt alive.

In the year 1499, one Badram, a pious man, was brought before the bishop of Norwich, having been accused by some of the priests, with holding the doctrines of Wickliffe. He confessed he did believe every thing that was objected against him. For this, he was condemned as an obstinate heretic, and a warrant was granted for his execution; accordingly he was brought to the stake at Norwich, where he suffered with great constancy.

In 1506, one William Tilfrey, a pious man, was burnt alive at Amersham, in a close called Stoneyprat, and at the same time, his daughter, Joan Clarke, a married woman, was obliged to light the fagots that were to burn her father.

This year also one father Roberts, a priest, was convicted of being a Lollard before the bishop of Lincoln, and burnt alive at Buckingham.

In 1507, one Thomas Norris was burnt alive for the testimony of the truth of the gospel, at Norwich. This man was a poor, inoffensive, harmless person, but his parish priest conversing with him one day conjectured he was a Lollard. In consequence of this supposition he gave information to the bishop, and Norris was apprehended.

In 1508, one Lawrence Guale, who had been kept in prison two years, was burnt alive at Salisbury, for denying the real presence in the sacrament. It appeared, that this man kept a shop in Salisbury and entertained some Lollards in his house; for which he was informed against to the bishop; but he abode by his first testimony, and was condemned to suffer as a heretic.

A pious woman was burnt at Chippen Sudburne, by order of the chancellor, Dr. Whittenham. After she had been consumed in the flames, and the people were returning home, a bull broke loose from a butcher and singling out the chancellor from all the rest of the company, he gored him through the body, and on his horns carried his entrails. This was seen by all the people, and it is remarkable, that the animal did not meddle with any other person whatever.

October 18, 1511, William Succling and John Bannister, who had formerly recanted, returned again to the profession of the faith, and were burnt alive in Smithfield.

In the year 1517, one John Brown, (who had recanted before in the reign of Henry VII. and borne a fagot round St. Paul's,) was condemned by Dr. Wonhaman, archbishop of Canterbury, and burnt alive at Ashford. Before he was chained to the stake, the archbishop Wonhaman, and Yester, bishop of Rochester, caused his feet to be burnt in a fire till all the flesh came off, even to the bones. This was done in order to make him again recant, but he persisted in his attachment to the truth to the last.

Much about this time one Richard Hunn, a merchant tailor of the city of

London, was apprehended, having refused to pay the priest his fees for the funeral of a child; and being conveyed to the Lollards' Tower, in the palace of Lambeth, was there privately murdered by some of the servants of the archbishop.

September 24, 1518, John Stilincen, who had before recanted, was apprehended, brought before Richard Fitz-James, bishop of London, and on the 25th of October was condemned as a heretic. He was chained to the stake in Smithfield amidst a vast crowd of spectators, and sealed his testimony to the truth with his blood. He declared that he was a Lollard, and that he had always believed the opinions of Wickliffe; and although he had been weak enough to recant his opinions, yet he was now willing to convince the world that he was ready to die for the truth.

In the year 1519, Thomas Mann was burnt in London, as was one Robert Celin, a plain honest man for speaking against image worship and pilgrimages.

Much about this time, was executed in Smithfield, in London, James Brewster, a native of Colchester. His sentiments were the same as the rest of the Lollards, or those who followed the doctrines of Wickliffe; but notwithstanding the innocence of his life, and the regularity of his manners, he was obliged to submit to papal revenge.

During this year, one Christopher, a shoemaker, was burnt alive at Newbury, in Berkshire, for denying those popish articles which we have already mentioned. This man had got some books in English, which were sufficient to render him obnoxious to the Romish clergy.

In 1521, Thomas Bernard was burnt alive at Norwich, for denying the real presence.

About the beginning of the year 1522, Mr. Wrigsham, a glover; Mr Langdale, a hosier; Thomas Bond, Robert Harchets, and William Archer, shoemaker, with Mrs. Smith, a widow, were apprehended on Ash Wednesday and committed to prison. After examination, the bishop of Litchfield declared them to be heretics, and they were all condemned and burnt alive at Coventry.

Robert Silks, who had been condemned in the bishop's court as a heretic, made his escape out of prison, but was taken two years afterward, and brought back to Coventry, where he was burnt alive.--The sheriffs always seized the goods of the martyrs for their own use, so that their wives and children were left to starve.

In 1532, Thomas Harding, who with his wife, had been accused of heresy, was brought before the bishop of Lincoln, and condemned for denying the real presence in the sacrament. He was then chained to a stake, erected for the purpose, at Chesham in the Pell, near Botely; and when they had set fire to the fagots, one of the spectators dashed out his brains with a billet. The priests told the people, that whoever brought fagots to burn heretics would have an indulgence to commit sins for forty days.

During the latter end of this year, Worham, archbishop of Canterbury, apprehended one Hitten, a priest at Maidstone; and after he had been long tortured in prison, and several times examined by the archbishop, and Fisher, bishop of Rochester, he was condemned as a heretic, and burnt alive before the door of his own parish church.

Thomas Bilney, professor of civil law at Cambridge, was brought before the bishop of London, and several other bishops, in the Chapter house, Westminster, and being several times threatened with the stake and flames, he was weak enough to recant; but he repented severely afterward.

For this he was brought before the bishop a second time, and condemned to death. Before he went to the stake he confessed his adherence to those opinions which Luther held; and, when at it, he smiled, and said, "I have had many storms in this world, but now my vessel will soon be on shore in heaven." He stood unmoved in the flames, crying out, "Jesus, I believe;" and these were the last words he was heard to utter.

A few weeks after Bilney had suffered, Richard Byfield was cast into prison, and endured some whipping, for his adherence to the doctrines of Luther: this Mr. Byfield had been some time a monk, at Barnes, in Surry, but was converted by reading Tindal's version of the New Testament. The sufferings this man underwent for the truth were so great, that it would require a volume to contain them. Sometimes he was shut up in a dungeon, where he was almost suffocated, by the offensive and horrid smell of filth and stagnated water. At other times he was tied up by the arms, till almost all his joints were dislocated. He was whipped at the post several times, till scarce any flesh was left on his back; and all this was done to make him recant. He was then taken to the Lollard's Tower in Lambeth palace, where he was chained by the neck to the wall, and once every day beaten in the most cruel manner by the archbishop's servants. At last he was condemned, degraded, and burnt in Smithfield.

The next person that suffered was John Tewkesbury. This was a plain simple man, who had been guilty of no other offence against what was called the holy mother church, than that of reading Tindal's translation of the New Testament. At first he was weak enough to abjure, but afterwards repented, and acknowledged the truth. For this he was brought before the bishop of London, who condemned him as an obstinate heretic. He suffered greatly during the time of his imprisonment, so that when they brought him out to execution he was almost dead. He was conducted to the stake in Smithfield, where he was burned, declaring his utter abhorrence of popery, and professing a firm belief that his cause was just in the sight of God.

Much about this time Valentine Treest, and his wife, were apprehended in Yorkshire, and having been examined by the archbishop, were deemed as obstinate heretics, and burnt.

The next person that suffered in this reign, was James Baynham, a reputable citizen in London, who had married the widow of a gentleman in the Temple. When chained to the stake he embraced the fagots, and said "Oh, ye papists, behold! ye look for miracles; here now may you see a miracle; for in this fire I feel no more pain than if I were in bed; for it is as sweet to me as a bed of roses." Thus he resigned his soul into the hands of his Redeemer.

Soon after the death of this martyr, one Traxnal, an inoffensive countryman, was burned alive at Bradford in Wiltshire, because he would not acknowledge the real presence in the sacrament, nor own the papal supremacy over the consciences of men.

In the year 1533, John Frith, a noted martyr, died for the truth. When brought to the stake in Smithfield, he embraced the fagots, and exhorted a young man named Andrew Hewit, who suffered with him, to trust his soul to that God who had redeemed it. Both these sufferers endured much torment, for the wind blew the flames away from them, so that they were above two hours in agony before they expired.

At the latter end of this year, Mr. Thomas Bennet, a school-master, was apprehended at Exeter, and being brought before the bishop, refused to recant his opinions, for which he was delivered over to the secular power, and burned alive near that city.

In the year 1538, one Collins, a madman, suffered death with his dog in Smithfield. The circumstances were as follow: Collins happened to be in church when the priest elevated the host; and Collins, in derision of the sacrifice of the Mass, lifted up his dog above his head. For this crime Collins, who ought to have been sent to a madhouse, or whipped at the cart's tail, was brought before the bishop of London; and although he was really mad, yet such was the force of popish power, such the corruption in church and state, that the poor madman, and his dog, were both carried to the stake in Smithfield, where they were burned to ashes, amidst a vast crowd of spectators.

There were some other persons who suffered the same year, of whom we shall take notice in the order they lie before us.

One Cowbridge suffered at Oxford; and although he was reputed to be a madman, yet he showed great signs of piety when he was fastened to the stake, and after the flames were kindled around him.

About the same time one Purderve was put to death, for saying privately to a priest, after he had drunk the wine, "He blessed the hungry people with the empty chalice."

At the same time was condemned William Letton, a monk of great age, in the county of Suffolk, who was burned at Norwich for speaking against an idol that was carried in procession; and for asserting, that the sacrament should be administered in both kinds.

Some time before the burning of these men, Nicholas Peke was executed at Norwich; and when the fire was lighted, he was so scorched that he was as black as pitch. Dr. Reading standing before him, with Dr. Hearne and Dr. Spragwell, having a long white wand in his hand, struck him upon the right shoulder, and said, "Peke, recant, and believe in the Sacrament." To this he answered, "I despise thee and it also;" and with great violence he spit blood, occasioned by the anguish of his sufferings. Dr. Reading granted forty days indulgence for the sufferer, in order that he might recant his opinions. But he persisted in his adherence to the truth, without paying any regard to the malice of his enemies; and he was burned alive, rejoicing that Christ had counted him worthy to suffer for his name's sake.

On July 28, 1540, or 1541, (for the chronology differs) Thomas Cromwell, earl of Essex, was brought to a scaffold on Tower-hill, where he was executed with some striking instances of cruelty. He made a short speech to the people, and then meekly resigned himself to the axe.

It is, we think, with great propriety, that this nobleman is ranked among the martyrs; for although the accusations preferred against him did not relate to any thing in religion, yet had it not been for his zeal to demolish popery, he might have to the last retained the king's favour. To this may be added, that the papists plotted his destruction, for he did more towards promoting the reformation, than any man in that age, except the good Dr. Cranmer.

Soon after the execution of Cromwell, Dr. Cuthbert Barnes, Thomas Garnet, and William Jerome, were brought before the ecclesiastical court of the bishop of London, and accused of heresy.

Being before the bishop of London, Dr. Barnes was asked whether the saints prayed for us? To this he answered, that he would leave that to God; but (said he) I will pray for you.

On the 13th of July, 1541, these men were brought from the Tower to Smithfield, where they were all chained to one stake; and there suffered death with a constancy that nothing less than a firm faith in Jesus Christ could inspire.

One Thomas Sommers, an honest merchant, with three others, was thrown into prison, for reading some of Luther's books; and they were condemned to carry those books to a fire in Cheapside; there they were to throw them in the flames; but Sommers threw his over, for which he was sent back to the Tower, where he was stoned to death.

Dreadful persecutions were at this time carried on at Lincoln, under Dr. Longland, the bishop of that diocess. At Buckingham, Thomas Bainard, and James Moreton, the one for reading the Lord's prayer in English, and the other for reading St. James' epistles in English, were both condemned and burnt alive.

Anthony Parsons, a priest, together with two others, were sent to Windsor, to be examined concerning heresy; and several articles were tendered to them to subscribe, which they refused. This was carried on by the bishop of Salisbury, who was the most violent persecutor of any in that age, except Bonner. When they were brought to the stake, Parsons asked for some drink, which being brought him, he drank to his fellow-sufferers, saying, "Be merry, my brethren, and lift up your hearts to God; for after this sharp breakfast I trust we shall have a good dinner in the kingdom of Christ, our Lord and Redeemer." At these words Eastwood, one of the sufferers, lifted up his eyes and hands to heaven, desiring the Lord above to receive his spirit. Parsons pulled the straw near to him, and then said to the spectators, This is God's armour, and now I am a christian soldier prepared for battle: I look for no mercy but through the merits of Christ; he is my only Saviour, in him do I trust for salvation; and soon after the fires were lighted, which burned their bodies, but could not hurt their precious and immortal souls. Their constancy triumphed over cruelty, and their sufferings will be held in everlasting remembrance.

In 1546, one Saitees, a priest, was, by order of bishop Gardiner, hanged in Southwark, without a council process; and all that was alleged against him was, that of reading Tindal's New Testament.

This year one Kirby was burned in Ipswich, for the testimony of the truth, for denying the real presence in the sacrament. When this martyr was brought to the stake, he said to one Mr. Wingfield, who attended him, "Ah! Mr. Wingfield, be at my death, and you shall say, there standeth a christian sufferer in the fire."

CHAPTER XII.

AN ACCOUNT OF THE PERSECUTION IN SCOTLAND DURING THE REIGN OF KING HENRY VIII.

The first person we meet with who suffered in Scotland on the score of religion, was one Patrick Hamilton, a gentleman of an independent fortune, and descended from a very ancient and honourable family.

Having acquired a liberal education, and being desirous of farther improving himself in useful knowledge, he left Scotland, and went to the university of Wirtemberg, in Germany, in order to finish his studies.

During his residence here, he became intimately acquainted with those eminent lights of the gospel, Martin Luther and Philip Melancthon; from whose writings and doctrines he strongly attached himself to the protestant religion.

The archbishop of St. Andrews (who was a rigid papist) hearing of Mr.

Hamilton's proceedings, caused him to be seized, and being brought before him, after a short examination relative to his religious principles, he committed him a prisoner to the castle, at the same time ordering him to be confined in the most loathsome part of the prison.

The next morning Mr. Hamilton was brought before the bishop, and several others, for examination, when the principal articles exhibited against him were, his publicly disapproving of pilgrimages, purgatory, prayers to saints, for the dead, &c.

These articles Mr. Hamilton acknowledged to be true, in consequence of which he was immediately condemned to be burnt; and that his condemnation might have the greater authority, they caused it to be subscribed by all those of any note who were present, and to make the number as considerable as possible, even admitted the subscription of boys who were sons of the nobility.

So anxious was this bigoted and persecuting prelate for the destruction of Mr. Hamilton, that he ordered his sentence to be put in execution on the afternoon of the very day it was pronounced. He was accordingly led to the place appointed for the horrid tragedy, and was attended by a prodigious number of spectators. The greatest part of the multitude would not believe it was intended he should be put to death, but that it was only done to frighten him, and thereby bring him over to embrace the principles of the Romish religion. But they soon found themselves mistaken.

When he arrived at the stake, he kneeled down, and, for some time, prayed with great fervency. After this he was fastened to the stake, and the fagots placed round him. A quantity of gunpowder having been placed under his arms was first set on fire which scorched his left hand and one side of his face, but did no material injury, neither did it communicate with the fagots. In consequence of this, more powder and combustible matter were brought, which being set on fire took effect, and the fagots being kindled, he called out, with an audible voice, "Lord Jesus, receive my spirit! How long shall darkness overwhelm this realm? And how long wilt thou suffer the tyranny of these men?"

The fire burning slow put him to great torment; but he bore it with christian magnanimity. What gave him the greatest pain was, the clamour of some wicked men set on by the friars, who frequently cried, "Turn, thou heretic; call upon our lady; say, Salve Regina, &c." To whom he replied, "Depart from me, and trouble me not, ye messengers of Satan." One Campbell, a friar, who was the ringleader, still continuing to interrupt him by opprobrious language; he said to him, "Wicked man, God forgive thee." After which, being prevented from farther speech by the violence of the smoke, and the rapidity of the flames, he resigned up his soul into the hands of Him who gave it.

This steadfast believer in Christ suffered martyrdom in the year 1527.

One Henry Forest, a young inoffensive Benedictine, being charged with speaking respectfully of the above Patrick Hamilton, was thrown into prison; and, in confessing himself to a friar, owned that he thought Hamilton a good man; and that the articles for which he was sentenced to die, might be defended. This being revealed by the friar, it was received as evidence; and the poor Benedictine was sentenced to be burnt.

Whilst consultation was held, with regard to the manner of his execution, John Lindsay, one of the archbishop's gentlemen, offered his advice, to burn friar Forest in some cellar; for, said be, the smoke of Patrick Hamilton hath infected all those on whom it blew.

This advice was taken, and the poor victim was rather suffocated than burnt.

The next who fell victims for professing the truth of the gospel, were David Stratton and Norman Gourlay.

When they arrived at the fatal spot, they both kneeled down, and prayed for some time with great fervency. They then arose, when Stratton, addressing himself to the spectators, exhorted them to lay aside their superstitious and idolatrous notions, and employ their time in seeking the true light of the gospel. He would have said more, but was prevented by the officers who attended.

Their sentence was then put into execution, and they cheerfully resigned up their souls to that God who gave them, hoping, through the merits of the great Redeemer, for a glorious resurrection to life immortal. They suffered in the year 1534.

The martyrdoms of the two before-mentioned persons, were soon followed by that of Mr. Thomas Forret, who, for a considerable time, had been dean of the Romish church; Killor and Beverage, two blacksmiths; Duncan Simson, a priest; and Robert Forrester, a gentleman. They were all burnt together, on the Castle-hill at Edinburgh, the last day of February, 1538.

The year following the martyrdoms of the before-mentioned persons, viz. 1539, two others were apprehended on a suspicion of heresy; namely, Jerom Russel, and Alexander Kennedy, a youth about eighteen years of age.

These two persons, after being some time confined in prison, were brought before the archbishop for examination. In the course of which, Russel, being a very sensible man, reasoned learnedly against his accusers; while they in return made use of very opprobrious language.

The examination being over, and both of them deemed heretics, the archbishop pronounced the dreadful sentence of death, and they were immediately delivered over to the secular power in order for execution.

The next day they were led to the place appointed for them to suffer; in their way to which, Russel, seeing his fellow-sufferer have the appearance of timidity in his countenance, thus addressed him: "Brother, fear not; greater is he that is in us, than he that is in the world. The pain that we are to suffer is short, and shall be light; but our joy and consolation shall never have an end. Let us, therefore, strive to enter into our Master and Saviour's joy, by the same straight way which he hath taken before us. Death cannot hurt us, for it is already destroyed by Him, for whose sake we are now going to suffer."

When they arrived at the fatal spot, they both kneeled down and prayed for some time; after which being fastened to the stake, and the fagots lighted, they cheerfully resigned their souls into the hands of Him who gave them, in full hopes of an everlasting reward in the heavenly mansions.

In 1543, the archbishop of St. Andrews made a visitation into various parts of his diocese, where several persons were informed against at Perth for heresy. Among these the following were condemned to die, viz. William Anderson, Robert Lamb, James Finlayson, James Hunter, James Raveleson, and Helen Stark.

The accusations laid against these respective persons were as follow:

The four first were accused of having hung up the image of St. Francis, nailing ram's horns on his head, and fastening a cow's tail to his rump; but the principal matter on which they were condemned was, having regaled themselves with a goose on fast day.

James Raveleson was accused of having ornamented his house with the three crowned diadem of Peter, carved in wood, which the archbishop conceived to be done in mockery to his cardinal's cap.

Helen Stark was accused of not having accustomed herself to pray to the Virgin Mary, more especially during the time she was in child bed.

On these respective accusations they were all found guilty, and immediately received sentence of death; the four men for eating the goose to be hanged; James Raveleson to be burnt; and the woman, with her sucking infant, to be put into a sack and drowned.

The four men, with the woman and child, suffered at the same time, but James Raveleson was not executed till some days after.

Besides the above-mentioned persons, many others were cruelly persecuted, some being banished, and others confined in loathsome dungeons. Among whom were Mr. John Knox, the celebrated Scottish reformist; and John Rogers, a pious and learned man, who was murdered in prison, and his body thrown over the walls into the street; after which a report was spread, that he had met with his death in attempting to make his escape.

An Account of the Life, Sufferings, and death of Mr. George Wishart, who was strangled and afterward burned, in Scotland, for professing the Truth of the Gospel.

Mr. George Wishart was born in Scotland, and after receiving a grammatical education at a private school, he left that place, and finished his studies at the university of Cambridge.

In order to improve himself as much as possible in the knowledge of literature, he travelled into various parts abroad, where he distinguished himself for his great learning and abilities, both in philosophy and divinity.

After being some time abroad he returned to England, and took up his residence at Cambridge, where he was admitted a member of Bennet college. Having taken up his degrees, he entered into holy orders, and expounded the gospel in so clear and intelligible a manner, as highly to delight his numerous auditors.

Being desirous of propagating the true gospel in his own country he left

Cambridge in 1544, and on his arrival in Scotland he first preached at Montrose, and afterwards at Dundee. In this last place he made a public exposition of the epistle to the Romans, which he went through with such grace and freedom, as greatly alarmed the papists.

In consequence of this, (at the instigation of cardinal Beaton, the archbishop of St. Andrews) one Robert Miln, a principal man at Dundee, went to the church where Wishart preached, and in the middle of his discourse publicly told him not to trouble the town any more, for he was determined not to suffer it.

This sudden rebuff greatly surprised Wishart, who, after a short pause, looking sorrowfully on the speaker and the audience, said, "God is my witness, that I never minded your trouble but your comfort; yea, your trouble is more grievous to me than it is to yourselves: but I am assured, to refuse God's word, and to chase from you his messenger, shall not preserve you from trouble, but shall bring you into it: for God shall send you ministers that shall fear neither burning nor banishment. I have offered you the word of salvation. With the hazard of my life, I have remained among you; now you yourselves refuse me; and I must leave my innocence to be declared by my God. If it be long prosperous with you, I am not led by the spirit of truth: but if unlooked-for trouble come upon you, acknowledge the cause and turn to God, who is gracious and merciful. But if you turn not at the first warning, he will visit you with fire and sword." At the close of this speech he left the pulpit, and retired.

After this he went into the west of Scotland, where he preached God's word, which was gladly received by many.

A short time after this, Mr. Wishart received intelligence, that the plague was broke out in Dundee. It began four days after he was prohibited from preaching there, and raged so extremely, that it was almost beyond credit how many died in the space of twenty-four hours. This being related to him, he, notwithstanding the importunity of his friends to detain him, determined to go there, saying, "They are now in troubles, and need comfort. Perhaps this hand of God will make them now to magnify and reverence the word of God, which before they lightly esteemed."

Here he was with joy received by the godly. He chose the eastgate for the place of his preaching; so that the healthy were within, and the sick without the gate. He took his text from these words, He sent his word and healed them, &c. In this sermon he chiefly dwelt upon the advantage and comfort of God's word, the judgments that ensue upon the contempt or rejection of it, the freedom of God's grace to all his people, and the happiness of those of his elect, whom he takes to himself out of this miserable world. The hearts of his hearers were so raised by the divine force of this discourse, as not to regard death, but to judge them the more happy who should then be called, not knowing whether he should have such comfort again with them.

After this the plague abated; though, in the midst of it, Wishart constantly visited those that lay in the greatest extremity, and comforted them by his exhortations.

When he took his leave of the people of Dundee, he said, "That God had almost put an end to that plague, and that he was now called to another place."

He went from thence to Montrose; where he sometimes preached, but spent most of his time in private meditation and prayer.

It is said, that before he left Dundee, and while he was engaged in the labours of love to the bodies, as well as to the souls, of those poor afflicted people, cardinal Beaton engaged a desperate popish priest, called John Weighton, to kill him; the attempt to execute which was as follows: one day, after Wishart had finished his sermon, and the people departed, a priest stood waiting at the bottom of the stairs, with a naked dagger in his hand under his gown.--But Mr. Wishart having a sharp, piercing eye, and seeing the priest as he came from the pulpit, said to him, "My friend, what would you have?" and immediately clapping his hand upon the dagger, took it from him. The priest being terrified, fell on his knees, confessed his intention, and craved pardon. A noise being hereupon raised, and it coming to the ears of those who were sick, they cried, "Deliver the traitor to us, we will take him by force;" and they burst in at the gate. But Wishart, taking the priest in his arms, said, "Whatsoever hurts him shall hurt me; for he hath done me no mischief, but much good, by teaching more heedfulness for the time to come." By this conduct he appeased the people and saved the life of the wicked priest.

Soon after his return to Montrose, the cardinal again conspired his death, causing a letter to be sent to him as if it had been from his familiar friend, the Laird of Kennier, in which he was desired with all possible speed to come to him, as he was taken with a sudden sickness. In the mean time the cardinal had provided sixty men armed to lie in wait within a mile and a half of Montrose, in order to murder him as he passed that way.

The letter coming to Wishart's hand by a boy, who also brought him a horse for the journey. Wishart, accompanied by some honest men, his friends, set forward; but something particular striking his mind by the way, he returned back, which they wondering at, asked him the cause; to whom he said, "I will not go; I am forbidden of God; I am assured there is treason. Let some of you go to yonder place, and tell me what you find." Which doing, they made the discovery; and hastily returning, they told Mr. Wishart; whereupon he said, "I know I shall end my life by that blood-thirsty man's hands, but it will not be in this manner."

A short time after this he left Montrose, and proceeded to Edinburgh in order to propagate the gospel in that city. By the way he lodged with a faithful brother, called James Watson of Inner-Goury. In the middle of the night he got up, and went into the yard, which two men hearing they privately followed him.

While in the yard, he fell on his knees, and prayed for some time with the greatest fervency, after which he arose, and returned to his bed. Those who attended him, appearing as though they were ignorant of all, came and asked him where he had been? But he would not answer them. The next day they importuned him to tell them, saying, "Be plain with us, for we heard your mourning, and saw your gestures."

On this he, with a dejected countenance, said, "I had rather you had been in your beds." But they still pressing upon him to know something, he said, "I will tell you; I am assured that my warfare is near at an end, and therefore pray to God with me, that I shrink not when the battle waxeth most hot."

Soon after, cardinal Beaton, archbishop of St. Andrews, being informed that Mr. Wishart was at the house of Mr. Cockburn, of Ormiston, in East Lothian, he applied to the regent to cause him to be apprehended; with which, after great persuasion, and much against his will, he complied.

In consequence of this the cardinal immediately proceeded to the trial of Wishart, against whom no less than eighteen articles were exhibited. Mr. Wishart answered the respective articles with great composure of mind, and in so learned and clear a manner, as greatly surprised most of those who were present.

After the examination was finished, the archbishop endeavoured to prevail on Mr. Wishart to recant; but he was too firmly fixed in his religious principles, and too much enlightened with the truth of the gospel, to be in the least moved.

On the morning of his execution there came to him two friars from the cardinal; one of whom put on him a black linen coat, and the other brought several bags of gunpowder, which they tied about different parts of his body.

As soon as he arrived at the stake, the executioner put a rope round his neck, and a chain about his middle; upon which he fell on his knees and thus exclaimed:

"O thou Saviour of the world, have mercy upon me! Father of heaven, I commend my spirit into Thy holy hands."

After this he prayed for his accusers, saying, "I beseech thee, Father of heaven, forgive them that have, from ignorance or an evil mind, forged lies of me: I forgive them with all my heart. I beseech Christ to forgive them, that have ignorantly condemned me."

He was then fastened to the stake, and the fagots being lighted, immediately set fire to the powder that was tied about him, and which blew into a flame and smoke.

The governor of the castle, who stood so near that he was singed with the flame, exhorted our martyr, in a few words, to be of good cheer, and to ask the pardon of God for his offences. To which he replied, "This flame occasions trouble to my body, indeed, but it hath in nowise broken my spirit. But he who now so proudly looks down upon me from yonder lofty place (pointing to the cardinal) shall, ere long, be as ignominiously thrown down, as now he proudly lolls at his ease." Which prediction was soon after fulfilled. The executioner then pulled the rope which was tied about his neck with great violence, so that he was soon strangled; and the fire getting strength, burnt with such rapidity that in less than an hour his body was totally consumed.

The next person who fell a martyr to popish bigotry, was one Adam Wallace, of Winton, in East-Lothian, who having obtained a true knowledge of the gospel of Christ, spent the greater part of his time in endeavouring to propagate it among his fellow-creatures.

His conduct being noticed by some bigoted papists, an information was laid against him for heresy, on which he was apprehended, and committed to prison.

After examination, sentence of death was passed upon him as heretic; and he was immediately delivered over to the secular power, in order for execution.

In the evening of the same day, Wallace was visited by several Romish priests, who endeavoured to prevail on him to recant; but he stood so steadfast in the faith he professed, and used such forcible arguments in vindication of the gospel, that they left him with some wrath, saying, "He was too abandoned to receive any impression."

The next morning he was conducted to the Castle-hill at Edinburgh, when, being chained to the stake, and the fagots lighted, he cheerfully resigned up his soul into the hands of him who gave it, in full assurance of receiving a crown of glory in the heavenly mansions.

The last who suffered martyrdom in Scotland, for the cause of Christ, was one Walter Mill, who was burnt at Edinburgh in the year 1558.

This person, in his younger years, had travelled into Germany, and on his return was installed a priest of the church of Lunan in Angus, but, on an information of heresy, in the time of cardinal Beaton, he was forced to abandon his charge and abscond. But he was soon apprehended, and committed to prison.

Being interrogated by Sir Andrew Oliphant, whether he would recant his opinions, he answered in the negative, saying, He would sooner forfeit ten thousand lives, than relinquish a particle of those heavenly principles he had received from the suffrages of his blessed Redeemer.

In consequence of this, sentence of condemnation was immediately passed on him, and he was conducted to prison in order for execution the following day.

This steadfast believer in Christ was eighty-two years of age, and exceedingly infirm; from whence it was supposed, that he could scarcely be heard. However, when he was taken to the place of execution, he expressed his religious sentiments with such courage, and at the same time composure of mind, as astonished even his enemies. As soon as he was fastened to the stake, and the fagots lighted, he addressed the spectators as follows:

The cause why I suffer this day is not for any crime, (though I acknowledge myself a miserable sinner) but only for the defence of the truth as it is in Jesus Christ; and I praise God who hath called me, by his mercy, to seal the truth with my life; which, as I received it from him, so I willingly and joyfully offer it up to his glory. Therefore, as you would escape eternal death, be no longer seduced by the lies of the seat of Antichrist: but depend solely on Jesus Christ, and his mercy, that you may be delivered from condemnation. And then added, "That he trusted he should be the last who would suffer death in Scotland upon a religious account."

Thus did this pious christian cheerfully give up his life, in defence of the truth of Christ's gospel, not doubting but he should be made a partaker of his heavenly kingdom.

CHAPTER XII.

PERSECUTIONS IN ENGLAND DURING THE REIGN OF QUEEN MARY.

The premature death of that celebrated young monarch, Edward the Sixth, occasioned the most extraordinary and wonderful occurrences, which had ever existed from the times of our blessed Lord and Saviour's incarnation in human shape. This melancholy event became speedily a subject of general regret. The succession to the British throne was soon made a matter of contention; and the scenes which ensued were a demonstration of the serious affliction which the kingdom was involved in. As his loss to the nation was more and more unfolded, the remembrance of his government was more and more the basis of grateful recollection. The very awful prospect, which was soon presented to the friends of Edward's administration, under the direction of his counsellors and servants, was a contemplation which the reflecting mind was compelled to regard with most alarming apprehensions. The rapid approaches which were made towards a total reversion of the proceedings of the young king's reign, denoted the advances which were thereby represented to an entire revolution in the management of public affairs both in church and state.

Alarmed for the condition in which the kingdom was likely to be involved by the king's death, an endeavour to prevent the consequences, which were but too plainly foreseen, was productive of the most serious and fatal effects. The king, in his long and lingering affliction, was induced to make a will, by which he bequeathed the English crown to lady Jane, the daughter of the duke of Suffolk, who had been married to the lord Guilford, the son of the duke of Northumberland, and was the grand-daughter of the second sister of king Henry, by Charles, duke of Suffolk. By this will, the succession of Mary and Elizabeth, his two sisters, was entirely superseded, from an apprehension of the returning system of popery; and the king's council, with the chief of the nobility, the lord-mayor of the city of London, and almost all the judges and the principal lawyers of the realm, subscribed their names to this regulation, as a sanction to the measure. Lord chief justice Hale, though a true protestant and an upright judge, alone declined to unite his name in favour of the lady Jane, because he had already signified his opinion, that Mary was entitled to assume the reins of government. Others objected to Mary's being placed on the throne, on account of their fears that she might marry a foreigner, and thereby bring the crown into considerable danger. Her partiality to popery also left little doubt on the minds of any, that she would be induced to revive the dormant interests of the pope, and change the religion which had been used both in the days of her father, king Henry, and in those of her brother Edward: for in all his time she had manifested the greatest stubbornness and inflexibility of temper, as must be obvious from her letter to the lords of the council, whereby she put in her claim to the crown, on her brother's decease.

When this happened, the nobles, who had associated to prevent Mary's succession, and had been instrumental in promoting, and, perhaps, advising the measures of Edward, speedily proceeded to proclaim lady Jane Gray, to be queen of England, in the city of London and various other populous cities of the realm. Though young, she possessed talents of a very superior nature, and her improvements under a most excellent tutor had given her many very great advantages.

Her reign was of only five days continuance, for Mary, having succeeded by false promises in obtaining the crown, speedily commenced the execution of her avowed intention of extirpating and burning every protestant. She was crowned at Westminister in the usual form, and her elevation was the signal for the commencement of the bloody persecution which followed.

Having obtained the sword of authority, she was not sparing in its exercise. The supporters of Lady Jane Gray were destined to feel its force. The duke of Northumberland was the first who experienced her savage resentment. Within a month after his confinement in the Tower, he was condemned, and brought to the scaffold, to suffer as a traitor. From his various crimes, resulting out of a sordid and inordinate ambition, he died unpitied and unlamented.

The changes, which followed with rapidity, unequivocally declared, that the queen was disaffected to the present state of religion.--Dr. Poynet was displaced to make room for Gardiner to be bishop of Winchester, to whom she also gave the important office of lord-chancellor. Dr. Ridley was dismissed from the see of London, and Bonne introduced. J. Story was put out of the bishopric of Chichester, to admit Dr. Day. J. Hooper was sent prisoner to the Fleet, and Dr. Heath put into the see of Worcester. Miles Coverdale was also excluded from Exeter, and Dr. Vesie placed in that diocess. Dr. Tonstall was also promoted to the see of Durham. "These things being marked and perceived, great heaviness and discomfort grew more and more to all good men's hearts; but to the wicked great rejoicing. They that could dissemble took no great care how the matter went; but such, whose consciences were joined with the truth, perceived already coals to be kindled, which after should be the destruction of many a true christian."

The words and behaviour of the lady Jane upon the Scaffold.

The next victim was the amiable lady Jane Gray, who, by her acceptance of the crown at the earnest solicitations of her friends, incurred the implacable resentment of the bloody Mary. When she first mounted the scaffold, she spake to the spectators in this manner: Good people, I am come hither to die, and by a law I am condemned to the same. The fact against the queen's highness was unlawful, and the consenting thereunto by me: but, touching the procurement and desire thereof by me, or on my behalf, I do wash my hands thereof in innocency before God, and the face of you, good christian people, this day: and therewith she wrung her hands, wherein she had her book. Then said she, I pray you all, good christian people, to bear me witness, that I die a good christian woman, and that I do look to be saved by no other mean, but only by the mercy of God in the blood of his only Son Jesus Christ: and I confess, that when I did know the word of God, I neglected the same, loved myself and the world, and therefore this plague and punishment is happily and worthily happened unto me for my sins; and yet I thank God, that of his goodness he hath thus given me a time and a respite to repent and now, good people, while I am alive, I pray you assist me with your prayers.

And then, kneeling down, she turned to Feckenham, saying, Shall I say this psalm? and he said, Yea. Then she said the psalm of Miserere mei Deus, in English, in a most devout manner throughout to the end; and then she stood up, and gave her maid, Mrs. Ellen, her gloves and handkerchief, and her book to Mr. Bruges; and then she untied her gown, and the executioner pressed upon her to help her off with it: but she, desiring him to let her alone, turned towards her two gentlewomen, who helped her off therewith, and also with her frowes, paaft, and neckerchief, giving to her a fair handkerchief to put about her eyes.

Then the executioner kneeled down, and asked her forgiveness whom she forgave most willingly. Then he desired her to stand upon the straw, which doing, she saw the block. Then she said, I pray you despatch me quickly. Then she kneeled down, saying, Will you take it off before I lay me down? And the executioner said, No madam. Then she tied a handkerchief about her eyes, and feeling for the block, she said, What shall I do? Where is it? Where is it? One of the standers-by guiding her thereunto, she laid her head upon the block, and then stretched forth her body, and said, Lord, into thy hands I commend my spirit; and so finished her life, in the year of our Lord 1554, the 12th day of February, about the 17th year of her age.

Thus died the Lady Jane; and on the same day the lord Guilford, her husband, one of the duke of Northumberland's sons, was likewise beheaded, two innocents in comparison of them that sat upon them. For they were both very young, and ignorantly accepted that which others had contrived, and by open proclamation consented to take from others, and give to them.

Touching the condemnation of this pious lady, it is to be noted, that Judge Morgan, who gave sentence against her, soon after he had condemned her, fell mad, and in his raving cried out continually, to have the lady Jane taken away from him, and so he ended his life.

On the 21st day of the same month, Henry, duke of Suffolk, was beheaded on Tower-hill, the fourth day after his condemnation: about which time many gentlemen and yeomen were condemned, whereof some were executed at London, and some in the country. In the number of whom was the lord Thomas Gray, brother to the said duke, being apprehended not long after in North-Wales, and executed for the same. Sir Nicholas Throgmorton, also, very narrowly escaped.

John Rogers, Vicar of St. Sepulchre's, and Reader of St. Paul's,

London.

John Rogers was educated at Cambridge, and was afterward many years chaplain to the merchants adventurers at Antwerp in Brabant. Here he met with the celebrated martyr William Tindal, and Miles Coverdale, both voluntary exiles from their country for their aversion to popish superstition and idolatry. They were the instruments of his conversion; and he united with them in that translation of the Bible into English, entitled "The Translation of Thomas Matthew." From the scriptures he knew that unlawful vows may be lawfully broken; hence he married, and removed to Wittenberg in Saxony, for the improvement of learning; and he there learned the Dutch language, and received the charge of a congregation, which he faithfully executed for many years. On king Edward's accession, he left Saxony, to promote the work of reformation in England; and, after some time, Nicholas Ridley, then bishop of London, gave him a prebend in St. Paul's Cathedral, and the dean and chapter appointed him reader of the divinity lesson there. Here he continued until queen Mary's succession to the throne, when the gospel and true religion were banished, and the Antichrist of Rome, with his superstition and idolatry, introduced.

The circumstance of Mr. Rogers having preached at Paul's cross, after queen Mary arrived at the Tower, has been already stated. He confirmed in his sermon the true doctrine taught in King Edward's time, and exhorted the people to beware of the pestilence of popery, idolatry, and superstition. For this he was called to account, but so ably defended himself, that, for that time, he was dismissed. The proclamation of the queen, however, to prohibit true preaching, gave his enemies a new handle against him. Hence he was again summoned before the council, and commanded to keep his house. He did so, though he might have escaped; and though he perceived the state of the true religion to be desperate. "He knew he could not want a living in Germany; and he could not forget a wife and ten children, and to seek means to succour them." But all these things were insufficient to induce him to depart and, when once called to answer in Christ's cause, he stoutly defended it, and hazarded his life for that purpose.

After long imprisonment in his own house, the restless Bonner, bishop of London, caused him to be committed to Newgate, there to be lodged among thieves and murderers.

After Mr. Rogers had been long and straitly imprisoned, and lodged in Newgate among thieves, often examined, and very uncharitably entreated, and at length unjustly and most cruelly condemned by Stephen Gardiner, bishop of Winchester: the 4th of February, in the year of our Lord 1555, being Monday in the morning, he was suddenly warned by the keeper of Newgates's wife, to prepare himself for the fire; who, being then sound asleep, could scarce be awaked. At length being raised and awaked, and bid to make haste, Then said he, if it be so, I need not tie my points. And so was had down, first to bishop Bonner to be degraded: which being done, he craved of Bonner but one petition; and Bonner asking what that should be? Mr. Rogers replied, that he might speak a few words with his wife before his burning. But that could not be obtained of him.

When the time came, that he should be brought out of Newgate to Smithfield, the place of his execution, Mr. Woodroofe, one of the sheriffs, first came to Mr. Rogers, and asked him, if he would revoke his abominable doctrine, and the evil opinion of the sacrament of the altar. Mr. Rogers answered that which I have preached I will seal with my blood. Then Mr. Woodroofe said, Thou art an heretic. That shall be known, quoth Mr. Rogers, at the day of judgment.--"Well, said Mr. Woodroofe, I will never pray for thee. But I will pray for you, said Mr. Rogers; and so was brought the same day, the 4th of February, by the sheriffs, towards Smithfield, saying the psalm Miserere by the way, all the people wonderfully rejoicing at his constancy with great praises and thanks to God for the same. And here, in the presence of Mr. Rochester, comptroller of the queen's household, sir Richard Southwell, both the sheriffs, and a great number of people he was burnt to ashes, washing his hands in the flame as he was burning. A little before his burning, his pardon was brought if he would have recanted; but he utterly refused it. He was the first martyr of all the blessed company that suffered in Queen Mary's time that gave the first adventure upon the fire. His wife and children, being eleven in number, ten able to go, and one sucking at her breast, met him by the way, as he went towards Smithfield: this sorrowful sight of his own flesh and blood could nothing move him but that he constantly and cheerfully took his death with wonderful patience, in the defence and quarrel of the gospel of Christ."

The Rev. Mr. Lawrence Saunders.

Mr. Saunders after passing some time in the school of Eaton, was chosen to go to King's college in Cambridge, where he continued three years, and profited in knowledge and learning very much for that time shortly after he quitted the university, and went to his parents, but soon returned to Cambridge again to his study, where he began to add to the knowledge of the Latin, the study of the Greek and Hebrew tongues, and gave himself up to the study of the holy scriptures, the better to qualify himself for the office of preacher.

In the beginning of king Edward's reign, when God's true religion was introduced, after license obtained, he began to preach, and was so well liked of them who then had authority, that they appointed him to read a divinity lecture in the college of Fothringham. The college of Fothringham being dissolved, he was placed to be a reader in the minster at Litchfield. After a certain space, he departed from Litchfield to a benefice in Leicestershire, called Church-langton, where he held a residence, taught diligently, and kept a liberal house. Thence he was orderly called to take a benefice in the city of London, namely, All-hallows in Bread-street.--After this he preached at Northampton, nothing meddling with the state, but boldly uttering his conscience against the popish doctrines which were likely to spring up again in England, as a just plague for the little love which the English nation then bore to the blessed word of God, which had been so plentifully offered unto them.

The queen's party, who were there, and heard him, were highly displeased with him for his sermon, and for it kept him among them as a prisoner. But partly for love of his brethren and friends, who were chief actors for the queen among them, partly because there was no law broken by his preaching, they dismissed him.

Some of his friends, perceiving such fearful menacing, counselled him to fly out of the realm, which he refused to do. But seeing he was with violence kept from doing good in that place, he returned towards London, to visit his flock.

In the afternoon of Sunday, Oct. 15, 1554, as he was reading in his church to exhort his people, the bishop of London interrupted him, by sending an officer for him.

His treason and sedition the bishop's charity was content to let slip until another time, but a heretic he meant to prove him, and all those, he said, who taught and believed that the administration of the sacraments, and all orders of the church, are the most pure, which come the nearest to the order of the primitive church.

After much talk concerning this matter, the bishop desired him to write what he believed of transubstantiation. Laurence Saunders did so, saying, "My Lord, you seek my blood, and you shall have it: I pray God that you may be so baptised in it that you may ever after loathe blood-sucking, and become a better man." Upon being closely charged with contumacy, the severe replies of Mr. Saunders to the bishop, (who had before, to get the favour of Henry VIII. written and set forth in print, a book of true obedience, wherein he had openly declared queen Mary to be a bastard) so irritated him, that he exclaimed, Carry away this frenzied fool to prison.

After this good and faithful martyr had been kept in prison one year and a quarter, the bishops at length called him, as they did his fellow-prisoners, openly to be examined before the queen's council.

His examination being ended, the officers led him out of the place, and staid until the rest of his fellow-prisoners were likewise examined, that they might lead them all together to prison.

After his excommunication and delivery over to the secular power, he was brought by the sheriff of London to the Compter, a prison in his own parish of Bread-street, at which he rejoiced greatly, both because he found there a fellow-prisoner, Mr. Cardmaker, with whom he had much christian and comfortable discourse; and because out of prison, as before in his pulpit, he might have an opportunity of preaching to his parishioners. The 4th of February, Bonner, bishop of London, came to the prison to degrade him; the day following, in the morning the sheriff of London delivered him to certain of the queen's guard, who were appointed to carry him to the city of Coventry, there to be burnt.

When they had arrived at Coventry, a poor shoemaker, who used to serve him with shoes, came to him, and said, O my good master, God strengthen and comfort you. Good shoemaker, Mr. Saunders replied, I desire thee to pray for me, for I am the most unfit man for this high office, that ever was appointed to it; but my gracious God and dear Father is able to make me strong enough. The next day, being the 8th of February, 1555, he was led to the place of execution, in the park, without the city; he went in an old gown and a shirt, bare-footed, and oftentimes fell flat on the ground, and prayed. When he was come nigh to the place, the officer, appointed to see the execution done, said to Mr. Saunders, that he was one of them who married the queen's realm, but if he would recant, there was pardon for him. "Not I," replied the holy martyr, "but such as you have injured the realm. The blessed gospel of Christ is what I hold; that do I believe, that have I taught, and that will I never revoke!" Mr. Saunders then slowly moved towards the fire, sank to the earth and prayed; he then rose up, embraced the stake, and frequently said, "Welcome, thou cross of Christ! welcome everlasting life!" Fire was then put to the fagots, and, he was overwhelmed by the dreadful flames, and sweetly slept in the Lord Jesus.

The history, imprisonment, and examinations, of Mr. John Hooper, Bishop of Worcester and Gloucester.

John Hooper, student and graduate in the university of Oxford, was stirred with such fervent desire to the love and knowledge of the scriptures, that he was compelled to remove from thence, and was retained in the house of Sir Thomas Arundel, as his steward, till Sir Thomas had intelligence of his opinions and religion, which he in no case did favour, though he exceedingly favoured his person and condition, and wished to be his friend. Mr. Hooper now prudently left Sir Thomas' house and arrived at Paris, but in a short time returned into England, and was retained by Mr. Sentlow, till the time that he was again molested and sought for, when he passed through France to the higher parts of Germany; where, commencing acquaintance with learned men, he was by them free and lovingly entertained, both at Basil, and especially at Zurich, by Mr. Bullinger, who was his singular friend; here also he married his wife, who was a Burgonian, and applied very studiously to the Hebrew tongue.

At length, when God saw it good to stay the bloody time of the six articles, and to give us king Edward to reign over this realm, with some peace and rest unto the church, amongst many other English exiles, who then repaired homeward, Mr. Hooper also, moved in conscience, thought not to absent himself, but seeing such a time and occasion, offered to help forward the Lord's work, to the uttermost of his ability.

When Mr. Hooper had taken his farewell of Mr. Bullinger, and his friends in Zurich, he repaired again into England in the reign of king Edward the Sixth, and coming to London, used continually to preach, most times twice, or at least once a day.

In his sermons, according to his accustomed manner, he corrected sin, and sharply inveighed against the iniquity of the world and the corrupt abuses of the church. The people in great flocks and companies daily came to hear his voice, as the most melodious sound and tune of Orpheus' harp, insomuch, that oftentimes when he was preaching, the church would be so full, that none could enter further than the doors thereof. In his doctrine, he was earnest, in tongue eloquent, in the scriptures, perfect, in pains indefatigable, in his life exemplary.

Having preached before the king's majesty, he was soon after made bishop of Gloucester. In that office he continued two years, and behaved himself so well, that his very enemies could find no fault with him, and after that he was made bishop of Worcester.

Dr. Hooper executed the office of a most careful and vigilant pastor for the space of two years and more, so long as the state of religion in king Edward's time was sound and flourishing.

After he had been cited to appear before Bonner and Dr. Heath, he was led to the Council, accused falsely of owing the queen money, and in the next year, 1554, he wrote an account of his severe treatment during near eighteen months' confinement to the Fleet, and after his third examination, January 28, 1555, at St. Mary Overy's, he, with the Rev. Mr. Rogers, was conducted to the Compter in Southwark, there to remain till the next day at nine o'clock, to see whether they would recant. Come, brother Rogers, said Dr. Hooper, must we two take this matter first in hand, and begin to fry in these fagots? Yes, Doctor, said Mr. Rogers, by God's grace. Doubt not, said Dr. Hooper, but God will give us strength; and the people so applauded their constancy, that they had much ado to pass.

January 29, bishop Hooper was degraded and condemned, and the Rev. Mr. Rogers was treated in like manner. At dark, Dr. Hooper was led through the city to Newgate; notwithstanding this secrecy, many people came forth to their doors with lights, and saluted him, praising God for his constancy.

During the few days he was in Newgate, he was frequently visited by Bonner and others, but without avail. As Christ was tempted, so they tempted him, and then maliciously reported that he had recanted. The place of his martyrdom being fixed at Gloucester, he rejoiced very much, lifting up his eyes and hands to heaven, and praising God that he saw it good to send him among the people over whom he was pastor, there to confirm with his death the truth which he had before taught them.

On Feb. 7th, he came to Gloucester, about five o'clock, and lodged at one Ingram's house. After his first sleep, he continued in prayer until morning; and all the day, except a little time at his meals, and when conversing with such as the guard kindly permitted to speak to him, he spent in prayer.

Sir Anthony Kingston, at one time Doctor Hooper's good friend, was appointed by the queen's letters to attend at his execution. As soon as he saw the bishop he burst into tears. With tender entreaties he exhorted him to live. "True it is," said the bishop, "that death is bitter, and life is sweet: but alas! consider that the death to come is more bitter, and the life to come is more sweet."

The same day a blind boy obtained leave to be brought into Dr. Hooper's presence. The same boy, not long before, had suffered imprisonment at Gloucester for confessing the truth. "Ah! poor boy," said the bishop, "though God hath taken from thee thy outward sight, for what reason he best knoweth, yet he hath endued thy soul with the eye of knowledge and of faith. God give thee grace continually to pray unto him, that thou lose not that sight, for then wouldst thou indeed be blind both in body and soul."

When the mayor waited upon him preparatory to his execution, he expressed his perfect obedience, and only requested that a quick fire might terminate his torments. After he had got up in the morning, he desired that no man should be suffered to come into the chamber, that he might be solitary till the hour of execution.

About eight o'clock, on February 9, 1555, he was led forth, and many thousand persons were collected, as it was market-day. All the way, being straitly charged not to speak, and beholding the people who mourned bitterly for him, he would sometimes lift up his eyes towards heaven, and look very cheerfully upon such as he knew: and he was never known, during the time of his being among them, to look with so cheerful and ruddy a countenance as he did at that time. When he came to the place appointed where he should die, he smilingly beheld the stake and preparation made for him, which was near unto the great elm-tree over against the college of priests, where he used to preach.

Now, after he had entered into prayer, a box was brought and laid before him upon a stool, with his pardon from the queen, if he would turn. At the sight whereof he cried, If you love my soul away with it. The box being taken away, lord Chandois said, Seeing there is no remedy, despatch him quickly.

Command was now given that the fire should be kindled. But because there were not more green fagots than two horses could carry, it kindled not speedily, and was a pretty while also before it took the reeds upon the fagots. At length it burned about him, but the wind having full strength at that place, and being a lowering cold morning, it blew the flame from him, so that he was in a manner little more than touched by the fire.

Within a space after, a few dry fagots were brought, and a new fire kindled with fagots, (for there were no more reeds) and those burned at the nether parts, but had small power above, because of the wind, saving that it burnt his hair, and scorched his skin a little. In the time of which fire, even as at the first flame, he prayed, saying mildly, and not very loud, but as one without pain, O Jesus, Son of David, have mercy upon me, and receive my soul! After the second fire was spent, he wiped both his eyes with his hands, and beholding the people, he said with an indifferent loud voice, For God's love, good people, let me have more fire! and all this while his nether parts did burn; but the fagots were so few, that the flame only singed his upper parts.

The third fire was kindled within a while after, which was more extreme than the other two. In this fire he prayed with a loud voice, Lord Jesus, have mercy upon me! Lord Jesus receive my spirit! And these were the last words he was heard to utter. But when he was black in the mouth, and his tongue so swollen that he could not speak, yet his lips went till they were shrunk to the gums: and he knocked his breast with his hands until one of his arms fell off, and then knocked still with the other, while the fat, water, and blood dropped out at his fingers' ends, until by renewing the fire, his strength was gone, and his hand clave fast in knocking to the iron upon his breast. Then immediately bowing forwards, he yielded up his spirit.

The life and conduct of Dr. Rowland Taylor of Hadley.

Dr. Rowland Taylor, vicar of Hadley, in Suffolk, was a man of eminent learning, and had been admitted to the degree of doctor of the civil and canon law.

His attachment to the pure and uncorrupted principles of christianity recommended him to the favour and friendship of Dr. Cranmer, archbishop of Canterbury, with whom he lived a considerable time, till through his interest he obtained the living of Hadley.

Dr. Taylor promoted the interest of the great Redeemer, and the souls of mankind, both by his preaching and example, during the time of king Edward VI. but on his demise, and the succession of queen Mary to the throne, he escaped not the cloud that burst on so many beside; for two of his parishioners, Foster, an attorney, and Clark, a tradesman, out of blind zeal, resolved that mass should be celebrated, in all its superstitious forms, in the parish church of Hadley, on Monday before Easter; this Dr. Taylor, entering the church, strictly forbade; but Clark forced the Doctor out of the church, celebrated mass, and immediately informed the lord-chancellor, bishop of Winchester of his behaviour, who summoned him to appear, and answer the complaints that were alleged against him.

The doctor upon the receipt of the summons, cheerfully prepared to obey the same; and rejected the advice of his friends to fly beyond sea. When Gardiner saw Dr. Taylor, he, according to his common custom, reviled him. Dr. Taylor heard his abuse patiently, and when the bishop said, How darest thou look me in the face! knowest thou not who I am? Dr. Taylor replied, You are Dr. Stephen Gardiner, bishop of Winchester, and lord-chancellor, and yet but a mortal man. But if I should be afraid of your lordly looks, why fear ye not God, the Lord of us all? With what countenance will you appear before the judgment-seat of Christ, and answer to your oath made first unto king Henry the Eighth, and afterward unto king Edward the Sixth, his son?

A long conversation ensued, in which Dr. Taylor was so piously collected and severe upon his antagonist, that he exclaimed, Thou art a blasphemous heretic! Thou indeed blasphemist the blessed sacrament, (here he put off his cap) and speakest against the holy mass, which is made a sacrifice for the quick and the dead. The bishop afterward committed him into the king's bench.

When Dr. Taylor came there, he found the virtuous and vigilant preacher of God's word, Mr. Bradford; who equally thanked God that he had provided him with such a comfortable fellow-prisoner; and they both together praised God, and continued in prayer, reading and exhorting one another.

After that Dr. Taylor had lain some time in prison, he was cited to appear in the arches of Bow-church.

Dr. Taylor being condemned, was committed to the Clink, and the keepers were charged to treat him roughly; at night he was removed to the Poultry Compter.

When Dr. Taylor had lain in the Compter about a week, on the 4th of February, Bonner came to degrade him, bringing with him such ornaments as appertained to the massing mummery; but the Doctor refused these trappings till they were forced upon him.

The night after he was degraded, his wife came with John Hull, his servant, and his son Thomas, and were by the gentleness of the keepers permitted to sup with him.

After supper, walking up and down, he gave God thanks for his grace, that had so called him and given him strength to abide by his holy word and turning to his son Thomas, he exhorted him to piety and filial obedience in the most earnest manner.

Dr. Taylor, about two o'clock in the morning, was conveyed to the Woolpack, Aldgate, and had an affecting interview with his wife and daughter, and a female orphan he had brought up who had waited all night in St. Botolph's porch, to see him pass, before being delivered to the sheriff of Essex. On coming out of the gates, John Hull, his good servant, stood at the rails with Thomas, (Dr. Taylor's son.) This, said he, is my own son. Then he lifted up his eyes to heaven, and prayed for his son and blessed him.

At Chelmsford the sheriff of Suffolk met them, there to receive him, and to carry him into Suffolk. Being at supper, the sheriff of Essex very earnestly besought him to return to the popish religion, thinking with fair words to persuade him. When they had all drunk to him, and the cup was come to him, he said, Mr. Sheriff, and my masters all, I heartily thank you for your good will. I have hearkened to your words, and marked well your counsels. And to be plain with you, I perceive that I have been deceived myself, and am like to deceive a great many in Hadley of their expectations. At these words they all rejoiced, but the Doctor had a meaning very remote from theirs. He alluded to the disappointment that the worms would have in not being able to feast upon his portly and goodly body, which they would have done if, instead of being burnt, he had been buried.

When the sheriff and his company heard him speak thus, they were amazed, marvelling at the constant mind that could thus without fear make a jest of the cruel torments and death now at hand, prepared for him. At Chelmsford he was delivered to the sheriff of Suffolk, and by him conducted to Hadley.

When Dr. Taylor had arrived at Aldham-Common, the place where he should suffer, seeing a great multitude of people, he asked, What place is this, and what meaneth it that so much people are gathered hither? It was answered, It is Aldham-Common, the place where you must suffer; and the people are come to look upon you. Then he said, Thanked be God, I am even at home; and he alighted from his horse and with both hands rent the hood from his head.

His head had been notched and clipped like as a man would clip a fool's; which cost the good bishop Bonner had bestowed upon him. But when the people saw his reverend and ancient face, with a long white beard, they burst out with weeping tears, and cried, saying, God save thee, good Dr. Taylor! Jesus Christ strengthen thee, and help thee! the Holy Ghost comfort thee! with such other like good wishes.

When he had prayed, he went to the stake and kissed it, and set himself into a pitch barrel, which they had put for him to stand in, and stood with his back upright against the stake, with his hands folded together, and his eyes towards heaven, and continually prayed.

They then bound him with the chains, and having set up the fagots, one Warwick cruelly cast a fagot at him which struck him on his head, and cut his face, so that the blood ran down. Then said Dr. Taylor, O friend, I have harm enough, what needed that?

Sir John Shelton standing by, as Dr. Taylor was speaking, and saying the psalm Miserere in English, struck him on the lips: You knave, said he, speak Latin: I will make thee. At last they kindled the fire; and Dr. Taylor holding up both his hands, calling upon God, and said, Merciful Father of heaven! for Jesus Christ, my Saviour's sake, receive my soul into thy hands! So he stood still without either crying or moving, with his hands folded together, till Soyce, with a halberd struck him on the head till his brains fell out, and the corpse fell down into the fire.

Thus rendered up this man of God his blessed soul into the hands of his merciful Father, and to his most dear Saviour Jesus Christ, whom he most entirely loved, faithfully and earnestly preached, obediently followed in living, and constantly glorified in death.

Martyrdom of Tomkins, Pygot, Knight, Lawrence, Hunter, and Higbed.

Thomas Tomkins was by trade a weaver in Shoreditch, till he was summoned before the inhuman Bonner, and confined with many others, who renounced the errors of popery, in a prison in that tyrant's house at Fulham.

Under his confinement, he was treated by the bishop not only unbecoming a prelate, but even a man; for the savage, because Tomkins would not assent to the doctrine of transubstantiation, bruised him in the face, and plucked off the greatest part of the hair of his beard.

On another occasion, this scandal to humanity, in the presence of many who came to visit at Fulham, took this poor honest man by the fingers, and held his hand directly over the flame of a wax candle having three or four wicks, supposing that, being terrified by the smart and pain of the fire, he would leave off the defence of the doctrine which he had received.

Tomkins thinking no otherwise, but there presently to die, began to commend himself unto the Lord, saying, O Lord, into thy hands I commend my spirit, &c. All the time that his hand was burning the same Tomkins afterward reported to one James Hinse, that his spirit was so rapt, that he felt no pain. In which burning he never shrank till the veins shrank, and the sinews burst and the water spurted into Mr. Harpsfield's face: insomuch that Mr. Harpsfield, moved with pity, desired the bishop to stay, saying, that he had tried him enough.

After undergoing two examinations, and refusing to swerve from his duty and belief, he was commanded to appear before the bishop.

Agreeably to this mandate, being brought before the bloody tribunal of bishops, and pressed to recant his errors and return to the mother church, he maintained his fidelity, nor would swerve in the least from the articles he had signed with his own hand. Having therefore declared him an obstinate heretic, they delivered him up to the secular power, and he was burned in Smithfield, March 16th, 1555, triumphant in the midst of the flames, and adding to the noble company of martyrs, who had preceded him through the path of the fiery trial to the realms of immortal glory.

William Hunter had been trained to the doctrines of the reformation from his earliest youth, being descended from religious parents, who carefully instructed him in the principles of the true religion.

Hunter, then nineteen years of age, refusing to receive the communion at mass, was threatened to be brought before the bishop; to whom this valiant young martyr was conducted by a constable.

Bonner caused William to be brought into a chamber, where he began to reason with him, promising him security and pardon if he would recant. Nay, he would have been content if he would have gone only to receive and to confession, but William would not do so for all the world.

Upon this the bishop commanded his men to put William in the stocks in his gate-house, where he sat two days and nights, with a crust of brown bread and a cup of water only, which he did not touch.

At the two days' end, the bishop came to him, and finding him steadfast in the faith, sent him to the convict prison, and commanded the keeper to lay irons upon him as many as he could bear. He continued in prison three quarters of a year, during which time he had been before the bishop five times, besides the time when he was condemned in the consistory in St. Paul's, February 9th, at which time his brother, Robert Hunter, was present.

Then the bishop, calling William, asked him if he would recant, and finding he was unchangeable, he pronounced sentence upon him, that he should go from that place to Newgate for a time, and thence to Brentwood, there to be burned.

About a month afterward, William was sent down to Brentwood, where he was to be executed. On coming to the stake, he knelt down and read the 51st psalm, till he came to these words, "The sacrifice of God is a contrite spirit; a contrite and a broken heart, O God, thou wilt not despise." Steadfast in refusing the queen's pardon, if he would become an apostate, at length one Richard Ponde, a bailiff, came, and made the chain fast about him.

William now cast his psalter into his brother's hand, who said William, think on the holy passion of Christ, and be not afraid of death. Behold, answered William, I am not afraid. Then he lifted up his hands to heaven, and said, Lord, Lord, Lord, receive my spirit and casting down his head again into the smothering smoke, he yielded up his life for the truth, sealing it with his blood to the praise of God.

About the same time William Pygot, Stephen Knight, and Rev. John Lawrence, were burnt as heretics, by order of the infamous Bonner. Thomas Higbed and Thomas Causton shared the same fate.

Dr. Robert Farrar.

This worthy and learned prelate, the bishop of St. David's in Wales, having in the former reign, as well as since the accession of Mary, been remarkably zealous to promoting the reformed doctrines, and exploding the errors of popish idolatry, was summoned, among others, before the persecuting bishop of Winchester, and other commissioners set apart for the abominable work of devastation and massacre.

His principal accusers and persecutors, on a charge of praemunire in the reign of Edward VI. were George Constantine Walter, his servant; Thomas Young, chanter of the cathedral, afterward bishop of Bangor, &c. Dr.

Farrar ably replied to the copies of information laid against him, consisting of fifty-six articles. The whole process of this trial was long and tedious. Delay succeeded delay, and after that Dr. Farrar had been long unjustly detained in custody under sureties, in the reign of king Edward, because he had been promoted by the duke of Somerset, whence after his fall he found fewer friends to support him against such as wanted his bishopric by the coming in of queen Mary, he was accused and examined not for any matter of praemunire, but for his faith and doctrine; for which he was called before the Bishop of Winchester with bishop Hooper, Mr. Rogers, Mr. Bradford, Mr. Saunders and others, Feb. 4, 1555; on which day he would also with them have been condemned, but his condemnation was deferred, and he sent to prison again, where he continued till Feb. 14, and then was sent into Wales to receive sentence. He was six times brought up before Henry Morgan, bishop of St. David's, who demanded if he would abjure; from which he zealously dissented, and appealed to cardinal Pole; notwithstanding which, the bishop, proceeding in his rage, pronounced him a heretic excommunicate, and surrendered him to the secular power.

Dr. Farrar, being condemned and degraded, was not long after brought to the place of execution in the town of Carmathen, in the market-place of which, on the south side of the market-cross, March 30, 1555, being Saturday next before Passion-Sunday, he most constantly sustained the torments of the fire.

Concerning his constancy, it is said that one Richard Jones, a knight's son, coming to Dr. Farrar a little before his death, seemed to lament the painfulness of the death he had to suffer; to whom the bishop answered, That if he saw him once stir in the pains of his burning, he ought then give no credit to his doctrine; and as he said, so did he maintain his promise, patiently standing without emotion, till one Richard Gravell with a staff struck him down.

Rawlins White.

Rawlins White was by his calling and occupation a fisherman, living and continuing in the said trade for the space of twenty years at least, in the town of Cardiff, where he bore a very good name amongst his neighbours.

Though the good man was altogether unlearned, and withal very simple, yet it pleased God to remove him from error and idolatry to a knowledge of the truth, through the blessed reformation in Edward's reign. He had his son taught to read English, and after the little boy could read pretty well, his father every night after supper, summer and winter, made the boy read a portion of the holy scriptures, and now and then a part of some other good book.

When he had continued in his profession the space of five years, king Edward died, upon whose decease queen Mary succeeded and with her all kind of superstition crept in. White was taken by the officers of the town, as a man suspected of heresy, brought before the bishop Llandaff, and committed to prison in Chepstow, and at last removed to the castle of Cardiff, where he continued for the space of one whole year. Being brought before the bishop in his chapel, he counselled him by threats and promises. But as Rawlins would in nowise recant his opinions, the bishop told him plainly, that he must proceed against him by law, and condemn him as a heretic.

Before they proceeded to this extremity, the bishop proposed that prayer should be said for his conversion. "This," said White, "is like a godly bishop, and if your request be godly and right, and you pray as you ought, no doubt God will hear you; pray you, therefore, to your God, and I will pray to my God." After the bishop and his party had done praying, he asked Rawlins if he would now revoke. "You find," said the latter, "your prayer is not granted, for I remain the same; and God will strengthen me in support of this truth." After this, the bishop tried what saying mass would do; but Rawlins called all the people to witness that he did not bow down to the host. Mass being ended Rawlins was called for again; to whom the bishop used many persuasions; but the blessed man continued so steadfast to his former profession, that the bishop's discourse was to no purpose.--The bishop now caused the definitive sentence to be read, which being ended, Rawlins was carried again to Cardiff, to a loathsome prison in the town, called Cockmarel, where he passed his time in prayer, and in singing of psalms. In about three weeks, the order came from town for his execution.

When he came to the place, where his poor wife and children stood weeping, the sudden sight of them so pierced his heart, that the tears trickled down his face. Being come to the altar of his sacrifice, in going towards the stake, he fell down upon his knees, and kissed the ground; and in rising again, a little earth sticking on his face, he said these words, Earth unto earth, and dust unto dust; thou art my mother, and unto thee I shall return.

When all things were ready, directly over against the stake, in the face of Rawlins White, there was a standing erected, whereon stept up a priest, addressing himself to the people, but, as he spoke of the Romish doctrines of the sacraments, Rawlins cried out, Ah, thou wicked hypocrite, dost thou presume to prove thy false doctrine by scripture? Look in the text that followeth; did not Christ say, "Do this in remembrance of me?"

Then some that stood by cried out, put fire! set on fire! which being done, the straw and reeds cast up a great and sudden flame. In which flame this good man bathed his hands so long, until such time as the sinews shrank, and the fat dropped away, saving that once he did, as it were, wipe his face with one of them. All this while, which was somewhat long, he cried with a loud voice, O Lord, receive my spirit! until he could not open his mouth. At last the extremity of the fire was so vehement against his legs, that they were consumed almost before the rest of his body was hurt, which made the whole body fall over the chain into the fire sooner than it would have done. Thus died this good old man for his testimony of God's truth, and is now rewarded, no doubt, with the crown of eternal life.

The Rev. Mr. George Marsh.

George Marsh, born in the parish of Deane, in the county of Lancaster, received a good education and trade from his parents; about his 25th year he married, and lived, blessed with several children, on his farm till his wife died. He then went to study at Cambridge, and became the curate of the Rev. Mr. Lawrence Saunders, in which duty he constantly and zealously set forth the truth of God's word, and the false doctrines of the modern Antichrist.

Being confined by Dr. Coles, the bishop of Chester, within the precincts of his own house, he was kept from any intercourse with his friends during four months: his friends and mother, earnestly wished him to have flown from "the wrath to come;" but Mr. Marsh thought that such a step would ill agree with that profession he had during nine years openly made. He, however, secreted himself, but he had much struggling, and in secret prayer begged that God would direct him, through the advice of his best friends, for his own glory and to what was best. At length, determined, by a letter he received, boldly to confess the faith of Christ, he took leave of his mother-in-law and other friends, recommending his children to their care and departed for Smethehills, whence he was, with others, conducted to Lathum, to undergo examination before the Earl of Derby, Sir William Nores Mr. Sherburn, the parson of Grapnal, and others. The various questions put to him he answered with a good conscience, but when Mr. Sherburn interrogated him upon his belief of the sacrament of the altar, Mr. Marsh answered like a true Protestant, that the essence of the bread and wine was not at all changed, hence, after receiving dreadful threats from some, and fair words from others, for his opinions, he was remanded to ward, where he lay two nights without any bed.--On Palm Sunday he underwent a second examination, and Mr. Marsh much lamented that his fear should at all have induced him to prevaricate, and to seek his safety, so long as he did not openly deny Christ; and he again cried more earnestly to God for strength that he might not be overcome by the subtleties of those who strove to overrule the purity of his faith. He underwent three examinations before Dr. Coles, who, finding him steadfast in the Protestant faith, began to read his sentence; but he was interrupted by the Chancellor, who prayed the bishop to stay before it was too late. The priest then prayed for Mr. Marsh, but the latter, upon being again solicited to recant, said he durst not deny his Saviour Christ, lest he lose his everlasting mercy, and so obtain eternal death. The bishop then proceeded in the sentence. He was committed to a dark dungeon, and lay deprived of the consolation of any one, (for all were afraid to relieve or communicate with him) till the day appointed came that he should suffer. The sheriffs of the city, Amry and Couper, with their officers, went to the north gate, and took out Mr. George Marsh, who walked all the way with the book in his hand, looking upon the same, whence the people said, This man does not go to his death as a thief, nor as one that deserveth to die.

When he came to the place of execution without the city, near Spittal-Boughton, Mr. Cawdry, deputy Chamberlain of Chester, showed Mr. Marsh a writing under a great seal, saying, that it was a pardon for him if he would recant. He answered, That he would gladly accept the same did it not tend to pluck him from God.

After that, he began to speak to the people, showing the cause of his death, and would have exhorted them to stick unto Christ, but one of the sheriffs prevented him. Kneeling down, he then said his prayers, put off his clothes unto his shirt, and was chained to the post, having a number of fagots under him, and a thing made like a firkin, with pitch and tar in it, over his head. The fire being unskilfully made, and the wind driving it in eddies, he suffered great extremity, which notwithstanding he bore with Christian fortitude.

When he had been a long time tormented in the fire without moving, having his flesh so broiled and puffed up, that they who stood before him could not see the chain wherewith he was fastened, and therefore supposed that he had been dead, suddenly he spread abroad his arms, saying. Father of heaven have mercy upon me! and so yielded his spirit into the hands of the Lord. Upon this, many of the people said he was a martyr and died gloriously patient. This caused the bishop shortly after to make a sermon in the cathedral church, and therein he affirmed, that the said Marsh was a heretic, burnt as such, and was a firebrand in hell.--Mr. Marsh suffered April 24, 1555.

Mr. William Flower.

William Flower, otherwise Branch, was born at Snow-hill, in the county of Cambridge, where he went to school some years, and then came to the abbey of Ely. After he had remained a while he became a professed monk, was made a priest in the same house, and there celebrated and sang mass. After that, by reason of a visitation, and certain injunctions by the authority of Henry VIII he took upon him the habit of a secular priest, and returned to Snow-hill, where he was born, and taught children about half a year.

He then went to Ludgate, in Suffolk, and served as a secular priest about a quarter of a year; from thence to Stoniland; at length to Tewksbury, where he married a wife, with whom he ever after faithfully and honestly continued: after marriage he resided at Tewksbury about two years, and from thence went to Brosley, where he practised physic and surgery; but departing from those parts, he came to London, and finally settled at Lambeth, where he and his wife dwelt together: however, he was generally abroad, excepting once or twice in a month, to visit and see his wife. Being at home upon Easter Sunday morning, he came over the water from Lambeth into St. Margaret's church at Westminster; when seeing a priest, named John Celtham, administering and giving the sacrament of the altar to the people, and being greatly offended in his conscience with the priest for the same, he struck and wounded him upon the head, and also upon the arm and hand, with his wood knife, the priest having at the same time in his hand a chalice with the consecrated host therein, which became sprinkled with blood.

Mr. Flower, for this injudicious zeal, was heavily ironed, and put into the gatehouse at Westminster; and afterward summoned before bishop Bonner and his ordinary, where the bishop, after he had sworn him upon a book, ministered articles and interrogations to him.

After examination, the bishop began to exhort him again to return to the unity of his mother the catholic church, with many fair promises. These

Mr. Flower steadfastly rejecting, the bishop ordered him to appear in the same place in the afternoon, and in the mean time to consider well his former answer; but he, neither apologizing for having struck the priest, nor swerving from his faith, the bishop assigned him the next day, April 20th, to receive sentence, if he would not recant. The next morning, the bishop accordingly proceeded to the sentence, condemning and excommunicating him for a heretic, and after pronouncing him to be degraded, committed him to the secular power.

April 24, St. Mark's eve, he was brought to the place of martyrdom, in St. Margaret's churchyard, Westminster, where the fact was committed: and there coming to the stake, he prayed to Almighty God, made a confession of his faith, and forgave all the world.

This done, his hand was held up against the stake, and struck off, his left hand being fastened behind him. Fire was then set to him and he burning therein, cried with it loud voice, O thou Son of God, have mercy upon me! O thou Son of God, receive my soul! three times; his speech being now taken from him, he spoke no more, but notwithstanding he lifted up the stump with his other arm as long as he could.

Thus he endured the extremity of the fire, and was cruelly tortured for the few fagots that were brought being insufficient to burn him, they were compelled to strike him down into the fire, where lying along upon the ground, his lower part was consumed in the fire, whilst his upper part was little injured, his tongue moving in his mouth for a considerable time.

The Rev. John Cardmaker and John Warne.

May 30, 1555, the Rev. John Cardmaker, otherwise called Taylor, prebendary of the church of Wells, and John Warne, upholsterer, of St. John's, Walbrook, suffered together in Smithfield. Mr. Cardmaker, who first was an observant friar before the dissolution of the abbeys, afterward was a married minister, and in King Edward's time appointed to be reader in St. Paul's; being apprehended in the beginning of Queen Mary's reign, with Dr. Barlow, bishop of Bath, he was brought to London, and put in the Fleet prison, King Edward's laws being yet in force. In Mary's reign, when brought before the bishop of Winchester, the latter offered them the queen's mercy, if they would recant.

Articles having been preferred against Mr. John Warne, he was examined upon them by Bonner, who earnestly exhorted him to recant his opinions.

To whom he answered, I am persuaded that I am in the right opinion, and I see no cause to recant; for all the filthiness and idolatry lies in the church of Rome.

The bishop then, seeing that all his fair promises and terrible threatenings could not prevail, pronounced the definitive sentence of condemnation, and ordered the 30th of May, 1555, for the execution of John Cardmaker and John Warne, who were brought by the sheriffs to Smithfield. Being come to the stake, the sheriffs called Mr. Cardmaker aside, and talked with him secretly, during which Mr. Warne prayed, was chained to the stake, and had wood and reeds set about him.

The people were greatly afflicted, thinking that Mr. Cardmaker would recant at the burning of Mr. Warne. At length Mr. Cardmaker departed from the sheriffs, and came towards the stake, knelt down, and made a long prayer in silence to himself. He then arose up, put off his clothes to his shirt, and went with a bold courage unto the stake and kissed it; and taking Mr. Warne by the hand, he heartily comforted him, and was bound to the stake, rejoicing. The people seeing this so suddenly done, contrary to their previous expectation, cried out, God be praised! the Lord strengthen thee, Cardmaker! the Lord Jesus receive thy spirit! And this continued while the executioner put fire to them, and both had passed through the fire to the blessed rest and peace among God's holy saints and martyrs, to enjoy the crown of triumph and victory prepared for the elect soldiers and warriors of Christ Jesus in his blessed kingdom, to whom be glory and majesty for ever. Amen.

John Simpson and John Ardeley.

John Simpson and John Ardeley were condemned on the same day with Mr. Cardmaker and John Warne, which was the 25th of May. They were shortly after sent down from London to Essex, where they were burnt in one day, John Simpson at Rochford, and John Ardeley at Railey, glorifying God in his beloved Son, and rejoicing that they were accounted worthy to suffer.

Thomas Haukes, Thomas Watts, Thomas Osmond, William Bamford, and Nicholas Chamberlain.

Mr. Thomas Haukes, with six others, were condemned on the 9th of February, 1555. In education he was erudite; in person, comely and of good stature; in manners, a gentleman, and a sincere Christian. A little before death, several of Mr. H's. friends, terrified by the sharpness of the punishment he was going to suffer, privately desired that in the midst of the flames he would show them some token, whether the pains of burning were so great that a man might not collectedly endure it. This he promised to do; and it was agreed, that if the rage of the pain might be suffered, then he should lift up his hands above his head towards heaven, before he gave up the ghost.

Not long after, Mr. Haukes was led away to the place appointed for slaughter, by lord Rich, and being come to the stake, mildly and patiently prepared himself for the fire, having a strong chain cast about his middle, with a multitude of people on every side compassing him about. Unto whom after he had spoken many things, and poured out his soul unto God, the fire was kindled.

When he had continued long in it, and his speech was taken away by violence of the flame, his skin drawn together, and his fingers consumed with the fire, so that it was thought that he was gone, suddenly and contrary to all expectation, this good man being mindful of his promise, reached up his hands burning in flames over his head to the living God, and with great rejoicings as it seemed, struck or clapped them three times together. A great shout followed this wonderful circumstance, and then this blessed martyr of Christ, sinking down in the fire, gave up his spirit, June 10, 1555.

Thomas Watts, of Billericay, in Essex, of the diocese of London, was a linen draper. He had daily expected to be taken by God's adversaries, and this came to pass on the 5th of April, 1555, when he was brought before lord Rich, and other commissioners at Chelmsford, and accused for not coming to the church.

Being consigned over to the bloody bishop, who gave him several hearings, and, as usual, many arguments, with much entreaty, that he would be a disciple of antichrist, but his preaching availed not, and he resorted to his last revenge--that of condemnation.

At the stake, after he had kissed it, he spake to lord Rich, charging him to repent, for the Lord would revenge his death. Thus did this good martyr offer his body to the fire, in defence of the true gospel of the Saviour.

Thomas Osmond, William Bamford, and Nicholas Chamberlain, all of the town of Coxhall, being sent up to be examined, Bonner, after several hearings, pronounced them obstinate heretics, and delivered them to the sheriffs, in whose custody they remained till they were delivered to the sheriff of Essex county, and by him were executed. Chamberlain at Colchester, the 14th of June; Thomas Osmond at Maningtree, and William Bamford, alias Butler, at Harwich, the 15th of June, 1555; all dying full of the glorious hope of immortality.

Rev. John Bradford, and John Leaf an apprentice.

Rev. John Bradford was born at Manchester, in Lancashire; he was a good Latin scholar, and afterward became a servant of Sir John Harrington, knight.

He continued several years in an honest and thriving way; but the Lord had elected him to a better function. Hence he departed from his master, quitting the Temple, at London, for the university of Cambridge, to learn, by God's law, how to further the building of the Lord's temple. In a few years after, the university gave him the degree of master of arts, and he became a fellow of Pembroke Hall.

Martin Bucer first urged him to preach, and when he modestly doubted his ability, Bucer was wont to reply, If thou hast not fine wheat bread, yet give the poor people barley bread, or whatsoever else the Lord hath committed unto thee. Dr. Ridley, that worthy bishop of London, and glorious martyr of Christ, first called him to take the degree of a deacon and gave him a prebend in his cathedral church of St. Paul.

In this preaching office Mr. Bradford diligently laboured for the space of three years. Sharply he reproved sin, sweetly he preached Christ crucified, ably he disproved heresies and errors, earnestly he persuaded to godly life. After the death of blessed king Edward VI. Mr. Bradford still continued diligent in preaching, till he was suppressed by queen Mary. An act now followed of the blackest ingratitude, and at which a Pagan would blush. It has been recited, that a tumult was occasioned by Mr. Bourne's (then bishop of Bath) preaching at St. Paul's Cross; the indignation of the people placed his life in imminent danger; indeed a dagger was thrown at him. In this situation he entreated Mr. Bradford, who stood behind him, to speak in his place, and assuage the tumult. The people welcomed Mr. Bradford, and the latter afterward kept close to him, that his presence might prevent the populace from renewing their assaults.

The same Sunday in the afternoon, Mr. Bradford preached at Bow church in Cheapside, and reproved the people sharply for their seditious misdemeanor. Notwithstanding this conduct, within three days after, he was sent for to the tower of London, where the queen then was, to appear before the council. There he was charged with this act of saving Mr. Bourne, which was called seditious, and they also objected against him for preaching. Thus he was committed, first to the Tower, then to other prisons, and, after his condemnation, to the Poultry Compter, where he preached twice a day continually, unless sickness hindered him. Such was his credit with the keeper of the king's Bench, that he permitted him in an evening to visit a poor, sick person near the Steel-yard, upon his promise to return in time, and in this he never failed.

The night before he was sent to Newgate, he was troubled in his sleep by foreboding dreams, that on Monday after he should be burned in Smithfield. In the afternoon the keeper's wife came up and announced this dreadful news to him, but in him it excited only thankfulness to God. At night, half a dozen friends came, with whom he spent all the evening in prayer and godly exercises.

When he was removed to Newgate, a weeping crowd accompanied him, and a rumor having been spread that he was to suffer at four the next morning, an immense multitude attended. At nine o'clock Mr. Bradford was brought into Smithfield. The cruelty of the sheriff deserves notice; for his brother-in-law, Roger Beswick, having taken him by the hand as he passed, Mr. Woodroffe, with his staff, cut his head open.

Mr. Bradford, being come to the place, fell flat on the ground, secretly making his prayers to Almighty God. Then, rising again, and putting off his clothes unto the shirt, he went to the stake, and there suffered with a young man of twenty years of age, whose name was John Leaf, an apprentice to Mr. Humphry Gaudy, tallow-chandler, of Christ-church, London. Upon Friday before Palm Sunday, he was committed to the Compter in Bread-street, and afterward examined and condemned by the bloody bishop.

It is reported of him, that, when the bill of his confession was read unto him, instead of pen, he took a pin, and pricking his hand, sprinkled the blood upon the said bill, desiring the reader thereof to show the bishop that he had sealed the same bill with his blood already.

They both ended this mortal life, July 12th, 1555, like two lambs, without any alteration of their countenances, hoping to obtain that prize they had long run for; to which may Almighty God conduct us all, through the merits of Christ our Saviour! We shall conclude this article with mentioning, that Mr. Sheriff Woodroffe, it is said, within half a year after, was struck on the right side with a palsy and for the space of eight years after, (till his dying day) he was unable to turn himself in his bed; thus he became at last a fearful object to behold.

The day after Mr. Bradford and John Leaf suffered in Smithfield, William Minge, priest, died in prison at Maidstone. With as great constancy and boldness he yielded up his life in prison, as if it had pleased God to have called him to suffer by fire, as other godly men had done before at the stake, and as he himself was ready to do, had it pleased God to have called him to this trial.

Rev. John Bland, Rev. John Frankesh, Nicholas Shetterden, and Humphrey Middleton.

These Christian persons were all burnt at Canterbury for the same cause. Frankesh and Bland were ministers and preachers of the word of God, the one being parson of Adesham, and the other vicar of Rolvindon. Mr. Bland was cited to answer for his opposition to antichristianism, and underwent several examinations before Dr. Harpsfield, archdeacon of Canterbury, and finally on the 25th of June, 1555, again withstanding the power of the pope, he was condemned, and delivered to the secular arm. On the same day were condemned, John Frankesh, Nicholas Shetterden, Humphrey Middleton, Thacker, and Cocker, of whom Thacker only recanted.

Being delivered to the secular power, Mr. Bland, with the three former, were all burnt together at Canterbury, July 12, 1555, at two several stakes, but in one fire, when they, in the sight of God and his angels, and before men, like true soldiers of Jesus Christ, gave a constant testimony to the truth of his holy gospel.

Nicholas Hall and Christopher Waid.

The same month of July, Nicholas Hall, bricklayer, and Christopher Waid, linendraper, of Dartford, suffered death, condemned by Maurice, bishop of Rochester, about the last day of June, 1555. At the same time three others were condemned, whose names were Joan Beach, widow, John Harpol, of Rochester, and Margery Polley.

Dirick Carver and John Launder.

The 22d of July, 1555, Dirick Carver, brewer, of Brighthelmstone, aged forty, was burnt at Lewes. And the day following John Launder, husbandman, aged twenty-five, of Godstone, Surry, was burnt at Stening.

Dirick Carver was a man whom the Lord had blessed as well with temporal riches as with his spiritual treasures. At his coming into the town of Lewes to be burnt, the people called to him, beseeching God to strengthen him in the faith of Jesus Christ; and, as he came to the stake, he knelt down, and prayed earnestly. Then his book was thrown into the barrel, and when he had stripped himself, he went into it. As soon as he was in, he took the book, and threw it among the people, upon which the sheriff commanded, in the name of the king and queen, on pain of death, to throw in the book again.--And immediately the holy martyr began to address the people. After he had prayed awhile, he said, "O Lord my God, thou hast written, he that will not forsake wife, children, house, and every thing that he hath, and take up thy cross and follow thee, is not worthy of thee!--but thou, Lord, knowest that I have forsaken all to come unto thee Lord have mercy upon me, for unto thee I commend my spirit! and my soul doth rejoice in thee!" These were the last words of this faithful servant of Christ before enduring the fire. And when the fire came to him, he cried, "O Lord have mercy upon me!" and sprang up in the fire, calling upon the name of Jesus, till he gave up the ghost.

Thomas Iveson, of Godstone, in the county of Surry, carpenter, was burnt about the same month at Chichester.

John Aleworth, who died in prison at Reading, July, 1555, had been imprisoned for the sake of the truth of the gospel.

James Abbes. This young man wandered about to escape apprehension, but was at last informed against, and brought before the bishop of Norwich, who influenced him to recant; to secure him further in apostasy, the bishop afterward gave him a piece of money; but the interference of Providence is here remarkable. This bribe lay so heavily upon his conscience, that he returned, threw back the money, and repented of his conduct. Like Peter, he was contrite, steadfast in the faith, and sealed it with his blood at Bury, August 2, 1555, praising and glorifying God.

John Denley, Gent., John Newman, and Patrick Packingham.

Mr. Denley and Newman were returning one day to Maidstone, the place of their abode, when they were met by E. Tyrrel, Esq. a bigoted justice of the peace in Essex, and a cruel persecutor of the protestants. He apprehended them merely on suspicion. On the 5th of July, 1555, they were condemned, and consigned to the sheriffs, who sent Mr. Denley to Uxbridge, where he perished, August the 8th, 1555. While suffering in agony, and singing a psalm, Dr. Story inhumanly ordered one of the tormentors to throw a fagot at him, which cut his face severely, caused him to cease singing, and to raise his hands to his face. Just as Dr. Story was remarking in jest that he had spoiled a good song, the pious martyr again chanted, spread his hands abroad in the flames, and through Christ Jesus resigned his soul into the hands of his Maker.

Mr. Packingham suffered at the same town on the 28th of the same month.

Mr. Newman, pewterer, was burnt at Saffron Waldon, in Essex, Aug. 31, for the same cause, and Richard Hook about the same time perished at Chichester.

W. Coker, W. Hooper, H. Laurence, R. Colliar, R. Wright and W. Stere.

These persons all of Kent, were examined at the same time with Mr. Bland and Shetterden, by Thornton, bishop of Dover, Dr. Harpsfield, and others. These six martyrs and witnesses of the truth were consigned to the flames in Canterbury, at the end of August, 1555.

Elizabeth Warne, widow of John Warne, upholsterer, martyr, was burnt at Stratford-le-bow, near London, at the end of August, 1555.

George Tankerfield, of London, cook, born at York, aged 27, in the reign of Edward VI. had been a papist; but the cruelty of bloody Mary made him suspect the truth of those doctrines which were enforced by fire and torture. Tankerfield was imprisoned in Newgate about the end of February, 1555, and on Aug. 26, at St. Alban's, he braved the excruciating fire, and joyfully died for the glory of his Redeemer.

Rev. Robert Smith was first in the service of Sir T. Smith, provost of Eton; and was afterward removed to Windsor, where he had a clerkship of ten pounds a year.

He was condemned, July 12, 1555, and suffered Aug. 8, at Uxbridge. He doubted not but that God would give the spectators some token in support of his own cause; this actually happened; for, when he was nearly half burnt, and supposed to be dead, he suddenly rose up, moved the remaining parts of his arms and praised God; then, hanging over the fire, he sweetly slept in the Lord Jesus.

Mr. Stephen Harwood and Mr. Thomas Fust suffered about the same time with Smith and Tankerfield, with whom they were condemned. Mr. William Hale, also, of Thorp, in Essex, was sent to Barnet, where about the same time he joined the ever-blessed company of Martyrs.

George King, Thomas Leyes, and John Wade, falling sick in Lollard's Tower, were removed to different houses, and died. Their bodies were thrown out in the common fields as unworthy of burial, and lay till the faithful conveyed them away by night.

Joan Lashford, daughter-in-law of John and Elizabeth Warne, martyr, was the last of the ten condemned before alluded to; her martyrdom took place in 1556, of which we shall speak in its date.

Mr. William Andrew of Horseley, Essex, was imprisoned in Newgate for heresy; but God chose to call him to himself by the severe treatment he endured in Newgate, and thus to mock the sanguinary expectations of his Catholic persecutors. His body was thrown into the open air, but his soul was received into the everlasting mansions of his heavenly Creator.

The Rev. Robert Samuel.

This gentleman was minister of Bradford, Suffolk, where he industriously taught the flock committed to his charge, while he was openly permitted to discharge his duty. He was first persecuted by Mr. Foster, of Copdock, near Ipswich, a severe and bigoted persecutor of the followers of Christ, according to the truth in the Gospel. Notwithstanding Mr. Samuel was ejected from his living, he continued to exhort and instruct privately; nor would he obey the order for putting away his wife, whom he had married in king Edward's reign; but kept her at Ipswich, where Foster, by warrant, surprised him by night with her. After being imprisoned in Ipswich jail, he was taken before Dr. Hopton, bishop of Norwich, and Dr. Dunnings, his chancellor, two of the most sanguinary among the bigots of those days. To intimidate the worthy pastor, he was in prison chained to a post in such a manner that the weight of his body was supported by the points of his toes: added to this his allowance of provision was reduced to a quantity so insufficient to sustain nature, that he was almost ready to devour his own flesh. From this dreadful extremity there was even a degree of mercy in ordering him to the fire. Mr. Samuel suffered August 31, 1555.

William Allen, a labouring servant to Mr. Houghton of Somerton suffered not long after Mr. Samuel, at Walsingham.

Roger Coo, was an aged man, and brought before the bishop of Norwich for contumacy, by whom he was condemned Aug. 12, 1555, and suffered in the following month at Yoxford, in Suffolk.

Thomas Cobb, was a butcher at Haverhill, and condemned by Dunnings, the furious chancellor of Norwich. Mr. Cobb suffered at Thetford, Sept. 1555.

G. Catmer, R. Streater, A. Burward, G. Brodbridge, and J. Tutty.

These five worthies, denying the real presence in the eucharist, were brought before Dr. Thornton, bishop of Dover, and condemned as heretics. They suffered in one fire, Sept. 6, 1555, at Canterbury, enduring all things for their faith in Christ Jesus.

About the same time William Glowd, Cornelius Bungey, William Wolsey, and Robert Pygot, suffered martyrdom.

Bishop Ridley and Bishop Latimer.

These reverend prelates suffered October 17, 1555, at Oxford, on the same day Wolsey and Pygot perished at Ely. Pillars of the church and accomplished ornaments of human nature, they were the admiration of the realm, amiably conspicuous in their lives, and glorious in their deaths.

Dr. Ridley was born in Northumberland, was first taught grammar at Newcastle, and afterward removed to Cambridge, where his aptitude in education raised him gradually till he came to be the head of Pembroke college, where he received the title of Doctor of Divinity. Having returned from a trip to Paris, he was appointed Chaplain to Henry VIII. and Bishop of Rochester, and was afterwards translated to the see of London in the time of Edward VI.

His tenacious memory, extensive erudition, impressive oratory, and indefatigable zeal in preaching, drew after him not only his own flock, but persons from all quarters, desirous of godly exhortation or reproof. His tender treatment of Dr. Heath, who was a prisoner with him during one year, in Edward's reign, evidently proves that he had no Catholic cruelty in his disposition. In person he was erect and well proportioned; in temper forgiving; in self-mortification severe. His first duty in the morning was private prayer: he remained in his study till 10 o'clock, and then attended the daily prayer used in his house. Dinner being done, he sat about an hour, conversing pleasantly, or playing at chess. His study next engaged his attention, unless business or visits occurred; about five o'clock prayers followed; and after he would recreate himself at chess for about an hour, then retire to his study till eleven o'clock, and pray on his knees as in the morning. In brief, he was a pattern of godliness and virtue, and such he endeavored to make men wherever he came.

His attentive kindness was displayed particularly to old Mrs. Bonner, mother of Dr. Bonner, the cruel bishop of London. Dr. Ridley, when at his manor at Fulham, always invited her to his house, placed her at the head of his table, and treated her like his own mother; he did the same by Bonner's sister and other relatives; but when Dr. Ridley was under persecution, Bonner pursued a conduct diametrically opposite, and would have sacrificed Dr. Ridley's sister and her husband, Mr. George Shipside, had not Providence delivered him by the means of Dr. Heath, bishop of Worcester. Dr. Ridley was first in part converted by reading Bertram's book on the sacrament, and by his conferences with archbishop Cranmer and Peter Martyr. When Edward VI. was removed from the throne, and the bloody Mary succeeded, bishop Ridley was immediately marked as an object of slaughter. He was first sent to the Tower, and afterward, at Oxford, was consigned to the common prison of Bocardo, with archbishop Cranmer and Mr. Latimer. Being separated from them, he was placed in the house of one Irish, where he remained till the day of his martyrdom, from 1554, till October 16, 1555. It will easily be supposed that the conversations of these chiefs of the martyrs were elaborate, learned, and instructive. Such indeed they were, and equally beneficial to all their spiritual comforts. Bishop Ridley's letters to various Christian brethren in bonds in all parts, and his disputations with the mitred enemies of Christ, alike prove the clearness of his head and the integrity of his heart. In a letter to Mr. Grindal, (afterward archbishop of Canterbury,) he mentions with affection those who had preceded him in dying for the faith, and those who were expected to suffer; he regrets that popery is re-established in its full abomination, which he attributes to the wrath of God, made manifest in return for the lukewarmness of the clergy and the people in justly appreciating the blessed light of the reformation.

Bishop Latimer was the son of Hugh Latimer, of Turkelson, in Leicestershire, a husbandman of repute, with whom he remained till he was four years old. His parents, finding him of acute parts, gave him a good education, and then sent him at fourteen to the university of

Cambridge, where he entered into the study of the school divinity of that day, and was from principle a zealous observer of the Romish superstitions of the time. In his oration when he commenced bachelor of divinity, he inveighed against the reformer Melancthon, and openly declaimed against good Mr. Stafford, divinity lecturer in Cambridge.

Mr. Thomas Bilney, moved by a brotherly pity towards Mr. Latimer, begged to wait upon him in his study, and to explain to him the groundwork of his (Mr. Bilney's) faith. This blessed interview effected his conversion: the persecutor of Christ became his zealous advocate, and before Dr. Stafford died he became reconciled to him.

Once converted, he became eager for the conversion of others, and commenced public preacher, and private instructer in the university. His sermons were so pointed against the absurdity of praying in the Latin tongue, and withholding the oracles of salvation from the people who were to be saved by belief in them, that he drew upon himself the pulpit animadversions of several of the resident friars and heads of houses, whom he subsequently silenced by his severe criticisms and eloquent arguments. This was at Christmas, 1529. At length Dr. West preached against Mr. Latimer at Barwell Abbey, and prohibited him from preaching again in the churches of the university, notwithstanding which, he continued during three years to advocate openly the cause of Christ, and even his enemies confessed the power of those talents he possessed. Mr. Bilney remained here some time with Mr. Latimer, and thus the place where they frequently walked together obtained the name of Heretics' Hill.

Mr. Latimer at this time traced out the innocence of a poor woman, accused by her husband of the murder of her child. Having preached before king Henry VIII. at Windsor, he obtained the unfortunate mother's pardon. This, with many other benevolent acts, served only to excite the spleen of his adversaries. He was summoned before Cardinal Wolsey for heresy, but being a strenuous supporter of the king's supremacy, in opposition to the pope's, by favour of lord Cromwell and Dr. Buts, (the king's physician,) he obtained the living of West Kingston, in Wiltshire. For his sermons here against purgatory, the immaculacy of the Virgin, and the worship of images, he was cited to appear before Warham, archbishop of Canterbury, and John, bishop of London. He was required to subscribe certain articles, expressive of his conformity to the accustomed usages; and there is reason to think, after repeated weekly examinations, that he did subscribe, as they did not seem to involve any important article of belief. Guided by Providence, he escaped the subtle nets of his persecutors, and at length, through the powerful friends before mentioned, became bishop of Worcester, in which function he qualified or explained away most of the papal ceremonies he was for form's sake under the necessity of complying with. He continued in this active and dignified employment some years, till the coming in of the Six Articles, when, to preserve an unsullied conscience, he, as well as Dr. Shaxton, bishop of Salisbury, resigned. He remained a prisoner in the Tower till the coronation of Edward VI. when he was again called to the Lord's harvest in Stamford, and many other places: he also preached at London in the convocation house, and before the young king; indeed he lectured twice every Sunday, regardless of his great age (then above sixty-seven years,) and his weakness through a bruise received from the fall of a tree. Indefatigable in his private studies, he rose to them in winter and in summer at two o'clock in the morning. By the strength of his own mind, or of some inward light from above, he had a prophetic view of what was to happen to the church in Mary's reign, asserting that he was doomed to suffer for the truth, and that Winchester, then in the Tower, was preserved for that purpose. Soon after queen Mary was proclaimed, a messenger was sent to summon Mr. Latimer to town, and there is reason to believe it was wished that he should make his escape. On entering Smithfield, he jocosely said, that the place had long groaned for him. After being examined by the council, he was committed to the Tower, where his cheerfulness is displayed in the following anecdote. Being kept without fire in severe frosty weather, his aged frame suffered so much, that he told the lieutenant's man, that if he did not look better after him he should deceive his master. The lieutenant, thinking he meant to effect his escape, came to him, to know what he meant by this speech; which Mr. Latimer replied to, by saying, "You, Mr. Lieutenant, doubtless suppose I shall *burn*; but, except you let me have some fire, I shall deceive your expectation, for here it is likely I shall be *starved with cold*."

Mr. Latimer, after remaining a long time in the Tower, was transported to Oxford, with Cranmer and Ridley, the disputations at which place have been already mentioned in a former part of this work. He remained imprisoned till October, and the principal objects of all his prayers were three--that he might stand faithful to the doctrine he had professed, that God would restore his gospel to England once again, and preserve the Lady Elizabeth to be queen; all which happened. When he stood at the stake without the Bocardo-gate, Oxford, with Dr. Ridley, and fire was putting to the pile of fagots, he raised his eyes benignantly towards heaven, and said, "God is faithful, who doth not suffer us to be tempted above our strength." His body was forcibly penetrated by the fire, and the blood flowed abundantly from the heart; as if to verify his constant desire that his heart's blood might be shed in defence of the gospel. His polemical and friendly letters are lasting monuments of his integrity and talents. It has been before said, that public disputation took place in April, 1554, new examinations took place in Oct. 1555, previous to the degradation and condemnation of Cranmer, Ridley, and Latimer. We now draw to the conclusion of the lives of the two last.

Dr. Ridley, the night before execution, was very facetious, had himself shaved, and called his supper a marriage feast; he remarked upon seeing Mrs. Irish (the keeper's wife) weep, "though my breakfast will be somewhat sharp, my supper will be more pleasant and sweet." The place of death was on the north side of the town opposite Baliol College:--Dr. Ridley was dressed in a black gown furred, and Mr. Latimer had a long shroud on, hanging down to his feet. Dr. Ridley, as he passed Bocardo, looked up to see Dr. Cranmer, but the latter was then engaged in disputation with a friar.--When they came to the stake, Dr. Ridley embraced Latimer fervently, and bid him be of good heart. He then knelt by the stake, and after earnestly praying together, they had a short private conversation. Dr. Smith then preached a short sermon against the martyrs, who would have answered him, but were prevented by Dr. Marshal, the vice-chancellor. Dr. Ridley then took off his gown and tippet, and gave them to his brother-in-law, Mr. Shipside. He gave away also many trifles to his weeping friends, and the populace were anxious to get even a fragment of his garments. Mr. Latimer gave nothing, and from the poverty of his garb, was soon stripped to his shroud, and stood venerable and erect, fearless of death. Dr. Ridley being unclothed to his shirt, the smith placed an iron chain about their waists, and Dr. Ridley bid him fasten it securely; his brother having tied a bag of gunpowder about his neck, gave some also to Mr. Latimer. Dr. Ridley then requested of Lord Williams, of Fame, to advocate with the queen the cause of some poor men to whom he had, when bishop, granted leases, but which the present bishop refused to confirm. A lighted fagot was now laid at Dr. Ridley's feet, which caused Mr. Latimer to say, "Be of good cheer, Ridley; and play the man. We shall this day, by God's grace, light up such a candle in England, as, I trust, will never be put out." When Dr. Ridley saw the flame approaching him, he exclaimed, "Into thy hands, O Lord, I commend my spirit!" and repeated often, "Lord receive my spirit!" Mr. Latimer, too, ceased not to say, "O Father of heaven receive my soul!" Embracing the flame, he bathed his hands in it, and soon died, apparently with little pain; but Dr. Ridley, by the ill-adjustment of the fagots, which were green, and placed too high above the furze was burnt much downwards. At this time, piteously entreating for more fire to come to him, his brother-in-law imprudently heaped the fagots up over him, which caused the fire more fiercely to burn his limbs, whence he literally leaped up and down under the fagots, exclaiming that he could not burn; indeed, his dreadful extremity was but too plain, for after his legs were quite consumed, he showed his body and shirt unsinged by the flame. Crying upon God for mercy, a man with a bill pulled the fagots down, and when the flames arose, he bent himself towards that side; at length the gunpowder was ignited, and then he ceased to move, burning on the other side, and falling down at Mr. Latimer's feet over the chain that had hitherto supported him.

Every eye shed tears at the afflicting sight of these sufferers, who were among the most distinguished persons of their time in dignity, piety, and public estimation. They suffered October 16, 1555.

In the following month died Stephen Gardiner, bishop of Winchester and Lord Chancellor of England. This papistical monster was born at Bury, in Suffolk, and partly educated at Cambridge. Ambitious, cruel, and bigoted, he served any cause; be first espoused the king's part in the affair of Anne Boleyn: upon the establishment of the Reformation, he declared the supremacy of the Pope an execrable tenet, and when queen Mary came to the crown, he entered into all her papistical bigoted views, and became a second time bishop of Winchester. It is conjectured it was his intention to have moved the sacrifice of Lady Elizabeth, but when he arrived at this point, it pleased God to remove him.

It was on the afternoon of the day when those faithful soldiers of Christ, Ridley and Latimer, perished, that Gardiner sat down with a joyful heart to dinner. Scarcely had he taken a few mouthfuls, when he was seized with illness, and carried to his bed, where he lingered fifteen days in great torment, unable in any wise to evacuate, and burnt with a devouring fever, that terminated in death. Execrated by all good Christians, we pray the Father of Mercies, that he may receive that mercy above he never imparted below.

Mr. John Webb, George Roper, and Gregory Parker.

These martyrs, after being brought before the bishop of Dover and Dr. Harpsfield, were finally examined, October 3, 1555, adjudged to be heretics, and at Canterbury, terminated their existence.

Wm. Wiseman, clothworker of London, died in Lollard's Tower, Dec. 13, 1555, not without suspicion of being made way with, for his love of the gospel. In December, died James Gore, at Colchester, imprisoned for the same cause.

Mr. John Philpot.

This martyr was the son of a knight, born in Hampshire, and brought up at New College, Oxford, where he several years studied the civil law, and became eminent in the Hebrew tongue. He was a scholar and a gentleman, zealous in religion, fearless in disposition, and a detester of flattery. After visiting Italy, he returned to England, affairs in King Edward's days wearing a more promising aspect. During this reign he continued to be archdeacon of Winchester under Dr. Poinet, who succeeded Gardiner. Upon the accession of Mary, a convocation was summoned, in which Mr. Philpot defended the Reformation against his ordinary, Gardiner, (again made bishop of Winchester,) and soon was conducted to Bonner and other commissioners for examination, Oct. 2, 1555, after being eighteen months imprisoned. Upon his demanding to see the commission, Dr. Story cruelly observed, "I will spend both my gown and my coat, but I will burn thee! Let him be in Lollard's tower, (a wretched prison,) for I will sweep the King's Bench and all other prisons of these heretics!" Upon Mr. Philpot's second examination, it was intimated to him, that Dr. Story had said that the Lord Chancellor had commanded that he should be made way with. It is easy to foretell the result of this inquiry; he was committed to Bonner's coal-house, where he joined company with a zealous minister of Essex, who had been induced to sign a bill of recantation; but afterward, stung by his conscience, he asked the bishop to let him see the instrument again, when he tore it to pieces; which induced Bonner in a fury to strike him repeatedly, and tear away part of his beard. Mr. Philpot had a private interview with Bonner the same night, and was then remanded to his bed of straw like other prisoners, in the coal-house. After seven examinations, Bonner ordered him to be set in the stocks, and on the following Sunday separated him from his fellow-prisoners as a sower of heresy, and ordered him up to a room near the battlements of St. Paul's, eight feet by thirteen, on the other side of Lollard's tower, and which could be overlooked by any one in the bishop's outer gallery. Here Mr. Philpot was searched, but happily he was successful in secreting some letters containing his examinations. In the eleventh investigation before various bishops, and Mr. Morgan, of Oxford, the latter was so driven into a corner by the close pressure of Mr. Philpot's arguments, that he said to him, "Instead of the spirit of the gospel which you boast to possess, I think it is the spirit of the buttery, which your fellows have had, who were drunk before their death, and went I believe drunken to it." To this unfounded and brutish remark, Mr. Philpot indignantly replied, "It appeareth by your communication, that you are better acquainted with that spirit than the spirit of God; wherefore I tell thee, thou painted wall and hypocrite, in the name of the living God, whose truth I have told thee, that God shall rain fire and brimstone upon such blasphemers as thou art!" He was then remanded by Bonner, with an order not to allow him his Bible nor candlelight. December 4th, Mr. Philpot had his next hearing, and this was followed by two more, making in all, fourteen conferences, previous to the final examination in which he was condemned; such were the perseverance and anxiety of the Catholics, aided by the argumentative abilities of the most distinguished of the papal bishops, to bring him into the pale of their church. Those examinations, which were very long and learned, were all written down by Mr. Philpot, and a stronger proof of the imbecility of the Catholic doctors, cannot, to an unbiassed mind, be exhibited. December 16th, in the consistory of St. Paul's bishop Bonner, after laying some trifling accusations to his charge such as secreting powder to make ink, writing some private letters, &c. proceeded to pass the awful sentence upon him, after he and the other bishops had urged him by every inducement to recant. He was afterward conducted to Newgate, where the avaricious Catholic keeper loaded him with heavy irons, which by the humanity of Mr. Macham were ordered to be taken off. December 17th, Mr. Philpot received intimation that he was to die next day, and the next morning about eight o'clock, he joyfully met the sheriffs, who were to attend him to the place of execution. Upon entering Smithfield the ground was so muddy, that two officers offered to carry him to the stake, but he replied, "Would you make me a pope? I am content to finish my journey on foot." Arrived at the stake, he said, "Shall I disdain to suffer at the stake, when my Redeemer did not refuse to suffer the most vile death upon the Cross for me?" He then meekly recited the cvii. and cviii. Psalms, and when he had finished his prayers, was bound to the post, and fire applied to the pile. On December 18th, 1555, perished this illustrious martyr, reverenced by man, and glorified in heaven! His letters arising out of the cause for which he suffered, are elegant, numerous, and elaborate.

Rev. T. Whittle, B. Green, T. Brown, J. Tudson, J. Ent, Isabel Tooster, and Joan Lashford.

These seven persons were summoned before Bonner's consistory, and the articles of the Romish church tendered for their approbation. Their refusal subjected them to the sentence of condemnation, and on January 27, 1556, they underwent the dreadful sentence of blood in Smithfield.

Mr. Bartlet Green was condemned the next day.

Mr. Thomas Brown, born at Histon, Ely, but afterward of St. Bride's, London, was presented by the parish constable to Bonner, for absenting himself from church. This faithful soldier of Christ suffered on the same day with the preceding.

Mr. John Tudson, of Ipswich by birth, was apprenticed in London to a Mr. Goodyear, of St. Mary Botolph. He was condemned January 15, 1556, and consigned to the secular power, which completed the fiery tyranny of the law, January 27, to the glory of God, and the immortal salvation of the meek sufferer.

Subsequently, John Hunt, Isabella Forster, and Joan Warne, were condemned and executed.

John Lomas, Agnes Snoth, Anne Wright, Joan Sole, and Joan Catmer.

These five martyrs suffered together, January 31, 1556. John Lomas was a young man of Tenterden. He was cited to appear at Canterbury, and was examined January 17. His answers being adverse to the idolatrous doctrine of the papacy, he was condemned on the following day, and suffered January 31.

Agnes Snoth, widow, of Smarden Parish, was several times summoned before the Catholic Pharisees, and rejecting absolution, indulgences, transubstantiation, and auricular confession, she was adjudged worthy to suffer death, and endured martyrdom, January 31, with Anne Wright and Joan Sole, who were placed in similar circumstances, and perished at the same time, with equal resignation. Joan Catmer, the last of this heavenly company, of the parish Hithe, was the wife of the martyr George Catmer.

Seldom in any country, for political controversy, have four women been led to execution, whose lives were irreproachable, and whom the pity of savages would have spared. We cannot but remark here that, when the Protestant power first gained the ascendency over the Catholic superstition, and some degree of force in the laws was necessary to enforce uniformity, whence some bigoted people suffered privation in their person or goods, we read of few burnings, savage cruelties, or poor women brought to the stake, but it is the nature of error to resort to force instead of argument, and to silence truth by taking away existence, of which the Redeemer himself is an instance. The above five persons were burnt at two stakes in one fire, singing hosannahs to the glorified Saviour, till the breath of life was extinct. Sir John Norton, who was present, wept bitterly at their unmerited sufferings.

Archbishop Cranmer.

Dr. Thomas Cranmer was descended from an ancient family, and was born at the village of Arselacton, in the county of Northampton. After the usual school education he was sent to Cambridge, and was chosen fellow of Jesus College. Here he married a gentleman's daughter, by which he forfeited his fellowship, and became a reader in Buckingham college, placing his wife at the Dolphin inn, the landlady of which was a relation of hers, whence arose the idle report that he was an ostler. His lady shortly after dying in childbed, to his credit he was re-chosen a fellow of the college before mentioned. In a few years after, he was promoted to be Divinity Lecturer, and appointed one of the examiners over those who were ripe to become Bachelors or Doctors in Divinity. It was his principle to judge of their qualifications by the knowledge they possessed of the Scriptures, rather than of the ancient fathers, and hence many popish priests were rejected, and others rendered much improved.

He was strongly solicited by Dr. Capon to be one of the fellows on the foundation of Cardinal Wolsey's college, Oxford, of which he hazarded the refusal. While he continued in Cambridge, the question of Henry VIII.'s divorce with Catharine was agitated. At that time, on account of the plague, Dr. Cranmer removed to the house of a Mr. Cressy, at Waltham Abbey, whose two sons were then educating under him. The affair of divorce, contrary to the king's approbation, had remained undecided above two or three years, from the intrigues of the canonists and civilians, and though the cardinals Campeius and Wolsey were commissioned from Rome to decide the question, they purposely protracted the sentence. It happened that Dr. Gardiner (secretary) and Dr. Fox, defenders of the king in the above suit, came to the house of Mr. Cressy to lodge, while the king removed to Greenwich. At supper, a conversation ensued with Dr. Cranmer, who suggested that the question, whether a man may marry his brother's wife or not, could be easily and speedily decided by the word of God, and this as well in the English courts as in those of any foreign nation. The king, uneasy at the delay, sent for Dr. Gardiner and Dr. Foxe, to consult them, regretting that a new commission must be sent to Rome, and the suit be endlessly protracted. Upon relating to the king the conversation which had passed on the previous evening with Dr. Cranmer, his majesty sent for him, and opened the tenderness of conscience upon the near affinity of the queen. Dr.

Cranmer advised that the matter should be referred to the most learned divines of Cambridge and Oxford, as he was unwilling to meddle in an affair of such weight; but the king enjoined him to deliver his sentiments in writing, and to repair for that purpose to the Earl of Wiltshire's, who would accommodate him with books, and every thing requisite for the occasion. This Dr. Cranmer immediately did, and in his declaration, not only quoted the authority of the Scriptures, of general councils and the ancient writers, but maintained that the bishop of Rome had no authority whatever to dispense with the word of God. The king asked him if he would stand by this bold declaration; to which replying in the affirmative, he was deputed ambassador to Rome, in conjunction with the Earl of Wiltshire, Dr. Stokesley, Dr. Carne, Dr. Bennet, and others, previous to which, the marriage was discussed in most of the universities of Christendom and at Rome; when the pope presented his toe to be kissed, as customary, the Earl of Wiltshire and his party refused. Indeed, it is affirmed, that a spaniel of the Earl's, attracted by the glitter of the pope's toe, made a snap at it, whence his holiness drew in his sacred foot, and kicked at the offender with the other. Upon the pope demanding the cause of their embassy, the Earl presented Dr. Cranmer's book, declaring that his learned friends had come to defend it. The pope treated the embassy honourably, and appointed a day for the discussion, which he delayed, as if afraid of the issue of the investigation. The Earl returned, and Dr. Cranmer, by the king's desire, visited the emperor, and was successful in bringing him over to his opinion. Upon the Doctor's return to England, Dr. Warham, archbishop of Canterbury, having quitted this transitory life, Dr. Cranmer was deservedly, and by Dr. Warham's desire, elevated to that eminent station.

In this function, it may be said that he followed closely the charge of St. Paul. Diligent in duty, he rose at five in the morning, and continued in study and prayer till nine: between then and dinner, he devoted to temporal affairs. After dinner, if any suitors wanted hearing, he would determine their business with such an affability, that even the defaulters were scarcely displeased. Then he would play at chess for an hour, or see others play, and at five o'clock he heard the Common Prayer read, and from this till supper he took the recreation of walking. At supper his conversation was lively and entertaining; again he walked or amused himself till nine o'clock, and then entered his study.

He ranked high in favour with king Henry and ever had the purity and the interest of the English church deeply at heart. His mild and forgiving disposition is recorded in the following instance--An ignorant priest, in the country, had called Cranmer an ostler, and spoken very derogatory of his learning. Lord Cromwell receiving information of it, the man was sent to the fleet, and his case was told to the archbishop by a Mr. Chertsey, a grocer, and a relation of the priest's. His grace, having sent for the offender, reasoned with him, and solicited the priest to question him on any learned subject. This the man, overcome by the bishop's good nature, and knowing his own glaring incapacity, declined, and entreated his forgiveness, which was immediately granted, with a charge to employ his time better when he returned to his parish. Cromwell was much vexed at the lenity displayed, but the bishop was ever more ready to receive injury than to retaliate in any other manner than by good advice and good offices.

At the time that Cranmer was raised to be archbishop, he was king's chaplain, and archdeacon of Taunton; he was also constituted by the pope, penitentiary general of England. It was considered by the king that Cranmer would be obsequious; hence the latter married the king to Anne Boleyn, performed her coronation, stood godfather to Elizabeth, the first child, and divorced the king from Catharine. Though Cranmer received a confirmation of his dignity from the pope, he always protested against acknowledging any other authority than the king's, and he persisted in the same independent sentiments when before Mary's commissioners in 1555. One of the first steps after the divorce was to prevent preaching throughout his diocess, but this narrow measure had rather a political view than a religious one, as there were many who inveighed against the king's conduct. In his new dignity Cranmer agitated the question of supremacy, and by his powerful and just arguments induced the parliament to "render to Caesar the things which are Caesar's." During Cranmer's residence in Germany, 1531, he became acquainted with Ossiander, at Nurenburgh, and married his niece, but left her with him while on his return to England; after a season he sent for her privately, and she remained with him till the year 1539, when the Six Articles compelled him to return her to her friends for a time.

It should be remembered that Ossiander, having obtained the approbation of his friend Cranmer, published the laborious work of the Harmony of the Gospels in 1537. In 1534 the archbishop completed the dearest wish of his heart, the removal of every obstacle to the perfection of the Reformation, by the subscription of the nobles and bishops to the king's sole supremacy. Only bishop Fisher and Sir Thomas More made objection; and their agreement not to oppose the succession, Cranmer was willing to consider as sufficient, but the monarch would have no other than an entire concession. Not long after, Gardiner, in a private interview with the king, spoke inimically of Cranmer, (whom he maliciously hated) for assuming the title of Primate of all England, as derogatory to the supremacy of the king, this created much jealousy against Cranmer, and his translation of the Bible was strongly opposed by Stokesley, bishop of London. It is said, upon the demise of queen Catharine, that her successor Anne Boleyn rejoiced--a lesson this to show how shallow is the human judgment! since her own execution took place in the spring of the following year, and the king, on the day following the beheading of this sacrificed lady, married the beautiful Jane Seymour, a maid of honour to the late queen. Cranmer was ever the friend of Anne Boleyn, but it was dangerous to oppose the will of the carnal tyrannical monarch.

In 1538, the holy Scriptures were openly exposed to sale; and the places of worship overflowed every where to hear its holy doctrines expounded. Upon the king's passing into a law the famous Six Articles, which went nearly again to establish the essential tenets of the Romish creed, Cranmer shone forth with all the lustre of a Christian patriot, in resisting the doctrines they contained, and in which he was supported by the bishops of Sarum, Worcester, Ely, and Rochester, the two former of whom resigned their bishoprics. The king, though now in opposition to Cranmer, still revered the sincerity that marked his conduct. The death of Lord Cromwell in the Tower, in 1540, the good friend of Cranmer, was a severe blow to the wavering protestant cause, but even now Cranmer, when he saw the tide directly adverse to the truth, boldly waited on the king in person, and by his manly and heartfelt pleading, caused the book of Articles to be passed on his side, to the great confusion of his enemies, who had contemplated his fall as inevitable.

Cranmer now lived in as secluded a manner as possible, till the rancour of Winchester preferred some articles against him, relative to the dangerous opinion he taught in his family, joined to other treasonable charges. These the king delivered himself to Cranmer, and believing firmly the fidelity and assertions of innocence of the accused prelate, he caused the matter to be deeply investigated, and Winchester and Dr. Lenden, with Thornton and Barber, of the bishop's household, were found by the papers to be the real conspirators. The mild forgiving Cranmer would have interceded for all remission of punishment, had not Henry, pleased with the subsidy voted by parliament, let them be discharged; these nefarious men, however, again renewing their plots against Cranmer, fell victims to Henry's resentment, and Gardiner forever lost his confidence. Sir G. Gostwick soon after laid charges against the archbishop, which Henry quashed, and the primate was willing to forgive.

In 1544, the archbishop's palace at Canterbury was burnt, and his brother-in-law with others perished in it. These various afflictions may serve to reconcile us to an humble state; for of what happiness could this great and good man boast? since his life was constantly harassed either by political, religious, or natural crosses. Again the inveterate Gardiner laid high charges against the meek archbishop and would have sent him to the tower; but the king was his friend, gave him his signet that he would defend him, and in the council not only declared the bishop one of the best affected men in his realm, but sharply rebuked his accusers for their calumny.

A peace having been made, Henry, and the French king Henry the Great, were unanimous to have the mass abolished in their kingdom, and Cranmer set about this great work; but the death of the English monarch, in 1546, suspended the procedure, and king Edward his successor continued Cranmer in the same functions, upon whose coronation he delivered a charge that will ever honour his memory, for its purity, freedom, and truth. During this reign he prosecuted the glorious reformation with unabated zeal, even in the year 1552, when he was seized with a severe ague, from which it pleased God to restore him that he might testify by his death the truth of that seed he had diligently sown.

The death of Edward, in 1553, exposed Cranmer to all the rage of his enemies. Though the archbishop was among those who supported Mary's accession, he was attainted at the meeting of parliament, and in November adjudged guilty of high treason at Guildhall, and degraded from his dignities. He sent an humble letter to Mary, explaining the cause of his signing the will in favor of Edward, and in 1554 he wrote to the council, whom he pressed to obtain a pardon from the queen, by a letter delivered to Dr. Weston, but which the latter opened, and on seeing its contents, basely returned. Treason was a charge quite inapplicable to Cranmer, who supported the queen's right; while others, who had favoured Lady Jane, upon paying a small fine were dismissed. A calumny was now spread against Cranmer, that he complied with some of the popish ceremonies to ingratiate himself with the queen, which he dared publicly to disavow, and justified his articles of faith. The active part which the prelate had taken in the divorce of Mary's mother had ever rankled deeply in the heart of the queen, and revenge formed a prominent feature in the death of Cranmer. We have in this work, noticed the public disputations at Oxford, in which the talents of Cranmer, Ridley, and Latimer, shone so conspicuously, and tended to their condemnation.--The first sentence was illegal, inasmuch as the usurped power of the pope had not yet been re-established by law. Being kept in prison till this was effected, a commission was despatched from Rome, appointing Dr. Brooks to sit as the representative of his Holiness, and Drs. Story and Martin as those of the queen. Cranmer was willing to bow to the authority of Drs. Story and Martin, but against that of Dr. Brooks he protested. Such were the remarks and replies of Cranmer, after a long examination, that Dr. Brooks observed, "We come to examine you, and methinks you examine us." Being sent back to confinement, he received a citation to appear at Rome within eighteen days, but this was impracticable, as he was imprisoned in England; and as he stated, even had he been at liberty, he was too poor to employ an advocate. Absurd as it must appear, Cranmer was condemned at Rome, and February 14, 1556, a new commission was appointed by which, Thirdly, bishop of Ely, and Bonner, of London, were deputed to sit in judgment at Christ-church, Oxford. By virtue of this instrument, Cranmer was gradually degraded, by putting mere rags on him to represent the dress of an archbishop; then stripping him of his attire, they took off his own gown, and put an old worn one upon him instead. This he bore unmoved, and his enemies, finding that severity only rendered him more determined, tried the opposite course, and placed him in the house of the dean of Christ-church, where he was treated with every indulgence. This presented such a contrast to the three years hard imprisonment he had received, that it threw him off his guard. His open, generous nature was more easily to be seduced by a liberal conduct than by threats and fetters. When satan finds the christian proof against one mode of attack, he tries another; and what form is so seductive as smiles, rewards, and power, after a long, painful imprisonment? Thus it was with Cranmer: his enemies promised him his former greatness if he would but recant, as well as the queen's favour, and this at the very time they knew that his death was determined in council. To soften the path to apostasy, the first paper brought for his signature was conceived in general terms; this one signed, five others were obtained as explanatory of the first, till finally he put his hand to the following detestable instrument:--

"I, Thomas Cranmer, late archbishop of Canterbury, do renounce, abhor, and detest all manner of heresies and errors of Luther and Zuinglius, and all other teachings which are contrary to sound and true doctrine. And I believe most constantly in my heart, and with my mouth I confess one holy and catholic church visible, without which there is no salvation; and therefore I acknowledge the bishop of Rome to be supreme head on earth, whom I acknowledge to be the highest bishop and pope, and Christ's vicar, unto whom all christian people ought to be subject.

"And as concerning the sacraments, I believe and worship in the sacrament of the altar the body and blood of Christ, being contained most truly under the forms of bread and wine; the bread, through the mighty power of God being turned into the body of our Saviour Jesus

Christ, and the wine into his blood.

"And in the other six sacraments, also, (alike as in this) I believe and hold as the universal church holdeth, and the church of Rome judgeth and determineth.

"Furthermore, I believe that there is a place of purgatory, where souls departed be punished for a time, for whom the church doth godlily and wholesomely pray, like as it doth honour saints and make prayers to them.

"Finally, in all things I profess, that I do not otherwise believe than the catholic church and the church of Rome holdeth and teacheth.--I am sorry that I ever held or thought otherwise. And I beseech Almighty God, that of his mercy he will vouchsafe to forgive me whatsoever I have offended against God or his church, and also I desire and beseech all christian people to pray for me.

"And all such as have been deceived either by mine example of doctrine, I require them by the blood of Jesus Christ that they will return to the unity of the church, that we may be all of one mind, without schism or division.

"And to conclude, as I submit myself to the catholic church of Christ, and to the supreme head thereof, so I submit myself unto the most excellent majesties of Philip and Mary, king and queen of this realm of England, &c. and to all other their laws and ordinances, being ready always as a faithful subject ever to obey them. And God is my witness, that I have not done this for favour or fear of any person, but willingly and of mine own conscience, as to the instruction of others."

"Let him that standeth take heed lest he fall!" said the apostle, and here was a falling off indeed! The papists now triumphed in their turn: they had acquired all they wanted short of his life. His recantation was immediately printed and dispersed, that it might have its due effect upon the astonished protestants; but God counter-worked all the designs of the catholics by the extent to which they carried the implacable persecution of their prey. Doubtless, the love of life induced Cranmer to sign the above declaration; yet death may be said to have been preferable to life to him who lay under the stings of a goaded conscience and the contempt of every gospel christian; this principle he strongly felt in all its force and anguish.

The queen's revenge was only to be satiated in Cranmer's blood, and therefore she wrote an order to Dr. Cole, to prepare a sermon to be preached March 21, directly before his martyrdom, at St. Mary's, Oxford; Dr. Cole visited him the day previous, and was induced to believe that he would publicly deliver his sentiments in confirmation of the articles to which he had subscribed. About nine in the morning of the day of sacrifice, the queen's commissioners, attended by the magistrates, conducted the amiable unfortunate to St. Mary's church. His torn, dirty garb, the same in which they habited him upon his degradation, excited the commisseration of the people. In the church he found a low, mean stage, erected opposite to the pulpit, on which being placed, he turned his face, and fervently prayed to God. The church was crowded with persons of both persuasions, expecting to hear the justification of the late apostacy: the catholics rejoicing, and the protestants deeply wounded in spirit at the deceit of the human heart. Dr. Cole, in his sermon, represented Cranmer as having been guilty of the most atrocious crimes; encouraged the deluded sufferer not to fear death, not to doubt the support of God in his torments, nor that masses would be said in all the churches of Oxford for the repose of his soul. The Doctor then noticed his conversion, and which he ascribed to the evident working of Almighty Power, and in order that the people might be convinced of its reality, asked the prisoner to give them a sign. This Cranmer did, and begged the congregation to pray for him, for he had committed many and grievous sins; but, of all, there was one which awfully lay upon his mind, of which he would speak shortly.

During the sermon Cranmer wept bitter tears: lifting up his hands and eyes to heaven, and letting them fall, as if unworthy to live: his grief now found vent in words: before his confession he fell upon his knees, and, in the following words unveiled the deep contrition and agitation which harrowed up his soul.

"O Father of heaven! O Son of God, Redeemer of the world! O Holy Ghost, three persons and one God! have mercy on me, most wretched caitiff and miserable sinner. I have offended both against heaven and earth, more than my tongue can express. Whither then may I go, or whither may I flee? To heaven I may be ashamed to lift up mine eyes, and in earth I find no place of refuge or succour. To thee, therefore, O Lord, do I run; to thee do I humble myself, saying, O Lord, my God, my sins be great, but yet have mercy upon me for thy great mercy. The great mystery that God became man, was not wrought for little or few offences. Thou didst not give thy Son, O Heavenly Father, unto death for small sins only, but for all the greatest sins of the world, so that the sinner return to thee with his whole heart, as I do at present. Wherefore, have mercy on me, O God, whose property is always to have mercy, have mercy upon me, O Lord, for thy great mercy. I crave nothing for my own merits, but for thy name's sake, that it may be hallowed thereby, and for thy dear Son Jesus Christ's sake. And now therefore, O Father of Heaven, hallowed be thy name," &c.

Then rising, he said he was desirous before his death to give them some pious exhortations by which God might be glorified and themselves edified. He then descanted upon the danger of a love for the world, the duty of obedience to their majesties of love to one another and the necessity of the rich administering to the wants of the poor. He quoted the three verses of the fifth chapter of James, and then proceeded, "Let them that be rich ponder well these three sentences: for if they ever had occasion to show their charity, they have it now at this present, the poor people being so many, and victual so dear.

"And now forasmuch as I am come to the last end of my life, whereupon hangeth all my life past, and all my life to come, either to live with my master Christ for ever in joy, or else to be in pain for ever with the wicked in hell, and I see before mine eyes presently, either heaven ready to receive me, or else hell ready to swallow me up; I shall therefore declare unto you my very faith how I believe, without any colour of dissimulation: for now is no time to dissemble, whatsoever I have said or written in times past.

"First, I believe in God the Father Almighty, maker of heaven and earth, &c. And I believe every article of the Catholic faith, every word and sentence taught by our Saviour Jesus Christ, his apostles and prophets, in the New and Old Testament.

"And now I come to the great thing which so much troubleth my conscience, more than any thing that ever I did or said in my whole life, and that is the setting abroad of a writing contrary to the truth, which now here I renounce and refuse, as things written with my hand contrary to the truth which I thought in my heart, and written for fear of death, and to save my life, if it might be; and that is, all such bills or papers which I have written or signed with my hand since my degradation, wherein I have written many things untrue. And forasmuch as my hand hath offended, writing contrary to my heart, therefore my hand shall first be punished; for when I come to the fire, it shall first be burned.

"And as for the Pope, I refuse him as Christ's enemy, and antichrist, with all his false doctrine.

"And as for the sacrament, I believe as I have taught in my book against the bishop of Winchester, which my book teacheth so true a doctrine of the sacrament, that it shall stand in the last day before the judgment of God, where the papistical doctrines contrary thereto shall be ashamed to show their face."

Upon the conclusion of this unexpected declaration, amazement and indignation were conspicuous in every part of the church. The catholics were completely foiled, their object being frustrated; Cranmer, like Sampson, having completed a greater ruin upon his enemies in the hour of death, than he did in his life.

Cranmer would have proceeded in the exposure of the popish doctrines, but the murmurs of the idolaters drowned his voice, and the preacher gave an order to lead the heretic away! The savage command was directly obeyed, and the lamb about to suffer was torn from his stand to the place of slaughter, insulted all the way by the revilings and taunts of the pestilent monks and friars. With thoughts intent upon a far higher object than the empty threats of man, he reached the spot dyed with the blood of Ridley and Latimer. There he knelt for a short time in earnest devotion, and then arose, that he might undress and prepare for the fire. Two friars who had been parties in prevailing upon him to abjure, now endeavoured to draw him off again from the truth, but he was steadfast and immoveable in what he had just professed, and before publicly taught. A chain was provided to bind him to the stake, and after it had tightly encircled him, fire was put to the fuel, and the flames began soon to ascend. Then were the glorious sentiments of the martyr made manifest;--then it was, that stretching out his right hand, he held it unshrinkingly in the fire till it was burnt to a cinder, even before his body was injured, frequently exclaiming, "This unworthy right hand!" Apparently insensible of pain, with a countenance of venerable resignation, and eyes directed to Him for whose cause he suffered, he continued, like St. Stephen, to say, "Lord Jesus receive my spirit!" till the fury of the flames terminated his powers of utterance and existence. He closed a life of high sublunary elevation, of constant uneasiness, and of glorious martyrdom, on March 21, 1556.

Thus perished the illustrious Cranmer, the man whom king Henry's capricious soul esteemed for his virtues above all other men. Cranmer's example is an endless testimony that fraud and cruelty are the leading characteristics of the catholic hierarchy. They first seduced him to live by recantation, and then doomed him to perish, using perhaps the sophistical arguments, that, being brought again within the catholic pale, he was then most fit to die. His gradual change from darkness to the light of the truth, proved that he had a mind open to conviction. Though mild and forgiving in temper, he was severe in church discipline, and it is only on this ground that one act of cruelty of his can in any way be excused. A poor woman was in Edward's reign condemned to be burnt for her religious opinions; the pious young monarch reasoned with the archbishop upon the impropriety of protestants resorting to the same cruel means they censured in papists, adding humanely, "What! would you have me send her quick to the devil in her error?" The prelate however was not to be softened, and the king signed the death warrant with eyes steeped in tears. There is however a shade in the greatest characters, and few characters, whether political or religious, were greater than Cranmer's.

Agnes Potten and Joan Trunchfield.

These godly women (before mentioned) were both of Ipswich, and suffered about the same time with Cranmer. When in prison together, Mrs. Trunchfield was less ardent and zealous than Mrs. Potten; but when at the stake, her hope in glory was brighter even than that of her fellow-sufferer.

John Maundrel, William Coberly, and John Spicer were burnt between Salisbury and Wilton, March 24, 1556. Two died without any particular retardation, but Coberly, from the current of wind as he stood, was a long time in perishing. His left arm was visible to the bone, while the right, but little injured, beat upon his breast softly, and the discharge from his mouth was considerable. Rising suddenly erect from hanging over the chain, as if dead, he gave up his mortal abode for one made without hands, eternal in the heavens!

Rev. Robert Drakes, Rev. William Tyms, Richard Spurge, Sheerman T. Spurge, Fuller; J. Cavel, Weaver; and G. Ambrose, Fuller.

These worthies were of Essex, and in the diocese of London.--They were all sent up to Gardiner, the chancellor, March 25, 1555; who imprisoned them some in the king's bench, and others in the Marshalsea.

March 28, the six were brought up for condemnation in the consistory of St. Paul's; after which sentence, they were delivered to the sheriff, to be sent to Newgate, where they remained, patiently waiting the Lord's time for deliverance, which took place about the 23d of April, 1556, in Smithfield.

In the same month, perished John Harpole, of Rochester, and Joan Beach, widow, (before mentioned) with Mr. N. Hall. They suffered under Maurice, bishop of Rochester, in whose diocess they lived.

Rev. John Hullier. This gentleman went from Eton school to king's college, Cambridge, and suffered under Dr. Thirlby, bishop of Ely. He died the 2d of April, 1556.

From Kent we now turn to Colchester in Essex, where six constant professors of the gospel were selected to witness the truth by the sacrifice of their lives. These were, C. Luyster, of Dagenham, husbandman; John Mace, apothecary; John Spencer, weaver; Simon Joyne, lawyer; Richard Nichols, weaver, and John Hammond, tanner; five of Colchester.

Hugh Laverick and John Aprice.

Here we perceive that neither the impotence of age nor the affliction of blindness, could turn aside the murdering fangs of these Babylonish monsters. The first of these unfortunates was of the parish of Barking, aged sixty-eight, a painter and a cripple. The other was blind,--dark indeed in his visual faculties, but intellectually illuminated with the radiance of the everlasting gospel of truth. Inoffensive objects like these were informed against by some of the sons of bigotry, and dragged before the prelatical shark of London, where they underwent examination, and replied to the articles propounded to them, as other christian martyrs had done before. On the 9th of May, in the consistory of St. Paul's, they were entreated to recant, and upon refusal, were sent to Fulham, where Bonner, by way of a dessert after dinner, condemned them to the agonies of the fire. Being consigned to the secular officers, May 15, 1556, they were taken in a cart from Newgate to Stratford-le-Bow, where they were fastened to the stake. When Hugh Laverick was secured by the chain, having no farther occasion for his crutch, he threw it away saying to his fellow-martyr, while consoling him, "Be of good cheer my brother; for my lord of London is our good physician; he will heal us both shortly--thee of thy blindness, and me of my lameness." They sank down in the fire, to rise to immortality!

The day after the above martyrdoms, Catharine Hut, of Bocking, widow; Joan Horns, spinster, of Billericay; Elizabeth Thackwel, spinster, of Great Burstead; suffered death in Smithfield.

Thomas Dowry. We have again to record an act of unpitying cruelty, exercised on this lad, whom bishop Hooper, had confirmed in the Lord and the knowledge of his word.

How long this poor sufferer remained in prison is uncertain. By the testimony of one John Paylor, register of Gloucester, we learn, that when Dowry was brought before Dr. Williams, then chancellor of Gloucester, the usual articles were presented him for subscription. From these he dissented; and, upon the doctor's demanding of whom and where he had learned his heresies, the youth replied, "Indeed, Mr. Chancellor, I learned from you in that very pulpit. On such a day (naming the day) you said, in preaching upon the sacrament, that it was to be exercised spiritually by faith, and not carnally and really, as taught by the papists." Dr. Williams then bid him recant, as he had done; but Dowry had not so learned his duty. "Though you," said he, "can so easily mock God, the world, and your own conscience, yet will I not do so."

After the death of the above, the following three persons suffered at Beccles, in Suffolk, May 21, 1556. Thomas Spicer, of Winston, labourer; John Denny, and Edmund Poole.

Preservation of George Crow and his Testament.

This poor man, of Malden, May 26, 1556, put to sea, to lade in Lent with Fuller's earth, but the boat, being driven on land, filled with water, and every thing was washed out of her; Crow, however, saved his Testament, and coveted nothing else. With Crow was a man and a boy, whose awful situation became every minute more alarming, as the boat was useless, and they were ten miles from land, expecting the tide should in a few hours set in upon them. After prayer to God, they got upon the mast, and hung there for the space of ten hours, when the poor boy, overcome by cold and exhaustion, fell off, and was drowned. The tide having abated, Crow proposed to take down the masts, and float upon them, which they did; and at ten o'clock at night they were borne away at the mercy of the waves. On Wednesday, in the night, Crow's companion died through fatigue and hunger, and he was left alone, calling upon God for succour. At length he was picked up by a Captain Morse, bound to Antwerp, who had nearly steered away, taking him for some fisherman's buoy floating in the sea. As soon as Crow was got on board, he put his hand in his bosom, and drew out his Testament, which indeed was wet, but no otherwise injured. At Antwerp he was well received, and the money he had lost was more than made good to him.

June 6, 1556, the following four martyrs suffered at Lewes, in Sussex: J. Harland, of Woodmancote, carpenter; John Oswald, of the same place, husbandmen; Thomas Avington, of Ardingly, turner; and Thomas Read.

June 20, at the same place, were burnt the Rev. Thomas Whood, and Thomas Mills. June 24, the Rev. Wm. Alderhall; and June 28, John Clement, wheelright, died in the King's Bench prison, and were buried on the dunghill in the backyard. June 21, a young man, the servant of a merchant, was burnt at Leicester.

Executions at Stratford-le-Bow.

At this sacrifice, which we are about to detail, no less than thirteen were doomed to the fire.

Each one refusing to subscribe contrary to conscience, they were condemned, and the 27th of June, 1556, was appointed for their execution at Stratford-le-Bow. Their constancy and faith glorified their Redeemer, equally in life and in death.

R. Bernard, A. Foster, and R. Lawson.

The first was a labourer, and a single man, of Framsden, Suffolk. He was a shrewd, undaunted professor, and fearlessly replied to the bishop's questions. Adam Foster was a husbandman, married, aged 26, of Mendlesham, Suffolk. Refusing to go to church, he was sent by Sir J. Tyrrel to Eye-Dungeon, and thence to bishop Hopton, who condemned him.

R. Lawson, of Bury, linen-weaver, a single man, aged 30, was sent to Eye-Dungeon, and after that to Bury, where they suffered in the same fire, praising God, and encouraging others to martyrdom.

Rev. Julius Palmer.

This gentleman's life presents a singular instance of error and conversion. In the time of Edward, he was a rigid and obstinate papist, so adverse to godly and sincere preaching, that he was even despised by his own party; that this frame of mind should be changed, and he suffer persecution and death in queen Mary's reign, are among those events of omnipotence at which we wonder and admire.

Mr. Palmer was born at Coventry, where his father had been mayor. Being afterward removed to Oxford, he became, under Mr. Harley, of Magdalen college, an elegant Latin and Greek scholar. He was fond of useful disputation, possessed of a lively wit, and a strong memory. Indefatigable in private study, he rose at four in the morning, and by this practice qualified himself to become reader in logic in Magdalen college. The times of Edward, however, favouring the reformation, Mr. Palmer became frequently punished for his contempt of prayer and orderly behaviour, and was at length expelled the house.

He afterwards embraced the doctrines of the reformation, which occasioned his arrest and final condemnation. He was tried on the 15th of July, 1556, together with one Thomas Askin, a fellow-prisoner. Askin and one John Guin had been sentenced the day before, and Mr. Palmer, on the 15th, was brought up for final judgment.--Execution was ordered to follow the sentence, and at five o'clock in the same afternoon, at a place called the Sand-pits, these three martyrs were fastened to a stake. After devoutly praying together, they sung the 31st psalm. When the fire was kindled, and it had seized their bodies, without an appearance of enduring pain, they continued to cry, Lord Jesus, strengthen us! Lord Jesus receive our souls! till animation was suspended and human suffering was past. It is remarkable, that, when their heads had fallen together in a mass as it were by the force of the flames, and the spectators thought Palmer was lifeless, his tongue and lips again moved, and were heard to pronounce the name of Jesus, to whom be glory and honour forever!

About this time, three women were burnt in the island of Guernsey, under circumstances of aggravated cruelty, whose names were, Catherine Cauches, and her two daughters, Mrs. Perotine Massey, and Guillemine Gilbert.

The day of execution having arrived, three stakes were erected: the middle post was assigned to the mother, the eldest daughter on her right hand, and the younger on the left. They were strangled previous to burning, but the rope breaking before they were dead, the poor women fell into the fire. Perotine, at the time of her inhuman sentence, was largely pregnant, and now, falling on her side upon the flaming fagots, presented a singular spectacle of horror!--Torn open by the tremendous pangs she endured, she was delivered of a fine male child, who was rescued from its burning bed by the humanity of one W. House, who tenderly laid it on the grass. The infant was taken to the provost, and by him presented to the bailiff, when the inhuman monster decreed it to be re-cast into the fire, that it might perish with its heretical mother! Thus was this innocent baptised in its own blood, to make up the very climax of Romish barbarity; being born and dying at the same time a martyr; and realizing again the days of Herodian cruelty, with circumstances of bigoted malice unknown even to that execrable murderer.

Their execution took place, July 18, 1556. On the same day, were burnt at Grinstead, in Sussex, Thomas Dungate, John Foreman, and Mother Tree.

June 26, 1556, at Leicester, was executed Thomas Moor, a servant, aged 24 years, who was taken up for saying that his Saviour was in Paradise, and not in the popish paste or wafer.

Joan Waste.

This poor honest woman, blind from her birth, and unmarried, aged 22, was of the parish of Allhallows, Derby. Her father was a barber, and also made ropes for a living: in which she assisted him, and also learned to knit several articles of apparel. Refusing to communicate with those who maintained doctrines contrary to those she had learned in the days of the pious Edward, she was called before Dr. Draicot, the chancellor of bishop Blaine, and Peter Finch, official of Derby.

With sophistical arguments and threats they endeavoured to confound the poor girl; but she proffered to yield to the bishop's doctrine, if he would answer for her at the day of judgment, (as pious Dr. Taylor had done in his sermons) that his belief of the real presence of the sacrament was true. The bishop at first answered that he would; but Dr. Draicot reminding him that he might not in any way answer for a heretic, he withdrew his confirmation of his own tenets; and she replied, that if their consciences would not permit them to answer at God's bar for that truth they wished her to subscribe to, she would answer no more questions. Sentence was then adjudged, and Dr. Draicot appointed to preach her condemned sermon, which took place August 1, 1556, the day of her martyrdom. His fulminating discourse being finished, the poor sightless object was taken to a place called Windmill Pit, near the town, where she for a time held her brother by the hand, and then prepared herself for the fire, calling upon the pitying multitude to pray with her, and upon Christ to have mercy upon her, till the glorious light of the everlasting sun of righteousness beamed upon her departed spirit.

September 8, 1556, Edward Sharp, aged 40, was condemned at Bristol.

September 24, Thomas Ravendale, a currier, and John Hart, suffered at Mayfield, in Essex; and on the day following, a young man, a carpenter, died at Bristol with joyous constancy. September 27, John Horn, and a female martyr suffered at Wooten-under-edge, Gloucestershire, professing abjurgation of popery.

In November, fifteen martyrs were imprisoned in Canterbury castle, of whom all were either burnt or famished. Among the latter were J. Clark, D. Chittenden, W. Foster of Stone, Alice Potkins, and J. Archer, of Cranbrooke, weaver. The two first of these had not received condemnation, but the others were sentenced to the fire. Foster, at his examination, observed upon the utility of carrying lighted candles about on Candlemas-day, that he might as well carry a pitch fork; and that a gibbet would have as good an effect as the cross.

We have now brought to a close the sanguinary proscriptions of the merciless Mary, in the year 1556, the number of which amounted to above EIGHTY-FOUR!

The beginning of the year 1557, was remarkable for the visit of Cardinal Pole to the University of Cambridge, which seemed to stand in need of much cleansing from heretical preachers and reformed doctrines. One object was also to play the popish farce of trying Martin Bucer and Paulus Phagius, who had been buried about three or four years; for which purpose the churches of St. Mary and St. Michael, where they lay, were interdicted as vile and unholy places, unfit to worship God in, until they were perfumed and washed with the Pope's holy water, &c. &c. The trumpery act of citing these dead reformers to appear, not having had the least effect upon them, on January 26, sentence of condemnation was passed, part of which ran in this manner, and may serve as a specimen of proceedings of this nature:--"We therefore pronounce the said Martin Bucer and Paulus Phagius excommunicated and anathematized, as well by the common law, as by letters of process; and that their memory be condemned, we also condemn their bodies and bones (which in that wicked time of schism, and other heresies flourishing in this kingdom, were rashly buried in holy ground) to be dug up, and cast far from the bodies and bones of the faithful, according to the holy canons; and we command that they and their writings, if any be there found, be publicly burnt; and we interdict all persons whatsoever of this university, town, or places adjacent, who shall read or conceal their heretical book, as well by the common law, as by our letters of process!"

After the sentence thus read, the bishop commanded their bodies to be dug out of their graves, and being degraded from holy orders, delivered them into the hands of the secular power; for it was not lawful for such innocent persons as they were, abhorring all bloodshed, and detesting all desire of murder, to put any man to death.

February 6, the bodies, enclosed as they were in chests, were carried into the midst of the market place at Cambridge, accompanied by a vast concourse of people. A great post was set fast in the ground, to which the chests were affixed with a large iron chain, and bound round their centres, in the same manner as if the dead bodies had been alive. When the fire began to ascend, and caught the coffins, a number of condemned books were also launched into the flames, and burnt. Justice, however, was done to the memories of these pious and learned men in queen Elizabeth's reign, when Mr. Ackworth, orator of the university, and Mr. J. Pilkington, pronounced orations in honour of their memory, and in reprobation of their catholic persecutors.

Cardinal Cole also inflicted his harmless rage upon the dead body of Peter Martyr's wife, who, by his command, was dug out of her grave, and buried on a distant dunghill, partly because her bones lay near St. Fridewide's relics, held once in great esteem in that college, and partly because he wished to purify Oxford of heretical remains as well as Cambridge. In the succeeding reign, however, her remains were restored to their former cemetary, and even intermingled with those of the catholic saint, to the utter astonishment and mortification of the disciples of his holiness the pope.

Cardinal Cole published a list of fifty-four Articles, containing instructions to the clergy of his diocess of Canterbury, some of which are too ludicrous and puerile to excite any other sentiment than laughter in these days.

Persecutions in the Diocess of Canterbury.

In the year 1557, fifteen were imprisoned in the castle of Canterbury, five of whom perished of hunger. We now proceed to the account of the other ten; whose names were--J. Philpot, M. Bradbridge, N. Final, all of Tenterden; W. Waterer and T. Stephens, of Beddington; J. Kempe, of Norgate; W. Hay, of Hithe; T. Hudson, of Salenge; W. Lowick, of Cranbrooke; and W. Prowting, of Thornham. Of these Kempe, Waterer, Prowting, Lowick, Hudson, and Hay, were burnt at Canterbury, January 15, 1557: Stephens and Philpot at Wye, about the same time; and Final and Bradbridge at Ashford, on the 16th. They were steadfast and immoveable in the faith.

In the month of February, the following persons were committed to prison:--R. Coleman, of Waldon, labourer; Joan Winseley, of Horsley Magna, spinster; S. Glover of Rayley; R. Clerk, of Much Holland, mariner; W. Munt, of Much Bentley, sawyer; Marg. Field, of Ramsey, spinster; R. Bongeor, currier; R. Jolley, mariner; Allen Simpson; Helen Ewing; C. Pepper, widow; Alice Walley, (who recanted;) W. Bongeor, glazier; all of Colchester; R. Atkin, of Halstead, weaver; R. Barcock, of Wilton, carpenter; R. George, of Westbarhoalt, labourer; R. Debnam, of Debenham, weaver; C. Warren, of Cocksall, spinster; Agnes Whitlock, of Dover-court, spinster; Rose Allen, spinster; and T. Feresannes, minor; both of Colchester.

These persons were brought before Bonner, who would have immediately sent them to execution, but Cardinal Pole was for more merciful measures, and Bonner, in a letter of his to the cardinal, seems to be sensible that he had displeased him, for he has this expression,--"I thought to have them all hither to Fulham, and to have given sentence against them; nevertheless, perceiving by my last doing that your grace was offended, I thought it my duty, before I proceeded farther, to inform your grace." This circumstance verifies the account that the cardinal was a humane man; and though a zealous catholic, we, as protestants, are willing to render him that honour which his merciful character deserves. Some of the bitter persecutors denounced him to the pope as a favourer of heretics, and he was summoned to Rome, but queen Mary, by particular entreaty, procured his stay. However, before his latter end, and a little before his last journey from Rome to England, he was strongly suspected of favouring the doctrine of Luther.

T. Loseby, H. Ramsey, T. Thirtell, Margaret Hide, and Agnes Stanley.

These persons were successively called up, condemned, delivered over to the sheriffs of London, in April 15, 1557, were conducted to Smithfield, there to exchange a temporal life for a life eternal with him for whose sake and truth they perished.

In May following, W. Morant, S. Gratwick, and ---- King, suffered in St. George's Field, Southwark.

Executions in Kent.

The following seven were arraigned for heresy: Joan Bainbridge, of

Staplehurst; W. Appleby, Petronella his wife, and the wife of John Manning, of Maidstone; B. Allin, and his wife Catherine, of Freytenden; and Elizabeth ----, a blind maiden. Allin was put in the stocks at night, and some advised him to compromise a little, and go for the form's sake to mass, which he did next day, but, just before the sacring, as it is termed, he went into the churchyard, and so reasoned with himself upon the absurdity of transubstantiation, that he staid away, and was soon after brought back again before Sir John Baker, and condemned for heresy. He was burnt with the six before mentioned at Maidstone, the 18th of June, 1557.

As in the last sacrifice four women did honour to the truth, so in the following auto-de-fe we have the like number of females and males, who suffered June 30, 1557, at Canterbury, and were J. Fishcock, F. White, N. Pardue, Barbary Final, widow; Bradbridge's widow; Wilson's wife; and Benden's wife.

Of this group we shall more particularly notice Alice Benden, wife of Edward Benden, of Staplehurst, Kent. She had been taken up in Oct. 1556, for non-attendance, and released upon a strong injunction to mind her conduct. Her husband was a bigoted catholic, and publicly speaking of his wife's contumacy, she was conveyed to Canterbury castle, where knowing, when she should be removed to the bishop's prison, she should be almost starved upon three farthings a day, she endeavoured to prepare herself for this suffering by living upon two-pence halfpenny per day. Jan. 22, 1557, her husband wrote to the bishop, that if his wife's brother, Roger Hall, were to be kept from consoling and relieving her, she might turn; on this account, she was moved to a prison called Monday's hole; her brother sought diligently for her, and at the end of five weeks providentially heard her voice in the dungeon, but could no otherwise relieve her, than by putting some money in a loaf, and sticking it on a long pole. Dreadful must have been the situation of this poor victim, lying on straw, between stone walls, without a change of apparel, or the meanest requisites of cleanliness, during a period of nine weeks!

March 25, she was summoned before the bishop, who, with rewards, offered her liberty if she would go home and be comfortable; but Mrs. Benden had been inured to suffering, and, showing him her contracted limbs and emaciated appearance, refused to swerve from the truth. She was however removed from this Black Hole to the West gate, whence, about the end of April, she was taken out to be condemned, and then committed to the castle prison till the 19th of June, the day of her burning. At the stake, she gave her handkerchief to one John Banks, as a memorial; and from her waist she drew a white lace, desiring him to give it her brother, and tell him, it was the last band that had bound her, except the chain; and to her father she returned a shilling he had sent her.

The whole of these seven martyrs undressed themselves with alacrity, and, being prepared, knelt down, and prayed with an earnestness and Christian spirit that even the enemies of the Cross were affected. After invocation made together, they were secured to the stake, and, being encompassed with the unsparing flames, they yielded their souls into the hands of the living Lord.

Matthew Plaise, weaver, a sincere and shrewd Christian, of Stone, Kent, was brought before Thomas, bishop of Dover, and other inquisitors, whom he ingeniously teazed by his indirect answers, of which the following is a specimen.

Dr. Harpsfield. Christ called the bread his body; what dost thou say it is?

Plaise. I do believe it was that which he gave them.

Dr. H. What was that?

P. That which he brake.

Dr. H. What did he break?

P. That which he took.

Dr. H. What did he take?

P. The text saith, "He took bread."

Dr. H. Well, then, thou sayest it was but bread which the disciples did eat.

P. I say, what he gave them, that did they eat indeed.

A very long disputation followed, in which Plaise was desired to humble himself to the bishop; but this he refused. Whether this zealous person died in prison, was executed, or delivered, history does not mention.

Execution of ten martyrs at Lewes.

Again we have to record the wholesale sacrifice of Christ's little flock, of whom five were women. On the 22d of June, 1557, the town of Lewes beheld ten persons doomed to perish by fire and persecution. The names of these worthies were, Richard Woodman; G. Stephens, W. Mainard, Alex. Hosman, and Thomasin Wood, servants; Margery Morris, and James Morris, her son; Dennis Burges, Ashdon's wife, and Grove's wife.

These nine persons were taken a few days only before their judgment, and suffered at Lewes, in Sussex, June 22, 1557. Of these, eight were prematurely executed, inasmuch as the writ from London could not have arrived for their burning. A person named Ambrose died in Maidstone prison about this time.

Rev. Mr. John Hullier was brought up at Eton college, and in process of time became curate of Babram, three miles from Cambridge and went afterward to Lynn; where, opposing the superstition of the papists, he was carried before Dr. Thirlby, bishop of Ely, and sent to Cambridge castle: here he lay for a time, and was then sent to the Tolbooth prison, where, after three months, he was brought to St. Mary's church, and condemned by Dr. Fuller. On Maunday Thursday, he was brought to the stake: while undressing, he told the people to bear witness that he was about to suffer in a just cause, and exhorted them to believe, that there was no other rock than Jesus Christ to build upon. A priest, named Boyes, then desired the mayor to silence him. After praying, he went meekly to the stake, and being bound with a chain, and placed in a pitch barrel, fire was applied to the reeds and wood; but the wind drove the fire directly to his back, which caused him under the severe agony to pray the more fervently. His friends directed the executioner to fire the pile to windward of his face, which was immediately done.

A quantity of books were now thrown into the fire, one of which (the Communion Service) he caught, opened it, and joyfully continued to read it, until the fire and smoke deprived him of sight; then even, in earnest prayer, he pressed the book to his heart, thanking God for bestowing on him in his last moments this precious gift.--The day being hot, the fire burnt fiercely; and at a time when the spectators supposed he was no more, he suddenly exclaimed, Lord Jesus, receive my spirit! And meekly resigned his life. He was burnt on Jesus Green, not far from Jesus College. He had gunpowder given him, but he was dead before it became ignited. This pious sufferer afforded a singular spectacle; for his flesh was so burnt from the bones, which continued erect, that he presented the idea of a skeleton figure chained to the stake. His remains were eagerly seized by the multitude, and venerated by all who admired his piety or detested inhuman bigotry.

Simon Miller and Elizabeth Cooper,

In the following month of July, received the crown of martyrdom. Miller dwelt at Lynn, and came to Norwich, where, planting himself at the door of one of the churches, as the people came out, he requested to know of them where he could go to receive the communion. For this a priest brought him before Dr. Dunning, who committed him to ward; but he was suffered to go home, and arrange his affairs; after which he returned to the bishop's house, and to his prison, where he remained till the 13th of July, the day of his burning.

Elizabeth Cooper, wife of a pewterer, of St. Andrews, Norwich, had recanted; but, tortured for what she had done by the worm which dieth not, she shortly after voluntarily entered her parish church during the time of the popish service, and standing up, audibly proclaimed that she revoked her former recantation, and cautioned the people to avoid her unworthy example. She was taken from her own house by Mr. Sutton the sheriff, who very reluctantly complied with the letter of the law, as they had been servants and in friendship together. At the stake, the poor sufferer, feeling the fire, uttered the cry of Oh! upon which Mr. Miller, putting his hand behind him towards her, desired her to be of good courage, "for (said he) good sister, we shall have a joyful and a sweet supper." Encouraged by this example and exhortation, she stood the fiery ordeal without flinching, and, with him, proved the power of faith over the flesh.

Executions at Colchester.

It was before mentioned that twenty-two persons had been sent up from Cholchester, who upon a slight submission, were afterward released. Of these, Wm. Munt, of Much-Bentley, husbandman, with Alice, his wife, and Rose Allin, her daughter, upon their return home, abstained from church, which induced the bigoted priest secretly to write to Bonner. For a short time they absconded, but returning again, March 7th, one Mr. Edmund Tyrrel, (a relation of the Tyrrel who murdered king Edward V. and his brother) with the officers, entered the house while Munt and his wife were in bed, and informed them that they must go to Colchester Castle. Mrs. Munt at that time very ill, requested her daughter to get her some drink; leave being permitted, Rose took a candle and a mug; and in returning through the house was met by Tyrrel, who cautioned her to advise her parents to become good catholics. Rose briefly informed him that they had the Holy Ghost for their adviser; and that she was ready to lay down her own life for the same cause. Turning to his company, he remarked that she was willing to burn; and one of them told him to prove her, and see what she would do by and by. The unfeeling wretch immediately executed this project; and, seizing the young woman by the wrist, he held the lighted candle under her hand, burning it crosswise on the back, till the tendons divided from the flesh, during which he loaded her with many opprobious epithets. She endured his rage unmoved, and then, when he had ceased the torture, she asked him to begin at her feet or head, for he need not fear that his employer would one day repay him. After this she took the drink to her mother.

This cruel act of torture does not stand alone on record. Bonner had served a poor blind harper in nearly the same manner, who had steadily maintained a hope that if every joint of him were to be burnt, he should not fly from the faith. Bonner, upon this, privately made a signal to his men, to bring a burning coal, which they placed in the poor man's hand, and then by force held it closed, till it burnt into the flesh deeply. But to return.--

In searching Munt's house, John Thurston and Margaret his wife were found, and conveyed to Colchester Castle; where lay J. Johnson, of Thorp, Essex, aged 34, widower, with his three young children, all indicted for heresy.

The following lay in Mote-hall, or town prison: Wm. Bongeor, of St. Nicholas, in Colchester; Thomas Penold, Colchester, tallow chandler; W. Pucras, of Bocking, Essex, fuller, 20; Agnes Silversides, Colchester, widow, 70; Helen Ewring, wife of John Ewring, miller, of Colchester, 45; and Eliz. Folks, a servant, Colchester.

Shortly after their condemnation, Bonner's writ arrived for their execution, which was fixed for the 2d of August, 1557. About seven o'clock in the morning, the town prisoners in the Mote-hall were brought to a plot of ground on the outside of the town wall, where the stake was erected, surrounded by fagots and fuel. Having prayed, and prepared themselves for the fiery torment, Elizabeth Folks, as she was standing at the stake, received a dreadful blow on the shoulder from the stroke of a hammer, which was aimed at the staple that secured the chain. This, however, in no wise discomposed her, but turning her head round, she continued to pray and exhort the people. Fire being put to the pile, these martyrs died amidst the prayers and commisseration of thousands who came to be witnesses of their fortitude and their faith.

In the same manner, in the afternoon, the county prisoners from Colchester castle were brought out, and executed, at different stakes, on the same spot; praising God, and exhorting the people to avoid idolatry and the church of Rome.

John Thurston, of whom mention was made before, died in May, in Colchester castle.

George Eagles, tailor, was indicted for having prayed that "God would turn queen Mary's heart, or take her away;" the ostensible cause of his death was his religion, for treason could hardly be imagined in praying for the reformation of such an execrable soul as that of Mary. Being condemned for this crime, he was drawn to the place of execution upon a sledge, with two robbers, who were executed with him. After Eagles had mounted the ladder, and been turned off a short time, he was cut down, before he was at all insensible; a bailiff, named Wm. Swallow, then dragged him to the sledge, and with a common blunt cleaver, hacked off the head: in a manner equally clumsy and cruel, he opened his body and tore out the heart.

In all this suffering the poor martyr repined not, but to the last called upon his Saviour. The fury of these bigots did not end here; the intestines were burnt, and the body was quartered, the four parts being sent to Colchester, Harwich, Chelmsford, and St. Rouse's.--Chelmsford had the honor of retaining his head, which was affixed to a long pole in the market-place. In time it was blown down, and lay several days in the streets, till it was buried at night in the church-yard. God's judgment not long after fell upon Swallow, who in his old age became a beggar, and affected with a leprosy that made him obnoxious even to the animal creation; nor did Richard Potts, who troubled Eagles in his dying moments, escape the visiting hand of God.

About this time, Richard Crashfield, of Wymundham, suffered at Norwich.

Nearly about this time a person named Fryer, and the sister of George Eagles, suffered martyrdom.

Mrs. Joyce Lewes.

This lady was the wife of Mr. T. Lewes, of Manchester. She had received the Romish religion as true, till the burning of that pious martyr, the Rev. Mr. Saunders, at Coventry. Understanding that his death arose from a refusal to receive the mass, she began to inquire into the ground of his refusal, and her conscience, as it began to be enlightened, became restless and alarmed. In this inquietude, she resorted to Mr. John Glover, who lived near, and requested that he would unfold those rich sources of gospel knowledge he possessed, particularly upon the subject of transubstantiation. He easily succeeded in convincing her that the mummery of popery and the mass were at variance with God's most holy word, and honestly reproved her for following too much the vanities of a wicked world. It was to her indeed a word in season, for she soon become weary of her former sinful life, and resolved to abandon the mass and idolatrous worship. Though compelled by her husband's violence to go to church, her contempt of the holy water and other ceremonies were so manifest, that she was accused before the bishop for despising the sacramentals.

A citation, addressed to her, immediately followed, which was given to Mr. Lewes, who, in a fit of passion, held a dagger to the throat of the officer, and made him eat it, after which he caused him to drink it down, and then sent him away. But for this the bishop summoned Mr. Lewes before him as well as his wife; the former readily submitted, but the latter resolutely affirmed, that, in refusing holy water, she neither offended God, nor any part of his laws. She was sent home for a month, her husband being bound for her appearance, during which time Mr. Glover impressed upon her the necessity of doing what she did, not from self-vanity, but for the honour and glory of God.

Mr. Glover and others earnestly exhorted Lewes to forfeit the money he was bound in, rather than subject his wife to certain death; but he was deaf to the voice of humanity, and delivered her over to the bishop, who soon found a sufficient cause to consign her to a loathsome prison, whence she was several times brought for examination. At the last time the bishop reasoned with her upon the fitness of her coming to mass, and receiving as sacred the sacrament and sacramentals of the Holy Ghost. "If these things were in the word of God," said Mrs. Lewes, "I would with all my heart receive, believe, and esteem them." The bishop, with the most ignorant and impious effrontery, replied, "If thou wilt believe no more than what is warranted by scripture, thou art in a state of damnation!" Astonished at such a declaration, this worthy sufferer ably rejoined, "that his words were as impure, as they were profane."

After condemnation, she lay a twelvemonth in prison, the sheriff not being willing to put her to death in his time, though he had been but just chosen. When her death warrant came from London, she sent for some friends, whom she consulted in what manner her death might be more glorious to the name of God, and injurious to the cause of God's enemies. Smilingly, she said, "As for death, I think but lightly of. When I know that I shall behold the amiable countenance of Christ my dear Saviour, the ugly face of death does not much trouble me." The evening before she suffered, two priests were anxious to visit her, but she refused both their confession and absolution, when she could hold a better communication with the High Priest of souls. About three o'clock in the morning, Satan began to shoot his fiery darts, by putting into her mind to doubt whether she was chosen to eternal life, and Christ died for her. Her friends readily pointed out to her those consolatory passages of Scripture which comfort the fainting heart, and treat of the Redeemer who taketh away the sins of the world.

About eight o'clock the sheriff announced to her that she had but an hour to live; she was at first cast down, but this soon passed away, and she thanked God that her life was about to be devoted to his service. The sheriff granted permission for two friends to accompany her to the stake--an indulgence for which he was afterward severely handled. Mr. Reniger and Mr. Bernher led her to the place of execution; in going to which, from its distance, her great weakness, and the press of the people, she had nearly fainted. Three times she prayed fervently that God would deliver the land from popery and the idolatrous mass; and the people for the most part, as well as the sheriff, said Amen.

When she had prayed, she took the cup, (which had been filled with water to refresh her,) and said, I drink to all them that unfeignedly love the gospel of Christ, and wish for the abolition of popery. Her friends, and a great many women of the place, drank with her, for which most of them afterward were enjoined penance.

When chained to the stake, her countenance was cheerful, and the roses of her cheeks were not abated. Her hands were extended towards heaven till the fire rendered them powerless, when her soul was received into the arms of the Creator. The duration of her agony was but short, as the under-sheriff, at the request of her friends, had prepared such excellent fuel that she was in a few minutes overwhelmed with smoke and flame. The case of this lady drew a tear of pity from every one who had a heart not callous to humanity.

Executions at Islington.

About the 17th of Sept. suffered at Islington the following four professors of Christ: Ralph Allerton, James Austoo, Margery Austoo, and Richard Roth.

James Austoo and his wife, of St. Allhallows, Barking, London, were sentenced for not believing in the presence. Richard Roth rejected the seven sacraments, and was accused of comforting the heretics by the following letter written in his own blood, and intended to have been sent to his friends at Colchester:--

"O dear Brethren and Sisters,

"How much reason have you to rejoice in God, that he hath given you such faith to overcome this blood-thirsty tyrant thus far! And no doubt he that hath begun that good work in you, will fulfil it unto the end. O dear hearts in Christ, what a crown of glory shall ye receive with Christ in the kingdom of God! O that it had been the good will of God that I had been ready to have gone with you; for I lie in my lord's Little-ease by day, and in the night I lie in the Coal-house, apart from Ralph Allerton, or any other; and we look every day when we shall be condemned; for he said that I should be burned within ten days before Easter; but I lie still at the pool's brink, and every man goeth in before me; but we abide patiently the Lord's leisure, with many bonds, in fetters and stocks, by which we have received great joy of God. And now fare you well, dear brethren and sisters, in this world, but I trust to see you in the heavens face to face.

"O brother Munt, with your wife and my sister Rose, how blessed are you in the Lord, that God hath found you worthy to suffer for his sake! with all the rest of my dear brethren and sisters known and unknown. O be joyful even unto death. Fear it not, saith Christ, for I have overcome death. O dear hearts, seeing that Jesus Christ will be our help, O tarry you the Lord's leisure. Be strong, let your hearts be of good comfort, and wait you still for the Lord. He is at hand. Yea, the angel of the Lord pitcheth his tent round about them that fear him, and delivereth them which way he seeth best. For our lives are in the Lord's hands; and they can do nothing unto us before God suffer them. Therefore give all thanks to God.

"O dear hearts, you shall be clothed in long white garments upon the mount of Sion, with the multitude of saints, and with Jesus Christ our Saviour, who will never forsake us. O blessed virgins, ye have played the wise virgins' part, in that ye have taken oil in your lamps that ye may go in with the bridegroom, when he cometh, into the everlasting joy with him. But as for the foolish, they shall be shut out, because they made not themselves ready to suffer with Christ, neither go about to take up his cross. O dear hearts, how precious shall your death be in the sight of the Lord! for dear is the death of his saints. O fare you well, and pray. The grace of our Lord Jesus Christ be with you all. Amen, Amen. Pray, pray, pray!

"Written by me, with my own blood,
"RICHARD ROTH."

This letter, so justly denominating Bonner the "blood-thirsty tyrant," was not likely to excite his compassion. Roth accused him of bringing them to secret examination by night, because he was afraid of the people by day. Resisting every temptation to recant, he was condemned, and, Sept. 17, 1557, these four martyrs perished at Islington, for the testimony of the Lamb, who was slain that they might be of the redeemed of God.

Agnes Bengeor and Margaret Thurston were doomed to the fire at Colchester, Sept. 17, 1557. Humbly they knelt to pray, and joyfully they arose to be chained to the stake, uttering invocations and hallelujahs, till the surrounding flames mounted to the seat of life, and their spirits ascended to the Almighty Saviour of all who truly believe!

About this time suffered, at Northampton, John Kurde, shoemaker of Syrsam, Northamptonshire.

John Noyes, a shoemaker, of Laxfield, Suffolk, was taken to Eye and at midnight, Sept. 21, 1557, he was brought from Eye to Laxfield to be burned. On the following morning he was led to the stake, prepared for the horrid sacrifice. Mr. Noyes, on coming to the fatal spot, knelt down, prayed, and rehearsed the 50th psalm. When the chain enveloped him, he said, "Fear not them that kill the body, but fear him that can kill both body and soul, and cast it into everlasting fire!" As one Cadman placed a fagot against him, he blessed the hour in which he was born to die for the truth: and while trusting only upon the all-sufficient merits of the Redeemer, fire was set to the pile, and the blazing fagots in a short time stifled his last words, Lord, have mercy on me!--Christ, have Mercy upon me!--The ashes of the body were buried in a pit, and with them one of his feet, whole to the ankle, with the stocking on.

Mrs. Cicely Ormes.

This young martyr, aged twenty-two, was the wife of Mr. Edmund Ormes, worsted weaver of St. Lawrence, Norwich. At the death of Miller and Elizabeth Cooper, before mentioned, she had said that she would pledge them of the same cup they drank of. For these words she was brought to the chancellor, who would have discharged her upon promising to go to church, and to keep her belief to herself. As she would not consent to this, the chancellor urged that he had shown more lenity to her than any other person, and was unwilling to condemn her, because she was an ignorant foolish woman; to this she replied, (perhaps with more shrewdness than he expected,) that, however great his desire might be to spare her sinful flesh, it could not equal her inclination to surrender it up in so great a quarrel. The chancellor then pronounced the fiery sentence, and, September 23, 1557, she was brought to the stake, at eight o'clock in the morning. After declaring her faith to the people, she laid her hand on the stake, and said, "Welcome thou cross of Christ." Her hand was sooted in doing this, (for it was the same stake at which Miller and Cooper were burnt,) and she at first wiped it; but directly after again welcomed and embraced it as the "sweet cross of Christ." After the tormentors had kindled the fire, she said, "My soul doth magnify the Lord, and my spirit doth rejoice in God my Saviour." Then crossing her hands upon her breast, and looking upwards with the utmost serenity, she stood the fiery furnace. Her hands continued gradually to rise till the sinews were dried, and then they fell. She uttered no sigh of pain, but yielded her life, an emblem of that celestial paradise in which is the presence of God, blessed for ever.

It might be contended that this martyr voluntarily sought her own death, as the chancellor scarcely exacted any other penance of her than to keep her belief to herself; yet it should seem in this instance as if God had chosen her to be a shining light, for a twelve-month before she was taken, she had recanted; but she was wretched till the chancellor was informed, by letter, that she repented of her recantation from the bottom of her heart. As if to compensate for her former apostacy, and to convince the catholics that she meant no more to compromise for her personal security, she boldly refused his friendly offer of permitting her to temporize. Her courage in such a cause deserves commendation--the cause of Him who has said, Whoever is ashamed of me on earth, of such will I be ashamed in heaven.

In November, Thomas Spurdance, one of queen Mary's servants, was brought before the chancellor of Norwich, who, among his interrogations, was severely recriminated upon by the prisoner. This good man was taken by two of his fellow-servants, dwelling at Codman, in Suffolk. He was sent to Bury where he remained some time in prison, and in November, 1557, braved the fiery indignation of the enemies of Christ with Christian fortitude and resignation.

J. Hallingdale, W. Sparrow, and R Gibson, suffered in Smithfield November 18th, 1557.

Rev. John Rough.

This pious martyr was a Scotchman: at the age of 17, he entered himself as one of the order of Black Friars, at Stirling, in Scotland. He had been kept out of an inheritance by his friends, and he took this step in revenge for their conduct to him. After being there sixteen years, Lord Hamilton, Earl of Arran, taking a liking to him, the archbishop of St. Andrew's induced the provincial of the house to dispense with his habit and order; and he thus became the Earl's chaplain. He remained in this spiritual employment a year, and in that time God wrought in him a saving knowledge of the truth; for which reason the Earl sent him to preach in the freedom of Ayr, where he remained four years; but finding danger there from the religious complexion of the times, and learning that there was much gospel freedom in England, he travelled up to the duke of Somerset, then Lord Protector of England, who gave him a yearly salary of twenty pounds, and authorized him, to preach at Carlisle, Berwick, and Newcastle, where he married. He was afterward removed to a benefice at Hull, in which he remained till the death of Edward VI.

In consequence of the tide of persecution then setting in, he fled with his wife to Friesland, and at Nordon they followed the occupation of knitting hose, caps, &c. for subsistence. Impeded in his business by the want of yarn, he came over to England to procure a quantity, and on Nov. 10th, arrived in London, where he soon heard of a secret society of the faithful, to whom he joined himself, and was in a short time elected their minister, in which occupation he strengthened them in every good resolution. Dec. 12th, through the information of one Taylor, a member of the society, Mr. Rough, with Cuthbert Symson and others, was taken up in the Saracen's Head, Islington, where, under the pretext of coming to see a play, their religious exercises were holden. The queen's vice-chamberlain conducted Rough and Symson before the council, in whose presence they were charged with meeting to celebrate the communion. The council wrote to Bonner and he lost no time in this affair of blood. In three days he had him up, and on the next (the 20th) resolved to condemn him. The charges laid against him were, that he, being a priest, was married, and that he had rejected the service in the Latin tongue. Rough wanted not arguments to reply to these flimsy tenets. In short, he was degraded and condemned.

Mr. Rough, it should be noticed, when in the north, in Edward the VIth's reign, had saved Dr. Watson's life, who afterward sat with bishop Bonner on the bench. This ungrateful prelate, in return for the kind act he had received, boldly accused Mr. Rough of being the most pernicious heretic in the country. The godly minister reproved him for his malicious spirit; he affirmed that, during the thirty years he had lived, he had never bowed the knee to Baal; and that twice at Rome he had seen the pope borne about on men's shoulders with the false-named sacrament carried before him, presenting a true picture of the very antichrist; yet was more reverence shown to him than to the wafer, which they accounted to be their God. "Ah?" said Bonner, rising up, and making towards him, as if he would have torn his garment, "hast thou been at Rome, and seen our holy father the pope, and dost thou blaspheme him after this sort?" This said, he fell upon him, tore off a piece of his beard, and, that the day might begin to his own satisfaction, he ordered the object of his rage to be burnt by half past five the following morning.

Cuthbert Symson.

Few professors of Christ possessed more activity and zeal than this excellent person. He not only labored to preserve his friends from the contagion of popery, but to guard them against the terrors of persecution. He was deacon of the little congregation over which Mr. Rough presided as minister.

Mr. Symson has written an account of his own sufferings, which we cannot detail better than in his own words:

"On the 13th of December, 1557, I was committed by the council to the tower of London. On the following Thursday, I was called into the ware-room, before the constable of the tower, and the recorder of London, Mr. Cholmly, who commanded me to inform them of the names of those who came to the English service. I answered, that I would declare nothing; in consequence of my refusal, I was set upon a rack of iron, as I judge for the space of three hours!

"They then asked me if I would confess: I answered as before. After being unbound, I was carried back to my lodging. The Sunday after I was brought to the same place again, before the lieutenant and recorder of London, and they examined me. As I had answered before, so I answered now. Then the lieutenant swore by God I should tell; after which my two fore-fingers were bound together, and a small arrow placed between them, they drew it through so fast that the blood followed, and the arrow brake.

"After enduring the rack twice again, I was retaken to my lodging, and ten days after the lieutenant asked me if I would not now confess that which they had before asked of me. I answered, that I had already said as much as I would. Three weeks after I was sent to the priest, where I was greatly assaulted, and at whose hand I received the pope's curse, for bearing witness of the resurrection of Christ. And thus I commend you to God, and to the word of his grace, with all those who unfeignedly call upon the name of Jesus; desiring God of his endless mercy, through the merits of his dear Son Jesus Christ, to bring us all to his everlasting kingdom, Amen. I praise God for his great mercy shown upon us. Sing Hosanna to the Highest with me, Cuthbert Symson. God forgive my sins! I ask forgiveness of all the world, and I forgive all the world, and thus I leave the world, in the hope of a joyful resurrection!"

If this account be duly considered, what a picture of repeated tortures does it present! But, even the cruelty of the narration is exceeded by the patient meekness with which it was endured. Here are no expressions of malice, no invocations even of God's retributive justice, not a complaint of suffering wrongfully! On the contrary, praise to God, forgiveness of sin, and a forgiving all the world, concludes this unaffected interesting narrative.

Bonner's admiration was excited by the steadfast coolness of this martyr. Speaking of Mr. Symson in the consistory, he said, "You see what a personable man he is, and then of his patience, I affirm, that, if he were not a heretic, he is a man of the greatest patience that ever came before me. Thrice in one day has he been racked in the tower: in my house also he has felt sorrow, and yet never have I seen his patience broken."

The day before this pious deacon was to be condemned, while in the stocks in the bishop's coal-house, he had the vision of a glorified form, which much encouraged him. This he certainly attested to his wife, Mr. Austen, and others, before his death; but Mr. Fox, in reciting this article, leaves it to the reader's judgment, to consider it either as a natural or supernatural circumstance.

With this ornament of the Christian reformation were apprehended Mr. Hugh Foxe and John Devinish; the three were brought before Bonner, March 19, 1558, and the papistical articles tendered. They rejected them, and were all condemned. As they worshipped together in the same society, at Islington, so they suffered together in Smithfield, March 28; in whose death the God of Grace was glorified, and true believers confirmed!

Wm. Nichol, of Haverfordwest, Wales, was taken up for reprobating the practice of the worshippers of antichrist, and April 9, 1558, bore testimony to the truth at Haverfordwest, in Wales, by enduring the fire.

Thomas Hudson, Thomas Carman, and William Seamen,

Were condemned by a bigoted vicar of Aylesbury, named Berry. The spot of execution was called Lollard's pit, without Bishopsgate, at Norwich. After joining together in humble petition to the throne of grace, they rose, went to the stake, and were encircled with their chains. To the great surprise of the spectators, Hudson slipped from under his chain, and came forward. A great opinion prevailed that he was about to recant; others thought that he wanted further time. In the mean time, his companions at the stake urged every promise and exhortation to support him. The hopes of the enemies of the cross, however, were disappointed: the good man, far from fearing the smallest personal terror at the approaching pangs of death, was only alarmed that his Saviour's face seemed to be hidden from him. Falling upon his knees, his spirit wrestled with God and God verified the words of his Son, "Ask, and it shall be given." The martyr rose in an ecstacy of joy, and exclaimed,

"Now, I thank God, I am strong! and care not what man can do to me!" With an unruffled countenance he replaced himself under the chain, joined his fellow-sufferers, and with them suffered death, to the comfort of the godly, and the confusion of antichrist.

Berry, unsatiated with this demoniacal act, summoned up two hundred persons in the town of Aylesham, whom he compelled to kneel to the cross at Pentecost, and inflicted other punishments. He struck a poor man for a trifling word, with a flail, which proved fatal to the unoffending object. He also gave a woman named Alice Oxes, so heavy a blow with his fist, as she met him entering the hall when he was in an ill-humour, that she died with the violence. This priest was rich, and possessed great authority; he was a reprobate, and, like the priesthood, he abstained from marriage, to enjoy the more a debauched and licentious life. The Sunday after the death of queen Mary, he was revelling with one of his concubines, before vespers; he then went to church, administered baptism, and in his return to his lascivious pastime, he was smitten by the hand of God. Without a moment given for repentance, he fell to the ground, and a groan was the only articulation permitted him. In him we may behold the difference between the end of a martyr and a persecutor.

In the month of May, William Harris, Richard Day, and Christiana George, suffered at Colchester, and there humbly made an offering of themselves to God.

Apprehensions at Islington.

In a retired close, near a field, in Islington, a company of decent persons had assembled, to the number of forty. While they were religiously engaged in praying and expounding the scripture, twenty-seven of them were carried before Sir Roger Cholmly. Some of the women made their escape, twenty-two were committed to Newgate, who continued in prison seven weeks. Previous to their examination, they were informed by the keeper, (Alexander,) that nothing more was requisite to procure their discharge, than to hear mass. Easy as this condition may seem, these martyrs valued their purity of conscience more than loss of life or property; hence, thirteen were burnt, seven in Smithfield, and six at Brentford; two died in prison, and the other seven were providentially preserved. The names of the seven who suffered were, H. Pond, R. Estland, R. Southain, M. Ricarby, J. Floyd, J. Holiday, and R. Holland. They were sent to Newgate June 16, 1558, and executed on the 27th.

The story of Roger Holland is the only one of these martyrs which has been handed down to us. He was first an apprentice to one Mr. Kempton, at the Black-Boy, Watling-street. He was, in every sense of the word, licentious, a lover of bad company, and, more than all, a stubborn determined papist--one of whom it might be said, that a miracle only could effect his conversion. Dissipated as he was, his master had the imprudent confidence to trust him with money; and, having received thirty pounds on his master's account, he lost it at the gaming table. Knowing it was impossible to regain his character, he determined to withdraw to France or Flanders.--With this resolution, he called early in the morning on a discreet servant in the house, named Elizabeth, who professed the gospel, and lived a life that did honour to her profession. To her he revealed the loss his folly had occasioned, regretted that he had not followed her advice, and begged her to give his master a note of hand from him acknowledging the debt, which he would repay if ever it were in his power; he also entreated his disgraceful conduct might be kept secret, lest it would bring the grey hairs of his father with sorrow to a premature grave.

The maid, with a generosity and Christian principle rarely surpassed, conscious that his imprudence might be his ruin, brought him the thirty pounds, which was part of a sum of money recently left her by legacy. "Here," said she, "is the sum requisite: you shall take the money, and I will keep the note; but expressly on this condition, that you abandon all lewd and vicious company; that you neither swear nor talk immodestly, and game no more; for, should I learn that you do, I will immediately show this note to your master. I also require, that you shall promise me to attend the daily lecture at Allhallows, and the sermon at St. Paul's every Sunday; that you cast away all your books of popery, and in their place substitute the Testament and the Book of Service, and that you read the Scriptures with reverence and fear, calling upon God for his grace to direct you in his truth. Pray also fervently to God, to pardon your former offences, and not to remember the sins of your youth, and would you obtain his favour, ever dread to break his laws or offend his majesty. So shall God have you in his keeping, and grant you your heart's desire." We must honour the memory of this excellent domestic, whose pious endeavours were equally directed to benefit the thoughtless youth in this life and that which is to come. May her example be followed by the present generation of servants, who seek rather to seduce by vain dress and loose manners the youth who are associated in servitude with them! God did not suffer the wish of this excellent domestic to be thrown upon a barren soil; within half a year after the licentious Holland became a zealous professor of the gospel, and was an instrument of conversion to his father and others whom he visited in Lancashire, to their spiritual comfort and reformation from popery.

His father, pleased with his change of conduct, gave him forty pounds to commence business with in London. Upon his return, like an honest man, he paid the debt of gratitude, and, rightly judging that she who had proved so excellent a friend and counsellor, would be no less amiable as a wife, he tendered her his hand. They were married in the first year of Mary, and a child was the fruit of their union, which Mr. Holland caused to be baptised by Mr. Ross in his own house. For this offence he was obliged to fly, and Bonner, with his accustomed implacability, seized his goods, and ill-treated his wife. After this, he remained secretly among the congregations of the faithful, till the last year of queen Mary, when he, with six others was taken not far from St. John's Wood, and brought to Newgate upon May-day, 1558.

He was called before the bishop, Dr. Chedsey, the Harpsfields, &c. Dr. Chedsey expressed much affection for him, and promised he should not want any favour that he or his friends could procure, if he would not follow his conceit. This was seconded by squire Eaglestone, a gentleman of Lancashire, and a near kinsman of Holland's, who said, "I am sure your honour means good to my cousin. I beseech God he may have the grace to follow your counsel." Holland directly replied, "Sir, you crave of God you know not what. I beseech of God to open your eyes to see the light of his blessed word." After some private communication among the commissioners, Bonner said, "I perceive, Roger, you will not be ruled by any counsel that I or my friends can give."

The following speech of Mr. Holland we are induced to give unabridged, as it contains a pointed charge, founded on the sins resulting from false doctrines; and, besides, is in itself a well-digested and just attack upon the tenets of popery.

"I may say to you, my lord, as Paul said to Felix and to the Jews, in the 22d of the Acts, and in the 15th of the first epistle to the Corinthians. It is not unknown to my master, to whom I was apprenticed, that I was of your blind religion--that which now is taught, and that I obstinately and wilfully remained in it, till the latter end of king Edward. Having liberty under your auricular confession, I made no conscience of sin, but trusted in the priests' absolution, who for money did also some penance for me; which after I had given, I cared no farther what offences I did, no more than he did after he had my money, whether he tasted bread and water for me, or not: so that lechery, swearing, and all other vices, I accounted no offence of danger, so long as I could for money have them absolved. So straitly did I observe your rules of religion, that I would have ashes upon Ash Wednesday, though I had used ever so much wickedness at night. Though I could not in conscience eat flesh upon the Friday, yet I made no conscience at all of swearing, drinking, or gaming all night long: thus I was brought up, and herein I have continued till now of late, when God hath opened the light of his word, and called me by his grace to repent of my former idolatry and wicked life; for in Lancashire their blindness and whoredom is much more, than may with chaste ears be heard. Yet these my friends, who are not clear in these notable crimes, think the priest with his mass can save them, though they blaspheme God, and keep concubines besides their wives, as long as they live. Yea, I know some priests, very devout, my lord, yet such have six or seven children by four or five sundry women.

"Mr. Doctor, as to your antiquity, unity, and universality, (for these Dr. Chedsey alleged as notes and tokens of their religion,) I am unlearned. I have no sophistry to shift my reasons with; but the truth I trust I have, which needs no painted colours to set her forth. The antiquity of our church is not from pope Nicholas, nor pope Joan, but our church is from the beginning, even from the time that God said unto Adam, that the seed of the woman should break the serpent's head; and so to faithful Noah; to Abraham, Isaac, and Jacob, to whom it was promised, that their seed should multiply as the stars in the sky; and so to Moses, David, and all the holy fathers that were from the beginning unto the birth of our Saviour Christ. All who believed these promises were of the church, though the number was oftentimes but few and small, as in Elias' days, who thought he was the only one that had not bowed the knee to Baal, when God had reserved seven thousand that never had bowed their knees to that idol: as I trust there be seven hundred thousand more than I know of, that have not bowed their knee to that idol your mass, and your God Maozim; in the upholding of which is your bloody cruelty while you daily persecute Elias and the servants of God, forcing them (as Daniel was in his chamber) closely to serve the Lord their God; and even as we by this your cruelty are forced in the fields to pray unto God, that his holy word may be once again truly preached amongst us, and that he would mitigate and shorten these idolatrous and bloody days wherein all cruelty reigns. Moreover, of our church have been the apostles and evangelists, the martyrs and confessors of Christ, who have at all times and in all ages been persecuted for the testimony of the word of God. But for the upholding of your church and religion, what antiquity can you show? The mass indeed, that idol and chief pillar of your religion, is not yet four hundred years old, and some of your masses are younger, as that of St. Thomas a Becket, the traitor, wherein you pray, That you may be saved by the blood of St. Thomas. And as for your Latin service, what are we of the laity the better for it? I think if any one were to hear your priests mumble up their service, although he well understood Latin, yet he would understand very few words of it, the priests so champ them and chew them, and post so fast, that they neither understand what they say, nor they that hear them; and in the mean time the people, when they should pray with the priest, are set to their beads to pray our Lady's Psalter. So crafty is Satan to devise these his dreams, (which you defend with fagot and fire,) to quench the light of the word of God; which, as David saith, should be a lantern to our feet. And again, Wherein shall a young man direct his way, but by the word of God? and yet you will hide it from us in a tongue unknown. St. Paul had rather have five words spoken with understanding, than ten thousand in an unknown tongue, and yet will you have your Latin service and praying in a strange tongue, whereof the people are utterly ignorant, to be of such antiquity.

"The Greek church, and a good part of Christendom besides, never received your service in an unknown tongue, but in their own natural language, which all the people understand; neither your transubstantiation, your receiving in one kind, your purgatory, your images, &c.

"As for the unity which is in your church, what is it but treason, murder, poisoning one another, idolatry, superstition, and wickedness? What unity was in your church, when there were three popes at once? Where was your head of unity when you had a woman pope?" Here he was interrupted, and was not suffered to proceed. The bishop said his words were blasphemous, and ordered the keeper to take him away. Bonner observing, on his second examination, that Holland said, he was willing to be instructed by the church, (meaning the true church,) he ordered the keeper to let him want for nothing, not even for money, by which conduct he hoped to inveigle him from the truth. This, however, upon his last examination did not produce the intended effect. Bonner spoke very handsomely to him, and assured him his former hasty answers should not operate against him, as he himself (the bishop) was sometimes too hasty, but it was soon over; he further said, that he should have consigned him to his own ordinary for examination, but for the particular interest he took in his welfare, for his and his friends' sake. From this exordium he proceeded to the touchstone question of the real presence in the mass.

"Do you not believe, that, after the priest hath spoken the words of consecration, there remains the body of Christ, really and corporeally under the forms of bread and wine? I mean the self-same body as was born of the Virgin Mary, that was crucified upon the cross, that rose again the third day." Holland replied, "Your lordship saith, the same body which was born of the Virgin Mary, which was crucified upon the cross, which rose again the third day: but you leave out 'which ascended into heaven;' and the Scripture saith, He shall remain until he come to judge the quick and the dead. Then he is not contained under the forms of bread and wine, by Hoc est corpus meum, &c."

Bonner, finding no impression could be made upon his firmness, and that he himself could not endure to hear the mass, transubstantiation, and the worshipping the sacrament, denominated impious and horrid idolatry, pronounced the condemnatory sentence, adjudging him to be burnt.

During this fulmination, Holland stood very quiet, and when he was about to depart, he begged permission to speak a few words. The bishop would not hear him, but, at the intercession of a friend, he was permitted. In the following speech, there is a spirit of prophecy which entitles it to particular attention; they were not the words of a random enthusiast, but of one to whom God seems to have given an assurance, that the present abject state of his faithful people should shortly be altered.

Holland. "Even now I told you that your authority was from God, and by his sufferance: and now I tell you God hath heard the voice of his servants, which hath been poured forth with tears for his afflicted saints, whom you daily persecute, as now you do us. But this I dare be bold in God to say, (by whose Spirit I am moved,) that God will shorten your hand of cruelty, that for a time you shall not molest his church. And this you shall in a short time well perceive, my dear brethren, to be most true. For *after this day, in this place*, there shall not be any by him put to the trial of fire and fagot;" and after that day there were none that suffered in Smithfield for the truth of the gospel.

In reply, Bonner said, "Roger, thou art, I perceive, as mad in these thy heresies as ever was Joan Butcher. In anger and fume thou would become a railing prophet. Though thou and all the rest of you would see me hanged, yet I *shall* live to burn, yea, and I *will* burn all the sort of you that come into my hands, that will not worship the blessed sacrament of the altar, for all thy prattling;" and so he went his way.

Then Holland began to exhort his friends to repentance, and to think well of them that suffered for the testimony of the gospel, upon which the bishop came back, charging the keeper that no man should speak to them without his license; if they did, they should be committed to prison. In the mean time, Henry Pond and Holland spake to the people, exhorting them to stand firm in the truth; adding, that God would shorten these cruel and evil days for his elect's sake.

The day they suffered, a proclamation was made, prohibiting every one from speaking or talking to, or receiving any thing from them, or touching them, upon pain of imprisonment without either bail or mainprize. Notwithstanding, the people cried out, "God strengthen them!" They also prayed for the people, and the restoration of his word. Embracing the stake and the reeds, Holland said these words:

"Lord, I most humbly thank thy Majesty, that thou hast called me from the state of death unto the light of thy heavenly word, and now unto the fellowship of thy saints, that I may sing and say, Holy, holy, holy, Lord God of Hosts! And, Lord, into thy hands I commit my spirit! Lord, bless these, thy people, and save them from idolatry." Thus he ended his life, looking towards heaven, praying to, and praising God, with the rest of his fellow saints. These seven martyrs were consumed, June 27, 1558.

The names of the six martyrs taken in company with those who were apprehended in the close, near Islington, were R. Mills, S. Cotton, R. Dynes, S. Wright, J. Slade, and W. Pikes, tanner. They were condemned by Bonner's chancellor in one day, and the next day a writ was sent to Brentford for their execution, which took place, July 14, 1558.

Flagellations by Bonner.

When this catholic hyena found that neither persuasions, threats, nor imprisonment, could produce any alteration in the mind of a youth named Thomas Hinshaw, he sent him to Fulham, and during the first night set him in the stocks, with no other allowance than bread and water. The following morning he came to see if this punishment had worked any change in his mind, and finding none, he sent Dr. Harpsfield, his archdeacon, to converse with him. The Doctor was soon out of humour at his replies, called him peevish boy, and asked him if he thought he went about to damn his soul? "I am persuaded," said Thomas, "that you labour to promote the dark kingdom of the devil, not for the love of the truth." These words the doctor conveyed to the bishop, who, in a passion that almost prevented articulation, came to Thomas, and said, "Dost thou answer my archdeacon thus, thou naughty boy? But I'll soon handle thee well enough for it, be assured!" Two willow twigs were then brought him, and causing the unresisting youth to kneel against a long bench, in an arbour in his garden, he scourged him till he was compelled to cease for want of breath and fatigue, being of a punchy and full-bellied make. One of the rods was worn quite away.

Many other conflicts did Hinshaw undergo from the bishop; who, at length, to remove him effectually, procured false witnesses to lay articles against him, all of which the young man denied, and, in short, refused to answer to any interrogatories administered to him. A fortnight after this, the young man was attacked by a burning ague, and at the request of his master, Mr. Pugson, of St. Paul's church-yard, he was removed, the bishop not doubting that he had given him his death in the natural way; he however remained ill above a year, and in the mean time queen Mary died, by which act of providence he escaped Bonner's rage.

John Willes was another faithful person, on whom the scourging hand of Bonner fell. He was the brother of Richard Willes, before mentioned, burnt at Brentford. Hinshaw and Willes were confined in Bonner's coal house together, and afterward removed to Fulham, where he and Hinshaw remained during eight or ten days, in the stocks. Bonner's persecuting spirit betrayed itself in his treatment of Willes during his examinations, often striking him on the head with a stick, seizing him by the ears, and filipping him under the chin, saying he held down his head like a thief. This producing no signs of recantation, he took him into his orchard, and in a small arbour there he flogged him first with a willow rod, and then with birch, till he was exhausted. This cruel ferocity arose from the answer of the poor sufferer, who, upon being asked how long it was since he had crept to the cross, replied, "Not since he had come to years of discretion, nor would he, though he should be torn to pieces by wild horses." Bonner then bade him make the sign of the cross on his forehead, which he refused to do, and thus was led to the orchard.

The communications that took place between Bonner and Willes are too tedious to give in detail. The reader would smile to read the infatuated simple reasons with which the bishop endeavoured to delude the ignorant. He strongly urged the impropriety of his meddling with matters of scripture; adding, "If thou wilt believe Luther, Zuinglius, and other protestant authors, thou canst not go right; but in believing me, there can be no error!--and, if there be, thy blood will be required at our hands. In following Luther, and the heretics of latter days, now wilt thou come to the place thou askest for?--They will lead thee to destruction, and burn thy body and soul in hell, like all those who have been burnt in Smithfield."

The bishop continued to afflict him in his examinations, in which, among other things, he said, "They call me bloody Bonner!--A vengeance on you all! I would fain be rid of you, but you have a delight in burning. Could I have my will, I would sew up your mouths, put you in sacks, and drown you!"

What a sanguinary speech was this, to proceed from the mouth of one who professed to be a minister of the gospel of peace, and a servant of the Lamb of God!--Can we have an assurance that the same spirit does not reign now, which reigned in this mitred catholic?

One day, when in the stocks, Bonner asked him how he liked his lodging and fare. "Well enough," said Willes, "might I have a little straw to sit or lie upon." Just at this time came in Willes' wife, then largely pregnant, and entreated the bishop for her husband, boldly declaring that she would be delivered in the house, if he were not suffered to go with her. To get rid of the good wife's importunity, and the trouble of a lying-in woman in his palace, he bade Willes make the sign of the cross, and say, In nomine Patris, et Filii, et Spiritus Sancti, Amen. Willes omitted the sign, and repeated the words, "in the name of the Father, and of the Son, and of the Holy Ghost, Amen." Bonner would have the words repeated in Latin, to which Willes made no objection, knowing the meaning of the words. He was then permitted to go home with his wife, his kinsman Robert Rouze being charged to bring him to St. Paul's the next day, whither he himself went, and, subscribing to a Latin instrument of little importance, was liberated. This is the last of the twenty-two taken at Islington.

Rev. Richard Yeoman.

This devout aged person was curate to Dr. Taylor, at Hadley, and eminently qualified for his sacred function. Dr. Taylor left him the curacy at his departure, but no sooner had Mr. Newall gotten the benefice, than he removed Mr. Yeoman, and substituted a Romish priest. After this he wandered from place to place, exhorting all men to stand faithfully to God's word, earnestly to give themselves unto prayer, with patience to bear the cross now laid upon them for their trial, with boldness to confess the truth before their adversaries, and with an undoubted hope to wait for the crown and reward of eternal felicity. But when he perceived his adversaries lay wait for him, he went into Kent, and with a little packet of laces, pins, points, &c. he travelled from village to village, selling such things, and in this manner subsisted himself, his wife, and children.

At last Justice Moile, of Kent, took Mr. Yeoman, and set him in the stocks a day and a night; but, having no evident matter to charge him with, he let him go again. Coming secretly again to Hadley, he tarried with his poor wife, who kept him privately, in a chamber of the town-house, commonly called the Guildhall, more than a year. During this time the good old father abode in a chamber locked up all the day, spending his time in devout prayer, in reading the Scriptures, and in carding the wool which his wife spun. His wife also begged bread for herself and her children, by which precarious means they supported themselves. Thus the saints of God sustained hunger and misery, while the prophets of Baal lived in festivity, and were costily pampered at Jezebel's table.

Information being at length given to Newall, that Yeoman was secreted by his wife, he came, attended by the constables, and broke into the room where the object of his search lay in bed with his wife. He reproached the poor woman with being a whore, and would have indecently pulled the clothes off, but Yeoman resisted both this act of violence and the attack upon his wife's character, adding that he defied the pope and popery. He was then taken out, and set in the stocks till day.

In the cage also with him was an old man, named John Dale, who had sat there three or four days, for exhorting the people during the time service was performing by Newall and his curate. His words were, "O miserable and blind guides, will ye ever be blind leaders of the blind? will ye never amend? will ye never see the truth of God's word? will neither God's threats nor promises enter into your hearts? will the blood of the martyrs nothing mollify your stony stomachs? O obdurate, hard-hearted, perverse, and crooked generation! to whom nothing can do good."

These words he spake in fervency of spirit against the superstitious religion of Rome; wherefore parson Newall caused him forthwith to be attached, and set in the stocks in a cage, where he was kept till Sir Henry Doile, a justice, came to Hadley.

When Yeoman was taken, the parson called earnestly upon Sir Henry Doile to send them both to prison. Sir Henry Doile as earnestly entreated the parson to consider the age of the men, and their mean condition; they were neither persons of note nor preachers; wherefore he proposed to let them be punished a day or two and to dismiss them, at least John Dale, who was no priest, and therefore, as he had so long sat in the cage, he thought it punishment enough for this time. When the parson heard this, he was exceedingly mad, and in a great rage called them pestilent heretics, unfit to live in the commonwealth of Christians. Sir Henry, fearing to appear too merciful, Yeoman and Dale were pinioned, bound like thieves with their legs under the horses' bellies, and carried to Bury jail, where they were laid in irons; and because they continually rebuked popery, they were carried into the lowest dungeon, where John Dale, through the jail-sickness and evil-keeping, died soon after: his body was thrown out, and buried in the fields. He was a man of sixty-six years of age, a weaver by occupation, well learned in the holy Scriptures, steadfast in his confession of the true doctrines of Christ as set forth in king Edward's time; for which he joyfully suffered prison and chains, and from this worldly dungeon he departed in Christ to eternal glory, and the blessed paradise of everlasting felicity.

After Dale's death, Yeoman was removed to Norwich prison, where, after strait and evil keeping, he was examined upon his faith and religion, and required to submit himself to his holy father the pope. "I defy him, (quoth he,) and all his detestable abomination: I will in no wise have to do with him." The chief articles objected to him, were his marriage and the mass sacrifice. Finding he continued steadfast in the truth, he was condemned, degraded, and not only burnt, but most cruelly tormented in the fire. Thus he ended this poor and miserable life, and entered into that blessed bosom of Abraham, enjoying with Lazarus that rest which God has prepared for his elect.

Thomas Benbridge.

Mr. Benbridge was a single gentleman, in the diocese of Winchester. He might have lived a gentleman's life, in the wealthy possessions of this world; but he chose rather to enter through the strait gate of persecution to the heavenly possession of life in the Lord's kingdom, than to enjoy present pleasure with disquietude of conscience. Manfully standing against the papists for the defence of the sincere doctrine of Christ's gospel, he was apprehended as an adversary to the Romish religion, and led for examination before the bishop of Winchester, where he underwent several conflicts for the truth against the bishop and his colleague; for which he was condemned, and some time after brought to the place of martyrdom by Sir Richard Pecksal, sheriff.

When standing at the stake he began to untie his points, and to prepare himself; then he gave his gown to the keeper, by way of fee. His jerkin was trimmed with gold lace, which he gave to Sir Richard Pecksal, the high sheriff. His cap of velvet he took from his head, and threw away. Then, lifting his mind to the Lord, he engaged in prayer.

When fastened to the stake, Dr. Seaton begged him to recant, and he should have his pardon; but when he saw that nothing availed, he told the people not to pray for him unless he would recant, no more than they would pray for a dog.

Mr. Benbridge, standing at the stake with his hands together in such a manner as the priest holds his hands in his Memento, Dr. Seaton came to him again, and exhorted him to recant, to whom he said, "Away, Babylon, away!" One that stood by said, Sir, cut his tongue out; another, a temporal man, railed at him worse than Dr. Seaton had done.

When they saw he would not yield, they bade the tormentors to light the pile, before he was in any way covered with fagots. The fire first took away a piece of his beard, at which he did not shrink. Then it came on the other side and took his legs, and the nether stockings of his hose being leather, they made the fire pierce the sharper, so that the intolerable heat made him exclaim, "I recant!" and suddenly he thrust the fire from him. Two or three of his friends being by, wished to save him; they stepped to the fire to help remove it, for which kindness they were sent to jail. The sheriff also of his own authority took him from the stake, and remitted him to prison, for which he was sent to the fleet, and lay there sometime. Before, however, he was taken from the stake, Dr. Seaton wrote articles for him to subscribe to. To these Mr. Benbridge made so many objections, that Dr. Seaton ordered them to set fire again to the pile. Then with much pain and grief of heart he subscribed to them upon a man's back.

This done, his gown was given him again, and he was led to prison. While there, he wrote a letter to Dr. Seaton, recanting those words he spake at the stake, and the articles which he had subscribed; for he was grieved that he had ever signed them. The same day se'night he was again brought to the stake, where the vile tormentors rather broiled than burnt him. The Lord give his enemies repentance!

Not long before the sickness of queen Mary, in the beginning of August, 1558, four inoffensive humble martyrs were burnt at St. Edmundsbury with very little examination. Neglect in attending the popish service at mass, which in vain they pleaded as a matter of conscience, was the cause of their untimely sufferings and deaths. Their heroic names were J. Crooke, sawyer; R. Miles, alias Plummer, sheerman; A. Lane, wheelright; and J. Ashley, a bachelor.

Alexander Gouch and Alice Driver.

These godly persons were apprehended by Mr. Noone, a justice in Suffolk.

They were brought to the stake at seven o'clock in the morning, notwithstanding they had come from Melton jail, six miles off. The sheriff, Sir Henry Dowell, was much dissatisfied with the time they took in prayer, and sent one of his men to bid them make an end. Gouch earnestly entreated for a little time, urging that they had but a little while to live: but the sheriff would grant no indulgence, and ordered the numerous friends who came to take the last farewell of them as they stood chained to the stake, to be forcibly torn away, and threatened them with arrest; but the indignation of the spectators made him revoke this order. They endured the terrific conflagration, and honoured God equally in their lives and deaths.

In the same month were executed at Bury, P. Humphrey, and J. and H. David, brothers. Sir Clement Higham, about a fortnight before the queen's death, issued out a warrant for their sacrifice, notwithstanding the queen's illness at that time rendered her incapable of signing the order for their execution.

Mrs. Prest.

From the number condemned in this fanatical reign, it is almost impossible to obtain the name of every martyr, or to embellish the history of all with anecdotes and exemplifications of Christian conduct. Thanks be to Providence, our cruel task begins to draw towards a conclusion, with the end of the reign of Papal terror and bloodshed. Monarchs, sit upon thrones possessed by hereditary right, should, of all others, consider that the laws of nature are the laws of God, and hence that the first law of nature is the preservation of their subjects. Maxims of persecutions, of torture, and of death, they should leave to those who have effected sovereignty by fraud or the sword; but where, except among a few miscreant emperors of Rome, and the Roman pontiffs, shall we find one whose memory is so "damned to everlasting fame" as that of queen Mary? Nations bewail the hour which separates them forever from a beloved governor, but, with respect to that of Mary, it was the most blessed time of her whole reign. Heaven has ordained three great scourges for national sins--plague, pestilence, and famine. It was the will of God in Mary's reign to bring a fourth upon this kingdom, under the form of Papistical Persecution. It was sharp, but glorious; the fire which consumed the martyrs has undermined the Popedom; and the Catholic states, at present the most bigoted and unenlightened, are those which are sunk lowest in the scale of moral dignity and political consequence. May they remain so, till the pure light of the gospel shall dissipate the darkness of fanaticism and superstition! But to return.

Mrs. Prest for some time lived about Cornwall, where she had a husband and children, whose bigotry compelled her to frequent the abominations of the church of Rome. Resolving to act as her conscience dictated, she quitted them, and made a living by spinning. After some time, returning home, she was accused by her neighbours, and brought to Exeter, to be examined before Dr. Troubleville, and his chancellor Blackston. As this martyr was accounted of inferior intellects, we shall put her in competition with the bishop, and let the reader judge which had the most of that knowledge conducive to everlasting life. The bishop bringing the question to issue, respecting the bread and wine being flesh and blood, Mrs. Prest said, "I will demand of you whether you can deny your creed, which says, that Christ doth perpetually sit at the right hand of his Father, both body and soul, until he come again; or whether he be there in heaven our Advocate, and to make prayer for us unto God his Father? If he be so, he is not here on earth in a piece of bread. If he be not here, and if he do not dwell in temples made with hands, but in heaven, what! shall we seek him here? If he did not offer his body once for all, why make you a new offering? If with one offering he made all perfect, why do you with a false offering make all imperfect? If he be to be worshipped in spirit and in truth, why do you worship a piece of bread? If he be eaten and drunken in faith and truth, if his flesh be not profitable to be among us, why do you say you make his flesh and blood, and say it is profitable for body and soul? Alas! I am a poor woman, but rather than do as you do, I would live no longer. I have said, Sir."

Bishop. I promise you, you are a jolly protestant. I pray you in what school have you been brought up?

Mrs. Prest. I have upon the Sundays visited the sermons, and there have I learned such things as are so fixed in my breast, that death shall not separate them.

B. O foolish woman, who will waste his breath upon thee, or such as thou art? But how chanceth it that thou wentest away from thy husband? If thou wert an honest woman, thou wouldst not have left thy husband and children, and run about the country like a fugitive.

Mrs. P. Sir, I laboured for my living; and as my master Christ counselleth me, when I was persecuted in one city, I fled into another.

B. Who persecuted thee?

Mrs. P. My husband and my children. For when I would have them to leave idolatry, and to worship God in heaven, he would not hear me, but he with his children rebuked me, and troubled me. I fled not for whoredom, nor for theft, but because I would be no partaker with him and his of that foul idol the mass; and wheresoever I was, as oft as I could, upon Sundays and holydays, I made excuses not to go to the popish church.

B. Belike then you are a good housewife, to fly from your husband and the church.

Mrs. P. My housewifery is but small; but God gave me grace to go to the true church.

B. The true church, what dost thou mean?

Mrs. P. Not your popish church, full of idols and abominations, but where two or three are gathered together in the name of God, to that church will I go as long as I live.

B. Belike then you have a church of your own. Well, let this mad woman be put down to prison till we send for her husband.

Mrs. P. No, I have but one husband, who is here already in this city, and in prison with me, from whom I will never depart.

Some persons present endeavouring to convince the bishop she was not in her right senses, she was permitted to depart. The keeper of the bishop's prisons took her into his house, where she either spun worked as a servant, or walked about the city, discoursing upon the sacrament of the altar. Her husband was sent for to take her home, but this she refused while the cause of religion could be served. She was too active to be idle, and her conversation, simple as they affected to think her, excited the attention of several catholic priests and friars. They teazed her with questions, till she answered them angrily, and this excited a laugh at her warmth.

Nay, said she, you have more need to weep than to laugh, and to be sorry that ever you were born, to be the chaplains of that whore of Babylon. I defy him and all his falsehood; and get you away from me, you do but trouble my conscience. You would have me follow your doings; I will first lose my life. I pray you depart.

Why, thou foolish woman, said they, we come to thee for thy profit and soul's health. To which she replied, What profit ariseth by you, that teach nothing but lies for truth? how save you souls, when you preach nothing but lies, and destroy souls?

How provest thou that? said they.

Do you not destroy your souls, when you teach the people to worship idols, stocks and stones, the works of men's hands? and to worship a false God of your own making of a piece of bread, and teach that the pope is God's vicar, and hath power to forgive sins? and that there is a purgatory, when God's Son hath by his passion purged all? and say you make God, and sacrifice him, when Christ's body was a sacrifice once for all? Do you not teach the people to number their sins in your ears, and say they will be damned if they confess not all; when God's word saith, Who can number his sins? Do you not promise them trentals and dirges, and masses for souls, and sell your prayers for money, and make them buy pardons, and trust to such foolish inventions of your imaginations? Do you not altogether act against God? Do you not teach us to pray upon beads, and to pray unto saints, and say they can pray for us? Do you not make holy water and holy bread to fray devils? Do you not do a thousand more abominations? And yet you say, you come for my profit, and to save my soul. No, no, one hath saved me. Farewell, you with your salvation.

During the liberty granted her by the bishop, before-mentioned, she went into St. Peter's church, and there found a skilful Dutchman, who was affixing new noses to certain fine images which had been disfigured in king Edward's time; to whom she said, What a madman art thou, to make them new noses, which within a few days shall all lose their heads? The Dutchman accused her and laid it hard to her change. And she said unto him, Thou are accursed, and so are thy images. He called her a whore. Nay, said she, thy images are whores, and thou art a whore-hunter; for doth not God say, You go a whoring after strange gods, figures of your own making? and thou art one of them. After this she was ordered to be confined, and had no more liberty.

During the time of her imprisonment, many visited her, some sent by the bishop, and some of their own will; among these was one Daniel, a great preacher of the gospel, in the days of king Edward, about Cornwall and Devonshire, but who, through the grievous persecution he had sustained, had fallen off. Earnestly did she exhort him to repent with Peter, and to be more constant in his profession.

Mrs. Walter Rauley and Mr. Wm. and John Kede, persons of great respectability, bore ample testimony of her godly conversation, declaring, that unless God were with her, it were impossible she could have so ably defended the cause of Christ. Indeed, to sum up the character of this poor woman, she united the serpent and the dove, abounding in the highest wisdom joined to the greatest simplicity. She endured imprisonment, threatenings, taunts, and the vilest epithets, but nothing could induce her to swerve; her heart was fixed; she had cast anchor; nor could all the wounds of persecution remove her from the rock on which her hopes of felicity were built.

Such was her memory, that, without learning, she could tell in what chapter any text of scripture was contained: on account of this singular property, one Gregory Basset, a rank papist, said she was deranged, and talked as a parrot, wild without meaning. At length, having tried every manner without effect to make her nominally a catholic, they condemned her. After this, one exhorted her to leave her opinions, and go home to her family, as she was poor and illiterate. "True, (said she) though I am not learned, I am content to be a witness of Christ's death, and I pray you make no longer delay with me; for my heart is fixed, and I will never say otherwise, nor turn to your superstitious doing."

To the disgrace of Mr. Blackston, treasurer of the church, he would often send for this poor martyr from prison, to make sport for him and a woman whom he kept; putting religious questions to her, and turning her answers into ridicule. This done, he sent her back to her wretched dungeon, while he battened upon the good things of this world.

There was perhaps something simply ludicrous in the form of Mrs. Prest, as she was of a very short stature, thick set, and about fifty-four years of age; but her countenance was cheerful and lively, as if prepared for the day of her marriage with the Lamb. To mock at her form was an indirect accusation of her Creator, who framed her after the fashion he liked best, and gave her a mind that far excelled the transient endowments of perishable flesh. When she was offered money, she rejected it, "because (said she) I am going to a city where money bears no mastery, and while I am here God has promised to feed me."

When sentence was read, condemning her to the flames, she lifted up her voice and praised God, adding, "This day have I found that which I have long sought." When they tempted her to recant,--"That will I not, (said she) God forbid that I should lose the life eternal, for this carnal and short life. I will never turn from my heavenly husband to my earthly husband; from the fellowship of angels to mortal children; and if my husband and children be faithful, then am I theirs. God is my father, God is my mother, God is my sister, my brother, my kinsman; God is my friend, most faithful."

Being delivered to the sheriff, she was led by the officer to the place of execution, without the walls of Exeter, called Sothenhey, where again the superstitious priests assaulted her. While they were tying her to the stake, she continued earnestly to exclaim "God be merciful to me, a sinner!" Patiently enduring the devouring conflagration, she was consumed to ashes, and thus ended a life which in unshaken fidelity to the cause of Christ, was not surpassed by that of any preceding martyr.

Richard Sharpe, Thomas Banion, and Thomas Hale.

Mr. Sharpe, weaver, of Bristol, was brought the 9th day of March, 1556, before Mr. Dalby, chancellor of the city of Bristol, and after examination concerning the sacrament of the altar, was persuaded to recant; and on the 29th, he was enjoined to make his recantation in the parish church. But, scarcely had he publicly avowed his backsliding, before he felt in his conscience such a tormenting fiend, that he was unable to work at his occupation; hence, shortly after, one Sunday, he came into the parish church, called Temple, and after high mass, stood up in the choir door, and said with a loud voice, "Neighbours, bear me record that yonder idol (pointing to the altar) is the greatest and most abominable that ever was; and I am sorry that ever I denied my Lord God!" Notwithstanding the constables were ordered to apprehend him, he was suffered to go out of the church; but at night he was apprehended and carried to Newgate. Shortly after, before the chancellor, denying the sacrament of the altar to be the body and blood of Christ, he was condemned to be burned by Mr. Dalby. He was burnt the 7th of May, 1558, and died godly, patiently, and constantly, confessing the protestant articles of faith.

With him suffered Thomas Hale, shoemaker, of Bristol, who was condemned by chancellor Dalby. These martyrs were bound back to back.

Thomas Banion, a weaver, was burnt on August 27th, of the same year, and died for the sake of the evangelical cause of his Saviour.

J. Corneford, of Wortham; C. Browne, of Maidstone; J. Herst, of Ashford; Alice Snoth, and Catharine Knight, an aged woman.

With pleasure we have to record that these five martyrs were the last who suffered in the reign of Mary for the sake of the protestant cause; but the malice of the papists was conspicuous in hastening their martyrdom, which might have been delayed till the event of the queen's illness was decided. It is reported that the archdeacon of Canterbury, judging that the sudden death of the queen would suspend the execution, travelled post from London, to have the satisfaction of adding another page to the black list of papistical sacrifices.

The articles against them were, as usual, the sacramental elements and the idolatry of bending to images. They quoted St. John's words, "Beware of images!" and respecting the real presence, they urged according to St. Paul, "the things that be seen are temporal." When sentence was about to be read against them, and excommunication take place in the regular form, John Corneford, illuminated by the Holy Spirit, awfully turned the latter proceeding against themselves, and in a solemn impressive manner, recriminated their excommunication in the following words: "In the name of our Lord Jesus Christ, the Son of the most mighty God, and by the power of his holy Spirit, and the authority of his holy catholic and apostolic church, we do here give into the hands of Satan to be destroyed, the bodies of all those blasphemers and heretics that maintain any error against his most holy word, or do condemn his most holy truth for heresy, to the maintenance of any false church or foreign religion, so that by this thy just judgment, O most mighty God, against thy adversaries, thy true religion may be known to thy great glory and our comfort and to the edifying of all our nation. Good Lord, so be it. Amen."

This sentence was openly pronounced and registered, and, as if Providence had awarded that it should not be delivered in vain, within six days after, queen Mary died, detested by all good men and accursed of God! Though acquainted with these circumstances, the archdeacon's implacability exceeded that of his great exemplary, Bonner, who, though he had several persons at that time under his fiery grasp, did not urge their deaths hastily, by which delay he certainly afforded them an opportunity of escape. Father Lining and his wife, with several others, thus saved their lives, who, had they been under the barbarous archdeacon, must inevitably have perished. At the queen's decease, many were in bonds: some just taken, some examined, and others condemned. The writs indeed were issued for several burnings, but by the death of the three instigators of protestant murder,--the chancellor, the bishop, and the queen, who fell nearly together, the condemned sheep were liberated, and lived many years to praise God for their happy deliverance.

These five martyrs, when at the stake, earnestly prayed that their blood might be the last shed, nor did they pray in vain. They died gloriously, and perfected the number God had selected to bear witness of the truth in this dreadful reign, whose names are recorded in the Book of Life;--though last, not least among the saints made meet for immortality through the redeeming blood of the Lamb!

Catharine Finlay, alias Knight, was first converted by her son's expounding the Scriptures to her, which wrought in her a perfect work that terminated in martyrdom. Alice Snoth at the stake sent for her grandmother and godfather, and rehearsed to them the articles of her faith, and the commandments of God, thereby convincing the world that she knew her duty. She died calling upon the spectators to bear witness that she was a Christian woman, and suffered joyfully for the testimony of Christ's gospel.

William Fetty scourged to death.

Among the numberless enormities committed by the merciless and unfeeling Bonner, the murder of this innocent and unoffending child may be ranked as the most horrid. His father, John Fetty, of the parish of Clerkenwell, by trade a tailor, and only twenty-four years of age, had made a blessed election; he was fixed secure in eternal hope, and depended on Him who so builds his church that the gates of hell shall not prevail against it. But alas! the very wife of his bosom, whose heart was hardened against the truth, and whose mind was influenced by the teachers of false doctrine, became his accuser. Brokenbery, a creature of the pope, and parson of the parish, received the information of this wedded Delilah, in consequence of which the poor man was apprehended. But here the awful judgment of an ever-righteous God, "who is of purer eyes than to behold iniquity," fell upon this stone-hearted and perfidious woman; for no sooner was the injured husband captured by her wicked contriving, than she also was suddenly seized with madness, and exhibited an awful and awakening instance of God's power to punish the evil doer. This dreadful circumstance had some effect upon the hearts of the ungodly hunters who had eagerly grasped their prey; but, in a relenting moment, they suffered him to remain with his unworthy wife, to return her good for evil, and to comfort two children, who, on his being sent to prison, would have been left without a protector, or have become a burden to the parish. As bad men act from little motives, we may place the indulgence shown him to the latter account.

We have noticed in the former part of our narratives of the martyrs, some whose affection would have led them even to sacrifice their own lives, to preserve their husbands; but here, agreeable to Scripture language, a mother proves, indeed, a monster in nature! Neither conjugal nor maternal affection could impress the heart of this disgraceful woman.

Although our afflicted Christian had experienced so much cruelty and falsehood from the woman who was bound to him by every tie, both human and divine, yet, with a mild and forbearing spirit, he overlooked her misdeeds, during her calamity endeavouring all he could to procure relief for her malady, and soothing her by every possible expression of tenderness: thus she became in a few weeks nearly restored to her senses. But, alas! she returned again to her sin, "as the dog returneth to his vomit." Malice against the saints of the Most High was seated in her heart too firmly to be removed; and as her strength returned, her inclination to work wickedness returned with it. Her heart was hardened by the prince of darkness; and to her may be applied these afflicting and soul-harrowing words, "can the Ethiopian change his skin, or the leopard his spots? then will they do good who are accustomed to do evil." Weighing this text duly with another, "I will have mercy on whom I will have mercy," how shall we presume to refine away the sovereignty of God, by arraigning Jehovah at the bar of human reason, which, in religious matters, is too often opposed by infinite wisdom? "Broad is the way which leadeth to death, and many walk therein. Narrow is the way which leadeth to life, and few there be who find it." The ways of heaven are indeed inscrutable, and it is our bounden duty to walk ever dependent on God, looking up to him with humble confidence, and hope in his goodness, and ever confess his justice; and where we "cannot unravel, there learn to trust." This wretched woman, pursuing the horrid dictates of a heart hardened and depraved, was scarcely confirmed in her recovery, when, stifling the dictates of honour, gratitude, and every natural affection, she again accused her husband, who was once more apprehended, and taken before Sir John Mordant, Knight, and one of queen Mary's commissioners.

Upon examination, his judge finding him fixed to opinions which militated against those nursed by superstition and maintained by cruelty he was sentenced to confinement and torture in Lollard's Tower. "Here (says honest Fox) he was put into the painful stocks, and had a dish of water set by him, with a stone put into it, to what purpose God knoweth, except it were to show that he should look for little other subsistence:

which is credible enough, if we consider their like practices upon divers before mentioned in this history; as, among others, upon Richard Smith, who died through their cruel imprisonment; touching whom, when a godly woman came to Dr. Story to have leave that she might bury him, he asked her if he had any straw or blood in his mouth; but what he means thereby, I leave to the judgment of the wise."

On the first day of the third week of our martyr's sufferings, an object presented itself to his view, which made him indeed feel his tortures with all their force, and to execrate, with bitterness only short of cursing, the author of his misery. To mark and punish the proceedings of his tormentors, remained with the Most High, who noteth even the fall of a sparrow, and in whose sacred word it is written, "Vengeance is mine, and I will repay." This object was his own son, a child of the tender age of eight years. For fifteen days, had its hapless father been suspended by his tormentor by the right arm and left leg, and sometimes by both, shifting his positions for the purpose of giving him strength to bear and to lengthen the date of his sufferings. When the unoffending innocent, desirous of seeing and speaking to its parent, applied to Bonner for permission so to do, the poor child being asked by the bishop's chaplain the purport of his errand, he replied, he wished to see his father. "Who is thy father?" said the chaplain. "John Fetty," returned the boy, at the same time pointing to the place where he was confined. The interrogating miscreant on this said, "Why, thy father is a heretic!" The little champion again rejoined, with energy sufficient to raise admiration in any breast, except that of this unprincipled and unfeeling wretch--this miscreant, eager to execute the behests of a remorseless queen--"My father is no heretic: for you have Balaam's mark."

Irritated by reproach so aptly applied, the indignant and mortified priest concealed his resentment for a moment, and took the undaunted boy into the house, where, having him secure, he presented him to others, whose baseness and cruelty being equal to his own, they stripped him to the skin, and applied their scourges to so violent a degree, that, fainting beneath the stripes inflicted on his tender frame, and covered with the blood that flowed from them, the victim of their ungodly wrath was ready to expire under his heavy and unmerited punishment.

In this bleeding and helpless state was the suffering infant, covered only with his shirt, taken to his father by one of the actors in the horrid tragedy, who, while he exhibited the heart-rending spectacle, made use of the vilest taunts, and exulted in what he had done. The dutiful child, as if recovering strength at the sight of his father, on his knees implored his blessing. "Alas! Will," said the afflicted parent, in trembling amazement, "who hath done this to thee!" The artless innocent related the circumstances that led to the merciless correction which had been so basely inflicted on him; but when he repeated the reproof bestowed on the chaplain, and which was prompted by an undaunted spirit, he was torn from his weeping parent, and conveyed again to the house, where he remained a close prisoner.

Bonner, somewhat fearful that what had been done could not be justified even among the bloodhounds of his own voracious pack, concluded in his dark and wicked mind, to release John Fetty, for a time at least, from the severities he was enduring in the glorious cause of everlasting truth! whose bright rewards are fixed beyond the boundaries of time, within the confines of eternity; where the arrow of the wicked cannot wound, even "where there shall be no more sorrowing for the blessed, who, in the mansion of eternal bliss shall glorify the Lamb forever and ever." He was accordingly by order of Bonner, (how disgraceful to all dignity, to say bishop!) liberated from the painful bonds, and led from Lollard's Tower, to the chamber of that ungodly and infamous butcher, where, says Fox, he found the bishop bathing himself before a great fire; and at his first entering the chamber, Fetty said, "God be here and peace!" "God be here and peace, (said Bonner,) that is neither God speed nor good morrow!" "If ye kick against this peace, (said Fetty,) then this is not the place that I seek for."

A chaplain of the bishop, standing by, turned the poor man about and thinking to abash him, said, in mocking wise, "What have we here--a player!" While Fetty was thus standing in the bishop's chamber, he espied, hanging about the bishop's bed, a pair of great black beads, whereupon he said, "My Lord, I think the hangman is not far off; for the halter (pointing to the beads) is here already!" At which words the bishop was in a marvellous rage. Then he immediately after espied also, standing in the bishop's chamber, in the window, a little crucifix. Then he asked the bishop what it was, and he answered, that it was Christ. "Was he handled as cruelly as he is here pictured?" said Fetty. "Yea, that he was," said the bishop. "And even so cruelly will you handle such as come before you; for you are unto God's people as Caiaphas was unto Christ!" The bishop, being in a great fury, said, "Thou art a vile heretic, and I will burn thee, or else I will spend all I have, unto my gown." "Nay, my Lord, (said Fetty) you were better to give it to some poor body, that he may pray for you." Bonner, notwithstanding his passion, which was raised to the utmost by the calm and pointed remarks of this observing Christian, thought it most prudent to dismiss the father, on account of the nearly murdered child. His coward soul trembled for the consequences which might ensue; fear is inseparable from little minds; and this dastardly pampered priest experienced its effects so far as to induce him to assume the appearance of that he was an utter stranger to, namely, MERCY.

The father, on being dismissed, by the tyrant Bonner, went home with a heavy heart, with his dying child, who did not survive many days the cruelties which had been inflicted on him. How contrary to the will of our great King and Prophet, who mildly taught his followers, was the conduct of this sanguinary and false teacher, this vile apostate from his God to Satan! But the arch-fiend had taken entire possession of his heart, and guided every action of the sinner he had hardened: who, given up to terrible destruction, was running the race of the wicked, marking his footsteps with the blood of the saints, as if eager to arrive at the goal of eternal death.

Deliverance of Dr. Sands.

This eminent prelate, vice-chancellor of Cambridge, at the request of the duke of Northumberland, when he came down to Cambridge in support of Lady Jane Grey's claim to the throne, undertook at a few hours notice, to preach before the duke and the university. The text he took was such as presented itself in opening the Bible, and a more appropriate one he could not have chosen, namely, the three last verses of Joshua. As God gave him the text, so he gave him also such order and utterance, that it excited the most lively emotions in his numerous auditors. The sermon was about to be sent to London to be printed, when news arrived that the duke had returned and queen Mary was proclaimed.

The duke was immediately arrested, and Dr. Sands was compelled by the university to give up his office. He was arrested by the queen's order, and when Mr. Mildmay wondered that so learned a man could wilfully incur danger, and speak against so good a princess as Mary, the doctor replied, "If I would do as Mr. Mildmay has done, I need not fear bonds. He came down armed against queen Mary; before a traitor--now a great friend. I cannot with one mouth blow hot and cold in this manner." A general plunder of Dr. Sands' property ensued, and he was brought to London upon a wretched horse. Various insults he met on the way from the bigoted catholics, and as he passed through Bishopsgate-street, a stone struck him to the ground. He was the first prisoner that entered the tower, in that day, on a religious account; his man was admitted with his Bible, but his shirts and other articles were taken from him.

On Mary's coronation-day, the doors of the dungeon were so laxly guarded, that it was easy to escape. A Mr. Mitchell, like a true friend, came to him, afforded him his own clothes as a disguise, and was willing to abide the consequence of being found in his place. This was a rare friendship: but he refused the offer; saying, "I know no cause why I should be in prison. To do thus, were to make myself guilty. I will expect God's good will, yet do I think myself much obliged to you:" and so Mr. Mitchell departed.

With doctor Sands was imprisoned Mr. Bradford; they were kept close in prison twenty-nine weeks. John Fowler, their keeper, was a perverse papist, yet, by often persuading him, at length he began to favour the gospel, and was so persuaded in the true religion, that on a Sunday, when they had mass in the chapel, Dr. Sands administered the communion to Bradford and to Fowler. Thus Fowler was their son begotten in bonds. To make room for Wyat and his accomplices, Dr. Sands and nine other preachers were sent to the Marshalsea.

The keeper of the Marshalsea appointed to every preacher a man to lead him in the street; he caused them to go on before, and he and Dr. Sands followed conversing together. By this time popery began to be unsavoury. After they had passed the bridge, the keeper said to Dr. Sands, "I perceive the vain people would set you forward to the fire. You are as vain as they, if you, being a young man, will stand in your own conceit, and prefer your own judgment before that of so many worthy prelates, ancient, learned, and grave men as be in this realm. If you do so, you shall find me a severe keeper, and one that utterly dislikes your religion." Dr. Sands answered, "I know my years to be young, and my learning but small; it is enough to know Christ crucified, and he hath learned nothing who seeth not the great blasphemy that is in popery. I will yield unto God, and not unto man; I have read in the Scriptures of many godly and courteous keepers: may God make you one! if not, I trust he will give me strength and patience to bear your hard usage." Then said the keeper, "Are you resolved to stand to your religion?" "Yes," quoth the doctor, "by God's grace!" "Truly," said the keeper, "I love you the better for it; I did but tempt you: what favour I can show you, you shall be assured of; and I shall think myself happy if I might die at the stake with you." He was as good as his word, for he trusted the doctor to walk in the fields alone, where he met with Mr. Bradford, who was also a prisoner in the King's Bench, and had found the same favour from his keeper. At his request, he put Mr. Saunders in along with him, to be his bed-fellow, and the communion was administered to a great number of communicants.

When Wyat with his army came to Southwark, he offered to liberate all the imprisoned protestants, but Dr. Sands and the rest of the preachers refused to accept freedom on such terms.

After Dr. Sands had been nine weeks prisoner in the Marshalsea, by the mediation of Sir Thomas Holcroft, knight marshal, he was set at liberty. Though Mr. Holcroft had the queen's warrant, the bishop commanded him not to set Dr. Sands at liberty, until he had taken sureties of two gentlemen with him, each one bound in L500, that Dr. Sands should not depart out of the realm without license. Mr. Holcroft immediately after met with two gentlemen of the north, friends and cousins to Dr. Sands, who offered to be bound for him.

After dinner, the same day, Sir Thomas Holcroft sent for Dr. Sands to his lodging at Westminster, to communicate to him all he had done. Dr. Sands answered, "I give God thanks, who hath moved your heart to mind me so well, that I think myself most bound unto you. God shall requite you, nor shall I ever be found unthankful. But as you have dealt friendly with me, I will also deal plainly with you. I came a freeman into prison; I will not go forth a bondman. As I cannot benefit my friends, so will I not hurt them. And if I be set at liberty, I will not tarry six days in this realm, if I may get out. If therefore I may not get free forth, send me to the Marshalsea again, and there you shall be sure of me."

This answer Mr. Holcroft much disapproved of; but like a true friend he replied, "Seeing you cannot be altered, I will change my purpose, and yield unto you. Come of it what will, I will set you at liberty; and seeing you have a mind to go over sea, get you gone as quick as you can. One thing I require of you, that, while you are there, you write nothing to me hither, for this may undo me."

Dr. Sands having taken an affectionate farewell of him, and his other friends in bonds, departed. He went by Winchester house, and there took boat, and came to a friend's house in London, called William Banks, and tarried there one night. The next night he went to another friend's house, and there he heard that strict search was making for him, by Gardiner's express order.

Dr. Sands now conveyed himself by night to one Mr. Berty's house, a stranger who was in the Marshalsea prison with him a while; he was a good protestant and dwelt in Mark-lake. There he was six days, and then removed to one of his acquaintances in Cornhill; he caused his man Quinton to provide two geldings for him, resolved on the morrow to ride into Essex, to Mr. Sands, his father-in-law, where his wife was, which after a narrow escape, he effected. He had not been there two hours, before Mr. Sands was told that two of the guards would that night apprehend Dr. Sands.

That night Dr. Sands was guided to an honest farmer's near the sea, where he tarried two days and two nights in a chamber without company. After that he removed to one James Mower's, a ship-master, who dwelt at Milton-Shore, where he waited for a wind to Flanders. While he was there, James Mower brought to him forty or fifty mariners, to whom he gave an exhortation; they liked him so well, that they promised to die rather than he should be apprehended.

The sixth of May, Sunday, the wind served. In taking leave of his hostess, who had been married eight years without having a child, he gave her a fine handkerchief and an old royal of gold, and said, "Be of good comfort; before that one whole year be past, God shall give you a child, a boy." This came to pass, for, that day twelvemonth, wanting one day, God gave her a son.

Scarcely had he arrived at Antwerp, when he learned that king Philip had sent to apprehend him. He next flew to Augsburgh, in Cleveland, where Dr. Sands tarried fourteen days, and then travelled towards Strasburgh, where, after he had lived one year, his wife came to him. He was sick of a flux nine months, and had a child which died of the plague. His amiable wife at length fell into a consumption, and died in his arms. When his wife was dead, he went to Zurich, and there was in Peter Martyr's house for the space of five weeks. As they sat at dinner one day, word was suddenly brought that queen Mary was dead, and Dr. Sands was sent for by his friends at Strasburgh, where he preached. Mr. Grindall and he came over to England, and arrived in London the same day that queen Elizabeth was crowned. This faithful servant of Christ, under queen Elizabeth, rose to the highest distinctions in the church, being successively bishop of Worcester, bishop of London, and archbishop of York.

Queen Mary's treatment of her sister the Princess Elizabeth.

The preservation of the princess Elizabeth may be reckoned a remarkable instance of the watchful eye which Christ had over his church. The bigotry of Mary regarded not the ties of consanguinity, of natural affection, of national succession. Her mind, physically morose was under the dominion of men who possessed not the milk of human kindness, and whose principles were sanctioned and enjoined by the idolatrous tenets of the Romish pontiff. Could they have foreseen the short date of Mary's reign, they would have imbrued their hands in the protestant blood of Elizabeth, and, as a *sine qua non* of the queen's salvation, have compelled her to bequeath the kingdom to some catholic prince. The contest might have been attended with the horrors incidental to a religious civil war, and calamities might have been felt in England similar to those under Henry the Great in France, whom queen Elizabeth assisted in opposing his priest-ridden catholic subjects. As if Providence had the perpetual establishment of the protestant faith in view, the difference of the durations of the two reigns is worthy of notice. Mary might have reigned many years in the course of nature, but the course of grace willed it otherwise. Five years and four months was the time of persecution allotted to this weak, disgraceful reign, while that of Elizabeth reckoned a number of years among the highest of those who have sat on the English throne, almost nine times that of her merciless sister!

Before Mary attained the crown, she treated her with a sisterly kindness, but from that period her conduct was altered, and the most imperious distance substituted. Though Elizabeth had no concern in the rebellion of Sir Thomas Wyat, yet she was apprehended, and treated as a culprit in that commotion. The manner too of her arrest was similar to the mind that dictated it: the three cabinet members, whom she deputed to see the arrest executed, rudely entered the chamber at ten o'clock at night, and, though she was extremely ill, they could scarcely be induced to let her remain till the following morning. Her enfeebled state permitted her to be moved only by short stages in a journey of such length to London; but the princess, though afflicted in person, had a consolation in mind which her sister never could purchase: the people, through whom she passed on her way, pitied her, and put up their prayers for her preservation. Arrived at court, she was made a close prisoner for a fortnight, without knowing who was her accuser, or seeing any one who could console or advise her. The charge however was at length unmasked by Gardiner, who, with nineteen of the council, accused her of abetting Wyat's conspiracy, which she religiously affirmed to be false. Failing in this, they placed against her the transactions of Sir Peter Carew in the west in which they were as unsuccessful as in the former. The queen now signified, it was her pleasure she should be committed to the Tower, a step which overwhelmed the princess with the greatest alarm and uneasiness. In vain she hoped the queen's majesty would not commit her to such a place; but there was no lenity to be expected; her attendants were limited, and a hundred northern soldiers appointed to guard her day and night.

On Palm-Sunday she was conducted to the Tower. When she came to the palace garden, she cast her eyes towards the windows, eagerly anxious to meet those of the queen, but she was disappointed. A strict order was given in London, that every one should go to church, and carry palms, that she might be conveyed without clamour or commiseration to her prison.

At the time of passing under London-bridge the fall of the tide made it very dangerous, and the barge some time stuck fast against the starlings. To mortify her the more, she was landed at Traitors' Stairs. As it rained fast, and she was obliged to step in the water to land, she hesitated; but this excited no complaisance in the lord in waiting. When she set her foot on the steps, she exclaimed, "Here lands as true a subject, being prisoner, as ever landed at these stairs; and before thee, O God, I speak it, having no friend but thee alone!"

A large number of the wardens and servants of the Tower were arranged in order, between whom the princess had to pass. Upon inquiring the use of this parade, she was informed it was customary to do so. "If," said she, "it is on account of me, I beseech you that they may be dismissed." On this the poor men knelt down, and prayed that God would preserve her grace, for which they were the next day turned out of their employments. The tragic scene must have been deeply interesting, to see an amiable and irreproachable princess sent like a lamb to languish in expectation of cruelty and death; against whom there was no other charge than her superiority in Christian virtues and acquired endowments. Her attendants openly wept as she proceeded with a dignified step to the frowning battlements of her destination. "Alas!" said Elizabeth, "what do you mean? I took you to comfort, not to dismay me; for my truth is such, that no one shall have cause to weep for me."

The next step of her enemies was to procure evidence by means which, in the present day, are accounted detestable. Many poor prisoners were racked, to extract, if possible, any matters of accusation which might affect her life, and thereby gratify Gardiner's sanguinary disposition. He himself came to examine her, respecting her removal from her house at Ashbridge to Dunnington castle a long while before. The princess had quite forgotten this trivial circumstance, and lord Arundel, after the investigation, kneeling down, apologized for having troubled her in such a frivolous matter. "You sift me narrowly," replied the princess, "but of this I am assured, that God has appointed a limit to your proceedings; and so God forgive you all."

Her own gentlemen, who ought to have been her purveyors, and served her provision, were compelled to give place to the common soldiers, at the command of the constable of the Tower, who was in every respect a servile tool of Gardiner,--her grace's friends, however, procured an order of council which regulated this petty tyranny more to her satisfaction.

After having been a whole month in close confinement, she sent for the lord Chamberlain and lord Chandois, to whom she represented the ill state of her health from a want of proper air and exercise. Application being made to the council, Elizabeth was with some difficulty admitted to walk in the queen's lodgings, and afterwards in the garden, at which time the prisoners on that side were attended by their keepers, and not suffered to look down upon her. Their jealousy was excited by a child of four years old, who daily brought flowers to the princess. The child was threatened with a whipping, and the father ordered to keep him from the princess' chambers.

On the 5th of May the constable was discharged from his office, and Sir Henry Benifield appointed in his room, accompanied by a hundred ruffian-looking soldiers in blue. This measure created considerable alarm in the mind of the princess, who imagined it was preparatory to her undergoing the same fate as lady Jane Gray, upon the same block. Assured that this project was not in agitation, she entertained an idea that the new keeper of the Tower was commissioned to make away with her privately, as his equivocal character was in conformity with the ferocious inclination of those by whom he was appointed.

A report now obtained that her grace was to be taken away by the new constable and his soldiers, which in the sequel proved to be true. An order of council was made for her removal to the manor of Woodstock, which took place on Trinity Sunday, May 13, under the authority of Sir Henry Benifield and Lord Tame. The ostensible cause of her removal was to make room for other prisoners. Richmond was the first place they stopped at, and here the princess slept, not however without much alarm at first, as her own servants were superseded by the soldiers, who were placed as guards at her chamber door. Upon representation, Lord Tame overruled this indecent stretch of power, and granted her perfect safety while under his custody.

In passing through Windsor, she saw several of her poor dejected servants waiting to see her. "Go to them," said she, to one of her attendants, "and say these words from me, tanquim ovis, that is, like a sheep to the slaughter."

The next night her grace lodged at the house of a Mr. Dormer, in her way to which the people manifested such tokens of loyal affection, that Sir Henry was indignant, and bestowed on them very liberally the names of rebels and traitors. In some villages they rang the bells for joy, imagining the princess's arrival among them was from a very different cause; but this harmless demonstration of gladness was sufficient with the persecuting Benefield to order his soldiers to seize and set these humble persons in the stocks.

The day following, her grace arrived at Lord Tame's house, where she staid all night, and was most nobly entertained. This excited Sir Henry's indignation, and made him caution Lord Tame to look well to his proceedings; but the humanity of Lord Tame was not to be frightened, and he returned a suitable reply. At another time, this official prodigal, to show his consequence and disregard of good manners, went up into a chamber, where was appointed for her grace a chair, two cushions, and a foot carpet, wherein he presumptuously sat and called his man to pull off his boots. As soon as it was known to the ladies and gentlemen, they laughed him to scorn. When supper was done, he called to his lordship, and directed that all gentlemen and ladies should withdraw home, marvelling much that he would permit such a large company, considering the great charge he had committed to him. "Sir Henry," said his lordship, "content yourself; all shall be avoided, your men and all." "Nay, but my soldiers," replied Sir Henry, "shall watch all night." Lord Tame answered, "There is no need." "Well," said he, "need or need not, they shall so do."

The next day her grace took her journey from thence to Woodstock, where she was enclosed, as before in the Tower of London, the soldiers keeping guard within and without the walls, every day, to the number of sixty; and in the night, without the walls were forty during all the time of her imprisonment.

At length she was permitted to walk in the gardens, but under the most severe restrictions, Sir Henry keeping the keys himself, and placing her always under many bolts and locks, whence she was induced to call him her jailer, at which he felt offended, and begged her to substitute the word officer. After much earnest entreaty to the council, she obtained permission to write to the queen; but the jailer, who brought her pen, ink, and paper stood by her while she wrote, and, when she left off, he carried the things away till they were wanted again. He also insisted upon carrying it himself to the queen, but Elizabeth would not suffer him to be the bearer, and it was presented by one of her gentlemen.

After the letter, doctors Owen and Wendy went to the princess, as the state of her health rendered medical assistance necessary. They staid with her five or six days, in which time she grew much better; they then returned to the queen, and spoke flatteringly of the princess' submission and humility, at which the queen seemed moved; but the bishops wanted a concession that she had offended her majesty. Elizabeth spurned this indirect mode of acknowledging herself guilty. "If I have offended," said she, "and am guilty, I crave no mercy but the law, which I am certain I should have had ere this, if any thing could have been proved against me. I wish I were as clear from the peril of my enemies; then should I not be thus bolted and locked up within walls and doors."

Much question arose at this time respecting the propriety of uniting the princess to some foreigner, that she might quit the realm with a suitable portion. One of the council had the brutality to urge the necessity of beheading her, if the king (Philip) meant to keep the realm in peace; but the Spaniards, detesting such a base thought, replied, "God forbid that our king and master should consent to such an infamous proceeding!" Stimulated by a noble principle, the Spaniards from this time repeatedly urged to the king that it would do him the highest honour to liberate the lady Elizabeth, nor was the king impervious to their solicitation. He took her out of prison, and shortly after she was sent for to Hampton court. It may be remarked in this place, that the fallacy of human reasoning is shown in every moment. The barbarian who suggested the policy of beheading Elizabeth little contemplated the change of condition which his speech would bring about. In her journey from Woodstock, Benefield treated her with the same severity as before; removing her on a stormy day, and not suffering her old servant, who had come to Colnbrook, where she slept, to speak to her.

She remained a fortnight strictly guarded and watched, before any one dared to speak with her; at length the vile Gardiner with three more of the council, came with great submission. Elizabeth saluted them, remarked that she had been for a long time kept in solitary confinement, and begged they would intercede with the king and queen to deliver her from prison. Gardiner's visit was to draw from the princess a confession of her guilt; but she was guarded against his subtlety, adding, that, rather than admit she had done wrong, she would lie in prison all the rest of her life. The next day Gardiner came again, and kneeling down, declared that the queen was astonished she should persist in affirming that she was blameless--whence it would be inferred that the queen had unjustly imprisoned her grace. Gardiner farther informed her that the queen had declared that she must tell another tale, before she could be set at liberty. "Then," replied the high-minded Elizabeth, "I had rather be in prison with honesty and truth, than have my liberty, and be suspected by her majesty. What I have said, I will stand to; nor will I ever speak falsehood!" The bishop and his friends then departed, leaving her locked up as before.

Seven days after the queen sent for Elizabeth at ten o'clock at night, two years had elapsed since they had seen each other. It created terror in the mind of the princess, who, at setting out, desired her gentlemen and ladies to pray for her, as her return to them again was uncertain.

Being conducted to the queen's bedchamber, upon entering it the princess knelt down, and having begged of God to preserve her majesty, she humbly assured her that her majesty had not a more loyal subject in the realm, whatever reports might be circulated to the contrary. With a haughty ungraciousness, the imperious queen replied, "You will not confess your offence, but stand stoutly to your truth. I pray God it may so fall out."

"If it do not," said Elizabeth, "I request neither favour nor pardon at your majesty's hands." "Well," said the queen, "you stiffly still persevere in your truth. Besides, you will not confess that you have not been wrongfully punished."

"I must not say so, if it please your majesty, to you."

"Why, then," said the queen, "belike you will to others."

"No, if it please your majesty: I have borne the burden, and must bear it. I humbly beseech your majesty to have a good opinion of me and to think me to be your subject, not only from the beginning hitherto, but for ever, as long as life lasteth." They departed without any heart-felt satisfaction on either side; nor can we think the conduct of Elizabeth displayed that independence and fortitude which accompanies perfect innocence. Elizabeth's admitting that she would not say neither to the queen nor to others, that she had been unjustly punished, was in direct contradiction to what she had told Gardiner, and must have arisen from some motive at this time inexplicable.--King Philip is supposed to have been secretly concealed during the interview, and to have been friendly to the princess.

In seven days from the time of her return to imprisonment, her severe jailer, and his men were discharged, and she was set at liberty, under the constraint of being always attended and watched by some of the queen's council. Four of her gentlemen were sent to the Tower without any other charge against them than being zealous servants of their mistress. This event was soon after followed by the happy news of Gardiner's death, for which all good and merciful men glorified God, inasmuch as it had taken the chief tiger from the den, and rendered the life of the protestant successor of Mary more secure.

This miscreant, while the princess was in the Tower, sent a secret writ, signed by a few of the council, for her private execution, and, had Mr. Bridges, lieutenant of the Tower, been as little scrupulous of dark assassination as this pious prelate was, she must have perished. The warrant not having the queen's signature, Mr. Bridges hastened to her majesty, to give her information of it, and to know her mind. This was a plot of Winchester's, who, to convict her of treasonable practices, caused several prisoners to be racked; particularly Mr. Edmund Tremaine and Smithwicke were offered considerable bribes to accuse the guiltless princess.

Her life was several times in danger. While at Woodstock, fire was apparently put between the boards and ceiling under which she lay. It was also reported strongly, that one Paul Penny, the keeper of Woodstock, a notorious ruffian was appointed to assassinate her, but, however this might be, God counteracted in this point the nefarious designs of the enemies of the reformation. James Basset was another appointed to perform the same deed: he was a peculiar favourite of Gardiner, and had come within a mile of Woodstock, intending to speak with Benefield on the subject. The goodness of God however so ordered it, that while Basset was travelling to Woodstock, Benefield, by an order of council, was going to London; in consequence of which, he left a positive order with his brother, that no man should be admitted to the princess during his absence, not even with a note from the queen; his brother met the murderer, but the latter's intention was frustrated, as no admission could be obtained.

When Elizabeth quitted Woodstock, she left the following lines written with her diamond on the window:--

> Much suspected by me,
> Nothing proved can be. Quoth Elizabeth, prisoner.

With the life of Winchester ceased the extreme danger of the princess, as many of her other secret enemies soon after followed him, and, last of all, her cruel sister, who outlived Gardiner but three years. The death of Mary was ascribed to several causes. The council endeavoured to console her in her last moments, imagining it was the absence of her husband that lay heavy at her heart, but though his treatment had some weight, the loss of Calais, the last fortress possessed by the English in France, was the true source of her sorrow. "Open my heart," said Mary, "when I am dead, and you shall find Calais written there." Religion caused her no alarm; the priests had lulled to rest every misgiving of conscience, which might have obtruded, on account of the accusing spirits of the murdered martyrs. Not the blood she had spilled, but the loss of a town, excited her emotions in dying, and this last stroke seemed to be awarded, that her fanatical persecution might be paralleled by her political imbecility. We earnestly pray that the annals of no country, catholic or pagan, may ever be stained with such a repetition of human sacrifices to papal power, and that the detestation in which the character of Mary is holden, may be a beacon to succeeding monarchs to avoid the rocks of fanaticism!

God's Punishments upon some of the Persecutors of his People in Mary's Reign.

After that arch-persecutor, Gardiner, was dead, others followed, of whom Dr. Morgan, bishop of St. David's, who succeeded bishop Farrar, is to be noticed. Not long after he was installed in his bishopric, he was stricken by the visitation of God; his food passed through the throat, but rose again with great violence. In this manner, almost literally starved to death, he terminated his existence.

Bishop Thornton, suffragan of Dover, was an indefatigable persecutor of the true church. One day after he had exercised his cruel tyranny upon a number of pious persons at Canterbury, he came from the chapter-house to Borne, where as he stood on a Sunday looking at his men playing at bowls, he fell down in a fit of the palsy, and did not long survive.

After the latter succeeded another bishop or suffragan, ordained by Gardiner, who not long after he had been raised to the see of Dover, fell down a pair of stairs in the cardinal's chamber at Greenwich, and broke his neck. He had just received the cardinal's blessing--he could receive nothing worse.

John Cooper, of Watsam, Suffolk, suffered by perjury; he was from private pique persecuted by one Fenning, who suborned two others to swear that they heard Cooper say, "If God did not take away queen Mary, the devil would." Cooper denied all such words, but Cooper was a protestant and a heretic, and therefore he was hung, drawn and quartered, his property confiscated, and his wife and nine children reduced to beggary. The following harvest, however, Grimwood of Hitcham, one of the witnesses before mentioned, was visited for his villany: while at work, stacking up corn, his bowels suddenly burst out, and before relief could be obtained he died. Thus was deliberate perjury rewarded by sudden death!

In the case of the martyr Mr. Bradford, the severity of Mr. Sheriff Woodroffe has been noticed--he rejoiced at the death of the saints, and at Mr. Rogers' execution, he broke the carman's head, because he stopped the cart to let the martyr's children take a last farewell of him. Scarcely had Mr. Woodroffe's sheriffalty expired a week, when he was struck with a paralytic affection, and languished a few days in the most pitiable and helpless condition, presenting a striking contrast to his former activity in the cause of blood.

Ralph Lardyn, who betrayed the martyr George Eagles, is believed to have been afterward arraigned and hanged in consequence of accusing himself. At the bar, he denounced himself in these words, "This has most justly fallen upon me, for betraying the innocent blood of that just and good man George Eagles, who was here condemned in the time of Queen Mary by my procurement, when I sold his blood for a little money."

As James Abbes was going to execution, and exhorting the pitying bystanders to adhere steadfastly to the truth, and like him to seal the cause of Christ with their blood, a servant of the sheriff's interrupted him, and blasphemously called his religion heresy, and the good man a lunatic. Scarcely however had the flames reached the martyr, before the fearful stroke of God fell upon this hardened wretch, in the presence of him he had so cruelly ridiculed. The man was suddenly seized with lunacy, cast off his clothes and shoes before the people, (as Abbes had done just before, to distribute among some poor persons,) at the same time exclaiming, "Thus did James Abbes, the true servant of God, who is saved but I am damned." Repeating this often, the sheriff had him secured, and made him put his clothes on, but no sooner was he alone, than he tore them off, and exclaimed as before. Being tied in a cart, he was conveyed to his master's house, and in about half a year he died; just before which a priest came to attend him, with the crucifix, &c. but the wretched man bade him take away such trumpery, and said that he and other priests had been the cause of his damnation, but that Abbes was saved.

One Clark, an avowed enemy of the protestants in king Edward's reign, hung himself in the Tower of London.

Froling, a priest of much celebrity, fell down in the street and died on the spot.

Dale, an indefatigable informer, was consumed by vermin, and died a miserable spectacle.

Alexander, the severe keeper of Newgate, died miserably, swelling to a prodigious size, and became so inwardly putrid, that none could come near him. This cruel minister of the law would go to Bonner, Story, and others, requesting them to rid his prison, he was so much pestered with heretics! The son of this keeper, in three years after his father's death, dissipated his great property, and died suddenly in Newgate market. "The sins of the father," says the decalogue, "shall be visited on the children." John Peter, son-in-law of Alexander, a horrid blasphemer and persecutor, died wretchedly. When he affirmed any thing, he would say, "If it be not true, I pray I may rot ere I die." This awful state visited him in all its loathsomeness.

Sir Ralph Ellerker was eagerly desirous to see the heart taken out of Adam Damlip, who was wrongfully put to death. Shortly after Sir Ralph was slain by the French, who mangled him dreadfully, cut off his limbs, and tore his heart out.

When Gardiner heard of the miserable end of Judge Hales, he called the profession of the gospel a doctrine of desperation; but he forgot that the judge's despondency arose after he had consented to the papistry. But with more reason may this be said of the catholic tenets, if we consider the miserable end of Dr. Pendleton, Gardiner, and most of the leading persecutors. Gardiner, upon his death bed, was reminded by a bishop of Peter denying his master. "Ah," said Gardiner, "I have denied with Peter, but never repented with Peter."

After the accession of Elizabeth, most of the Catholic prelates were imprisoned in the Tower or the fleet; Bonner was put into the Marshalsea.

Of the revilers of God's word, we detail, among many others, the following occurrence. One William Maldon, living at Greenwich in servitude, was instructing himself profitably in reading an English primer one winter's evening. A serving man, named John Powell, sat by, and ridiculed all that Maldon said, who cautioned him not to make a jest of the word of God. Powell nevertheless continued, till Maldon came to certain English Prayers, and read aloud, Lord, have mercy upon us,

Christ have mercy upon us, &c. Suddenly the reviler started, and exclaimed, Lord, have mercy upon us! He was struck with the utmost terror of mind, said the evil spirit could not abide that Christ should have any mercy upon him, and sunk into madness. He was remitted to Bedlam, and became an awful warning that God will not always be insulted with impunity.

Henry Smith, a student in the law, had a pious protestant father, of Camden, in Gloucestershire, by whom he was virtuously educated. While studying law in the middle temple, he was induced to profess catholicism, and, going to Louvain, in France, he returned with pardons, crucifixes, and a great freight of popish toys. Not content with these things, he openly reviled the gospel religion he had been brought up in; but conscience one night reproached him so dreadfully, that in a fit of despair he hung himself in his garters. He was buried in a lane, without the Christian service being read over him.

Dr. Story, whose name has been so often mentioned in the preceding pages, was reserved to be cut off by public execution, a practice in which he had taken great delight when in power. He is supposed to have had a hand in most of the conflagrations in Mary's time, and was even ingenious in his invention of new modes of inflicting torture. When Elizabeth came to the throne, he was committed to prison, but unaccountably effected his escape to the continent, to carry fire and sword there among the protestant brethren. From the duke of Alva, at Antwerp, he received a special commission to search all ships for contraband goods, and particularly for English heretical books.

Dr. Story gloried in a commission that was ordered by Providence to be his ruin, and to preserve the faithful from his sanguinary cruelty. It was contrived that one Parker, a merchant, should sail to Antwerp and information should be given to Dr. Story that he had a quantity of heretical books on board. The latter no sooner heard this, than he hastened to the vessel, sought every where above, and then went under the hatches, which were fastened down upon him. A prosperous gale brought the ship to England, and this traitorous, persecuting rebel was committed to prison, where he remained a considerable time, obstinately objecting to recant his anti-christian spirit, or admit of queen Elizabeth's supremacy. He alleged, though by birth and education an Englishman, that he was a sworn subject of the king of Spain, in whose service the famous duke of Alva was. The doctor being condemned, was laid upon a hurdle, and drawn from the Tower to Tyburn, where after being suspended about half an hour, he was cut down, stripped, and the executioner displayed the heart of a traitor. Thus ended the existence of this Nimrod of England.

CHAPTER XIV.

THE SPANISH ARMADA.

Philip, king of Spain, husband to the deceased queen Mary of England, was no less an enemy than that princess to the protestants. He had always disliked the English, and after her death, determined, if possible, to crown that infamous cruelty which had disgraced the whole progress of her reign, by making a conquest of the island, and putting every protestant to death.

The great warlike preparations made by this monarch, though the purpose was unknown, gave a universal alarm to the English nation; as, though he had not declared that intention, yet it appeared evident that he was taking measures to seize the crown of England. Pope Sixtus V. not less ambitious than himself, and equally desirous of persecuting the protestants, urged him to the enterprise. He excommunicated the queen, and published a crusade against her, with the usual indulgences. All the ports of Spain resounded with preparations for this alarming expedition; and the Spaniards seemed to threaten the English with a total annihilation.

Three whole years had been spent by Philip in making the necessary preparations for this mighty undertaking; and his fleet, which on account of its prodigious strength, was called the "Invincible Armada," was now completed. A consecrated banner was procured from the pope, and the gold of Peru was lavished on the occasion.

The duke of Parma, by command of the Spaniards, built ships in Flanders, and a great company of small broad vessels, each one able to transport thirty horses, with bridges fitted for them severally; and hired mariners from the east part of Germany, and provided long pieces of wood sharpened at the end, and covered with iron, with hooks on one side; and 20,000 vessels, with a huge number of fagots; and placed an army ready in Flanders, of 103 companies of foot and 4000 horsemen. Among these 700

English vagabonds, who were held of all others in most contempt. Neither was Stanley respected or obeyed who was set over the English; nor Westmoreland, nor any other who offered their help, but for their unfaithfulness to their own country were shut out from all consultations, and as men unanimously rejected with detestation. And because Pope Sixtus the Fifth in such a case would not be wanting, he sent Cardinal Allen into Flanders, and renewed the bulls declaratory of Pope Pius the Fifth, and Gregory the Thirteenth.

He excommunicated and deposed queen Elizabeth, absolved her subjects from all allegiance, and, as if it had been against the Turks or infidels, he set forth in print a conceit, wherein he bestowed plenary indulgences, out of the treasure of the church, besides a million of gold, or ten hundred thousand ducats, to be distributed (the one half in hand, the rest when either England, or some famous haven therein, should be won) upon all them that would join their help against England. By which means the Marquis of Bergau, of the house of Austria, the duke of Pastrana, Amadis, duke of Savoy, Vespasian, Gonzaga, John Medicis, and divers other noblemen, were drawn into these wars.

Queen Elizabeth, that she might not be surprised unawares, prepared as great a navy as she could, and with singular care and providence, made all things ready necessary for war. And she herself, who was ever most judicious in discerning of men's wits and aptness, and most happy in making choice, when she made it out of her own judgment, and not at the discretion of others, designed the best and most serviceable to each several employment. Over the whole navy she appointed the Lord Admiral Charles Howard, in whom she reposed much trust; and sent him to the west part of England, where Captain Drake, whom she made vice-admiral, joined with him. She commanded Henry Seimor, the second son to the duke of Somerset, to watch upon the Belgic shore, with forty English and Dutch ships, that the duke of Parma might not come out with his forces; although some were of opinion, that the enemy was to be expected and set upon by land forces, accordingly as it was upon deliberation resolved, in the time of Henry the Eighth, when the French brought a great navy on the English shore.

For the land fight, there were placed on the south shore twenty thousand; and two armies beside were mustered of the choicest men for war. The one of these, which consisted of 1000 horse and twenty two thousand foot was commanded by the earl of Leicester, and encamped at Tilbury, on the side of the Thames. For the enemy was resolved first to set upon London. The other army was commanded by the Lord Hunsdon, consisting of thirty-four thousand foot, and two thousand horse, to guard the queen.

The Lord Gray, Sir Francis Knowles, Sir John Norris, Sir Richard Bingham, Sir Roger Williams, men famously known for military experience, were chosen to confer of the land-fight. These commanders thought fit that all those places should be fortified, with men and ammunition, which were commodious to land in, either out of Spain or out of Flanders, as Milford-Haven, Falmouth, Plymouth, Portland, the Isle of Wight, Portsmouth, the open side of Kent, called the Downs, the Thames' mouth, Harwich, Yarmouth, Hull, &c. That trained soldiers through all the maratime provinces should meet upon warning given, to defend the places; that they should by their best means, hinder the enemy from landing; and if they did happen to land, then they were to destroy the fruits of the country all about, and spoil every thing that might be of any use to the enemy, that so they might find no more victuals than what they brought with them. And that, by continued alarms, the enemy should find no rest day or night. But they should not try any battle until divers captains were met together with their companies. That one captain might be named in every shire which might command.

Two years before, the duke of Parma, considering how hard a matter it was to end the Belgic war, so long as it was continually nourished and supported with aid from the queen, he moved for a treaty of peace, by the means of Sir James Croft, one of the privy council, a man desirous of peace, and Andrew Loe, a Dutchman, and professed that the Spaniard had delegated authority to him for this purpose. But the queen fearing that the friendship between her and the confederate princes might be dissolved, and that so they might secretly be drawn to the Spaniard, she deferred that treaty for some time. But now, that the wars on both sides prepared might be turned away, she was content to treat for peace; but so as still holding the weapons in her hand.

For this purpose, in February, delegates were sent into Flanders, the earl of Derby, the lord Cobham, Sir James Croft, Dr. Dale, and Dr. Rogers. These were received with all humanity on the duke's behalf, and a place appointed for their treating, that they might see the authority delegated to him by the Spanish king. He appointed the place near to Ostend, not in Ostend, which at that time was held by the English against the Spanish king. His authority delegated, he promised them to show, when they were once met together. He wished them to make good speed in the business, lest somewhat might fall out in the mean time, which might trouble the motions of peace. Richardotus, spoke somewhat more plainly, That he knew not what in this interim should be done against England.

Not long after, Dr. Rogers was sent to the prince, by an express commandment from the queen, to know the truth, whether the Spaniards had resolved to invade England, which he and Richardotus seemed to signify. He affirmed, that he did not so much as think of the invasion of England, when he wished that the business might proceed with speed; and was in a manner offended with Richardotus, who denied that such words fell from him.

The 12th of April, the count Aremberg, Champigny, Richardotus, Doctor Maesius, and Garnier, delegated from the prince of Parma, met with the English, and yielded to them the honour both in walking and sitting.

This conference, however, came to nothing; undertaken by, the queen, as the wiser then thought, to avert the Spanish fleet; continued by the Spaniard that he might oppress the queen, being as he supposed unprovided, and not expecting the danger. So both of them tried to use time to their best advantages.

At length the Spanish fleet, well furnished with men, ammunition, engines, and all warlike preparations, the best, indeed, that ever was seen upon the ocean, called by the arrogant title, The Invincible Armada, consisted of 130 ships, wherein there were in all, 19,290. Mariners, 8,350. Chained rowers, 11,080. Great ordnance, 11,630. The chief commander was Perezius Guzmannus, duke of Medina Sidonia; and under him Joannes Martinus Ricaldus, a man of great experience in sea affairs.

The 30th of May they loosed out of the river Tagus, and bending their course to the Groin, in Gallicia, they were beaten and scattered by a tempest, three galleys, by the help of David Gwin, an English servant, and by the perfidiousness of the Turks which rowed, were carried away into France. The fleet, with much ado, after some days came to the Groin, and other harbours near adjoining. The report was, that the fleet was so shaken by this tempest, that the queen was persuaded, that she was not to expect that fleet this year. And Sir Francis Walsingham, sec'y, wrote to the lord admiral, that he might send back four of the greatest ships, as if the war had been ended. But the lord admiral did not easily give credit to that report; yet with a gentle answer entreated him to believe nothing hastily in so important a matter: as also that he might be permitted to keep those ships with him which he had, though it were upon his own charges. And getting a favourable wind, made sail towards Spain, to surprise the enemy's damaged ships in their harbours. When he was close in with the coast of Spain, the wind shifting, and he being charged to defend the English shore, fearing that the enemy might unseen, by the same wind, sail for England, he returned unto Plymouth.

Now with the same wind, the 12th of July, the duke of Medina with his fleet departed from the Groin. And after a few days he sent Rodericus Telius into Flanders, to advertise the duke of Parma, giving him warning that the fleet was approaching, and therefore he was to make himself ready. For Medina's commission was to join himself with the ships and soldiers of Parma; and under the protection of his fleet to bring them into England, and to land his forces upon the Thames side.

The sixteenth, day, (saith the relator,) there was a great calm, and a thick cloud was upon the sea till noon; then the north wind blowing roughly; and again the west wind till midnight, and after that the east; the Spanish navy was scattered, and hardly gathered together until they came within sight of England the nineteenth day of July. Upon which day, the lord admiral was certified by Fleming, (who had been a pirate) that the Spanish fleet was entered into the English sea, which the mariners call the Channel, and was descried near to the Lizard. The lord admiral brought forth the English fleet into the sea, but not without great difficulty, by the skill, labour, and alacrity of the soldiers and mariners, every one labouring; yea, the lord admiral himself putting his hand to this work.

The next day the English fleet viewed the Spanish fleet coming along like the towering castles in height, her front crooked like the fashion of the moon, the wings of the fleet were extended one from the other about seven miles, or as some say eight miles asunder, sailing with the labour of the winds, the ocean as it were groaning under it, their sail was but slow, and yet at full sail before the wind. The English were willing to let them hold on their course, and when they were passed by, got behind them, and so got to windward of them.

Upon the 21st of July, the lord admiral of England sent a cutter before, called the Defiance, to denounce the battle by firing off pieces. And being himself in the Royal-Arch, (the English admiral ship) he began the engagement with a ship which he took to be the Spanish admiral, but which was the ship of Alfonsus Leva. Upon that he expended much shot. Presently Drake, Hawkins, and Forbisher, came in upon the rear of the Spaniards which Ricaldus commanded.--Upon these they thundered. Ricaldus endeavoured, as much as in him lay, to keep his men to their quarters, but all in vain, until his ship, much beaten and battered with many shot, hardly recovered the fleet. Then the duke of Medina gathered together his scattered fleet, and setting more sail, held on his course. Indeed they could do no other, for the English had gotten the advantage of the wind, and their ships being much easier managed, and ready with incredible celerity to come upon the enemy with a full course, and then to tack and retack and be on every side at their pleasure. After a long fight, and each of them had taken a trial of their courage, the lord admiral thought proper to continue the fight no longer, because there were forty ships more, which were then absent, and at that very time were coming out of Plymouth Sound.

The night following, the St. Catharine, a Spanish ship, being sadly torn in the battle, was taken into the midst of the fleet to be repaired. Here a great Cantabrian ship, of Oquenda, wherein was the treasurer of the camp, by force of gunpowder took fire, yet it was quenched in time by the ships that came to help her. Of those which came to assist the fired ship, one was a galleon, commanded by one Petrus Waldez; the fore-yard of the galleon was caught in the rigging of another ship, and carried away. This was taken by Drake, who sent Waldez to Dartmouth, and a great sum of money, viz. 55,000 ducats, which he distributed among the soldiers. This Waldez coming into Drake's presence, kissed his hand, and told him they had all resolved to die, if they had not been so happy as to fall into his hands whom they knew to be noble. That night he was appointed to set forth a light, but neglected it; and some German merchant ships coming by that night, he, thinking them to be enemies, followed them so far, that the English fleet lay to all night, because they could see no light set forth. Neither did he nor the rest of the fleet find the admiral until the next evening. The admiral all the night proceeding with the Bear and the Mary Rose, carefully followed the Spaniards with watchfulness. The duke was busied in ordering his squadron. Alfonsus Leva was commanded to join the first and last divisions. Every ship had its proper station assigned, according to that prescribed form which was appointed in Spain; it was present death to any one who forsook his station. This done, he sent Gliclius and Anceani to Parma, which might declare to them in what situation they were, and left that Cantabrian ship, of Oquenda, to the wind and sea, having taken out the money and mariners, and put them on board of other ships. Yet it seemed that he had not care for all; for that ship the same day, with fifty mariners and soldiers wounded and half-burned, fell into the hands of the English, and was carried to Weymouth.

The 23d of the same month, the Spaniards having a favourable north wind, tacked towards the English; but they being more expert in the management of their ships, tacked likewise, and kept the advantage they had gained, keeping the Spaniards to leeward, till at last the fight became general on both sides. They fought awhile confusedly with variable success: whilst on the one side the English with great courage delivered the London ships which were enclosed about by the Spaniards; and on the other side, the Spaniards by valour freed Ricaldus from the extreme danger he was in; great and many were the explosions, which, by the continued firing of great guns, were heard this day. But the loss (by the good providence of God,) fell upon the Spaniards, their ships being so high, that the shot went over our English ships, and the English, having such a fair mark at their large ships, never shot in vain. During this engagement, Cock, an Englishman, being surrounded by the Spanish ships, could not be recovered, but perished; however, with great honour he revenged himself. Thus a long time the English ships with great agility were sometimes upon the Spaniards, giving them the fire of one side, and then of the other, and presently were off again, and still kept the sea, to make themselves ready to come in again. Whereas the Spanish ships, being of great burden, were troubled and hindered, and stood to be the marks for the English shot. For all that the English admiral would not permit his people to board their ships, because they had such a number of soldiers on board, which he had not; their ships were many in number, and greater, and higher, that if they had come to grapple, as many would have had it, the English being much lower than the Spanish ships, must needs have had the worst of them that fought from the higher ships. And if the English had been overcome, the loss would have been greater than the victory could have been; for our being overcome would have put the kingdom in hazard.

The 24th day of July they gave over fighting on both sides. The admiral sent some small barks to the English shore for a supply of provisions, and divided his whole fleet into four squadrons; the first whereof he took under his own command, the next was commanded by Drake, the third by Hawkins, and the last by Forbisher. And he appointed out of every squadron certain little ships, which, on divers sides might set upon the Spaniards in the night, but a sudden calm took them so that expedition was without effect.

The 25th, the St. Anne, a galleon of Portugal, not being able to keep up with the rest, was attacked by some small English ships. To whose aid came in Leva, and Didacus Telles Enriques, with three galeasses; which the admiral, and the Lord Thomas Howard, espying, made all the sail they could against the galeasses, but the calm continuing, they were obliged to be towed along with their boats; as soon as they reached the galeasses, they began to play away so fiercely with their great guns, that with much danger, and great loss, they hardly recovered their galleon. The Spaniards reported that the Spanish admiral was that day in the rear of their fleet, which, being come nearer to the English ships than before, got terribly shattered with their great guns, many men were killed aboard, and her masts laid over the side. The Spanish admiral, after this, in company with Ricaldus, and others, attacked the English admiral, who, having the advantage of the wind, suddenly tacked and escaped. The Spaniards holding on their course again, sent to the duke of Parma, that with all possible speed he should join his ships with the king's fleet. These things the English knew not, who write that they had carried away the lantern from one of the Spanish ships, the stern from another, and sore mauled the third very much disabling her. The Non-Parigly, and the Mary Rose, fought awhile with the Spaniards, and the Triumph being in danger, other ships came in good time to help her.

The next day the lord admiral knighted the Lord Thomas Howard, the Lord Sheffield, Roger Townsend, John Hawkins, and Martin Forbisher, for their valour in the last engagement. After this, they agreed not to attack the enemy until they came into the straits of Calais, where Henry Seimor, and William Winter, waited for their coming. Thus with a fair gale the Spanish fleet went forward, and the English followed. This great Spanish Armada was so far from being esteemed invincible in the opinion of the English, that many young men and gentlemen, in hope to be partakers of a famous victory against the Spaniards, provided ships at their own expense, and joined themselves to the English fleet; among whom were the earls of Essex, Northumberland, and Cumberland, Thomas and Robert Cecil, Henry Brooks, William Hatton, Robert Cary, Ambrose Willoughby, Thomas Gerard, Arthur George, and other gentlemen of good note and quality.

The 27th day, at even, the Spaniards cast anchor near to Calais, being admonished by their skilful seamen, that if they went any further they might be in danger, through the force of the tide, to be driven into the North Ocean. Near to them lay the English admiral with his fleet, within a great gun's shot. The admiral, Seimor and Winter, now join their ships; so that now there were a hundred and forty ships in the English fleet, able, and well furnished for fighting, for sailing, and every thing else which was requisite; and yet there were but fifteen of these which bore the heat of the battle, and repulsed the enemy. The Spaniard, as often as he had done before, so now with great earnestness sent to the duke of Parma, to send forty fly-boats, without which they could not fight with the English, because of the greatness and slowness of their ships, and the agility of the English, entreating him by all means now to come to sea with his army, which army was now to be protected as it were, under the wings of the Spanish Armada, until they should land in England.

But the duke was unprovided, and could not come out in an instant. The broad ships with flat bottoms being then full of chinks must be mended. Victuals wanted, and must be provided. The mariners being long kept against their wills, began to shrink away. The ports of Dunkirk and Newport, by which he must bring his army to the sea, were now so beset with the strong ships of Holland and Zealand, which were furnished with great and small munition, that he was not able to come to sea, unless he would come upon his own apparent destruction, and cast himself and his men wilfully into a headlong danger. Yet he omitted nothing that might be done, being a man eager and industrious, and inflamed with a desire of overcoming England.

But queen Elizabeth's providence and care prevented both the diligence of this man, and the credulous hope of the Spaniard; for by her command the next day the admiral took eight of their worst ships, charging the ordnance therein up to the mouth with small shot, nails, and stones, and dressed them with wild fire, pitch, and rosin, and filling them full of brimstone, and some other matter fit for fire, and these being set on fire by the management of Young and Prowse, were secretly in the night, by the help of the wind, set full upon the Spanish fleet, which, on Sunday, the seventh of August, they sent in among them as they lay at anchor.

When the Spanish saw them come near, the flames giving light all over the sea, they supposing those ships, besides the danger of fire, to have been also furnished with deadly engines, to make horrible destruction among them; lifting up a most hideous cry, some pull up anchors, some for haste cut their cables, they set up their sails, they apply their oars, and stricken with extreme terror, in great haste they fled most confusedly. Among them the Pretorian Galleass floating upon the seas, her rudder being broken, in great danger and fear drew towards Calais, and striking in the sand, was taken by Amias Preston, Thomas Gerard, and Harvey; Hugh Moncada the governor was slain, the soldiers and mariners were either killed or drowned; in her there was found great store of gold, which fell to be the prey of the English. The ship and ordnance went to the governor of Calais.

The Spaniards report, that the duke, when he saw the fire ships coming, commanded all the fleet to heave up their anchors, but so as the danger being past, every ship might return again to his own station; and he himself returned, giving a sign to the rest by shooting off a gun; which was heard but by a few, for they were far off scattered some into the open ocean, some through fear were driven upon the shallows of the coast of Flanders.

Over against Gravelling the Spanish fleet began to gather themselves together. But upon them came Drake and Fenner, and battered them with great ordnance: to these Fenton, Southwel, Beeston, Cross, Riman, and presently after the lord admiral, and Sheffield, came in. The Duke Medina, Leva, Oquenda, Ricaldus, and others, with much ado in getting themselves out of the shallows, sustained the English ships as well as they might, until most of their ships were pierced and torn; the galleon St. Matthew, governed by Diego Pimentellas, coming to aid Francis Toleton, being in the St. Philip, was pierced and shaken with the reiterated shots of Seimor and Winter, and driven to Ostend, and was at last taken by the Flushingers. The St. Philip came to the like end; so did the galleon of Biscay, and divers others.

The last day of this month, the Spanish fleet striving to recover the straits again, were driven towards Zealand. The English left off pursuing them, as the Spaniards thought, because they saw them in a manner cast away; for they could not avoid the shallows of Zealand. But the wind turning, they got them out of the shallows, and then began to consult what were best for them to do. By common consent they resolved to return into Spain by the Northern Seas, for they wanted many necessaries, especially shot; their ships were torn, and they had no hope that the duke of Parma could bring forth his forces. And so they took the sea, and followed the course toward the north. The English navy followed, and sometimes the Spanish turned upon the English, insomuch that it was thought by many that they would turn back again.

Queen Elizabeth caused an army to encamp at Tilbury. After the army had come thither, her majesty went in person to visit the camp, which then lay between the city of London and the sea, under the charge of the earl of Leicester, where placing herself between the enemy and her city, she viewed her army, passing through it divers times, and lodging in the borders of it, returned again and dined in the army. Afterwards when they were all reduced into battle, prepared as it were for fight, she rode round about with a leader's staff in her hand, only accompanied with the general, and three or four others attending upon her.[A]

I could enlarge the description hereof with many more particulars of mine own observation, (says the author,) for I wandered, as many others did, from place to place, all the day, and never heard a word spoke of her, but in praising her for her stately person and princely behaviour, in praying for her long life, and earnestly desiring to venture their lives for her safety. In her presence they sung psalms of praise to Almighty God, for which she greatly commended them, and devoutly praised

God with them. This that I write, you may be sure I do not with any comfort, but to give you these manifest arguments that neither this queen did discontent her people, nor her people show any discontent in any thing they were commanded to do for her service, as heretofore hath been imagined.

This account was related by a popish spy, in a letter written here in England to Mendea. The copy of which letter was found upon Richard Leigh, a seminary priest in French and English: which priest was executed for high treason while the Spanish Armada was at sea.

The same day whereon the last fight was, the duke of Parma, after his vows offered to the lady of Halla, came somewhat late to Dunkirk, and was received with very opprobrious language by the Spaniards, as if in favour of queen Elizabeth he had slipped the fairest opportunity that could be to do the service. He, to make some satisfaction, punished the purveyors that had not made provision of beer, bread, &c. which was not yet ready nor embarked, secretly smiling at the insolence of the Spaniards, when he heard them bragging that what way soever they came upon England, they would have an undoubted victory; that the English were not able to endure the sight of them. The English admiral appointed Seimor and the Hollanders to watch upon the coast of Flanders that the duke of Parma should not come out; whilst he himself close followed the Spaniards until they were past Edinburgh Frith.

The Spaniards, seeing all hopes fail, fled amain; and so this great navy, being three years preparing with great expense, was within one month overthrown, and, after many were killed, being chased again, was driven about all England, by Scotland, the Oreades, and Ireland, tossed and damaged with tempests, much diminished, and went home without glory. There were not a hundred men of the English lost, and but one ship. Whereupon money was coined with a navy fleeing away in full sail, with this inscription, **Venit, Vidit, Fugit**. Others were coined with the ships on fire, the navy confounded, inscribed, in honour of the queen, **Dux Faemina Facti**. As they fled, it is certain that many of their ships were cast away upon the shores of Scotland and Ireland. About seven hundred soldiers and mariners were cast away upon the Scottish shore, who, at the duke of Parma's intercession with the Scotch king, the queen of England consenting, were after a year sent into Flanders. But they that were cast upon the Irish shore came to more miserable fortunes, for some were killed by the wild Irish, and others were destroyed for fear they should join themselves with the wild Irish, (which cruelty queen Elizabeth much condemned,) and the rest being afraid, sick and hungry, with their disabled ships, committed themselves to the sea, and many were drowned.

The queen went to public thanksgiving in St. Paul's church, accompanied by a glorious train of nobility, through the streets of London, which were hung with blue cloth, the companies standing on both sides in their liveries; the banners that were taken from the enemies were spread; she heard the sermon, and public thanks were rendered unto God with great joy. This public joy was augmented when Sir Robert Sidney returned from Scotland, and brought from the king assurances of his noble mind and affection to the queen, and to religion; which as in sincerity he had established, so he purposed to maintain with all his power. Sir Robert Sidney was sent to him when the Spanish fleet was coming, to congratulate and return thanks for his great affection towards the maintenance of the common cause, and to declare how ready she would be to help him if the Spaniards should land in Scotland; and that he might recal to memory with what strange ambition the Spaniards had gaped for all Britain, urging the pope to excommunicate him, to the end that he might be thrust from the kingdom of Scotland, and from the succession in England: and to give him notice of the threatening of Mendoza, and the pope's nuncio, who threatened his ruin if they could effect it: and therefore warned him to take special heed to the Scottish papists.

The king pleasantly answered that he looked for no other benefit from the Spaniards, than that which Polyphemus promised to Ulysses, to devour him last after his fellows were devoured.

It may not be improper here to subjoin a list of the different articles taken on board the Spanish ships, designed for the tormenting of the protestants, had their scheme taken effect.

1. The common soldiers' pikes, eighteen feet long, pointed with long sharp spikes, and shod with iron, which were designed to keep off the horse, to facilitate the landing of the infantry.

2. A great number of lances used by the Spanish officers. These were formerly gilt, but the gold is almost worn off by cleaning.

3. The Spanish ranceurs, made in different forms, which were intended either to kill the men on horseback, or pull them off their horses.

4. A very singular piece of arms, being a pistol in a shield, so contrived as to fire the pistol, and cover the body at the same time, with the shield. It is to be fired by a match-lock, and the sight of the enemy is to be taken through a little grate in the shield, which is

pistol proof.

5. The banner, with a crucifix upon it, which was to have been carried before the Spanish general. On it is engraved the pope's benediction before the Spanish fleet sailed: for the pope came to the water side, and, on seeing the fleet, blessed it, and styled it ***invincible***.

6. The Spanish cravats, as they are called. These are engines of torture, made of iron, and put on board to lock together the feet, arms and heads of Englishmen.

7. Spanish bilboes, made of iron likewise, to yoke the English prisoners two and two.

8. Spanish shot, which are of four sorts: pike-shot, star-shot, chain-shot, and link-shot, all admirably contrived, as well for the destruction of the masts and rigging of ships, as for sweeping the decks of their men.

9. Spanish spadas poisoned at the points, so that if a man received the slightest wound with one of them, certain death was the consequence.

10. A Spanish poll-axe, used in boarding of ships.

11. Thumb-screws, of which there were several chests full on board the Spanish fleet. The use they were intended for is said to have been to extort confession from the English where their money was hid.

12. The Spanish morning star; a destructive engine resembling the figure of a star, of which there were many thousands on board, and all of them with poisoned points; and were designed to strike at the enemy as they came on board, in case of a close attack.

13. The Spanish general's halberd, covered with velvet. All the nails of this weapon are double gilt with gold; and on its top is the pope's head, curiously engraved.

14. A Spanish battle-axe, so contrived, as to strike four holes in a man's head at once; and has besides a pistol in its handle, with a match-lock.

15. The Spanish general's shield, carried before him as an ensign of honour. On it are depicted, in most curious workmanship, the labours of Hercules, and other expressive allegories.

When the Spanish prisoners were asked by some of the English what their intentions were, had their expedition succeeded, they replied, "To extirpate the whole from the island, at least all heretics (as they called the protestants,) and to send their souls to hell." Strange infatuation! Ridiculous bigotry! How prejudiced must the minds of those men be, who would wish to destroy their fellow-creatures, not only in this world, but, if it were possible, in that which is to come, merely because they refused to believe on certain subjects as the Spaniards themselves did.

A conspiracy by the Papists for the destruction of James I., the royal family, and both houses of Parliament; commonly known by the name of the Gunpowder Plot.

The papists (of which there were great numbers in England at the time of the intended Spanish invasion) were so irritated at the failure of that expedition, that they were determined, if possible, to project a scheme at home, that might answer the purposes, to some degree, of their blood-thirsty competitors. The vigorous administration of Elizabeth, however, prevented their carrying any of their iniquitous designs into execution, although they made many attempts with that view. The commencement of the reign of her successor was destined to be the era of a plot, the barbarity of which transcends every thing related in ancient or modern history.

In order to crush popery in the most effectual manner in this kingdom, James soon after his succession, took proper measures for eclipsing the power of the Roman Catholics, by enforcing those laws which had been made against them by his predecessors. This enraged the papists to such a degree, that a conspiracy was formed, by some of the principal leaders, of the most daring and impious nature; namely, to blow up the king, royal family, and both houses of parliament, while in full session, and thus to involve the nation in utter and inevitable ruin.

The cabal who formed the resolution of putting in practice this horrid scheme, consisted of the following persons:--Henry Garnet, an Englishman, who, about the year 1586, had been sent to England as superior of the English Jesuits; Catesby, an English gentleman; Tesmond, a Jesuit; Thomas Wright; two gentlemen of the name of Winter; Thomas Percy, a near relation of the earl of Northumberland; Guido Fawkes, a bold and enterprising soldier of fortune; Sir Edward Digby; John Grant, Esq.; Francis Tresham, Esq.; Robert Keyes and Thomas Bates, gentlemen.

Most of these were men both of birth and fortune; and Catesby, who had a large estate, had already expended two thousand pounds in several voyages to the court of Spain, in order to introduce an army of Spaniards into England, for overturning the protestant government, and restoring the Roman Catholic religion; but, being disappointed in this project of an invasion, he took an opportunity of disclosing to Percy (who was his intimate friend, and who, in a sudden fit of passion, had hinted a design of assassinating the king) a nobler and more extensive plan of treason, such as would include a sure execution of vengeance, and, at one blow, consign over to destruction all their enemies.

Percy assented to the project proposed by Catesby, and they resolved to impart the matter to a few more, and, by degrees, to all the rest of their cabal, every man being bound by an oath, and taking the sacrament (the most sacred rite of their religion), not to disclose the least syllable of the matter, or to withdraw from the association, without the consent of all persons concerned.

These consultations were held in the spring and summer of the year 1604, and it was towards the close of that year that they began their operations; the manner of which, and the discovery, we shall relate with as much brevity as is consistent with perspicuity.

It had been agreed that a few of the conspirators should run a mine below the hall in which the parliament was to assemble, and that they should choose the very moment when the king should deliver his speech to both houses, for springing the mine, and thus, by one blow cut off the king, the royal family, lords, commons, and all the other enemies of the catholic religion in that very spot where that religion has been most oppressed. For this purpose, Percy, who was at that time a gentleman-pensioner undertook to hire a house adjoining to the upper house of parliament with all diligence. This was accordingly done, and the conspirators expecting the parliament would meet on the 17th of February following, began, on the 11th of December, to dig in the cellar, through the wall of partition, which was three yards thick. There was seven in number joined in this labour: they went in by night, and never after appeared in sight, for, having supplied themselves with all necessary provisions, they had no occasion to go out. In case of discovery, they had provided themselves with powder, shot, and fire arms, and formed a resolution rather to die than be taken.

On Candlemas-day, 1605, they had dug so far through the wall as to be able to hear a noise on the other side: upon which unexpected event, fearing a discovery, Guido Fawkes, (who personated Percy's footman,) was despatched to know the occasion, and returned with the favourable report, that the place from whence the noise came was a large cellar under the upper house of parliament, full of sea-coal which was then on sale, and the cellar offered to be let.

On this information, Percy immediately hired the cellar, and bought the remainder of the coals: he then sent for thirty barrels of gunpowder from Holland, and landing them at Lambeth, conveyed them gradually by night to this cellar, where they were covered with stones, iron bars, a thousand billets, and five hundred fagots; all which they did at their leisure, the parliament being prorogued to the 5th of November.

This being done, the conspirators next consulted how they should secure the duke of York,[B] who was too young to be expected at the parliament house, and his sister, the Princess Elizabeth, educated at Lord Harrington's, in Warwickshire. It was resolved, that Percy and another should enter into the duke's chamber, and a dozen more, properly disposed at several doors, with two or three on horseback at the court-gate to receive him, should carry him safe away as soon as the parliament-house was blown up; or, if that could not be effected, that they should kill him, and declare the princess Elizabeth queen, having secured her, under pretence of a hunting-match, that day.

Several of the conspirators proposed obtaining foreign aid previous to the execution of their design; but this was over-ruled, and it was agreed only to apply to France, Spain, and other powers for assistance after the plot had taken effect; they also resolved to proclaim the princess Elizabeth queen, and to spread a report, after the blow was given, that the puritans were the perpetrators of so inhuman an action.

All matters being now prepared by the conspirators, they, without the least remorse of conscience, and with the utmost impatience, expected the 5th of November. But all their counsels were blasted by a happy and providential circumstance. One of the conspirators, having a desire to save William Parker, Lord Monteagle, sent him the following letter:

"My Lord,

"Out of the love I bear to some of your friends, I
have a care for your preservation; therefore I
advise you, as you tender your life, to devise you
some excuse to shift off your attendance at this

parliament; for God and man have concurred to punish the wickedness of this time: and think not slightly of this advertisement, but retire yourself into the country, where you may expect the event with safety, for though there be no appearance of any stir, yet I say they shall receive a terrible blow, this parliament, and yet they shall not see who hurts them. This counsel is not to be contemned, because it may do you good, and can do you no harm; for the danger is past so soon (or as quickly) as you burn this letter; and I hope God will give you the grace to make good use of it, to whose holy protection I commend you."

The Lord Monteagle was, for some time, at a loss what judgment to form of this letter, and unresolved whether he should slight the advertisement or not; and fancying it a trick of his enemies to frighten him into an absence from parliament, would have determined on the former, had his own safety been only in question: but apprehending the king's life might be in danger, he took the letter at midnight to the earl of Salisbury, who was equally puzzled about the meaning of it; and though he was inclined to think it merely a wild and waggish contrivance to alarm Monteagle, yet he thought proper to consult about it with the earl of Suffolk, lord chamberlain. The expression, "that the blow should come, without knowing who hurt them," made them imagine that it would not be more proper than the time of parliament, nor by any other way likely to be attempted than by gunpowder, while the king was sitting to that assembly: the lord chamberlain thought this the more probable, because there was a great cellar under the parliament-chamber, (as already mentioned,) never used for any thing but wood or coal, belonging to Wineyard, the keeper of the palace; and having communicated the letter to the earls of Nottingham, Worcester, and Northampton, they proceeded no farther till the king came from Royston, on the 1st of November.

His majesty being shown the letter by the earls, who, at the same time acquainted him with their suspicions, was of opinion that either nothing should be done, or else enough to prevent the danger: and that a search should be made on the day preceding that designed for this execution of the diabolical enterprise.

Accordingly, on Monday, the 4th of November, in the afternoon, the lord chamberlain, whose office it was to see all things put in readiness for the king's coming, accompanied by Monteagle, went to visit all places about the parliament-house, and taking a slight occasion to see the cellar, observed only piles of billets and fagots, but in greater number than he thought Wineyard could want for his own use. On his asking who owned the wood, and being told it belonged to one Mr. Percy, he began to have some suspicions, knowing him to be a rigid papist, and so seldom there, that he had no occasion for such a quantity of fuel; and Monteagle confirmed him therein, by observing that Percy had made him great professions of friendship.

Though there was no other materials visible, yet Suffolk thought it was necessary to make a further search; and, upon his return to the king, a resolution was taken that it should be made in such a manner as should be effectual, without scandalizing any body, or giving any alarm.

Sir Thomas Knevet, steward of Westminster, was accordingly ordered, under the pretext of searching for stolen tapestry hangings in that place, and other houses thereabouts, to remove the wood, and see if anything was concealed underneath. This gentleman going at midnight, with several attendants, to the cellar, met Fawkes, just coming out of it, booted and spurred, with a tinder-box and three matches in his pockets, and seizing him without any ceremony, or asking him any questions, as soon as the removal of the wood discovered the barrels of gunpowder, he caused him to be bound, and properly secured.

Fawkes, who was a hardened and intrepid villain, made no hesitation of avowing the design, and that it was to have been executed on the morrow. He made the same acknowledgment at his examination before a committee of the council; and though he did not deny having some associates in this conspiracy, yet no threats of torture could make him discover any of them, he declaring that "he was ready to die, and had rather suffer ten thousand deaths, than willingly accuse his master, or any other."

By repeated examinations, however, and assurances of his master's being apprehended, he at length acknowledged, "that whilst he was abroad, Percy had kept the keys of the cellar, had been in it since the powder had been laid there, and, in effect, that he was one of the principal actors in the intended tragedy."

In the mean time it was found out, that Percy had come post out of the north on Saturday night, the 2d of November, and had dined on Monday at Sion-house, with the earl of Northumberland; that Fawkes had met him on the road, and that, after the lord chamberlain had been that evening in the cellar, he went, about six o'clock, to his master, who had fled immediately, apprehending the plot was detected.

The news of the discovery immediately spreading, the conspirators fled different ways, but chiefly into Warwickshire, where Sir Everard Digby had appointed a hunting-match, near Dunchurch, to get a number of recusants together, sufficient to seize the princess Elizabeth; but this design was prevented by her taking refuge in Coventry; and their whole party, making about one hundred, retired to Holbeach, the seat of Sir Stephen Littleton, on the borders of Staffordshire, having broken open stables, and taken horses from different people in the adjoining counties.

Sir Richard Walsh, high sheriff of Worcestershire, pursued them to Holbeach, where he invested them, and summoned them to surrender. In preparing for their defence, they put some moist powder before a fire to dry, and a spark from the coals setting it on fire, some of the conspirators were so burned in their faces, thighs, and arms, that they were scarcely able to handle their weapons. Their case was desperate, and no means of escape appearing, unless by forcing their way through the assailants, they made a furious sally for that purpose. Catesby (who first proposed the manner of the plot) and Percy were both killed. Thomas Winter, Grant, Digby, Rockwood, and Bates, were taken and carried to London, were the first made a full discovery of the conspiracy. Tresham, lurking about the city, and frequently shifting his quarters, was apprehended soon after, and having confessed the whole matter, died of the strangury, in the Tower. The earl of Northumberland, suspected on account of his being related to Thomas Percy, was, by way of precaution, committed to the custody of the archbishop of Canterbury, at Lambeth; and was afterwards fined thirty thousand pounds, and sent to the Tower, for admitting Percy into the band of gentlemen pensioners, without tending him the oath of supremacy.

Some escaped to Calais, and arriving there with others, who fled to avoid a persecution which they apprehended on this occasion, were kindly received by the governor; but one of them declaring before him, that he was not so much concerned at his exile, as that the powder plot did not take effect, the governor was so much incensed at his glorying in such an execrable piece of iniquity, that, in a sudden impulse of indignation, he endeavoured to throw him into the sea.

On the 27th of January, 1606, eight of the conspirators were tried and convicted, among whom was Sir Everard Digby, the only one that pleaded guilty to the indictment, though all the rest had confessed their guilt before. Digby was executed on the 30th of the same month, with Robert Winter, Grant, and Bates, at the west end of St. Paul's churchyard;

Thomas Winter, Keyes, Rockwood, and Fawkes, were executed the following day in Old Palace yard.

Garnet was tried on the 28th of March, "for his knowledge and concealment of the conspiracy; for administering an oath of secrecy to the conspirators, for persuading them of the lawfulness of the treason, and for praying for the success of the great action in hand at the beginning of the parliament." Being found guilty,[C] he received sentence of death, but was not executed till the 3d of May, when, confessing his own guilt, and the iniquity of the enterprise, he exhorted all Roman Catholics to abstain from the like treasonable practices in future. Gerard and Hall, two Jesuits, got abroad; and Littleton, with several others, were executed in the country.

The Lord Monteagle had a grant of two hundred pounds a year in land, and a pension of five hundred pounds for life, as a reward for discovering the letter which gave the first hint of the conspiracy; and the anniversary of this providential deliverance was ordered to be for ever commemorated by prayer and thanksgiving.

Thus was this diabolical scheme happily rendered abortive, and the authors of it brought to that condign punishment which their wickedness merited. In this affair Providence manifestly interposed in behalf of the protestants, and saved them from that destruction which must have taken place had the scheme succeeded according to the wishes of a bigoted, superstitious, and blood-thirsty faction.

NOTES:

[A] The queen made the following animated speech to the troops assembled at Tilbury:

"My loving people, we have been persuaded by some, that are careful of our safety, to take heed how we commit ourselves to armed multitudes, for fear of treachery, but I assure you, I do not desire to live to distrust my faithful and loving people.--Let tyrants fear: I have always so behaved myself, that under God, I have placed my chiefest strength and safeguard in the loyal hearts and good will of my subjects. And therefore I am come among you at this time, not as for my recreation or sport, but being resolved, in the midst and heat of the battle, to live or die among you all, to lay down, for my God, and for my kingdom, and for my people, my honour and my blood, even in the dust. I know I have but the body of a weak and feeble woman, but I have the heart of a king, and of a king of England too; and think foul scorn that Parma or Spain, or any prince of Europe, should dare to invade the borders of my realms: To which rather than any dishonour should grow by me, I myself will take up arms; I myself will be your general, judge, and rewarder of every one of your virtues in the field. I know already, by your forwardness, that you have deserved rewards and crowns; and I do assure you, on the word of a prince, they shall be duly paid you. In the mean time my lieutenant-general shall be in my stead, than whom never prince commanded a more noble and worthy subject; not doubting by your obedience to my general, by your concord in the camp, and your valour in the field, we shall shortly have a famous victory over those enemies of my God, of my kingdom, and of my people."

[B] Afterward Charles I.

CHAPTER XV.

RISE AND PROGRESS OF THE PROTESTANT RELIGION IN IRELAND; WITH AN ACCOUNT OF THE BARBAROUS MASSACRE OF 1641.

The gloom of popery had overshadowed Ireland from its first establishment there till the reign of Henry VIII. when the rays of the gospel began to dispel the darkness, and afford that light which till then had been unknown in that island. The abject ignorance in which the people were held, with the absurd and superstitious notions they entertained, were sufficiently evident to many; and the artifices of their priests were so conspicuous, that several persons of distinction, who had hitherto been strenuous papists, would willingly have endeavoured to shake off the yoke, and embrace the protestant religion; but the natural ferocity of the people, and their strong attachment to the ridiculous doctrines which they had been taught, made the attempt dangerous. It was, however, at length undertaken, though attended with the most horrid and disastrous consequences.

The introduction of the protestant religion into Ireland may be principally attributed to George Browne, an Englishman, who was consecrated archbishop of Dublin on the 19th of March, 1535. He had formerly been an Augustine friar, and was promoted to the mitre on account of his merit.

After having enjoyed his dignity about five years, he, at the time that Henry VIII. was suppressing the religious houses in England, caused all the relics and images to be removed out of the two cathedrals in Dublin, and the other churches in his diocese; in the place of which he caused to be put up the Lord's prayer, the creed, and the ten commandments.

A short time after this he received a letter from Thomas Cromwell, lord-privy seal, informing him that Henry VIII. having thrown off the papal supremacy in England, was determined to do the like in Ireland; and that he thereupon had appointed him (archbishop Browne) one of the commissioners for seeing this order put in execution. The archbishop answered, that he had employed his utmost endeavours at the hazard of his life, to cause the Irish nobility and gentry to acknowledge Henry as their supreme head, in matters both spiritual and temporal; but had met with a most violent opposition, especially from George, archbishop of Armagh; that this prelate had, in a speech to his clergy, laid a curse on all those who should own his highness'[D] supremacy: adding, that their isle, called in the Chronicles *Insula Sacra*, or the Holy Island, belonged to none but the bishop of Rome, and that the king's progenitors had received it from the pope. He observed likewise, that the archbishop and clergy of Armagh, had each despatched a courier to Rome; and that it would be necessary for a parliament to be called in Ireland, to pass an act of supremacy, the people not regarding the king's commission without the sanction of the legislative assembly. He concluded with observing, that the popes had kept the people in the most profound ignorance; that the clergy were exceedingly illiterate; that the common people were more zealous, in their blindness, than the saints and martyrs had been in the defence of truth at the beginning of the gospel; and that it was to be feared Shan O'Neal, a chieftain of great power in the northern part of the island, was decidedly opposed to the king's commission.

In pursuance of this advice, the following year a parliament was summoned to meet at Dublin, by order of Leonard Grey, at that time lord-lieutenant. At this assembly archbishop Browne made a speech in which he set forth, that the bishops of Rome used, anciently, to acknowledge emperors, kings, and princes, to be supreme in their own dominions, and, therefore, that he himself would vote king Henry VIII. as supreme in all matters, both ecclesiastical and temporal. He concluded with saying, that whosoever should refuse to vote for this act, was not a true subject of the king. This speech greatly startled the other bishops and lords; but at length, after violent debates, the king's supremacy was allowed.

Two years after this, the archbishop wrote a second letter to lord Cromwell, complaining of the clergy, and hinting at the machinations which the pope was then carrying on against the advocates of the gospel. This letter is dated from Dublin, in April, 1538; and among other matters, the archbishop says, "A bird may be taught to speak with as much sense as many of the clergy do in this country. These, though not scholars, yet are crafty to cozen the poor common people and to dissuade them from following his highness' orders. The country folk here much hate your lordship, and despitefully call you, in their Irish tongue, the Blacksmith's Son. As a friend, I desire your lordship to look well to your noble person. Rome hath a great kindness for the duke of Norfolk, and great favors for this nation, purposely to oppose his highness."

A short time after this, the pope sent over to Ireland (directed to the Archbishop of Armagh and his clergy) a bull of excommunication against all who had, or should own the king's supremacy within the Irish nation; denouncing a curse on all of them, and theirs, who should not, within forty days, acknowledge to their confessors, that they had done amiss in so doing.

Archbishop Browne gave notice of this in a letter, dated, Dublin, May, 1538. Part of the form of confession, or vow, sent over to these Irish papists, ran as follows; "I do farther declare him or her, father or mother, brother or sister, son or daughter, husband or wife, uncle or aunt, nephew or niece, kinsman or kinswoman, master or mistress, and all others, nearest or dearest relations, friend or acquaintance whatsoever, accursed, that either do or shall hold, for the time to come, any ecclesiastical or civil power above the authority of the mother church; or that do or shall obey, for the time to come, any of her the mother of churches' opposers or enemies, or contrary to the same, of which I have here sworn unto: so God, the Blessed Virgin, St. Peter, St. Paul, and the Holy Evangelists, help me, &c." This is an exact agreement with the doctrines promulgated by the councils of Lateran and Constance, which expressly declare, that no favour should be shown to heretics, nor faith kept with them; that they ought to be excommunicated and condemned, and their estates confiscated; and that princes are obliged, by a solemn oath, to root them out of their respective dominions.

How abominable a church must that be, which thus dares to trample upon

all authority! how besotted the people who regard the injunctions of
such a church!

In the archbishop's last-mentioned letter, dated May, 1538, he says,
"His highness' viceroy of this nation is of little or no power with the
old natives. Now both English and Irish begin to oppose your lordship's
orders, and to lay aside their national quarrels, which I fear will (if
any thing will) cause a foreigner to invade this nation."

Not long after this, Archbishop Browne seized one Thady O'Brian, a
Franciscan friar, who had in his possession a paper sent from Rome dated
May, 1538, and directed to O'Neal. In this letter were the following
words: "His holiness, Paul, now pope, and the council of the fathers,
have lately found, in Rome, a prophecy of one St. Lacerianus, an Irish
bishop of Cashel, in which he saith, that the mother church of Rome
falleth, when, in Ireland, the catholic faith is overcome. Therefore,
for the glory of the mother church, the honour of St. Peter, and your
own secureness, suppress heresy, and his holiness' enemies."

This Thady O'Brian, after farther examination and search made, was
pilloried, and kept close prisoner, till the king's orders arrived in
what manner he should be farther disposed of. But order coming over from
England that he was to be hanged, he laid violent hands on himself in
the castle of Dublin. His body was afterwards carried to Gallows-green,
where, after being hanged up for some time, it was interred.

After the accession of Edward VI. to the throne of England, an order was
directed to Sir Anthony Leger, the lord-deputy of Ireland, commanding
that the liturgy in English be forthwith set up in Ireland, there to be
observed within the several bishoprics, cathedrals, and parish churches;
and it was first read in Christ-church, Dublin, on Easter day, 1551,
before the said Sir Anthony, Archbishop Browne, and others. Part of the
royal order for this purpose was as follows: "Whereas, our gracious
father, King Henry VIII. taking into consideration the bondage and heavy
yoke that his true and faithful subjects sustained, under the
jurisdiction of the bishop of Rome; how several fabulous stories and
lying wonders misled our subjects; dispensing with the sins of our
nations, by their indulgences and pardons, for gain; purposely to
cherish all evil vices, as robberies, rebellions, theft, whoredoms,
blasphemy, idolatry, &c. our gracious father hereupon dissolved all
priories, monasteries, abbeys, and other pretended religious houses; as
being but nurseries for vice or luxury, more than for sacred learning,"
&c.

On the day after the common-prayer was first used in Christ-church, Dublin, the following wicked scheme was projected by the papists:

In the church was left a marble image of Christ, holding a reed in his hand, with a crown of thorns on his head. Whilst the English service (the Common Prayer) was being read before the lord-lieutenant, the archbishop of Dublin, the privy-council, the lord-mayor, and a great congregation, blood was seen to run through the crevices of the crown of thorns, and to trickle down the face of the image. On this, some of the contrivers of the imposture cried aloud: "See how our Saviour's image sweats blood! But it must necessarily do this, since heresy is come into the church." Immediately many of the lower order of people, indeed the *vulgar of all ranks*, were terrified at the sight of so *miraculous* and *undeniable* an evidence of the divine displeasure; they hastened from the church, convinced that the doctrines of protestantism emanated from an infernal source, and that salvation was only to be found in the bosom of their own *infallible* church.

This incident, however ludicrous it may appear to the enlightened reader, had great influence over the minds of the ignorant Irish, and answered the ends of the impudent imposters who contrived it, so far as to check the progress of the reformed religion in Ireland very materially; many persons could not resist the conviction that there were many errors and corruptions in the Romish church, but they were awed into silence by this pretended manifestation of Divine wrath, which was magnified beyond measure by the bigoted and interested priesthood.

We have very few particulars as to the state of religion in Ireland during the remaining portion of the reign of Edward VI. and the greater part of that of Mary. Towards the conclusion of the barbarous sway of that relentless bigot, she attempted to extend her inhuman persecutions to this island; but her diabolical intentions were happily frustrated in the following providential manner, the particulars of which are related by historians of good authority.

Mary had appointed Dr. Cole (an agent of the blood-thirsty Bonner) one of the commissioners for carrying her barbarous intentions into effect. He having arrived at Chester with his commission, the mayor of that city, being a papist, waited upon him; when the doctor taking out of his cloak-bag a leathern case, said to him, "Here is a commission that shall lash the heretics of Ireland." The good woman of the house being a protestant, and having a brother in Dublin, named John Edmunds, was greatly troubled at what she heard. But watching her opportunity, whilst the mayor was taking his leave, and the doctor politely accompanying him

down stairs, she opened the box, took out the commission, and in its
stead laid a sheet of paper, with a pack of cards, and the knave of
clubs at top. The doctor, not suspecting the trick that had been played
him, put up the box, and arrived with it in Dublin, in September, 1558.

Anxious to accomplish the intentions of his "*pious*" mistress, he
immediately waited upon Lord Fitz-Walter, at that time viceroy, and
presented the box to him; which being opened, nothing was found in it
but a pack of cards. This startling all the persons present, his
lordship said, "We must procure another commission; and in the mean time
let us shuffle the cards!"

Dr. Cole, however, would have directly returned to England to get
another commission; but waiting for a favourable wind, news arrived that
queen Mary was dead, and by this means the protestants escaped a most
cruel persecution. The above relation as we before observed, is
confirmed by historians of the greatest credit, who add, that queen
Elizabeth settled a pension of forty pounds per annum upon the above
mentioned Elizabeth Edmunds, for having thus saved the lives of her
protestant subjects.

During the reigns of Elizabeth and James I. Ireland was almost
constantly agitated by rebellions and insurrections, which, although not
always taking their rise from the difference of religious opinions
between the English and Irish, were aggravated and rendered more bitter
and irreconcilable from that cause. The popish priests artfully
exaggerated the faults of the English government, and continually urged
to their ignorant and prejudiced hearers the lawfulness of killing the
protestants, assuring them that all catholics who were slain in the
prosecution of so *pious* an enterprise, would be immediately received
into everlasting felicity. The naturally ungovernable dispositions of
the Irish, acted upon by these designing men, drove them into continual
acts of barbarous and unjustifiable violence; and it must be confessed
that the unsettled and arbitrary nature of the authority exercised by
the English governors, was but little calculated to gain their
affections. The Spaniards, too, by landing forces in the south, and
giving every encouragement to the discontented natives to join their
standard, kept the island in a continual state of turbulence and
warfare. In 1601, they disembarked a body of 4000 men at Kinsale, and
commenced what they called "the holy war for the preservation of the
faith in Ireland;" they were assisted by great numbers of the Irish,
but were at length totally defeated by the deputy, lord Mountjoy, and
his officers.

This closed the transactions of Elizabeth's reign with respect to Ireland; an interval of apparent tranquility followed, but the popish priesthood, ever restless and designing, sought to undermine by secret machinations, that government and that faith which they durst no longer openly attack. The pacific reign of James afforded them the opportunity of increasing their strength and maturing their schemes, and under his successor, Charles I. their numbers were greatly increased by titular Romish archbishops, bishops, deans, vicars-general, abbots, priests, and friars; for which reason, in 1629, the public exercise of the popish rites and ceremonies was forbidden.

But notwithstanding this, soon afterwards, the Romish clergy erected a new popish university in the city of Dublin. They also proceeded to build monasteries and nunneries in various parts of the kingdom; in which places these very Romish clergy, and the chiefs of the Irish, held frequent meetings; and from thence, used to pass to and fro, to France, Spain, Flanders, Lorrain, and Rome; where the detestable plot of 1641 was hatching by the family of the O'Neals and their followers.

A short time before the horrid conspiracy broke out, which we are now going to relate, the papists in Ireland had presented a remonstrance to the lords-justices of that kingdom, demanding the free exercise of their religion, and a repeal of all laws to the contrary, to which both houses of parliament in England, solemnly answered, that they would never grant any toleration to the popish religion in that kingdom.

This farther irritated the papists to put in execution the diabolical plot concerted for the destruction of the protestants; and it failed not of the success wished for by its malicious and rancorous projectors.

The design of this horrid conspiracy was, that a general insurrection should take place at the same time throughout the kingdom, and that all the protestants, without exception, should be murdered. The day fixed for this horrid massacre, was the 23d of October, 1641, the feast of Ignatius Loyola, founder of the Jesuits; and the chief conspirators, in the principal parts of the kingdom, made the necessary preparations for the intended conflict.

In order that this detested scheme might the more infallibly succeed, the most distinguished artifices were practised by the papists; and their behaviour in their visits to the protestants, at this time, was with more seeming kindness than they had hitherto shown, which was done the more completely to effect the inhuman and treacherous designs then meditating against them.

The execution of this savage conspiracy was delayed till the approach of winter, that sending troops from England might be attended with greater difficulty. Cardinal Richelieu, the French minister, had promised the conspirators a considerable supply of men and money; and many Irish officers had given the strongest assurances that they would heartily concur with their catholic brethren, as soon as the insurrection took place.

The day preceding that appointed for carrying this horrid design into execution, was now arrived, when, happily for the metropolis of the kingdom, the conspiracy was discovered by one Owen O'Connelly, an Irishman, for which most signal service the English parliament voted him 500*l.* and a pension of 200*l.* during his life.

So very seasonably was this plot discovered, even but a few hours before the city and castle of Dublin were to have been surprised, that the lords-justices had but just time to put themselves, and the city, in a proper posture of defence. The lord M'Guire, who was the principal leader here, with his accomplices, were seized the same evening in the city; and in their lodgings were found swords, hatchets, pole-axes, hammers, and such other instruments of death as had been prepared for the destruction and extirpation of the protestants in that part of the kingdom.

Thus was the metropolis happily preserved; but the bloody part of the intended tragedy was past prevention. The conspirators were in arms all over the kingdom early in the morning of the day appointed, and every protestant who fell in their way was immediately murdered. No age, no sex, no condition, was spared. The wife weeping for her butchered husband, and embracing her helpless children, was pierced with them, and perished by the same stroke. The old, the young, the vigorous, and the infirm, underwent the same fate, and were blended in one common ruin. In vain did flight save from the first assault, destruction was every where let loose, and met the hunted victims at every turn. In vain was recourse had to relations, to companions, to friends; all connexions were dissolved; and death was dealt by that hand from which protection was implored and expected. Without provocation, without opposition, the astonished English, living in profound peace, and, as they thought, full security, were massacred by their nearest neighbours, with whom they had long maintained a continued intercourse of kindness and good offices. Nay, even death was the slightest punishment inflicted by these monsters in human form; all the tortures which wanton cruelty could invent, all the lingering pains of body, the anguish of mind, the agonies of despair, could not satiate revenge excited without injury, and cruelly derived from no just cause whatever. Depraved nature, even perverted religion, though encouraged by the utmost license, cannot reach to a greater pitch of ferocity than appeared in these merciless barbarians. Even the weaker sex themselves, naturally tender to their own sufferings, and compassionate to those of others, have emulated their robust companions in the practice of every cruelty. The very children, taught by example, and encouraged by the exhortation of their parents, dealt their feeble blows on the dead carcasses of the defenceless children of the English.

Nor was the avarice of the Irish sufficient to produce the least restraint on their cruelty. Such was their frenzy, that the cattle they had seized, and by rapine had made their own, were, because they bore the name of English, wantonly slaughtered, or, when covered with wounds, turned loose into the woods, there to perish by slow and lingering torments.

The commodious habitations of the planters were laid in ashes, or levelled with the ground. And where the wretched owners had shut themselves up in the houses, and were preparing for defence, they perished in the flames together with their wives and children.

Such is the general description of this unparalleled massacre; but it now remains, from the nature of our work, that we proceed to particulars.

The bigoted and merciless papists had no sooner begun to imbrue their hands in blood, than they repeated the horrid tragedy day after day, and the protestants in all parts of the kingdom fell victims to their fury by deaths of the most unheard of cruelty.

The ignorant Irish were more strongly instigated to execute the infernal business by the jesuits, priests, and friars, who, when the day for the execution of the plot was agreed on, recommended in their prayers, diligence in the great design, which they said would greatly tend to the prosperity of the kingdom, and to the advancement of the Catholic cause. They every where declared to the common people, that the protestants were heretics, and ought not to be suffered to live any longer among them; adding, that it was no more sin to kill an Englishman than to kill a dog; and that the relieving or protecting them was a crime of the most unpardonable nature.

The papists having besieged the town and castle of Longford, and the inhabitants of the latter, who were protestants, surrendering on condition of being allowed quarter, the besiegers, the instant the towns-people appeared, attacked them in a most unmerciful manner, their priest, as a signal for the rest to fall on, first ripping open the belly of the English protestant minister; after which his followers murdered all the rest, some of whom they hung, others were stabbed or shot and great numbers knocked on the head with axes provided for the purpose.

The garrison at Sligo was treated in like manner by O'Connor Slygah; who, upon the protestants quitting their holds, promised them quarter, and to convey them safe over the Curlew mountains, to Roscommon. But he first imprisoned them in a most loathsome jail, allowing them only grains for their food. Afterward, when some papists were merry over their cups, who were come to congratulate their wicked brethren for their victory over these unhappy creatures, those protestants who survived were brought forth by the White-friars, and were either killed, or precipitated over the bridge into a swift river, where they were soon destroyed. It is added, that this wicked company of White-friars went, some time after, in solemn procession, with holy water in their hands, to sprinkle the river; on pretence of cleansing and purifying it from the stains and pollution of the blood and dead bodies of the heretics, as they called the unfortunate protestants who were inhumanly slaughtered at this very time.

At Kilmore, Dr. Bedell, bishop of that see, had charitably settled and supported a great number of distressed protestants, who had fled from their habitations to escape the diabolical cruelties committed by the papists. But they did not long enjoy the consolation of living together; the good prelate was forcibly dragged from his episcopal residence, which was immediately occupied by Dr. Swiney, the popish titular bishop of Kilmore, who said mass in the church the Sunday following, and then seized on all the goods and effects belonging to the persecuted bishop.

Soon after this, the papists forced Dr. Bedell, his two sons, and the rest of his family, with some of the chief of the protestants whom he had protected, into a ruinous castle, called Lochwater, situated in a lake near the sea. Here he remained with his companions some weeks, all of them daily expecting to be put to death. The greatest part of them were stripped naked, by which means, as the season was cold, (it being in the month of December) and the building in which they were confined open at the top, they suffered the most severe hardships. They continued in this situation till the 7th of January, when they were all released. The bishop was courteously received into the house of Dennis O'Sheridan, one of his clergy, whom he had made a convert to the church of England; but he did not long survive this kindness. During his residence here, he spent the whole of his time in religious exercises, the better to fit and prepare himself and his sorrowful companions, for their great change as not but certain death was perpetually before their eyes. He was at this time in the 71st year of his age, and being afflicted with a violent ague caught in his late cold and desolate habitation on the lake, it soon threw him into a fever of the most dangerous nature. Finding his dissolution at hand, he received it with joy, like one of the primitive martyrs just hastening to his crown of glory. After having addressed his little flock, and exhorted them to patience, in the most pathetic manner, as they saw their own last day approaching, after having solemnly blessed his people, his family, and his children, he finished the course of his ministry and life together, on the 7th day of February, 1642. His friends and relations applied to the intruding bishop for leave to bury him, which was with difficulty obtained; he, at first telling them that the churchyard was holy ground, and should be no longer defiled with heretics: however, leave was at last granted, and though the church funeral service was not used at the solemnity, (for fear of the Irish papists) yet some of the better sort, who had the highest veneration for him while living, attended his remains to the grave. At his interment, they discharged a volley of shot, crying out, "Requiescat in pace ultimas Anglorum;" that is, May the last of the English rest in peace. Adding, that as he was one of the best so he should be the last English bishop found among them. His learning was very extensive; and he would have given the world a greater proof of it, had he printed all he wrote. Scarce any of his writings were saved; the papists having destroyed most of his papers and his library. He had gathered a vast heap of critical expositions of scripture, all which with a great trunk full of his manuscripts, fell into the hands of the Irish. Happily his great Hebrew MS. was preserved, and is now in the library of Emanuel college, Oxford.

In the barony of Terawley, the papists, at the instigation of the friars, compelled above forty English protestants, some of whom were women and children, to the hard fate either of falling by the sword, or of drowning in the sea. These choosing the latter, were accordingly forced, by the naked weapons of their inexorable persecutors, into the deep, where, with their children in their arms, they first waded up to their chins, and afterwards sunk down and perished together.

In the castle of Lisgool upwards of one hundred and fifty men, women, and children, were all burnt together; and at the castle of Moneah not less than one hundred were all put to the sword.--Great numbers were also murdered at the castle of Tullah, which was delivered up to M'Guire on condition of having fair quarter; but no sooner had that base villain got possession of the place, than he ordered his followers to murder the people, which was immediately done with the greatest cruelty.

Many others were put to deaths of the most horrid nature, and such as could have been invented only by demons instead of men. Some of them were laid with the centre of their backs on the axle-tree of a carriage, with their legs resting on the ground on one side, and then arms and head on the other. In this position one of the savages scourged the wretched object on the thighs, legs, &c. while another set on furious dogs, who tore to pieces the arms and upper parts of the body; and in this dreadful manner were they deprived of their existence. Great numbers were fastened to horses' tails, and the beasts being set on full gallop by their riders, the wretched victims were dragged along till they expired. Others were hung on lofty gibbets, and a fire being kindled under them, they finished their lives, partly by hanging, and partly by suffocation.

Nor did the more tender sex escape the least particle of cruelty that could be projected by their merciless and furious persecutors. Many women, of all ages, were put to deaths of the most cruel nature. Some, in particular, were fastened with their backs to strong posts, and being stripped to their waists, the inhuman monsters cut off their right breasts with shears, which, of course, put them to the most excruciating torments; and in this position they were left, till, from the loss of blood, they expired.

Such was the savage ferocity of these barbarians, that even unborn infants were dragged from the womb to become victims to their rage. Many unhappy mothers were hung naked on the branches of trees, and their bodies being cut open, the innocent offsprings were taken from them, and thrown to dogs and swine. And to increase the horrid scene, they would oblige the husband to be a spectator before suffered himself.

At the town of Issenskeath they hanged above a hundred Scottish protestants, showing them no more mercy than they did to the English. M'Guire, going to the castle of that town, desired to speak with the governor, when being admitted, he immediately burnt the records of the county, which were kept there. He then demanded L1000 of the governor, which having received, he immediately compelled him to hear mass, and to swear that he would continue so to do. And to complete his horrid barbarities, he ordered the wife and children of the governor to be hung before his face; besides massacring at least one hundred of the inhabitants. Upwards of one thousand men, women and children, were driven, in different companies, to Porterdown bridge, which was broken in the middle, and there compelled to throw themselves into the water, and such as attempted to reach the shore were knocked on the head.

In the same part of the country, at least four thousand persons were drowned in different places. The inhuman papists, after first stripping them, drove them like beasts to the spot fixed on for their destruction; and if any, through fatigue, or natural infirmities, were slack in their pace, they pricked them with their swords and pikes; and to strike terror on the multitude, they murdered some by the way.--Many of these poor wretches, when thrown into the water, endeavoured to save themselves by swimming to the shore; but their merciless persecutors prevented their endeavors taking effect by shooting them in the water.

In one place one hundred and forty English, after being driven for many miles stark naked, and in the most severe weather, were all murdered on the same spot, some being hanged, others burnt, some shot, and many of them buried alive; and so cruel were their tormentors, that they would not suffer them to pray before they robbed them of their miserable existence.

Other companies they took under pretence of safe conduct, who, from that consideration, proceeded cheerfully on their journey; but when the treacherous papists had got them to a convenient spot, they butchered them all in the most cruel manner.

One hundred and fifteen men, women, and children, were conducted, by order of Sir Phelim O'Neal, to Porterdown bridge, where they were all forced into the river, and drowned. One woman, named Campbell, finding no probability of escaping, suddenly clasped one of the chief of the papists in her arms, and held him so fast, that they were both drowned together.

In Killoman they massacred forty-eight families, among whom twenty-two were burnt together in one house. The rest were either hanged, shot, or drowned.

In Kilmore the inhabitants, which consisted of about two hundred families, all fell victims to their rage. Some of them sat in the stocks till they confessed where their money was; after which they put them to death. The whole county was one common scene of butchery, and many thousands perished, in a short time, by sword, famine, fire, water, and other the most cruel deaths, that rage and malice could invent.

These bloody villains showed so much favour to some as to despatch them immediately; but they would by no means suffer them to pray. Others they imprisoned in filthy dungeons, putting heavy bolts on their legs, and keeping them there till they were starved to death.

At Casel they put all the protestants into a loathsome dungeon, where they kept them together, for several weeks, in the greatest misery. At length they were released, when some of them were barbarously mangled, and left on the highways to perish at leisure; others were hanged, and some were buried in the ground upright, with their heads above the earth, and the papists, to increase their misery, treating them with derision during their sufferings. In the county of Antrim they murdered nine hundred and fifty-four protestants in one morning; and afterward about twelve hundred more in that county.

At a town called Lisnegary, they forced twenty-four protestants into a house, and then setting fire to it, burned them together, counterfeiting their outcries in derision to the others.

Among other acts of cruelty they took two children belonging to an English woman, and dashed out their brains before her face; after which they threw the mother into a river, and she was drowned. They served many other children in the like manner, to the great affliction of their parents, and the disgrace of human nature.

In Kilkenny all the protestants, without exception, were put to death; and some of them in so cruel a manner, as, perhaps, was never before thought of.

They beat an English woman with such savage barbarity, that she had scarce a whole bone left; after which they threw her into a ditch; but not satisfied with this, they took her child, a girl about six years of age and after ripping up its belly, threw it to its mother, there to languish till it perished. They forced one man to go to mass, after which they ripped open his body, and in that manner left him. They sawed another asunder, cut the throat of his wife, and after having dashed out the brains of their child, an infant, threw it to the swine, who greedily devoured it.

After committing these, and several other horrid cruelties, they took the heads of seven protestants, and among them that of a pious minister, all which they fixed up at the market cross. They put a gag into the minister's mouth, then slit his cheeks to his ears, and laying a leaf of a Bible before it, bid him preach, for his mouth was wide enough. They did several other things by way of derision, and expressed the greatest satisfaction at having thus murdered and exposed the unhappy protestants.

It is impossible to conceive the pleasure these monsters took in exercising their cruelty, and to increase the misery of those who fell into their hands, when they butchered them they would say, "Your soul to the devil." One of these miscreants would come into a house with his hands imbued in blood, and boast that it was English blood, and that his sword had pricked the white skins of the protestants, even to the hilt. When any one of them had killed a protestant, others would come and receive a gratification in cutting and mangling the body; after which they left it exposed to be devoured by dogs; and when they had slain a number of them they would boast, that the devil was beholden to them for sending so many souls to hell. But it is no wonder they should thus treat the innocent christians, when they hesitated not to commit blasphemy against God and his most holy word.

In one place they burnt two protestant Bibles, and then said they had burnt hell-fire. In the church at Powerscourt they burnt the pulpit, pews, chests, and Bibles belonging to it. They took other Bibles, and after wetting them with dirty water, dashed them in the faces of the protestants, saying, "We know you love a good lesson; here is an excellent one for you; come to-morrow, and you shall have as good a sermon as this."

Some of the protestants they dragged by the hair of their heads into the church, where they stripped and whipped them in the most cruel manner, telling them, at the same time, "That if they came to-morrow, they should hear the like sermon."

In Munster they put to death several ministers in the most shocking manner. One, in particular, they stripped stark naked, and driving him before them, pricked him with swords and darts till he fell down, and expired.

In some places they plucked out the eyes, and cut off the hands of the protestants, and in that manner turned them into the fields, there to wander out their miserable existence. They obliged many young men to force their aged parents to a river, where they were drowned; wives to assist in hanging their husbands; and mothers to cut the throats of their children.

In one place they compelled a young man to kill his father, and then immediately hanged him. In another they forced a woman to kill her husband, then obliged the son to kill her, and afterward shot him through the head.

At a place called Glaslow, a popish priest, with some others, prevailed on forty protestants to be reconciled to the church of Rome. They had no sooner done this, than they told them they were in good faith, and that they would prevent their falling from it, and turning heretics, by sending them out of the world, which they did by immediately cutting their throats.

In the county of Tipperary upwards of thirty protestants, men, women, and children, fell into the hands of the papists, who, after stripping them naked, murdered them with stones, pole-axes, swords, and other weapons.

In the county of Mayo about sixty protestants, fifteen of whom were ministers, were, upon covenant, to be safely conducted to Galway, by one Edmund Burke and his soldiers; but that inhuman monster by the way drew his sword, as an intimation of his design to the rest, who immediately followed his example, and murdered the whole, some of whom they stabbed, others were run through the body with pikes, and several were drowned.

In Queen's county great numbers of protestants were put to the most shocking deaths. Fifty or sixty were placed together in one house, which being set on fire, they all perished in the flames. Many were stripped naked, and being fastened to horses by ropes placed round their middles, were dragged through bogs till they expired. Some were hung by the feet to tenter-hooks driven into poles; and in that wretched posture left till they perished. Others were fastened to the trunk of a tree, with a branch at top. Over this branch hung one arm, which principally supported the weight of the body; and one of the legs was turned up, and fastened to the trunk, while the other hung straight. In this dreadful and uneasy posture did they remain, as long as life would permit, pleasing spectacles to their blood-thirsty persecutors.

At Clownes seventeen men were buried alive; and an Englishman, his wife, five children, and a servant maid, were all hung together and afterward thrown into a ditch. They hung many by the arms to branches of trees, with a weight to their feet; and others by the middle, in which postures they left them till they expired. Several were hung on windmills, and before they were half dead, the barbarians cut them in pieces with their swords. Others, both men, women, and children, they cut and hacked in various parts of their bodies, and left them wallowing in their blood to perish where they fell. One poor woman they hung on a gibbet, with her child, an infant about a twelve-month old, the latter of whom was hung by the neck with the hair of its mother's head, and in that manner finished its short but miserable existence.

In the county of Tyrone no less than three hundred protestants were drowned in one day; and many others were hanged, burned, and otherwise put to death. Dr. Maxwell, rector of Tyrone, lived at this time near Armagh, and suffered greatly from these merciless savages. This person, in his examination, taken upon oath before the king's commissioners, declared, that the Irish papists owned to him, that they, at several times, had destroyed, in one place, 12,000 protestants, whom they inhumanly slaughtered at Glynwood, in their flight from the county of Armagh.

As the river Bann was not fordable, and the bridge broken down, the Irish forced thither at different times, a great number of unarmed, defenceless protestants, and with pikes and swords violently thrust above one thousand into the river, where they miserably perished.

Nor did the cathedral of Armagh escape the fury of these barbarians, it being maliciously set on fire by their leaders, and burnt to the ground. And to extirpate, if possible, the very race of those unhappy protestants, who lived in or near Armagh, the Irish first burnt all their houses, and then gathered together many hundreds of those innocent people, young and old, on pretence of allowing them a guard and safe conduct to Colerain; when they treacherously fell on them by the way, and inhumanly murdered them.

The like horrid barbarities with those we have particularized, were practised on the wretched protestants in almost all parts of the kingdom; and, when an estimate was afterward made of the number who were sacrificed to gratify the diabolical souls of the papists, it amounted to one hundred and fifty thousand. But it now remains that we proceed to the particulars that followed.

These desperate wretches, flushed and grown insolent with success, (though by methods attended with such excessive barbarities as perhaps not to be equalled) soon got possession of the castle of Newry, where the king's stores and ammunition were lodged; and, with as little difficulty, made themselves masters of Dundalk. They afterward took the town of Ardee, where they murdered all the protestants, and then proceeded to Drogheda. The garrison of Drogheda was in no condition to sustain a siege, notwithstanding which, as often as the Irish renewed their attacks they were vigorously repulsed by a very unequal number of the king's forces, and a few faithful protestant citizens under sir Henry Tichborne, the governor, assisted by the lord viscount Moore. The siege of Drogheda began on the 30th of November, 1641, and held till the 4th of March, 1642, when sir Phelim O'Neal, and the Irish miscreants under him were forced to retire.

In the mean time ten thousand troops were sent from Scotland to the remaining protestants in Ireland, which being properly divided in the most capital parts of the kingdom, happily eclipsed the power of the Irish savages; and the protestants for a time lived in tranquility.

In the reign of king James II. they were again interrupted, for in a parliament held at Dublin in the year 1689, great numbers of the protestant nobility, clergy, and gentry of Ireland, were attainted of high treason. The government of the kingdom was, at that time, invested in the earl of Tyrconnel, a bigoted papist, and an inveterate enemy to the protestants. By his orders they were again persecuted in various parts of the kingdom. The revenues of the city of Dublin were seized, and most of the churches converted into prisons. And had it not been for the resolution and uncommon bravery of the garrisons in the city of Londonderry, and the town of Inniskillin, there had not one place remained for refuge to the distressed protestants in the whole kingdom; but all must have been given up to king James, and to the furious popish party that governed him.

The remarkable siege of Londonderry was opened on the 18th of April, 1689, by twenty thousand papists, the flower of the Irish army. The city was not properly circumstanced to sustain a siege, the defenders consisting of a body of raw undisciplined protestants, who had fled thither for shelter, and half a regiment of lord Mountjoy's disciplined soldiers, with the principal part of the inhabitants, making in all only seven thousand three hundred and sixty-one fighting men.

The besieged hoped, at first, that their stores of corn, and other necessaries, would be sufficient; but by the continuance of the siege their wants increased; and these became at last so heavy, that for a considerable time before the siege was raised, a pint of coarse barley, a small quantity of greens, a few spoonfuls of starch, with a very moderate proportion of horse flesh, were reckoned a week's provision for a soldier. And they were, at length, reduced to such extremities, that they ate dogs, cats, and mice.

Their miseries increasing with the siege, many, through mere hunger and want, pined and languished away, or fell dead in the streets. And it is remarkable, that when their long expected succours arrived from England, they were upon the point of being reduced to this alternative, either to preserve their existence by eating each other, or attempting to fight their way through the Irish, which must have infallibly produced their destruction.

These succours were most happily brought by the ship Mountjoy of Derry, and the Phoenix of Colerain, at which time they had only nine lean horses left with a pint of meal to each man. By hunger, and the fatigues of war, their seven thousand three hundred and sixty-one fighting men, were reduced to four thousand three hundred, one-fourth part of whom were rendered unserviceable.

As the calamities of the besieged were great, so likewise were the terrors and sufferings of their protestant friends and relations; all of whom (even women and children) were forcibly driven from the country thirty miles round, and inhumanly reduced to the sad necessity of continuing some days and nights without food or covering, before the walls of the town; and were thus exposed to the continual fire both of the Irish army from without, and the shot of their friends from within.

But the succours from England happily arriving put an end to their affliction; and the siege was raised on the 31st of July, having been continued upwards of three months.

The day before the siege of Londonderry was raised, the Inniskillers engaged a body of six thousand Irish Roman catholics, at Newton, Butler, or Crown-Castle, of whom near five thousand were slain. This, with the defeat at Londonderry, dispirited the papists, and they gave up all farther attempts to persecute the protestants.

The year following, viz. 1690; the Irish took up arms in favour of the abdicated prince, king James II. but they were totally defeated by his successor king William the Third. That monarch, before he left the country, reduced them to a state of subjection, in which they have ever since continued; and it is to be hoped will so remain as long as time shall be.

By a report made in Ireland, in the year 1731, it appeared that a great number of ecclesiastics had, in defiance of the laws, flocked into that kingdom: that several convents had been opened by jesuits, monks, and friars; that many new and pompous mass-houses had been erected in some of the most conspicuous parts of their great cities, where there had not been any before; and that such swarms of vagrant, immoral Romish priests had appeared, that the very papists themselves considered them as a burthen.

But notwithstanding all this, the protestant interest at present stands upon a much stronger basis than it did a century ago. The Irish, who formerly led an unsettled and roving life, in the woods, bogs, and mountains, and lived on the depredation of their neighbours, they who, in the morning seized the prey, and at night divided the spoil, have, for many years past, become quiet and civilized. They taste the sweets of English society, and the advantages of civil government. They trade in our cities, and are employed in our manufactories. They are received also into English families; and treated with great humanity by the protestants.

The heads of their clans, and the chiefs of the great Irish families, who cruelly oppressed and tyrannized over their vassals, are now dwindled in a great measure to nothing; and most of the ancient popish nobility and gentry of Ireland have renounced the Romish religion.

It is also to be hoped, that inestimable benefits will arise from the establishment of protestant schools in various parts of the kingdom, in which the children of the Roman catholics are instructed in religion and reading, whereby the mist of ignorance is dispelled from their eyes, which was the great source of the cruel transactions that have taken place, at different periods, in that kingdom.

In order to preserve the protestant interest in Ireland upon a solid basis, it behooves all in whom that power is invested, to discharge it with the strictest assiduity and attention; for should it once again lose ground, there is no doubt but the papists would take those advantages they have hitherto done, and thousands might yet fall victims to their malicious bigotry.

NOTES:

[C] Although Garnet was convicted for this horrible crime, yet the bigoted papists were so besotted as to look upon him as an object of devotion; they fancied that miracles were wrought by his blood; and regarded him as a martyr! Such is the deadening and perverting influence of popery.

[D] The king of England was at that time called *highness*, not *majesty*, as at present.

CHAPTER XVI.

THE RISE, PROGRESS, PERSECUTIONS, AND SUFFERINGS OF THE QUAKERS.

In treating of these people in a historical manner, we are obliged to have recourse to much tenderness. That they differ from the generality of protestants in some of the capital points of religion, cannot be denied, and yet, as protestant dissenters, they are included under the description of the toleration act. It is not our business to inquire whether people of similar sentiments had any existence in the primitive ages of Christianity: perhaps, in some respects, they had not, but we are to write of them not as what they were, but what they now are. That they have been treated by several writers in a very contemptuous manner, is certain; that they did not deserve such treatment, is equally certain.

The appellation *Quakers*, was bestowed upon them as a term of reproach, in consequence of their apparent convulsions which they laboured under when they delivered their discourses, because they imagined they were the effect of divine inspiration.

It is not our business, at present, to inquire whether the sentiments of these people are agreeable to the gospel, but this much is certain, that the first leader of them, as a separate body, was a man of obscure birth, who had his first existence in Leicestershire, about the year 1624. In speaking of this man we shall deliver our own sentiments in a historical manner, and joining these to what have been said by the Friends themselves, we shall endeavour to furnish out a complete narrative.

He was descended of honest and respected parents, who brought him up in the national religion: but from a child he appeared religious, still, solid, and observing, beyond his years, and uncommonly knowing in divine things. He was brought up to husbandry, and other country business, and was particularly inclined to the solitary occupation of a shepherd; "an employment," says our author, "that very well suited his mind in several respects, both for its innocency and solitude; and was a just emblem of his after ministry and service." In the year 1646, he entirely forsook the national church, in whose tenets he had been brought up, as before observed; and in 1647, he travelled into Derbyshire and Nottinghamshire, without any set purpose of visiting particular places, but in a solitary manner he walked through several towns and villages, which way soever his mind turned. "He fasted much," said Sewell, "and walked often in retired places, with no other companion than his Bible." "He visited the most retired and religious people in those parts," says Penn, "and some there were, short of few, if any, in this nation, who waited for the consolation of Israel night and day; as Zacharias, Anna, and Simeon, did of old time." To these he was sent, and these he sought out in the neighbouring counties, and among them he sojourned till his more ample ministry came upon him. At this time he taught, and was an example of silence, endeavouring to bring them from self-performances; testifying of, and turning them to the light of Christ within them, and encouraging them to wait in patience, and to feel the power of it to stir in their hearts, that their knowledge and worship of God might stand in the power of an endless life which was to be found in the light, as it was obeyed in the manifestation of it in man: for in the word was life, and that life is the light of men. Life in the word, light in men; and life in men too, as the light is obeyed; the children of the light living by the life of the word, by which the word begets them again to God, which is the generation and new birth, without which there is no coming into the kingdom of God, and to which whoever comes is greater than John: that is, than John's dispensation, which was not that of the kingdom, but the consummation of the legal, and forerunning of the gospel times, the time of the kingdom. Accordingly several meetings were gathering in those parts; and thus his time was employed for some years.

In the year 1652, "he had a visitation of the great work of God in the earth, and of the way that he was to go forth, in a public ministry, to begin it." He directed his course northward, "and in every place where he came, if not before he came to it, he had his particular exercise and service shown to him, so that the Lord was his leader indeed." He made great numbers of converts to his opinions, and many pious and good men joined him in his ministry. These were drawn forth especially to visit the public assemblies to reprove, reform, and exhort them; sometimes in markets, fairs, streets, and by the highway-side, "calling people to repentance, and to return to the Lord, with their hearts as well as their mouths; directing them to the light of Christ within them, to see, examine, and to consider their ways by, and to eschew the evil, and to do the good and acceptable will of God."

They were not without opposition in the work they imagined themselves called to, being often set in the stocks, stoned, beaten, whipped and imprisoned, though, as our author observes, honest men of good report, that had left wives, children, houses, and lands, to visit them with a living call to repentance. But these coercive methods rather forwarded than abated their zeal, and in those parts they brought over many proselytes, and amongst them several magistrates, and others of the better sort. They apprehended the Lord had forbidden them to pull off their hats to any one, high or low, and required them to speak to the people, without distinction, in the language of thou and thee. They scrupled bidding people good-morrow, or good-night, nor might they bend the knee to any one, even in supreme authority. Both men and woman went in a plain and simple dress, different from the fashion of the times. They neither gave nor accepted any titles of respect or honour, nor would they call any man master on earth. Several texts of scripture they quoted in defence of these singularities; such as, Swear not at all. How can ye believe who receive honour one of another, and seek not the honour which comes from God only? &c. &c. They placed the basis of religion in an inward light, and an extraordinary impulse of the Holy Spirit.

In 1654, their first separate meeting in London was held in the house of Robert Dring, in Watling-street, for by that time they spread themselves into all parts of the kingdom, and had in many places set up meetings or assemblies, particularly in Lancashire, and the adjacent parts, but they were still exposed to great persecutions and trials of every kind. One of them in a letter to the protector, Oliver Cromwell, represents, though there are no penal laws in force obliging men to comply with the established religion, yet the Quakers are exposed upon other accounts; they are fined and imprisoned for refusing to take an oath; for not paying their tithes; for disturbing the public assemblies, and meeting in the streets, and places of public resort; some of them have been whipped for vagabonds, and for their plain speeches to the magistrate.

Under favour of the then toleration, they opened their meetings at the Bull and Mouth, in Aldersgate-street, where women, as well as men, were moved to speak. Their zeal transported them to some extravagancies, which laid them still more open to the lash of their enemies, who exercised various severities upon them throughout the next reign. Upon the suppression of Venner's mad insurrection, the government, having published a proclamation, forbidding the Anabaptists, Quakers, and Fifth

Monarchy Men, to assemble or meet together under pretence of worshipping God, except it be in some parochial church, chapel, or in private houses, by consent of the persons there inhabiting, all meetings in other places being declared to be unlawful and riotous, &c. &c. the Quakers thought it expedient to address the king thereon, which they did in the following words:

"*O king Charles!*

"Our desire is, that thou mayest live for ever in the fear of God, and thy council. We beseech thee and thy council, to read these following lines in tender bowels, and compassion for our souls, and for your good.

"And this consider, we are about four hundred imprisoned, in and about this city, of men and women from their families, besides, in the county jails, about ten hundred; we desire that our meetings may not be broken up, but that all may come to a fair trial, that our innocency may be cleared up.

"London, 16th day, eleventh month, 1660."

On the 28th of the same month, they published the declaration referred to in their address, entitled, "A declaration from the harmless and innocent people of God, called Quakers, against all sedition, plotters, and fighters in the world, for removing the ground of jealousy and suspicion, from both magistrates and people in the kingdom, concerning wars and fightings." It was presented to the king the 21st day of the eleventh month, 1660, and he promised them upon his royal word, that they should not suffer for their opinions, as long as they lived peaceably; but his promises were very little regarded afterward.

In 1661, they assumed courage to petition the house of Lords for a toleration of their religion, and for a dispensation from taking the oaths, which they held unlawful, not from any disaffection to the government, or a belief that they were less obliged by an affirmation, but from a persuasion that all oaths were unlawful; and that swearing upon the most solemn occasions was forbidden in the New Testament. Their petition was rejected, and instead of granting them relief, an act was passed against them, the preamble to which set forth, "That whereas several persons have taken up an opinion that an oath, even before a magistrate, is unlawful, and contrary to the word of God: and whereas, under pretence of religious worship, the said persons do assemble in great numbers in several parts of the kingdom, separating themselves from the rest of his majesty's subjects, and the public congregations and usual places of divine worship; be it therefore enacted, that if any such persons, after the 24th of March, 1661-2, shall refuse to take an oath when lawfully tendered, or persuade others to do it, or maintain in writing or otherwise, the unlawfulness of taking an oath; or if they shall assemble for religious worship, to the number of five or more, of the age of fifteen, they shall for the first offence forfeit five pounds; for the second, ten pounds; and for the third shall abjure the realm, or be transported to the plantations: and the justices of peace at their open sessions may hear and finally determine in the affair."

This act had a most dreadful effect upon the Quakers, though it was well known and notorious that these conscientious persons were far from sedition or disaffection to the government. George Fox, in his address to the king, acquaints him, that three thousand and sixty-eight of their friends had been imprisoned since his majesty's restoration; that their meetings were daily broken up by men with clubs and arms, and their friends thrown into the water, and trampled under foot till the blood gushed out, which gave rise to their meeting in the open streets. A relation was printed, signed by twelve witnesses, which says, that more than four thousand two hundred Quakers were imprisoned; and of them five hundred were in and about London, and the suburbs; several of whom were dead in the jails.

However, they even gloried in their sufferings, which increased every day; so that in 1665, and the intermediate years, they were harassed without example. As they persisted resolutely to assemble, openly, at the Bull and Mouth, before mentioned, the soldiers, and other officers, dragged them from thence to prison, till Newgate was filled with them, and multitudes died of close confinement, in that and other jails.

Six hundred of them, says an account published at this time, were in prison, merely for religion's sake, of whom several were banished to the plantations. In short, says Mr. Neale, the Quakers gave such full employment to the informers, that they had less leisure to attend the meetings of other dissenters.

Yet, under all these calamities, they behaved with patience and modesty towards the government, and upon occasion of the Rye-house plot in 1682, thought proper to declare their innocence of that sham plot, in an address to the king, wherein, appealing to the Searcher of all hearts, they say, their principles do not allow them to take up defensive arms, much less to avenge themselves for the injuries they received from others: that they continually pray for the king's safety and preservation; and therefore take this occasion humbly to beseech his majesty to compassionate their suffering friends, with whom the jails are so filled, that they want air, to the apparent hazard of their lives, and to the endangering an infection in divers places. Besides, many houses, shops, barns, and fields are ransacked, and the goods, corn, and cattle swept away, to the discouraging trade and husbandry, and impoverishing great numbers of quiet and industrious people; and this, for no other cause, but for the exercise of a tender conscience in the worship of Almighty God, who is sovereign Lord and King of men's consciences.

On the accession of James II. they addressed that monarch honestly and plainly, telling him, "We are come to testify our sorrow for the death of our good friend Charles, and our joy for thy being made our governor. We are told thou art not of the persuasion of the church of England, no more than we; therefore we hope thou wilt grant us the same liberty which thou allowest thyself, which doing, we wish thee all manner of happiness."

When James, by his dispensing power, granted liberty to the dissenters, they began to enjoy some rest from their troubles; and indeed it was high time, for they were swelled to an enormous amount. They, the year before this, to them one of glad release, in a petition to James for a cessation of their sufferings, set forth, "that of late above one thousand five hundred of their friends, both men and women, and that now there remain one thousand three hundred and eighty-three; of which two hundred are women, many under sentence of praemunire; and more than three hundred near it, for refusing the oath of allegiance, because they could not swear. Three hundred and fifty have died in prison since the year 1680; in London, the jail of Newgate has been crowded, within these two years sometimes with near 20 in a room, whereby several have been suffocated, and others, who have been taken out sick, have died of malignant fevers within a few days. Great violences, outrageous distresses, and woful havock and spoil, have been made upon people's goods and estates, by a company of idle, extravagant, and merciless informers, by persecutions on the conventicle-act, and others, also on *qui tam* writs, and on other processes, for twenty pounds a month, and two-thirds of their estates seized for the king. Some had not a bed to rest on, others had no cattle to till the ground, nor corn for feed or bread, nor tools to work with, the said informers and bailiffs in some places breaking into houses, and making great waste and spoil, under pretence of serving the king and the church. Our religious assemblies have been charged at common law with being rioters and disturbers of the public peace, whereby great numbers have been confined in prison without regard to age, and many confined in holes and dungeons. The seizing for

L20 a month has amounted to many thousands, and several who have employed some hundreds of poor people in manufactures, are disabled to do so any more, by reason of long imprisonment. They spare neither widow nor fatherless, nor have they so much as a bed to lie on. The informers are both witnesses and prosecutors, to the ruin of great numbers of sober families; and justices of the peace have been threatened with the forfeiture of one hundred pounds, if they do not issue out warrants upon their informations." With this petition they presented a list of their friends in prison, in the several counties, amounting to four hundred and sixty.

During the reign of king James II. these people were, through the intercession of their friend Mr. Penn, treated with greater indulgence than ever they had been before. They were now become extremely numerous in many parts of the country, and the settlement of Pennsylvania taking place soon after, many of them went over to America. There they enjoyed the blessings of a peaceful government, and cultivated the arts of honest industry.

As the whole colony was the property of Mr. Penn, so he invited people of all denominations to come and settle with him. A universal liberty of conscience took place; and in this new colony the natural rights of mankind were, for the first time, established.

These Friends are, in the present age, a very harmless, inoffensive body of people; but of that we shall take more notice hereafter. By their wise regulations, they not only do honour to themselves, but they are of vast service to the community.

It may be necessary here to observe, that as the Friends, commonly called Quakers, will not take an oath in a court of justice, so their affirmation is permitted in all civil affairs; but they cannot prosecute a criminal, because, in the English courts of justice, all evidence must be upon oath.

An account of the persecution of Friends, commonly called Quakers in the United States.

About the middle of the seventeenth century, much persecution and suffering were inflicted on a sect of protestant dissenters, commonly called Quakers: a people which arose at that time in England some of whom sealed their testimony with their blood.

For an account of the above people, see Sewell's, or Gough's history of them.

The principal points upon which their conscientious nonconformity rendered them obnoxious to the penalties of the law, were,

1. The Christian resolution of assembling publicly for the worship of God, in a manner most agreeable to their consciences.

2. Their refusal to pay tithes, which they esteemed a Jewish ceremony, abrogated by the coming of Christ.

3. Their testimony against wars and fighting, the practice of which they judged inconsistent with the command of Christ: "Love your enemies," &c. Matt. v. 44.

4. Their constant obedience to the command of Christ: "Swear not at all," &c. Matt. v. 34.

5. Their refusal to pay rates or assessments for building and repairing houses for a worship which they did not approve.

6. Their use of the proper and Scriptural language, "thou," and "thee," to a single person: and their disuse of the custom of uncovering their heads, or pulling off their hats, by way of homage to man.

7. The necessity many found themselves under, of publishing what they believed to be the doctrine of truth; and sometimes even in the places appointed for the public national worship.

Their conscientious noncompliance in the preceding particulars, exposed them to much persecution and suffering, which consisted in prosecutions, fines, cruel beatings, whippings, and other corporeal punishments; imprisonment, banishment, and even death.

To relate a particular account of their persecutions and sufferings, would extend beyond the limits of this work: we shall therefore refer, for that information, to the histories already mentioned, and more particularly to Besse's Collection of their sufferings; and shall confine our account here, mostly to those who sacrificed their lives, and evinced, by their disposition of mind, constancy, patience, and faithful perseverance, that they were influenced by a sense of religious duty.

Numerous and repeated were the persecutions against them; and sometimes for transgressions or offences which the law did not contemplate or embrace.

Many of the fines and penalties exacted of them, were not only unreasonable and exorbitant, but as they could not consistently pay them, were sometimes distrained to several times the value of the demand; whereby many poor families were greatly distressed, and obliged to depend on the assistance of their friends.

Numbers were not only cruelly beaten and whipped in a public manner, like criminals, but some were branded and others had their ears cut off.

Great numbers were long confined in loathsome prisons; in which some ended their days in consequence thereof.

Many were sentenced to banishment; and a considerable number were transported. Some were banished on pain of death; and four were actually executed by the hands of the hangman, as we shall here relate, after inserting copies of some of the laws of the country where they suffered.

"At a General Court held at Boston, the 14th of October, 1656.

"Whereas, there is a cursed sect of heretics, lately risen up in the world, which are commonly called Quakers, who take upon them to be immediately sent from God, and infallibly assisted by the Spirit, to speak and write blasphemous opinions, despising government, and the order of God, in the church and commonwealth, speaking evil of dignities, reproaching and reviling magistrates and ministers, seeking to turn the people from the faith, and gain proselytes to their pernicious ways: this court taking into consideration the premises, and to prevent the like mischief, as by their means is wrought in our land, doth hereby order, and by authority of this court, be it ordered and enacted, that what master or commander of any ship, bark, pink, or ketch, shall henceforth bring into any harbour, creek, or cove, within this jurisdiction, any Quaker or Quakers, or other blasphemous heretics, shall pay, or cause to be paid, the fine of one hundred pounds to the treasurer of the country, except it appear he want true knowledge or information of their being such; and, in that case, he hath liberty to clear himself by his oath, when sufficient proof to the contrary is wanting: and, for default of good payment, or good security for it, shall be cast into prison, and there to continue till the said sum be satisfied to the treasurer as aforesaid. And the commander of any ketch, ship, or vessel, being legally convicted, shall give in sufficient security to the governor, or any one or more of the magistrates, who have power to determine the same, to carry them back to the place whence he brought them; and, on his refusal so to do, the governor or one or more of the magistrates, are hereby empowered to issue out his or their warrants to commit such master or commander to prison, there to continue, till he give in sufficient security to the content of the governor, or any of the magistrates, as aforesaid. And it is hereby further ordered and enacted, that what Quaker soever shall arrive in this country from foreign parts, or shall come into this jurisdiction from any parts adjacent, shall be forthwith committed to the house of correction; and, at their entrance, to be severely whipped, and by the master thereof be kept constantly to work, and none suffered to converse or speak with them, during the time of their imprisonment, which shall be no longer than necessity requires. And it is ordered, if any person shall knowingly import into any harbour of this jurisdiction, any Quakers' books or writings, concerning their devilish opinions, shall pay for such book or writing, being legally proved against him or them the sum of five pounds; and whosoever shall disperse or conceal any such book or writing, and it be found with him or her, or in his or her house and shall not immediately deliver the same to the next magistrate; shall forfeit or pay five pounds, for the dispersing or concealing of any such book or writing. And it is hereby further enacted, that if any person within this colony, shall take upon them to defend the heretical opinions of the Quakers, or any of their books or papers, shall be fined for the first time forty shillings; if they shall persist in the same, and shall again defend it the second time, four pounds; if notwithstanding they again defend and maintain the said Quakers' heretical opinions, they shall be committed to the house of correction till there be convenient passage to send them out of the land, being sentenced by the court of Assistants to banishment. Lastly, it is hereby ordered, that what person or persons soever, shall revile the persons of the magistrates or ministers, as is usual with the Quakers, such person or persons shall be severely whipped or pay the sum of five pounds.

"This is a true copy of the court's order, as attests

"EDWARD RAWSON, Sec."

"*At a General Court held at Boston, the 14th of October, 1657.*

"As an addition to the late order, in reference to the coming or bringing of any of the cursed sect of the Quakers into this jurisdiction, it is ordered, that whosoever shall from henceforth bring, or cause to be brought, directly or indirectly, any known Quaker or Quakers, or other blasphemous heretics, into this jurisdiction, every such person shall forfeit the sum of one hundred pounds to the country, and shall by warrant from any magistrate be committed to prison, there to remain till the penalty be satisfied and paid; and if any person or persons within this jurisdiction, shall henceforth entertain and conceal any such Quaker or Quakers, or other blasphemous heretics, knowing them so to be, every such person shall forfeit to the country forty shillings for every hours' entertainment and concealment of any Quaker or Quakers, &c. as aforesaid, and shall be committed to prison as aforesaid, till the forfeiture be fully satisfied and paid. And it is further ordered, that if any Quaker or Quakers shall presume, after they have once suffered what the law requires, to come into this jurisdiction, every such male Quaker shall, for the first offence, have one of his ears cut off, and be kept at work in the house of correction, till he can be sent away at his own charge; and for the second offence, shall have his other ear cut off; and every woman Quaker, that has suffered the law here, that shall presume to come into this jurisdiction, shall be severely whipped, and kept at the house of correction at work, till she be sent away at her own charge, and so also for her coming again, she shall be alike used as aforesaid. And for every Quaker, he or she, that shall a third time herein again offend, they shall have their tongues bored through with a hot iron, and be kept at the house of correction close to work, till they be sent away at their own charge. And it is further ordered, that all and every Quaker arising from among ourselves, shall be dealt with, and suffer the like punishment as the law provides against foreign Quakers.

"EDWARD RAWSON, Sec."

"An Act made at a General Court, held at Boston, the 20th of October, 1658.

"Whereas, there is a pernicious sect, commonly called Quakers, lately risen, who by word and writing have published and maintained many dangerous and horrid tenets, and do take upon them to change and alter the received laudable customs of our nation, in giving civil respect to equals, or reverence to superiors; whose actions tend to undermine the civil government, and also to destroy the order of the churches, by denying all established forms of worship, and by withdrawing from orderly church fellowship, allowed and approved by all orthodox professors of truth, and instead thereof, and in opposition thereunto, frequently meeting by themselves, insinuating themselves into the minds of the simple, or such as are at least affected to the order and government of church and commonwealth, whereby divers of our inhabitants have been infected, notwithstanding all former laws, made upon the experience of their arrogant and bold obtrusions, to disseminate their principles amongst us, prohibiting their coming into this jurisdiction, they have not been deterred from their impious attempts to undermine our peace, and hazard our ruin.

"For prevention thereof, this court doth order and enact, that any person or persons, of the cursed sect of the Quakers, who is not an inhabitant of, but is found within this jurisdiction, shall be apprehended without warrant, where no magistrate is hand, by any constable commissioner, or select-man, and conveyed from constable to constable, to the next magistrate, who shall commit the said person to close prison, there to remain (without bail) until the next court of Assistants, where they shall have legal trial. And being convicted to be of the sect of the Quakers, shall be sentenced to banishment, on pain of death. And that every inhabitant of this jurisdiction, being convicted to be of the aforesaid sect, either by taking up, publishing, or defending the horrid opinions of the Quakers, or the stirring up mutiny, sedition, or rebellion against the government, or by taking up their abusive and destructive practices, viz. denying civil respect to equals and superiors, and withdrawing from the church assemblies; and instead thereof, frequenting meetings of their own, in opposition to our church order; adhering to, or approving of any known Quaker, and the tenets and practices of Quakers, that are opposite to the orthodox received opinions of the godly; and endeaving to disaffect others to civil government and church order, or condemning the practice and proceedings of this court against the Quakers, manifesting thereby their complying with those, whose design is to overthrow the order established in church and state: every such person, upon conviction before the said court of Assistants, in manner aforesaid, shall be committed to close prison for one month, and then, unless they choose voluntarily to depart this jurisdiction, shall give bond for their good behaviour and appear at the next court, where, continuing obstinate, and refusing to retract and reform the aforesaid opinions, they shall be sentenced to banishment, upon pain of death. And any one magistrate, upon information given him of any such person, shall cause him to be apprehended, and shall commit any such person to prison, according to his discretion, until he come to trial as aforesaid."

It appears there were also laws passed in both of the then colonies of New-Plymouth and New-Haven, and in the Dutch settlement at

New-Amsterdam, now New-York, prohibiting the people called Quakers, from coming into those places, under severe penalties; in consequence of which, some underwent considerable suffering.

The two first who were executed were William Robinson, merchant, of London, and Marmaduke Stevenson, a countryman, of Yorkshire. These coming to Boston, in the beginning of September, were sent for by the court of Assistants, and there sentenced to banishment, on pain of death. This sentence was passed also on Mary Dyar, mentioned hereafter, and Nicholas Davis, who were both at Boston. But William Robinson, being looked upon as a teacher, was also condemned to be whipped severely; and the constable was commanded to get an able man to do it. Then Robinson was brought into the street, and there stripped; and having his hands put through the holes of the carriage of a great gun, where the jailer held him, the executioner gave him twenty stripes, with a three-fold cord-whip. Then he and the other prisoners were shortly after released, and banished, as appears from the following warrant:

"You are required by these, presently to set at liberty William Robinson, Marmaduke Stevenson, Mary Dyar, and Nicholas Davis, who, by an order of the court and council, had been imprisoned, because it appeared by their own confession, words, and actions, that they are Quakers: wherefore, a sentence was pronounced against them, to depart this jurisdiction, on pain of death; and that they must answer it at their peril, if they, or any of them, after the 14th of this present month, September, are found within this jurisdiction, or any part thereof.

"EDWARD RAWSON"

"Boston, September 12, 1659."

Though Mary Dyar and Nicholas Davis left that jurisdiction for that time, yet Robinson and Stevenson, though they departed the town of Boston, could not yet resolve (not being free in mind) to depart that jurisdiction, though their lives were at stake. And so they went to Salem, and some places thereabout, to visit and build up their friends in the faith. But it was not long before they were taken, and put again into prison at Boston, and chains locked to their legs. In the next month, Mary Dyar returned also. And as she stood before the prison, speaking with one Christopher Holden, who was come thither to inquire for a ship bound for England, whither he intended to go, she was also taken into custody. Thus, they had now three persons, who, according to their law, had forfeited their lives. And, on the 20th of October, these three were brought into court, where John Endicot and others were assembled. And being called to the bar, Endicot commanded the keeper to pull off their hats; and then said, that they had made several laws to keep the Quakers from amongst them, and neither whipping, nor imprisoning, nor cutting off ears, nor banishing upon pain of death, would keep them from amongst them. And further, he said, that he or they desired not the death of any of them. Yet, notwithstanding, his following words, without more ado, were, "Give ear, and hearken to your sentence of death." Sentence of death was also passed upon Marmaduke Stevenson, Mary Dyar, and William Edrid. Several others were imprisoned, whipped, and fined. We have no disposition to justify the Pilgrims for these proceedings, but we think, considering the circumstances of the age in which they lived, their conduct admits of much palliation. The following remarks of Mr. Hawes, in his tribute to the memory of the Pilgrims, are worthy of serious consideration.

"It is alleged that they enacted laws which were oppressive to other denominations, and, moreover, that they were actually guilty of persecution. This, indeed, is a serious charge, and to some extent must be admitted to be true. And yet whoever candidly examines the facts in the case, will find abundant evidence that our fathers, in this respect, were far from being sinners above all who have dwelt on the earth. Many of the laws that are complained of were enacted when there were few or none of any other denomination in the land. They were designed to protect and support their own ecclesiastical and civil order; and not to operate at all as persecuting or oppressive enactments against christians belonging to other sects. It is also true that most of those persons who are said to have been persecuted and oppressed, suffered not so much for their religious opinions, as for their offences against the state. Some of them outraged all decency and order, and committed such acts as would unquestionably, at the present day, subject a man to imprisonment, if not to severer punishment.

"This, according to Winthrop, was the ground of the sentence of banishment, passed on Roger Williams. 'He broached and divulged divers new opinions against the authority of magistrates, as also wrote letters of defamation both of the magistrates and churches.'"--Winthrop's Hist. of N. E. edit. by Savage, vol. 1, p. 167.

"For a particular account of the causes for which Mr. Williams was banished, see Hutchinson's History of Massachusetts, vol. 1, p. 41;

Dwight's Travels, vol. 1, p. 142; Magnalia, vol. 2, p. 430. As for the laws subsequently enacted against the Baptists and Quakers, no one most certainly can justify them. They were oppressive and wrong. But let no one reproach, too severely, the memory of our fathers, in this matter, till he is certain, that *in similar circumstances*, he would have shown a better temper.

"It is allowed that they were culpable; but we do not concede, that in the present instance, they stood alone, or that they merited all the censure bestowed on them. 'Laws similar to those of Massachusetts were passed elsewhere against the Quakers and also against the Baptists, particularly in Virginia. If no execution took place here, it was not owing to the moderation of the church.'"--Jefferson Virg. Query, XVIII.

"The prevalent opinion among most sects of christians, at that day, that toleration is sinful, ought to be remembered; nor should it be forgotten, that the first Quakers in New England, besides speaking and writing what was deemed blasphemous, reviled magistrates and ministers, and disturbed religious assemblies; and that the tendency of their opinions and practices was to the subversion of the commonwealth in the period of its infancy."--*Holmes' Am. Annals. Hutch. vol. 1, p. 180-9.*

"It should be added, that in Massachusetts the law which enacted that all Quakers returning into the state after banishment, should be punished with death, and under which four persons were executed, met with great, and at first, successful opposition. The deputies, who constituted the popular branch of the legislature, at first rejected it; but afterwards, on reconsideration, concurred with the magistrates, (by whom it was originally proposed,) by a majority of only one."--Chr. Spect. 1830, p. 266.

"The fathers of New England, endured incredible hardships in providing for themselves a home in the wilderness; and to protect themselves in the undisturbed enjoyment of rights, which they had purchased at so dear a rate, they sometimes adopted measures which, if tried by the more enlightened and liberal views of the present day, must at once be pronounced altogether unjustifiable. But shall they be condemned without mercy for not acting up to principles which were unacknowledged and unknown throughout the whole of christendom? Shall they alone be held responsible for opinions and conduct which had become sacred by antiquity, and which were common to christians of all other denominations? Every government then in existence assumed to itself the right to legislate in matters of religion; and to restrain heresy by penal statutes. This right was claimed by rulers, admitted by subjects, and is sanctioned by the names of Lord Bacon and Montesquieu, and many others equally famed for their talents and learning. It is unjust then, to 'press upon one poor persecuted sect, the sins of all christendom?' The fault of our fathers was the fault of the age; and though this cannot justify, it certainly furnishes an extenuation of their conduct. As well might you condemn them for not understanding the art of navigating by steam, as for not understanding and acting up to the principles of religious toleration. At the same time, it is but just to say, that imperfect as were their views of the rights of conscience, they were nevertheless far in advance of the age to which they belonged; and it is to them more than to any other class of men on earth, the world is indebted for the more rational views that now prevail on the subject of civil and religious liberty."

CHAPTER XVII.

PERSECUTIONS OF THE FRENCH PROTESTANTS IN THE SOUTH OF FRANCE, DURING THE YEARS 1814 AND 1820.

The persecution in this protestant part of France continued with very little intermission from the revocation of the edict of Nantes, by Louis XIV. till a very short period previous to the commencement of the late French revolution. In the year 1785, M. Rebaut St. Etienne and the celebrated M. de la Fayette were among the first persons who interested themselves with the court of Louis XVI., in removing the scourge of persecution from this injured people, the inhabitants of the south of France.

Such was the opposition on the part of the catholics and the courtiers, that it was not till the end of the year 1790, that the protestants were freed from their alarms. Previously to this, the catholics at Nismes in particular, had taken up arms; Nismes then presented a frightful spectacle; armed men ran through the city, fired from the corners of the streets, and attacked all they met with swords and forks. A man named Astuc was wounded and thrown into the aqueduct; Baudon fell under the repeated strokes of bayonets and sabres, and his body was also thrown into the water; Boucher, a young man only 17 years of age, was shot as he was looking out of his window; three electors wounded, one dangerously; another elector wounded, only escaped death by repeatedly declaring he was a catholic; a third received four sabre wounds, and was taken home dreadfully mangled. The citizens that fled were arrested by the catholics upon the roads, and obliged to give proofs of their religion before their lives were granted. M. and Madame Vogue, were at their country house, which the zealots broke open, where they massacred both, and destroyed their dwelling. M. Blacher, a protestant seventy years of age, was cut to pieces with a sickle; young Pyerre, carrying some food to his brother, was asked, "Catholic or protestant?" "Protestant," being the reply, a monster fired at the lad, and he fell. One of the murderer's companions said, "you might as well have killed a lamb." "I have sworn," replied he, "to kill four protestants for my share, and this will count for one." However, as these atrocities provoked the troops to unite in defence of the people, a terrible vengeance was retaliated upon the catholic party that had used arms, which with other circumstances, especially the toleration exercised by Napoleon Buonaparte, kept them down completely till the year 1814, when the unexpected return of the ancient government rallied them all once more round the old banners.

The arrival of King Louis XVIII. at Paris.

This was known at Nismes on the 13th of April, 1814. In a quarter of an hour, the white cockade was seen in every direction, the white flag floated on the public buildings, on the splendid monuments of antiquity, and even on the tower of Mange, beyond the city walls. The protestants, whose commerce had suffered materially during the war, were among the first to unite in the general joy, and to send in their adhesion to the senate, and the legislative body; and several of the protestant departments sent addresses to the throne, but unfortunately, M. Froment was again at Nismes at the moment when many bigots being ready to join him, the blindness and fury of the sixteenth century rapidly succeeded the intelligence and philanthropy of the nineteenth. A line of distinction was instantly traced between men of different religious opinions; the spirit of the old catholic church was again to regulate each person's share of esteem and safety. The difference of religion was now to govern every thing else; and even catholic domestics who had served protestants with zeal and affection, began to neglect their duties, or to perform them ungraciously, and with reluctance. At the fetes and spectacles that were given at the public expense, the absence of the protestants was charged on them as a proof of their disloyalty; and in the midst of the cries of "*Vive le Roi*," the discordant sounds of "*A bas le Maire*," down with the mayor, were heard. M. Castletan was a protestant; he appeared in public with the prefect M. Ruland, a catholic, when potatoes were thrown at him, and the people declared that he ought to resign his office. The bigots of Nismes even succeeded in procuring an address to be presented to the king, stating that there ought to be in France but one God, one king, and one faith. In this they were imitated by the catholics of several towns.

The History of the Silver Child.

About this time, M. Baron, counsellor of the Cour Royale of Nismes, formed the plan of dedicating to God a silver child, if the Duchess d'Angouleme would give a prince to France. This project was converted into a public religious vow, which was the subject of conversation both in public and private, whilst persons, whose imaginations were inflamed by these proceedings, run about the streets crying Vivent les Bourbons, or the Bourbons forever. In consequence of this superstitious frenzy, it is said that, at Alais, women were advised and instigated to poison their protestant husbands, and at length it was found convenient to accuse them of political crimes. They could no longer appear in public without insults and injuries. When the mobs met with protestants, they seized them, and danced round them with barbarous joy, and amidst repeated cries of *Vive le Roi*, they sung verses, the burden of which was, "We will wash our hands in protestant blood, and make black puddings of the blood of Calvin's children." The citizens who came to the promenades for air and refreshment, from the close and dirty streets, were chased with shouts of *Vive le Roi*, as if those shouts were to justify every excess. If protestants referred to the charter, they were directly assured it would be of no use to them, and that they had only been managed to be more effectually destroyed. Persons of rank were heard to say in the public streets, "All the Huguenots must be killed; this time their children must be killed, that none of the accursed race may remain." Still, it is true, they were not murdered, but cruelly treated, protestant children could no longer mix in the sports of catholics, and were not even permitted to appear without their parents. At dark their families shut themselves up in their apartments; but even then stones were thrown against their windows. When they arose in the morning, it was not uncommon to find gibbets drawn on their doors or walls; and in the streets the catholics held cords already soaped before their eyes, and pointed out the instruments by which they hoped and designed to exterminate them. Small gallows or models were handed about, and a man who lived opposite to one of the pastors, exhibited one of these models in his window, and made signs sufficiently intelligible when the minister passed. A figure representing a protestant preacher was also hung up on a public crossway, and the most atrocious songs were sung under his window. Towards the conclusion of the carnival, a plan had even been formed to make a caricature of the four ministers of the place, and burn them in effigy; but this was prevented by the mayor of Nismes, a protestant. A dreadful song presented to the prefect, in the country dialect, with a false translation, was printed by his approval, and had a great run before he saw the extent of the error into which he had been betrayed. The sixty-third regiment of the line was publicly censured and insulted, for having, according to order, protected protestants. In fact, the protestants seemed to be as sheep destined for the slaughter.

Napoleon's Return from the Isle of Elba.

Soon after this event, the duke d'Angouleme was at Nismes, and remained there some time; but even his influence was insufficient to bring about a reconciliation between the catholics and the protestants of that city. During the hundred days betwixt Napoleon's return from the Isle of Elba, and his final downfall, not a single life was lost in Nismes, not a single house was pillaged; only four of the most notorious disturbers of the peace were punished, or rather prevented from doing mischief, and even this was not an act of the protestant but the *arrete* of the catholic prefect, announced every where with the utmost publicity. Some time after, when M. Baron, who proposed the vow of the silver child in favour of the Duchess d'Angouleme, who was considered as the chief of the catholic royalists, was discovered at the bottom of an old wine tun, the populace threw stones at his carriage, and vented their feelings in abusive language. The protestant officers protected him from injury.

The Catholic arms at Beaucaire.

In May, 1815, a federative association, similar to those of Lyons, Grenoble, Paris, Avignon, and Montpelier, was desired by many persons at Nismes; but this federation terminated here after an ephemeral and illusory existence of fourteen days. In the mean while a large party of catholic zealots were in arms at Beaucaire, and who soon pushed their patroles so near the walls of Nismes, "as to alarm the inhabitants." These catholics applied to the English off Marseilles for assistance, and obtained the grant of 1000 muskets, 10,000 cartouches, &c. General Gilly, however, was soon sent against these partizans, who prevented them from coming to extremes, by granting them an armistice; and yet when Louis XVIII. had returned to Paris, after the expiration of Napoleon's reign of a hundred days, and peace and party spirit seemed to have been subdued, even at Nismes, bands from Beaucaire joined Trestaillon in this city, to glut the vengeance they had so long premeditated. General Gilly had left the department several days: the troops of the line left behind had taken the white cockade, and waited farther orders, whilst the new commissioners had only to proclaim the cessation of hostilities, and the complete establishment of the king's authority. In vain, no commissioners appeared, no despatches arrived to calm and regulate the public mind; but towards evening the advanced guard of the banditti, to the amount of several hundreds, entered the city, undesired but unopposed. As they marched without order or discipline, covered with clothes or rags of all colours, decorated with cockades not *white*, but *white* and *green*, armed with muskets, sabres, forks, pistols and reaping hooks, intoxicated with wine, and stained with the blood of the protestants whom they had murdered on their route, they presented a most hideous and appalling spectacle. In the open place in the front of the barracks, this banditti was joined by the city armed mob, headed by Jaques Dupont, commonly called Trestaillon. To save the effusion of blood, this garrison of about 500 men consented to capitulate, and marched out sad and defenceless; but when about fifty had passed, the rabble commenced a tremendous fire on their confiding and unprotected victims; nearly all were killed or wounded, and but very few could re-enter the yard before the garrison gates were again closed. These were again forced in an instant, and all were massacred who could not climb over roofs, or leap into the adjoining gardens. In a word, death met them in every place and in every shape and this catholic massacre rivalled in cruelty, and surpassed in treachery, the crimes of the September assassins of Paris and the Jacobinical butcheries of Lyons and Avignon. It was marked, not only by the fervour of the revolution, but by the subtlety of the league, and will long remain a blot upon the history of the second restoration.

Massacre and Pillage at Nismes.

Nismes now exhibited a most awful scene of outrage and carnage, though many of the protestants had fled to the Convennes and the Gardonenque.

The country houses of Messrs. Rey, Guiret, and several others, had been pillaged, and the inhabitants treated with wanton barbarity. Two parties had glutted their savage appetites on the farm of Madame Frat: the first, after eating, drinking, and breaking the furniture, and stealing what they thought proper, took leave by announcing the arrival of their comrades, "compared with whom," they said, "they should be thought merciful." Three men and an old woman were left on the premises: at the sight of the second company two of the men fled. "Are you a catholic?" said the banditti to the old woman. "Yes." "Repeat, then, your Pater and Ave." Being terrified she hesitated, and was instantly knocked down with a musket. On recovering her senses, she stole out of the house, but met Ladet, the old *valet de ferme*, bringing in a salad which the depredators had ordered him to cut. In vain she endeavoured to persuade him to fly. "Are you a protestant?" they exclaimed; "I am." A musket being discharged at him, he fell wounded, but not dead. To consummate their work, the monsters lighted a fire with straw and boards, threw their yet living victim into the flames, and suffered him to expire in the most dreadful agonies. They then ate their salad, omelet, &c. The next day, some labourers, seeing the house open and deserted, entered and discovered the half consumed body of Ladet. The prefect of the Gard, M. Darbaud Jouques, attempting to palliate the crimes of the catholics, had the audacity to assert that Ladet was a catholic; but this was publicly contradicted by two of the pastors at Nismes.

Another party committed a dreadful murder at St. Cezaire, upon Imbert la Plume, the husband of Suzon Chivas. He was met on returning from work in the fields. The chief promised him his life, but insisted that he must be conducted to the prison at Nismes. Seeing, however, that the party was determined to kill him, he resumed his natural character, and being a powerful and courageous man advanced and exclaimed, "You are brigands--fire!" Four of them fired, and he fell, but he was not dead; and while living they mutilated his body and then passing a cord round it, drew it along, attached to a cannon of which they had possession. It was not till after eight days that his relatives were apprized of his death. Five individuals of the family of Chivas, all husbands and fathers, were massacred in the course of a few days.

Near the barracks at Nismes is a large and handsome house, the property of M. Vitte, which he acquired by exertion and economy. Besides comfortable lodgings for his own family, he let more than twenty chambers, mostly occupied by superior officers and commissaries of the army. He never inquired the opinion of his tenants, and of course his guests were persons of all political parties; but, under pretence of searching for concealed officers, his apartments were overrun, his furniture broken, and his property carried off at pleasure. The houses of Messrs. Lagorce, most respectable merchants and manufacturers M. Matthieu, M. Negre, and others, shared the same fate: many only avoided by the owners paying large sums as commutation money, or escaping into the country with their cash.

Interference of Government against the Protestants.

M. Bernis, extraordinary royal commissioner, in consequence of these abuses, issued a proclamation which reflects disgrace on the authority from whence it emanated. "Considering," it said, "that the residence of citizens in places foreign to their domicile, can only be prejudicial to the *communes* they have left, and to those to which they have repaired, it is ordered, that those inhabitants who have quitted their residence since the commandment of July, return home by the 28th at the latest, otherwise they shall be deemed accomplices of the evil-disposed persons who disturb the public tranquility, and their property shall be placed under provisional *sequestration*."

The fugitives had sufficient inducements to return to their hearths, without the fear of sequestration. They were more anxious to embrace their fathers, mothers, wives, and children, and to resume their ordinary occupations, than M. Bernis could be to insure their return. But thus denouncing men as criminals who fled for safety from the sabres of assassins, was adding oil to the fire of persecution. Trestaillon, one of the chiefs of the brigands, was dressed in complete uniform and epaulettes which he had stolen; he wore a sabre at his side, pistols in his belt, a cockade of white and green, and a sash of the same colours on his arm. He had under him, Truphemy, Servan, Aime, and many other desperate characters. Some time after this M. Bernis ordered all parties and individuals, armed or unarmed, to abstain from searching houses, without either an order, or the presence of an officer. On suspicion of arms being concealed, the commandant of the town was ordered to furnish a patrol to make search and seizure; and all persons carrying arms in the streets, without being on service, were to be arrested. Trestaillon, however, who still carried arms, was not arrested till some months after, and then not by these authorities, but by General La Garde, who was afterwards assassinated by one of his comrades. On this occasion it was remarked, that "the system of specious and deceptive proclamations was perfectly understood, and had long been practised in Languedoc; it was *not too late* to persecute the protestants simply for their religion. Even in the good times of Louis XIV. there was public opinion enough in Europe to make that arch tyrant have recourse to the meanest stratagems." The following single specimen of the plan pursued by the authors of the Dragonades may serve as a key to all the plausible proclamations which, in 1815, covered the perpetration of the most deliberate and extensive crimes:--

Letters from Louvois to Marillac.

"The king rejoices to learn from your letters, that there are so many conversions in your department; and he desires that you would continue your efforts, and employ the same means that have been hitherto so successful. His majesty has ordered me to send a regiment of cavalry, the greatest part of which he wishes to be quartered upon the protestants, but he does not think it **prudent** that they should be all lodged with them; that is to say, of twenty-six masters, of which a company is composed, if, by a judicious distribution, ten ought to be received by the protestants, give them twenty, and put them all on the rich, making this pretence, that when there are not soldiers enough in a town for all to have some, the poor ought to be exempt, and the rich burdened. His majesty has also thought proper to order, that all converts be exempted from lodging soldiers for two years. This will occasion numerous conversions if you take care that it is rigorously executed, and that in all the distributions and passage of troops, by far the greatest number are quartered on the rich protestants. His majesty particularly enjoins that your orders on this subject, either by yourself or your sub-delegates, be given by word of mouth to the mayors and sheriffs, without letting them know that his majesty intends by these means to force to become converts, and only explaining to them, that you give these orders on the information you have received, that in these places the rich are excepted by their influence, to the prejudice of the poor."

The merciless treatment of the women, in this persecution at Nismes, was such as would have disgraced any savages ever heard of. The widows Rivet and Bernard, were forced to sacrifice enormous sums; and the house of Mrs. Lecointe was ravaged, and her goods destroyed. Mrs. F. Didier had her dwelling sacked and nearly demolished to the foundation. A party of these bigots visited the widow Perrin, who lived on a little farm at the windmills; having committed every species of devastation, they attacked even the sanctuary of the dead, which contained the relics of her family. They dragged the coffins out, and scattered the contents over the adjacent grounds. In vain this outraged widow collected the bones of her ancestors and replaced them: they were again dug up; and, after several useless efforts, they were reluctantly left spread over the surface of the fields.

Till the period announced for the sequestration of the property of the fugitives by *authority*, murder and plunder were the daily employment of what was called the army of Beaucaire, and the catholics of Nismes. M. Peyron, of Brossan, had all his property carried off; his wine, oil, seed, grain, several score of sheep, eight mules, three carts, his furniture and effects, all the cash that could be found and he had only to congratulate himself that his habitation was not consumed, and his vineyards rooted up. A similar process against several other protestant farmers, was also regularly carried on during several days. Many of the protestants thus persecuted were well known as staunch royalists; but it was enough for their enemies to know that they belonged to the reformed communion; these fanatics were determined not to find either royalists or citizens worthy the common protection of society. To accuse, condemn, and destroy a protestant, was a matter that required no hesitation. The house of M. Vitte, near the barracks at Nismes, was broken open, and every thing within the walls demolished. A Jew family of lodgers was driven out, and all their goods thrown out of the windows. M. Vitte was seized, robbed of his watch and money, severely wounded, and left for dead. After he had been fourteen hours in a state of insensibility, a commissary of police, touched by his misfortunes, administered some cordials to revive him; and, as a measure of safety, conducted him to the citadel, where he remained many days, whilst his family lamented him as dead. At length, as there was not the slightest charge against him, he obtained his liberation from M. Vidal; but when the Austrians arrived, one of the aids-de-camp, who heard of his sufferings and his respectability, sought him out, and furnished an escort to conduct his family to a place of safety. Dalbos, the only city beadle who was a protestant, was dragged from his home and led to prison. His niece threw herself on the neck of one of them and begged for mercy; the ruffian dashed her to the ground. His sister was driven away by the mob; and he being shot, his body remained a long time exposed to the insults of the rabble.

Royal Decree in favour of the Persecuted.

At length the decree of Louis XVIII., which annulled all the extraordinary powers conferred either by the king, the princes, or subordinate agents, was received at Nismes, and the laws were now to be administered by the regular organs, and a new prefect arrived to carry them into effect; but in spite of proclamations, the work of destruction, stopped for a moment, was not abandoned, but soon renewed with fresh vigour and effect. On the 30th of July, Jacques Combe, the father of a family, was killed by some of the national guards of Rusau, and the crime was so public, that the commander of the party restored to the family the pocket-book and papers of the deceased. On the following day tumultuous crowds roamed about the city and suburbs, threatening the wretched peasants; and on the 1st of August they butchered them without opposition. About noon on the same day, six armed men, headed by Truphemy, the butcher, surrounded the house of Monot, a carpenter; two of the party, who were smiths, had been at work in the house the day before, and had seen a protestant who had taken refuge there, M. Bourillon, who had been a lieutenant in the army, and had retired on a pension. He was a man of an excellent character, peaceable and harmless, and had never served the emperor Napoleon. Truphemy not knowing him, he was pointed out partaking of a frugal breakfast with the family. Truphemy ordered him to go along with him, adding, "Your friend, Saussine, is already in the other world." Truphemy placed him in the middle of his troop, and artfully ordered him to cry *Vive l'Empereur*: he refused, adding, he had never served the emperor. In vain did the women and children of the house intercede for his life, and praise his amiable and virtuous qualities. He was marched to the Esplanade and shot, first by Truphemy and then by the others. Several persons attracted by the firing, approached, but were threatened with a similar fate. After some time the wretches departed, shouting *Vive le Roi*. Some women met them, and one of them appeared affected, said one, "I have killed seven to-day, for my share and if you say a word, you shall be the eighth." Pierre Courbet, a stocking weaver, was torn from his loom by an armed band, and shot at his own door. His eldest daughter was knocked down with the butt end of a musket; and a poignard was held at the breast of his wife while the mob plundered her apartments. Paul Heraut, a silk weaver, was literally cut in pieces, in the presence of a large crowd, and amidst the unavailing cries and tears of his wife and four young children. The murderers only abandoned the corpse to return to Heraut's house and secure every thing valuable. The number of murders on this day could not be ascertained. One person saw six bodies at the *Cours Neuf*, and nine were carried to the hospital.

If murder some time after, became less frequent for a few days, pillage and forced contributions were actively enforced. M. Salle d'Hombro, at several visits was robbed of 7000 francs; and on one occasion, when he pleaded the sacrifices he had made, "Look," said a bandit, pointing to his pipe, "this will set fire to your house; and this," brandishing his sword, "will finish you." No reply could be made to these arguments. M. Feline, a silk manufacturer, was robbed of 32,000 francs in gold, 3000 francs in silver, and several bales of silk.

The small shopkeepers were continually exposed to visits and demands of provisions, drapery, or whatever they sold; and the same hands that set fire to the houses of the rich, and tore up the vines of the cultivator, broke the looms of the weaver, and stole the tools of the artizan. Desolation reigned in the sanctuary and in the city. The armed bands, instead of being reduced, were increased; the fugitives, instead of returning received constant accessions, and their friends who sheltered them were deemed rebellious. Those protestants who remained, were deprived of all their civil and religious rights, and even the advocates and huissiers entered into a resolution to exclude all of "the pretended reformed religion" from their bodies. Those who were employed in selling tobacco were deprived of their licenses. The protestant deacons who had the charge of the poor were all scattered. Of five pastors only two remained; one of these was obliged to change his residence, and could only venture to administer the consolations of religion, or perform the functions of his ministry, under cover of the night.

Not content with these modes of torment, calumnious and inflamatory publications charged the protestants with raising the proscribed standard in the communes, and invoking the fallen Napoleon; and, of course, as unworthy the protection of the laws and the favour of the monarch.

Hundreds after this were dragged to prison without even so much as a *written order*; and though an official newspaper, bearing the title of the *Journal du Gard*, was set up for five months, while it was influenced by the prefect, the mayor, and other functionaries, the word *charter* was never once used in it. One of the first numbers, on the contrary, represented the suffering protestants as "Crocodiles only weeping from rage and regret that they had no more victims to devour; as persons who had surpassed Danton, Marat, and Robespierre, in doing mischief: and as having prostituted their daughters to the garrison to gain it over to Napoleon." An extract from this article, stamped with the crown and the arms of the Bourbons, was hawked about the streets, and the vender was adorned with the medal of the police.

Petition of the Protestant Refugees.

To these reproaches it is proper to oppose the petition which the Protestant Refugees in Paris presented to Louis XVIII. in behalf of their brethren at Nismes.

"We lay at your feet, sire, our acute sufferings. In your name our fellow-citizens are slaughtered, and their property laid waste. Misled peasants, in pretended obedience to your orders, had assembled at the command of a commissioner appointed by your august nephew. Although ready to attack us, they were received with the assurances of peace. On the 15th of July, 1815, we learnt your majesty's entrance into Paris, and the white flag immediately waved on our edifices. The public tranquility had not been disturbed, when armed peasants introduced themselves. The garrison capitulated, but were assailed on their departure, and almost totally massacred. Our national guard was disarmed, the city filled with strangers, and the houses of the principal inhabitants, professing the reformed religion, were attacked and plundered. We subjoin the list. Terror has driven from our city the most respectable inhabitants.

"Your majesty has been deceived if there has not been placed before you the picture of the horrors which make a desert of your good city of Nismes. Arrests and proscriptions are continually taking place, and difference of *religious* opinions is the real and only cause. The calumniated protestants are the defenders of the throne. Your nephew has beheld our children under his banners; our fortunes have been placed in his hands. Attacked without reason, the protestants have not, even by a just resistance, afforded their enemies the fatal pretext for calumny. Save us, sire! extinguish the brand of civil war; a single act of your

will would restore to political existence a city interesting for its population and its manufactures. Demand an account of their conduct from the chiefs who have brought our misfortunes upon us. We place before your eyes all the documents that have reached us. Fear paralizes the hearts, and stifles the complaints of our fellow-citizens. Placed in a more secure situation, we venture to raise our voice in their behalf," &c. &c.

Monstrous outrage upon Females.

At Nismes it is well known that the women wash their clothes either at the fountains, or on the banks of streams. There is a large basin near the fountain, where numbers of women may be seen every day, kneeling at the edge of the water, and beating the clothes with heavy pieces of wood in the shape of battledoors. This spot became the scene of the most shameful and indecent practices. The catholic rabble turned the women's petticoats over their heads, and so fastened them as to continue their exposure, and their subjection to a newly invented species of chastisement; for nails being placed in the wood of the *battoirs* in the form of *fleur-de-lis*, they beat them till the blood streamed from their bodies, and their cries rent the air. Often was death demanded as a commutation of this ignominious punishment, but refused with a malignant joy. To carry their outrage to the highest possible degree, several who were in a state of pregnancy were assailed in this manner. The scandalous nature of these outrages prevented many of the sufferers from making them public, and, especially, from relating the most aggravating circumstances. "I have seen," says M. Durand, "a catholic avocat, accompanying the assassins in the fauxbourg Bourgade, arm a battoir with sharp nails in the form of *fleur-de-lis*; I have seen them raise the garments of females, and apply, with heavy blows, to the bleeding body this *battoir* or battledoor, to which they gave a name which my pen refuses to record. The cries of the sufferers--the streams of blood--the murmurs of indignation which were suppressed by fear--nothing could move them. The surgeons who attended on those women who are dead, can attest, by the marks of their wounds, the agonies which they must have endured, which, however horrible, is most strictly true."

Nevertheless, during the progress of these horrors and obscenities, so disgraceful to France and the catholic religion, the agents of government had a powerful force under their command, and by honestly employing it they might have restored tranquility. Murder and robbery, however, continued, and were winked at, by the catholic magistrates, with very few exceptions; the administrative authorities, it is true, used words in their proclamations, &c. but never had recourse to actions to stop the enormities of the persecutors, who boldly declared that, on the 24th, the anniversary of St. Bartholomew, they intended to make a general massacre. The members of the reformed church were filled with terror, and, instead of taking part in the election of deputies, were occupied as well as they could in providing for their own personal safety.

Arrival of the Austrians at Nismes.

About this time, a treaty between the French court and the allied sovereigns, prohibited the advance of the foreign troops beyond the line of territory already occupied, and traced by the course of the Loire, and by the Rhone, below the Ardeche. In violation of this treaty, 4000 Austrians entered Nismes on the 24th of August; under pretence of making room for them, French troops, bearing the *feudal* title of Royal Chasseurs, followed by the murdering bands of the Trestaillons and

Quatretaillons, who continued their march to Alais, where a fair was to be held, and carried disorder and alarm into all the communes on that route. Nothing now was heard but denunciations of fusillading, burning, razing, and annihilating; and while the catholics were feasting and murdering at Nismes, the flames of the country houses of the protestants, rising one hundred feet in the air, rendered the spectacle still more awful and alarming. Unfortunately, some of the peasants, falsely charged with the murder of two protestants, were brought to Nismes while the prefect was celebrating the fete of St. Louis. At a splendid dinner given to the Austrian commanders, and even without quitting the table, it appears, that the French prefect placed the fate and fortune of these unfortunate prisoners at the disposal of Count Stahremberg, who, of course, believing the representations made to him ordered the accused to be immediately shot. To mortify and exhaust the protestant communes, the Austrians were directed to occupy them, where they completely disarmed the inhabitants without the least opposition. In fact, these foreigners were soon undeceived. They expected to meet the most perfidious and brutal enemies in arms, and in open rebellion against their king; but, on the contrary, they found them all in peace, and experienced the most kind and respectful treatment; and though their duty was a most vexatious and oppressive one, they performed it in general with moderation. On this account they could not refrain from expressing their astonishment at the reports made to them by the authorities at Nismes, declaring, "They had found a population suffering great misfortunes, but no rebels; and that compassion was the only feeling that prevailed in their minds." The commander himself was so convinced of the good disposition of the people of the Cevennes, that he visited those districts without an escort, desiring, he said, to travel in that country as he would in his own. Such confidence was a public reproach on the authorities at Nismes, and a sentence of condemnation on all their proceedings.

As the persecution of the protestants was spreading into other departments, strong and forcible representations were secretly printed and made to the king. All the ordinary modes of communication had been stopped; the secrecy of letters violated, and none circulated but those relative to private affairs. Sometimes these letters bore the postmark of places very distant, and arrived without signatures, and enveloped in allegorical allusions. In fact, a powerful resistance on the part of the outraged protestants was at length apprehended, which, in the beginning of September excited the proclamation of the king, on which it was observed, "that if his majesty had been correctly and fully informed of all that had taken place, he surely would not have contented himself with announcing his severe displeasure to a misled people, who took justice into their own hands, and avenged the crimes committed against royalty." The proclamation was dictated as though there had not been a protestant in the department; it assumed and affirmed throughout the guilt of the sufferers; and while it deplored the atrocious outrages endured by the followers of the duke d'Angouleme, (outrages which never existed,) the plunder and massacre of the reformed were not even noticed.

Still disorders kept pace with the proclamations that made a show of suppressing them, and the force of the catholic faction also continued to increase. The catholic populace, notwithstanding the decrees of the magistrates, were allowed to retain the arms they had illegally seized, whilst the protestants in the departments were disarmed. The members of the reformed churches wished at this period to present another memorial to the government, descriptive of the evils they still suffered, but this was not practicable. On the 26th of September, the president of the consistory wrote as follows: "I have only been able to assemble two or three members of the consistory pastors or elders. It is impossible to draw up a memoir, or to collect facts; so great is the terror, that every one is afraid to speak of his own sufferings, or to mention those he has been compelled to witness."

Outrages committed in the Villages, &c.

We now quit Nismes to take a view of the conduct of the persecutors in the surrounding country. After the re-establishment of the royal government, the local authorities were distinguished for their zeal and forwardness in supporting their employers, and, under pretence of rebellion, concealment of arms, non-payment of contributions, &c. troops, national guards, and armed mobs, were permitted to plunder, arrest, and murder peaceable citizens, not merely with impunity, but with encouragement and approbation. At the village of Milhaud, near Nismes, the inhabitants were frequently forced to pay large sums to avoid being pillaged. This, however, would not avail at Madame Teulon's: On Sunday, the 16th of July, her house and grounds were ravaged; the valuable furniture removed or destroyed, the hay and wood burnt, and the corpse of a child, buried in the garden, taken up and dragged round a fire made by the populace. It was with great difficulty that M. Teulon escaped with his life. M. Picherol, another protestant, had deposited some of his effects with a catholic neighbour; this house was attacked, and though all the property of the latter was respected, that of his friend was seized and destroyed. At the same village, one of a party doubting whether M. Hermet, a tailor, was the man they wanted, asked, "Is he a protestant?" this he acknowledged. "Good," said they, and he was instantly murdered. In the Canton of Vauvert, where there was a consistory church, 80,000 francs were extorted. In the communes of Beauvoisin and Generac similar excesses were committed by a handful of licentious men, under the eye of the catholic mayor and to the cries of "Vive le Roi." St. Gilles was the scene of the must unblushing villainy. The protestants, the most wealthy of the inhabitants, were disarmed, whilst their houses were pillaged. The mayor was appealed to:--the mayor laughed and walked away. This officer had, at his disposal, a national guard of several hundred men, organised by his own orders. It would be wearisome to read the lists of the crimes that occurred during many months. At Clavisson the mayor prohibited the protestants the practice of singing the psalms commonly used in the temple, that, as he said, the catholics might not be offended or disturbed.

At Sommieres, about ten miles from Nismes, the catholics made a splendid procession through the town, which continued till evening and was succeeded by the plunder of the protestants. On the arrival of foreign troops at Sommieres, the pretended search for arms was resumed; those who did not possess muskets were even compelled to buy them on purpose to surrender them up, and soldiers were quartered on them at six francs per day till they produced the articles in demand. The protestant church which had been closed, was converted into barracks for the Austrians. After divine service had been suspended for six months at Nismes, the church, by the protestants called the Temple, was re-opened, and public worship performed on the morning of the 24th of December. On examining the belfry, it was discovered that some persons had carried off the clapper of the bell. As the hour of service approached, a number of men, women, and children, collected at the house of M. Ribot, the pastor, and threatened to prevent the worship. At the appointed time, when he proceeded towards the church, he was surrounded; the most savage shouts were raised against him; some of the women seized him by the collar; but nothing could disturb his firmness, or excite his impatience: he entered the house of prayer, and ascended the pulpit; stones were thrown in and fell among the worshippers; still the congregation remained calm and attentive, and the service was concluded amidst noise, threats, and outrage. On retiring many would have been killed but for the chasseurs of the garrison, who honourably and zealously protected them. From the captain of these chasseurs, M. Ribot soon after received the following letter.

"January 2, 1816.

"I deeply lament the prejudices of the catholics

against the *protestants*, who they pretend do not love the king. Continue to act as you have hitherto done, and time and your conduct will convince the catholics to the contrary: should any tumult occur similar to that of Saturday last inform me. I preserve my reports of these acts, and if the agitators prove incorrigible, and forget what they owe to the best of kings and the *charter*, I will do my duty and inform the government of their proceedings. Adieu, my dear sir; assure the consistory of my esteem, and of the sense I entertain of the moderation with which they have met the provocations of the evil-disposed at Sommieres. I have the honor to salute you with respect.

SUVAL DE LAINE."

Another letter to this worthy pastor from the Marquis de Montlord, was received on the 6th of January, to encourage him to unite with all good men who believe in God to obtain the punishment of the assassins, brigands, and disturbers of public tranquility, and to read the instructions he had received from government to this effect publicly. Notwithstanding this, on the 20th of January, 1816, when the service in commemoration of the death of Louis XVI. was celebrated, a procession being formed, the National Guards fired at the white flag suspended from the windows of the protestants, and concluded the day by plundering their houses. In the Commune of Angargues, matters were still worse; and in that of Fontanes, from the entry of the king in 1815, the catholics broke all terms with the protestants; by day they insulted them, and in the night broke open their doors, or marked them with chalk to be plundered or burnt. St. Mamert was repeatedly visited by these robberies; and at Montmiral, as lately as the 16th of June, 1816, the protestants were attacked, beaten, and imprisoned, for daring to celebrate the return of a king who had sworn to preserve religious liberty and to maintain the charter. In fact, to continue the relation of the scenes that took place in the different departments of the south of France, would be little better than a repetition of those we have already described, excepting a change of names: but the most sanguinary of all seems that which was perpetrated at Uzes, at the latter end of August, and the burning of several protestants places of worship. These shameful persecutions continued till after the dissolution of the Chamber of Deputies at the close of the year 1816. After a review of these anti-protestant proceedings, the British reader will not think of comparing them with the riots of London in 1780, or with those of Birmingham about 1793; as it is evident that where governments possess absolute power, such events could not have been prolonged for many months and even for years over a vast extent of country, had it not been for the systematic and powerful support of the higher department of the state.

Farther account of the proceedings of the Catholics at Nismes.

The excesses perpetrated in the country it seems did not by any means divert the attention of the persecutors from Nismes. October, 1815, commenced without any improvement in the principles or measures of the government, and this was followed by corresponding presumption on the part of the people. Several houses in the Quartier St. Charles were sacked, and their wrecks burnt in the streets amidst songs, dances, and shouts of Vive le Roi. The mayor appeared, but the merry multitude pretended not to know him, and when he ventured to remonstrate, they told him, "his presence was unnecessary, and that he might retire." During the 16th of October, every preparation seemed to announce a night of carnage; orders for assembling and signals for attack were circulated with regularity and confidence; Trestaillon reviewed his satellites, and urged them on to the perpetration of crimes, holding with one of those wretches the following dialogue:

Satellite. "If all the protestants, without one exception, are to be killed, I will cheerfully join; but as you have so often deceived me, unless they are all to go I will not stir."

Trestaillon. "Come along, then, for this time not a single man shall escape." This horrid purpose would have been executed had it not been for General La Garde, the commandant of the department. It was not till ten o'clock at night that he perceived the danger; he now felt that not a moment could be lost. Crowds were advancing through the suburbs, and the streets were filling with ruffians, uttering the most horrid imprecations. The generale sounded at eleven o'clock, and added to the confusion that was now spreading through the city. A few troops rallied round the Count La Garde, who was wrung with distress at the sight of the evil which had arrived at such a pitch. Of this M. Durand, a catholic advocate, gave the following account:

"It was near midnight, my wife had just fallen asleep; I was writing by her side, when we were disturbed by a distant noise; drums seemed crossing the town in every direction. What could all this mean! To quiet her alarm, I said it probably announced the arrival or departure of some troops of the garrison. But firing and shouts were immediately audible; and on opening my window I distinguished horrible imprecations mingled with cries of *vive le Roi!* I roused an officer who lodged in the house, and M. Chancel, Director of the Public Works. We went out together, and gained the Boulevarde. The moon shone bright, and almost every object was nearly as distinct as day; a furious crowd was pressing on vowing extermination, and the greater part half naked, armed with knives, muskets, sticks, and sabres. In answer to my inquiries I was told the massacre was general, that many had been already killed in the suburbs. M. Chancel retired to put on his uniform as captain of the *Pompiers*; the officers retired to the barracks, and anxious for my wife I returned home. By the noise I was convinced that persons followed. I crept along in the shadow of the wall, opened my door, entered, and closed it, leaving a small aperture through which I could watch the movements of the party whose arms shone in the moonlight. In a few moments some armed men appeared conducting a prisoner to the very spot where I was concealed. They stopped, I shut my door gently, and mounted on an alder tree planted against the garden wall. What a scene! a man on his knees imploring mercy from wretches who mocked his agony, and loaded him with abuse. In the name of my wife and children, he said, spare me! What have I done? Why would you murder me for nothing? I was on the point of crying out and menacing the murderers with vengeance. I had not long to deliberate, the discharge of several fusils terminated my suspense; the unhappy supplicant, struck in the loins and the head, fell to rise no more. The backs of the assassins were towards the tree; they retired immediately, reloading their pieces. I descended and approached the dying man, uttering some deep and dismal groans. Some National Guards arrived at the moment, I again retired and shut the door. "I see," said one, "a dead man." "He sings still," said another. "It will be better," said a third, "to finish him and put him out of his misery." Five or six muskets were fired instantly, and the groans ceased. On the following day crowds came to inspect and insult the deceased. A day after a massacre was always observed as a sort of fete, and every occupation was left to go and gaze upon the victims. This was Louis Lichare, the father of four children; and four years after the event, M. Durand verified this account by his oath upon the trial of one of the murderers."

Attack upon the Protestant Churches.

Some time before the death of general La Garde, the duke d'Angouleme had visited Nismes, and other cities in the south, and at the former place honoured the members of the protestant consistory with an interview, promising them protection, and encouraging them to reopen their temple so long shut up. They have two churches at Nismes, and it was agreed that the small one should be preferred on this occasion, and that the ringing of the bell should be omitted, general La Garde declared that he would answer with his head for the safety of his congregation. The protestants privately informed each other that worship was once more to be celebrated at ten o'clock, and they began to assemble silently and cautiously. It was agreed that M. Juillerat Chasseur should perform the service, though such was his conviction of danger that he entreated his wife, and some of his flock, to remain with their families. The temple being opened only as a matter of form, and in compliance with the orders of the duke d'Angouleme, this pastor wished to be the only victim. On his way to the place he passed numerous groupes who regarded him with ferocious looks. "This is the time," said some, "to give them the last blow." "Yes," added others, "and neither women nor children must be spared." One wretch, raising his voice above the rest, exclaimed, "Ah, I will go and get my musket, and ten for my share." Through these ominous sounds M. Juillerat pursued his course, but when he gained the temple the sexton had not the courage to open the door, and he was obliged to do it himself. As the worshippers arrived they found strange persons in possession of the adjacent streets, and upon the steps of the church, vowing their worship should not be performed, and crying, "Down with the protestants! kill them! kill them!" At ten o'clock the church being nearly filled, M. J. Chasseur commenced the prayers; a calm that succeeded was of short duration. On a sudden the minister was interrupted by a violent noise, and a number of persons entered, uttering the most dreadful cries, mingled with **Vive le Roi!** but the gens-d'armes succeeded in excluding these fanatics, and closing the doors. The noise and tumult without now redoubled, and the blows of the populace trying to break open the doors, caused the house to resound with shrieks and groans. The voice of the pastors who endeavoured to console their flock, was inaudible; they attempted in vain to sing the 42d psalm.

Three quarters of an hour rolled heavily away. "I placed myself," says Madame Juillerat, "at the bottom of the pulpit, with my daughter in my arms; my husband at length joined and sustained me; I remembered that it was the anniversary of my marriage; after six years of happiness, I said, I am about to die with my husband and my daughter; we shall be slain at the altar of our God, the victims of a sacred duty, and heaven will open to receive us and our unhappy brethren. I blessed the Redeemer, and without cursing our murderers, I awaited their approach."

M. Oliver, son of a pastor, an officer in the royal troops of the line, attempted to leave the church, but the friendly sentinels at the door advised him to remain besieged with the rest. The national guards refused to act, and the fanatical crowd took every advantage of the absence of general La Garde, and of their increasing numbers. At length the sound of martial music was heard, and voices from without called to the besieged, "Open, open and save yourselves." Their first impression was a fear of treachery, but they were soon assured that a detachment returning from mass was drawn up in front of the church to favour the retreat of the protestants. The door was opened, and many of them escaped among the ranks of the soldiers, who had driven the mob before them; but this street, as well as others through which the fugitives had to pass, was soon filled again. The venerable pastor, Olivier Desmond, between 70 and 80 years of age, was surrounded by murderers; they put their fists in his face, and cried, "Kill the chief of brigands." He was preserved by the firmness of some officers, among whom was his own son; they made a bulwark round him with their bodies, and amidst their naked sabres conducted him to his house. M. Juillerat, who had assisted at divine service with his wife at his side and his child in his arms, was pursued and assailed with stones, his mother received a blow on the head, and her life was some time in danger. One woman was shamefully whipped, and several wounded and dragged along the streets; the number of protestants more or less ill treated on this occasion amounted to between seventy and eighty.

Murder of General La Garde.

At length a check was put to these excesses by the report of the murder of Count La Garde, who, receiving an account of this tumult, mounted his horse, and entered one of the streets, to disperse a crowd. A villain seized his bridle; another presented the muzzle of a pistol close to his body, and exclaimed, "Wretch, you make me retire!" He immediately fired. The murderer was Louis Boissin, a serjeant in the national guard; but, though known to every one, no person endeavoured to arrest him, and he effected his escape. As soon as the general found himself wounded, he gave orders to the gendarmerie to protect the protestants, and set off on a gallop to his hotel; but fainted immediately on his arrival. On recovering, he prevented the surgeon from searching his wound till he had written a letter to the government, that, in case of his death, it might be known from what quarter the blow came, and that none might dare to accuse the protestants of this crime. The probable death of this general produced a small degree of relaxation on the part of their enemies, and some calm; but the mass of the people had been indulged in licentiousness too long to be restrained even by the murder of the representative of their king. In the evening they again repaired to the temple, and with hatchets broke open the door; the dismal noise of their blows carried terror into the bosom of the protestant families sitting in their houses in tears. The contents of the poor's box, and the clothes prepared for distribution, were stolen; the minister's robes rent in pieces; the books torn up or carried away; the closets were ransacked, but the rooms which contained the archives of the church, and the synods, was providentially secured; and had it not been for the numerous patrols on foot, the whole would have become the prey of the flames, and the edifice itself a heap of ruins. In the mean while, the fanatics openly ascribed the murder of the general to his own self-devotion, and said "that it was the will of God." Three thousand francs were offered for the apprehension of Boissin; but it was well known that the protestants dared not arrest him, and that the fanatics would not. During these transactions, the systems of forced conversions to catholicism was making regular and fearful progress.

Interference of the British Government.

To the credit of England, the reports of these cruel persecutions carried on against our protestant brethren in France, produced such a sensation on the part of the government as determined them to interfere; and now the persecutors of the protestants made this spontaneous act of humanity and religion the pretext for charging the sufferers with a treasonable correspondence with England; but in this state of their proceedings, to their great dismay, a letter appeared, sent some time before to England by the duke of Wellington, stating "that much information existed on the events of the south."

The ministers of the three denominations in London, anxious not to be misled, requested one of their brethren to visit the scenes of persecution, and examine with impartiality the nature and extent of the evils they were desirous to relieve. The Rev. Clement Perot undertook this difficult task, and fulfilled their wishes with a zeal, prudence, and devotedness, above all praise. His return furnished abundant and incontestible proof of a shameful persecution, materials for an appeal to the British Parliament, and a printed report which was circulated through the continent, and which first conveyed correct information to the inhabitants of France.

Foreign interference was now found eminently useful; and the declarations of tolerance which it elicited from the French government, as well as the more cautious march of the catholic persecutors, operated as decisive and involuntary acknowledgments of the importance of that interference, which some persons at first censured and despised but though the stern voice of public opinion in England and elsewhere produced a reluctant suspension of massacre and pillage, the murderers and plunderers were still left unpunished, and even caressed and rewarded for their crimes; and whilst protestants in France suffered the most cruel and degrading pains and penalties for alleged trifling crimes, *catholics*, covered with blood, and guilty of numerous and horrid murders, were acquitted.

Perhaps the virtuous indignation expressed by some of the more enlightened catholics against these abominable proceedings, had no small share in restraining them. Many innocent protestants had been condemned to the galleys and otherwise punished, for supposed crimes, upon the oaths of wretches the most unprincipled and abandoned. M. Madier de Montgau, judge of the *cour royale* of Nismes, and president of the *cour d'assizes* of the Gard and Vaucluse, upon one occasion felt himself compelled to break up the court, rather than take the deposition of that notorious and sanguinary monster Truphemy: "In a hall," says he, "of the Palace of Justice, opposite that in which I sat, several unfortunate persons persecuted by the faction were upon trial, every deposition tending to their crimination was applauded with the cries of '*Vive le Roi*.' Three times the explosion of this atrocious joy became so terrible, that it was necessary to send for reinforcements from the barracks, and two hundred soldiers were often unable to restrain the people. On a sudden the shouts and cries of '*Vive le Roi*' redoubled: a man arrives, caressed, applauded, borne in triumph--it is the horrible Truphemy; he approaches the tribunal--he comes to depose against the prisoners--he is admitted as a witness--he raises his hand to take the oath! Seized with horror at the sight, I rush from my seat, and enter the hall of council; my colleagues follow me; in vain they persuade me to resume my seat; 'No!' exclaimed I, 'I will not consent to see that wretch admitted to give evidence in a court of justice in the city which he has filled with murders; in the palace, on the steps of which he has murdered the unfortunate Bourillon. I cannot admit that he should kill his victims by his testimonies no more than by his poignards. He an accuser! he a witness! No, never will I consent to see this monster rise, in the presence of magistrates, to take a sacrilegious oath, his hand still reeking with blood.' These words were repeated out of doors; the witness trembled; the factious also trembled; the factious who guided the tongue of Truphemy as they had directed his arm, who dictated calumny after they had taught him murder. These words penetrated the dungeons of the condemned, and inspired hope; they gave another courageous advocate the resolution to espouse the cause of the persecuted; he carried the prayers of innocence and misery to the foot of the throne; there he asked if the evidence of a Truphemy was not sufficient to annul a sentence. The king granted a full and free pardon."

Perjury in the case of General Gilly, &c.

This catholic system of subornation and perjury was carried to such an infamous degree, that twenty-six witnesses were found to sign and swear, that on the 3d of April, 1815, general Gilly, with his own hand and *before their eyes*, took down the white flag at Nismes; though it was proved that at the time when the tri-coloured flag was raised in its room, the general was fifteen leagues from Nismes, and that he did not arrive there till *three* days after that event. Before tribunals thus constructed, even innocence had not the least chance for protection. General Gilly knew better than to appear before them, and was condemned to death for contempt of court. But when he left Nismes, he thought either of passing into a foreign country, or of joining the army of the Loire; and it was long supposed that he had actually escaped. As it was impossible to gain any point, or find any security, his only hope was in concealment, and a friend found him an asylum in the cottage of a peasant; but that peasant was a protestant, and the general was a catholic: however, he did not hesitate; he confided in this poor man's honour. This cottage was in the canton of Anduze; the name of its keeper, Perrier; he welcomed the fugitive, and did not even ask his name: it was a time of proscription, and his host would know nothing of him, it was enough that he was unfortunate, and in danger. He was disguised and he passed for Perrier's cousin. The general is naturally amiable, and he made himself agreeable, sat by the fire, ate potatoes, and contented himself with miserable fare. Though subject to frequent and many painful alarms, he preserved his retreat several months, and often heard the visiters of his host boast of the concealment of general Gilly, or of being acquainted with the place of his retreat. Patrols were continually searching for arms in the houses of protestants; and often in the night the general was obliged to leave his mattress, half naked, and hide himself in the fields. Perrier, to avoid these inconveniences, made an under-ground passage, by which his guest could pass to an outhouse. The wife of Perrier could not endure that one who had seen better days should live as her family did, on vegetables and bread, and occasionally bought meat to regale the melancholy stranger. These unusual purchases excited attention; it was suspected that Perrier had some one concealed; nightly visits were more frequent. In this state of anxiety he often complained of the hardness of his lot. Perrier one day returned from market in a serious mood; and after some inquiries from his guest, he replied, "Why do you complain? you are fortunate compared with the poor wretches whose heads were cried in the market to-day. Bruguier, the pastor, at 2400 francs; Bresse, the mayor, at the same, and general Gilly at 10,000!"--"Is it possible?" "Aye, it is certain." Gilly concealed his emotion, a momentary suspicion passed his mind; he appeared to reflect. "Perrier," said he, "I am weary of life; you are poor and want money: I know Gilly and the place of his concealment; let us denounce him; I shall, no doubt, obtain my liberty, and you shall have the 10,000 francs." The old man stood speechless, and as if petrified. His son, a gigantic peasant, 27 years of age, who had served in the army, rose from his chair, in which he had listened to the conversation, and in a tone not to be described, said, "Sir, hitherto we thought you unfortunate, but honest; we have respected your sorrow, and kept your secret; but since you are one of those wretched beings who would inform of a fellow creature, and insure his death to save yourself, there is the door; and if you do not retire, I will throw you out of the window." Gilly hesitated; the peasant insisted; the general wished to explain, but he was seized by the collar. "Suppose I should be general Gilly," said the fugitive. The soldier paused. "And it is even so," continued he, "denounce me, and the 10,000 francs are yours." The soldier threw himself on his neck; the family were dissolved in tears; they kissed his hands, his clothes, protested they would never let him leave them, and that they would die rather than he should be arrested. In their kindness he was more secure than ever; but their cottage was more suspected, and he was ultimately obliged to seek another asylum. The family refused any indemnity for the expense he had occasioned them, and it was not till long after that he could prevail upon them to accept an acknowledgement of their hospitality and fidelity. In 1820, when the course of justice was more free, general Gilly demanded a trial; there was nothing against him; and the duke d'Angouleme conveyed to Madame Gilly the permission of the king for the return of her husband to the bosom of his country.

But, even when the French government was resolved to bring the factions of the department of the Gard, under the laws, the same men continued to exercise the public functions. The society, called *Royale*, and its secret committee, maintained a power superior to the laws. It was impossible to procure the condemnation of an assassin though the evidence against him was incontestible, and for whom, in other times, there would have been no hope. The Truphemys, and others of his stamp, appeared in public, wearing immense mustachios, and white cockades embroidered with green. Like the brigands of Calabria, they had two pistols and a poignard at their waists. Their appearance diffused an air of melancholy mixed with indignation. Even amidst the bustle of the day there was the silence of fear, and the night was disturbed by atrocious songs, or vociferations like the sudden cry of ferocious wild beasts.

Ultimate resolution of the Protestants at Nismes.

With respect to the conduct of the protestants, these highly outraged citizens, pushed to extremities by their persecutors, felt at length that they had only to choose the manner in which they were to perish. They unanimously determined that they would die fighting in their own defence. This firm attitude apprised their butchers that they could no longer murder with impunity. Every thing was immediately changed. Those, who for four years had filled others with terror, now felt it in their turn. They trembled at the force which men, so long resigned, found in despair, and their alarm was heightened when they heard that the inhabitants of the Cavennes, persuaded of the danger of their brethren, were marching to their assistance. But, without waiting for these reinforcements, the protestants appeared at night in the same order and armed in the same manner as their enemies. The others paraded the Boulevards, with their usual noise and fury, but the protestants remained silent and firm in the posts they had chosen. Three days these dangerous and ominous meetings continued; but the effusion of blood was prevented by the efforts of some worthy citizens distinguished by their rank and fortune. By sharing the dangers of the protestant population, they obtained the pardon of an enemy who now trembled while he menaced.

But though the protestants were modest in their demands, only asking present safety, and security for the future, they did not obtain above half of their requests. The dissolution of the National Guard at Nismes was owing to the prudence and firmness of M. Laine. The re-organization of the **Cour Royale** was effected by M. Pasquier, then Keeper of the Seals; and these measures certainly ensured them a present safety but no more. M. Madier de Montgau, the generous champion of the protestants at Nismes, was officially summoned before the Court of Cassation at Paris, over which M. de Serre, Keeper of the Seals, presided, to answer for an alleged impropriety of conduct as a magistrate, in making those public appeals to the Chamber which saved the protestants, and increased the difficulties of renewing those persecutions of which he complained. The French attorney general demanded the erasure of his name from the list of magistrates, but this the court refused. Unfortunately since the law of elections in France has been changed, two of the bitterest enemies of the protestants had been chosen Deputies at Nismes. The future, therefore, is not without its dangers, and the condition of the persecuted may fluctuate with the slightest political alteration; but which, it is to be hoped, may be prevented from any acts that may again disgrace the catholic religion, by the powerful expression of the public mind, actuated with better principles, or by the interference of the protestant influence in this or other countries. Happily, since the year 1820, no fresh complaints have issued from the south of France on the score of religion.

CHAPTER XVIII.

ASAAD SHIDIAK.

NARRATIVE OF THE CONVERSION, IMPRISONMENT, AND SUFFERINGS OF ASAAD SHIDIAK, A NATIVE OF PALESTINE, WHO HAS BEEN CONFINED FOR SEVERAL YEARS IN THE CONVENT OF MT. LEBANON.

The following narrative illustrates two points. 1st. The usefulness of Christian Missions. 2d. The unchanging persecuting spirit of the papal church. The subject of the following narrative has now been in confinement about five years; during which time he has suffered almost every indignity and vexation which the malice of his enemies could impose upon him. Up to the present time, however, he has remained steadfast in his adherence to the principles of the gospel. We give the narrative of his trials and sufferings in the simple and affecting language of the missionaries, which excited such powerful interest in the bosoms of Christians, at the time of its first publication. The principal facts are taken from the Missionary Herald published by the American Board of Commissioners for Foreign Missions.

Biographical Notices of Asaad Shidiak.

The following account of the remarkable convert from the Maronite Roman Catholic church, whose name has, of late, appeared frequently on the pages of the Missionary Herald, is compiled chiefly from the journal of Mr. Bird, American Missionary in Syria. The other matter which is inserted, is derived from authentic sources, and is designed to connect, or to illustrate the extracts from the journal, or to render the biography more complete and satisfactory.

His early History.

Asaad Shidiak was born in the district north of Beyroot, called Kesruan, where, and at Hadet, a small village five miles south-east of Beyroot, his family have ever since lived. This family now consists of the widowed mother, five sons, (of whom Asaad is the third) and two or three daughters. At about the age of 16, he entered the college of Ain Warka, and spent a year and a half in studying grammar, (Arabic and Syriac,) logic and theology. After this he passed two years teaching theology to the monks of a convent near Hadet.

He has also been some considerable time scribe to the bishop of Beyroot, and to the patriarch, the latter of whom was a teacher in the college when Asaad was a student. During the late rebellion, headed by the shekh Besir, a mere complimentary letter of Asaad's to one of the disaffected party, being intercepted, and shown to the emir Beshir, his suspicion was excited, and he wrote immediately to the patriarch, in whose employ he then was, to dismiss him from his service. The letter of Asaad was produced, and though it was seen to contain nothing exceptionable, the patriarch thought proper to dismiss him without ceremony.

Connexion with Mr. King.

The dispensations of Providence often seem afflictive when they happen, and most kind and benevolent afterwards, when their design is perceived. So it was in the case of Asaad. Being thus cast out upon the world, by those who ought to have befriended him, he applied to Mr. King for employment as his instructer in Syriac, and was accepted. Though a young man, Mr. King pronounced him to be one of the most intelligent natives of the country, whom he had met with on Mount Lebanon. From morning until night, for several weeks, they were together, and hours were spent by them, almost every day, in discussing religious subjects, and upon a mind so candid, so shrewd, so powerful in its conceptions, and so comprehensive in its surveys, as that of Asaad, an impression favorable to protestant christianity could not but be made.

Having completed his engagements with Mr. King, he, at the recommendation of Mr. Fisk, set up a school in Beyroot, for teaching

Arabic grammatically, but soon found himself obliged to relinquish it, at the command of his patriarch. He was also forbidden, as is stated by Mr. Bird, to give any further instruction to the ***Bible-men***, as the missionaries are called, because the patriarch "had received fresh instructions from Rome to ***persecute*** these men by every means in his power, so long as one of them should remain in the country."

When Mr. King was about to leave Syria, he wrote the farewell letter to his friends in that country. The letter was designed, by the writer, to show the reasons which prevented his becoming a member of the Roman catholic church. This letter Asaad attempted to answer but his answer, so far from being satisfactory to himself, was the occasion of raising strong doubts in his mind, as to the general correctness of the Romish faith.

Connexion with Mr. Bird.

Under the influence of these doubts, which seem to have distressed him greatly, he entered the service of Mr. Bird as his instructer in Arabic. His doubts continued to increase; for he now began in earnest the study of the Bible and of his own heart, and made constant progress in the knowledge of both. At length he became a protestant in faith, and, as there is reason to believe, a truly pious man. Immediately he commenced reformer; and though young, his matured judgment, his vigorous intellect, his intrepidity, and his acquisitions, great for his age and his nation, soon drew towards him the general attention.

Visits his Relations.

On the 12th of November, 1825,--says Mr. Bird--Shidiak received a letter from the patriarch, in which he threatens him, with his brother Tannoos and another Maronite youth, with immediate excommunication, unless they cease from all connexion with the Bible-men.

15. After mature deliberation it was thought advisable, for the present, that he should go home to his friends in Hadet, until the fever of alarm and opposition should subside a little.

His return to Mr. Bird.

Dec. 12. Shidiak returned, after nearly a month's absence, to continue

with me for a year, risking whatever obloquy and violence might come
upon him. He has just been obliged to give up an advantageous contract
of marriage, into which he had some months ago entered, because, since
suspicions were afloat that he is heretical in his notions, the father
of the girl required him to bring a letter from the patriarch,
specifying what office he would give him. He now gives up all intentions
of marriage. For his greater security, I am to procure for him the usual
written protection of the English consul, which shall insure to him,
while in my immediate employ, all the safety and liberty of an English
resident.

Progress of His Opinions.

13. Spent most of the day in conversation with Asaad on the subject of
religion. He had lately been much in company with the emir Sulman, and
observed, that his prejudices against christianity were evidently much
softened.

14. Conversed with Asaad on the books of the Apocrypha.[E] He seemed
satisfied with the proofs that they were not given by inspiration of
God. He is now searching the scriptures with such an intensity of
interest, as to leave him neither time nor relish for any thing else.

We have a copy of the Arabic bible, printed at Rome, at the end of which
is an appendix which he has discovered to contain a copious list of
popish doctrines, with their appropriate references to scripture proofs.
These proofs he has found so weak, that he expresses his astonishment
how such doctrines could be inferred from them; and nothing has occurred
of late, which has more strengthened his conviction that the church of
Rome is radically wrong. What seems to have affected him most sensibly,
is, the expression he has found, "We are under obligation to kill
heretics."--Proof,--'False prophets God commanded to be slain. Jehu and
Elijah killed the worshippers and prophets of Baal.' This passage he
shows to all who visit him, priests and people, and calls upon them to
judge whether such sweeping destruction is according to the spirit of
the gospel.

In this country, where the pope cannot do all he could wish, the right
of murdering every one who differs from him, has not been so publicly
asserted of late, and some, when they hear it, are a little startled.
But most of the good children of "the church" are soon quieted again, by
the recollection, that their kind and compassionate "mother" *means*
well, even in murder. The common mode of reasoning, is, in this case,

inverted. It is not said, "the action is right, therefore the church does it;" but, "the church does it, therefore it is right."

Jan. 1, 1826. Twelve or fourteen individuals were present at the Arabic service at Mr. Goodell's. After this service, we questioned Asaad closely with regard to the state of his heart, and were rather disappointed at the readiness, with which he replied, that he thought he was born again. For ourselves, we chose rather to suspend our opinion. He can hardly be supposed to have acquired yet, even ***speculatively***, very clear notions of what is regeneration; and it would seem quite as consistent with christian humility, and with a true knowledge of his sinfulness, if he should speak of himself with more doubt and caution.

In the evening, an acquaintance of his, one who has heretofore expressed great friendship to him, and to us; who had said that there was no true religion to be found in the whole country, and pretended to lament very much that the patriarch and priests had so much sway; came to give Asaad a last serious admonition.

"This," said he, "is the last time I intend ever to say a word to you on the subject of religion. I wish, therefore, before you go any further, that you would pause and think whether you can meet all the reproach of the world, and all the opposition of the patriarch and priests."

Asaad replied, that he had made up his mind to meet all these things. "And now," said he, "if, as you say, you intend never to hold any more conversation with me on the subject of religion, I have one request to make of you, and that is, that you will go, and make the subject of religion a matter of serious prayer and inquiry, and see where the path of life is; I then leave you with your conscience and with God."

After relating the substance of this conversation to us, Asaad remarked, that these people reminded him of the late patriarch such an one, who had a moderate share of understanding, but was ambitious to appear very well. This patriarch had a bishop who was really an acute and learned man, and whose opinions were always received with the greatest deference on all matters relative to religion. The bishop being on a visit one day at the patriarch's, the latter called him to his presence, and proposed to him the interpretation of a passage of scripture. The bishop gave the explanation according to the best of his judgment. "No," said his holiness, "that is not the meaning of the passage;" and proposed to have a second. When the bishop had again given his opinions and reasons, the patriarch answered as before, "That is not the meaning of the passage." In a third and fourth case, the bishop was equally unfortunate, all his arguments being swept away by the single sage remark of his holiness, "That is not the meaning of the passage." At last the bishop, in a fit of discouragement, said, "Your holiness has put me upon the solution of a number of questions, in all which, it seems, I have been *wrong*. I would now thank your holiness to tell me what is *right*." The patriarch being startled at the new ground he was on, changed the conversation. "So," said Asaad, "these people can all tell me I am mistaken; but when I ask them what is *right*, they are silent."

Asaad has often remarked, that he is full of anxiety, and finds no rest for the sole of his foot. In many things he sees the Romish church to be wrong, and in some things he thinks *we* are so. Our apparent tranquility of mind, as to our religious views, is a matter of surprise to him. This evening he conversed on the subject with more than usual feeling. "I seem," said he, "to be alone among men. There is nobody like me, and I please nobody. I am not quite in harmony with the English in my views, and therefore do not please *you*. My own countrymen are in so much error, I cannot please *them*. *God* I have no reason to think I please; nor do I please *myself*. What shall I do?"

It was not altogether unpleasant to hear these professions of diffidence in himself, and I endeavoured to turn off his attention from all other sources of consolation than that of the "Comforter, which is the Holy Ghost."

Asaad observed, that whatever might be said, and whatever might be true, of our *object*, in coming to this country he saw that the *doctrines* we taught were according to truth, and he was more than ever determined to hold to them.

Asaad says, that wherever he goes, and to whomsoever he addresses himself on the subject of religion, people say, "Ah, it is very well for you to go about and talk in this manner: you have, no doubt, been well paid for it all." These insinuations wear upon his spirit, and he sometimes says, "O that I were in some distant land, where nobody had ever known me, and I knew nobody, that I might be able to fasten men's attention to the truth, without the possibility of their flying off to these horrid suspicions."

He wishes also to have another interview with the patriarch, that he may tell him his whole heart, and see what he will say. The patriarch is not, he says, of a bad disposition by nature, and perhaps if he could be persuaded that he was neither acting from revenge nor from love of money, but simply from a conviction of the truth, he would be softened in his feelings, and something might be done with him to the benefit of religion. He desired, among other things, to propose, that an edition of the New Testament should be printed under the patriarch's inspection at Schooair, the expense of which, (if he chose) should be borne by the English.[F]

Visits the Patriarch.

6. For some time, we had been looking daily for a regular excommunication to be published by the patriarch's order against Asaad; but instead of this, a letter arrived from his holiness to-day, brought by his own brother, priest Nicholas, containing his apostolic blessing, inviting him to an interview, and promising him a situation in some office. The messenger said, that the patriarch, his brother, had heard that the English had given Asaad 40 purses, (2000 dollars) to unite him with them, and that he had thought of giving Asaad the same sum, that no obstacle might remain to his leaving them. "This money," said he, "with which the English print books, and hire men into their service is but the pelf of the man of sin, and could you but be present to hear what the people say of you, through the whole country, for your associating with the English, you would never be in their company again."

When we were informed of what occurred between this priest and Asaad, and of Asaad's intention to go and see the patriarch, we all expressed our fears that he would be ill-treated, but he did not anticipate it. He said, he had known an instance of a vile infidel and blasphemer, who was simply excommunicated, and that it was not the custom of the Maronites to kill, as we suggested, on account of religion. We assured him that he had not yet learned how much men hate the truth, and that his church would not feel herself half as much in danger from an open blasphemer, as from an active lover of the gospel. But he was so confident that good would result from such a visit, that we ceased from urging our objections, and commended him to the will of God.

It was during this visit, that most of the conversations happened which are so admirably narrated in the public statement made by himself, which will be found in the sequel. He manifested throughout, as the reader will discover, the spirit of the early christian confessors. He denied the infallibility of popes and councils; asserted and defended the great doctrines of the gospel, and besought, that the scriptures might be circulated, and read, and be made the only standard of faith, and rule of practice, and that evangelists might be sent through the land.

Against such a formidable innovator, the patriarch and his bishops rose up in wrath, and Asaad was threatened with imprisonment and death.

Two days after his departure, he thus wrote to Mr. Bird.

"I am now at Der Alma, (convent of Alma,) and thanks to God, I arrived in good health. But as yet I have not seen the patriarch. I pray God the Father, and his only Son Jesus Christ our Lord, that he would establish me in his love, that I may never exchange it for any created thing--that neither death, nor life, nor things present, nor things to come, nor height, nor depth, nor riches, nor honour, nor dignity, nor office, nor any thing in creation, shall separate me from this love. I hope you will pray to God for me; which request I also make to all the brethren and sisters, (all the saints,) after giving them, especially Mr. Goodell, abundant salutations."

24. Heard that Asaad had been sent to the Armenian convent Bzumar, to confess, and that he would probably be sent to Aleppo as a priest. Another said, he was seen at the college of Ain Warka.

Is forcibly detained.

Feb. 22. Fearing for the safety of Asaad, since hearing that he has not written to his friends, we this morning sent a messenger with a short note, to find him, and ascertain his state.

23. The messenger returned, saying, that he yesterday went to the village, where he understood the patriarch was, and found that he had just gone with a train of twenty men, and Asaad in company, to Der Alma. In the morning, he rose, went to that convent, and chanced to find Asaad alone. After some conversation, in which they were providentially not interrupted, Asaad handed him a hasty line, and he returned. The line was as follows:

"Much respected brother,--Your note has reached me, and has added another proof to the many I have had already, of your kind regard to me. I now beseech you once more, to pray for me, that I may be delivered from the dark devices of men. I find myself reduced to quite an extremity. One or more of three things are before me; either to be thought mad, or to commit sin, or to offer up my life I call upon God for deliverance. I cannot now write fully, but the bearer will tell you of all."

The messenger said, that the emir of that district had threatened to send him to Bteddeen, to be imprisoned. Asaad replied, that he was ready to go to prison and to death. He was engaged in daily disputations with the patriarch and others. His countenance wore a shade of melancholy, and his eyes were red with weeping.

When it was proposed by the messenger to interfere with English authority for his rescue, he said such a course might exasperate his enemies, and cost him his life: it would be better to wait a while, and leave it for Providence to open a way for his escape.

This assurance of his steadfastness was like a cordial to our spirits, and was not without a good influence on some that are about us. By the grace of God, he will witness a good confession before the dignitaries both of church and state, and by the same grace, he may open the eyes of some of them to the truth as it is in Jesus. To him that was with Daniel and with the three children in their dangers, we commend him.

24. Called on the consul to inquire what could be done for the protection or relief of Asaad. He recommended a course of moderation and forbearance, and said it was not customary to extend English protection to natives, when abroad on their own business.

26. Two young emirs from Hadet called. I asked one of them "Where is Asaad Shidiak at present?"

He replied, "He is with the patriarch."

"And is he contented there?"

"Not very well contented. But what should he do, poor fellow, necessity is laid upon him."

This remark proves to us, that it is not a secret among the priests and emirs, that Asaad is detained against his will.

March 1. A youth called this morning, and said Asaad Shidiak sent me salutation. He showed me a line he had received from Asaad the day before, saying, "If you will pass this way about midnight, I will go with you to Beyroot." Owing to some circumstance, the young man did not go to the convent, and now he proposed to take a horse, by which Asaad may escape to-night.

As we had not perfect confidence in the youth, we did nothing, but having ascertained his plan, left him to go on as he chose. In the evening, we had a season of prayer, particularly on his account.

Escapes and returns to Beyroot.

2. Rose early, and repaired to the room, where Asaad would have been, had he come; but there were no tidings from him. Little expectation remained of his coming to-day, and we were not without our fears that the attempt had miscarried. It was not long, however, before it was announced, that Asaad was at the door.

The meeting was one of great joy and thanksgiving to us all.--After a little rest and refreshment, he gave us a brief account of his escape.

He had not seen the youth, who had undertaken to befriend him, but finding he did not call the night before, as he expected, he resolved not to wait another day. Therefore, at about twelve o'clock last night, having written a paper and left it on his bed, with the quotation, "Come out of her my people," &c. he set off on foot, committing himself to God for strength and protection. The darkness was such, that he often found himself out of his road, sometimes miring in mud, and sometimes wading in rivers. After some hours of weariness and anxiety, he came to the shore of the sea, where he found a large boat thrown up, under which he cast himself, and obtained a little rest. After this, he continued his walk without interruption, till he reached Beyroot.

In the course of the forenoon, a messenger came from the neighbouring shekh, or sheriff, requesting Asaad to come and see him; adding, that if he did not come, he would watch an opportunity to take his life. The messenger came a second time, and returned without accomplishing his object. We afterwards wrote a line to the shekh to say, that if he would favour us with a call in person and take a cup of coffee, he could have the privilege of an interview with Asaad. Just as the note was sent, the consul providentially came in, and the shekh found him ready to give him a seasonable reprimand for presuming to threaten a person under English protection. The shekh declared, that he had never sent such a message; that the man who brought it was but an ass, and said it from his own brain; that having heard of Asaad's arrival, he merely wished to see whether the reports respecting his insanity were true or false; that Asaad was his bosom friend, his own son, and that whatever he had was his; and that as for church, and priests, and patriarch, he cared for none of them.

Towards evening, the youth already mentioned entered the house, ready to faint with excessive fear and fatigue. He had fled from the mountains in all haste, under the absurd apprehension, that he should be suspected and taken up as an accomplice with Asaad. Having thrown himself upon a seat, and taken a little breath, he began to relate what had happened. He was at the convent, when it was first discovered that Asaad had fled. The patriarch and his train were occupied in the religious services of the morning, so that no great sensation was at first apparent among them. One individual spoke boldly in favour of Asaad, saying, "Why should he not leave you? What inducement had he to remain here? What had he here to do? What had he to enjoy? Books he had none; friendly society none; conversation against religion abundant; insults upon his opinions and his feelings abundant. Why should he not leave you?"

Others, especially the great ones, pitied the poor maniac, (as they called him,) and sent in quest of him to every direction, lest peradventure, he might be found starving in some cavern, or floating in the sea, or dashed in pieces at the bottom of a precipice.

On learning of Asaad all that had passed during his absence, we requested him to write a statement of the facts somewhat in the form of a journal. We wished this not only for our own information, but to produce it to those who shall inquire on the subject of Asaad's lunacy hereafter.

Public Statement of Asaad Shidiak.

Beyroot, March 1826.

Respected Brethren and Friends,--Since many have heard a report, that I have become insane; and others, that I have become a heretic; I have wished to write an account of myself in few words, and then let every reflecting man judge for himself, whether I am mad, or am slandered; whether following after heresy, or after the truth of the orthodox faith. Every serious man of understanding will concede, that true religion is not that of compulsion, nor that which may be bought and sold; but that which proceeds from attending to the word of God, believing it, and endeavouring to walk according to it to the glory of God, and that every one, whose object is solely contention, and who does not obey the truth, but follows after unrighteousness, is far distant from the true religion. This is the standard, by which I would be judged by every one who reads this narrative.

About eight or nine months ago, I was employed, by an American by the name of J. King, in teaching him the Syriac language. At that time, I was very fond of engaging with him in disputatious conversations, to prove him to be in error; but with none but worldly motives, to display my talents and knowledge, and acquire the praise of men. After this, I applied myself to reading of the word of God with intense interest. Now this person wrote a farewell letter to his friends, in which he excuses himself from uniting himself with the Roman Catholic church. After reading this letter, I found, in the Holy scriptures, many passages, which made against the opinions of the writer. These passages I selected, and from them and other evidences, composed a reply to him. But when I was copying the first rough draught of the same, and had arrived to the answer to the last of the objections, which he said prevented his becoming a member of the Roman Catholic church, viz: that the Roman Catholic church teaches, that it is wrong for the common people to possess or read the word of God but that they ought to learn from the popes and councils, I observed the writer brings a proof against the doctrine from the prophet Isaiah, viz: "To the law and to the testimony, if they speak not according to my word, it is because there is no light in them."

While I was endeavouring to explain this passage also, according to the views of the Roman Catholic church, with no other object than the praise of men, and other worldly motives, I chanced to to read the 29th chapter of Isaiah, from the 15th verse to the end. I read, and was afraid. I meditated upon the chapter a long while, and feared that I was doing what I did, with a motive far different from the only proper one, viz. the glory and the pleasure of God. I therefore threw by my paper without finishing the copy, and applied myself diligently to the reading of the prophecy of Isaiah. I had wished to find, in the prophets, plain proofs, by which to establish, beyond contradiction, that Jesus Christ is the Messiah, so long expected from ancient days; proofs that might be made use of in answer to Moslems and Jews. While I was thus searching, I found various passages, that would *bear* an explanation according to my views, but did not find them sufficient to enforce conviction on others, until I finally came to the 52d chapter 14th verse, and onward to the end of the next chapter.

On finding this testimony, my heart rejoiced, and was exceeding glad, for it removed many dark doubts from my *own* mind also. From that time, my desire to read the New Testament, that I might discover the best means of acting according to the doctrines of Jesus, was greatly increased. I endeavoured to divest myself of all selfish bias, and loved more and more to inquire into religious subjects. I saw, and continue to see, many of the doctrines of the Roman Catholic church, which I could not believe, and which I found opposed to the truths of the Gospel; and I wished much to find some of her best teachers to explain them to me, that I might see how they proved them from the Holy scriptures. As I was reading an appendix to a copy of the sacred scriptures, printed at Rome by the Propaganda, and searching out the passages referred to, for proving the duty of worshipping saints, and other similar doctrines, I found that these proofs failed altogether of establishing the points in question, and that to infer such doctrines from such premises, was even worthy of ridicule. Among other things, in this appendix, I found the very horrible *Neronian* doctrines, that it is our duty to destroy heretics. Now every one knows, that whoever does not believe that the pope is infallible, is a heretic in his opinions.

This doctrine is not merely that it is **allowable** to kill heretics, but that we are **bound** to do it. From this I was the more established in my convictions against the doctrines of the pope, and saw that they were the doctrines of the ravenous beast, and not of the gentle lamb. After I had read this, I asked one of the priests in Beyroot respecting this doctrine, and he assured me, that it was even so as I had read. I then wished to go to some place, though it might be a distant country, that I might find some man of the Roman Catholic church sufficiently learned to prove the doctrine above alluded to.

After this, as I was at Beyroot teaching a few Greek youths the Arabic grammar, I received a letter from his holiness the Maronite patriarch, saying, that if I did not cease from all assistance whatever to the English, and that if I did not leave them within one day, I should, *ipso facto*, fall under the heaviest excommunication.

Thinking, as I did, that obeying my superiors, in all things not sinful, was well and good, I did not delay to leave, and so went to my friends at Hadet; but still thinking very much on the subject of religion, so that some people thought me melancholy. I loved exceedingly to converse on religious subjects, indeed I took no pleasure in any worldly concerns, and found all worldly possessions vain. After this, I received a second letter from his holiness the patriarch, in which he said thus: "After we had written you the first letter, we wrote you a second; see that you act according to it. And if you fulfil all that was commanded in it, and come up to us when we come to Kesran, we will provide you a situation." But I saw that nothing, in which I was accustomed to take delight, pleased me any longer. I returned again, after some time, to Beyroot; and after I had been there no long time, Hoory Nicolas arrived, brother to his holiness the rev. patriarch, with a request from the latter, to come and see him, which I hastened to do. Hoory Nicolas then began to converse with me, in the way of reprimand, for being in connexion with the English. I replied that, as we ought not to deny the unity of God, because the Musselmans believe it, so we ought not to hate the gospel because the English love it. He then began to tell me of the wish of his holiness, the rev. patriarch, that I should come out to him, and of his great love to me; and said that he (the patriarch) had heard, that I had received thirty or forty purses of money from the English; and he assured me of their readiness not to suffer this to be any hindrance to my coming out from them.

Now if my object were money, as some seemed to think, I had then a fair opportunity to tell him a falsehood, and say, "I indeed received from the English that sum, but I have expended so and so, and cannot leave them unless I restore the whole." In this way I might have contrived to take what I wished. Yet I did not so answer him, but declared to him the truth, how much wages I had received, and which was nothing extraordinary.

He then gave me a paper from his holiness the patriarch, in which he says, "You will have received from us an answer, requesting that when we come to Alma, you will come up and see us. We expect your presence, and, if God please, we will provide you some proper situation, with an income that shall be sufficient for your sustenance. Delay not your coming, lest the present happy opportunity should pass by." Knowing, as I did, that many people supposed my object, in continuing with the English, to be gain, I did not delay fulfilling the request of his reverence, hoping to remove this suspicion, and to enjoy an opportunity of speaking the truth without being hired to do it.

So, about the 7th of January, I left Beyroot, with Hoory Nicolas, and arrived at Der Alma the same night. His holiness, the patriarch, was not there. On the next day, when he came, I met him, and saluted him in the road. In the evening he called me into his chamber, and began to ask me questions, that he might discover what I was; and I answered him telling him the whole truth, although this course was opposed to my personal convenience. At this he seemed surprised, for he must have perceived it was contrary to what he had been accustomed to see in me. Afterwards, when I declared to him, that I never had before been a believer, according to the true living faith, he was probably still more astonished. He then asked me if I believed as the Romish church believed. I again told him the truth, that I did not. He asked then what was my faith, and I answered to the following purport, "True and living faith must be divine, connected with hope, love and repentance, and that all these virtues are the gift of God &c.; that I believed the truth as God had inspired it; and that it would be but a lie, if I should say that I believed as the Romish church does, while in fact I do not. I must have proofs."

After some conversation like this, he told me that this doctrine of mine was heretical, and that as long as I remained in this state of opinion, he would suffer no one to have intercourse with me in buying and selling, &c. This prohibition of his brought to my mind the words in the Revelation, xiii, 17.[G] Then he gave me to understand, that if, after three days, I did not get back out of this state, I must no more enter the church. At other times, he wished me to swear by the eucharist and by the gospel, that my faith was like the faith of the Roman catholic church. He asked me if I was a Bible man; I replied, "I do not follow the opinions of the Bible men; but if you think me a Bible man on account of the opinions I have advanced, very well."

The sum of what I said was, that without evidence I could not believe what the Romish church believes. From that time, after three days, I did not enter the church for a space. Some time passed again, and the patriarch inquired of me my faith. I then explained to him what I believed respecting the unity and trinity of God, and that the Messiah was one person with two natures, and that the Holy Spirit proceeds from the Father and Son. Then arose a disputation about, who is the Vicar that Christ has appointed to explain his law. I answered in substance as I afterwards did in writing, that by reason, and learning, and prayer to God, with purity of motive, we may know, from the holy scriptures, every thing necessary to our salvation. This was the purport of my reply, which perhaps was not expressed with sufficient clearness, or perhaps I was not able to say it in the manner that was appropriate, for such a tumult and storm were excited in the company that they seemed to me to be intent on overcoming me by dint of vociferation, rather than by argument, and to drown my voice, rather than to understand my opinions.

When, after some days, came bishop Abdalla Blabul and Padre Bernardus of Gzir, the patriarch one day called me to them in his chamber, and asked me what I wished, whether money or office, or whatever it might be, promising to gratify me, speaking of his love to me and of his great interest in my welfare. These professions I know to be sincere, but they are according to the world, and not according to the Gospel. I assured him that I wanted nothing of the things he had mentioned; that I was submissive and obedient to him; and that if he thought of me, that I had taken money of the English, he was welcome to shut me up in my chamber as to a prison, and take from me every thing that I possessed;

that I wished from them merely my necessary food and clothing, and that I would give them this assurance in writing. The bishop and priest then begged me, in presence of the patriarch, to say that my faith was like that of the Romish church. I replied, that I feared to tell a falsehood by saying a thing, while actually, in my reason, I did not believe it.

"But," said they, "the patriarch here will absolve you from the sin of the falsehood." I turned to the Patriarch and put the question whether he would so absolve me. He answered, that he would. I said, "What the law of nature itself condemns, it is out of the power of any man to make lawful." He then again asked me what I wished to do. I said, I wish to go and see the Armenian patriarch Gregory, and inquire of him what I ought to do. He consented, and requested me, when I had done this, to return to him, to which I agreed. I was accompanied by a priest from the station of the patriarch to the College of Ain Warka, where I found Hoory Joseph Shaheen, with whom I conversed a considerable time, and with great pleasure; for I found that for himself, he did not believe that the pope was infallible in matters of faith, that is to say, unless in concert with the congregated church. I then began to confess to him: but when I saw that he held steadfastly some opinions for no other reason than that the church so believed, and without bringing any proper evidence of the fact, viz. from councils or from the fathers, and burst out upon me with exceeding bitter words, saying, "Know that the church neither deceives, nor is deceived, and be quiet;" and when I wished him to instruct me according to the word of God, with the simple object of glorifying God and fulfilling his will, I saw that he was not disposed to support any opinion because it was according to the word of God, but because so thought the church; and I saw him also ready to retain these opinions, although I should bring the strongest evidences against them from the holy Scriptures. He told me that it was impossible for him to teach any thing contrary to the council of Trent. So I found I could not receive his system, because, though you should shew him that it was wrong, he would not give it up, lest with it he should be obliged to give up his office. I therefore told him, you are bound, i. e. shut up as between walls, by the doctrines of the pope and the council of Trent.

In conversation on the images, he would have proved their propriety from Baronius' church history. We found this author quoting the sacred scriptures to prove that our Saviour sent a picture of himself to the king of Abgar. I declared that it was false, in so far as he stated that the *Gospel* made any such statement, and on that account I could not believe the story. To this he gave me no answer. After this, as we were reading the book, and found a statement respecting the bishops collected in Constantinople, to the number of 313; that they decreed the abolition of the use of images, because it was idolatrous, and that in the clearest terms,--I asked him the question, "If an assembly composed of the bishops of the church were infallible, how is it that this council is said to have committed an error?"

About this time, I heard that a certain individual wished to converse with me on the subject of religion, which rejoiced me exceedingly, and I was impatient for an interview. He came on a Sabbath day to Ain Warka, for the study of the Arabic grammar, according to his custom, and we had a short conversation together on works unlawful on the Sabbath day, and other subjects. He then excused himself from further conversation for want of time; but promised that when we should meet again, he hoped to have a sufficient opportunity to dwell on these subjects at large. I continued at Ain Warka the whole week, reading with the rest at prayers and confessing to Hoory Joseph above mentioned; and on the next Lord's day, the Armenian priest aforesaid came again, and I fully expected to have time and opportunity to ascertain his opinions; but I was disappointed again; for he wished to have the dispute carried on in writing, and to have an assistant with him, with other conditions.

In these circumstances I failed of my object; but was on the whole more inclined than before to receive the doctrines of the Romish church; since the priest had promised to bring his evidence, on all points, from the word of God, that they (the papists) were walking in light and not in darkness.

At this time one informed me that his holiness, bishop Jacob, superior of the convent of Bzumar, wished to see me. And because Hoory Joseph, at first told me that this state in which I had fallen was a temptation of Satan, and at one time shewed me that it was usual for people, when they came to the age of manhood, to be tempted on the subject of their religion, and at another, assured me, that this was a state of delirium:--and again, because I had heard formerly that this bishop Jacob had himself been delirious, and that he was a man of information, I wished very much to see him; and on the same day I went to Hoory Joseph and declared to him plainly my opinions, and shewed him that the beast mentioned in the Revelation was a figure, as the lamb evidently was, and how dreadful must be the torments of those who worship the image of the beast. I then disclosed to him my intention of going up to the convent of Bzumar, where were the patriarch Gregory, bishop Jacob, and the Armenian priest already mentioned.

I set off the same day, and on my arrival saluted the patriarch, and on the same night reasoned on the subjects of faith, hope and love. It appeared that the patriarch's opinion was, that a man may be possessed of living faith, faith unto salvation, although he should feel nothing in his heart. I answered him with a quotation from St. Paul, "With the heart man believeth unto righteousness, and with the mouth confession is made unto salvation." But this did not convince him. He explained the *heart* to mean the *will*. It then appeared to me that he was not a true believer, and from that time forward I could not believe him, as I would believe a real Christian, but I wished to hear his worldly arguments. On the following day, I asked him how it can he said, that the pope was infallible if there were no proofs of the fact to be brought. I asked him if this pretension of the pope was that of an apostle, or a prophet? if an apostle, or a prophet, he could not be believed without miracles, and that we christians were not to believe any one, though he were to bring down fire from Heaven.[H] His replies to me were weak; and after considerable conversation on what is the church of Christ, on the ignorance that is pardonable, &c. he began to prove that if the pope is not infallible, then there is *no religion*, *no gospel*, and even *no God*. But I observed all his proofs so weak, that I could not be convinced, and I fell into deep perplexity as to what I should do. For sometimes I greatly endeavoured to submit my judgment to his rules and opinions, and made these efforts until my very head would ache. The next day I asked him what was that *great city*, ruling over the kings of the earth, mentioned in the Rev. xvii, 18? After he had brought his book of commentaries, he answered that it was Rome, which is also called spiritual Babylon, or Babel, and after wishing me to yield to his opinion or that of the book, he said nothing more. From this time I was with the patriarch every day for three or four hours, and his best advice to me was, to pray to St. Antony of Padua, together with one repetition of the Lord's prayer, and one of Hail Mary, &c. every day for three days. When I was thus in doubt from the weakness of their proofs, one of the monks said to me, "If you wish to know *good tobacco*, ask the patriarch." I hoped that this priest would explain to me those doctrines of the Romish church, which I could not believe; so I went into his chamber and questioned him very particularly on all points. He expressed his wish that we might discuss together all the points one by one, but on condition that the patriarch Joseph should appoint him to do so. He told me he had in his possession a book refuting the opinions of Luther and Calvin. I begged permission to read it; but he refused, telling me that the doctrines of the church all remained unrefuted. He wished me to go down to the patriarch Joseph on this business. So after a stay of four days from my arrival, I departed for Ain Warka according to my promise to Hoory Joseph.

Here I found one of my friends of whom I had heard that he had been very much astonished at my connexion with the Bible men. After I had seen him, and had conversed with him a little on some points, he would no longer hear me, fearing among other things lest he should be crazed. When we touched on the subject of the great city above mentioned, he told me that he had seen a book of commentaries on the Revelation, which made the city clearly to be Rome. At this I wondered greatly, since the meaning was so clear that not even the teachers of the Romish church herself could deny it. I then finished my confession to Hoory Joseph Shaheen, and about sunset the same day, went down to the patriarch to the convent Alma. He requested me again to write a paper stating that my faith was according to the faith of the Romish church. From this I excused myself, begging that such a thing might not be required of me, for the council of Trent had added nothing to the rule of faith, which was established by that of Nice, which begins, "I believe in one God," &c. A short space after, I gave him my advice, with modest arguments, and mild suggestions, on his duty to cause the gospel to be preached in the church among the Maronite people; and offered him the opinion that this should be done by the priests in the vulgar language, every Sabbath day, for the space of one or two hours; and if this should appear too burthensome to the people, to take off from them some of the feast days. After this, I remained silent in my chamber near to his own; and as there came to me a few of the deacons of the patriarch, and others, I read to them at their request in the New Testament printed in Rome. But in a little time after, I entered my room, and found in it none of all the books that had been there, neither New Testament nor any other, and I knew that the patriarch had given the order for this purpose, for he reproved me for reading the gospel to them, but he could accuse me of no false or erroneous explanations, or that I taught them any thing heretical.

One day after this, he called me to his presence and began to threaten me in a most unusual manner. I said, "What do you wish of me, your reverence? What have I done, and what would you have me do? What is my sin, except that I conversed with some individuals, shewing them the errors of the church of Rome?" Then he requested me again, to say, that I believed as did that church, and said, grasping me firmly by the chin, "see how I will take you if you do not repent." I begged him to appoint some one to shew me the truth, by way of discussion, but he would not, and continued expressing his own sentiment, that we are bound to hold fast to the church, even to such a length, that if she should even reject the gospel, we should reject it too.

And here I wish to say a word to every reader that regards and loves the truth; how does such doctrine appear to you? and how could I believe in all which the Romish church holds, without *knowing* all of it? and how could I say, without a lie, that I believe, when I do not believe?

When I saw the patriarch breaking out with an exceeding loud and unusual voice, I was afraid that I should be found among "*the fearful*," (Rev. xxi. 8.) and rose to depart. When I reached the door, I turned and said to him, "I will hold fast the religion of Jesus Christ, and I am ready for the sake of it to shed my blood; and though you should all become infidels, yet will not I;" and so left the room.

One of my friends told me, that he had suggested to the patriarch the grand reason why I did not believe in the pope, which was, that among other doctrines of his, he taught, that he could not commit an error, and that now, though a pope should see any one of his predecessors had erred, he could not say this, for fear that *he* also should appear to be an unbeliever. This friend also told me, that the patriarch wondered how I should pretend that I held to the Christian religion, and still converse in such abusive terms against it; and *I* also wondered, that after he saw this, he should not be willing so much as to ask me, in mildness, and self-possession, and forbearance, *for what reasons* I was unwilling to receive the doctrines of the pope, or to say I believed as he did; but he would not consent that the above mentioned Armenian priest should hold a discussion with me, and more than this, laid every person, and even his own brother, under excommunication, if he should presume to dispute or converse with me on the subject of religion.

Under this prohibition from conversation, and this bereavement of books, from what quarter could I get the necessary evidence to believe in their opinion?

Another cause I had of wonder, which was, that not one of all with whom I conversed, after he saw me to be heretical and declining from the truth, thought proper to advise me to use the only means of becoming strong in the faith, viz. prayer to God the Most High, and searching his Holy Word, which a child may understand. I wondered, too, that they should ridicule me, and report me abroad as one mad and after all this, be so fearful to engage in a dispute with the madman, lest he should vanquish them in argument, or spoil their understandings, or turn them away from the truth.

After some time came the bishop of Beyroot. I gave him the usual salutation, and was greatly rejoiced to see him, as I knew the excellency of his understanding, and his quickness of apprehension, and hoped that, after some discussion between us, he would explain the truth, and that he would rest on clear evidence to support his views. But in this case also, I was disappointed; for one day, when I asked him a question, and during the whole short conversation which followed, whenever I began to bring evidence against him, he was angry, and finally drove me from my chamber in a fury, and that with no other cause, as he pretended, than that he did not wish to converse with a heretic.

Some time after this, Hoory Joseph Shaheen came down to the convent of Alma, and I endeavoured to get him to unite with me in persuading the patriarch to send out among the people preachers of the gospel, or that there should be preaching in the churches as before mentioned. But he would not co-operate with me in this, and I was again disappointed.

Then, when the patriarch and the bishop of Beyroot wished to dispute with me, I expressed the hope that the discussion might be in meekness, and without anger. It was concluded that the discussion should be in writing, that no one afterwards should be able to alter what he had once said. They then commenced by asking me questions; the first question was, in amount, this, "Has the Messiah given us a new law?" At first, I did not grant that he had, strictly speaking, given us a new law, and quoted the words of John, that "the law was given by Moses, but grace and truth came by Jesus Christ;" but when I afterwards saw that by "a new law," they meant merely the gospel, or the New Testament, I answered in the affirmative. They then asked me if there was not to be found in this new law some obscurities. I answered, "Yes." They then asked me, Suppose any difference of sentiment should arise between the teachers of Christianity, how are we to distinguish the truth from the error? I answered thus;--"We have no other means of arriving at the truth, than searching the word of God, with learning, and reason, and inquiry of learned spiritual teachers, with purity of motive, and with disinterestedness of inclination. If the obscurities of the word of God cannot be understood by these means, our ignorance is excusable, and will not prevent our salvation. If the passages, which still remain obscure, concern faith, it is sufficient for a man to say, I believe according as the truth is in itself before God, or I believe in the thing as God inspired it to the writer. And if the obscurity respects our practice, after making use of the means above mentioned, if that branch of our practice be forbidden, or under a doubt, desist from it, but if it is not forbidden, do it, and Blessed is he that condemneth not himself in the thing which he alloweth."

After I had given them this answer, they brought no evidence to prove any error in it, and moreover afterwards never put to me any question to writing.

Once, as I was walking with the bishop of Beyroot, he began to tell me how much they all felt for me; and how unwilling they should be to put me in chains to die a lingering death; and that were it not for the sympathy and their love towards me, there were people who had conversed with them, who were ready to take my life. Some further conversation passed, and I began to introduce the subject of religion, and to ask how we could believe in the pope that he was infallible. He quoted for proof the words of our Saviour, *Thou art Peter, &c.* I asked him if it was proper to suppose that all things bestowed on Peter, were also given to the pope? If so, why does not the pope speak with tongues; and why is he not secure from the evil effects of poison, &c.? He answered, that these last things were not necessary. "But how do you prove it necessary," said I, "that the pope should not err? Is it not sufficient if any one has doubts, to ask his teacher who is not infallible? if you say *yes*, then the opinion of the fallible man will answer. But if you say *no*, and that we *must* go to the pope, what must become of the man who dies before the answer of the pope can reach him?"

He then resorted to another mode of proof, saying, "Is it not desirable that the pope should be infallible?" I assured him I wished he might be so. "Well, is not God able to render him so?" "Yes, He is able to do all things." He wished to infer his point from these two premises. But I said, "your reasoning with regard to the *pope*, may be applied to all the bishops of the church; for it is desirable that they should all be infallible, and God is able to make them so." He said, "No, for the bishops feeling less their need of the pope, would not look to him, or submit to him as their head, and then there would be divisions and contentions in the church." But why, said I, did not divisions and contentions arise among the apostles? Were they not all infallible as well as Peter? He would not say they *were* infallible. I told him, that was an opinion that could not be believed, that the pope was infallible, and the apostles not; for it was well known to all, that the Holy Spirit descended upon the apostles in a peculiar manner. I asked him again, how it could be made to appear that divisions would be produced if all bishops were infallible, for if they were all of one opinion, as they of course would be, their union must be the more perfect. We conversed farther at some length, when he concluded by saying, "You are possessed of a devil."

The next day, as the patriarch and the bishop of Beyroot were seated under a tree without the convent, I went out to them, and said, "Your holiness sent to me to come hither for employment, and I came, and have remained here a considerable time. What do you wish me to do for you, for I cannot remain here in idleness?" He said, "What do you wish to do?" If your holiness pleases, that I teach in the school of Ain Warka, I will do that. "No, I cannot have you go to Ain Warka, to corrupt the minds of those who are studying science, and to contradict my opinions." But I will instruct in grammar. "No, the youths of the college are now attending to *moral* science." Well, I only beg you will let me know what I am to do, and if you have no employment for me, I wish to return home. The bishop here broke in upon the conversation, saying, I will not suffer you to go back among my flock to deceive them, and turn them away to heresy. Will you then debar me, said I, from my home? If so, let me know where I shall go, what I shall do? The bishop then said to the patriarch, "Indeed I will not suffer this man to go abroad among my people, for he is even attempting to make heretics of us also." Yes replied the patriarch, it will not do after this, to afford him a residence in any part of the land. The bishop then turned to me, in the bitterest anger and rage, reviling me and saying, "If you go among my people again, I will send and take your life, though it be in the bosom of your own house." I said, "Well, what would you have me to do, and what will you do with me? If you wish to kill me, or shut me up in prison, or give me up to the government, or whatever it may be, I wish to know it." "You must wait here till spring or summer," said the patriarch, "and then we shall see how you are." I answered him in the words of that christian who was given by his judge ten days to deliberate whether he would worship an image: "Consider the time already past, and do what you please."

I asked the bishop his reasons for wishing to kill me. What evil had I done? He was filled with high and bitter indignation, saying, "What, miscreant! Shall we let you go forth to corrupt my flock for me? Is not what has passed enough?" I rose and said to them, "God at least is with me," and left them. The patriarch sent after me his nephew, requesting me, in soothing words to return, and saying that he would do what I wished.

But when I contemplated the hardness of heart manifested by the bishop, I could not restrain myself from reproving him, hoping that he would grow mild. I said, therefore, "Our Lord Jesus Christ said, out of the abundance of the heart the mouth speaketh, and that Satan, who was in his heart, wished to kill me, for Satan was a murderer from the beginning." I told him, moreover, that he was not a true disciple of Christ. And when I had left them a second time, the patriarch again sent his nephew to enquire of me what I wished; whether it was money, or what else, promising that he would answer my enquiries.

I returned and told him, that I had a request to make of one thing only, and that I hoped he would answer me, not as to a little child, who would ask a childish thing. He asked me what it was. I said I have to ask of you the favour to send from your priests two faithful men to preach the gospel through the country, and I am ready, if necessary, to sell all that I possess to give to them as part of their wages. He promised me it should be done. But I had reason to expect that he would receive such a request as from the mouth of one out of his reason. Now there was at the convent a man called Hoory Gabriel, who was said to be insane, and was known to all his acquaintance as a man that never would say a word on the subject of religion, and he was a scribe of the patriarch, and from the time of my arrival until that day, had never asked me a single question about my faith, or opinions, nor had given me the least word of advice about any of my errors. The same night, as this priest was passing the evening in company with the patriarch, bishop, and other individuals, as if they had been conversing on my idiocy in making the request of to-day, the patriarch sent for me to come and sit with them. I came. The patriarch then asked this priest and the others present, if two proper men could be found to go and preach the gospel. They then answered one to another, such an one, and such an one, would be the fittest persons, some mentioning one and some another, looking at me in the mean time laughing, to see what I would say.

I smiled in a pleasant manner at all this, and when one asked me, why I laughed? I said to the patriarch, "Have you not perfect confidence in the integrity of the priest Gabriel?" He said, "Yes." I then said, pray let this priest then examine me for the space of a few days, and if he does not conclude that I am a heretic, I will for *one*, take upon myself this duty of preaching. This remark put an immediate end to the conversation.

The third day, when the bishop wished to mock me before the patriarch and a shekh of the country, I answered his questions according to his own manner; but in a little time he began to revile me, and rebuke me for blasphemy against the eucharist, against the virgin Mary and the pictures, and that because I had said before one of his deacons, that were it not for fear of the patriarch, I would tear all the pictures to pieces and burn them. I gave him answer to every particular by itself, and when he found that he could produce against me no accusation, he increased in wrath. I then said, if this is your pleasure, I will say no more. I told him that I had said, that pictures were not Gods; that such was my opinion always; and that I wished to tell all the common people so, that they might understand it. But to this he would not consent. He then began to accuse me of saying of the eucharist, "Let them smell the scent of it, and know that it is but bread and wine still." I told him that if he would give me leave to speak, or if he wished to hear my views, I would speak; "but how is it that you bring against me accusations, and do not suffer me to make my defence?" Here again he was not willing that I should speak, but the patriarch said to me, "*Speak*." I then observed, that St. Ephraim says, "Come, eat the fire of the bread, and drink the spirit of the wine;" and began to say from this, that our eating the body of Christ was not natural, but spiritual. Then again he fell into a rage against me. I said to him, "It is written, *be ye angry and sin not*. I told you before, that I would keep silence and not speak without your consent, and whatever you wish, tell me that I may act or refrain accordingly." At this the patriarch smiled. But the bishop fell into a passion still more violent, against the patriarch as well as myself, and rose and went away. I also left the room. In the evening, when were collected together the patriarch and bishop and all the monks, with priest Nicholas, whom they were about to ordain bishop on the morrow, the patriarch began to ask me questions respecting my faith. When I saw that their object was neither to benefit me, nor receive benefit, I gave them answers calculated to continue the conversation in a trifling strain, saying, "My faith is the faith of Peter, and the faith of Peter is my faith. I believe all that God has given by inspiration to the one only holy catholic church." He asked me, What is the church? I answered, "The church is the whole company of those who believe in the Messiah and his law, on all the face of the earth." But where is the place of the church? "The place of the church is the whole world, it is made up of every nation and people." "What," said he "the *English* among the rest?" "Yes, of the English also." Afterwards, when he continued to question me, and I saw that he had no other object than to try me, I assured him, this is my faith, and to this faith will I hold, whether it is worth any thing in your estimation or not. I then asked him if he was willing to hold a discussion on the subject; but he would not permit it in any shape. He afterwards requested me to tell my faith again without fear and without concealment. I referred them to the priest that was about to be ordained, saying, that I had conversed with him on all points particularly, and that he was able to make answer for me. The priest then bore testimony on the spot, that I had said before him that I believed the pope to be infallible, while I never said this to him at any time. Afterward, when I was in his company privately, I inquired how he could bear such testimony as he had done. He confessed in the fullest terms, that he knew it was a falsehood, but that he said what he did, that they might cease talking with me. The same night I had resolved on quitting them; so at about midnight I left the convent, committing myself to the protection of God, who never deserts them who put their trust in him, and arrived at Beyroot, on the morning of Thursday, March 2, 1826.

Here then I remain at present, not that I may take my views from the English, or from the Bible men, nor that I may receive my religion from them. No, by no means; for I hold to the word of God. This is beyond all danger of error. In this I believe; in this is my faith; and according to it I desire to regulate my life, and enjoy all my consolations. By this I wish to show what I believe and not to confer with flesh and blood, that I may not run now nor hereafter in vain; for I know and am persuaded, that the true religion is not according to the teaching of men, but according to the inspiration of God: not according to the custom of education, but according to the truth, which is made manifest by the word of God. I therefore say to myself now, as I did in the convent with the patriarch, where I wrote thus:

"Far from me be all the commandments of men. Nothing is to come into comparison with the teaching of Jesus by reading the New Testament. If our *hearts are not transformed*, there is the greatest danger that we die in our sins. If any thing in the doctrine of Jesus seems burdensome, let us pray that he may make it light; and if there is any thing that we do not understand, let us pray that he would instruct us and reveal the obscurity to all who truly believe in Jesus. There is nothing more delightful to the soul than he. O taste and see that the Lord is good! Blessed are all that put their trust in him! Cast thy burthen on the Lord and he will sustain thee. Sweet is the sorrow produced by his word; for it gives us an aversion to all the consolations of time. Let us therefore seek refuge in God. Alas for thee, O thou that trustest to the doctrines of men, especially if they give rest to your conscience, for that rest is false and deceitful, proceeding from the thoughts of men, and preventing you from attaining that true rest, of which the Apostles speak, saying, *We do rest from our labours.* Take heed lest there be in any of you an evil heart of unbelief in departing from the living God. Read the word and it shall teach you all things necessary to your salvation. If you say you do not understand it, behold the promise of St. James, If any may lack wisdom, let him ask of God, who giveth to all men liberally and upbraideth not, and it shall be given him. The divine word is a most precious treasure, from which all wise men are enriched. Drink from the fountain itself. Again, I say, vain is the philosophy of men; for it recommends to us doctrines newly invented, and prevents our increase in virtue, rather than promotes it. Cast it far from you."

This is what I wrote some time since, and I would revolve these thoughts in my mind at all times. The object in all that I have done, or attempted, or written, in this late occurrence, is, that I may act as a disciple and servant of Christ. I could not, therefore, receive any advice, which should direct me to hide my religion under a bushel. I cannot regulate myself by any rules contrary to those of Christ; for I believe that all who follow his word in truth, are the good grain, and that all those who add to his word, are the tares sown by the enemy, which shall soon be gathered in bundles and cast into the fire unquenchable. And I beg every member of my sect, i. e. of the Maronite church, who loves truth, if he sees me in an error to point it out to me, that I may leave it, and cleave to the truth. But I must request those who would rectify my views, not to do as did a priest at Beyroot, who after a considerable discussion, denied the inspiration of the New Testament. Men like him I do not wish to attempt to point out my errors; for such men, it is evident, need rather to be preached to, than to preach; and to be guided, rather than to guide. But if any understanding man will take the word of God and prove to me from it any doctrine whatever, I will respect him and honour him with all pleasure. But if a doctrine cannot be established thus, it is not only opposed to the doctrines of Christ, but to the views of the early christians, the fathers of the church; such as St. Ephraim and others. Such doctrines I cannot confess to be correct, although it should cost me the shedding of my blood. Be it known, that I am not seeking money, nor office; nor do I fear any thing from contempt, nor from the cross, nor from the persecution of men, nor from their insults, nor their evil accusations, so far as they are false. For I am ready for the sake of Christ to die daily, to be accounted as a sheep for the slaughter, for he, in that he suffered being tempted, is able to succour those that are tempted. I consider that the sufferings of this present time are not worthy to be compared with the glory that shall be revealed in us. I believe that Jesus is our High Priest for ever and hath an unchangeable priesthood, wherefore he is able to save them to the uttermost that come unto God by him, for he is the one Mediator between God and man, and he ever liveth to make intercession with the Father for us; and he is the propitiation for our sins, and to him be glory with the Father and his Holy Spirit of life for ever and ever--*Amen.*

I would only add, if there is any one, whoever he may be, that will shew me to be under a mistake, and that there is no salvation for me unless I submit to the pope, or at least shew me that it is lawful to do so, I am ready to give up all my peculiar views and submit in the Lord. But without evidence that my views are thus mistaken, I cannot give them up, and yield a blind obedience, until it shall be not only *told* that I am mad, but until I shall be so in *fact*, and all my understanding leaves me. Not until men shall have burned not only the Bibles printed by the English, but all the Bibles of the world. But these two things, understanding and the Bible, I pray God to preserve both to me and to all the followers of Christ, and that he will preserve and save all you, my friends, in the Lord.

ASAAD SHIDIAK.

Interview with several of his Relatives.

6. Among those who came to see Asaad to-day, were three of his brothers and an uncle. Mansoor, the oldest of the brothers, we had never before seen. He is a furious bigot, and perfectly ignorant and regardless of the first principles of religion. The second, Tannoos, or Antony, has lived among us as a teacher, and has good native and acquired talents; but, though he might be a protestant if he were left at liberty, he thinks it altogether preposterous to attempt to quarrel with bishops and patriarchs on the subject of religion.

These two brothers, and the uncle, (the last worse than the first,) came and conversed together with Asaad in his chamber a considerable time. Hearing them very earnest, I took the liberty also to go in. They continued their rebukes and arguments, (especially the uncle,) in so harsh and unfeeling a manner, that it made me tremble to hear them. They contradicted Asaad, scoffed at and threatened him, calling him possessed, mad, under the power of Satan, and so on. Asaad consented to go home and leave the English, which was the great point they wished to gain, provided they would get an assurance from the patriarch in writing, to say, on the faith of a christian, that he would not molest him.

"But," said they, "then you must hold your tongue, and not broach your new opinions among the people."

"What," replied Asaad, "must I go and live like a *dumb* man? No, that I will never do. My religion binds me not to do it. I must love my neighbour as myself."

"Why do you not go," said they, "to the Druses, and the Moslems, and preach the gospel to them? You answer, because there is danger. So there is danger in the present case; this is not a land of liberty, therefore be silent."

Asaad.--"Secure me but the free exercise of my conscience, and I will go with you. My religion is my all, and I must be free in it."

They.--"We can give you no such security. Nobody dares go to the patriarch with such a request. You cannot be permitted to publish your notions abroad among the people."

"Then," said Asaad, "there is no more to be said;"--rising, and with clasped hands walking the room;--"Religion unshackled--Religion unshackled, is my doctrine."

They rose and left the room in an angry despair. Mansoor returned, and wished to speak a word with Asaad at the door. In a moment, Asaad returned. "Do you know what Mansoor has told me?" said he. "His last words were, 'Even if the patriarch and the emir should do nothing; if they make no attempts to take your life; be assured, *we ourselves* will do the work: so take heed to your self accordingly.'"

Asaad was much affected by the interview. As soon as he found himself at liberty, he stepped up into the loft where he sleeps, and threw himself on his couch in prayer.

While in this attitude his next younger brother, Galed, knocked at the door. I called to Asaad to inform him of the fact; but he gave me no answer. I then invited Galed to another room, where Asaad soon joined us with a full and heavy heart. The two brothers saluted each other with embarrassment. Asaad evidently wished to be alone, and the brother, after a few mild, unmeaning inquiries, left him.

Begins to converse more pointedly with the People.

7. I yesterday advised Asaad to direct his conversations with the people, as much as possible to their hearts, and say little or nothing on the corruption of their church. He objected to the counsel. I referred him to similar advice he gave me some months ago. "Ah," said he, "I thought so then, but I now see that you cannot stir a step, but you meet some of their corruptions." However, he to-day made the experiment, and held an hour's conversation with two visiters on the subject of regeneration. They both thought themselves renewed, but took too little interest in the subject to confine their attention to it. "You see," said Asaad, after they had gone, "how little they feel on such a subject. It is painful to talk with such men. I would rather see

them contradict, and dispute, and get angry, or any thing, than to appear so dead."

Interview with a younger Brother.

Asaad's brother Galed came again to-day, and discovered more feeling than yesterday on the subject of his brother's leaving the English. He said he had brought an insupportable shame upon the family. Asaad insisted, that such shame was no argument whatever for his leaving us; that all the disciples of Christ were to expect it as a thing of course. Galed assured him, that nobody would think of molesting him, if he were at Hadet. I asked Galed if his brother Mansoor did not threaten yesterday to kill him. He turned away, colored, and muttered something that I did not understand; but the whole was a full acknowledgment of the fact.

Asaad said, "I cannot confide in you."

"But," said Galed, "if any one were disposed to take your life, could they not do it as well here, as at home?"

I answered, "no; that the emir Beshir himself could not enter my house without my permission, and that if the relatives of Asaad did not cease from their threats, I should feel myself bound to shut them out of it."

After a long conversation, at the end of which he found Asaad as inflexible as ever, he rose abruptly, and was going out without a compliment, when Asaad started up, and asked, "Well, what do you conclude to do? Do you really intend to send some assassin to take my life in my room?" The youth, without deigning to look at him, closed the door in sullen grief, and departed.

Asaad turning to me, said, "I cannot please these people. Whatever I say, they are sure to be angry. Soft words, or hard words, it makes no difference to them. They come as if I were under their kingly authority. They lay hold of my cloak, and say, 'Give me this.' If I say, 'I will not give it,' they are angry; and if I reason with them with all the mildness of which I am capable, and say, 'Cannot you be accommodated elsewhere? Can you not wait upon me in a few days?' &c. they are equally angry."

Correspondence with his family.

8. A messenger called this morning with the following note.

"To our brother Asaad Esh Shidiak: May God bless you.--We beg you to come home to-night, and not wait till Sunday. We have pledged our mother that you shall come. If you fail to do so, you will trouble us all. Your brother,

GALED."

To this letter, Asaad sat down, and instantly wrote the following reply:

"To our much honoured and very dear brother Galed: God preserve him.--Your note has reached us, in which you speak of our coming home to-night, and say, that if we do not come, we trouble you all.

"Now if we were in some distant land, your longing after us in this manner might be very proper; but we are near you, and you have been here, and seen us in all health, and we have seen you. Then quiet our mother, that we, through the bounty of God, are in perfect health, and that we have great peace in the Lord Jesus Christ, peace above all that the world can afford, and abundant joy in the Holy Ghost above all earthly joy. But as to our coming up this evening, we do not find it convenient, not even though we had the strongest desire to see our mother and you.

"I beg you all to love God, and to serve him in our Lord Jesus Christ. This is of all things the most important; for if we love God, if he but renew our hearts by the holy Ghost, we shall enjoy each other's society for ever and ever.

"And now we are prevented from coming to you, and you know we are not void of all desire to see you, but the hindrances to which we have alluded, are, we think, a sufficient apology. We beg you to accept our excuse, and to apologize for us to our mother, and we pray God to pour out his grace richly on you all, and lengthen your days.

"Your brother, ASAAD.

"P. S. Tell our mother not to think so much of these earthly things but rather of God our Saviour."

Is visited by his Mother.

This letter had been gone scarcely time sufficient to reach Hadet, when the mother herself was announced at the door. We welcomed her with all cordiality, and treated her with all the respect and attention we could. But all we could do or say did not alter her resolution to get her son away, if in her power. She besought him by the honour he owed her, by the love he professed for her, by his regard for the reputation of her family, for religion itself, and for his own personal safety, that he would immediately accompany her home; and when she found him inflexible, she declared she would never stir out of the house unless he went with her.

To all this Asaad replied, "To what purpose would it be, that I should go home? You wish me to go, you say, that people may be convinced that I am not mad. But you, who come hither, and see, and converse with me, say, after all, that I *am* mad. How can it be expected that I should convince others that I am *not* mad, when my own mother will not believe it. Or do you think that if I once get out among you, the air of Hadet will change my opinions, or induce me to be silent? All these are vain expectations. I see no object to be gained. If I should go to Hadet, and be constantly disputing with the people, and telling them, that you are all going astray; that you are worshipping idols instead of the living God; that I could wish to tear down every picture in your churches; that the bread and wine of the Lord's Supper are not Jesus Christ; that I believe the pope to be the beast in the revelation,[I] whose business is to deceive the people and ruin their souls;--by all this, I should injure your feelings, enrage the people, excite the opposition of the emirs, and bishops, and patriarchs, and then return here just in the state I am in now."

The youngest brother, Phares, who accompanied his mother, conversed freely and in good temper, and listened with attention to all Asaad's arguments, by which he endeavoured to justify his views and determinations. But no argument or evidence could convince the disconsolate mother. Asaad had repeated the name of Christ, and the word of God so often, that she, at last, in a fit of impatience exclaimed, "Away, with Christ, and the word of God; what have we to do with them!" and when we pointed out to Asaad some text of Scripture, which we thought applicable in any case, she would endeavour to close the book, or catch it from him, as if it taught paganism, or witchcraft. During her stay we dined, and as Asaad took the meat upon his plate, and ate it without a scruple, in this season of Lent, it was remarked with what a gaze of wonder she regarded him. She seemed to say in her heart, "All is over--my son is lost!"

After some hours of troublesome expostulation and entreaty, during which
Asaad once said he could bear it no longer, and rose, and shook my hand
to go, it was finally settled that the mother should go home without
him, but that to save the family from the insupportable shame, which
threatened it, Asaad should give her a paper, stating, in effect, that
he was not a follower of the English. When the paper was finished,
"Now," said Asaad, "go to your home in peace;" and walked away; but
suddenly recollecting himself, he called his brother back, and said,
"Phares, I wish you fully to understand, that I love you, and I have one
request to make of you, which is, that you will take the New Testament,
and read it attentively."--"Give me a New Testament," said Phares,
quickly. We gave him the book, and he went his way, evidently affected
and softened by the interview.

9. The shekh before mentioned communicated to Asaad, through the medium
of a priest, the offer of his daughter in marriage, on condition he
should leave the English.

10. Set apart a day of fasting and prayer on Asaad's account. He was
observed not to be in a happy temper. Towards evening he spoke of going
home. I hoped he would finish writing the statement we had requested of
him, "for," said I, "if you go home I shall not see you again for
months." "No," said he, "perhaps not for years." His manner was very
peculiar. I knew not what was the matter, till, in the evening, after a
long conversation on the evidences of inspiration, he said, "I have been
in deep darkness to-day. My heart has been full of blasphemy, such as I
have scarcely ever known. I have even doubted the existence of God. But
now I am relieved, and I would just say, I shall not go home to-morrow,
as I hinted."

This temptation seems to have arisen chiefly from a discrepancy in the
scriptures, which I had shewed him, and which I knew not how to
reconcile. He begged that, for the present, I would by no means shew him
another such.

Suspects himself to have been poisoned.

11. One of the neighbours brought Shidiak a letter, cautioning him, if
he went to the shekh's house, not to smoke or drink with him.

12. Word came to Asaad, that the shekh was with the family below, and
would be glad to see him. Asaad went down, but in a few minutes came up,

pale and trembling, and said he was exceedingly dizzy and faint. He had just taken coffee below, attended with suspicious circumstances, and begged to know if he might not be poisoned. We opened a medical book we had, and explained to him, as rapidly as possible, the symptoms of a poisoned person. "Oh! these are my feelings," said he, and fell upon his knees before his seat in silent prayer. We immediately gave him an emetic, which operated well, and before night he was relieved of every alarming symptom. The youth who gave the coffee, being sent for, gave good evidence of having had no bad intentions; and notwithstanding many suspicious circumstances, we did not think the evidence of an attempt at poison sufficiently strong, to prosecute any public inquiry into the matter.

16. A youth from Der el Kamer called to see Asaad. He remarked, that he once saw a priest at his village tear in pieces five of these books of ours, but he could not tell for what reasons. He had, apparently, never seen the ten commandments before, and was very much surprised to find image-worship so expressly condemned in them. A letter was received by Asaad from the patriarch, written in very plausible terms.

Visits his Relatives at Hadet.

17. Four of the relatives of Asaad came down, and succeeded in persuading him to accompany them home. He said he could not believe, after all that has been said, that they would do him violence, and he strongly expected that his visit to Hadet would do good. A majority of us opposed his going with all we could say; but he thinks he knows the people here better than we do. He left us toward evening, expecting to be absent only a few days.

Their violence, and the consequent proceedings of Phares Shidiak.

24. Phares Shidiak came to my house to day, and wished to speak with me in private.

"Yesterday morning," said he, "as I was in my room reading the New Testament, my brother Mansoor entered, drew a sword he had, and gave me a blow upon the neck. I continued with the book in my hand, until one snatched it from me. Mansoor afterwards drew up his musket, threatening to shoot me; but my mother interfered to prevent him. My brother Tannoos hearing a bustle, came in with a cane, and began cudgelling me, without stopping to inquire at all into the merits of the case, calling out,

'Will you leave off your heresy, and go to church like other people, or not?' Mansoor not finding Asaad present, as he seemed to have expected, went to Asaad's chest which stood near me, seized all the books he had received of you, Hebrew, Syriac, Italian, and Arabic, tore them, one by one, in pieces, and strewed them on the floor.

"In the course of the day, I came down near where the soldiers of the emir are encamped, and passed the night in company with my brother Galeb. This morning *he* returned, with a line from me to Asaad, and *I* came off to Beyroot, with the full determination never to go home again. And now I will either go to some place in this country where I can enjoy my liberty or I will take ship, and leave the country altogether."

As he wished my advice, I counselled him neither to go from the country, nor from his home, but to return, and at least make a further trial of doing good to his relatives, and bearing their persecutions. He, however, continued inflexible.

In the space of a few hours, Galeb came in search of Phares, with a letter from Asaad, of which the following is a copy.

Asaad's letter to his brother Phares.

"To my beloved brother Phares; the Lord Most High preserve him. Your departure caused me great grief. *First*, because you were impatient when trial and persecution came upon you. It is a thing we are regularly to expect, that if we hope in God in this world, we shall give universal offence. But we have another city, for which we hope. Do not lose your courage, for you have not yet resisted unto blood, striving against sin. Remember, we cannot share in the glory of Christ, if we share not also in his sufferings. Therefore, rejoice whenever you are tried; rejoice, and never be sad; for our faith is sure.

"*Secondly*, I was grieved because you gave me no information where you were going, and what you intended to do. Now, it is not becoming, that we should do any thing rashly, that is, till we have prayed to God for direction. Come home, then, and let us set apart a season of fasting and prayer to God, and do what is most agreeable to him. Perhaps it is best to let our works preach in silence, in these evil days.

"You must know, that if you fail to come home, you will give us great pain, and this, you know, would be inconsistent with love. Jesus says,

'By this shall all men know that ye are my disciples, if ye have love one to another.' You well know how much joy and consolation it would give us to see you; do not then deny us this pleasure, but come at all events. If you do not come, it may be an injury both to yourself and me. I wish to see you, if it be only to say to you two words, and then act your pleasure; for not every word can be said with paper and pen. Farewell.

"Your brother and companion in tribulation,

ASAAD."

Galeb took me aside, and begged me to urge his brother to go home. I said I had already advised him to do so, but that I could not force him to go--that if he found he could not enjoy liberty of conscience, and the privilege of reading the word of God, in Hadet, he was welcome to stay with me as long as he pleased. "You are a man," said Galeb, "that speaks the truth and acts uprightly, but Asaad and Phares are not like you; they talk very improper things." Among these things, he mentioned a report to which Asaad had given circulation, respecting the patriarch, to which I was obliged to reply, that instead of taking it for granted to be a *false* report, he ought to believe it to be true, and that such a report was not abroad respecting the patriarch alone, but respecting a majority of patriarchs and bishops of the whole land.

After some further conversation on the wickedness of treating brothers, as they had done Phares and Asaad, we went to Phares, and endeavoured to persuade him to go home with his brother. But it was all in vain. "If I leave this house," said he, "instead of going to Hadet, I will go in the opposite direction." The brother returned without him.

Conversation of Phares with the Bishop of Beyroot.

After Galeb had gone, we put a great many questions to Phares, and he communicated some interesting particulars. Among others was the following:

"The day that Asaad and myself left you, (the 17th,) the bishop of Beyroot was at the next house, and I went to salute him.

"He said to me, 'I understand *you* have become English, too. You *reason on the subject of religion*.'

"But," said I, "is every one English, if he *reasons* on that subject?"

Bishop.--"But you read in the Bibles of the English."

Phares.--"Yes, and from whom is the Bible? is it from the English, or from God?"

B.--"But it is *printed* by the English."

P.--"Well, is it altered in any place?"

B.--"See, now you have begun again to argue on the subject of religion. I tell you, young man, cease this heretical habit, or you are excommunicated."

Phares informed us of three or four Bibles and New Testaments, that we had given at different times to individuals in Hadet, which had lately been destroyed by order of the bishop. This news, together with a discovery we yesterday made in the neighbouring house, of two covers of the New Testament, whose contents had long ago been torn out, shews us anew, if new evidence were wanting, that if the Gospel is ever introduced again in its power and purity into this country, it will be with a desperate struggle.

Two brothers of Phares, Mansoor and Galeb, came to converse with him anew. We saw them seated together on the ground, at a little distance from the house, but afterwards saw them no more. It is singular that Phares should have left without coming either to take his cloak, or bid us farewell.[J]

28. Having heard nothing particular directly from Asaad since he left, especially since the affair of the books, I yesterday sent him a line, and to-day received the following reply:

Letter from Asaad to Mr. Bird.

"Dear Sir,--After expressing imperfectly the love I bear you, and the desire I have to see you in all health, I have to say, that in due time your letter came to hand, and I read and understood it. You ask respecting our health. I answer, I am in a state of anxiety, but not so great as some days ago.

"On Thursday last, having come home from a visit to the emir Sulman, I found the remnants of the Holy Scriptures, torn in pieces, as there is reason to believe, by order of the bishop. When I was told, that my brother Mansoor had done this mischief, I returned to the emir, and informed him of the affair. He sent to call Mansoor, while I returned again to our house. I now learned, that my brother Phares had gone off. After searching for him some time, I went down to the inn in quest of him, but he was not to be found. As I was on my way returning from the inn, where I had gone in search of my brother, I prayed to God, that he would take every thing from me, if necessary, only let faith and love towards him remain in my heart.

"As I proceeded on, a man came up, and gave me information that all the consuls of Beyroot were slain, and that you also were slain with them. The report came from a man, who said he had deposited goods with you for safety. In order to be the more sure, I asked the man if it were really true, and he again assured me, that it was. Ask me not the state of my feelings at that moment.

"On reaching home, I heard this terrible news confirmed; at the same time looking out, and seeing the heap of ashes near the house, all that remained of the 11 copies of the holy scriptures which my brothers had destroyed, I burst into tears, and committed all my concerns into the hands of God, saying, 'Blessed be his holy name: the Lord gave, and the Lord hath taken away;'--and so I prayed on, with tears and groanings, which I cannot describe.

"I afterwards heard, that Phares was probably in the neighbourhood, and set off to search after him by night, but found him not. When I heard the news of your death confirmed, I sent off a messenger, that, wherever Phares might be found, he might return; and when I received his letter, saying that he had gone to your house, I could not yet believe that the report respecting you was false.

"But when the truth on this subject began to appear, then I heard by a person who came to the yesterday evening, that the patriarch and the emir had made an agreement to kill *me*, and that they had sent men to lie in wait for that purpose. I was afterwards told, by another person, that some of the servants of the emir were appointed to accomplish this end.

"Here I am, then, in a sort of imprisonment, enemies within, and enemies without.

"One of my brothers, the other day, advised me to surrender my self entirely to the mercy of the bishop, whereupon I wrote the bishop a letter, (of which I send you the enclosed copy,) and gave it to my brother Tannoos, begging him to carry it to the bishop, and bring me his reply. Tannoos read the letter, and without saying a word, threw it down in contempt. I then gave it to my uncle with the same request, but as yet I have got no reply.[K]

"All my concerns I commit into the hands of God, who created me. Through the blood of our Lord Jesus Christ, I hope that all my distresses will be for the best.

"I accept with pleasure all your kind wishes, and send you many salutations in the Lord, and pray for you length of days.

"Yours, &c. ASAAD."

"March 27, 1826."

His relatives deliver him up to the Patriarch.

31. Information is received, that Asaad has been taken away against his will, to the patriarch.

April 4. Phares Shidiak arrived here in the evening direct from Der Alma, and said he had accompanied Asaad to that convent a week ago, that Asaad was still there, and that the patriarch, having in the morning set off for Cannobeen, would send down for Assad after a few days. He then handed me the following line from Asaad.

"If you can find a vessel setting off for Malta, in the course of four or five days, send me word; if not, pray for your brother.

ASAAD."

We were disposed to send off a messenger this very evening, but Phares said it would not be necessary.

Had some serious conversation with Phares, in which I exhorted him to continue reading the New Testament, and take particular notice of the general spirit of it; and then to judge, if all this deceit, confining, beating, and threatening to kill, was consistent with that spirit. We observed, that we supposed the patriarch and the bishop were well pleased with all the violence that Mansoor had used in this affair. "Yes," said Phares, "priest Hanna Stambodi, at Ain Warka, told me yesterday, that none of us had any religion, except Mansoor."

In a subsequent part of his journal, Mr. Bird records the following particulars respecting Asaad, during his last visit to Hadet, and when about to be violently removed from thence. They were received from Phares.

A neighbouring emir being sick, one day, Asaad carried him a paper of medicine, on the outside of which he had written how it was to be taken. While Asaad stood without, a servant took in this medicine, and gave it to the prince, saying, "This is from Asaad Esh Shidiak, and here he has written the directions on the paper." The prince, who is not remarkable for mildness, and perhaps was not conscious that Asaad overheard him, spoke out angrily, "A fig for the paper and writing; 'tis the medicine I want." "Your lordship is in the right," replied Asaad, "the truth is with you. The *medicine* is the thing; the *paper* that holds it, is nothing. So we ought to say of the gospel, the great medicine for the soul. 'Tis the *pure gospel* we want, and not the *church* that holds it."

After Mansoor, in his catholic zeal, had torn up and burned all his Bibles and Testaments, Asaad could not remain without the scriptures, but sent and obtained a copy from the little church, which he daily read, marking the most striking and important passages.

When his relatives, to the number of twenty or more, had assembled, and

Asaad perceived they were come to take him to the patriarch by force, he began to expostulate with Tannoos, and besought him to desist from a step so inconsistent with fraternal love. He besought in vain. Tannoos turned away from him with a cold indifference. Affected with his hardness, Asaad went aside, and wept and prayed aloud.

The evening before he was taken away, he said to those who had assembled, "If I had not read the gospel, I should have been surprised at this new movement of yours. But now it is just what I might have expected. In this blessed book, I am told, the brother shall deliver up the brother to death, and a man's foes shall be they of his own household. Here you see it is just so. You have come together to fulfil this prophecy of the gospel. What have I done against you? What is my crime? Allowing that I do take the Bible as my only and sufficient guide to heaven, what sin is there in this?" During the evening, he laid himself down to sleep, as he was to set off early in the morning. But he was often interrupted; for, whenever he caught a word of false doctrine from the lips of those who continued their conversation, he would rise up, refute them, and again compose himself to rest. One of his uncles, speaking of his going to the patriarch, said in a great rage, "If you don't go off with us peaceably, we will take your life." Asaad replied, "Softly, softly, my dear uncle, don't be hasty. **Blessed are the meek.**"

Phares wrote a letter this evening to Asaad, in a hand that had been agreed on between them, saying, that if he would come to Beyroot, he need not fear, and that it might be a matter for further consideration whether he should leave the country.

5. The letter of Phares was sent off by a moslem, who returned at evening, saying that when he arrived at the convent, he was accosted by two or three men, inquiring his business, telling him he was a Greek, and had letters from the English. They then seized him, and took the letter by force, and, had he not shewn them that he was a moslem, would have probably sent him to the emir of the district for further examination. They then asked him some questions about the English, and assured him that after eight days Asaad would no longer be a living man. Thus were our hopes of a second deliverance of this sufferer of persecution, for the present, blasted. After all the threats, which have been thrown out without being put in execution, we rather hope, that this last will prove like the rest; yet we cannot tell how far their hatred of the truth may, with the divine forbearance, carry them. We leave all with him, in whose hands our life and breath are, and whose are all our ways, with the humble hope, that light may yet arise out of darkness, and that much glory may be added to his name, from this

evident work of Satan.

6. Sent word, in a blind hand, on a torn scrap of paper, to Phares respecting the fate of our message to his brother. He returns answer that he is coming to Beyroot to-morrow.

7. Phares came, according to his notice of yesterday, saying, that if the patriarch should get his letter to Asaad, there would be danger in his staying at Hadet. He should be glad to go to Malta, or almost any other place out of the Maronite influence, lest his brothers should seize him, and deliver him up to the fury of the patriarch, as they had done his brother Asaad. Mansoor, the eldest and most violent of them, when he heard, yesterday, that a letter had arrived for Phares from Beyroot, breathed out threatenings and slaughter, not only against Phares, but against the innocent messenger himself.

8. Wrote to ----, a friendly Maronite bishop, to give me whatever information he might be able to procure respecting Shidiak.

May 10. A messenger whom we sent to Cannobeen, returned with the report that he was denied the privilege of seeing Asaad, under pretence that he was going through a course of confession, during which the rule is, that the person so confessing, shall pass his time, for a number of days, alone, and see no company.

14. We were, to-day, credibly informed, that Shidiak is still firm in his adherence to the gospel, but that he was kept under rigid inspection, not being permitted to step out of his room without an attendant.

17. Phares Shidiak informed us to-day, that he had been told that his brother Asaad had been at the college of Ain Warka. He thought it might be true, as one object in delivering him up to the patriarch was, to give the people the general impression, that he had no longer any thing to do with the English. He had now been a sufficient time absent from us to give general currency to the report, that he was no longer with us, and now, perhaps, the patriarch had let him go free.

Asaad is cruelly treated.

27. The messenger, who went before to Cannobeen, had set out to go for us a second time, and this morning early returned with the following story:--Being met by a man near Batroon, whom he suspected to be from

Cannobeen, he inquired him out, and found him to be a messenger sent by Asaad himself to his uncles and other connexions, to beg them to come and deliver him. Asaad saw the man, and gave him his commission from the window of the convent, without the knowledge of the patriarch, or the others in his service. This messenger said, that Asaad was in close confinement, in chains, and was daily beaten; and that the great cause of complaint against him was, that he refused to worship either the pictures, or the virgin Mary.

I had written a letter of mere salutation to Shidiak by my messenger, which letter he enclosed in one from himself, and sent it on by his brother, returning himself with the messenger from Asaad. This brother of his, he is much afraid, may be ill-treated by the patriarch.

28. J., the messenger, called, and said, that he himself should not go to Cannobeen, but twelve or fifteen of his other relatives would go and endeavour at least to save him from chains and stripes. J. had been to the emir Beshir the less, who lives at Hadet, begging him, (with a present) to save his brother, if it should prove that he had suffered by the suspicion or the resentment of the patriarch. The emir promised to interfere--"But why," said he, "should Asaad go and join the English? they are a people I do not love."

June 2. A youth of the neighbourhood said it was reported that Asaad was a complete maniac; that he rent his garments, raved, reviled, &c. and that he had been sent to the convent at Koshia, like other lunatics, for a miraculous cure. This news was brought by priest Bernardus, of Gzir, mentioned in Shidiak's statement.

3. The brother of J. about whom he was so solicitous, returned last evening in safety, with the following letter in Asaad's own hand writing.

"To our respected brother J. ----. After expressing my love to you, I have to say, that your letter by your brother ----, arrived in safety, and I have understood it. In it you and ----, inquire after my health. May the Lord pour out his grace upon you, and follow you with his blessings. As to me, I am at present in health, with regard to my *body*, but as to other circumstances, your brother will give you information. Love to cousin ----, your wife. Pray send me word respecting you every opportunity, and may the Lord lengthen your days. From your brother.

"ASAAD ESH SHIDIAK."

This letter is certainly genuine, and is a full proof of what nature the insanity is, under which he labours. It has greatly relieved the anxiety we felt from the report of yesterday.

From the verbal account, given by the lad who brought the letter, the following are selected as the most important particulars. He entered the convent on his arrival, and seeing nobody but the keeper of the prison-room, obtained leave to go in, and see Asaad alone. He found him sitting on the bare floor, with a heavy chain around his neck, and firmly fastened at the other end into the wall. His bed had been removed together with all his books and writing materials, and (what is considered here the extreme of privation,) he was left without a pipe.

The lad continued with him an hour or two, without being discovered by any one but the keeper. During the conversation, Asaad observed, that not long since he was sent to Koshia, as a man possessed of a devil, and that he escaped from that place and had arrived near Tripoli, when he was taken by a party of Maronites, and brought back to the patriarch. He had, since that time, been kept regularly at Cannobeen, subject occasionally to beating and insult, from such as might call in to see the heretic. We understood the man to say, that the patriarch even instructed the common people to spit in his face, and call him by odious names, in order to shame him into submission. Asaad gave his advice that we should either send some one with a horse, and get him away by stealth, or get the consul to interfere by writing to the pasha. The letter written by Asaad was done through the contrivance of his keeper for a small reward.

Attempts made to procure his release.

After hearing all this, we went directly to the consul to inform him of the case, and to urge him to an interference. He consented, that we should first procure some one to write a firm and consistent letter to the patriarch, demanding by what right he had taken a man from an English employer, and under English protection, and imprisoned him unheard, &c. intimating, that if the man was not soon given up, something more would be done.

Toward evening, J. came again to inquire what we had concluded on. When he found what step we had taken, he seemed much alarmed for his own safety, and begged us not to proceed, for he should be immediately suspected as the mediator of the affair, and should be in danger of being persecuted as such. He mentioned, as a justification of his fears, that the keeper overheard Asaad when he recommended that course to his brother, and that the keeper, when inquired of, would of course mention the fact to the patriarch. Instead of the measure we were about taking, he recommended to apply to the emir, through one of his relatives, who was our mutual friend, and to this we consented. It is, however, probable, that the object of J. is not so much to avoid danger, as to put his friend the emir in a way to get a small present.

5. J. has been to see the emir, in order to persuade him to intercede with his uncle, the emir Beshir, but the former was not at home, and therefore the latter was not consulted. J. then went to the emir M. but found him quite averse to do any thing, saying, that to liberate a man, who had become English, would never do. He next saw Mansoor, the brother, and asked him if he knew that Asaad was in close confinement. "Yes," answered he, "and he may end his days there, unless he can learn to behave himself better." One characteristic mark of a heathen is, that he is "*without natural affection, implacable, unmerciful.*"

J. says, that his brother has told him in addition, that Asaad himself, on the whole, wished not to have the consul interfere, but that some one might, for the present, be sent every week or two, to see how he got along, and in the mean time, he hoped to make his own escape, for that only a few days before, he had loosed himself from his chains, and got out of the convent, but not understanding the path, he became afraid to proceed, and returned of his own accord.

6. Went again to confer with the consul with regard to Asaad. When we mentioned the fact, that Asaad was under a sort of oath of obedience to the patriarch, an agreement which all make who are educated from the funds of the Ain Warka college, he seemed to think differently of the case, because, though an oath to bind the conscience, as in this case, can never be binding, and is neither acknowledged by Turks or English, yet, in the opinion of all Maronites, it justifies what the patriarch has done. This English protection, they would say, is of no avail, since he was under a previous engagement to serve the patriarch. The consul thinks the case, if presented to the chief emir, would be rejected without consideration, on the ground, that it was ecclesiastical, and not civil; and if presented to the pasha, he would exact fines from many innocent convents, and other wise oppress them, without perhaps, after all, procuring the release of the prisoner. He would prefer some secret mode of effecting the object.

Priest Bernardus, of Gzir, already mentioned was on a visit to the family below, and sent up to beg the favour of a sight at Shidiak's statement. I at first refused, but on a second application, and being assured that the priest was a friend of Shidiak, I consented, and invited the man to come and take with me a cup of coffee, which he did. It will be observed, that this Bernardus was one of those, who wished Shidiak to say that his faith was like that of the Roman catholic church, although it should be a falsehood, saying that the patriarch would bestow on him a pardon for the lie. The priest acknowledged to the family below, that Shidiak's statement of that affair was correct.

14. Received a line from the friendly Maronite bishop, to whom I had written, (April 8,) who says that he has been assured, probably afresh, that Shidiak is in prison, and suffers beating.

15. The emir A. came and conversed a length of time on the case of Shidiak. I offered to reward him well for his trouble, if he would procure his release, which he has promised to attempt.

21. J. came to say, that he had never seen the emir A. who had endeavoured to persuade his uncle to write to the patriarch. The uncle, however, refused, but added, "*You* may write in my name, and say, that it is my pleasure, that Shidiak should be liberated." The messenger has, therefore, gone with such a letter.

22. This morning, came Tannoos Shidiak, accompanied by a young emir, saying, that they had knowledge of our attempt to liberate Asaad, through the medium of the emir A. "It will not do," said he, "you will not accomplish your object so." They both said, that the emir A. was a great liar, had a little mind, and little, if any, influence with his uncle. In short, *they* proposed *a more excellent way*, viz. that we should give *them* also a good reward to engage in this noble work of brotherly love.

24. The messenger from the emir A. arrived from Cannobeen, with the following letter from the patriarch, in answer to his own.

"After kissing the hands of your honourable excellency, &c. &c. With regard to your slave, **Asaad Esh Shidiak**, the state into which he is fallen, is not unknown to your excellency. His understanding is subverted. In some respects he is a demoniac, in others not. Every day his malady increases upon him, until I have been obliged to take severe measures with him, and put him under keepers, lest he should escape from here, and grow worse, and infuse his poison into others. Two days ago, he succeeded in getting away in the night, and obliged me to send men to bind him and bring him back; and after he was come, he showed signs of returning sanity, and begged to be forgiven. But he does not abide by his word, for he is very fickle; and the most probable opinion respecting him is, that he is possessed of the devil. However, as he was, to appearance, disposed to yield me obedience, I treated him kindly and humanely, and used every means to promote his permanent cure. This is what I have to communicate to your excellency, and the bearer will inform you further. Whatever your excellency commands, I obey, and the Lord lengthen your life.

JOSEPH, *Patriarch of Antioch.*"

27. A youth from Ain Warka informed us, that he had seen a letter in Asaad's own hand-writing, saying, that he had yielded obedience to the patriarch, and professed again the faith of the Roman catholic church. This report, excited great joy, he says, at the college. We are rather pained by the news, because, if Asaad has done this, we are almost sure it has been done insincerely, and merely to escape the pains of his persecution. The same person says, that a relative of the patriarch at Cannobeen, has been in the habit of writing, every week or two, to the college, to give the news of what was done with Asaad from time to time, in which he spoke of his *chains* and *stripes*, and so on. He also observes, that many people have boldly questioned the right of the patriarch to proceed to such extremities with the members of his church, saying, they saw not, at this rate, which was chief governor of the mountains, the prince, or the patriarch.

July 1. One who seemed certain of delivering Shidiak, if he should set about it, went, with our recommendation to Tripoli, from which place he hopes to have a convenient communication with Cannobeen.

14. The youth who went to Tripoli to attempt something, came back unsuccessful.

17. Application has been made by Phares to the emir M., but he refused to do any thing for Asaad, alleging that it is an affair of religion, and belongs exclusively to the patriarch. Phares says, that notwithstanding the superstition and anger, which his mother exhibited when here, she has more than once said, that the English are better than the Maronites, for they take an interest in the fate of Asaad, while the Maronites all seem to care nothing about him, whether he is dead or alive, happy or wretched.

Phares, as well as others, says, that Tannoos is Asaad's enemy from jealousy. Asaad is younger than Tannoos, but has been much more noticed. This Tannoos could not bear, and has therefore been quite willing to see him disgraced and punished.

Phares observes, that Tannoos was quite as favourably disposed to protestant principles as Asaad, but the moment Asaad took the start of him, he fell back, and is a much firmer Maronite than ever. He seemed to be affected at the death of Mr. Fisk, but inferred from it, that God did not approve the efforts of the protestants in this country. The death of Mr. Dalton, also, his former pupil, probably confirmed this feeling.

Great difficulties in the way of Asaad's release.

18. Tannoos came to converse about his brother Asaad. He had just received a letter in Asaad's own hand-writing, saying, that he was reduced to a great extremity of distress, and perhaps had not long to live, and begging Tannoos to come up and see if nothing could be done to end or mitigate his sufferings. Tannoos declares that he would be very glad to get him away from Cannobeen, if he could be safe, but that in any other place in the dominions of the emir Beshir, he would be killed. He might be safe at the consul's, but with me, he would ***not*** be. "There are men in these mountains," said he, "that can kill and ***have*** killed patriarchs and emirs, and that in their own houses; and why could they not kill Asaad with you, if they chose? Is your house more secure than the convent of the patriarch, or the palace of the emir? A man in entering your house, would violate all law, but the English would not make war for the killing of a single man."

I observed, that an application would very possibly be made to the pasha, by the consul, if Asaad was not soon delivered up. "An application of that sort," replied T. "would be quite useless. The pasha would send the application to the emir, and do you not think the emir would arrange the affair as he pleased? He knows well this sort of dealing. He has known how to manage these mountains for forty years, and do you think he would be at a loss about such a trifle as this? For example, what would be more easy for the emir, if he chose to detain the man, than to say he had committed murder, and therefore could not be given up?" "But," said I, "such a charge must be established by competent witnesses, and under the consul's inspection." "True," replied he, "and where would be the difficulty in that? The emir would bring 500 witnesses to-morrow to establish any crime he was pleased to allege. And as to his fearing the pasha, though he holds his office under him, yet his power is even superior to the pasha's."----"The patriarch," continued Tannoos, "can do just what he chooses, in spite of the English. You have brought books here, and the patriarch has burned them in spite of you. He has issued to all denominations a proclamation full of lies against you, and what have you been able to do? You have indeed written a reply to the proclamation, and hold it up to the people, and say, 'Look how the patriarch lies about us;' but what does he care for all that."

So talks a Lebanon mountaineer, of more sense, information and truth, than most others, respecting the moral character and godly fear of his patriarch and prince.

His family attempt his liberation.

19. Phares brought us a letter, which had just been received by the family at Hadet, from the patriarch, wishing them to come immediately to Cannobeen. Tannoos and his mother have gone, and intend, if possible, to bring Asaad away, either to Kesroan, or to Hadet. The mother insisted on going, and wished to pass through Beyroot on her way, that she might consult us before she went; but this was not permitted her.

The above mentioned letter, in English, runs thus:--"After telling you how much I desire to see you in all health and prosperity, I send you news respecting the wretch Asaad Esh Shidiak, otherwise called lord of hell. His obduracy, with which you are acquainted, has exceedingly increased. It is not unknown to you, how much care I have bestowed on him for his good, how much I have laboured for his salvation, and under what severe discipline I have put him; and all to no effect. And now, as might be expected, he has fallen ill, and therefore can no longer run away, according to his custom, and we have been thus constrained to take off the severity of our treatment. But fearing lest his disease should increase upon him, I have sent you word, that you may come and see how he is, and consult what is best to be done with him. Make no delay, therefore, in coming, and the apostolic blessing be upon you."

This attempt of his family to effect his liberation failed, for some reason unknown; and he continued immured in prison, suffering persecution. He was confined in a small room with an iron collar round his neck fastened to the wall with a strong chain. In October, 1826, another attempt was made to effect the liberation of Asaad. The civil authorities were consulted, but could not be prevailed upon to enlist in his behalf. In November, 1826, however, he effected his escape, but was soon arrested, and treated more cruelly than ever.

In the Herald for April, 1828, we find the following history of Asaad from the time he was betrayed into the hands of the patriarch till the spring of 1826. It is thus prefaced by Mr. Bird, one of the missionaries.

"This account of our suffering friend, though by no means complete, may nevertheless be relied on as authentic, and is by far the most full and satisfactory account which we have been able to obtain. It was sent us, as you will see in the journal, by the friendly young shekh, Naami Latoof, who, some time previous, spent a few weeks in our families, and whose heart seems to have been touched with the truths of the gospel. The priest, who has proved so great a benefactor to Asaad, is a relative of the shekh, and they have grown up together from childhood on the most intimate terms of familiarity and friendship. Many of the occurrences here related, the priest found written among the monks, who pass their time idly with the patriarch, and to many he was an eye-witness. The account was drawn up under his own inspection. He seems a man unusually conscientious for an Arab, unusually open to conviction in argument, and has promised to do his utmost to save Asaad from further abuse, and in the end to deliver him from his state of confinement. Thus, while all our own efforts have failed of essentially benefitting the poor man, the Lord, without any of our instrumentality, has raised up a friend from the midst of his persecutors, who has already saved him from impending death, and we hope and pray, will soon open the way for his complete deliverance from this Syrian Inquisition."

Brief history of Asaad Esh Shidiak, from the time of his being betrayed into the hands of the Maronite Patriarch, in the spring of 1826.

=Translated from the Arabic of Naami Latoof.=

When the relatives of Asaad brought him to the convent of Alma in the district of Kesroan, and gave him up to the patriarch, the latter began by way of flattery to promise him all the worldly advantages he could bestow; but withal demanding that he should put away all the heretical notions, and all the corrupt knowledge, which the Bible-men, those enemies of the pope, had taught him. He replied, "These things which you hold out to me, are to me of no value. I no longer trouble myself about them, for they are vain and of short duration. Every christian is bound to think, and labour, and strive to be accounted worthy to hear that blessed welcome, 'Come ye blessed of my Father, inherit the kingdom prepared for you from the foundation of the world.' As to rejecting from my mind those things which I have learned from the Bible-men, I have to say, that, for many years, I had read, occasionally, the holy scriptures, which are able to make us wise unto salvation, but could not live according to them; for I was given to the indulgence of all wicked passions: but since my acquaintance with these men, I see myself, through the merits of my Saviour, possessed of a new heart, though it is not yet, I confess, in all respects such as I could wish it to be."

During the few days they remained in the Kesroan, the patriarch shewed him every attention, and suffered no one to oppose his opinions saying, "The protestants, by the great sums they have given him, have blinded his eyes, and inclined him to join them, and diffuse their poisonous sentiments, so that he cannot, at once, be brought to leave them. Let him alone for the present, do nothing to oppose or to offend him, until we shall arrive at Cannobeen, where we may examine into his faith and state at our leisure, and if we find that he still clings to his heresy, we then can do with him as circumstances may require." After a short time they proceeded with him to Cannobeen, and there began to use arguments to convince him of his errors, and persuade him to confess and forsake them, and embrace whatever the councils and the church had enacted;--requiring that he should surrender his conscience to the holy catholic church, and bless all whom she blessed, and curse all whom she cursed; and this they did in the most stern and threatening manner. He replied, "It has been said, by the mouth of the Holy One, Bless and curse not." They still pressed him to yield his opinions, but he said, "I can give up nothing, nor can I believe any thing but as it is written in the holy scriptures; for in these is contained all doctrines necessary to salvation."--"But," said they, "is every thing then, worthless, that has been ordained by the councils and the fathers?" He answered, "The councils may have enacted laws good for themselves, but we are not bound to follow them."

After urging him, day after day, to no purpose, they finally asked in despair, "Are you then still of the same sentiment?" "Of the same sentiment," said he; "I still believe and hold whatever is written in the holy scriptures, and neither more nor less." "Will every one, then, who reads the gospel, be saved?" "By no means;--but as it is written, 'he that hath my commands and *keepeth* them, he it is that loveth me.'" "It is the duty of every person to possess the gospel, and read it?" "Yes, it is the duty of every one. 'For,' said Paul, 'if our gospel be hid, it is hid to them that are lost, in whom the god of this world hath blinded the minds of them which believe not, lest the light of the glorious gospel should shine unto them.'" They then reviled him, and spurned him away from their sight, and began to meditate measures of violence against him. He was separated from all around him, and compelled to take his meals by himself; and lest he should attempt to escape, a person was set over him to keep him under a constant watch. He was made to feel himself in the lowest state of disgrace, all taking the fullest liberty to reproach and ridicule him.

From this state of debasement he soon began to meditate his escape. Accordingly, one evening, just as the sun had set, and while his keeper's eye was off him, he fled. An immediate and diligent search was made for him, but he could not be found until the second day, when he was discovered still hiding in a grove near by, for he was totally ignorant of the way he ought to take. They brought him immediately to the patriarch. When he arrived, he was met by reproaches and revilings, and the servants, by order of the patriarch beat him, and put him into confinement. This was at Diman, a pleasant, airy situation belonging to Cannobeen, and about an hour's distance from it. Soon after this, he was taken up to the latter place, when he was left a little more at large, but was always under the watch of a keeper.

One evening, when all had gone in the chapel for prayers, he lay as if he had been asleep, and the monk, his keeper, thinking him really so, went in with the rest, but took with him, as a precaution, Asaad's silver inkhorn, supposing that if he should wake, and think of escaping, he would not be willing to leave behind him so valuable an article. When Asaad saw that all were gone, knowing the length of their prayers, he at once left the convent, and ran about an hour's distance. People were despatched in search of him with all diligence, but they returned without finding him. On account of his ignorance of the way, he remained secreted near the road till the day broke, when he continued his flight until he had reached the distance of three hours or more from his prison, when a couple of men in the service of the patriarch, having been apprized of his escape by the pursuers during the night, discovered him, and called out, "Who are you? Are you Asaad?" He replied, "I am Asaad." They at once took him into custody, and brought him back, but without any violence or indignity, to the patriarch. A different treatment, however, awaited him at the convent. He had no sooner reached it, than they covered him with insult, beating him, and mocking him, and saying, "fool that you are, why did you answer to your name?" He replied, "God has laid a curse upon the lying mouth, and therefore I cannot use it." They said, "If you do not return to your faith, and hold to all that has been ordained by the church and the fathers, you are ruined. You will die under your tortures, and go to perdition." He replied, "Whoever shall call on the name of the Lord shall be saved. I am willing to expose myself to every indignity and suffering for the sake of Him who loved us, and shed his precious blood for our salvation. These things I am bound to say and do, and I am bound to exhort you also, as beloved friends." When he had said this, they all laughed him to scorn, called him a madman, and were about to beat him for attempting, as they pretended, to make heretics of them also. When he saw their anger, he cried out, "Why are you enraged at me, and what are you about to do to me? I am a dying man like yourselves, and preach unto you that you should turn from your vanities unto the living God, who made heaven, and earth, and the sea, and all that are therein." They then renewed their cries that he was mad, and thrust him into his prison room, and locked the door upon him, and strict orders were given that no one should say any thing to him more or less. In this state he remained for some days. The patriarch then sent to him to inquire after his faith, especially respecting his trust in the images of the church, declaring to him that without faith in these, he could not be saved. He replied, "Let no man beguile you of your reward in a voluntary humility and worshipping of angels." They brought him proofs from the councils, that images were used by the fathers, and ought to be set up and worshipped in the churches, in honour of the saints, and to obtain their intercession. He answered, "I will also bring you proof from the councils, that the worship of images, and all use of them in the churches, was forbidden and reprobated by the fathers." Here they contradicted him. "Be it as it may," said he, "it is impossible for me to follow the opinions of any man or set of men., and leave the word of God behind me. This word tells me, that 'forasmuch as we are the offspring of God, we ought not to think that the Godhead is like unto gold, or silver, or stone, graven by art or man's device.'" The messengers then quit him, and made their report to the patriarch, who left him in his prison for a considerable time, in the most abject and suffering state.

In process of time, certain individuals, possessed of a little humanity, became interested in his situation, sympathized in his sufferings, interceded for him, and procured liberty to open the prison door, so that any one who chose could go in and see him without restraint. Again he began to meditate an attempt to escape, and on a certain evening, set off from the convent. But, as before, his ignorance of the proper path to escape in, prevented the accomplishment of his purpose. He soon saw the lighted torches streaming off in every direction in search of him, and to avoid his pursuers, turned aside a short distance, and climbed into a tree. From this situation he did not dare to come down till the night was fairly gone, when he shifted the position of his clothes, turning his cloak inside out, using his turban for a girdle and his girdle for a turban, and took his way. He had, however, not proceeded far, when one of the patriarch's men discovered him, and called out, "Asaad is it you?" He answered, "it is I." The man immediately caught him, like a greedy wolf, bound him, beat him, and drove him before him, as a slave, or a brute, to Cannobeen. On their way they were met by many others who had been sent off in quest of him, who all united with the captor in his brutal treatment. On his arrival, the patriarch gave immediate orders for his punishment, and they fell upon him with reproaches, caning him and smiting him with their hands; and so it was, that as often as they struck him on one cheek, he turned to them the other also. "This," said he, "is a joyful day to me. My blessed Lord and Master has said, 'Bless them that curse you, and if they strike you on the right cheek turn to them the left also.' This I have been enabled to do, and I am ready to suffer even more than this for him, who was beaten, and spit upon, and led as a sheep to the slaughter, on our account." When they heard this, they fell to beating him anew saying, "Have we need of your preaching, thou deceiver? Of what avail are such pretensions in one who is in the broad way to perdition?" He replied, "he that believeth that Jesus Christ is the Son of God, hath eternal life." "Ah," said they, "this is what blinds you. Your salvation is by faith alone in Christ; thus you cast contempt on his mother, and his saints; you deny the presence of his holy body on earth;"--and they threw him on the ground, overwhelmed with the multitude of their blows. For three successive days, he was subjected to the bastinado, by order of the patriarch, who, after that, summoned him to his presence, and demanded of him his faith. "I am a Christian, a follower of Jesus of Nazareth." Those present exhorted him to acknowledge the intercession of the saints, and to repair to them for help in this hour of trial. But he refused, saying, "My help is in him who shed his blood for sinners." "But have the saints," said they, "no intercession, and is it vain to worship them, and pray to them?" He said, "We are not taught to seek help or protection from any, but from him who is the Great Shepherd, who has said with his own blessed mouth, 'Come unto me, all ye that labour and are heavy laden, and I will give you rest.' To any other than God, we are not commanded to pray or seek for refuge."

They then returned him to his prison as before. Those who sympathized with him, went and begged him to confess that the canons of the councils were binding on all Christians, and that the images were very properly made use of in the churches. He answered, "Professing themselves to be wise, they became fools, and changed the glory of the incorruptible God into an image made like unto corruptible man." At this they turned away from him in despair and disgust, and reported to the patriarch that he was in the most settled state of obstinacy, and was doubtless possessed of a devil.

Upon this, the patriarch ordered him to be put in chains, and the door to be barred upon him, as formerly, and his food to be given him in short allowance. In this condition he remained till he was much reduced, and began to entreat them to have pity on him and take off the irons from his feet, and open the door of his prison. Some were moved by his supplications, interceded for him, unbarred the door, took off his chains, and left him. He arose, walked out, and sat down with one of them and conversed. He then begged the patriarch to give him some books to copy, to rid himself of the tedium of his idleness. But he refused, nor would he suffer any to hold conversation with him.

After some days, there came into the convent two men, in the character of beggars, and wished to pass the night, but were turned away. That same night Asaad made another attempt to escape. As soon as it was discovered that he was gone, a vigorous search was made to find him, but all to no purpose. The universal cry now was, that the two men already mentioned had been sent by the protestants to steal him away for a large reward. Immediately his holiness, the patriarch, sent letters to the emeer Abdallah informing him of Asaad's escape, and requesting him to guard the roads of the Kesroan, and search the neighbourhood, if possibly Asaad might still be found lurking in that district. Accordingly search was made, Asaad was discovered among his relatives by a couple of soldiers, was bound, and taken off to the emeer, who sent him direct to the patriarch.

On his arrival, he was loaded with chains, cast into a dark, filthy room, and bastinadoed, every day, for eight days, sometimes fainting under the operation, until he was near death. He was then left in his misery, his bed a thin flag mat, his covering his common clothes. The door of his prison was filled up with stone and mortar, and his food was six thin cakes of bread a day, and a scanty cup of water. In this loathsome dungeon, from which there was no access but a small loop hole, through which they passed his food, he lay for several days; and he would lift up his voice, and cry, "Love ye the Lord Jesus Christ according as he hath loved us, and given himself to die for us. Think of me, O ye that pass by, have pity upon me, and deliver me from these sufferings."

Now when his groans and cries were thus heard, a certain priest, who had been a former friend of Asaad, was touched with compassion. His former friendship revived, his bowels yearned over his suffering brother, and he besought every one who could speak with the patriarch, that they would intercede and endeavour to soften his feelings towards his prisoner. By dint of perseverance, the priest at length succeeded, and obtained permission to open the prison door of his friend and take off his irons. The first request he made of the priest on his entering, was, that he would give him a little food, for he was famishing with hunger. The priest immediately brought him a little bread and cooked victuals, which he ate, and said, "The name of the Lord be blessed."

Those present began to exhort him to turn to the mother of God, if, peradventure, she would have mercy upon him, and bring him back to the way of salvation. He answered, "If she has the power of intercession, let her intercede for us with her beloved Son." The priest was very assiduous in supplying him with every thing necessary for his comfort; in particular he obtained the return of his clothes, of which he had been partly stripped; for the snow was upon the ground, and the cold filled him with pains.

Now when the others saw the care and attention of the priest, they said, "You have become a convert to his heretical opinions." But he replied, "God has said, 'Blessed are the merciful;'" and continued firm in his purpose. His assiduity was such, that whenever he left the convent for any time, he would give money to the cook to prevail on him to supply Asaad with proper food, and to attend upon him in whatever he might need. The enemies of the priest accused him to the patriarch, but they could not succeed in their object, for the priest is of blameless morals, and has a good name among all.

The priest now passed much of his time in company with Asaad, and conversed with him freely. On a certain occasion they began to converse on the subject of the cross, the priest saying it ought to be worshipped. Asaad replied, "For what reason? and where is the use of it?" The priest said, "In memory of the Saviour." Asaad,--"Why do you kiss the cross, and who has commanded it?" Priest,--"We kiss it in honour of him who hung upon it." Asaad.--"But why then do you not paint the *ass* also, and pay it all obeisance, and all honours, for our Saviour, when he rode upon the ass, was in all honour, and all paid him obeisance; but when he was on the cross, he was in sorrow and disgrace." The priest reproved him gently for returning such an answer, and when he saw that the priest was displeased, he said, "On account of your love to me, and the favour you have done me, I wish to prove to you this point, that all religious reverence and worship and service to any but God, is vain; for it is said, 'He that heareth my word, and believeth on him that sent me, hath everlasting life,' and I have to beg of you, that you will continually search the holy scriptures, and pray as David prayed, 'Create in me a clean heart, O God, and renew a right spirit within me.'" During this time, one of their enemies was standing without the door, and listened to the whole conversation. This man went immediately, to the patriarch, and told him all that he had heard, and that the priest was conversing with Asaad in so gentle a manner, that he was likely soon to be won over to heresy. His holiness was startled at the intelligence, and hastening down inquired the truth of the report. Asaad concealed nothing. The patriarch, however, at first, repressed his own feelings, and exhorted him in the most winning manner he could assume, promising that if he would but return to the holy church and fathers and councils, worship the images, and saints, and the mother of God, he would again immediately make him his secretary. He replied, "With regard to the opinions which I hold, I assure you I wish to hold none which are opposed to the word of God; and as to resorting to the virgin Mary, I say, as I have before said, that if she has any power of intercession, let her intercede for us. As to giving up my opinions to the church and councils, how can I do it, so long as I am possessed of satisfactory evidence that these councils are opposed to one another? We are in no need of the councils, but have sufficient light without them to guide us in the way of salvation. Moreover I can say, that *I do* surrender my opinions to the holy catholic church, for I profess the faith of the church of Christ, and unite my conscience with it."

The patriarch could no longer restrain his feelings, but broke out in the language of reproach, saying, "You are a worthless fellow, obstinately bent on maintaining your folly. I give you to understand that I am clear of your guilt. You will not be taught, but love to shew your contempt of the cross, and of the worship of the images, whose worship is only in honour of those to whose memory they are set up, and who laboured and died in the service of Christ." Asaad replied, "With regard to worshipping such things as these, it is said, 'Thou shalt worship the Lord thy God, and him only shalt thou serve;' and as to those who laboured and shed their blood for the Saviour, they are above our honours, for they have gone to inherit unspeakable glory in their master's presence." The patriarch was more angry than ever, and taking off his slipper, beat both him and the priest, and drove the latter from the room, and locked the door.

After six days of additional confinement, the friendly priest again procured his release from his prison, and obtained the favour of taking the entire oversight of him. In this condition the persecuted man remains. May the Most High grant him speedy deliverance.

Feb. 15th, 1827.

* * * * *

The latest accounts from Palestine state that Asaad is still in confinement, but remains firm to the principles he has embraced. In a letter from Mr. Goodell, dated April, 1830, we find the following sentence.--"Asaad Shidiak is still alive, and there is every reason to believe that he loves and obeys the truth, that he is sanctified by it, rooted and grounded in it, and ready to suffer for it." We take our leave of this interesting narrative, commending the suffering subject of it to God, and the word of his grace, accounting him more blessed if he perseveres steadfast unto the end, than if his brows were endowed with an imperial diadem.

NOTES:

[E] The Papists receive these books as of equal divine authority with the books of the Old Testament.--ED.

[F] This he actually proposed, but the patriarch would not listen to the proposal a moment.

[G] "He causeth all--to receive a mark," &c. "and no man might buy or sell save he that had the mark or the name of the beast." The patriarch was also clothed in scarlet, like the woman on the scarlet coloured beast.

[H] See Rev. xiii. 13

[I] When he first came to Beyroot, this same sentence was dictated to him, and it appeared in his eyes so much like blasphemy, that he refused to write it.

[J] We afterwards ascertained, that he was decoyed off to a distance, as if for walk, and when he would have returned, was prevented by force.

[K] This letter was a mere tissue of testimonies, brought from the fathers, and from the scriptures, condemning the worship of images.

CHAPTER IX.

PERSECUTIONS OF THE BAPTIST MISSIONARIES IN INDIA, DURING THE YEAR 1824.

Account of the Scenes at Ava during the War.

Mr. and Mrs. Judson were among the number of the first missionaries who left this country for India. After labouring for some time in Hindostan they finally established themselves at Rangoon in the Burman Empire, in 1813. In 1824 war broke out between the British East India Company and the emperor of Burmah. Mr. and Mrs. Judson and Dr. Price, who were at Ava, the capital of the Burman Empire, when the war commenced, were immediately arrested and confined for several months. The account of the sufferings of the missionaries was written by Mrs. Judson, and is given in her own words.

The sufferings of the missionaries, during this long and disastrous period, surpassed all that the most alarmed and fertile imagination had conceived. Of the dreadful scenes at Ava, a minute account was written by Mrs. Judson to Dr. Elnathan Judson. It will be read with strong and painful interest. Fiction itself has seldom invented a tale more replete with terror.

"*Rangoon, May 26, 1826.*

"My beloved Brother,

"I commence this letter with the intention of giving you the particulars of our captivity and sufferings at Ava. How long my patience will allow my reviewing scenes of disgust and horror, the conclusion of this letter will determine. I had kept a journal of every thing that had transpired from our arrival at Ava, but destroyed it at the commencement of our difficulties.

"The first certain intelligence we received of the declaration of war by the Burmese, was on our arrival at Tsenpyoo-kywon, about a hundred miles this side of Ava, where part of the troops, under the command of the celebrated Bandoola, had encamped. As we proceeded on our journey, we met Bandoola himself, with the remainder of his troops, gaily equipped, seated on his golden barge, and surrounded by a fleet of gold war boats, one of which was instantly despatched the other side of the river to hail us, and make all necessary inquiries. We were allowed to proceed quietly on, when he had informed the messenger that we were Americans, *not English*, and were going to Ava in obedience to the command of his Majesty.

"On our arrival at the capital, we found that Dr. Price was out of favour at court, and that suspicion rested on most of the foreigners then at Ava. Your brother visited at the palace two or three times, but found the king's manner toward him very different from what it formerly had been; and the queen, who had hitherto expressed wishes for my speedy arrival, now made no inquiries after me, nor intimated a wish to see me. Consequently, I made no effort to visit at the palace, though almost daily invited to visit some of the branches of the royal family, who were living in their own houses, out of the palace enclosure. Under these circumstances, we thought our most prudent course lay in prosecuting our original intention of building a house, and commencing missionary operations as occasion offered, thus endeavouring to convince the government that we had really nothing to do with the present war.

"In two or three weeks after our arrival, the king, queen, all the members of the royal family, and most of the officers of government, returned to Amarapora, in order to come and take possession of the new palace in the customary style. As there has been much misunderstanding relative to Ava and Amarapora, both being called the capital of the Burmese Empire, I will here remark, that present Ava was formerly the seat of government; but soon after the old king had ascended the throne, it was forsaken, and a new palace built at Amarapora, about six miles from Ava, in which he remained during his life. In the fourth year of the reign of the present king, Amarapora was in its turn forsaken, and a new and beautiful palace built at Ava, which was *then* in ruins, but is *now the capital* of the Burmese Empire, and the residence of the Emperor. The king and royal family had been living in the temporary buildings at Ava, during the completion of the new palace, which gave occasion for their returning to Amarapora.

"I dare not attempt a description of that splendid day, when majesty with all its attendant glory entered the gates of the golden city, and amid the acclamations of millions, I may say, took possession of the palace. The saupwars of the provinces bordering on China, all the Viceroys and high officers of the kingdom, were assembled on the occasion, dressed in their robes of state, and ornamented with the insignia of their office. The white elephant, richly adorned with gold and jewels, was one of the most beautiful objects in the procession. The king and queen alone were unadorned, dressed in the simple garb of the country; they, hand in hand, entered the garden in which we had taken our seats, and where a banquet was prepared for their refreshment. All the riches and glory of the empire were on this day exhibited to view. The number and immense size of the elephants, the numerous horses, and great variety of vehicles of all descriptions, far surpassed any thing I have ever seen or imagined. Soon after his majesty had taken possession of the new palace, an order was issued that no foreigner should be allowed to enter, excepting Lansago. We were a little alarmed at this, but concluded it was from political motives, and would not, perhaps, essentially affect us.

"For several weeks nothing took place to alarm us, and we went on with our school. Mr. J. preached every Sabbath, all the materials for building a brick house were procured, and the masons had made considerable progress in raising the building.

"On the 23d of May, 1824, just as we had concluded worship at the Doctor's house, the other side of the river, a messenger came to inform us that Rangoon was taken by the English. The intelligence produced a shock, in which was a mixture of fear and joy. Mr. Gouger, a young merchant residing at Ava, was then with us, and had much more reason to fear than the rest of us. We all, however, immediately returned to our house, and began to consider what was to be done. Mr. G. went to prince Thar-yar-wa-dee, the king's most influential brother, who informed him he need not give himself any uneasiness, as he had mentioned the subject to his majesty, who had replied, that 'the few foreigners residing at Ava, had nothing to do with the war, and should not be molested.'

"The government were now all in motion. An army of ten or twelve thousand men, under the command of the Kyee-woon-gyee, were sent off in three or four days, and were to be joined by the Sakyer-woon-gyee, who had previously been appointed Viceroy of Rangoon, and who was on his way thither, when the news of its attack reached him. No doubt was entertained of the defeat of the English; the only fear of the king was, that the foreigners hearing of the advance of the Burmese troops, would be so alarmed, as to flee on board their ships and depart, before there would be time to secure them as slaves. 'Bring for me,' said a wild young buck of the palace, 'six kala pyoo, (white strangers,) to row my boat;' and 'to me,' said the lady of a Woongyee, 'send four white strangers to manage the affairs of my house, as I understand they are trusty servants.' The war boats, in high glee, passed our house, the soldiers singing and dancing, and exhibiting gestures of the most joyous kind. Poor fellows! said we, you will probably never dance again. And it so proved, for few if any ever saw again their native home.

"As soon as the army were despatched, the government began to inquire the cause of the arrival of the strangers at Rangoon. There must be spies in the country, suggested some, who have invited them over. And who so likely to be spies, as the Englishmen residing at Ava? A report was in circulation, that Captain Laird, lately arrived, had brought Bengal papers which contained the intention of the English to take Rangoon, and it was kept a secret from his Majesty. An inquiry was instituted. The three Englishmen, Gouger, Laird, and Rogers, were called and examined. It was found they had seen the papers, and were put in confinement, though not in prison. We now began to tremble for ourselves, and were in daily expectation of some dreadful event.

"At length Mr. Judson and Dr. Price were summoned to a court of examination, where strict inquiry was made relative to all they knew. The great point seemed to be whether they had been in the habit of making communications to foreigners, of the state of the country, &c. They answered, they had always written to their friends in America, but had no correspondence with English officers, or the Bengal government. After their examination, they were not put in confinement as the Englishmen had been, but were allowed to return to their houses. In examining the accounts of Mr. G. it was found that Mr. J. and Dr. Price had taken money of him to a considerable amount. Ignorant, as were the Burmese, of our mode of receiving money, by orders on Bengal, this circumstance, to their suspicious minds, was a sufficient evidence, that the missionaries were in the pay of the English, and very probably spies. It was thus represented to the king, who, in an angry tone, ordered the immediate arrest of the 'two teachers.'

"On the 8th of June, just as we were preparing for dinner, in rushed an officer, holding a black book, with a dozen Burmans, accompanied by *one*, whom, from his spotted face, we knew to be an executioner, and a 'son of the prison.' 'Where is the teacher?' was the first inquiry. Mr. Judson presented himself. 'You are called by the king,' said the officer; a form of speech always used when about to arrest a criminal. The spotted man instantly seized Mr. Judson, threw him on the floor, and produced the small cord, the instrument of torture. I caught hold of his arm; 'Stay, (said I,) I will give you money.' 'Take her too,' said the officer; 'she also is a foreigner.' Mr. Judson, with an imploring look, begged they would let me remain till further orders. The scene was now shocking beyond description. The whole neighbourhood had collected--the masons at work on the brick house threw down their tools, and ran--the little Burman children were screaming and crying--the Bengalee servants stood in amazement at the indignities offered their master--and the hardened executioner, with a hellish joy, drew tight the cords, bound

Mr. Judson fast, and dragged him off, I knew not whither. In vain I begged and entreated the spotted face to take the silver, and loosen the ropes, but he spurned my offers, and immediately departed. I gave the money, however, to Moung Ing to follow after, to make some further attempt to mitigate the torture of Mr. Judson; but instead of succeeding, when a few rods from the house, the unfeeling wretches again threw their prisoner on the ground, and drew the cords still tighter, so as almost to prevent respiration.

"The officer and his gang proceeded on to the court house, where the Governor of the city and officers were collected, one of whom read the order of the king, to commit Mr. Judson to the death prison, into which he was soon hurled, the door closed--and Moung Ing saw no more. What a night was now before me! I retired into my room, and endeavoured to obtain consolation from committing my case to God, and imploring fortitude and strength to suffer whatever awaited me. But the consolation of retirement was not long allowed me, for the magistrate of the place had come into the verandah, and continually called me to come out, and submit to his examination. But previously to going out, I destroyed all my letters, journals, and writings of every kind, lest they should disclose the fact that we had correspondents in England, and had minuted down every occurrence since our arrival in the country. When this work of destruction was finished, I went out and submitted to the examination of the magistrate, who inquired very minutely of everything I knew; then ordered the gates of the compound to be shut, no person be allowed to go in or out, placed a guard of ten ruffians, to whom he gave a strict charge to keep me safe, and departed.

"It was now dark. I retired to an inner room with my four little Burman girls, and barred the doors. The guard instantly ordered me to unbar the doors and come out, or they would break the house down. I obstinately refused to obey, and endeavoured to intimidate them by threatening to complain of their conduct to higher authorities on the morrow. Finding me resolved in disregarding their orders, they took the two Bengalee servants, and confined them in the stocks in a very painful position. I could not endure this; but called the head man to the window, and promised to make them all a present in the morning, if they would release the servants. After much debate, and many severe threatenings, they consented, but seemed resolved to annoy me as much as possible. My unprotected, desolate state, my entire uncertainty of the fate of Mr. Judson, and the dreadful carousings and almost diabolical language of the guard, all conspired to make it by far the most distressing night I had ever passed. You may well imagine, my dear brother, that sleep was a stranger to my eyes, and peace and composure to my mind.

"The next morning, I sent Moung Ing to ascertain the situation of your brother, and give him food, if still living. He soon returned, with the intelligence, that Mr. Judson, and all the white foreigners, were confined in the ***death prison***, with three pairs of iron fetters each, and fastened to a long pole, to prevent their moving! The point of my anguish now was, that I was a prisoner myself, and could make no efforts for the release of the Missionaries. I begged and entreated the magistrate to allow me to go to some member of government to state my case; but he said he did not dare to consent, for fear I should make my escape. I next wrote a note to one of the king's sisters, with whom I had been intimate, requesting her to use her influence for the release of the teachers. The note was returned with this message--She 'did not understand it,'--which was a polite refusal to interfere; though I afterwards ascertained, that she had an anxious desire to assist us, but dared not on account of the queen. The day dragged heavily away, and another dreadful night was before me. I endeavoured to soften the feelings of the guard by giving them tea and segars for the night; so that they allowed me to remain inside of my room, without threatening as they did the night before. But the idea of your brother being stretched on the bare floor in irons and confinement, haunted my mind like a spectre, and prevented my obtaining any quiet sleep, though nature was almost exhausted.

"On the third day, I sent a message to the governor of the city, who has the entire direction of prison affairs, to allow me to visit him with a present. This had the desired effect; and he immediately sent orders to the guards, to permit my going into town. The governor received me pleasantly, and asked me what I wanted. I stated to him the situation of the foreigners, and particularly that of the teachers, who were Americans, and had nothing to do with the war. He told me it was not in his power to release them from prison or irons, but that he could make their situation more comfortable; there was his head officer, with whom I must consult, relative to the means. The officer, who proved to be one of the city writers, and whose countenance at the first glance presented the most perfect assemblage of all the evil passions attached to human nature, took me aside, and endeavoured to convince me, that myself, as well as the prisoners, was entirely at his disposal--that our future comfort must depend on my liberality in regard to presents--and that these must be made in a private way and unknown to any officer in the government! What must I do, said I, to obtain a mitigation of the present sufferings of the two teachers? 'Pay to me,' said he, 'two hundred tickals, (about a hundred dollars,) two pieces of fine cloth, and two pieces of handkerchiefs.' I had taken money with me in the morning, our house being two miles from the prison--I could not easily return. This I offered to the writer, and begged he would not insist on the other articles, as they were not in my possession. He hesitated for some time, but fearing to lose the sight of so much money, he concluded to take it, promising to relieve the teachers from their most painful situation.

"I then procured an order from the governor, for my admittance into prison; but the sensations, produced by meeting your brother in that *wretched, horrid* situation, and the affecting scene which ensued, I will not attempt to describe. Mr. Judson crawled to the door of the prison--for I was never allowed to enter--gave me some directions relative to his release; but before we could make any arrangement, I was ordered to depart, by those iron hearted jailers, who could not endure to see us enjoy the poor consolation of meeting in that miserable place. In vain I pleaded the order of the governor for my admittance; they again, harshly repeated, 'Depart, or we will pull you out.' The same evening, the missionaries, together with the other foreigners, who had paid an equal sum, were taken out of the common prison, and confined in an open shed in the prison enclosure. Here I was allowed to send them food, and mats to sleep on; but was not permitted to enter again for several days.

"My next object was to get a petition presented to the queen; but no person being admitted into the palace, who was in disgrace with his Majesty, I sought to present it through the medium of her brother's wife. I had visited her in better days, and received particular marks of her favour. But now times were altered: Mr. Judson was in prison, and I in distress, which was a sufficient reason for giving me a cold reception. I took a present of considerable value. She was lolling on her carpet as I entered, with her attendants around her. I waited not for the usual question to a suppliant, 'What do you want?' but in a hold, earnest, yet respectful manner, stated our distresses and our wrongs, and begged her assistance. She partly raised her head, opened the present I had brought, and coolly replied, 'Your case is not singular; all the foreigners are treated alike.' 'But it is singular,' said I, 'the teachers are Americans; they are ministers of religion, have nothing to do with war or politics, and came to Ava in obedience to the king's command. They have never done any thing to deserve such treatment; and is it right they should be treated thus?' 'The king does as he pleases,' said she; 'I am not the king, what can I do?' 'You can state their case to the queen, and obtain their release,' replied I. 'Place yourself in my situation,--were you in America, your husband, innocent of crime, thrown into prison, in irons, and you a solitary, unprotected female--what would you do?' With a slight degree of feeling, she said, 'I will present your petition,--come again to-morrow.' I returned to the house, with considerable hope, that the speedy release of the missionaries was at hand. But the next day Mr. Gouger's property, to the amount of fifty thousand dollars, was taken and carried to the palace. The officers, on their return, politely informed me, they should *visit our house* on the morrow. I felt obliged for this information, and accordingly made preparations to receive them, by secreting as many little articles as possible; together with considerable silver, as I knew, if the war should be protracted, we should be in a state of starvation without it. But my mind was in a dreadful state of agitation, lest it should be discovered, and cause my being thrown into prison. And had it been possible to procure money from any other quarter, I should not have ventured on such a step.

"The following morning, the royal treasurer, prince Tharyawadees, chief Woon, and Koung-tone Myoo-tsa, who was in future our steady friend, attended by forty or fifty followers, came to take possession of all we had. I treated them civilly, gave them chairs to sit on, tea and sweetmeats for their refreshment; and justice obliges me to say, that they conducted the business of confiscation with more regard to my feelings than I should have thought it possible for Burmese officers to exhibit. The three officers, with one of the royal secretaries, alone entered the house; their attendants were ordered to remain outside. They saw I was deeply affected, and apologized for what they were about to do, by saying, that it was painful for them to take possession of property not their own, but they were compelled thus to do by order of the king. 'Where is your silver, gold, and jewels?' said the royal treasurer. 'I have no gold or jewels; but here is the key of a trunk which contains the silver--do with it as you please.' The trunk was produced, and the silver weighed. 'This money,' said I, 'was collected in America, by the disciples of Christ, and sent here for the purpose of building a kyoung, (the name of a priest's dwelling) and for our support while teaching the religion of Christ. Is it suitable that you should take it? (The Burmans are averse to taking what is offered in a religious point of view, which was the cause of my making the inquiry.) 'We will state this circumstance to the king,' said one of them, 'and perhaps he will restore it. But this is all the silver you have?' I could not tell a falsehood: 'The house is in your possession,' I replied, 'search for yourselves.' 'Have you not deposited silver with some person of your acquaintance?' 'My acquaintances are all in prison, with whom should I deposit silver? They next ordered my trunk and drawers to be examined. The secretary only was allowed to accompany me in this search. Everything nice or curious, which met his view, was presented to the officers, for their decision, whether it should be taken or retained. I begged they would not take our wearing apparel, as it would be disgraceful to take clothes partly worn, into the possession of his majesty, and to us they were of unspeakable value. They assented, and took a list only, and did the same with the books, medicines, &c. My little work table and rocking chair, presents from my beloved brother, I rescued from their grasp, partly by artifice, and partly through their ignorance. They left also many articles, which were of inestimable value, during our long imprisonment.

"As soon as they had finished their search and departed, I hastened to the queen's brother, to hear what had been the fate of my petition; when, alas! all my hopes were dashed, by his wife's coolly saying, 'I stated your case to the queen; but her majesty replied,--'The teachers will not die: let them remain as they are.' My expectations had been so much excited, that this sentence was like a thunderbolt to my feelings. For the truth at one glance assured me, that if the queen refused assistance, who would dare to intercede for me? With a heavy heart I departed, and on my way home, attempted to enter the prison gate, to communicate the sad tidings to your brother but was harshly refused admittance: and for the ten days following notwithstanding my daily efforts, I was not allowed to enter. We attempted to communicate by writing, and after being successful for a few days, it was discovered; the poor fellow who carried the communications was beaten and put in the stocks; and the circumstance cost me about ten dollars, besides two or three days of agony, for fear of the consequences.

"The officers who had taken possession of our property, presented it to his majesty, saying, 'Judson is a true teacher; we found nothing in his house, but what belongs to priests. In addition to this money, there are an immense number of books, medicines, trunks of wearing apparel, &c. of which we have only taken a list. Shall we take them, or let them remain?' 'Let them remain,' said the king, 'and put this property by itself, for it shall be restored to him again, if he is found innocent.' This was an allusion to the idea of his being a spy.

"For two or three months following, I was subject to continual harassments, partly through my ignorance of police management and partly through the insatiable desire of every petty officer to enrich himself through our misfortunes. When the officers came to our house, to confiscate our property, they insisted on knowing how much I had given the governor and prison officers, to release the teachers from the inner prison. I honestly told them, and they demanded the sum from the governor, which threw him into a dreadful rage, and he threatened to put all the prisoners back into their original place. I went to him the next morning, and the first words with which he accosted me, were, 'You are very bad; why did you tell the royal treasurer that you had given me so much money?' 'The treasurer inquired; what could I say!' I replied. 'Say that you had given nothing,' said he, 'and I would have made the teachers comfortable in prison; but now I know not what will be their fate.' 'But I cannot tell a falsehood,' I replied. 'My religion differs from yours, it forbids prevarication; and had you stood by me with your knife raised, I could not have said what you suggested.' His wife, who sat by his side, and who always, from this time, continued my firm friend, instantly said, 'Very true--what else could she have said? I like such straight-forward conduct; you must not (turning to the governor) be angry with her.' I then presented the governor with a beautiful opera glass, I had just received from England, and begged his anger at me would not influence him to treat the prisoners with unkindness, and I would endeavour, from time to time, to make him such presents, as would compensate for his loss. 'You may intercede for your husband only; for your sake, he shall remain where he is; but let the other prisoners take care of themselves.' I pleaded hard for Dr. Price; but he would not listen, and the same day had him returned to the inner prison, where he remained ten days. He was then taken out, in consequence of the Doctor's promising a piece of broad cloth, and my sending two pieces of handkerchiefs.

"About this period, I was one day summoned to the Tlowtdan, in an official way. What new evil was before me, I knew not, but was obliged to go. When arrived, I was allowed to ***stand*** at the bottom of the stairs, as no female is permitted to ascend the steps, or even to stand, but sit on the ground. Hundreds were collected around. The officer who presided, in an authoritative voice, began; 'Speak the truth in answer to the questions I shall ask. If you speak true, no evil will follow; but if not, your life will not be spared. It is reported that you have committed to the care of a Burmese officer, a string of pearls, a pair of diamond ear-rings, and a silver tea-pot. Is it true? 'It is not,' I replied; 'and if you or any other person can produce these articles, I refuse not to die.' The officer again urged the necessity of 'speaking true.' I told him I had nothing more to say on this subject, but begged he would use his influence to obtain the release of Mr. Judson from prison.

"I returned to the house, with a heart much lighter than I went, though conscious of my perpetual exposure to such harassments. Notwithstanding the repulse I had met in my application to the queen, I could not remain without making continual effort for your brother's release, while there was the least probability of success. Time after time my visits to the queen's sister-in-law were repeated, till she refused to answer a question, and told me by her looks, I had better keep out of her presence. For the seven following months, hardly a day passed, that I did not visit some one of the members of government, or branches of the royal family, in order to gain their influence in our behalf; but the only benefit resulting was, their encouraging promises preserved us from despair, and induced a hope of the speedy termination of our difficulties, which enabled us to bear our distresses better than we otherwise should have done. I ought, however, to mention, that by my repeated visits to the different members of government, I gained several friends, who were ready to assist me with articles of food, though in a private manner, and who used their influence in the palace to destroy the impression of our being in any way engaged in the present war. But no one dared to speak a word to the king or queen in favor of a foreigner, while there were such continual reports of the success of the English arms.

"During these seven months, the continual extortions and oppressions to which your brother, and the other white prisoners were subject, are indescribable. Sometimes sums of money were demanded, sometimes pieces of cloth and handkerchiefs; at other times, an order would be issued, that the white foreigners should not speak to each other, or have any communication with their friends without. Then again, the servants were forbidden to carry in their food, without an extra fee. Sometimes, for days and days together, I could not go into the prison till after dark, when I had two miles to walk, in returning to the house. O how many, many times, have I returned from that dreary prison at nine o'clock at night, solitary and worn out with fatigue and anxiety, and thrown myself down in that same rocking chair which you and Deacon L. provided for me in Boston and endeavoured to invent some new scheme for the release of the prisoners. Sometimes, for a moment or two, my thoughts would glance toward America, and my beloved friends there--but for nearly a year and a half, so entirely engrossed was every thought with present scenes and sufferings, that I seldom reflected on a single occurrence of my former life, or recollected that I had a friend in existence out of Ava.

"You, my dear brother, who know my strong attachment to my friends, and how much pleasure I have hitherto experienced from retrospect, can judge from the above circumstances, how intense were my sufferings. But the point, the acme of my distresses, consisted in the awful uncertainty of our final fate. My prevailing opinion was, that my husband would suffer violent death; and that I should, of course, become a slave, and languish out a miserable though short existence, in the tyrannic hands of some unfeeling monster. But the consolations of religion, in these trying circumstances, were neither 'few nor small.' It taught me to look beyond this world, to that rest, that peaceful, happy rest, where Jesus reigns, and oppression never enters. But how have I digressed from my relation. I will again return.

"The war was now prosecuted with all the energy the Burmese government possessed. New troops were continually raised and sent down the river, and as frequent reports returned of their being all cut off. But that part of the Burmese army stationed at Arracan, under the command of Bandoola, had been more successful. Three hundred prisoners, at one time, was sent to the capital, as an evidence of the victory that had been gained. The king began to think that none but Bandoola understood the art of fighting with foreigners; consequently his majesty recalled him with the design of his taking command of the army that had been sent to Rangoon. On his arrival at Ava, he was received at court in the most flattering manner, and was the recipient of every favour in the power of the king and queen to bestow. He was, in fact, while at Ava, the acting king. I was resolved to apply to him for the release of the missionaries, though some members of government advised me not, lest he, being reminded of their existence, should issue an immediate order for their execution. But it was my last hope, and as it proved, my last application.

"Your brother wrote a petition privately, stating every circumstance that would have a tendency to interest him in our behalf. With fear and trembling I approached him, while surrounded by a crowd of flatterers, and one of his secretaries took the petition, and read it aloud. After hearing it, he spake to me in an obliging manner--asked several questions relative to the teachers--said he would think of the subject--and bade me come again. I ran to the prison to communicate the favourable reception to Mr. Judson; and we both had sanguine hopes that his release was at hand. But the governor of the city expressed his amazement at my temerity, and said he doubted not it would be the means of destroying all the prisoners. In a day or two, however, I went again, and took a present of considerable value. Bandoola was not at home; but his *lady*, after ordering the present to be taken into another room, modestly informed me that she was ordered by her husband to make the following communication--that he was now very busily employed in making preparations for Rangoon; but that when he had re-taken that place and expelled the English, he would return and release all the prisoners.

"Thus again were all our hopes dashed; and we felt that we could do nothing more, but sit down and submit to our lot. From this time we gave up all idea of being released from prison, till the termination of the war; but I was still obliged to visit constantly some of the members of government, with little presents, particularly the governor of the city, for the purpose of making the situation of the prisoners tolerable. I generally spent the greater part of every other day at the governor's house, giving him all the information relative to American manners, customs, government, &c. He used to be so much gratified with my communications, as to feel greatly disappointed, if any occurrence prevented my spending the usual hours at his house.

"Some months after your brother's imprisonment, I was permitted to make a little bamboo room in the prison enclosures, where he could be much by himself, and where I was sometimes allowed to spend two or three hours. It so happened that the two months he occupied this place, was the coldest part of the year, when he would have suffered much in the open shed he had previously occupied. After the birth of your little niece, I was unable to visit the prison and the governor as before, and found I had lost considerable influence, previously gained; for he was not so forward to hear my petitions when any difficulty occurred, as he formerly had been. When Maria was nearly two months old, her father one morning sent me word that he and all the white prisoners were put into the inner prison in five pairs of fetters each, that his little room had been torn down, and his mat, pillow, &c. been taken by the jailers. This was to me a dreadful shock, as I thought at once it was only a prelude to greater evils.

"I should have mentioned before this, the defeat of Bandoola, his escape to Danooboo, the complete destruction of his army and loss of ammunition, and the consternation this intelligence produced at court. The English army had left Rangoon, and were advancing towards Prome, when these severe measures were taken with the prisoners.

"I went immediately to the governor's house. He was not at home, but had ordered his wife to tell me, when I came, not to ask to have the additional fetters taken off, or the prisoners released, for it could not be done. I went to the prison gate, but was forbid to enter. All was as still as death--not a white face to be seen, or a vestige of Mr. J.'s little room remaining. I was determined to see the governor and know the cause of this additional oppression; and for this purpose returned to town the same evening, at an hour I knew he would be at home. He was in his audience room, and, as I entered, looked up without speaking, but exhibited a mixture of shame and affected anger in his countenance. I began by saying--Your Lordship has hitherto treated us with the kindness of a father. Our obligations to you are very great. We have looked to you for protection from oppression and cruelty. You have in many instances mitigated the sufferings of those unfortunate, though innocent beings, committed to your charge. You have promised me particularly, that you would stand by me to the last, and though you should receive an order from the king, you would not put Mr. J. to death. What crime has he committed to deserve such additional punishment? The old man's hard heart was melted, for he wept like a child. 'I pity you, Tsa-yar-ga-dau, (a name by which he always called me) I knew you would make me feel; I therefore forbade your application. But you must believe me when I say, I do not wish to increase the sufferings of the prisoners. When I am ordered to execute them, the least that I can do is, to put them out of sight. I will now tell you (continued he) what I have never told you before, that three times I have received intimations from the queen's brother, to assassinate all the white prisoners privately; but I would not do it. And I now repeat it, though I execute all the others, I will never execute your husband. But I cannot release him from his present confinement, and you must not ask it.' I had never seen him manifest so much feeling, or so resolute in denying me a favour, which circumstance was an additional reason for thinking dreadful scenes were before us.

"The situation of the prisoners was now distressing beyond description. It was at the commencement of the hot season. There were above a hundred prisoners shut up in one room, without a breath of air excepting from the cracks in the boards. I sometimes obtained permission to go to the door for five minutes, when my heart sickened at the wretchedness exhibited. The white prisoners, from incessant perspiration and loss of appetite, looked more like the dead than the living. I made daily applications to the governor, offering him money, which he refused; but all that I gained, was permission for the foreigners to eat their food outside, and this continued but a short time.

"It was at this period that the death of Bandoola was announced in the palace. The king heard it with silent amazement, and the queen, in eastern style, smote upon her breast, and cried, ama! ama! (alas, alas.) Who could be found to fill his place? who would venture since the invincible Bandoola had been cut off? Such were the exclamations constantly heard in the streets of Ava. The common people were speaking *low* of a rebellion, in case more troops should be levied. For as yet the common people had borne the weight of the war, not a tickal had been taken from the royal treasury. At length the Pakan Woon, who a few months before had been so far disgraced by the king as to be thrown into prison and irons, now offered himself to head a new army that should be raised on a different plan from those which had been hitherto raised; and assured the king in the most confident manner, that he would conquer the English, and restore those places that had been taken, in a very short time. He proposed that every soldier should receive a hundred tickals in advance, and he would obtain security for each man, as the money was to pass through his hands. It was afterwards found that he had taken, for his own use, ten tickals from every hundred. He was a man of enterprise and talents, though a violent enemy to all foreigners. His offers were accepted by the king and government, and all power immediately committed to him. One of the first exercises of his power was, to arrest Lansago and the Portuguese priest, who had hitherto remained unmolested, and cast them into prison, and to subject the native Portuguese and Bengalees to the most menial occupations. The whole town was in alarm, lest they should feel the effects of his power; and it was owing to the malignant representations of this man, that the white prisoners suffered such a change in their circumstances, as I shall soon relate.

"After continuing in the inner prison for more than a month, your brother was taken with a fever. I felt assured he would not live long, unless removed from that noisome place. To effect this, and in order to be near the prison, I removed from our house and put up a small bamboo room in the governor's enclosure, which was nearly opposite the prison gate. Here I incessantly begged the governor to give me an order to take Mr. J. out of the large prison, and place him in a more comfortable situation; and the old man, being worn out with my entreaties, at length gave me the order in an official form; and also gave orders to the head jailer, to allow me to go in and out, all times of the day, to administer medicines, &c. I now felt happy indeed, and had Mr. J. instantly removed into a little bamboo hovel, so low, that neither of us could stand upright--but a palace in comparison with the place he had left.

Removal of the prisoners to Oung-pen-la--Mrs. Judson follows them.

"Notwithstanding the order the governor had given for my admittance into prison, it was with the greatest difficulty that I could persuade the under jailer to open the gate. I used to carry Mr. J's. food myself, for the sake of getting in, and would then remain an hour or two, unless driven out. We had been in this comfortable situation but two or three days, when one morning, having carried in Mr. Judson's breakfast, which, in consequence of fever, he was unable to take, I remained longer than usual, when the governor in great haste sent for me. I promised him to return as soon as I had ascertained the governor's will, he being much alarmed at this unusual message. I was very agreeably disappointed, when the governor informed, that he only wished to consult me about his watch, and seemed unusually pleasant and conversable. I found afterwards, that his only object was, to detain me until the dreadful scene, about to take place in the prison, was over. For when I left him to go to my room, one of the servants came running, and with a ghastly countenance informed me, that all the white prisoners were carried away. I would not believe the report, but instantly went back to the governor, who said he had just heard of it, but did not wish to tell me. I hastily ran into the street, hoping to get a glimpse of them before they were out of sight, but in this was disappointed. I ran first into one street, then another, inquiring of all I met, but none would answer me. At length an old woman told me the white prisoners had gone towards the little river; for they were to be carried to Amarapora. I then ran to the banks of the little river, about half a mile, but saw them not, and concluded the old woman had deceived me. Some of the friends of the foreigners went to the place of execution, but found them not. I then returned to the governor to try to discover the cause of their removal, and the probability of their future fate. The old man assured me that he was ignorant of the intention of government to remove the foreigners till that morning. That since I went out, he had learned that the prisoners were to be sent to Amarapora; but for what purpose, he knew not. 'I will send off a man immediately,' said he, 'to see what is to be done with them. You can do nothing more for your husband,' continued he, '*take care of yourself.*' With a heavy heart I went to my room, and having no hope to excite me to exertion, I sunk down almost in despair. For several days previous, I had been actively engaged in building my own little room, and making our hovel comfortable. My thoughts had been almost entirely occupied in contriving means to get into prison. But now I looked towards the gate with a kind of melancholy feeling, but no wish to enter. All was the stillness of death; no preparation of your brother's food, no expectation of meeting him at the usual dinner hour, all my employment, all my occupations seemed to have ceased, and I had nothing left but the dreadful recollection that Mr. Judson was carried off, I knew not whither. It was one of the most insupportable days I ever passed. Towards night, however, I came to the determination to set off the next morning for Amarapora; and for this purpose was obliged to go to our house out of town.

"Never before had I suffered so much from fear in traversing the streets of Ava. The last words of the governor, 'Take care of yourself,' made me suspect there was some design with which I was unacquainted. I saw, also, he was afraid to have me go into the streets, and advised me to wait till dark, when he would send me in a cart, and a man to open the gates. I took two or three trunks of the most valuable articles, together with the medicine chest, to deposit in the house of the governor; and after committing the house and premises to our faithful Moung Ing and a Bengalee servant, who continued with us, (though we were unable to pay his wages,) I took leave, as I then thought probable, of our house in Ava forever.

"On my return to the governor's, I found a servant of Mr. Gouges, who happened to be near the prison when the foreigners were led out, and followed on to see the end, who informed me, that the prisoners had been carried before the Lamine Woon, at Amarapora, and were to be sent the next day to a village he knew not how far distant. My distress was a little relieved by the intelligence that our friend was yet alive, but still I knew not what was to become of him. The next morning I obtained a pass from government, and with my little Maria, who was then only three months old, Mary and Abby Hasseltine, (two of the Burman children) and our Bengalee cook, who was the only one of the party who could afford me any assistance, I set off for Amarapora. The day was dreadfully hot; but we obtained a covered boat, in which we were tolerably comfortable, till within two miles of the government house. I then procured a cart; but the violent motion, together with the dreadful heat and dust; made me almost distracted. But what was my disappointment on my arriving at the court house, to find that the prisoners had been sent on two hours before, and that I must go in that uncomfortable mode four miles further with little Maria in my arms, whom I held all the way from Ava. The cart man refused to go any further; and after waiting an hour in the burning sun, I procured another, and set off for that never to be forgotten place, Oung-pen-la. I obtained a guide from the governor and was conducted directly to the prison-yard. But what a scene of wretchedness was presented to my view! The prison was an old shattered building, without a roof; the fence was entirely destroyed; eight or ten Burmese were on the top of the building, trying to make something like a shelter with the leaves; while under a little low projection outside of the prison sat the foreigners, chained together two and two, almost dead with suffering and fatigue. The first words of your brother were, 'Why have you come? I hoped you would not follow, for you cannot live here.' It was now dark. I had no refreshment for the suffering prisoners, or for myself, as I had expected to procure all that was necessary at the market of Amarapora, and I had no shelter for the night. I asked one of the jailers if I might put up a little bamboo house near the prisoners; he said no, it was not customary. I then begged he would procure me a shelter for the night, when on the morrow I could find some place to live in. He took me to his house, in which there were only two small rooms--one in which he and his family lived--the other, which was then half full of grain, he offered to me; and in that little filthy place, I spent the next six months of wretchedness. I procured some half boiled water, instead of my tea, and, worn out with fatigue, laid myself down on a mat spread over the paddy, and endeavoured to obtain a little refreshment from sleep. The next morning your brother gave me the following account of the brutal treatment he had received on being taken out of prison.

"As soon as I had gone out at the call of the governor, one of the jailers rushed into Mr. J's little room--roughly seized him by the arm--pulled him out--stripped him of all his clothes, excepting shirt and pantaloons--took his shoes, hat, and all his bedding--tore off his chains--tied a rope round his waist, and dragged him to the court house, where the other prisoners had previously been taken. They were then tied two and two, and delivered into the hands of the Lamine Woon, who went on before them on horseback, while his slaves drove the prisoners, one of the slaves holding the rope which connected two of them together. It was in May, one of the hottest months in the year, and eleven o'clock in the day, so that the sun was intolerable indeed. They had proceeded only half a mile, when your brother's feet became blistered, and so great was his agony, even at this early period, that as they were crossing the little river, he longed to throw himself into the water to be free from misery. But the sin attached to such an act alone prevented. They had then eight miles to walk. The sand and gravel were like burning coals to the feet of the prisoners, which soon became perfectly destitute of skin; and in this wretched state they were goaded on by their unfeeling drivers. Mr. J.'s debilitated state, in consequence of fever, and having taken no food that morning, rendered him less capable of bearing such hardships than the other prisoners. When about half way on their journey, as they stopped for water, your brother begged the Lamine Woon to allow him to ride his horse a mile or two, as he could proceed no farther in that dreadful state. But a scornful, malignant look, was all the reply that was made. He then requested captain Laird, who was tied with him, and who was a strong, healthy man, to allow him to take hold of his shoulder, as he was fast sinking. This the kind-hearted man granted for a mile or two, but then found the additional burden insupportable. Just at that period, Mr. Gouger's Bengalee servant came up to them, and seeing the distresses of your brother, took off his head dress, which was made of cloth, tore it in two, gave half to his master, and half to Mr. Judson, which he instantly wrapt round his wounded feet, as they were not allowed to rest even for a moment. The servant then offered his shoulder to Mr. J. and was almost carried by him the remainder of the way. Had it not been for the support and assistance of this man, your brother thinks he should have shared the fate of the poor Greek, who was one of their number, and when taken out of prison that morning was in perfect health. But he was a corpulent man, and the sun affected him so much that he fell down on the way. His inhuman drivers beat and dragged him until they themselves were wearied, when they procured a cart, in which he was carried the remaining two miles. But the poor creature expired in an hour or two after their arrival at the court house. The Lamine Woon seeing the distressing state of the prisoners, and that one of their number was dead, concluded they should go no farther that night, otherwise they would have been driven on until they reached Oung-pen-la the same day. An old shed was appointed for their abode during the night, but without even a mat or pillow, or any thing to cover them. The curiosity of the Lamine Woon's wife, induced her to make a visit to the prisoners, whose wretchedness considerably excited her compassion, and she ordered some fruit, sugar, and tamarinds, for their refreshment; and the next morning rice was prepared for them, and as poor as it was, it was refreshing to the prisoners, who had been almost destitute of food the day before. Carts were also provided for their conveyance, as none of them were able to walk. All this time the foreigners were entirely ignorant of what was to become of them; and when they arrived at Oung-pen-la, and saw the dilapidated state of the prison, they immediately, all as one, concluded that they were there to be burnt, agreeably to the report which had previously been in circulation at Ava. They all endeavoured to prepare themselves for the awful scene anticipated, and it was not until they saw preparations making for repairing the prison, that they had the least doubt that a cruel lingering death awaited them. My arrival was in an hour or two after this.

"The next morning I arose and endeavoured to find something like food. But there was no market, and nothing to be procured. One of Dr. Price's friends, however, brought some cold rice and vegetable curry, from Amarapora, which, together with a cup of tea from Mr. Lansago, answered for the breakfast of the prisoners; and for dinner, we made a curry of dried salt fish, which a servant of Mr. Gouger had brought. All the money I could command in the world, I had brought with me, secreted about my person; so you may judge what our prospects were, in case the war should continue long. But our heavenly Father was better to us than our fears; for notwithstanding the constant extortions of the jailers, during the whole six months we were at Oung-pen-la, and the frequent straits to which we were brought, we never really suffered for the want of money, though frequently for want of provisions, which were not procurable. Here at this place my personal bodily sufferings commenced. While your brother was confined in the city prison, I had been allowed to remain in our house, in which I had many conveniences left, and my health continued good beyond all expectations. But now I had not a single article of convenience--not even a chair or seat of any kind, excepting a bamboo floor. The very morning after my arrival, Mary Hasseltine was taken with the small pox, the natural way. She, though very young, was the only assistant I had in taking care of little Maria. But she now required all the time I could spare from Mr. Judson, whose fever still continued in prison, and whose feet were so dreadfully mangled, that for several days he was unable to move. I knew not what to do, for I could procure no assistance from the neighbourhood, or medicine for the sufferers, but was all day long going backwards and forwards from the house to the prison, with little Maria in my arms. Sometimes I was greatly relieved by leaving her, for an hour, when asleep, by the side of her father, while I returned to the house to look after Mary, whose fever ran so high as to produce delirium. She was so completely covered with the small pox, that there was no distinction in the pustules. As she was in the same little room with myself, I knew Maria would take it; I therefore inoculated her from another child, before Mary's had arrived at such a state as to be infectious. At the same time, I inoculated Abby, and the jailer's children, who all had it so lightly as hardly to interrupt their play. But the inoculation in the arm of my poor little Maria did not take--she caught it of Mary, and had it the natural way. She was then only three months and a half old, and had been a most healthy child; but it was above three months before she perfectly recovered from the effects of this dreadful disorder.

"You will recollect I never had the small pox, but was vaccinated previously to leaving America. In consequence of being for so long a time constantly exposed, I had nearly a hundred pustules formed, though no previous symptoms of fever, &c. The jailer's children having had the small pox so lightly, in consequence of inoculation, my fame was spread all over the village, and every child, young and old, who had not previously had it, was brought for inoculation. And although I knew nothing about the disorder, or the mode of treating it, I inoculated them all with a needle, and told them to take care of their diet,--all the instructions I could give them. Mr. Judson's health was gradually restored, and he found himself much more comfortably situated, than when in the city prison.

"The prisoners were at first chained two and two; but as soon as the jailers could obtain chains sufficient, they were separated, and each prisoner had but one pair. The prison was repaired, a new fence made, and a large airy shed erected in front of the prison, where the prisoners were allowed to remain during the day, though locked up in the little close prison at night. All the children recovered from the small pox; but my watchings and fatigue, together with my miserable food, and more miserable lodgings, brought on one of the diseases of the country, which is almost always fatal to foreigners. My constitution seemed destroyed, and in a few days I became so weak as to be hardly able to walk to Mr. Judson's prison. In this debilitated state, I set off in a cart for Ava, to procure medicines, and some suitable food, leaving the cook to supply my place. I reached the house in safety, and for two or three days the disorder seemed at a stand; after which it attacked me so violently, that I had no hopes of recovery left--and my only anxiety now was, to return to Oung-pen-la to die near the prison. It was with the greatest difficulty that I obtained the medicine chest from the governor, and then had no one to administer medicine. I however got at the laudanum, and by taking two drops at a time for several hours, it so far checked the disorder, as to enable me to get on board a boat, though so weak that I could not stand, and again set off for Oung-pen-la. The last four miles was in that painful conveyance, the cart, and in the midst of the rainy season, when the mud almost buries the oxen. You may form some idea of a Burmese cart, when I tell you their wheels are not constructed like ours; but are simply round thick planks with a hole in the middle, through which a pole that supports the body is thrust.

"I just reached Oung-pen-la when my strength seemed entirely exhausted. The good native cook came out to help me into the house but so altered and emaciated was my appearance, that the poor fellow burst into tears at the first sight. I crawled on to the mat in the little room, to which I was confined for more than two months, and never perfectly recovered, until I came to the English camp. At this period, when I was unable to take care of myself, or look after Mr. Judson, we must both have died, had it not been for the faithful and affectionate care of our Bengalee cook. A common Bengalee cook will do nothing but the simple business of cooking: But he seemed to forget his cast, and almost his own wants, in his efforts to serve us. He would provide, cook, and carry your brother's food, and then return and take care of me. I have frequently known him not to taste of food till near night, in consequence of having to go so far for wood and water, and in order to have Mr. Judson's dinner ready at the usual hour. He never complained, never asked for his wages, and never for a moment hesitated to go any where, or to perform any act we required. I take great pleasure in speaking of the faithful conduct of this servant, who is still with us, and I trust has been well rewarded for his services.

"Our dear little Maria was the greatest sufferer at this time, my illness depriving her of her usual nourishment, and neither a nurse nor a drop of milk could be procured in the village. By making presents to the jailers, I obtained leave for Mr. Judson to come out of prison, and take the emaciated creature around the village, to beg a little nourishment from those mothers who had young children. Her cries in the night were heart-rending, when it was impossible to supply her wants. I now began to think the very afflictions of Job had come upon me. When in health, I could bear the various trials and vicissitudes through which I was called to pass. But to be confined with sickness, and unable to assist those who were so dear to me, when in distress, was almost too much for me to bear; and had it not been for the consolations of religion, and an assured conviction that every additional trial was ordered by infinite love and mercy, I must have sunk under my accumulated sufferings. Sometimes our jailers seemed a little softened at our distress, and for several days together allowed Mr. Judson to come to the house, which was to me an unspeakable consolation. Then again they would be as iron-hearted in their demands, as though we were free from sufferings, and in affluent circumstances. The annoyance, the extortions, and oppressions, to which we were subject, during our six months residence in Oung-pen-la, are beyond enumeration or description.

"It was some time after our arrival at Oung-pen-la, that we heard of the execution of the Pakan Woon, in consequence of which our lives were still preserved. For we afterwards ascertained, that the white foreigners had been sent to Oung-pen-la, for the express purpose of sacrificing them, and that he himself intended witnessing the horrid scene. We had frequently heard of his intended arrival at Oung-pen-la; but we had no idea of his diabolical purposes. He had raised an army of fifty thousand men, (a tenth part of whose advanced pay was found in his house,) and expected to march against the English army in a short time, when he was suspected of high treason, and instantly executed without the least examination. Perhaps no death in Ava ever produced such universal rejoicings, as that of the Pakan Woon. We never, to this day, hear his name mentioned, but with an epithet of reproach or hatred. Another brother of the king was appointed to the command of the army now in readiness, but with no very sanguine expectations of success. Some weeks after the departure of these troops, two of the Woongyees were sent down for the purpose of negotiating. But not being successful, the queen's brother, the *acting king* of the country, was prevailed on to go. Great expectations were raised in consequence; but his cowardice induced him to encamp his detachment of the army at a great distance from the English, and even at a distance from the main body of the Burmese army, whose head-quarters were then at Maloun. Thus he effected nothing, though reports were continually reaching us, that peace was nearly concluded.

"The time at length arrived for our release from that detested place, the Oung-pen-la prison. A messenger from our friend, the governor of the north gate of the palace, who was formerly Koung-tone, Myoo-tsa, informed us that an order had been given, the evening before, in the palace, for Mr. Judson's release. On the same evening an official order arrived; and with a joyful heart I set about preparing for our departure early the following morning. But an unexpected obstacle occurred, which made us fear that *I* should still be retained as a prisoner. The avaricious jailers, unwilling to lose their prey, insisted, that as my name was not included in the order, I should not go. In vain I urged that I was not sent there as a prisoner, and that they had no authority over me--they still determined I should not go, and forbade the villagers from letting me a cart. Mr. Judson was then taken out of prison, and brought to the jailer's house, where, by promises and threatenings, he finally gained their consent, on condition that we would leave the remaining part of our provisions we had recently received from Ava. It was noon before we were allowed to depart. When we reached Amarapora, Mr. Judson was obliged to follow the guidance of the jailer, who conducted him to the governor of the city. Having made all necessary inquiries, the governor appointed another guard, which conveyed Mr. Judson to the court-house in Ava, to which place he arrived some time in the night. I took my own course, procured a boat, and reached our house before dark.

"My first object the next morning, was to go in search of your brother, and I had the mortification to meet him again in prison, though not the death prison. I went immediately to my old friend the governor of the city, who now was raised to the rank of a Woongyee. He informed me that Mr. Judson was to be sent to the Burmese camp, to act as translator and interpreter; and that he was put in confinement for a short time only, till his affairs were settled. Early the following morning I went to this officer again, who told me that Mr. Judson had that moment received twenty tickals from government, with orders to go immediately on board a boat for Maloun, and that *he* had given him permission to stop a few moments at the house, it being on his way. I hastened back to the house, where Mr. Judson soon arrived; but was allowed to remain only a short time, while I could prepare food and clothing for future use. He was crowded into a little boat, where he had not room sufficient to lie down, and where his exposure to the cold damp nights threw him into a violent fever, which had nearly ended all his sufferings. He arrived at Maloun on the third day, where, ill as he was, he was obliged to enter immediately on the work of translating. He remained at Maloun six weeks, suffering as much as he had at any time in prison, excepting he was not in irons, nor exposed to the insults of those cruel jailers.

"For the first fortnight after his departure, my anxiety was less than it had been at any time previous, since the commencement of our difficulties. I knew the Burmese officers at the camp would feel the value of Mr. Judson's services too much to allow their using any measures threatening his life. I thought his situation, also, would be much more comfortable than it really was--hence my anxiety was less. But my health, which had never been restored, since that violent attack at Oung-pen-la, now daily declined, till I was seized with the spotted fever, with all its attendant horrors. I knew the nature of the fever from its commencement; and from the shattered state of my constitution, together with the want of medical attendants, I concluded it must be fatal. The day I was taken, a Burmese nurse came and offered her services for Maria. This circumstance filled me with gratitude and confidence in God; for though I had so long and so constantly made efforts to obtain a person of this description, I had never been able; when at the very time I most needed one, and with out any exertion, a voluntary offer was made. My fever raged violently and without any intermission. I began to think of settling my worldly affairs, and of committing my dear little Maria to the care of a Portuguese woman, when I lost my reason, and was insensible to all around me. At this dreadful period, Dr. Price was released from prison; and hearing of my illness, obtained permission to come and see me. He has since told me that my situation was the most distressing he had ever witnessed, and that he did not then think I should survive many hours. My hair was shaved, my head and feet covered with blisters, and Dr. Price ordered the Bengalee servant who took care of me, to endeavour to persuade me to take a little nourishment, which I had obstinately refused for several days. One of the first things I recollect was, seeing this faithful servant standing by me, trying to induce me to take a little wine and water. I was in fact so far gone, that the Burmese neighbours who had come in to see me expire, said, 'She is dead; and if the king of angels should come in, he could not recover her.'

"The fever, I afterwards understood, had run seventeen days when the blisters were applied. I now began to recover slowly; but it was more than a month after this before I had strength to stand. While in this weak, debilitated state, the servant who had followed your brother to the Burmese camp, came in, and informed me that his master had arrived, and was conducted to the court-house in town. I sent off a Burman to watch the movements of government, and to ascertain, if possible, in what way Mr. Judson was to be disposed of. He soon returned with the sad intelligence, that he saw Mr. Judson go out of the palace yard, accompanied by two or three Burmans, who conducted him to one of the prisons; and that it was reported in town, that he was to be sent back to the Oung-pen-la prison. I was too weak to bear ill tidings of any kind; but a shock so dreadful as this, almost annihilated me. For some time, I could hardly breathe; but at last gained sufficient composure to dispatch Moung Ing to our friend, the governor of the north gate, and begged him to make *one more effort* for the release of Mr. Judson, and prevent his being sent back to the country prison, where I knew he must suffer much, as I could not follow. Moung Ing then went in search of Mr. Judson; and it was nearly dark when he found him in the interior of an obscure prison. I had sent food early in the afternoon, but being unable to find him, the bearer had returned with it, which added another pang to my distresses, as I feared he was already sent to Oung-pen-la.

"If I ever felt the value and efficacy of prayer, I did at this time. I could not rise from my couch; I could make no efforts to secure my husband; I could only plead with that great and powerful Being who has said, 'Call upon me in the day of trouble, and *I will hear*, and thou shalt glorify me;'" and who made me at this time feel so powerfully this promise, that I became quite composed, feeling assured that my prayers would be answered.

"When Mr. Judson was sent from Maloun to Ava, it was within five minutes' notice, and without his knowledge of the cause. On his way up the river, he accidently saw the communication made to government respecting him, which was simply this: 'We have no further use for Yoodathan, we therefore return him to the golden city.' On arriving at the court-house, there happened to be no one present who was acquainted with Mr. J. The presiding officer inquired from what place he had been sent to Maloun. He was answered from Oung-pen-la. Let him then, said the officer, be returned thither--when he was delivered to a guard and conducted to the place above-mentioned, there to remain until he could be conveyed to Oung-pen-la. In the mean time the governor of the north gate presented a petition to this high court of the empire, offered himself as Mr. Judson's security, obtained his release, and took him to his house, where he treated him with every possible kindness, and to which I was removed as soon as returning health would allow.

"The rapid strides of the English army towards the capital at this time, threw the whole town into the greatest state of alarm, and convinced the government that some speedy measures must be taken to save the golden city. They had hitherto rejected all the overtures of Sir Archibald Campbell, imagining, until this late period, that they could in some way or other, drive the English from the country. Mr. Judson and Dr. Price were daily called to the court-house and consulted; in fact, nothing was done without their approbation. Two English officers, also, who had lately been brought to Ava as prisoners, were continually consulted, and their good offices requested in endeavouring to persuade the British General to make peace on easier terms. It was finally concluded that Mr. Judson and one of the officers above-mentioned, should be sent immediately to the English camp, in order to negotiate. The danger attached to a situation so responsible, under a government so fickle as the Burmese, induced your brother to use every means possible to prevent his being sent. Dr. Price was not only willing, but desirous of going; this circumstance Mr. Judson represented to the members of government, and begged he might not be compelled to go, as Dr. Price could transact this business equally as well as himself. After some hesitation and deliberation, Dr. Price was appointed to accompany Dr. Sandford, one of the English officers, on condition that Mr. Judson would stand security for his return; while the other English officer, then in irons, should be security for Dr. Sandford. The king gave them a hundred tickals each, to bear their expenses, (twenty-five of which Dr. Sandford generously sent to Mr. Gouger, still a prisoner at Oung-pen-la,) boats, men, and a Burmese officer, to accompany them, though he ventured no farther than the Burman camp. With the most anxious solicitude the court waited the arrival of the messengers, but did not in the least relax in their exertions to fortify the city. Men and beasts were at work night and day, making new stockades and strengthening old ones, and whatever buildings were in their way were immediately torn down. Our house, with all that surrounded it, was levelled to the ground, and our beautiful little compound turned into a road and a place for the erection of cannon. All articles of value were conveyed out of town and safely deposited in some other place.

"At length the boat in which the ambassadors had been sent was seen approaching a day earlier than was expected. As it advanced towards the city, the banks were lined by thousands, anxiously inquiring their success. But no answer was given--the government must first hear the news. The palace gates were crowded, the officers at the Tlowtdau were seated, when Dr. Price made the following communication: 'The general and commissioners will make no alteration in their terms, except the hundred lacks (a lack is a hundred thousand) of rupees, may be paid at four different times. The first twenty-five lacks to be paid within twelve days, or the army will continue their march.' In addition to this, the prisoners were to be given up immediately. The general had commissioned Dr. Price to demand Mr. Judson and myself and little Maria. This was communicated to the king, who replied, 'They are not English, they are my people, and shall not go.' At this time, I had no idea that we should ever be released from Ava. The government had learned the value of your brother's services, having employed him the last three months; and we both concluded they would never consent to our departure. The foreigners were again called to a consultation, to see what could be done. Dr. Price and Mr. Judson told them plainly that the English would never make peace on any other terms than those offered, and that it was in vain to go down again without the money. It was then proposed that a third part of the first sum demanded should he sent down immediately. Mr. Judson objected, and still said it would be useless. Some of the members of government then intimated that it was probable the teachers were on the side of the English, and did not try to make them take a smaller sum; and also threatened if they did not make the English comply, they and their families should suffer.

"In this interval, the fears of the government were considerably allayed, by the offers of a general, by name Layarthoo-yah, who desired to make one more attempt to conquer the English, and disperse them. He assured the king and government, that he could so fortify the ancient city of Pagan, as to make it impregnable; and that he would there defeat and destroy the English. His offers were heard, he marched to Pagan with a very considerable force, and made strong the fortifications. But the English took the city with perfect ease, and dispersed the Burmese army; while the general fled to Ava, and had the presumption to appear in the presence of the king, and demand new troops. The king being enraged that he had ever listened to him for a moment, in consequence of which the negotiation had been delayed, the English general provoked, and the troops daily advancing, that he ordered the general to be immediately executed! The poor fellow was soon hurled from the palace, and beat all the way to the court-house--when he was stripped of his rich apparel, bound with cords, and made to kneel and bow towards the palace. He was then delivered into the hands of the executioners, who, by their cruel treatment, put an end to his existence, before they reached the place of execution.

"The king caused it to be reported, that this general was executed, in consequence of disobeying his commands, '*not to fight the English*.'

"Dr. Price was sent off the same night, with part of the prisoners, and with instructions to persuade the general to take six lacks instead of twenty-five. He returned in two or three days with the appalling intelligence, that the English general was very angry, refused to have any communication with him, and was now within a few days' march of the capital. The queen was greatly alarmed, and said the money should be raised immediately, if the English would only stop their march. The whole palace was in motion, gold and silver vessels were melted up, the king and queen superintended the weighing of a part of it, and were determined, if possible, to save their city. The silver was ready in the boats by the next evening; but they had so little confidence in the English, that after all their alarm, they concluded to send down six lacks only, with the assurance that if the English would stop where they then were, the remainder should be forthcoming immediately.

"The government now did not even ask Mr. Judson the question whether he would go or not; but some officers took him by the arm as he was walking in the street, and told him he must go immediately on board the boat, to accompany two Burmese officers, a Woongyee and Woondouk, who were going down to make peace. Most of the English prisoners were sent at the same time. The general and commissioners would not receive the six lacks, neither would they stop their march; but promised, if the sum complete reached them before they should arrive at Ava, they would make peace. The general also commissioned Mr. Judson to collect the remaining foreigners, of whatever country, and ask the question before the Burmese government, whether they wished to go or stay. Those who expressed a wish to go should be delivered up immediately, or peace would not be made.

"Mr. Judson reached Ava at midnight; had all the foreigners called the next morning, and the question asked. Some of the members of government said to him, 'You will not leave us--you shall become a great man if you will remain.' He then secured himself from the odium of saying that he wished to leave the service of his majesty by recurring to the order of Sir Archibald, that whoever wished to leave Ava should be given up, and that I had expressed a wish to go, so that he of course must follow. The remaining part of the twenty-five lacks was soon collected; the prisoners at Oung-pen-la were all released, and either sent to their houses, or down the river to the English; and in two days from the time of Mr. Judson's return, we took an affectionate leave of the good natured officer who had so long entertained us at his house, and who now accompanied us to the water side, and we then left forever the banks of Ava.

It was on a cool, moonlight evening, in the month of March, that with hearts filled with gratitude to God, and overflowing with joy at our prospects, we passed down the Irrawaddy, surrounded by six or eight golden boats, and accompanied by all we had on earth. The thought that we had still to pass the Burman camp, would sometimes occur to damp our joy, for we feared that some obstacle might there arise to retard our progress. Nor were we mistaken in our conjectures. We reached the camp about midnight, where we were detained two hours; the Woongyee, and high officers, insisting that *we* should wait at the camp, while Dr. Price, (who did not return to Ava with your brother, but remained at the camp,) should go on with the money and first ascertain whether peace would be made. The Burmese government still entertained the idea, that as soon as the English had received the money and prisoners, they would continue their march, and yet destroy the capital. We knew not but that some circumstance might occur to break off the negotiations; Mr. Judson, therefore strenuously insisted that he would not remain, but go on immediately. The officers were finally prevailed on to consent, hoping much from Mr. Judson's assistance in making peace.

"We now, for the first time, for more than a year and a half, felt that we were free, and no longer subject to the oppressive yoke of the Burmese. And with what sensations of delight, on the next morning, did I behold the masts of the steam-boat, the sure presage of being within the bounds of civilized life. As soon as our boat reached the shore, brigadier A. and another officer came on board, congratulated us on our arrival, and invited us on board the steam-boat, where I passed the remainder of the day; while your brother went on to meet the general, who, with a detachment of the army, had encamped at Yandaboo, a few miles further down the river. Mr. Judson returned in the evening, with an invitation from Sir Archibald, to come immediately to his quarters, where I was the next morning introduced, and received with the greatest kindness by the general, who had a tent pitched for us near his own--took us to his own table, and treated us with the kindness of a father, rather than as strangers of another country.

"We feel that our obligations to general Campbell can never be cancelled. Our final release from Ava, and our recovering all the property that had there been taken, was owing entirely to his efforts. This subsequent hospitality and kind attention to the accommodations for our passage to Rangoon, have left an indelible impression on our minds, which can never be forgotten. We daily received the congratulation of the British officers, whose conduct towards us formed a striking contrast to that of the Burmese. I presume to say, that no persons on earth were ever happier than we were, during the fortnight we passed at the English camp. For several days, this single idea wholly occupied my mind, that we were out of the power of the Burmese government, and once more under the protection of the English. Our feelings continually dictated expressions like these: What shall we render to the Lord for all his benefits towards us?

"The treaty of peace was soon concluded, signed by both parties, and a termination of hostilities publicly declared. We left Yandaboo, after a fortnight's residence, and safely reached the mission house in Rangoon, after an absence of two years and three months.

"A review of our trip to, and adventures in, Ava, often, excites the inquiry, Why were we permitted to go? What good has been effected? Why did I not listen to the advice of friends in Bengal, and remain there till the war was concluded? But all that we can say is, It is not in man that walketh to direct his steps. So far as my going round to Rangoon, at the time I did, was instrumental in bringing those heavy afflictions upon us, I can only say, that if I ever acted from a sense of duty in my life, it was at that time; for my conscience would not allow me any peace, when I thought of sending for your brother to come to Calcutta, in prospect of the approaching war. Our society at home have lost no property in consequence of our difficulties; but two years of precious time have been lost to the mission, unless some future advantage may be gained, in consequence of the severe discipline to which we ourselves have been subject. We are sometimes induced to think, that the lesson we found so very hard to learn, will have a beneficial effect through our lives; and that the mission may, in the end, be advanced rather than retarded.

"We should have had no hesitation about remaining in Ava, if no part of the Burmese empire had been ceded to the British. But as it was, we felt it would be an unnecessary exposure, besides the missionary field being much more limited, in consequence of intoleration. We now consider our future missionary prospects as bright indeed; and our only anxiety is, to be once more in that situation where our time will be exclusively devoted to the instruction of the heathen."

In a concluding paragraph, dated Amherst, July 27, she adds:

"From the date at the commencement of this long letter, you see, my dear brother, that my patience has continued for two months. I have frequently been induced to throw it aside altogether, but feeling assured that you and my other friends are expecting something of this kind I am induced to send it with all its imperfections. This letter, dreadful as are the scenes herein described, gives you but a faint idea of the awful reality. The anguish, the agony of mind, resulting from a thousand little circumstances impossible to delineate on paper, can be known by those only who have been in similar situations. Pray for us, my dear brother and sister, that these heavy afflictions may not be in vain, but may be blessed to our spiritual good, and the advancement of Christ's church among the heathen."

At the close of this long and melancholy narrative, we may appropriately introduce the following tribute to the benevolence and talents of Mrs. Judson, written by one of the English prisoners, who were confined at Ava with Mr. Judson. It was published in a Calcutta paper after the conclusion of the war:

"Mrs. Judson was the author of those eloquent and forcible appeals to the government, which prepared them by degrees for submission to terms of peace, never expected by any, who knew the hauteur and inflexible pride of the Burman court.

"And while on this subject, the overflowing of grateful feelings, on behalf of myself and fellow-prisoners, compel me to add a tribute of public thanks to that amiable and humane female, who, though living at a distance of two miles from our prison, without any means of conveyance, and very feeble in health, forgot her own comfort and infirmity, and almost every day visited us, sought out and administered to our wants, and contributed in every way to alleviate our misery.

"While we were left by the government destitute of food, she, with unwearied perseverance, by some means or other, obtained for us a constant supply.

"When the tattered state of our clothes evinced the extremity of our distress, she was ever ready to replenish our scanty wardrobe.

"When the unfeeling avarice of our keepers confined us inside, or made our feet fast in the stocks, she, like a ministering angel, never ceased her applications to the government, until she was authorized to communicate to us the grateful news of our enlargement, or of a respite from our galling oppressions.

"Besides all this, it was unquestionably owing, in a chief degree, to the repeated eloquence, and forcible appeals of Mrs. Judson, that the untutored Burman was finally made willing to secure the welfare and happiness of his country, by a sincere peace."

CHAPTER XX.

PERSECUTION OF THE WESLEYAN MISSIONARIES IN THE WEST INDIES.

The exertions of Christians to spread the truths of the gospel among the Africans in the West Indies, have met with much opposition from the white population. Moravian missionaries, at first, sold themselves as slaves, and laboured with the negroes on the plantations for the purpose of preaching the gospel during the intervals of labour. The Methodist missionaries have been treated with much indignity, and have had their lives endangered by the violence of the white mob. In 1816, the white rabble of Barbadoes, collected together, and totally destroyed the Methodist chapel. The destruction of the chapel occupied two successive nights, and so listless were the authorities, that no attempt was made to prevent it. And when the governor issued a proclamation, offering a reward to any person who should apprehend the leaders in this outrageous proceeding, the mob immediately issued a counter proclamation, threatening with death any one who should dare to comply with the governor's orders.

In August, 1823, an insurrection took place at Demerara, among the negroes, which was most unjustly attributed to the efforts of the missionaries. The principal events in relation to this affair are detailed in the subjoined account from the Missionary Herald.

Various accounts have, from time to time, appeared in the public prints, of the insurrection of the slaves in the colony of Demerara, and of the condemnation of the Rev. Mr. Smith, a missionary from the London Missionary Society, on an accusation of having been accessary to the plot. We have collected and embodied such of the leading facts, relative to these transactions, as have come to our knowledge.

The slaves of many plantations on the eastern coast of Demerara had formed a conspiracy to obtain their freedom. The plot was disclosed by a servant to his master on the 18th of August; not till the conspiracy was thoroughly organized, and arrangements made to secure simultaneous movements; and only a few hours before the time appointed for action. Information was immediately communicated to the commander-in-chief, and the most efficient measures taken; but before a sufficient force could be assembled to resist a large body of negroes, who were immediately under arms, the evening, which was the time for executing the first grand enterprise, had arrived. This was simultaneously to seize upon the whites at the different plantations, confine them in the stocks, and take possession of their arms. This was effected on nearly fifty plantations, containing, inclusive of women and children, 10 or 12,000 negroes. The whites, to the number of about 250, were imprisoned. In some places an ineffectual resistance was made, and several lives lost on both sides.

On the morning of the 19th, the governor issued a proclamation, declaring the colony under martial law, and ordered all who were capable of bearing arms, without distinction, to be immediately enrolled. The most vigorous measures were pursued; and in the course of a few days, after several skirmishes, in which a considerable number of negroes lost their lives, the insurrection was subdued.

A court martial was then constituted, and many of the negroes brought to trial, condemned and executed. Subsequent accounts state that more than 1000 had suffered death, in consequence of the insurrection, and that many of their heads had been fixed up on poles in various parts of the country.

We might easily be more particular in regard to the circumstances of the insurrection, but our object is chiefly to relate what concerns the missionary who was accused of having a part in the scheme, and the other missionaries in the colony. On these points we have to regret that the information which has yet been received is very scanty and in many respects indefinite.

The extract which follows is from the Missionary Chronicle, and was published in the name of the Directors of the London Missionary Society.

The insurrection it should seem, manifested itself first in Mahaica, the district to the east of that in which Mr. Smith resides. Its appearance on the Le Ressouvenir estate, where Mr. Smith resides, was on Monday, the 18th August, in consequence of an order to take into custody two slaves belonging to an adjoining plantation, whom the negroes of the Le Ressouvenir, as the prisoners had to pass over it, rose to rescue. Mr.

Smith was at home. He successfully used his endeavours, on perceiving the tumult, to rescue the manager from the negroes, and continued his exertions to induce them to return to their duty, till he himself was driven with violence, and with a weapon held to his body, from the estate.

Mr. Smith was taken into custody on the evening of the 21st August, and all his papers seized. He is kept a prisoner in the Colony-house, and has, since the 24th of August, had a guard stationed over him.

Mr. Elliot, another missionary, who laboured about 20 miles from Mr. Smith, was also taken into custody, on the ground of disobedience of orders, "which he had not understood to be such," in visiting Mr. Smith in his confinement. He was kept about ten days, and then released. No charge was preferred against him. The estates on which he labours had been quiet, and none of the negroes under his instructions were implicated in the rebellion.

In a letter to the Directors of the London Missionary Society, Mr Elliot writes thus:

Numerous false reports have been sent forth against Mr. Smith, but assure yourself and all the directors, that whatever reports you may hear, the only crime the missionaries have committed is their zeal for the conversion of the negroes. They have neither been so weak nor so wicked as to excite the negroes to rebellion. The missionaries want justice only; they have no favour to ask; they have nothing to fear. The missionaries have not degraded their holy calling, nor dishonoured the society of which they are members, by sowing the seeds of rebellion instead of the Word of Life. The real causes of the rebellion are far, very far from being the instructions given by the missionaries.

On the 13th of October, Mr. Smith was brought to trial before a court martial. All the accounts which we have yet seen of the charges brought against him are very obscure and imperfect. The January number of the Missionary Chronicle, from which we have already quoted, says,--

The public papers have stated four charges as forming the indictment against him, but of their accuracy the directors are not enabled to judge. They trust that, under the direction of Divine Providence, he has been able to prove himself *guiltless* of them all.

It is not, however, to be concealed, that he will have had much to contend with from the violence of public prejudice in the Colony, and it is to be feared from the false assertions of some of the unhappy negroes, whom the hope of favour towards themselves may have led to bring against him "things that he knew not." Indeed, the directors are informed, upon authority on which they can rely, that some of the condemned negroes, finding the hope of life taken away, had in the most solemn manner declared that they had been induced so to act; and that others, on being questioned whether they had not been induced to rebellion by Mr. Smith, had in the strongest terms which their broken language could supply, denied the imputation. It is stated by the writer of one letter, that he has often heard charges circulated against the missionaries, as if spoken by the negroes at the time of their execution, which he knew, (for he was a near spectator,) that they never had uttered.

We can as yet learn little more respecting the evidence which was produced before the court than that some of the negroes testified that the instructions of Mr. Smith had a tendency to make them dissatisfied with their condition, and that he knew of the plot before it was carried into execution.

He was condemned, and sentenced to **death**. The sentence was however transmitted by the governor, to England, for the consideration and ultimate decision of the king. What we know of the decision will be seen in the following paragraph, copied from the New-York Observer of March 27th.

It appears from the London papers, that "the king has remitted the sentence of death of the court martial on Mr. Smith, the missionary of the London Society in Demerara, (which sentence was accompanied by a recommendation for mercy on the part of the court,) but has given orders that he should be dismissed from the colony, and should come under obligations not to reside within any of his majesty's colonial possessions in the West Indies." The charges against Mr. Smith appear to have originated in the perjury of some of the negroes engaged in the insurrection.

In the mean time Mr. Smith was languishing under the influence of disease, which rendered the stroke of the executioner unnecessary to remove him from the earth. He died in prison, before the intelligence had arrived that his sentence was reversed. The following notice of his death appeared in the Demerara Courant.

Died,--In the Colonial Jail, at Demerara, February 9th, where he had been confined, as a state prisoner since the 26th of November last, on the termination of his trial by the general court martial, on a charge of high treason, sentence thereon having been transmitted to his majesty for his final decision--JOHN SMITH, missionary; he had been in a poor state of health, and had been attended regularly by skilful physicians. We are happy to state, from personal inquiry and inspection, that this unhappy man had the utmost attention and kindness shewn to him, by the humane keeper of the prison, (Mr. Padmore,) all the time of his confinement. His apartment was airy and commodious, he had always at his command every comfort which his taste fancied or his necessities required. He has left a widow to deplore his fate, and deplore his loss.

The conviction which results from the present state of our information on this subject, is that, through prejudice and exasperated feeling, Mr. Smith was condemned, being innocent. The directors of the society under which he laboured, have, however, given us reason to look for further intelligence in a future number of the Missionary Chronicler, which we hope will soon arrive.

It appears that none of the negroes under the instruction of any missionary, either of the London or Wesleyan Missionary Society except Mr. Smith, were implicated in the insurrection. Respecting the Methodists in the colony we quote the following statement from the Wesleyan Methodist Magazine:

We stated in our last number, that Messrs. Mortier and Cheesewright, our missionaries in Demerara were safe, and that *only* two of the members of our society there had been apprehended on suspicion of being implicated in the late revolt. We have received a second letter from Mr. Mortier, dated Demerara, September seventeenth, which communicated the gratifying intelligence that these two persons, who were servants of the governor, had been liberated upon full conviction of their entire innocence, and that *no one* of the members of our large society of twelve hundred and sixteen, chiefly slaves, had been in the least concerned in the revolt: and that the slaves of another estate, under the care of Mr. Cheesewright, had not only refused to join the rebels, but had conducted their master to a vessel, by which he reached Georgetown in safety.

Case of Rev. John Smith.

The London Missionary Chronicle for March contains a statement respecting Mr. Smith's case, occupying, with accompanying documents nearly twelve pages, which confirms the impression that Mr. Smith was innocent. The Directors of the London Missionary Society, after stating some circumstances relative to his trial, says.

The Directors having stated these points of serious objection (and more might easily be found,) to the proceedings on the trial, conclude that the members of the society, and the candid beyond its circle, will approve of their declaring that they retain the conviction formerly expressed, of the moral and legal innocence of their missionary, Smith; that they do not withdraw from him their confidence; and that they are "not ashamed of his bonds." They regard him as an unmerited sufferer, in the diligent and faithful, and it may be added, useful discharge of his duties, as a missionary; and they earnestly wish the Divine forgiveness may be extended to those who may have been instrumental in causing his sufferings.

The Rev. Mr. Austin, a clergyman of the church of England, and Chaplain of the Colony, thus expresses his opinion in a private letter.

"I feel no hesitation in declaring, from the intimate knowledge which my most anxious inquiries have obtained, that in the late scourge which the hand of an all-wise Creator has inflicted on this ill-fated country, nothing but those religious impressions which, under Providence, Mr. Smith has been instrumental in fixing--nothing but those principles of the gospel of peace which he has been proclaiming--could have prevented a dreadful effusion of blood here, and saved the lives of these very persons who are now (I shudder to write it,) seeking his."

The following extract of a letter from William Arrindell, Esq. of Demerara, Mr. Smith's counsel, addressed to Mrs. Smith, after the trial, is also inserted.

"It is almost presumptuous in me to differ from the sentence of a Court, but, before God, I do believe Mr. Smith to be innocent; nay, I will go further, and defy any minister, of any sect whatever, to have shewn a more faithful attention to his sacred duties, than he has been proved, by the evidence on his trial, to have done."

The Directors had resolved to take further measures for obtaining, in England the reversal of his sentence.

This subject was brought before the English parliament, and after a full and fair discussion, the innocence of Mr. Smith was established beyond a question. The following from the London Christian Observer gives an account of the proceedings in Parliament.

A debate of two days' continuance on the case of the missionary Smith has taken place in the House of Commons. A motion was made by Mr. Brougham, to express the serious alarm and deep sorrow with which the house contemplated the violation of law and justice, manifested in the unexampled proceedings against Mr. Smith in Demerara, and their sense of the necessity of adopting measures to secure a just and humane administration of law in that colony, and to protect the voluntary instruction of the negroes, as well as the negroes themselves, and the rest of his Majesty's subjects from oppression. This motion was supported by Mr. Brougham with a power of argument and eloquence which has seldom been equalled; and he was followed on the same side by Sir James Mackintosh, Dr. Lushington, Mr. J Williams, Mr. Wilberforce, Mr. Denman, and Sir Joseph Yorke. The motion was opposed by Mr. Horton, Mr. Scarlett, Mr. Tindal, the Attorney General, and Mr. Canning, on the ground, not of the legality of the proceedings, or of the justice of the sentence, but that the motion went to condemn unheard the governor of Demerara, and the court that tried Mr. Smith. On this ground the previous question was moved and carried by 193 to 146, the largest minority in the present session. The division, under all the circumstances of the case may be considered as a triumph. Not an individual attempted to defend the proceedings. In short, nothing could have been more decisive of the innocence of Mr. Smith, and the injustice of his condemnation.

Persecutions of the Wesleyan Methodists in St. Domingo.

We extract from the publications of the Wesleyan Missionary Society, the following account of the aggressions committed upon the Protestant population of Hayti, by the Roman Catholics of that Island, during the year 1824.

Persecutions at Port au Prince.

The following extracts from the journal of Mr. St. Denis, and letters of Mr. Pressoir, members of the Methodist Society at Port au Prince, we copied from the Wesleyan Magazine. The first extracts are from the journal of Mr. St. Denis.

On Sunday, Feb. 2d, our assembly was held at Belair. During the morning service several stones were thrown.

Feb. 4. Whilst we were singing, a shower of stones was thrown, but no one received any injury.

That evening (Feb. 7th) we had a small assembly of thirty-two persons. A plan had been laid for apprehending us, which was put in execution. We had time to sing a hymn, read a chapter, and a homily; but whilst singing the second hymn, the noise of the soldiers was so great in approaching our house of prayer, that we were obliged to cease singing. Wishing, however, to continue our meeting, an officer of the police said, "In the name of the law, leave off that prayer!" Then we left off. Not finding J. C. Pressoir, they made me his second. We were taken to general Thomas's, who pretended to be ignorant of the matter. Colonel Victor pretended to be ignorant also. When we reached the house of the *Juge de Paix*, we were ordered to halt for a moment. Colonel Victor knocked at his door, the *Juge de Paix* asked who we were, and was answered, "A band of methodists." The *Juge de Paix* said, "Ha! ha! take them to the jail!" Col. Victor replied, "Yes!" We were led to prison, and each of our names was taken. The sisters were put in the debtor's place, and the men were shut up in close confinement.

The next morning, the person who keeps the keys of the prison under the jailer told us, that the Juge de Paix would not allow our door to be opened; but the jailer went and spoke respecting it, and our door was opened about nine o'clock. A moment after the Juge de Paix came to visit us, and addressing himself to me in anger, I wished to reply: he would not listen to me; but began to blaspheme religion, despising the Lord. He withdrew in anger, without being able to do any thing with us. A moment after he left us, we were taken into the debtor's prison, near to the sisters, in a separate chamber.

When Mr. Pressoir heard of this event, he visited his brethren at the prison. The following extract is from one of his letters.

I would not run into prison of my own accord, but having waited, and finding nothing was said to us, I went to see my brethren and sisters. I found there were thirty-two, and St. Denis preparing to write to the president, which he did, and I carried this letter to his excellency, by which we requested him to cause us to be judged, and punished, if we were found guilty by the law. When I arrived under the piazza of the palace, I asked an officer on duty if I could see the president, who answered, Yes. I entered the hall, where I found the president seated, and surrounded by a circle, as well of officers as civilians. After saluting them, I presented the letter to the president, who asked me from whence it came. I replied, "From the methodists who are in prison."

His good humour was immediately changed. "Methodists," said he, "I did not know that." Colonel Victor, who was present, thinking that through fear I would wish to conceal myself, addressed himself to the president, saying, "President, this is a methodist," as if the president did not know it. Immediately the president replied, "You are fanatics." "Pardon me, president, we are not." "Why, you have changed your religion." "If I have changed my religion, president, it is the government which has made me do it." "How is that?" said he. "It was the late president who sent for the missionaries. I heard the letter read, and saw the late president's signature: this is what I can tell you." "Enough, enough," said he, "I will send an answer." I went to the prison and waited till it was late; but hearing nothing, and being ill of the fever, I returned to my mother's.

The next day orders were given for the brethren and sisters to appear before the chief judge. A dollar was demanded of each on leaving prison, and they were conducted by a single serjeant. On their arrival the chief judge forbade them, in the name of the president, to assemble together again. "No one can hinder you from worshipping God as you please; but let every one abide at home, for as often as you are found assembled you shall be put in prison; and if you unhappily persist, I have received orders to disperse you every where." Several wished to reply, but he refused to listen, saying, "It is not from me; it is not my fault; these orders are given me." All our brethren and sisters went out, animated with a holy zeal, determining not to abandon their assemblies. The next day we were assembled. After an exhortation we sung a hymn which being finished, we kneeled down to pray: a shower of stones came, as if they would have demolished the house, and have stoned us like Stephen. With one accord we commended ourselves to our faithful Creator, and continued in prayer till they had ceased.

In a subsequent letter, dated July 31st, he writes:--

Since the Lord has granted us the favour of meeting again, we have continued our assemblies without intermission, although forbidden to do this under pain of prison and exile. The only interruption we meet with is bad words, and a few stones now and then; and I am become so marked, that I cannot go out without people crying after me, "Methodist! Parson!"--with a contemptuous sneer, and a thousand other things not fit to write, but which serve only to strengthen my faith in the promises of Him who is faithful; till last Sunday some foolish young women came to revile us; and on Tuesday evening, whilst reading, stones were thrown, and whilst we were at prayer a great number rushed in, armed with sabres, sticks, and, if I mistake not, with stones, crying out, "In the name of the law," as if they had been authorized by the heads of the people to arrest us. This band consisted of boys, led on to commit disorders by a set of idle, good-for-nothing persons, of the worst class, who had armed themselves with sabres, and were disguised with old cocked hats; trying thus to show their bravery over those who would make no resistance. But the hairs of our head are all numbered; nor have they been permitted to hurt any of us to the present. It would be useless for us to ask or hope for the protection of the law; and we are thus led to place all our confidence in God, who can and will deliver us in his time. And if the Lord is for me, of whom should I be afraid? He that spared not his own Son, but delivered him up for me, will he not with him freely give me all things? I have already experienced that all my sufferings for his name are great blessings to me. All my care is about His church; and what wisdom does it require to conduct so many persons of such different dispositions! I feel new wants daily.

The following brief view of the persecutions of the methodists, in Hayti, is taken from "Missionary Notices," published by the Wesleyan Missionary Society. This account gave some particulars in addition to those narrated in the details inserted above:

We regret to find,--say the committee of that society,--from the following letter received from Mr. Pressoir, that our poor persecuted society at Port-au-Prince, so long the object of popish rancour, has again had to sustain the brutal outrages of an ignorant mob, incited it would seem, in another place, by persons calling themselves "respectable," and without experiencing any protection from the local authorities. The committee have endeavoured to obtain for them the common protection of the laws of their own country, by applications through various quarters, and hope they may be ultimately successful. In the mean time this excellent and suffering people are entitled to the special sympathies, and earnest prayers, of the friends of missions. We trust that they may yet, by their meek and patient suffering, and heroic perseverance, obtain that liberty of worship which they so earnestly desire.

The letter from Mr. Pressoir is dated about a year since. The following extracts describe the violence of the mob:

I have read of many instances of martyrdom for the testimony of Jesus Christ, but I have not yet read a passage which relates that the people of a city rose up like murderers, with a very few exceptions, to stone a few persons met together in a house, as our fathers, mothers, brethren, and children have done unto us not long ago. O cruel people! They began to throw stones at us at five o'clock in the afternoon, and continued their assaults till ten o'clock, committing all kinds of violence. They broke down the doors, broke open the windows, destroyed the first and second partitions in the upper chambers; in a word, every thing that was in the house, and beat with their cowskin-whips the brethren and sisters there, without showing compassion for either age or youth or even infancy. I believe I suffered the least of any. Only a great emissary of Satan, seized my left hand, and lifting up his whip declared he would knock me down, if I did not say "Almighty God, the Virgin Mary." My only answer was, turning my back. Several times he even brought his whip to my neck, and afterwards laid it on my shoulder, raging and abusing me with all the fury of Anti-christ. But he that numbered my hairs did not allow one of them to fall to the ground. Thanks be to him for confidence in his holy word, which is firmer than heaven on earth. When the populace entered to knock down our sisters I was in the first chamber, and hearing their cries, I tried to force my way to them, to try if I could render them any assistance; then the tyrant persecutor struck me several times on my hat, but I received no injury. But we were in great danger; those who wished to go out were stoned, beaten, torn, outraged, and brought back to the house, where they exercised their dark cruelty. It appeared as if Satan was unchained, and had come forth to make war against those whom the truth of the gospel had made free, and to crush those who had believed the testimony of the Son of God.

I ask, then, by whom have we been protected, and delivered unto this day? Was it by magistrates, judges, and police officers? Or by the other guards appointed to appease riots and defend the law? It is true, they were present in great numbers, but it was rather to advise and direct others. Some brought barrows full of stones, and others threw them, and said to the cruel populace, that, since we were so obstinate, the government had given us into their hands, and they might do to us whatever they pleased; and they did treat us with inhumanity and the greatest violence.

It was impossible to go out without being beaten, stoned, dragged, abused, and covered with dirt, and in the end we could neither buy nor sell without being dragged before a magistrate, beat, and covered with spitting and mud, and all kinds of outrages. They went beyond Porte Marchant to brother Floran's, sister Claire's, and J. P. J. Lusant's. At brother Floran's they destroyed every thing in the garden, and treated his wife, already broken with age, with the greatest inhumanity; dragging sister Claire by her feet out of the house, as also her god-daughter. And at J. P. J. Lusant's what disorders have they not committed amongst those poor persons, who have fled from the town to have some tranquility. I must tell you one circumstance which J. P. J. L. told me, to show you the cowardice of persecutors; five or six of them entered his gate, concealing their swords, making up to him with loud vociferations; seeing them coming, he went into his house, took an old rusty musket without flint, and levelling it at them, they all instantly fled with all speed, saying, "The Quakers don't carry arms, and see this old Quaker hero intends killing us."

Alluding to the letter of Mr. Pressoir, above noticed, and to other communications received about the same time, the Wesleyan Committee remark, in their publication for July, 1824.

In a recent number we laid before our readers some extracts of letters from our afflicted and persecuted society at Port-au-Prince, Hayti; from which it appeared that several of them had again been called to suffer bonds for the cause of Christ; that the house in which they were in the habit of assembling for religious worship was demolished; and that they themselves were delivered up to the will of a blind and infuriated populace, the magistrates refusing to afford them any protection against the outrages to which they were daily exposed. From later communications we learn, that, on an appeal being made by letter to the president, those in prison were set at liberty; and that a proclamation was made by his excellency's orders, forbidding any one to stone, injure, or otherwise persecute the methodists, but at the same time prohibiting all meetings of our society for religious worship; on pain of being arrested.

Notwithstanding the above proclamation, our people have still to suffer, in various ways, the insults and persecutions of the rabble. They continue, as they are able, and can find opportunity, to meet together for prayer, &c.

The letter to president Boyer shows very clearly the pacific character and object of these protestants. It is too important a part of these documents to be omitted.

President,--You are acquainted with our society, formed here six years ago. The end of our meeting together is, to invoke the blessing of God, not only on ourselves, but also on the government, its magistrates, and even on those who evil entreat us without cause; for we do not hate them, nor render evil for evil. This is what our religion commands. It is not that we wish by our meetings to disobey our president; but our desire is to obey God our sovereign, and his law requires that we should love the head that he has placed over us.

We know that your excellency will not approve the conduct of those who have stoned and evil entreated us without cause. We have been treated as enemies to the government, yet are not such. Yesterday we were arrested and put in prison, by order of general Thomas, who at once without examination, pronounced our sentence. And we know this was not by order of the president, which renders it our indisputable duty to give you information thereof.

President, let our society be narrowly examined, and if fault is found in us, we are willing to suffer the punishment we merit.

Confidently expecting your favourable reply, we have the honour of saluting you most respectfully.

To this letter the president did not reply, but ordered those, who had been arrested, to be set at liberty. Ten days after the date of the letter to the president, a letter was written, from which the following paragraphs are taken. The concluding sentences open the way for putting a favourable construction on the intentions of the president.

A proclamation was made in the name of general Thomas, commandant of the place, to prevent any one from throwing stones at the methodists, forbidding every one to evil entreat them, or to go before their houses to insult them. But by that proclamation we were also forbidden to meet together, and informed that should we meet, the police is ordered to arrest us; but as for the people, they ought not to interfere, nor throw stones, because we are citizens of the republic. This is the substance of the proclamation.

Although this proclamation was made, yet the people did not cease to ill treat us, and cry after us, as we went along. General Thomas gets out of that affair by saying, that they only made use of his name when he had nothing to do in it. "But, take care," said he, "if that continue, that it do not cost the life of some one."

One of our sisters visited the president, to whom she made her complaints, and informed him that it was said, that it was by his order that these things were done. He received her very politely, assured her that this was not so, but that he was exceedingly sorry that we should be improperly treated, and that he had written to general Thomas to that effect, and if the general did not attend to his orders he could not hold any command in the republic. In consequence of this the general made the above proclamation. The president also told her, that he could not allow us to hold our meetings, because we were not in peace; that France was proposing to march upon us, &c. &c. Since the last persecution, we enjoy, by the grace of God, the means of praying, when several of us meet together.

CHAPTER XXI.

PERSECUTIONS IN SWITZERLAND FROM 1813 TO 1830.

The information contained in the following account of the persecution in Switzerland, is derived principally from the Christian Spectator and the London Christian Observer.

Scarcely any country of Continental Europe, has excited so deep an interest in the minds of Americans, as Switzerland. Its valleys and lakes, its streams and cataracts, its lofty mountains and the seas of ice and deserts of snow which crown their summits, have been the Ultima Thule of the traveller, from whatever land. But *we* have dwelt upon them from the very days of boyhood, with an interest belonging to scarcely any thing earthly, because we regarded all this magnificent and beautiful display, as the mere scenery and decoration of the stage, on which an important act in the great drama of liberty, was exhibited. In the christian, these magnificent objects awaken emotions perhaps less tumultuous, but deeper and more elevating; for it is here that another scene of that great drama was early opened, involving interests incomparably more valuable, and a struggle far more deadly, not for the civil liberty of Switzerland, but to free the world from a tyranny, in comparison with which, that of Austrian dukes was paternal kindness,--a despotism that held the soul itself chained to the papal throne, and assumed the triple crown of heaven and earth and hell, which its representative still wears. To the christian, the names of Tell and Winkelreid, sink into insignificance beside those of Zuingle and Calvin; and the war of Swiss independence scarcely deserves a thought, in comparison with that struggle for the moral reformation of the world, in which these men were such distinguished actors, and to whose influence we ourselves owe that religious liberty, which is the most precious part of our birthright.

But it is an humbling reflection, that the palladium of liberty could not be kept inviolate, even in the fastnesses of the Alps. A few years only have elapsed, since some of the fairest portions of this "land of the free," were held as conquered tributaries by other cantons, and were governed by a bailiff residing in his castle, and exercising a power like that of a feudal baron. A considerable portion of Switzerland is still subject to an aristocracy, as absolute in its sway, and as much opposed to the extension of light and liberty, as any other branch of the holy alliance. The press is, in many cantons, under severe restrictions, and industry and enterprise are checked by the regulations of the incorporated *trades*, which place the rod of oppression in the hands of ignorance and self-interest; and which bring home its influence to the work-bench of the mechanic, and too often paralyze the arm of laborious poverty. Within ten years, and in one of the most enlightened cantons, men and women have been arrested, and fined, and imprisoned, in the most cruel manner, for assembling to read the word of God; have even been banished under pain of death, and without any passport to secure them from imprisonment as vagrants in the neighbouring countries, merely for preaching and hearing the gospel, out of the established church.

In the protestant churches of German Switzerland, the Helvetic confession and the Heidelberg catechism, both in the strictest sense orthodox, are recognized as standards of faith. This, however, is the *only* bond of union between the different portions of the Helvetic church. The spiritual concerns of each canton are under the direction of what is called the "church council," established by the government, and composed of some of its members united with some of the clergy. This body license, locate and pay the clergy; and form the court of appeal in the affairs of the church. A congregation have no voice in the selection of their pastor. Baptism and confirmation, or admission to the Lord's supper, in the established church, are required by law, as indispensable to the exercise of civil rights; and the latter ceremony is generally regarded as a mere introduction into life. In the canton of Berne, no person can enter the most menial station as a domestic, without exhibiting his certificate of communion; and so far is this from being an obsolete law, that we have known a person incur its penalty, because he delayed for a few days the exhibition of this certificate to the police. In this canton, (and we believe in most others,) no person can be excluded from the communion, except by government; and, as a necessary consequence, no discipline exists in the church. The Lord's supper is received with great regularity by the whole parish; and in some districts at least, the opinion prevails, that this ordinance is a seal of the pardon of their sins.

Such is the external state of the church in German Switzerland. In regard to its spiritual condition, we have little encouraging to present. The mercenary troops which Switzerland has so long been accustomed to sell to France, Spain and Italy, have usually brought back corrupt principles and licentious habits; and the young men of patrician families, from whom the rulers are ultimately chosen, have been prepared, by serving as officers to these troops, to exert a baneful influence upon their country. Those who were destined to the ministry, or to the learned professions, were accustomed to seek an education, if possible, in the German universities, where they would imbibe a taste for any thing but evangelical principles. Rousseau, Voltaire, and Gibbon, during their residence in Switzerland, contributed not a little to the increase of infidelity; and the French revolution seemed to sweep away the landmarks of religion and morality, and to banish whatever might have remained, of the character of Switzerland, from the portions to which its emissaries had immediate access.

It will not be supposed that the church escaped untainted, amidst all these causes of corruption. The feeling which we found extensively prevalent, that it was indecorous to inquire into the opinions of the clergy and the doctrines actually maintained in the church, and which presented a serious obstacle to investigation on this subject, sufficiently indicates, that there is something which will not bear a comparison with the public standard. But more unequivocal evidence of the change of opinion is found in the fact, that candidates for the ministry are now only required to avow their belief in the new testament, and these regulations are avowedly adopted, in order not to exclude those who are called "liberal" or "rational" in their opinions.

We trust indeed, that there are many thousands in Switzerland, who have not bowed the knee to Baal, in any form. We believe especially, that in the cantons of Basle, Zurich, Appenzell, and Schaffhausen, as well as Geneva and Vaud, there are many faithful ministers of the gospel. We know that in the midst of decayed churches, there are little bands, who, without separating themselves, or exciting public attention, have adopted the principles and the devotional habits of the United Brethren, or Moravians. The missionary seminary at Basle is a radiating point, from which divine truth is going forth to the ends of the earth; and there is a cluster of christian institutions around it, which are a monument of love and zeal. Light is springing up in various directions in the midst of darkness and these first gleamings of the dawn are a sure and delightful presage, that the Sun of righteousness is about to arise upon Switzerland, with healing in its beams.

For several years past, two or three of the clergy of the established church in the city of Berne, have preached the doctrines of the gospel, as exhibited in the standards of the church, with simplicity and faithfulness. Much interest was thus excited in a small number of persons, several of whom were among the class of patricians, and the result might be termed a little revival. Public attention was called to it, by the change of conduct in those who were its subjects. Their consciences would no longer allow them to partake in those violations of the Sabbath, and those questionable amusements which were customary in the world around them; and they felt the need of assembling themselves for social devotion and christian intercourse, during the week. Those who felt reproved by such conduct, spared neither censure nor ridicule. The names of "*priest*," "*methodist*," "*mummer*," etc., were unsparingly applied to them; and in one instance, the windows of a person who was obnoxious on this account, were broken. It is but justice to the government to state, that immediate and vigorous measures were taken to repress all violence; and no one was suffered to interrupt them, so long as they continued in connexion with the established church. Much hostility was indeed expressed against these private assemblies; but so much patrician influence was exerted in their favour, that the government did not venture to execute the threats, sometimes thrown out, of prohibiting them. Pietism continued to increase, from the increased action produced by these social meetings; and the flame was undoubtedly nourished by the conversation and correspondence of pious British travellers, whose influence may now be traced in every part of the continent, from Calais to Naples, and exhibits one of these remarkable traits in the divine government, by which the seed of the word is scattered over the world, often by the consent of those who wish to destroy it. The wealth of the English gives them access every where. Even the court of Rome, rather than lose this source of revenue, allows heresy to rear its standard of rebellion on the banks of the Tiber; and the efforts of such as are piously disposed to spread light around them, are winked at, to avoid offending or alarming the *national* spirit, even of those who are devoted to the pleasures of the world.

During the year 1828, a small number of the persons who were thus awakened, felt it their duty to separate themselves entirely from the established church. Their consciences were wounded by the prostitution of the ordinance of the supper, in admitting all who chose to come; since many of the openly vicious, and a multitude who had no apparent interest in religion, belonged to the number. They urged the necessity of discipline from Matt. xvi. and xviii., 1 Cor. v., etc., and maintained that that could not be deemed a church of Christ, which tolerated vice in its very bosom. They felt themselves bound by the precept, 2 Thess. iii. 6, 14, 15, and 2 John 10, 11, to withdraw from a church in which the gospel was not generally preached; and which cherished in its bosom, so many who crucified Christ afresh, and whom they considered themselves as recognizing as brethren, by partaking of the same bread and the same cup. This measure was promoted by a person who had been banished from the canton de Vaud; and who was received at Berne, under a pledge to the police, that he would not speak of separation. The violation of this pledge led to his expulsion, which was the first act of the government on this subject. This excited no serious opposition, since those who agreed with him in sentiment, did not approve of his violation of truth. It did not however prevent the continuance of the assemblies of separatists, and their distinct avowal of their sentiments; and they obtained from a member of the government belonging to the established church, the use of a room to his own house, on condition that nothing should be said there in direct promotion of separatism.

This decided course of conduct, notwithstanding many hints and threats, placed the government in an embarrassing situation. Eight years before, the canton of Vaud had treated a similar sect (of which indeed, some of these very individuals had been members) with great severity; but with so little effect, that their number had been constantly increasing, and their spirit had been diffused through a large number of the established churches; to the great annoyance of those who did not love the gospel. Thus warned of the danger of violent measures, and yet anxious to find reasons for expelling the leaders of the obnoxious party, they directed the superintendent of the police to keep them and their assemblies under constant and rigid inspection; and all who were concerned with them, were watched with the same view. At the same time, one of the evangelical clergymen was sent for, and warned to alter his mode of preaching; and although he did not approve or preach separation, he was accused of contributing to the excitement of feeling, which gave rise to it, by his mode of exhibiting the doctrines of the bible. We need scarcely add, that the warning was without effect on this faithful minister of Christ.

In the year 1813, a few pious individuals began to meet in private, for the purpose of seeking and cherishing that holy truth which was banished from the public assemblies. These persons were directed by some students of theology, among whom was M. Empaytaz. The venerable company of pastors soon heard of these unauthorized proceedings, and lost no time in evincing their disapprobation respecting them. M. Empaytaz, was especially marked out as the object of their displeasure; and they refused to ordain him, unless he would avoid every religious assembly which had not their sanction. He chose rather to incur their anathema than to wound his conscience, and departed from the city.

But the light had broke forth, and it was not easy again to extinguish it. The honourable company seem to have been extremely troubled as to the course to be pursued. To sit still, however, was to yield to the rising spirit of reformation, and they determined to bestir themselves. Accordingly, after due deliberation, they issued certain regulations, bearing date May 3, 1817, which they hoped would be received as articles.

These articles however, did not produce the anticipated effect. The doctrine of the divinity of Christ, and others equally offensive to Unitarians, continued to be preached. In 1818, M. Malan, a pious orthodox divine, was deprived of his place of regent of the college; and another, M. Mejanel, was ordered to quit Geneva.

For some time, however, the individuals who retained their allegiance to the Helvetic Confession, and remained at Geneva, still held their meetings, with little other provocation than that of a few hard names, such as "enthusiasts," "Nazarenes," "advocates for exploded doctrines," &c., which the Unitarians, in the exuberance of their wit, and the overflowing of their liberality, had the gratification to bespatter them. These attacks produced very little impression upon the persons assailed. The arguments next adopted, were calculated to supply the defect. About the beginning of July, 1818, the place of meeting being changed, when the persons assembled, they found a large mob prepared to insult them. These enlightened and worthy abettors of the reformed church of Geneva, and citizens of that free republic, assembled at the house of meeting, and vociferated amidst other expressions of hostility--we transcribe the words with shame and horror,--A bas Jesus Christ! A bas les Moraves! A mort, a la lanterne, &c. and pursued the obnoxious ministers as they came out, with similar cries. Neither did they stop here: their valour and zeal, as is the case with all mobs, became more impetuous as they were not resisted. "Our silence," says one who was present, "in the midst of these insults, did not satisfy them: we had to suffer menaces, maledictions; stoning through the streets, and the violation of our houses." Had not the police exerted themselves to suppress these disorders, the consequences would probably have been still more fearful.

Persecution in the Pays de Vaud.

In the month of December, 1823, a letter was addressed by three young men, ministers of that canton, and subsequently signed by a few others, to the council of state, intimating a determination to withdraw from the established church, and requesting permission to constitute places of worship independent of it. The cause assigned was, that the Helvetic Confession had been virtually set aside, both by pastors and people; and that the discipline of the church was annihilated. Their plan was to preach according to that Confession, and to restore the discipline.

The petition to the council of state is dated Dec. 24, 1823. The official answer bears date Jan. 15, 1824; and has all the formalities with which the spirit of intolerance and persecution generally invests itself, and is signed, Le Landamman en Charge, F. Clavel, Le Chandelier, Boisot. In this instrument, the ministers and their friends are called "Momiers;" and it is summarily decreed, that those who separate themselves from the national church shall not be tolerated; that the justices of the peace, &c. are specially charged instantly to dissolve their meetings, and to report their proceedings to the council of state, and every person who attends these prohibited assemblies, and who has disobeyed the orders to leave them, and rendered it necessary to employ force, shall be imprisoned three days, besides the possible infliction of other pains and penalties; and that all persons whose measures shall have tended to gain proselytes, shall be fined 600 livres, or imprisoned two years; the same punishment to be awarded to him who furnishes a place of meeting, or who has called or directed a prohibited assembly, or who has taken any part whatever in quality of a chief or director. The above decree was accompanied by a circular, dated Jan. 16, 1824, emanating from the same high quarter, addressed to the justices of the peace, municipalities, &c. and conceived in the same spirit with its *respectable* associate.

This iniquitous and anti-christian enactment has been carried into effect in several instances. M. Charles Rochat, minister of the gospel, of the Canton de Vaud, of a respectable family, and whose brother is one of the national clergy, of the Canton, is the first on whom the severity of the law has fallen. Five persons were found seated round a table in his own house, with the bible open before them: the wife of M. Rochat, a common friend, with two of his sisters, and a young person, a stranger. This was the whole crime. M. Rochat was found guilty of reading in his own house, before his wife and four friends, a chapter of the New Testament! For this he was at first condemned to three year's banishment, which, however, the tribunal of appeal reduced to one year.

Next, M. Olivier was banished for two years, by the sentence of the same law.

Like judgments have been pronounced against M. M. Chavannes, Juvet, and Fivas, of whom, the two former, were previously confined ten weeks in prison.

Two females also were banished by the judgment de premiere instant, of the tribunal of Orbe and Yverden, on the charge of similar meetings being held at their houses; one of whom, however, has been since acquitted at Lausanne, as it was proved that she lived with her mother, and consequently that it was at her house, and not at hers, that some friends, after dinner, read the bible together.

But it is not merely in the Canton de Vaud that these enormous instances of injustice have occurred: at Neufchatel, an act of arbitrary power has just been committed, almost incredible from its severity. An old law, long obsolete, has been discovered, which, it seems, was passed two or three hundred years back. An agriculturer has been made the first victim of its revived powers. He received into his house M. Juvet, one of the condemned ministers of the Canton de Vaud, and allowed him to administer the sacrament. For this crime he was thrown into prison for three months, and was then brought up in chains, and with a rope drawn tight round his neck, to receive sentence. Ten years banishment was the punishment pronounced; and that if he shall attempt to return before the expiration of this term, he is to be marked with a hot iron for the first offence, and for the second to be *hanged*. No passport was given him, so that he was left to be hunted about from place to place, like the most degraded criminal. This worthy man, whose name was Maguin, has a wife and three children, for whom he has now no means of procuring a support. [Wilson's Tour, 2d ed. page 325.]

These atrocities were practised by those who claim to be the only enlightened and liberal characters of our day--by Unitarians and Socinians--by men too, whose complaints respecting bigotry and intolerance, have been the burden of many a long article, expressly designed to represent orthodoxy as peculiarly relentless and cruel.

A large number of Swiss pastors have been driven into banishment, by the inquisitorial proceedings of those who style themselves the *liberal* party in Switzerland. Many of the exiles are now residing in different parts of France, mostly near the frontiers of their own country--others have found a home in different parts of Switzerland.

One of them is now in that place where the wicked cease from troubling--and another seems rapidly advancing to it. M. Juvet, who signed, with two other ministers, the letter to the "Council of State," having been banished from his own canton, sought an asylum in another canton: this was refused. He then retired to Ferney Voltaire, and pursued his labors. He was at that time weak from a pulmonary consumption; but he ventured on an excursion to L'Isle of Mantrichen, to visit those who were disposed to hear the word of God. "He was insulted, attacked and pursued by the populace, from town to town; and at Le Isle, where he arrived quite exhausted, and in profuse perspiration, he was thrown into a cold dungeon, with only a chair and some chopped straw, on which to pass the night. His friends were not permitted to give him either food, fire, or clothing, and in this state he was detained fifteen hours." For two months he was confined in the prison of Yverden, under circumstances of severe illness and medical attendance was denied him. After leaving the prison, he was presently arrested and expelled the commune. Under such accumulated sufferings, nature at length gave way: he slept in the Lord; and among his last prayers were petitions for his persecutors whether the magistrates or the mob.

Recent information from Geneva, and the other cantons of Switzerland, inform us that the spirit of persecution is still exhibited by the *liberal* party in that country. Those who adhere to the Helvetic Confession, and preach conformably to the doctrines of the creed of the established church, are called "Momiers," "enthusiasts," and other terms equally, unkind and unchristian. The *liberal*, or infidel party, do not confine themselves simply to reproaches. They disturb the places of public worship--they stone the people as they return from their devotions--they arraign them before civil tribunals for preaching Christ and him crucified--they impose fines upon them, subject them to imprisonment, banishment, and even death itself. All this is done too, in the 19th century, and by those who claim to be the only enlightened and liberal party on the continent.

CHAPTER XXII.

SKETCHES OF THE LIVES OF SOME OF THE MOST EMINENT REFORMERS.

It will not be inappropriate to devote a few pages of this work to a brief detail of the lives of some of those men who first stepped forward, regardless of the bigoted power which opposed all reformation, to stem the tide of papal corruption, and to seal the pure doctrines of the gospel with their blood. Among these, Great Britain has the honor of taking the lead, and first maintaining that freedom in religious controversy which astonished Europe, and demonstrated that political and religious liberty are equally the growth of that favored island. Among the earliest of these eminent persons was

John Wickliffe.

This celebrated reformer, denominated the Morning Star of the Reformation, was born about the year 1324, in the reign of Edward II. Of his extraction we have no certain account. His parents designing him for the church, sent him to Queen's College, Oxford, about that period founded by Robert Eaglesfield, confessor to queen Philippi. But not meeting with the advantages for study in that newly established house which he expected, he removed to Merton College, which was then esteemed one of the most learned societies in Europe.

The first thing which drew him into public notice, was his defence of the University against the begging friars, who about this time, from their settlement in Oxford in 1230, had been troublesome neighbours to the University. Feuds were continually fomented; the friars appealing to the pope, the scholars to the civil power; and sometimes one party, and sometimes the other, prevailed. The friars became very fond of a notion that Christ was a common beggar; that his disciples were beggars also; and that begging was of gospel institution. This doctrine they urged from the pulpit and wherever they had access.

Wickliffe had long held these religious friars in contempt for the laziness of their lives, and had now a fair opportunity of exposing them. He published a treatise against able beggary, in which he lashed the friars, and proved that they were not only a reproach to religion, but also to human society. The University began to consider him one of her first champions, and he was soon promoted to the mastership of Baliol College.

About this time, archbishop Islip founded Canterbury Hall, in Oxford, where he established a warden and eleven scholars. To this wardenship Wickliffe was elected by the archbishop, but upon his demise, he was displaced by his successor, Stephen Langham, bishop of Ely. As there was a degree of flagrant injustice in the affair, Wickliffe appealed to the pope, who subsequently gave it against him from the following cause: Edward the Third, then king of England, had withdrawn the tribute, which from the time of king John had been paid to the pope. The pope menaced; Edward called a parliament. The parliament resolved that king John had done an illegal thing, and given up the rights of the nation, and advised the king not to submit, whatever consequences might follow.

The clergy now began to write in favour of the pope, and a learned monk published a spirited and plausible treatise, which had many advocates. Wickliffe, irritated at seeing so bad a cause so well defended, opposed the monk, and did it in so masterly a way, that he was considered no longer as unanswerable. His suit at Rome was immediately determined against him; and nobody doubted but his opposition to the pope, at so critical a period, was the true cause of his being non-suited at Rome.

Wickliffe was afterward elected to the chair of the divinity professor: and now fully convinced of the errors of the Romish church, and the vileness of its monastic agents, he determined to expose them. In public lectures he lashed their vices and opposed their follies. He unfolded a variety of abuses covered by the darkness of superstition. At first he began to loosen the prejudices of the vulgar, and proceeded by slow advances; with the metaphysical disquisitions of the age, he mingled opinions in divinity apparently novel. The usurpations of the court of Rome was a favourite topic. On these he expatiated with all the keenness of argument, joined to logical reasoning. This soon procured him the clamour of the clergy, who, with the archbishop of Canterbury, deprived him of his office.

At this time, the administration of affairs was in the hands of the duke of Lancaster, well known by the name of John of Gaunt. This prince had very free notions of religion, and was at enmity with the clergy. The exactions of the court of Rome having become very burdensome, he determined to send the bishop of Bangor and Wickliffe to remonstrate against these abuses, and it was agreed that the pope should no longer dispose of any benifices belonging to the church of England. In this embassy, Wickliffe's observant mind penetrated into the constitution and policy of Rome, and he returned more strongly than ever determined to expose its avarice and ambition.

Having recovered his former situation, he inveighed, in his lectures, against the pope--his usurpation--his infallibility--his pride--his avarice--and his tyranny. He was the first who termed the pope Antichrist. From the pope, he would turn to the pomp, the luxury and trappings of the bishops, and compared them with the simplicity of primitive bishops. Their superstitions and deceptions were topics that he urged with energy of mind and logical precision.

From the patronage of the duke of Lancaster, Wickliffe received a good benefice; but he was no sooner settled in his parish, than his enemies and the bishops began to persecute him with renewed vigor. The duke of Lancaster was his friend in this persecution, and by his presence and that of Lord Percy, earl marshal of England, he so overawed the trial, that the whole ended in disorder.

After the death of Edward III. his grandson Richard II. succeeded, in the eleventh year of his age. The duke of Lancaster not obtaining to be the sole regent, as he expected, his power began to decline, and the enemies of Wickliffe, taking advantage of this circumstance, renewed their articles of accusation against him. Five bulls were despatched in consequence by the pope to the king and certain bishops, but the regency and the people manifested a spirit of contempt at the haughty proceedings of the pontiff, and the former at that time wanting money to oppose an expected invasion of the French, proposed to apply a large sum, collected for the use of the pope to that purpose. The question was submitted to the decision of Wickliffe. The bishops, however, supported by the papal authority, insisted upon bringing Wickliffe to trial, and he was actually undergoing examination at Lambeth, when, from the riotous behaviour of the populace without, and awed by the command of sir Lewis Clifford, a gentleman of the court, that they should not proceed to any definitive sentence, they terminated the whole affair in a prohibition to Wickliffe, not to preach those doctrines which were obnoxious to the pope; but this was laughed at by our reformer, who, going about barefoot, and in a long frieze gown, preached more vehemently than before.

In the year 1378, a contest arose between two popes, Urban VI. and Clement VII. which was the lawful pope, and true vicegerent of God. This was a favourable period for the exertion of Wickliffe's talents: he soon produced a tract against popery, which was eagerly read by all sorts of people.

About the end of the year, Wickliffe was seized with a violent disorder, which it was feared might prove fatal. The begging friars, accompanied by four of the most eminent citizens of Oxford, gained admittance to his bed-chamber, and begged of him to retract, for his soul's sake, the unjust things he had asserted of their order. Wickliffe surprised at the solemn message, raised himself in his bed, and with a stern countenance replied, "I shall not die, but live to declare the evil deeds of the friars."

When Wickliffe recovered, he set about a most important work, the translation of the bible into English. Before this work appeared, he published a tract, wherein he showed the necessity of it. The zeal of the bishops to suppress the scriptures, greatly promoted its sale, and they who were not able to purchase copies, procured transcripts of particular gospels or epistles. Afterward, when Lollardy increased, and the flames kindled, it was a common practice to fasten about the neck of the condemned heretic such of these scraps of scripture as were found in his possession, which generally shared his fate.

Immediately after this transaction, Wickliffe ventured a step further, and affected the doctrine of transubstantiation. This strange opinion was invented by Paschade Radbert, and asserted with amazing boldness. Wickliffe, in his lecture before the university of Oxford, 1381, attacked this doctrine, and published a treatise on the subject. Dr. Barton, at this time vice-chancellor of Oxford, calling together the heads of the university, condemned Wickliffe's doctrines as heretical, and threatened their author with excommunication. Wickliffe could now derive no support from the duke of Lancaster, and being cited to appear before his former adversary, William Courteney, now made archbishop of Canterbury, he sheltered himself under the plea, that, as a member of the university, he was exempt from episcopal jurisdiction. This plea was admitted, as the university were determined to support their member.

The court met at the appointed time, determined, at least to sit in judgment upon his opinions, and some they condemned as erroneous, others as heretical. The publication on this subject was immediately answered by Wickliffe, who had become a subject of the archbishop's determined malice. The king, solicited by the archbishop, granted a license to imprison the teacher of heresy, but the commons made the king revoke this act as illegal. The primate, however, obtained letters from the king, directing the head of the university of Oxford to search for all heresies and the books published by Wickliffe; in consequence of which order, the university became a scene of tumult. Wickliffe is supposed to have retired from the storm, into an obscure part of the kingdom. The seeds, however, were scattered, and Wickliffe's opinions were so prevalent, that it was said, if you met two persons upon the road, you might be sure that one was a Lollard. At this period, the disputes between the two popes continued. Urban published a bull, in which he earnestly called upon all who had any regard for religion, to exert themselves in its cause; and to take up arms against Clement and his adherents in defence of the holy see.

A war, in which the name of religion was so vilely prostituted, roused Wickliffe's inclination, even in his declining years. He took up his pen once more, and wrote against it with the greatest acrimony. He expostulated with the pope in a very free manner, and asks him boldly, "How he durst make the token of Christ on the cross (which is the token of peace, mercy and charity) a banner to lead us to slay christian men, for the love of two false priests, and to oppress Christendom worse than Christ and his apostles were oppressed by the Jews? When, said he, will the proud priest of Rome grant indulgences to mankind to live in peace and charity, as he now does to fight and slay one another?"

This severe piece drew upon him the resentment of Urban; and was likely to have involved him in greater troubles than he had before experienced, but providentially he was delivered out of their hands. He was struck with the palsy, and though he lived some time yet in such a way, that his enemies considered him as a person below their resentment. To the last he attended divine worship, and received the fatal stroke of his disorder in his church at Lutterworth, in the year 1384.

Martin Luther.

This illustrious German divine and reformer of the church, was the son of John Luther and Margaret Lindeman, and born at Isleben, a town of Saxony, in the county of Mansfield, November 10, 1483. His father's extraction and condition were originally but mean, and his occupation that of a miner: it is probable, however, that by his application and industry he improved the fortunes of his family, as he afterward became a magistrate of rank and dignity. Luther was early initiated into letters, and at the age of thirteen was sent to school at Madgeburg, and thence to Eysenach, in Thuringia, where he remained four years, producing the early indications of his future eminence.

In 1501 he was sent to the university of Erfurt, where he went through the usual courses of logic and philosophy. When twenty, he took a master's degree, and then lectured on Aristotle's physics, ethics, and other parts of philosophy. Afterward, at the instigation of his parents, he turned himself to the civil law, with a view of advancing himself to the bar, but was diverted from this pursuit by the following accident. Walking out into the fields one day, he was struck by lightning so as to fall to the ground, while a companion was killed by his side; and this affected him so sensibly, that, without communicating his purpose to any of his friends, he withdrew himself from the world, and retired into the order of the hermits of St. Augustine.

Here he employed himself in reading St. Augustine and the school men; but, in turning over the leaves of the library, he accidentally found a copy of the Latin Bible, which he had never seen before. This raised his curiosity to a high degree: he read it over very greedily, and was amazed to find what a small portion of the scriptures was rehearsed to the people. He made his profession in the monastery of Erfurt, after he had been a novice one year; and he took priest's orders, and celebrated his first mass in 1507. The year after, he was removed from the convent of Erfurt to the university of Wittemberg; for this university being just founded, nothing was thought more likely to bring it into immediate repute and credit, than the authority and presence of a man so celebrated, for his great parts and learning, as Luther. In 1512, seven convents of his order having a quarrel with their vicar-general, Luther was chosen to go to Rome to maintain their cause. At Rome he saw the pope and the court, and had an opportunity of observing also the manners of the clergy, whose hasty, superficial, and impious way of celebrating mass, he has severely noted. As soon as he had adjusted the dispute which was the business of his journey, he returned to Wittemberg, and was created doctor of divinity, at the expense of Frederic, elector of Saxony; who had often heard him preach, was perfectly acquainted with his merit, and reverenced him highly. He continued in the university of Wittemberg, where, as professor of divinity, he employed himself in the business of his calling. Here then he began in the most earnest manner to read lectures upon the sacred books: he explained the epistle to the Romans, and the Psalms, which he cleared up and illustrated in a manner so entirely new, and so different from what had been pursued by former commentators, that "there seemed, after a long and dark night, a new day to arise, in the judgment of all pious and prudent men." The better to qualify himself for the task he had undertaken, he applied himself attentively to the Greek and Hebrew languages; and in this manner was he employed, when the general indulgences were published in 1517. Leo X. who succeeded Julius II. in March, 1513, formed a design of building the magnificent church of St. Peter's at Rome, which was, indeed, begun by Julius, but still required very large sums to be finished. Leo, therefore, 1517 published general indulgences throughout all Europe, in favour of those who contribute any sum to the building of St. Peter's; and appointed persons in different countries to preach up these indulgences, and to receive money for them. These strange proceedings gave vast offence at Wittemberg, and particularly inflamed the pious zeal of Luther; who, being naturally warm and active, and in the present case unable to contain himself, was determined to declare against them at all adventures. Upon the eve of All-saints, therefore, in 1517, he publicly fixed up, at the church next to the castle of that town, a thesis upon indulgences; in the beginning of which, he challenged any one to oppose it either by writing or disputation. Luther's propositions about indulgences, were no sooner published, than Tetzel, the Dominican friar, and commissioner for selling them, maintained and published at Francfort, a thesis, containing a set of propositions directly contrary to them. He did more; he stirred up the clergy of his order against Luther; anathematized him from the pulpit, as a most damnable heretic; and burnt his thesis publicly at Francfort. Tetzel's thesis was also burnt, in return, by the Lutherans at Wittemburg; but Luther himself disowned having had any hand in that procedure. In 1518, Luther, though dissuaded from it by his friends, yet, to show obedience to authority, went to the monastery of St. Augustine, at Heidelberg, while the chapter was held; and here maintained, April 26, a dispute concerning "justification by faith," which Bucer, who was present at, took down in writing, and afterward communicated to Beatus Rhenanus, not without the highest commendations. In the meantime, the zeal of his adversaries grew every day more and more active against him; and he was at length accused to Leo X. as a heretic. As soon as he returned therefore from Heidelberg, he wrote a letter to that pope, in the most submissive terms; and sent him, at the same time, an explication of his propositions about indulgences. This letter is dated on Trinity-Sunday, 1518, and was accompanied with a protestation, wherein he declared, that "he did not pretend to advance or defend any thing contrary to the holy scriptures, or to the doctrine of the fathers, received and observed by the church of Rome, or to the canons and decretals of the popes: nevertheless, he thought he had the liberty either to approve or disapprove the opinions of St. Thomas, Bonaventure, and other school-men and canonists, which are not grounded upon any text."

The emperor Maximilian was equally solicitous with the pope about putting a stop to the propagation of Luther's opinions in Saxony; troublesome both to the church and empire. Maximilian, therefore, applied to Leo, in a letter dated August 5, 1518, and begged him to forbid, by his authority, these useless, rash, and dangerous disputes; assuring him also, that he would strictly execute in the empire whatever his holiness should enjoin. In the meantime Luther, as soon an he understood what was transacting about him at Rome, used all imaginable means to prevent his being carried thither, and to obtain a hearing of his cause in Germany. The elector was also against Luther's going to Rome, and desired of cardinal Cajetan, that he might be heard before him, as the pope's legate in Germany. Upon these addresses, the pope consented that the cause should be tried before cardinal Cajetan, to whom he had given power to decide it. Luther, therefore, set off immediately for Augsburg, and carried with him letters from the elector. He arrived here in October, 1518, and, upon an assurance of his safety, was admitted into the cardinal's presence. But Luther was soon convinced that he had more to fear from the cardinal's power, than from disputations of any kind; and, therefore, apprehensive of being seized, if he did not submit, withdrew from Augsburg upon the 20th. But, before his departure, he published a formal appeal to the pope, and finding himself protected by the elector, continued to teach the same doctrines at Wittemberg, and sent a challenge to all the inquisitors to come and dispute with him.

As to Luther, Miltitius, the pope's chamberlain, had orders to require the elector to oblige him to retract, or to deny him his protection; but things were not now to be carried with so high a hand, Luther's credit being too firmly established. Besides, the emperor Maximilian happened to die upon the 12th of this month, whose death greatly altered the face of affairs, and made the elector more able to determine Luther's fate. Miltitius thought it best, therefore, to try what could be done by fair and gentle means, and to that end came to some conference with Luther. During all these treaties, the doctrine of Luther spread, and prevailed greatly; and he himself received great encouragement at home and abroad. The Bohemians about this time sent him a book of the celebrated John Huss, who had fallen a martyr in the work of reformation; and also letters, in which they exhorted him to constancy and perseverance, owning, that the divinity which he taught was the pure, sound, and orthodox divinity. Many great and learned men had joined themselves to him. In 1519, he had a famous dispute at Leipsic with John Eccius. But this dispute ended at length like all others, the parties not the least nearer in opinion, but more to enmity with each other's persons. About the end of this year, Luther published a book, in which he contended for the communion being celebrated in both kinds; which was condemned by the bishop of Misnia, January 24, 1520. While Luther was labouring to excuse himself to the new emperor and the bishops of Germany, Eccius had gone to Rome, to solicit his condemnation; which, it may easily be conceived, was now become not difficult to be attained. Indeed the continual importunities of Luther's adversaries with Leo, caused him at length to publish a formal condemnation of him, and he did so accordingly, in a bull, dated June 15, 1520; this was carried into Germany, and published there by Eccius, who had solicited it at Rome; and who, together with Jerom Alexander, a person eminent for his learning and eloquence, was entrusted by the pope with the execution of it. In the meantime, Charles V. of Spain, after he had set things to rights in the Low Countries, went into Germany, and was crowned emperor, October the 21st, at Aix-la-Chapelle. The diet of Worms was held in the beginning of 1521; which ended at length in this single and peremptory declaration of Luther, that "unless he was convinced by texts of scripture or evident reason (for he did not think himself obliged to submit to the pope or his councils,) he neither could nor would retract any thing, because it was not lawful for him to act against his conscience." Before the diet of Worms was dissolved, Charles V. caused an edict to be drawn up, which was dated the 8th of May, and decreed that Martin Luther be, agreeably to the sentence of the pope, henceforward looked upon as a member separated from the church, a schismatic, and an obstinate and notorious heretic. While the bull of Leo X. executed by Charles V. was thundering throughout the empire, Luther was safely shut up in the castle of Wittemberg; but weary at length of his retirement, he appeared publickly again at Wittemberg, March 6, 1522, after he had been absent about ten months. Luther now made open war with the pope and bishops; and, that he might make the people despise their authority as much as possible, he wrote one book against the pope's bull, and another against the order falsely called "the order of bishops." He published also, a translation of the "New Testament" in the German tongue, which was afterward corrected by himself and Melancthon. Affairs were now in great confusion in Germany; and they were not less so in Italy, for a quarrel arose between the pope and the emperor, during which Rome was twice taken, and the pope imprisoned. While the princes were thus employed in quarrelling with each other, Luther persisted in carrying on the work of the reformation, as well by opposing the papists, as by combating the Anabaptists and other fanatical sects; which, having taken the advantage of his contest with the church of Rome, had sprung up and established themselves in several places.

In 1527, Luther was suddenly seized with a coagulation of the blood about the heart, which had like to have put an end to his life. The troubles of Germany being not likely to have any end, the emperor was forced to call a diet at Spires, in 1529, to require the assistance of the princes of the empire against the Turks. Fourteen cities, viz. Stratsburg, Nuremberg, Ulm, Constance, Retlingen, Windsheim, Memmingen, Lindow, Kempten, Hailbron, Isny, Weissemburg, Nortlingen, S. Gal, joined against the decree of the diet protestation, which was put into writing, and published the 19th of April, 1529. This was the famous protestation, which gave the name of Protestants to the reformers in Germany.

After this, the protestant princes laboured to make a firm league and enjoined the elector of Saxony and his allies to approve of what the diet had done; but the deputies drew up an appeal, and the protestants afterwards presented an apology for their "Confession"--that famous confession which was drawn up by the temperate Melancthon, as also the apology. These were signed by a variety of princes, and Luther had now nothing else to do, but to sit down and contemplate the mighty work he had finished: for that a single monk should be able to give the church of Rome so rude a shock, that there needed but such another entirely to overthrow it, may be well esteemed a mighty work.

In 1533, Luther wrote a consolatory epistle to the citizens of Oschatz, who had suffered some hardships for adhering to the Augsburg confession of faith: and in 1534, the Bible translated by him into German was first printed, as the old privilege, dated at Bibliopolis, under the elector's own hand, shows; and it was published in the year after. He also published this year a book "against masses and the consecration of priests." In February, 1537, an assembly was held at Smalkald about matters of religion, to which Luther and Melancthon were called. At this meeting Luther was seized with so grievous an illness, that there was no hope of his recovery. As he was carried along he made his will, in which he bequeathed his detestation of popery to his friends and brethren. In this manner was he employed till his death, which happened in 1546. That year, accompanied by Melancthon, he paid a visit to his own country, which he had not seen for many years, and returned again in safety. But soon after, he was called thither again by the earls of Mansfelt, to compose some differences which had arisen about their boundaries, where he was received by 100 horsemen, or more, and conducted in a very honourable manner; but was at the same time so very ill, that it was feared he would die. He said, that these fits of sickness often came upon him, when he had any great business to undertake; of this, however, he did not recover, but died February 18, in his 63d year. A little before he expired, he admonished those that were about him to pray to God for the propagation of the gospel; "because," said he, "the council of Trent, which had sat once or twice, and the pope, will devise strange things against it." Soon after, his body was put into a leaden coffin, and carried with funeral pomp to the church at Iselbein, when Dr. Jonas preached a sermon upon the occasion. The earls of Mansfelt desired that his body should be interred in their territories; but the elector of Saxony insisted upon his being brought back to Wittemberg, which was accordingly done; and there he was buried with the greatest pomp that perhaps ever happened to any private man. Princes, earls, nobles, and students without number, attended the procession of this extraordinary reformer; and Melancthon made his funeral oration.

We will close this account of the great founder of the reformation, by subjoining a few opinions, which have been passed upon him, by both papists and Protestants. "Luther," says Father Simon, "was the first Protestant who ventured to translate the Bible into the vulgar tongue from the Hebrew text, although he understood Hebrew but very indifferently. As he was of a free and bold spirit, he accuses St Jerom of ignorance in the Hebrew tongue; but he had more reason to accuse himself of this fault, and for having so precipitately undertaken a work of this nature, which required more time than he employed about it. There is nothing great or learned in his commentaries upon the Bible; every thing low and mean: and though he had studied divinity, he has rather composed a rhapsody of theological questions, than a commentary upon the scripture text: to which we may add, that he wanted understanding, and usually followed his senses instead of his reason."

This is the language of those in the church of Rome who speak of Luther with any degree of moderation; for the generality allow him neither parts, nor learning, nor any attainment intellectual or moral. But let us leave these impotent railers, and attend a little to more equitable judges. "Luther," says Wharton, in his appendix to Cave's Historia Literaria, "was a man of prodigious sagacity and acuteness, very warm, and formed for great undertakings; being a man, if ever there was one, whom nothing could daunt or intimidate. When the cause of religion was concerned, he never regarded whose love he was likely to gain, or whose displeasure to incur." He is also highly spoken of by Atterbury and others.

John Calvin.

This reformer was born at Noyon in Picardy, July 10, 1409. He was instructed in grammar learning at Paris under Maturinus Corderius, and studied philosophy in the college of Montaign under a Spanish professor. His father, who discovered many marks of his early piety, particularly in his reprehensions of the vices of his companions, designed him at first for the church, and got him presented, May 21, 1521, to the chapel of Notre Dame de la Gesine, in the church of Noyon. In 1527 he was presented to the rectory of Marieville, which he exchanged in 1529 for the rectory of Pont l'Eveque, near Noyon. His father afterward changed his resolution, and would have him study law; to which Calvin, who, by reading the scriptures, had conceived a dislike to the superstitions of popery, readily consented, and resigned the chapel of Gesine and the rectory of Pont l'Eveque, in 1534. He made a great progress in that science, and improved no less in the knowledge of divinity by his private studies. At Bourges he applied to the Greek tongue, under the direction of professor Wolmar. His father's death having called him back to Noyon, he stayed there a short time, and then went to Paris, where a speech of Nicholas Cop, rector of the university of Paris, of which Calvin furnished the materials, having greatly displeased the Sarbonne and the parliament, gave rise to a persecution against the protestants, and Calvin, who narrowly escaped being taken in the college of Forteret, was forced to retire to Xaintonge, after having had the honour to be introduced to the queen of Navarre, who had raised this first storm against the protestants. Calvin returned to Paris in 1534. This year the reformed met with severe treatment, which determined him to leave France, after publishing a treatise against those who believe that departed souls are in a kind of sleep. He retired to Basil, where he studied Hebrew: at this time he published his Institutions of the Christian religion; a work well adapted to spread his fame, though he himself was desirous of living in obscurity. It is dedicated to the French king, Francis I. Calvin next wrote an apology for the protestants who were burnt for their religion in France. After the publication of this work, Calvin went to Italy to pay a visit to the duchess of Ferrara, a lady of eminent piety, by whom he was very kindly received.

From Italy he came back to France, and having settled his private affairs, he proposed to go to Strasbourg or Basil, in company with his sole surviving brother, Antony Calvin; but as the roads were not safe on account of the war, except through the duke of Savoy's territories, he chose that road. "This was a particular direction of Providence," says Bayle; "it was his destiny that he should settle at Geneva, and when he was wholly intent upon going farther, he found himself detained by an order from heaven, if I may so speak." At Geneva, Calvin therefore was obliged to comply with the choice which the consistory and magistrates made of him, with the consent of the people, to be one of their ministers, and professor of divinity. He wanted to undertake only this last office, and not the other; but in the end he was obliged to take both upon him, in August, 1536. The year following, he made all the people declare, upon oath, their assent to the confession of faith, which contained a renunciation of popery. He next intimated, that he could not submit to a regulation which the canton of Berne had lately made. Whereupon the syndics of Geneva, summoned an assembly of the people; and it was ordered that Calvin, Farel, and another minister, should leave the town in a few days, for refusing to administer the sacrament.

Calvin retired to Strasbourg, and established a French church in that city, of which he was the first minister: he was also appointed to be professor of divinity there. Meanwhile the people of Geneva entreated him so earnestly to return to them, that at last he consented and arrived September 13, 1541, to the great satisfaction both of the people and the magistrates; and the first thing he did, after his arrival, was to establish a form of church discipline, and a consistorial jurisdiction, invested with power of inflicting censures and canonical punishments, as far as excommunication, inclusively.

Agency of Calvin in the death of Michael Servetus.

It has long been the delight of both infidels and some professed christians, when they wish to bring odium upon the opinions of Calvin, to refer to his agency in the death of Michael Servetus. This action is used on all occasions by those who have been unable to overthrow his opinions, as a conclusive argument against his whole system. Calvin burnt Servetus!--Calvin burnt Servetus! is good proof with a certain class of reasoners, that the doctrine of the Trinity is not true--that divine sovereignty is anti-scriptural,--and christianity a cheat. We have no wish to palliate any act of Calvin's which is manifestly wrong. All his proceedings, in relation to the unhappy affair of Servetus, we think, cannot be defended. Still it should be remembered that the true principles of religious toleration were very little understood in the time of Calvin. All the other reformers then living, approved of Calvin's conduct. Even the gentle and amiable Melancthon expressed himself in relation to this affair, in the following manner. In a letter addressed to Bullinger, he says, "I have read your statement respecting the blasphemy of Servetus, and praise your piety and judgment; and am persuaded that the Council of Geneva has done right in putting to death this obstinate man, who would never have ceased his blasphemies. I am astonished, that any one can be found to disapprove of this proceeding." Farel expressly says, that "Servetus deserved a capital punishment." Bucer did not hesitate to declare, that "Servetus deserved something worse than death." The truth is, although Calvin had some hand in the arrest and imprisonment of Servetus, he was unwilling that he should be burnt at all. "I desire," says he, "that the severity of the punishment should be remitted." "We endeavoured to commute the kind of death, but in vain." "By wishing to mitigate the severity of the punishment," says Farel to Calvin, "you discharge the office of a friend towards your greatest enemy." "That Calvin was the instigator of the magistrates that Servetus might be burned," says Turritine, "historians neither any where affirm, nor does it appear from any considerations. Nay, it is certain, that he, with the college of pastors, dissuaded from that kind of punishment."

It has been often asserted, that Calvin possessed so much influence with the magistrates of Geneva, that he might have obtained the release of Servetus, had he not been desirous of his destruction. This however, is not true. So far from it, that Calvin was himself once banished from Geneva, by these very magistrates, and often opposed their arbitrary measures in vain. So little desirous was Calvin of procuring the death of Servetus, that he warned him of his danger and suffered him to remain several weeks at Geneva, before he was arrested. But his language, which was then accounted blasphemous, was the cause of his imprisonment. When in prison, Calvin visited him, and used every argument to persuade him to retract his horrible blasphemies, without reference to his peculiar sentiments. This was the extent of Calvin's agency in this unhappy affair.

It cannot, however, be denied, that in this instance, Calvin acted contrary to the benignant spirit of the gospel. It is better to drop a tear over the inconsistency of human nature, and to bewail those infirmities which cannot be justified. He declares he acted conscientiously, and publicly justified the act. Cranmer acted the same part towards the poor Anabaptists in the reign of Edward VI. This doctrine they had learned at Rome, and it is certain, that, with a very few exceptions, it was at this time the opinion of all parties. The author of the Memoirs of Literature says, "If the religion of protestants depended on the doctrine and conduct of the reformers, he should take care how he published his account of Servetus; but as the protestant religion is entirely founded on Holy Scripture, so the defaults of the reformers ought not to have any ill influence on the reformation. The doctrine of non-toleration, which obtained to the sixteenth century, among some protestants, was that pernicious error which they had imbibed in the Church of Rome; and I believe, I can say, without doing any injury to that church, that she is, in a great measure, answerable for the execution of Servetus. If the Roman catholics had never put any person to death for the sake of religion, I dare say that Servetus had never been condemned to die in any protestant city. Let us remember, that Calvin, and all the magistrates of Geneva, in the year 1553, were born and bred up in the church of Rome: this is the best apology that can be made for them."--*Biographia Evangelica*, vol. II. p. 42.

The apostles John and James would have called down fire from heaven; Calvin and Cranmer kindled it on earth. This, however, is the only fault alleged against Calvin; but "Let him that is without sin cast the first stone."

"It ought, however," says a sensible writer, "to be acknowledged that persecution for religious principles was not at that time peculiar to any party of christians, but common to all, whenever they were invested with civil power." It was a detestable error; but it was the error of the age. They looked upon heresy in the same light as we look upon those crimes which are inimical to the peace of civil society; and, accordingly, proceeded to punish heretics by the sword of the civil magistrate. If Socinians did not persecute their adversaries so much as Trinitarians, it was because they were not equally invested with the power of doing so. Mr. Lindsay acknowledges, that Faustus Socinus himself was not free from persecution in the case of Francis David, superintendent of the Unitarian churches in Transylvania. David had disputed with Socinus on the invocation of Christ, and died in prison in consequence of his opinion, and some offence taken at his supposed indiscreet propagation of it from the pulpit. "I wish I could say," adds Mr. Lindsay, "that Socinus, or his friend Blandrata, had done all in their power to prevent his commitment, or procure his release afterwards." The difference between Socinus and David was very slight. They both held Christ to be a mere man. The former, however, was for praying to him; which the latter, with much greater consistency, disapproved. Considering this, the persecution to which Socinus was accessary was as great as that of Calvin; and there is no reason to think, but that if David had differed as much from Socinus, as Servetus did from Calvin, and if the civil magistrates had been for burning him, Socinus would have concurred with them. To this it might be added, that the conduct of Socinus was marked with disingenuity: in that he considered the opinion of David in no very heinous point of light; but was afraid of increasing the odium under which he and his party already lay, among other Christian churches.

It was the opinion, that erroneous religious principles are punishable by the civil magistrate, that did the mischief, whether at Geneva, in Transylvania, or in Britain; and to this, rather than to Trinitarianism, or Unitarianism, it ought to be imputed.

The inflexible rigour with which Calvin asserted, on all occasions, the rights of his consistory, procured him many enemies: but nothing daunted him; and one would hardly believe, if there were not unquestionable proofs of it, that, amidst all the commotions at home, he could take so much care as he did of the churches abroad, in France, Germany, England, and Poland, and write so many books and letters. He did more by his pen than his presence; nevertheless on some occasions, he acted in person, particularly at Frankfort, in 1556, whither he went to put an end to the disputes which divided the French church in that city. He was always employed, having almost constantly his pen in his hand, even when sickness confined him to his bed; and he continued the discharge of all those duties, which his zeal for the general good of the churches imposed on him, till the day of his death, May 27, 1564. He was a man whom God had endowed with very eminent talents; a clear understanding, a solid judgment, and a happy memory: he was a judicious, elegant, and indefatigable writer, and possessed of very extensive learning and a great zeal for truth. Joseph Scaliger, who was not lavish of his praise, could not forbear admiring Calvin; none of the commentators, he said, had so well hit the sense of the prophets; and he particularly commended him for not attempting to give a comment on the Revelation. We understand from Guy Patin, that many of the Roman catholics would do justice to Calvin's merit, if they dared to speak their minds. It must excite a laugh at those who have been so stupid as to accuse him of being a lover of wine, good cheer, company, money, &c. Artful slanderers would have owned that he was sober by constitution, and that he was not solicitous to heap up riches.

That a men who had acquired so great a reputation and such an authority, should yet have had but a salary of 100 crowns, and refuse to accept more; and after living 55 years with the utmost frugality, should leave but 300 crowns to his heirs, including the value of his library, which sold very dear, is something so heroical, that one must have lost all feeling not to admire. When Calvin took his leave of Strasbourg, to return to Geneva, they wanted to continue to him the privileges of a freeman of their town, and the revenues of a prebend, which had been assigned to him; the former he accepted, but absolutely refused the other. He carried one of the brothers with him to Geneva, but he never took any pains to get him preferred to an honourable post, as any other possessed of his credit would have done. He took care indeed of the honour of his brother's family, by getting him freed from an adultress, and obtaining leave for him to marry again; but even his enemies relate that he made him learn the trade of a bookbinder, which he followed all his life after.

Calvin as a friend of civil liberty.

The Rev. Dr. Wisner, in his late discourse at Plymouth, on the anniversary of the landing of the pilgrims, makes the following assertion:--"Much as the name of Calvin has been scoffed at and loaded with reproach by many sons of freedom, there is not an historical proposition more susceptible of complete demonstration than this, that no man has lived to whom the world is under greater obligations for the freedom it now enjoys, than John Calvin." In a note appended to the sermon, Dr. Wisner gives the following testimonies, from history, of the truth of this proposition--testimonies which deserve the more attention, as they come from Calvin's opposers. We copy the note from the Boston Recorder.

"It may not be unacceptable to the reader, to add a few particulars in confirmation of the statement in reference to the influence of Calvin in forming the opinions and character of the Puritans, and thus contributing to the discovery and establishment of the principles of religious and civil liberty.

"The peculiarities of the religious doctrines of the Puritans had an important influence in producing in them determined and persevering resistance to arbitrary power, and a successful vindication of their religious and political rights. The fact is sufficiently illustrated in the quotation in the sermon from the Edinburg Review. It is admitted by Hume, and by all, whatever their religious opinions, who have thoroughly investigated the springs of action in those discoverers, and founders of religious and civil freedom. But the doctrinal views of the Puritans were derived from Calvin.

"Their disapprobation of the rites and ceremonies enjoined by the English government was a prominent means of leading them to the discovery, and stimulating to the successful vindication of the principles of religious and civil liberty. And that disapprobation may be directly traced to the influence of Calvin. With him many of the leading Puritan divines studied theology, and were taught the importance of laying aside the whole mass of popish additions to the simplicity of apostolic worship. When the difficulties arose among the exiles at Frankfort, in Mary's reign, about the use of King Edward's Liturgy, they asked advice of Calvin, "who having perused the English Liturgy, took notice, 'that there were many tolerable weaknesses in it, which, because at first they could not be amended, were to be suffered; but that it behooved the learned, grave, and godly ministers of Christ to enterprise farther, and to set up something more filed from rust, and purer.' 'If religion,' says he 'had flourished till this day in England, many of these things would have been corrected. But since the reformation is overthrown and a church is to be set up in another place where you are at liberty to establish what order is most for edification, I cannot tell what they mean, who are so fond of the leavings of popish dregs.'" When the conformist party had triumphed at Frankfort, they "wrote to Mr. Calvin to countenance their proceedings; which that great divine could not do; but after a modest excuse for intermeddling in their affairs, told them, that, 'in his opinion, they were too much addicted to the English ceremonies; nor could he see to what purpose it was to burden the church with such hurtful and offensive things, when there was liberty to have simple and more pure order.'" The puritan part of the exiles retired to Geneva, and there prepared and published a service book, in the dedication of which they say, that "they had set up such an order as, in the judgment of Mr. Calvin and other learned divines, was most agreeable to scripture, and the best reformed churches. And when, subsequently, the important step was taken, by several puritans in and about London, of breaking off from the established churches and setting up a separate congregation, they adopted for use, (as they say in their 'agreement' thus to separate) a book and order of preaching, administration of sacraments and discipline, that the great Mr. Calvin had approved of, and which was free from the superstitions of the English service."--*Neal, i. 152, 153, 154, 155, 252.*

But most important of all, in its influence on religious and civil liberty, was the attachment of the puritans to a popular church government. And of the origin of this system, we have the following account from 'the judicious Hooker,' prefixed to his famous work on Ecclesiastical Polity, written expressly against it. "A founder it had, whom, for mine own part, I think incomparably the wisest man that ever the French (protestant) church, did enjoy, since the hour it enjoyed him. His bringing up was in the civil law. Divine knowledge he gathered, not by hearing or reading, so much as by teaching others. For thousands were debtors to him, as touching knowledge in that kind, yet he to none, but only to God, the author of that most blessed fountain the Book of Life, and of the admirable dexterity of wit, together with the helps of other learning, which were his guides. Two things of principal moment there are, which have deservedly procured him honour throughout the world; the one, his exceeding pains in composing the institutions of the christian religion; this other, his no less industrious travels for the exposition of holy scripture, according to the same institutions. In which two things, whosoever they were that after him bestowed their labour, he gained the advantage, of prejudice against them if they gainsayed, and of glory above them if they consented. Of what account the Master of Sentences was in the church of Rome, the same, and more, among the preachers of the reformed churches, Calvin had purchased; so that the perfectest divines were judged they who were skilfulest in Calvin's writings; his books being almost the very canon to judge both doctrine and discipline by."

"These statements are confirmed by abundant testimony from writers of authority who had no good opinion of Calvin or his principles. Says Hume, (History of England, iii. 57,) "These disputes [about ceremonies, &c.] which had been started during the reign of Edward, were carried abroad by the protestants who fled from the persecutions of Mary; and as the zeal of these men had received an increase from the pious zeal of their enemies, they were generally inclined to carry their opposition to the utmost extremity against the practices of the church of Rome. Their communication with Calvin, and the other reformers who followed the discipline and worship of Geneva, confirmed them in this obstinate reluctance; and though some of the refugees, particularly those who were established at Frankfort, still adhered to king Edward's Liturgy, the prevailing spirit carried these confessors to seek a still further reformation."

"The celebrated Dean Swift, in a sermon preached on what tories and high churchmen in England, have styled, "the martyrdom of king Charles I." makes the following statements:--Upon the cruel persecution raised against the protestants under queen Mary, among great numbers who fled the kingdom to seek for shelter, several went and resided at Geneva, which is a commonwealth, governed without a king, where the religion contrived by Calvin is without the order of bishops. When the protestant faith was restored by queen Elizabeth, those who fled to Geneva returned, among the rest, home to England, and were grown so fond of the government and religion of the place they had left, that they used all possible endeavours to introduce both into their own country; at the same time continually preaching and railing against ceremonies and distinct habits of the clergy, taxing whatever they disliked as a remnant of popery; and continued exceedingly troublesome to the church and state, under that great queen, as well as her successor, king James I. These people called themselves puritans, as pretending to a purer faith than those of the established church. And these were the founders of our dissenters. They did not think it sufficient to leave all the errors of popery; but threw off many laudable and edifying institutions of the primitive church, and at last even the government of bishops, which, having been ordained by the apostles themselves, had continued without interruption, in all christian churches, for above fifteen hundred years. And all this they did, not because those things were evil, but because they were kept by the papists. From hence they proceeded, by degrees, to quarrel with the kingly government, because, as I have already said, the city of Geneva, to which their fathers had flown for refuge, was a commonwealth, or government of the people." Having thus stated the foundation and principles of puritanism, the Dean proceeds with an account of its growth till the breaking out of the civil war, and concludes the narrative as follows: "That odious parliament had early turned the bishops out of the House of Lords, in a few years after they murdered their king; then immediately abolished the whole House of Lords; and so, at last obtained their wishes of having a government of the people, and a new religion, both after the manner of Geneva, without a king, a bishop, or a nobleman; and this they blasphemously called, 'The kingdom of Christ and His Saints.'"

"In the same way, Dryden traced the origin of republicanism in England, as appears from his political poem called the ***Hind and the Panther***; in which he characterizes the Romish church under the name of the Hind, the English church under that of the Panther, and the Presbyterian under that of the Wolf. In the following extract, the 'kennel' means the city of Geneva; the 'puddle' its lake, and the 'wall' its rampart.

>"The last of all the litter scap'd by chance,
>And from Geneva first invested France.
>Some authors thus his pedigree will trace;
>But others write him of an upstart race,
>Because of Wickliffe's brood no mark he brings
>***But his innate antipathy to kings.***

>*   *   *   *   *

>What though your native kennel still be small,
>Bounded betwixt a puddle and a wall?
>Yet your victorious colonies are sent,
>Where the north ocean girds the continent.
>Quicken'd with fire below, your monster's breed,
>In fenny Holland, and in fruitful Tweed;
>And like the first, the last effects to be
>Drawn to the dregs of a ***democracy***.

>*   *   *   *   *

> But as the poisons of the deadliest kind
> Are to their own unhappy coasts confined,
> So Presbyt'ry and pestilential zeal,
> *Can only flourish in a* COMMONWEAL."

The Life of the Rev. John Fox.

John Fox, was born at Boston, in Lincolnshire, in 1517, where his parents are stated to have lived in respectable circumstances. He was deprived of his father at an early age; and notwithstanding his mother soon married again, he still remained under the parental roof. From an early display of talents and inclination to learning, his friends were induced to send him to Oxford, in order to cultivate and bring them to maturity. During his residence at this place, he was distinguished for the excellence and acuteness of his intellect, which was improved by the emulation of his fellow-collegians, united to an indefatigable zeal and industry on his part. These qualities soon gained him the admiration of all; and as a reward for his exertions and amiable conduct, he was chosen fellow of Magdalen college; which was accounted a great honour in the university, and seldom bestowed unless in cases of great distinction. It appears that the first display of his genius was in poetry; and that he composed some Latin comedies, which are still extant. But he soon directed his thoughts to a more serious subject, the study of the sacred scriptures: to divinity, indeed, he applied himself with more fervency than circumspection, and discovered his partiality to the reformation, which had then commenced, before he was known to its supporters, or to those who protected them; a circumstance which proved to him the source of his first troubles.

He is said to have often affirmed, that the first matter which occasioned his search into the popish doctrine, was, that he saw divers things, most repugnant in their nature to one another, forced upon men at the same time; upon this foundation his resolution and intended obedience to that church were somewhat shaken, and by degrees a dislike to the rest took place.

His first care was to look into both the ancient and modern history of the church; to ascertain its beginning and progress; to consider the causes of all those controversies which in the meantime had sprung up, and diligently to weigh their effects, solidity, infirmities, &c.

Before he had attained his thirtieth year, he had studied the Greek and Latin fathers, and other learned authors, the transactions of the councils, and decrees of the consistories, and had acquired a very competent skill in the Hebrew language. In these occupations, he frequently spent a considerable part, or even the whole of the night, and in order to unbend his mind after such incessant study, he would resort to a grove near the college, a place much frequented by the students in the evening, on account of its sequestered gloominess. In these solitary walks, he has been heard to ejaculate heavy sobs and sighs, and with tears to pour forth his prayers to God. These nightly retirements, in the sequel, gave rise to the first suspicion of his alienation from the church of Rome. Being pressed for an explanation of this alteration in his conduct, he scorned to call in fiction to his excuse; he stated his opinions; and was, by the sentence of the college ***convicted, condemned as a heretic, and expelled***.

His friends, upon the report of this circumstance, were highly offended, and especially his father-in-law, who was now grown altogether implacable, either through a real hatred conceived against him for this cause, or pretending himself aggrieved, that he might now, with more show of justice, or at least with more security, withhold from Mr. Fox his paternal estate; for he knew it could not be safe for one publicly hated, and in danger of the law, to seek a remedy for his injustice.

When he was thus forsaken by his own friends, a refuge offered itself in the house of Sir Thomas Lucy, of Warwickshire, by whom he was sent for to instruct his children. In this house he afterwards married. But the fear of the popish inquisitors hastened his departure thence; as they were not contented to pursue public offences, but began also to dive into the secrets of private families. He now began to consider what was best to be done to free himself from further inconvenience, and resolved either to go to his wife's father or to his father in-law.

His wife's father was a citizen of Coventry, whose heart was not alienated from him, and he was more likely to be well entreated, for his daughter's sake. He resolved first to go to him; and, in the meanwhile, by letters, to try whether his father-in-law would receive him or not. This he accordingly did, and he received for answer, "that it seemed to him a hard condition to take one into his house whom he knew to be guilty and condemned for a capital offence; neither was he ignorant what hazard he should undergo in so doing; he would, however, show himself a kinsman, and neglect his own danger." If he would alter his mind, he might come, on condition to stay as long as he himself desired; but if he could not be persuaded to that, he must content himself with a shorter stay, and not bring him and his mother into danger.

No condition was to be refused; besides, he was secretly advised by his mother to come, and not to fear his father-in-law's severity; "for that, perchance, it was needful to write as he did, but when occasion should be offered, he would make recompense for his words with his actions." In fact he was better received by both of them than he had hoped for.

By these means he kept himself concealed for some time, and afterwards made a journey to London, in the latter part of the reign of Henry, VIII. Here, being unknown, he was in much distress, and was even reduced to the danger of being starved to death, had not Providence interfered in his favour in the following manner:

One day as Mr. Fox was sitting in St. Paul's church, exhausted with long fasting, a stranger took a seat by his side, and courteously saluted him, thrust a sum of money into his hand, and bade him cheer up his spirits; at the same time informing him, that in a few days new prospects would present themselves for his future subsistence. Who this stranger was, he could never learn, but at the end of three days he received an invitation from the dutchess of Richmond to undertake the tuition of the children of the earl of Surry who, together with his father, the duke of Norfolk, was imprisoned in the Tower, by the jealousy and ingratitude of the king. The children thus confided to his care were, Thomas, who succeeded to the dukedom; Henry, afterwards earl of Northampton; and Jane who became countess to Westmoreland. In the performance of his duties, he fully satisfied the expectations of the dutchess, their aunt.

These halcyon days continued during the latter part of the reign of Henry VIII. and the five years of the reign of Edward VI. till Mary came to the crown, who, soon after her accession, gave all power into the hands of the papists.

At this time Mr. Fox, who was still under the protection of his noble pupil, the duke, began to excite the envy and hatred of many, particularly Dr. Gardiner, then bishop of Winchester, who in the sequel became his most violent enemy.

Mr. Fox, aware of this, and seeing the dreadful persecutions then commencing, began to think of quitting the kingdom. As soon as the duke knew his intention, he endeavoured to persuade him to remain; and his arguments were so powerful, and given with so much sincerity, that he gave up the thought of abandoning his asylum for the present.

At that time the bishop of Winchester was very intimate with the duke (by the patronage of whose family he had risen to the dignity he then enjoyed,) and frequently waited on him to present his service when he several times requested that he might see his old tutor. At first the duke denied his request, at one time alleging his absence, at another, indisposition. At length it happened that Mr. Fox, not knowing the bishop was in the house, entered the room where the duke and he were in discourse; and seeing the bishop, withdrew. Gardiner asked who that was; the duke answered, "his physician, who was somewhat uncourtly, as being new come from the university." "I like his countenance and aspect very well," replied the bishop "and when occasion offers, I will send for him." The duke understood that speech as the messenger of some approaching danger; and now himself thought it high time for Mr. Fox to quit the city, and even the country. He accordingly caused every thing necessary for his flight to be provided in silence, by sending one of his servants to Ipswich to hire a bark, and prepare all the requisites for his departure. He also fixed on the house of one of his servants, who was a farmer, where he might lodge till the wind became favourable; and every thing being in readiness, Mr. Fox took leave of his noble patron, and with his wife, who was pregnant at the time, secretly departed for the ship.

The vessel was scarcely under sail, when a most violent storm came on, which lasted all day and night, and the next day drove them back to the port from which they had departed. During the time that the vessel had been at sea, an officer, despatched by the bishop of Winchester, had broken open the house of the farmer with a warrant to apprehend Mr. Fox wherever he might be found, and bring him back to the city. On hearing this news he hired a horse, under the pretence of leaving the town immediately; but secretly returned the same night, and agreed with the captain of the vessel to sail for any place as soon as the wind should shift, only desiring him to proceed, and not to doubt that God would prosper his undertaking. The mariner suffered himself to be persuaded, and within two days landed his passengers in safety at Nieuport.

After spending a few days in that place, Mr. Fox set out for Basle, where he found a number of English refugees, who had quitted their country to avoid the cruelty of the persecutors, with these he associated, and began to write his "History of the Acts and Monuments of the Church," which was first published in Latin at Basle, and shortly after in English.

In the meantime the reformed religion began again to flourish in England, and the popish faction much to decline, by the death of Queen Mary; which induced the greater number of the protestant exiles to return to their native country.

Among others, on the accession of Elizabeth to the throne, Mr. Fox returned to England; where, on his arrival, he found a faithful and active friend in his late pupil, the duke of Norfolk, till death deprived him of his benefactor: after which event, Mr. Fox inherited a pension bequeathed to him by the duke, and ratified by his son, the earl of Suffolk.

Nor did the good man's successes stop here. On being recommended to the queen by her secretary of state, the great Cecil, her majesty granted him the prebendary of Shipton, in the cathedral of Salisbury, which was in a manner forced upon him; for it was with difficulty that he could be persuaded to accept it.

On his resettlement in England, he employed himself in revising and enlarging his admirable Martyrology. With prodigious pains and constant study he completed that celebrated work in eleven years. For the sake of greater correctness, he wrote every line of this vast book with his own hand, and transcribed all the records and papers himself. But, in consequence of such excessive toil, leaving no part of his time free from study, nor affording himself either the repose or recreation which nature required, his health was so reduced, and his person became so emaciated and altered, that such of his friends and relations as only conversed with him occasionally, could scarcely recognise his person. Yet, though he grew daily more exhausted, he proceeded in his studies as briskly as ever, nor would he be persuaded to diminish his accustomed labours. The papists, forseeing how detrimental his history of their errors and cruelties would prove to their cause, had recourse to every artifice to lessen the reputation of his work; but their malice was of signal service, both to Mr. Fox himself, and to the church of God at large, as it eventually made his book more intrinsically valuable, by inducing him to weigh, with the most scrupulous attention, the certainty of the facts which he recorded, and the validity of the authorities from which he drew his information.

But while he was thus indefatigably employed in promoting the cause of truth, he did not neglect the other duties of his station; he was charitable, humane, and attentive to the wants, both spiritual and temporal, of his neighbours. With the view of being more extensively useful, although he had no desire to cultivate the acquaintance of the rich and great on his own account, he did not decline the friendship of those in a higher rank who proffered it, and never failed to employ his influence with them in behalf of the poor and needy. In consequence of his well known probity and charity, he was frequently presented with sums of money by persons possessed of wealth, which he accepted and distributed among those who were distressed. He would also occasionally attend the table of his friends, not so much for the sake of pleasure, as from civility, and to convince them that his absence was not occasioned by a fear of being exposed to the temptations of the appetite. In short, his character as a man and as a christian, was without reproach.

Of the esteem in which he was held, the names of the following respectable friends and noble patrons, will afford ample proof. It has been already mentioned that the attachment of the duke of Norfolk was so great to his tutor, that he granted him a pension for life; he also enjoyed the patronage of the earls of Bedford and Warwick, and the intimate friendship of Sir Francis Walsingham, (secretary of state,) Sir Thomas, and Mr. Michael Hennage, of whom he was frequently heard to observe, that Sir Thomas had every requisite for a complete courtier, but that Mr. Michael possessed all the merits of his brother, besides his own, still untainted by the court. He was on very intimate and affectionate terms with Sir Drue Drury, Sir Francis Drake, Dr. Grindal, archbishop of Canterbury, Dr. Elmar, bishop of London, Dr. Pilkington, bishop of Durham, and Dr. Nowell, dean of St. Paul's. Others of his most intimate acquaintances and friends were, Doctors Umphrey, Whitaker, and Fulk, Mr. John Crowly, and Mr. Baldwin Collins. Among the eminent citizens, we find he was much venerated by Sir Thomas Gresham, Sir Thomas Roe, Alderman Bacchus, Mr. Smith, Mr. Dale, Mr. Sherrington, &c. &c. &c.

At length, having long served both the church and the world by his ministry, by his pen, and by the unsullied lustre of a benevolent useful, and holy life, he meekly resigned his soul to Christ, on the 18th of April, 1587, being then in the seventieth year of his age. He was interred in the chancel of St Giles', Cripplegate; of which parish he had been, in the beginning of Elizabeth's reign, for some time vicar.

The Lord had given him a foresight of his departure; and so fully was he assured that the time was just at hand when his soul should quit the body, that (probably to enjoy unmolested communion with God, and to have no worldly interruptions in his last hours) he purposely sent his two sons from home, though he loved them with great tenderness; and before they returned, his spirit, as he had foreseen would be the case, had flown to heaven.

His death occasioned great lamentations throughout the city, and his funeral was honoured with a great concourse of people, each of whom appeared to bewail the loss of a father or a brother.

In his able martyrology he has elaborately treated of the vices and absurdities of papal hierarchy, of which the following is a brief enumeration.

Errors, Rites, Ceremonies, and Superstitious Practices, of the Romish Church.

TRADITIONS.] The church of Rome having deprived the laity of the Bible, substitutes in its stead apostolic and ecclesiastical traditions; and obliges her disciples to admit for truth whatever she teaches them: but what do the holy scriptures say? "Why do ye transgress the commandment of God by your tradition?" Matt. xv. 3, 9, &c. They also command us "to call no man master (in spiritual concerns;) to try the spirit, and beware of false teachers."

PRAYERS AND DIVINE SERVICES IN LATIN.] The Roman Catholics will not interpret the scriptures otherwise than according to the sense of holy mother church, and the pretended unanimous consent of the fathers: they assert also, that the scriptures ought not to be read publicly, nor indifferently by all; and, that the common people may be enslaved by gross ignorance, they perform public worship in an unknown tongue, contrary to the rule laid down by the apostle, "That all things should be done to edification." St. Paul says, "If I pray in an unknown tongue, my spirit prayeth, but my understanding is unfruitful."

SEVEN SACRAMENTS.] Two only were instituted by Christ, to which the Romish church has added five more, making in all seven, necessary to salvation, namely, the eucharist, baptism, confirmation, penance, extreme unction, orders, and matrimony. To those two which Christ instituted, she has added a mixture of her own inventions; for in the sacrament of baptism, she uses, salt, oil, or spittle; and in the sacrament of the Lord's supper, the laity have only the bread administered to them; and even that not after the manner ordained by Christ, who broke the bread and gave it to his disciples; instead of which the church of Rome administers to her members not bread, but a wafer, and the priests only drink the wine, though our blessed Lord said, "Drink ye ALL of this." Matt. xxvi. 27.

THE MASS.] Roman catholics believe it to be a true, proper, and propitiatory sacrifice, and therefore call it the sacrament of the altar; whereas, the death of Christ was a full and complete sacrifice, "in which he hath, by one suffering, perfected for ever them that are sanctified. He himself is a priest for ever; who, being raised from the dead, died no more; and who, through the eternal Spirit, offered himself without spot to God." Paul's Epist. to the Hebrews, ch. ix. 10. It was on account of this gross absurdity, and the irreligious application of it, that our first reformers suffered, and so many were put to death in the reign of queen Mary.

TRANSUBSTANTIATION.] Roman catholics profess, that in the most holy sacrament of the Lord's supper, there is really and substantially the body and blood, together with the soul and divinity, of Christ, and that the whole substance of the bread is turned into his body, and the whole substance of the wine into his blood; which conversion, so contradictory to our senses, they call transubstantiation, but at the same time they affirm, that, under either kind or species, only one whole entire Christ, and the true sacrament, is received. But why are those words, "This is my body," to be taken in a literal sense, any more than those concerning the cup? Our Saviour says, "I am the true vine, I am the door." St. Paul says, "Our fathers drank of the rock that followed them, and that rock was Christ;" and writing to the Corinthians, he affirms, that, "he had fed them with milk." Can these passages be taken literally? Why then must we be forced to interpret our Saviour's words in a literal sense, when the apostle has explained the intention of the sacrament to be "to show forth the Lord's death till he come!"

PURGATORY.] This, they say, is a certain place, in which, as in a prison, after death, those souls, by the prayers of the faithful, are purged, which in this life could not be fully cleansed; no not by the blood of Christ: and notwithstanding it is asserted in the scriptures, "if we confess our sins, he is faithful and just to forgive us, and to cleanse us from all unrighteousness." 1 John i. 9. This place of purgatory is in the power of the pope, who dispenses the indulgences, and directs the treasury of his merits, by which the pains are mitigated, and the deliverance hastened. For the tormented sufferers, in this ideal inquisition, his monks and friars say masses, all of whom must be paid for their trouble; because, no penny, no pater-noster; by which bubble the church of Rome amasses great wealth.

IDOLATRY AND CREATURE-WORSHIP.] In all the Romish worship the blessed virgin is a principal object of adoration. She is styled the queen of Heaven, lady of the world, the only hope of sinners, queen of angels, patroness of men, advocate for sinners, mother of mercies, under which titles they desire her, by the power of a mother, to command her Son. In some prayers, they invoke God to bring them to heaven by the merits and mediation of the Virgin Mary and all her saints, and that they may enjoy perpetual soundness both of body and mind by her glorious intercession. Hence it might be imagined by a papist, that the sacred writings were full of encomiums on this pretended mother of God; whereas, on the contrary, we do not find Christ in any part of scripture called the Son of Mary, nor that he at any time calls her mother; and when the woman cried, "Blessed is the womb that bore thee, and the paps that thou hast sucked." "Yea, (returns our Lord) rather blessed are they that hear the word of God, and keep it." Nor does our Saviour own any relation but that of a disciple; for when his mother and brethren stood without, desiring to speak with him, Jesus answered, "Who are my mother and brethren?" And looking round upon his disciples, he saith, "Behold my mother and my brethren; for whosoever shalt do the will of my Father who is in heaven, the same is my brother, sister, and mother." Of the same nature are their prayers to other saints and angels, by which they derogate from the honour of our Christ, and transfer his offices to others; though the scriptures expressly assert, there is but one mediator between God and man. Nor must we omit under this head the idolatry of the mass, in the elevation of the host. Thus is the second commandment infringed, which the Romish church has endeavoured as much as possible to suppress, and in many of their little manuals it is altogether omitted.

PAPAL SOVEREIGNTY.] This is politically supported by a pretended infallibility; auricular confession, founded upon the priest's power to forgive sins; indulgences; pretended relics; penance; strings of beads for Ave-Marys and pater-nosters; celibacy; merits and works of supererogations; restrictions; monkish austerities; religious vows and orders; palms; candles; decorated images; holy water; christening of bells; hallowed flowers and branches; agnus dei; oblations; consecrations, &c., &c.

LUDICROUS FORMS AND CEREMONIES.] At the feast of Christmas, the Roman catholics have exhibited in their churches a cradle, with an image of an infant in it, which is rocked with great seeming devotion; and on Good-Friday they have the figure of our Saviour on the cross, and then they perform the service which they call the Tenebres; having abundance of lighted candles, all of which they extinguish one by one, after which the body is taken down from the cross and put into a sepulchre, and men stand to watch it.

CRUEL MAXIMS.] Papists hold that heretics may not be termed children and kindred; that no faith is to be kept with heretics; and that it is lawful to torture or kill them for the good of their souls.

CHAPTER XXIII.

SKETCH OF THE FRENCH REVOLUTION OF 1789, AS CONNECTED WITH THE HISTORY OF PERSECUTION.

The design of those who were the primary agents in originating the causes of the French Revolution, was the utter subversion of the christian religion. Voltaire, the leader in this crusade against religion, boasted that "with one hand he would pull down, what took twelve Apostles to build up." The motto on the seal of his letters was, "Crush the wretch," having reference to Jesus Christ, and the system of religion, which he promulgated. To effect his object he wrote and published a great variety of infidel tracts, containing the most licentious sentiments and the most blasphemous attacks upon the religion of the Bible. Innumerable copies of these tracts were printed, and gratuitously circulated in France and other countries. As they were adapted to the capacity of all classes of persons, they were eagerly sought after, and read with avidity. The doctrines inculcated in them were subversive of every principle of morality and religion. The everlasting distinctions between virtue and vice, were completely broken down. Marriage was ridiculed--obedience to parents treated as the most abject slavery--subordination to civil government, the most odious despotism--and the acknowledgement of a God, the height of folly and absurdity. Deeply tinged with such sentiments, the revolution of 1789, found the popular mind in France prepared for all the atrocities which followed. The public conscience had become so perverted, that scenes of treachery, cruelty and blood were regarded with indifference, and sometimes excited the most unbounded applause in the spectators. Such a change had been effected in the French character, by the propagation of Infidel and Atheistical opinions, "that from being one of the most light hearted and kind tempered of nations," says Scott, "the French seemed upon the revolution to have been animated, not merely with the courage, but with the rabid fury of wild beasts." When the Bastile was stormed "Fouton and Berthier, two individuals whom they considered as enemies of the people, were put to death, with circumstances of cruelty and insult fitting only at the death stake of an Indian encampment; and in imitation of literal cannibals, there were men, or rather monsters found, not only to tear asunder, the limbs of their victims, but to eat their hearts, and drink their blood."

Croly, in his new interpretation of the Apocalypse, holds the following language.

The primary cause of the French revolution was the exile of Protestantism.

Its decency of manners had largely restrained the licentious tendencies of the higher orders; its learning had compelled the Romish Ecclesiastics to similar labours; and while christianity could appeal to such a church in France, the progress of the infidel writers was checked by the living evidence of the purity, peacefulness and wisdom of the Gospel. It is not even without sanction of scripture and history to conceive that, the presence of such a body of the servants of God was a divine protection to their country.

But the fall of the church was followed by the most palpable, immediate, and ominous change. The great names of the Romish priesthood, the vigorous literature of Bossnett, the majestic oratory of Massillon, the pathetic and classic elegance of Fenelon, the mildest of all enthusiasts; a race of men who towered above the genius of their country and of their religion; passed away without a successor. In the beginning of the 18th century, the most profligate man in France was an ecclesiastic, the Cardinal Dubois, prime minister to the most profligate prince in Europe, the Regent Orleans. The country was convulsed with bitter personal disputes between Jesuit and Jansenist, fighting even to mutual persecution upon points either beyond or beneath the human intellect. A third party stood by, unseen, occasionally stimulating each, but equally despising both, a potential fiend, sneering at the blind zealotry and miserable rage that were doing its unsuspected will. Rome, that boasts of her freedom from schism should blot the 18th century from her page.

The French mind, subtle, satirical, and delighting to turn even matters of seriousness into ridicule, was immeasurably captivated by the true burlesque of those disputes, the childish virulence, the extravagant pretensions, and the still more extravagant impostures fabricated in support of the rival pre-eminence in absurdity; the visions of half-mad nuns and friars; the Convulsionaries; the miracles at the tomb of the Abbe Paris, trespasses on the common sense of man, scarcely conceivable by us if they had not been renewed under our eyes by popery. All France was in a burst of laughter.

In the midst of this tempest of scorn an extraordinary man arose, to guide and deepen it into public ruin, VOLTAIRE; a personal profligate; possessing a vast variety of that superficial knowledge which gives importance to folly; frantic for popularity, which he solicited at all hazards; and sufficiently opulent to relieve him from the necessity of any labours but those of national undoing. Holding but an inferior and struggling rank in all the manlier provinces of the mind, in science, poetry, and philosophy; he was the prince of scorners. The splenetic pleasantry which stimulates the wearied tastes of high life; the grossness which half concealed captivates the loose, without offence to their feeble decorum; and the easy brilliancy which throws what colours it will on the darker features of its purpose; made Voltaire, the very genius of France. But under this smooth and sparkling surface, reflecting like ice all the lights flung upon it, there was a dark fathomless depth of malignity. He hated government; he hated morals; he hated man, he hated religion. He sometimes bursts out into exclamations of rage and insane fury against all that we honour as best and holiest, that sound less the voice of human lips than the echoes of the final place of agony and despair.

A tribe worthy of his succession, showy, ambitious, and malignant, followed; each with some vivid literary contribution, some powerful and popular work, a new despotic of combustion in that mighty mine on which stood in thin and fatal security the throne of France. Rousseau, the most impassioned of all romancers, the great corrupter of the female mind. Buffon, a lofty and splendid speculator, who dazzled the whole multitude of the minor philosophers, and fixed the creed of Materialism. Moutesquieu, eminent for knowledge and sagacity in his "Spirit of Laws" striking all the establishments of his country into contempt; and in his "Persian Letters," levelling the same blow at her morals. D'Alembert, the first mathematician of his day, an eloquent writer, the declared pupil of Voltaire, and, by his secretary-ship of the French academy, furnished with all the facilities for propagating his master's opinions. And Diderot, the projector and chief conductor of the Encyclopedia, a work justly exciting the admiration of Europe, by the novelty and magnificence of its design, and by the comprehensive and solid extent of its knowledge; but in its principles utterly evil, a condensation of all the treasons of the school of anarchy, the lex scripta of the Revolution.

All those men were open infidels; and their attacks on religion, such as they saw it before them, roused the Gallican church. But the warfare was totally unequal. The priesthood came armed with the antiquated and unwieldy weapons of old controversy, forgotten traditions and exhausted legends. They could have conquered them only by the bible; they fought them only with the breviary. The histories of the saints, and the wonders of images were but fresh food for the most overwhelming scorn. The bible itself, which popery has always laboured to close, was brought into the contest, and used resistlessly against the priesthood. They were contemptuously asked, in what part of the sacred volume had they found the worship of the Virgin, of the Saints, or of the Host? where was the privilege that conferred Saintship at the hands of the pope? where was the prohibition of the general use of scripture by every man who had a soul to be saved? where was the revelation of that purgatory, from which a monk and a mass could extract a sinner? where was the command to imprison, torture, and slay men for their difference of opinion with an Italian priest and the college of cardinals? To those formidable questions the clerics answered by fragments from the fathers, angry harangues, and more legends of more miracles. They tried to enlist the nobles and the court in a crusade. But the nobles were already among the most zealous, though secret, converts to the Encyclopedia; and the gentle spirit of the monarch was not to be urged into a civil war. The threat of force only inflamed contempt into vengeance. The populace of Paris, like all mobs, licentious, restless, and fickle; but beyond all, taking an interest in public matters, had not been neglected by the deep designers who saw in the quarrel of the pen the growing quarrel of the sword. The Fronde was not yet out of their minds; the barrier days of Paris; the municipal council which in 1648, had levied war against the government; the mob-army which had fought, and terrified that government into forgiveness; were the strong memorials on which the anarchists of 1793 founded their seduction. The perpetual ridicule of the national belief was kept alive among them. The populace of the provinces, whose religion was in their rosary, were prepared for rebellion by similar means and the terrible and fated visitation of France began.

After passing through many scenes from the recital of which the mind turns away with loathing and disgust, the reign of terror commenced. Previous to this, however, there had been dreadful riots, and disorders in Paris. The Swiss Guards had been cut to pieces, and the king and royal family imprisoned. The priests had nearly all perished or been banished from France. The national assembly was divided into desperate

factions, which often turned their arms against one another. When one
party triumphed, proscription followed, and the guillotine was put in
requisition, and blood flowed in torrents. The grossest irreligion
likewise prevailed. Leaders of the atheistical mob would extend their
arms to heaven and dare a God, if he existed, to vindicate his insulted
majesty, and crush them with his thunderbolts. Over the entrance of
their grave yards was placed this inscription, "DEATH AN ETERNAL SLEEP."
Men who dared to think differently from the dominant faction, were
immediately executed, in mockery, often, of all the forms of justice.
The most ferocious of the bloody factions, were the jacobins, so called
from their place of meeting. The leaders of this party were Danton,
Robespierre, and Marat. They are thus described by Scott in his life of
Napoleon.

Three men of terror, whose names will long remain, we trust, unmatched
in history by those of any similar miscreants, had now the unrivalled
leading of the jacobins, and were called the Triumvirate.

Danton deserves to be named first, as unrivalled by his colleagues in
talent and audacity. He was a man of gigantic size, and possessed a
voice of thunder. His countenance was that of an Ogre on the shoulders
of a Hercules. He was as fond of the pleasures of vice as of the
practice of cruelty; and it was said there were times when he became
humanized amidst his debauchery, laughed at the terror which his furious
declamation excited, and might be approached with safety like the
Maelstrom at the turn of tide. His profusion was indulged to an extent
hazardous to his popularity, for the populace are jealous of a lavish
expenditure, as raising their favourites too much above their own
degree; and the charge of peculation finds always ready credit with
them, when brought against public men.

Robespierre possessed this advantage over Danton, that he did not seem
to seek for wealth, either for hoarding or expending, but lived in
strict and economical retirement, to justify the name of the
Incorruptible, with which he was honoured by his partisans. He appears
to have possessed little talent, saving a deep fund of hypocrisy,
considerable powers of sophistry, and a cold exaggerated strain of
oratory, as foreign to good taste, as the measures he recommended were
to ordinary humanity. It seemed wonderful, that even the seething and
boiling of the revolutionary cauldron should have sent up from the
bottom, and long supported on the surface, a thing so miserably void of
claims to public distinction; but Robespierre had to impose on the minds
of the vulgar, and he knew how to beguile them, by accommodating his
flattery to their passions and scale of understanding, and by acts of

cunning and hypocrisy, which weigh more with the multitude than the words of eloquence, or the arguments of wisdom. The people listened as to their Cicero, when he twanged out his apostrophes of Pauvre Peuple, Peuple verteueux! and hastened to execute whatever came recommended by such honied phrases, though devised by the worst of men for the worst and most inhuman of purposes.

Vanity was Robespierre's ruling passion, and though his countenance was the image of his mind, he was vain even of his personal appearance, and never adopted the external habits of a sans culotte. Amongst his fellow jacobins he was distinguished by the nicety with which his hair was arranged and powdered; and the neatness of his dress was carefully attended to, so as to counterbalance, if possible, the vulgarity of his person. His apartments, though small, were elegant, and vanity had filled them with representations of the occupant. Robespierre's picture at length hung in one place, his miniature in another, his bust occupied a niche, and on the table were disposed a few medallions exhibiting his head in profile. The vanity which all this indicated was of the coldest and most selfish character, being such as considers neglect as insult, and receives homage merely as a tribute; so that, while praise is received without gratitude, it is withheld at the risk of mortal hate. Self-love of this dangerous character is closely allied with envy, and Robespierre was one of the most envious and vindictive men that ever lived. He never was known to pardon any opposition, affront, or even rivalry; and to be marked in his tablets on such an account was a sure, though perhaps not an immediate sentence of death. Danton was a hero, compared with this cold, calculating, creeping miscreant; for his passions, though exaggerated, had at least some touch of humanity, and his brutal ferocity was supported by brutal courage. Robespierre was a coward, who signed death-warrants with a hand that shook, though his heart was relentless. He possessed no passions on which to charge his crimes; they were perpetrated in cold blood, and upon mature deliberation.

Marat, the third of this infernal triumvirate, had attracted the attention of the lower orders, by the violence of his sentiments in the journal which he conducted from the commencement of the revolution, upon such principles that it took the lead in forwarding its successive changes. His political exhortations began and ended like the howl of a blood-hound for murder; or, if a wolf could have written a journal, the gaunt and famished wretch could not have ravined more eagerly for slaughter. It was blood which was Marat's constant demand, not in drops from the breast of an individual, not in puny streams from the slaughter of families, but blood in the profusion of an ocean. His usual calculation of the heads which he demanded amounted to two hundred and sixty thousand; and though he sometimes raised it as high as three hundred thousand, it never fell beneath the smaller number. It may be hoped, and, for the honour of human nature, we are inclined to believe, there was a touch of insanity in this unnatural strain of ferocity; and the wild and squalid features of the wretch appear to have intimated a degree of alienation of mind. Marat was, like Robespierre, a coward. Repeatedly denounced in the Assembly, he skulked instead of defending himself, and lay concealed in some obscure garret or cellar, among his cut-throats, until a storm appeared, when, like a bird of ill omen, his death-screech was again heard. Such was the strange and fatal triumvirate, in which the same degree of cannibal cruelty existed under different aspects. Danton murdered to glut his rage; Robespierre to avenge his injured vanity, or to remove a rival whom he envied! Marat, from the same instinctive love of blood, which induces a wolf to continue his ravage of the flocks long after his hunger is appeased.

These monsters ruled France for a time with the most despotic sway. The most sanguinary laws were enacted--and the most vigilant system of police maintained. Spies and informers were employed--and every murmur, and every expression unfavourable to the ruling powers was followed with the sentence of death and its immediate execution.

"Men," says Scott, "read Livy for the sake of discovering what degree of private crime might be committed under the mask of public virtue. The deed of the younger Brutus, served any man as an apology to betray to ruin and to death, a friend or a patron, whose patriotism might not be of the pitch which suited the time. Under the example of the elder Brutus, the nearest ties of blood were repeatedly made to give way before the ferocity of party zeal--a zeal too often assumed for the most infamous and selfish purposes. As some fanatics of yore studied the old testament for the purpose of finding examples of bad actions to vindicate those which themselves were tempted to commit, so the republicans of France, we mean the desperate and outrageous bigots of the revolution, read history to justify, by classical instances, their public and private crimes. Informers, those scourges of a state, were encouraged to a degree scarce known in ancient Rome in the time of the emperors, though Tacitus has hurled his thunders against them, as the poison and pest of his time. The duty of lodging such informations was unblushingly urged as indispensable. The safety of the republic being the supreme charge of every citizen, he was on no account to hesitate in *denouncing*, as it was termed, any one whomsoever, or howsoever connected with him,--the friend of his counsels, or the wife of his bosom,--providing he had reason to suspect the devoted individual of the crime of *incivism*,--a crime the more mysteriously dreadful, as no one knew exactly its nature."

In this place we shall give an account of some of the scenes to which France was subject during this awful period. In order to render the triumph complete, the leaders of the Jacobins determined upon a general massacre of all the friends of the unfortunate Louis and the constitution in the kingdom. For this purpose, suspected persons of all ranks were collected in the prisons and jails, and on the 2d of September, 1792, the work of death commenced.

Massacre of Prisoners.

The number of individuals accumulated in the various prisons of Paris had increased by the arrests and domiciliary visits subsequent to the 10th of August, to about eight thousand persons. It was the object of this infernal scheme to destroy the greater part of these under one general system of murder, not to be executed by the sudden and furious impulse of an armed multitude, but with a certain degree of cold blood and deliberate investigation. A force of armed banditti, Marsellois partly, and partly chosen ruffians of the Fauxbourgs, proceeded to the several prisons, into which they either forced their passage, or were admitted by the jailers, most of whom had been apprised of what was to take place, though some even of these steeled officials exerted themselves to save those under their charge. A revolutionary tribunal was formed from among the armed ruffians themselves, who examined the registers of the prison, and summoned the captives individually to undergo the form of a trial. If the judges, as was almost always the case, declared for death, their doom, to prevent the efforts of men in despair, was expressed in the words "Give the prisoner freedom." The victim was then thrust out into the street, or yard; he was despatched by men and women, who, with sleeves tucked up, arms dyed elbow-deep in blood, hands holding axes, pikes, and sabres, were executioners of the sentence; and, by the manner in which they did their office on the living, and mangled the bodies of the dead, showed that they occupied the post as much from pleasure as from love of hire. They often exchanged places; the judges going out to take the executioners' duty, the executioners, with reeking hands, sitting as judges in their turn. Mailard, a ruffian alleged to have distinguished himself at the siege of the Bastile, but better known by his exploits on the march to Versailles, presided during these brief and sanguinary investigations. His companions on the bench were persons of the same stamp. Yet there were occasions when they showed some transient gleams of humanity, and it is not unimportant to remark, that boldness had more influence on them than any appeal to mercy or compassion. An avowed royalist was occasionally dismissed uninjured, while the constitutionalists were sure to be massacred. Another trait of a singular nature is, that two of the ruffians who were appointed to guard one of these intended victims home in safety, as if they were acquitted, insisted on seeing his meeting with his family, seemed to share in the transports of the moment, and on taking leave, shook the hand of their late prisoner, while their own were clotted with the gore of his friends, and had been just raised to shed his own. Few, indeed, and brief, were these symptoms of relenting. In general, the doom of the prisoner was death, and that doom was instantly accomplished.

In the meanwhile, the captives were penned up in their dungeons like cattle in a shambles, and in many instances might, from windows which looked outwards, mark the fate of their comrades, hear their cries, and behold their struggles, and learn from the horrible scene, how they might best meet their own approaching fate. They observed, according to St. Meard, who, in his well-named Agony of Thirty-Six Hours, has given the account of this fearful scene, that those who intercepted the blows of the executioners, by holding up their hands, suffered protracted torment, while those who offered no show of struggle were more easily despatched; and they encouraged each other to submit to their fate, in the manner least likely to prolong their sufferings.

Many ladies, especially those belonging to the court, were thus murdered. The Princess de Lamballe, whose only crime seems to have been her friendship for Marie Antoinette, was literally hewn to pieces, and her head, and that of others, paraded on pikes through the metropolis. It was carried to the temple on that accursed weapon, the features yet beautiful in death, and the long fair curls of the hair floating around the spear. The murderers insisted that the King and Queen should be compelled to come to the window to view this dreadful trophy. The municipal officers who were upon duty over the royal prisoners, had difficulty, not merely in saving them from this horrible inhumanity, but also in preventing their prison from being forced. Three-coloured ribbons were extended across the street, and this frail barrier was found sufficient to intimate that the Temple was under the safeguard of the nation. We do not read that the efficiency of the three-coloured ribbons was tried for the protection of any of the other prisoners. No doubt the executioners had their instructions where and when they should be respected.

The clergy, who had declined the constitutional oath from pious scruples, were, during the massacre, the peculiar objects of insult and cruelty, and their conduct was such as corresponded with their religious and conscientious professions. They were seen confessing themselves to each other, or receiving the confessions of their lay companions in misfortune, and encouraging them to undergo the evil hour, with as much calmness as if they had not been to share its bitterness. As protestants, we cannot abstractedly approve of the doctrines which render the established clergy of one country dependant upon the sovereign pontiff, the prince of an alien state. But these priests did not make the laws for which they suffered; they only obeyed them; and as men and christians we must regard them as martyrs, who preferred death to what they considered as apostacy.

In the brief intervals of this dreadful butchery, which lasted four days, the judges and executioners ate, drank, and slept: and awoke from slumber, or arose from their meal, with fresh appetite for murder. There were places arranged for the male, and for the female murderers, for the work had been incomplete without the intervention of the latter. Prison after prison was invested, entered, and under the same form of proceeding made the scene of the same inhuman butchery. The Jacobins had reckoned on making the massacre universal over France. But the example was not generally followed. It required, as in the case of St. Bartholomew, the only massacre which can be compared to this in atrocity, the excitation of a large capital, in a violent crisis, to render such horrors possible.

The community of Paris were not in fault for this. They did all they could to extend the sphere of murder. Their warrant brought from Orleans near sixty persons, including the Duke de Cosse-Brissac, De Lesart the late minister, and other royalists of distinction, who were to have been tried before the high court of that department. A band of assassins met them, by appointment of the community, at Versailles, who, uniting with their escort, murdered almost the whole of the unhappy men.

From the 2d to the 6th of September, these infernal crimes proceeded uninterrupted, protracted by the actors for the sake of the daily pay of a louis to each, openly distributed amongst them, by order of the Commune. It was either from a desire to continue as long as possible a labour so well requited, or because these beings had acquired an insatiable lust of murder, that, when the jails were emptied of state criminals, the assassins attacked the Bicetre, a prison where ordinary delinquents were confined. These unhappy wretches offered a degree of resistance which cost the assailants more dear than any they had experienced from their proper victims. They were obliged to fire on them with cannon, and many hundreds of the miserable creatures were in thus way exterminated, by wretches worse than themselves.

No exact account was ever made of the number of persons murdered during this dreadful period; but not above two or three hundred of the prisoners arrested for state offences were known to escape, or be discharged, and the most moderate computation raises the number of those who fell to two or three thousand, though some carry it to twice the extent. Truchod announced to the Legislative Assembly, that four thousand had perished. Some exertion was made to save the lives of those imprisoned for debt, whose numbers, with those of common felons, may make up the balance betwixt the number slain and eight thousand who were prisoners when the massacre began. The bodies were interred in heaps, in immense trenches, prepared beforehand by order of the community of Paris; but their bones have since been transferred to the subterranean catacombs, which form the general charnel-house of the city. In those melancholy regions, while other relics of mortality lie exposed all around, the remains of those who perished in the massacres of September, are alone secluded from the eye. The vault in which they repose is closed with a screen of freestone, as if relating to crimes unfit to be thought of even in the proper abode of death; and which France would willingly hide in oblivion.

After this dreadful massacre, the Jacobins eagerly demanded the life of Louis XVI. He was accordingly tried by the convention and condemned to be beheaded.

Death of Louis XVI. and other Members of the Royal Family.

On the 21st of January, 1793, Louis XVI. was publicly beheaded in the midst of his own metropolis, in the ***Place Louis Quinze***, erected to the memory of his grandfather. It is possible, for the critical eye of the historian, to discover much weakness in the conduct of this unhappy monarch; for he had neither the determination to fight for his rights, nor the power of submitting with apparent indifference to circumstances where resistance inferred danger. He submitted, indeed, but with so bad a grace, that he only made himself suspected of cowardice, without getting credit for voluntary concession. But yet his behaviour on many trying occasions effectually vindicate him from the charge of timidity, and showed that the unwillingness to shed blood, by which he was peculiarly distinguished, arose from benevolence, not from pusillanimity.

Upon the scaffold, he behaved with the firmness which became a noble spirit, and the patience beseeming one who was reconciled to heaven. As one of the few marks of sympathy with which his sufferings were softened, the attendance of a confessor, who had not taken the constitutional oath, was permitted to the dethroned monarch. He who undertook the honourable but dangerous office, was a gentleman of gifted family of Edgeworth of Edgeworthstown; and the devoted zeal with which he rendered the last duties to Louis, had like in the issue to have proved fatal to himself. As the instrument of death descended, the confessor pronounced the impressive words,--"Son of Saint Louis, ascend to heaven!"

There was a last will of Louis XVI. circulated upon good authority, bearing this remarkable passage:--"I recommend to my son, should you have the misfortune to become king, to recollect that his whole faculties are due to the service of the public; that he ought to consult the happiness of his people, by governing according to the laws, forgetting all injuries and misfortunes, and in particular those which I may have sustained. But while I exhort him to govern under the authority of the laws, I cannot but add, that this will be only in his power, in so far as he shall be endowed with authority to cause right to be respected, and wrong punished; and that without such authority, his situation in the government must be more hurtful than advantageous to the state."

Not to mingle the fate of the illustrious victim of the royal family with the general tale of the sufferers under the reign of terror, we must here mention the deaths of the rest of that illustrious house, which closed for a time a monarchy, that existing through three dynasties, had given sixty-six kings to France.

It was not to be supposed, that the queen was to be long permitted to survive her husband. She had been even more than he the object of revolutionary detestation; nay, many were disposed to throw on Marie Antoinette, almost exclusively, the blame of those measures which they considered as counter-revolutionary.

The terms of her accusation were too basely depraved to be even hinted at here. She scorned to reply to it, but appealed to all who had been mothers, against the very possibility of the horrors which were stated against her. The widow of a king, the sister of an emperor, was condemned to death, dragged in an open tumbril to the place of execution, and beheaded on the 16th October, 1793. She suffered death in her 39th year.

The princess Elizabeth, sister of Louis, of whom it might he said, in the words of lord Clarendon, that she resembled a chapel in a king's palace, into which nothing but piety and morality enter, while all around is filled with sin, idleness, and folly, did not, by the most harmless demeanour and inoffensive character, escape the miserable fate in which the Jacobins had determined to involve the whole family of Louis XVI. Part of the accusation redounded to the honour of her character. She was accused of having admitted to the apartments of the Tuilleries some of the national guards, of the section of Filles de Saint Thomas, and causing the wounds to be looked to which they had received in a skirmish with the Marsellois, immediately before the 10th of August. The princess admitted her having done so, and it was exactly in consistence with her whole conduct. Another charge stated the ridiculous accusation, that she had distributed bullets chewed by herself and her attendants, to render then more fatal, to the defenders of the castle of the Tuilleries; a ridiculous fable, of which there was no proof whatever. She was beheaded in May, 1794, and met her death as became the manner in which her life had been spent.

We are weary of recounting these atrocities, as others must be of reading them. Yet it is not useless that men should see how far human nature can be carried, in contradiction to every feeling the most sacred, to every pleading, whether of justice or of humanity. The Dauphin we have already described as a promising child of seven years old, an age at which no offence could have been given, and from which no danger could have been apprehended. Nevertheless, it was resolved to destroy the innocent child, and by means to which ordinary murders seem deeds of mercy.

The unhappy boy was put in charge of the most hard-hearted villain whom the community of Paris, well acquainted where such agents were to be found, were able to select from their band of Jacobins. This wretch, a shoemaker called Simon, asked his employers, "what was to be done with the young wolf-whelp; Was he to be slain?"--"No?"--"Poisoned?"--"No."--"Starved to death?"--"No." "What then?"--"He was to be got rid of." Accordingly, by a continuance of the most severe treatment--by beating, cold, vigils, fasts, and ill usage of every kind, so frail a blossom was soon blighted. He died on the 8th June, 1795.

After this last horrible crime, there was a relaxation in favour of the daughter, and now the sole child of this unhappy house. The princess royal, whose qualities have honoured even her birth and blood, experienced from this period a mitigated captivity. Finally, on the

19th December, 1795, this last remaining relic of the family of Louis, was permitted to leave her prison and her country, in exchange for La Fayette and others, whom, on that condition, Austria delivered from captivity. She became afterwards the wife of her cousin, the duke d'Angouleme, eldest son of the reigning monarch of France, and obtained, by the manner in which she conducted herself at Bourdeaux in 1815, the highest praise for gallantry and spirit.

Dreadful scenes in La Vendee.

In La Vendee, one of the departments of France, an insurrection broke out against the Jacobinical government, in 1793.

Upwards of two hundred battles and skirmishes were fought in this devoted country. The revolutionary fever was in its access; the shedding of blood seemed to have become positive pleasure to the perpetrators of slaughter, and was varied by each invention which cruelty could invent to give it new zest. The habitations of the Vendeans were destroyed, their families subjected to violation and massacre, their cattle houghed and slaughtered, and their crops burnt and wasted. One republican column assumed and merited the name of the Infernal, by the horrid atrocities which they committed. At Pilau, they roasted the women and children in a heated oven. Many similar horrors could be added, did not the heart and hand recoil from the task. Without quoting any more special instances of horror, we use the words of a republican eye witness, to express the general spectacle presented by the theatre of public conflict.

"I did not see a single male being at the towns of St. Hermand, Chantonnay, or Herbiers. A few women alone had escaped the sword. Country-seats, cottages, habitations of whichever kind, were burnt. The herds and flocks were wandering in terror around their usual places of shelter, now smoking in ruins. I was surprised by night, but the wavering and dismal blaze of conflagration afforded light over the country. To the bleating of the terrified flocks, and bellowing of the terrified cattle, was joined the deep hoarse notes of carrion crows, and the yells of wild animals coming from the recesses of the woods to prey upon the carcasses of the slain. At length a distant colume of fire, widening and increasing as I approached, served me as a beacon. It was the town of Mortagne in flames. When I arrived there, no living creatures were to be seen, save a few wretched women who were striving to save some remnants of their property from the general conflagration."--Les Memoires d'un Ancien Administrateur des Armees Republicaines.

Scenes at Marseilles and Lyons.

Marseilles, Toulon, and Lyons, had declared themselves against the Jacobin supremacy. Rich from commerce and their maratime situation, and, in the case of Lyons, from their command of internal navigation, the wealthy merchants and manufacturers of those cities foresaw the total insecurity of property, and in consequence of their own ruin, in the system of arbitrary spoliation and murder upon which the government of the Jacobins was founded. But property, for which they were solicitous, though, if its natural force is used in time, the most powerful barrier to withstand revolution, becomes, after a certain period of delay, its helpless victim. If the rich are in due season liberal of their means, they have the power of enlisting in their cause, and as adherents, those among the lower orders, who, if they see their superiors dejected and despairing, will be tempted to consider them as objects of plunder. But this must be done early, or those who might be made the most active defenders of property, will join with such as are prepared to make a prey of it.

Marseilles showed at once her good will and her impotency of means. The utmost exertions of that wealthy city, whose revolutionary band had contributed so much to the downfall of the monarchy in the attack on the Tuilleries, were able to equip only a small and doubtful army of about 3000 men, who were despatched to the relief of Lyons. This inconsiderable army threw themselves into Avignon, and were defeated with the utmost ease, by the republican general Cartaux, despicable as a military officer, and whose forces would not have stood a single *engaillement* of Vendean sharp-shooters. Marseilles received the victors, and bowed her head to the subsequent horrors which it pleased Cartaux, with two formidable Jacobins, Barras and Ferron, to inflict on that flourishing city. The place underwent the usual terrors of Jacobin purifaction, and was for a time affectedly called "nameless commune."

Lyons made a more honourable stand. That noble city had been subjected for some time to the domination of Chalier, one of the most ferocious, and at the same time one of the most extravagantly absurd, of the Jacobins. He was at the head of a formidable club, which was worthy of being affiliated with the mother society, and ambitious of treading in its footsteps; and he was supported by a garrison of two revolutionary regiments, besides a numerous artillery, and a large addition of volunteers, amounting in all to about ten thousand men, forming what was called a revolutionary army. This Chalier, was an apostate priest, an atheist, and a thorough-paced pupil in the school of terror. He had been procureur of the community, and had imposed on the wealthy citizens a tax, which was raised from six to thirty millions of livres. But blood as well as gold was his object. The massacre of a few priests and aristocrats confined in the fortress of Pierre-Scixe, was a pitiful sacrifice; and Chalier, ambitious of deeds more decisive, caused a general arrest of an hundred principal citizens, whom he destined as a hecatomb more worthy of the demon whom he served.

This sacrifice was prevented by the courage of the Lyonnois; a courage which, if assumed by the Parisians, might have prevented most of the horrors which disgraced the revolution. The meditated slaughter was already announced by Chalier to the Jacobin club. "Three hundred heads," he said, "are marked for slaughter. Let us lose no time in seizing the members of the departmental office-bearers, the presidents and secretaries of the sections, all the local authorities who obstruct our revolutionary measures. Let us make one fagot of the whole, and deliver them at once to the guillotine."

But ere he could execute his threat, terror was awakened into the courage of despair. The citizens rose in arms and besieged the Hotel de Ville, in which Chalier, with his revolutionary troops, made a desperate, and for some time a successful, yet ultimately a vain defence. But the Lyonnois unhappily knew not how to avail themselves of their triumph. They were not sufficiently aware of the nature of the vengeance which they had provoked, or of the necessity of supporting the bold step which they had taken, by measures which precluded a compromise. Their resistance to the violence and atrocity of the Jacobins had no political character, any more than that offered by the traveller against robbers who threaten him with plunder and murder. They were not sufficiently aware, that, having done so much, they must necessarily do more. They ought, by declaring themselves royalists, to have endeavoured to prevail on the troops of Savoy, if not on the Swiss, (who had embraced a species of neutrality, which, after the 10th of August, was dishonourable to their ancient reputation,) to send in all haste, soldiery to the assistance of a city which had no fortifications or regular troops to defend it; but which possessed, nevertheless, treasures to pay their auxiliaries, and strong hands and able officers to avail themselves of the localities of their situation, which, when well defended, are sometimes as formidable as the regular protection erected by scientific engineers.

The people of Lyons vainly endeavoured to establish a revolutionary character for themselves upon the system of Gironde; two of whose proscribed deputies tried to draw them over to their unpopular and hopeless cause: and they inconsistently sought protection by affecting a republican zeal, even while resisting the decrees, and defeating the troops of the Jacobins. There were undoubtedly many of royalist principles among the insurgents, and some of their leaders were decidedly such; but these were not numerous or influential enough to establish the true principle of open resistance, and the ultimate chance of rescue, by a bold proclamation of the king's interest. They still appealed to the convention as their legitimate sovereign, in whose eyes they endeavoured to vindicate themselves, and at the same time tried to secure the interest of two Jacobin deputies, who had countenanced every violation attempted by Chalier, that they might prevail upon them to represent their conduct favourably. Of course they had enough of promises to this effect, while Messrs. Guathier and Nioche, the deputies in question, remained in their power; promises, doubtless the more readily given, that the Lyonnois, though desirous to conciliate the favour of the convention, did not hesitate in proceeding to the punishment of the Jacobin Chalier. He was condemned and executed, along with one of his principal associates, termed Reard.

To defend these vigourous proceedings, the unhappy insurgents placed themselves under the interim government of a council, who, still desirous to temporize and maintain the revolutionary character, termed themselves "the popular and republican commission of public safety of the department of the Rhine and Loire;" a title which, while it excited no popular enthusiasm, and attracted no foreign aid, no ways soothed, but rather exasperated, the resentment of the convention, now under the absolute domination of the Jacobins, by whom every thing short of complete fraternization was accounted presumptuous defiance. Those who were not with them, it was their policy to hold as their most decided enemies.

The Lyonnois had indeed letters of encouragement, and promised concurrence, from several departments; but no effectual support was ever directed to their city, excepting the petty reinforcement from Marseilles, which we have seen was intercepted and dispersed with little trouble by the Jacobin general, Cartaux.

Lyons had expected to become the patroness and focus of an Anti-Jacobin league, formed by the great commercial towns, against Paris and the predominant part of the convention. She found herself isolated and unsupported, and left to oppose her own proper forces and means of defence, to an army of sixty thousand men, and to the numerous Jacobins contained within her own walls. About the end of July, after a lapse of an interval of two months, a regular blockade was formed around the city, and in the first week of August, hostilities took place. The besieging army was directed in its military character by general Kellerman, who, with other distinguished soldiers, had now began to hold an eminent rank in the republican armies. But for the purpose of executing the vengeance for which they thirsted, the Jacobins relied chiefly on the exertions of the deputies they had sent along with the commander, and especially of the representative, Dubois Crance, a man whose sole merit appears to have been his frantic Jacobinism. General Percy, formerly an officer in the royal service, undertook the almost hopeless task of defence, and by forming redoubts on the most commanding situations around the town, commenced a resistance against the immensely superior force of the besiegers, which was honourable if it could have been useful. The Lyonnois, at the same time, still endeavoured to make fair weather with the besieging army, by representing themselves as firm republicans. They celebrated as a public festival the anniversary of the 10th of August, while Dubois Crance, to show the credit he gave them for their republican zeal, fixed the same day for commencing his fire on the place, and caused the first gun to be discharged by his own concubine, a female born in Lyons. Bombs and red-hot bullets were next resorted to, against the second city of the French empire; while the besieged sustained the attack with a constancy, and on many parts repelled it with a courage highly honourable to their character. But their fate was determined. The deputies announced to the convention their purpose of pouring their instruments of havoc on every quarter of the town at once, and when it was on fire in several places, to attempt a general storm. "The city," they said, "must surrender, or there shall not remain one stone upon another, and this we hope to accomplish in spite of the suggestions of false compassion. Do not then be surprised when you hear that Lyons exists no longer." The fury of the attack threatened to make good these promises.

The sufferings of the citizens became intolerable. Several quarters of the city were on fire at the same time, immense magazines were burnt to the ground, and a loss incurred, during two night's bombardment, which was calculated at two hundred millions of livres. A black flag was hoisted by the besieged on the Great Hospital, as a sign that the fire of the assailants should not be directed on that asylum of hopeless misery. The signal seemed only to draw the republican bombs to the spot where they could create the most frightful distresses, and outrage in the highest degree the feelings of humanity. The devastations of famine were soon added to those of slaughter; and after two months of such horrors had been sustained, it became obvious that farther resistance was impossible.

The parylitic Couthon, with Collot D'Herbois, and other deputies were sent to Lyons by the committee of public safety, to execute the vengeance which the Jacobins demanded; while Dubois Crance was recalled, for having put, it was thought, less energy to his proceedings than the prosecution of the siege required. Collot D'Herbois had a personal motive of a singular nature for delighting in the task intrusted to him and his colleagues. In his capacity of a play-actor, he had been hissed from the stage at Lyons, and the door to revenge was now open. The instructions of this committee enjoined them to take the most satisfactory revenge for the death of Chalier and the insurrection of Lyons, not merely on the citizens, but on the town itself. The principal streets and buildings were to be levelled with the ground, and a monument erected where they stood, was to record the cause:--"Lyons rebelled against the Republic--Lyons is no more." Such fragments of the town as might be permitted to remain, were to bear the name of Ville Affranchie. It will scarce be believed that a doom like that which might have passed the lips of some eastern despot, in all the frantic madness of arbitrary power and utter ignorance, could have been seriously pronounced, and as seriously enforced, in one of the most civilized nations in Europe; and that to the present enlightened age, men who pretended to wisdom and philosophy, should have considered the labours of the architect as a proper subject of punishment. So it was, however; and to give the demolition more effect, the impotent Couthon was carried from house to house, devoting each to ruin, by striking the door with a silver hammer, and pronouncing these words--"House of a rebel. I condemn thee in the name of the law." Workmen followed in great multitudes, who executed the sentence by pulling the house down to the foundations. This wanton demolition continued for six months, and is said to have been carried on at an expense equal to that which the superb military hospital, the Hotel des Invalides, cost its founder, Louis XIV. But republican vengeance did not waste itself exclusively upon senseless lime and stone--it sought out sentient victims.

The deserved death of Chalier had been atoned by an apotheosis executed after Lyons had surrendered; but Collot D'Herbois declared that every drop of that patriotic blood fell as if scalding his own heart, and that the murder demanded atonement. All ordinary process, and every usual mode of execution, was thought too tardy to avenge the death of a Jacobin proconsul. The judges of the revolutionary commission were worn out with fatigue--the arm of the executioner was weary--the very steel of the guillotine was blunted. Collot D'Herbois devised a more summary mode of slaughter. A number of from two to three hundred victims at once were dragged from prison to the place de Baotteaux, one of the largest squares in Lyons, and there subjected to a fire of grape-shot. Efficacious as this mode of execution may seem, it was neither speedy nor merciful. The sufferers fell to the ground like singed flies, mutilated but not slain, and imploring their executioners to despatch them speedily. This was done with sabres and bayonets, and with such haste and zeal, that some of the jailers and assistants were slain along with those whom they had assisted in dragging to death; and the mistake was not discerned, until, upon counting the dead bodies, the military murderers found them to amount to more than the destined tale. The bodies of the dead were thrown into the Rhone, to carry news of the republican vengeance, as Collot D'Herbois expressed himself, to Toulon, then also in a state of revolt. But the sullen stream rejected the office imposed on it, and headed back the dead in heaps upon the banks; and the committee of Representatives was compelled at length to allow the relics of their cruelty to be interred, to prevent the risk of contagion.

The Installation of the Goddess of Reason.

At length the zeal of the infuriated Atheists in France hurried them to the perpetration of one of the most ridiculous, and at the same time impious transactions which ever disgraced the annals of any nation. It was no less than a formal renunciation of the existence of a Supreme Being, and the installation of the **Goddess of Reason**, in 1793.

"There is," says Scott, "a fanaticism of atheism, as well as of superstitious belief; and a philosopher can harbour and express as much malice against those who persevere in believing what he is pleased to denounce as unworthy of credence, as an ignorant and bigoted priest can bear against a man who cannot yield faith to dogmata which he thinks insufficiently proved." Accordingly, the throne being totally annihilated, it appeared to the philosophers of the school of Hebert, (who was author of the most gross and beastly periodical paper of the time, called the **Pere du Chene**) that in totally destroying such vestiges of religion and public worship as were still retained by the people of France, there was room for a splendid triumph of liberal opinions. It was not enough, they said, for a regenerate nation to have dethroned earthly kings, unless she stretched out the arm of defiance towards those powers which superstition had represented as reigning over boundless space.

An unhappy man, named Gobet, constitutional bishop of Paris, was brought forward to play the principal part in the most impudent and scandalous farce ever acted in the face of a national representation.

It is said that the leaders of the scene had some difficulty in inducing the bishop to comply with the task assigned him, which, after all, he executed, not without present tears and subsequent remorse. But he did play the part prescribed. He was brought forward in full procession, to declare to the convention, that the religion which he had taught so many years, was, in every respect, a piece of priestcraft, which had no foundation either in history or sacred truth. He disowned, in solemn and explicit terms, the existence of the Deity to whose worship he had been consecrated, and devoted himself in future to the homage of liberty, equality, virtue, and morality. He then laid on the table his episcopal decorations, and received a fraternal embrace from the president of the convention. Several apostate priests followed the example of this prelate.

The gold and silver plate of the churches was seized upon and desecrated, processions entered the convention, travestied in priestly garments, and singing the most profane hymns; while many of the chalices and sacred vessels were applied by Chaumette and Hebert to the celebration of their own impious orgies. The world for the first time, heard an assembly of men, born and educated in civilization, and assuming the right to govern one of the finest of the European nations, uplift their united voice to deny the most solemn truth which man's soul receives, and renounce unanimously the belief and worship of a Deity. For a short time the same mad profanity continued to be acted upon.

One of the ceremonies of this insane time stands unrivalled for absurdity, combined with impiety. The doors of the convention were thrown open to a band of musicians; preceded by whom, the members of the municipal body entered in solemn procession, singing a hymn in praise of liberty, and escorting, as the object of their future worship, a veiled female, whom they termed the Goddess of Reason. Being brought within the bar, she was unveiled with great form, and placed on the right hand of the president; when she was generally recognized as a dancing-girl of the opera, with whose charms most of the persons present were acquainted from her appearance on the stage, while the experience of individuals was farther extended. To this person, as the fittest representative of that reason whom they worshipped the national convention of France rendered public homage.

This impious and ridiculous mummery had a certain fashion; and the installation of the Goddess of reason was renewed and imitated throughout the nation, in such places where the inhabitants desired to show themselves equal to all the heights of the revolution. The churches were, in most districts of France, closed against priests and worshippers--the bells were broken and cast into cannon--the whole ecclesiastical establishment destroyed--and the republican inscription over the cemeteries, declaring death to be perpetual sleep, announced to those who lived under that dominion, that they were to hope no redress even in the next world.

Intimately connected with these laws affecting religion, was that which reduced the union of marriage, the most sacred engagement which human beings can form, and the permanence of which leads most strongly to the consolidation of society, to the state of a mere civil contract of a transitory character, which any two persons might engage in, and cast loose at pleasure, when their taste was changed, or their appetite gratified. If fiends had set themselves to work, to discover a mode of most effectually destroying whatever is venerable, graceful, or permanent in domestic life, and of obtaining at the same time an assurance that the mischief which it was their object to create should be perpetuated from one generation to another, they could not have invented a more effectual plan than the degradation of marriage into a state of mere occasional co-habitation, or licensed concubinage. Sophie Arnoult, an actress famous for the witty things she said, described the republican marriage as the sacrament of adultery.

Fall of Danton, Robespierre, Marat and other Jacobins.

These monsters fell victims by the same means they had used for the destruction of others. Marat was poignarded in 1793, by Charlotte Corday, a young female, who had cherished in a feeling between lunacy and heroism, the ambition of ridding the world of a tyrant. Danton was guillotined in 1794. Robespierre followed soon after. His fall is thus described by Scott in his life of Napoleon.

At length his fate urged him on to the encounter. Robespierre descended to the convention, where he had of late but rarely appeared, like the far nobler dictator of Rome; and in his case also, a band of senators was ready to poignard the tyrant on the spot, had they not been afraid of the popularity he was supposed to enjoy, and which they feared might render them instant victims to the revenge of the Jacobins. The speech which Robespierre addressed to the convention was as menacing as the first distant rustle of the hurricane, and dark and lurid as the eclipse which announces its approach. Anxious murmurs had been heard among the populace who filled the tribunes, or crowded the entrances of the hall of the convention, indicating that a second 31st of May (being the day on which the Jacobins proscribed the Girondists) was about to witness a similar operation.

The first theme of the gloomy orator was the display of his own virtues and his services as a patriot, distinguishing as enemies to their country all whose opinions were contrary to his own. He then reviewed successively the various departments of the government, and loaded them in turn with censure and contempt. He declaimed against the supineness of the committees of public safety and public security, as if the guillotine had never been in exercise; and he accused the committee of finance of having *counter-revolutionized* the revenues of the republic. He enlarged with no less bitterness on withdrawing the artillery-men (always violent Jacobins) from Paris, and on the mode of management adopted in the conquered countries of Belgium. It seemed as if he wished to collect within the same lists all the functionaries of the state, and in the same breath to utter defiance to them all.

The usual honorary motion was made to print the discourse; but then the storm of opposition broke forth, and many speakers vociferously demanded, that before so far adopting the grave inculpations which it contained, the discourse should be referred to the two committees. Robespierre in his turn, exclaimed, that this was subjecting his speech to the partial criticism and revision of the very parties whom he had accused. Exculpations and defences were heard on all sides against the charges which had been thus sweepingly brought forward; and there were many deputies who complained in no obscure terms of individual tyranny, and of a conspiracy on foot to outlaw and murder such part of the convention as might be disposed to offer resistance. Robespierre was but feebly supported, save by Saint Just, Couthon, and by his own brother. After a stormy debate, in which the convention were alternately swayed by their fear and their hatred of Robespierre, the discourse was finally referred to the committees, instead of being printed; and the haughty and sullen dictator saw in the open slight, thus put on his measures and opinions, the sure mark of his approaching fall.

He carried his complaints to the Jacobin Club, to repose, as he expressed it, his patriotic sorrows in their virtuous bosoms, where alone he hoped to find succour and sympathy. To this partial audience he renewed, in a tone of yet greater audacity, the complaints with which he had loaded every branch of the government, and the representative body itself. He reminded those around him of various heroic eras, when their presence and their pikes had decided the votes of the trembling deputies. He reminded them of their pristine actions of revolutionary vigour--asked them if they had forgot the road to the convention, and concluded by pathetically assuring them, that if they forsook him, "he stood resigned to his fate; and they should behold with what courage he would drink the fatal hemlock." The artist David, caught him by the hand as he closed, exclaiming, in rapture at his elocution, "I will drink it with thee."

The distinguished painter has been reproached, as having, on the subsequent day, declined the pledge which he seemed so eagerly to embrace. But there were many of his original opinion, at the time he expressed it so boldly; and had Robespierre possessed either military talents, or even decided courage, there was nothing to have prevented him from placing himself that very night at the head of a desperate insurrection of the Jacobins and their followers.

Payan, the successor of Hebert, actually proposed that the Jacobins should instantly march against the two committees, which Robespierre charged with being the focus of the anti-revolutionary machinations, surprise their handful of guards, and stifle the evil with which the state was menaced, even in the very cradle. This plan was deemed too hazardous to be adopted, although it was one of those sudden and master strokes of policy which Machiavel would have recommended. The fire of the Jacobins spent itself in tumult, and threatening, and in expelling from the bosom of their society Collot d'Herbois, Tallien, and about thirty other deputies of the mountain party, whom they considered as specially leagued to effect the downfall of Robespierre, and whom they drove from their society with execration and even blows.

Collot d'Herbois, thus outraged, went straight from the meeting of the Jacobins to the place where the committee of public safety was still sitting, in consultation on the report which they had to make to the convention the next day upon the speech of Robespierre. Saint Just, one of their number, though warmly attached to the dictator, had been intrusted by the committee with the delicate task of drawing up that report. It was a step towards reconciliation; but the entrance of Collot d'Herbois, frantic with the insults he had received, broke off all hope of accommodation betwixt the friends of Danton and those of Robespierre. D'Herbois exhausted himself in threats against Saint Just, Couthon, and their master, Robespierre, and they parted on terms of mortal and avowed enmity. Every exertion now was used by the associated conspirators against the power of Robespierre, to collect and combine against him the whole forces of the convention, to alarm the deputies of the plain with fears for themselves, and to awaken the rage of the mountaineers, against whose throat the dictator now waved the sword, which their short sighted policy had placed in his hands. Lists of proscribed deputies were handed around, said to have been copied from the tablets of the dictator; genuine or false, they obtained universal credit and currency; and these whose names stood on the fatal scrolls, engaged themselves for protection in the league against their enemy. The opinion that his fall could not be delayed now became general.

This sentiment was so commonly entertained in Paris on the 9th Thermidor, or 27th July, that a herd of about eighty victims, who were in the act of being dragged to the guillotine, were nearly saved by means of it. The people, in a generous burst of compassion, began to gather in crowds, and interrupted the melancholy procession, as if the power which presided over these hideous exhibitions had already been deprived of energy. But the hour was not come. The vile Henriot, commandant of the national guards, came up with fresh forces also on the day destined to be the last of his own life, proved the means of carrying to execution this crowd of unhappy and doubtless innocent persons.

On this eventful day, Robespierre arrived in the convention, and beheld the mountain in close array and completely manned, while, as in the case of Catiline, the bench on which he himself was accustomed to sit, seemed purposely deserted. Saint Just, Couthon, Le Bas (his brother-in-law,) and the younger Robespierre, were the only deputies of name who stood prepared to support him. But could he make an effectual struggle, he might depend upon the aid of the servile Barrere, a sort of Belial in the convention, the meanest, yet not the least able, amongst those fallen spirits, who, with great adroitness and ingenuity, as well as wit and eloquence, caught opportunities as they arose, and was eminently dexterous in being always strong upon the strongest, and safe upon the safest side. There was a tolerably numerous party ready, in times so dangerous, to attach themselves to Barrere, as a leader who professed to guide them to safety if not to honour; and it was the existence of this vacillating and uncertain body, whose ultimate motions could never be calculated upon, which rendered it impossible to presage with assurance the event of any debate in the convention during this dangerous period.

Saint Just arose, in the name of the committee of public safety, to make, after his own manner, not theirs, a report on the discourse of Robespierre on the previous evening. He had begun a harangue in the tone of his patron, declaring that, were the tribune which he occupied the Tarpeian rock itself, he would not the less, placed as he stood there, discharge the duties of a patriot. "I am about," he said, "to lift the veil."--"I tear it asunder," said Tallien, interrupting him. "The public interest is sacrificed by individuals, who come hither exclusively in their own name, and conduct themselves as superior to the whole convention." He forced Saint Just from the tribune, and a violent debate ensued.

Billaud Varennes called the attention of the assembly to the sitting of the Jacobin club on the preceding evening. He declared the military force of Paris was placed under the command of Henriot, a traitor and a parricide, who was ready to march the soldiers whom he commanded, against the convention. He denounced Robespierre himself as a second Catiline, artful as well as ambitious, whose system it had been to nurse jealousies and inflame dissentions in the convention, so as to disunite parties, and even individuals from each other, attack them in detail, and thus destroy those antagonists separately, upon whose combined and united strength he dared not have looked.

The convention echoed with applause every violent expression of the orator, and when Robespierre sprung to the tribune, his voice was drowned by a general shout of "down with the tyrant!" Tallien moved the denunciation of Robespierre, with the arrest of Henriot, his staff-officers, and of others connected with the meditated violence on the convention. He had undertaken to lead the attack upon the tyrant he said, and to poignard him in the convention itself, if the members did not show courage enough to enforce the law against him. With these words he brandished an unsheathed poignard, as if about to make his purpose good. Robespierre still struggled hard to obtain audience, but the tribune was adjudged to Barrere; and the part taken against the fallen dictator by that versatile and self-interested statesman, was the most absolute sign that his overthrow was irrecoverable. Torrents of invective were now uttered from every quarter of the hall, against him whose single word was wont to hush it into silence.

This scene was dreadful; yet not without its use to those who may be disposed to look at it as an extraordinary crisis, in which human passions were brought so singularly into collision. While the vaults of the hall echoed with exclamations from those who had hitherto been the accomplices, the flatterers, the followers, at least the timid and overawed assentors to the dethroned demagogue--he himself, breathless, foaming, exhausted, like the hunter of classical antiquity when on the point of being overpowered and torn to pieces by his own hounds, tried in vain to raise those screech-owl notes, by which the convention had formerly been terrified and put to silence. He appealed for a hearing from the president of the assembly, to the various parties of which it was composed. Rejected by the mountaineers, his former associates, who now headed the clamour against him, he applied to the Girondists, few and feeble as they were, and to the more numerous but equally helpless deputies of the plain, with whom they sheltered. The former shook him from them with disgust, the last with horror. It was in vain he reminded individuals that he had spared their lives, while at his mercy. This might have been applied to every member in the house; to every man in France; for who was it during two years that had lived on other terms than under Robespierre's permission? and deeply must he internally have regretted the clemency, as he might term it, which had left so many with ungashed throats to bay at him. But his agitated and repeated appeals were repulsed by some with indignation, by others with sullen, or embarrassed and timid silence.

A British historian might say, that even Robespierre ought to have been heard in his defence; and that such calmness would have done honour to the convention, and dignified their final sentence of condemnation. As it was, they no doubt treated the guilty individual according to his deserts: but they fell short of that regularity and manly staidness of conduct which was due to themselves and to the law, and which would have given to the punishment of the demagogue the effect and weight of a solemn and deliberate sentence, in place of its seeming the result of the hasty and precipitate seizure of a temporary advantage.

Haste was, however, necessary, and must have appeared more so at such a crisis, than perhaps it really was. Much must be pardoned to the terrors of the moment, the horrid character of the culprit, and the necessity of hurrying to a decisive conclusion. We have been told that his last audible words, contending against the exclamations of hundreds, and the bell which the president was ringing incessantly, had uttered in the highest tones which despair could give to a voice naturally shrill and discordant, dwelt long on the memory, and haunted the dreams of many who heard him:--"President of assassins," he screamed, "for the last time I demand privilege of speech!" After this exertion, his breath became short and faint; and while he still uttered broken murmurs and hoarse ejaculations, the members of the mountain called out, that the blood of Danton choked his voice.

The tumult was closed by a decree of arrest against Robespierre, his brother, Couthon, and Saint Just; Le Bas was included on his own motion, and indeed could scarce have escaped the fate of his brother-in-law, though his conduct then, and subsequently, showed more energy than that of the others. Couthon hugging in his bosom the spaniel upon which he was wont to exhaust the overflowing of his affected sensibility, appealed to his decrepitude, and asked whether, maimed of proportion and activity as he was, *he* could be suspected of nourishing plans of violence or ambition. "Wretch," said Legendre, "thou hast the strength of Hercules for the perpetration of crime." Dumas, president of the revolutionary tribunal, with Henriot, commandant of the national guards, and other satellites of Robespierre, were included in the doom of arrest.

The convention had declared their sitting permanent, and had taken all precautions for appealing for protection to the large mass of citizens, who, wearied out by the reign of terror, were desirous to close it at all hazards. They quickly had deputations from several of the neighbouring sections, declaring their adherence to the national representatives, in whose defence they were arming, and (many undoubtedly prepared beforehand) were marching in all haste to the protection of the convention. But they heard also the less pleasing tidings, that Henriot, having effected the dispersion of those citizens who had obstructed, as elsewhere mentioned, the execution of the eighty condemned persons, and consummated that final act of murder, was approaching the Tuilleries, where they had held their sitting, with a numerous staff, and such of the Jacobinical forces as could hastily be collected.

Happily for the convention, this commandant of the national guards, on whose presence of mind and courage the fate of France perhaps for the moment depended, was as stupid and cowardly as he was brutally ferocious. He suffered himself without resistance, to be arrested by a few gens d'armes, the immediate guards of the convention, headed by two of its members, who behaved in the emergency with equal prudence and spirit.

But fortune, or the demon whom he had served, afforded Robespierre another chance for safety, perhaps even for empire; for moments which a man of self-possession might have employed for escape, one of desperate courage might have used for victory, which, considering the divided and extremely unsettled state of the capital, was likely to be gained by the boldest competitor.

The arrested deputies had been carried from one prison to another, all the jailers refusing to receive under their official charge Robespierre, and those who had aided him in supplying their dark habitations with such a tide of successive inhabitants. At length the prisoners were secured in the office of the committee of public safety. But by this time all was in alarm amongst the commune of Paris, where Fleuriot the mayor, and Payan the successor of Hebert, convoked the civic body, despatched municipal officers to raise the city and the Fauxbourgs in their name, and caused the tocsin to be rung. Payan speedily assembled a force sufficient to liberate Henriot, Robespierre, and the other arrested deputies, and to carry them to the Hotel de Ville, where about two thousand men were congregated, consisting chiefly of artillerymen, and of insurgents from the suburb of Saint Antoine, who already expressed their resolution of marching against the convention. But the selfish and cowardly character of Robespierre was unfit for such a crisis. He appeared altogether confounded and overwhelmed with what had passed and was passing around him; and not one of all the victims of the reign of terror felt its disabling influence so completely as he, the despot who had so long directed its sway. He had not, even though the means must have been in his power, the presence of mind to disperse money in considerable sums, which of itself would not have failed to insure the support of the revolutionary rabble.

Meantime the convention continued to maintain the bold and commanding front which they had so suddenly and critically assumed. Upon learning the escape of the arrested deputies, and hearing of the insurrection at the Hotel de Ville, they instantly passed a decree outlawing Robespierre and his associates, inflicting a similar doom upon the mayor of Paris, the procureur, and other members of the commune, and charging twelve of their members, the boldest that could be selected, to proceed with the armed force to the execution of the sentence. The drums of the national guards now beat to arms in all the sections under authority of the convention, while the tocsin continued to summon assistance with its iron voice to Robespierre and the civic magistrates. Every thing appeared to threaten a violent catastrophe, until it was seen clearly that the public voice, and especially amongst the national guards, was declaring itself generally against the terrorists.

The Hotel de Ville was surrounded by about fifteen hundred men, and cannon turned upon the doors. The force of the assailants was weakest in point of number, but their leaders were men of spirit, and night concealed their inferiority of force.

The deputies commissioned for the purpose read the decree of the assembly to those whom they found assembled in front of the city hall, and they shrunk from the attempt of defending it, some joining the assailants, others laying down their arms and dispersing. Meantime the deserted group of terrorists within conducted themselves like scorpions, which, when surrounded by a circle of fire, are said to turn their stings on each other, and on themselves. Mutual and ferocious upbraiding took place among these miserable men. "Wretch, were these the means you promised to furnish?" said Payan to Henriot, whom he found intoxicated and incapable of resolution or exertion; and seizing on him as he spoke, he precipitated the revolutionary general from a window. Henriot survived the fall only to drag himself into a drain, in which he was afterwards discovered and brought out to execution. The younger Robespierre threw himself from the window, but had not the good fortune to perish on the spot. It seemed as if even the melancholy fate of suicide, the last refuge of guilt and despair, was denied to men who had so long refused every species of mercy to their fellow-creatures. Le Bas alone had calmness enough to despatch himself with a pistol shot. Saint Just, after imploring his comrades to kill him, attempted his own life with an irresolute hand, and failed. Couthon lay beneath the table brandishing a knife, with which he repeatedly wounded his bosom, without daring to add force enough to reach his heart. Their chief, Robespierre, in an unsuccessful attempt to shoot himself, had only inflicted a horrible fracture on his under-jaw.

In this situation they were found like wolves in their lair, foul with blood, mutilated, despairing, and yet not able to die. Robespierre lay on a table in an anti-room, his head supported by a deal box, and his hideous countenance half hidden by a bloody and dirty cloth bound round the shattered chin.

The captives were carried in triumph to the convention, who, without admitting them to the bar, ordered them, as outlaws, for instant execution. As the fatal cars passed to the guillotine, those who filled them, but especially Robespierre, were overwhelmed with execrations from the friends and relatives of victims whom he had sent on the same melancholy road. The nature of his previous wound, from which the cloth had never been removed till the executioner tore it off, added to the torture of the sufferer. The shattered jaw dropped, and the wretch yelled aloud to the horror of the spectators. A masque taken from that dreadful head was long exhibited in different nations of Europe, and appalled the spectator by its ugliness, and the mixture of fiendish expression with that of bodily agony.

Thus fell Maximilian Robespierre, after having been the first person in the French republic for nearly two years, during which time he governed it upon the principles of Nero or Caligula. His elevation to the situation which he held, involved more contradictions than perhaps attach to any similar event in history. A low-born and low-minded tyrant was permitted to rule with the rod of the most frightful despotism a people, whose anxiety for liberty had shortly before rendered them unable to endure the rule of a humane and lawful sovereign. A dastardly coward arose to the command of one of the bravest nations in the world; and it was under the auspices of a man who dared scarce fire a pistol, that the greatest generals in France began their careers of conquest. He had neither eloquence nor imagination; but substituted in their stead a miserable, affected, bombastic style, which, until other circumstances gave him consequence, drew on him general ridicule. Yet against so poor an orator, all the eloquence of the philosophical Girondists, all the terrible powers of his associate Danton, employed in a popular assembly, could not enable them to make an effectual resistance. It may seem trifling to mention, that in a nation where a good deal of prepossession is excited by amiable manners and beauty of external appearance, the person who ascended to the highest power was not only ill-looking, but singularly mean in person, awkward and constrained in his address, ignorant how to set about pleasing even when he most desired to give pleasure, and as tiresome nearly as he was odious and heartless.

To compensate all these deficiencies, Robespierre had but an insatiable ambition, founded on a vanity which made him think himself capable of filling the highest situation; and therefore gave him daring, when to dare is frequently to achieve. He mixed a false and overstrained, but rather fluent species of bombastic composition, with the grossest flattery to the lowest classes of the people; in consideration of which, they could not but receive as genuine the praises which he always bestowed on himself. His prudent resolution to be satisfied with possessing the essence of power, without seeming to desire its rank and trappings, formed another art of cajoling the multitude. His watchful envy, his long-protracted but sure revenge, his craft, which to vulgar minds supplies the place of wisdom, were his only means of competing with his distinguished antagonists. And it seems to have been a merited punishment of the extravagances and abuses of the French revolution, that it engaged the country in a state of anarchy which permitted a wretch such as we have described, to be for a long period master of her destiny. Blood was his element, like that of the other terrorists and he never fastened with so much pleasure on a new victim; as when he was at the same time an ancient associate. In an epitaph, of which the following couplet may serve as a translation, his life was represented as incompatible with the existence of the human race:--

"Here lies Robespierre--let no tear be shed:
Reader, if he had lived, thou hadst been dead."

The fall of Robespierre ended the "***Reign of Terror***." Most of the leaders who had acted a conspicuous part in these horrid scenes, met a doom similar to that of their leaders. It is impossible to convey to the reader any adequate conception of the atrocities committed in France during this gloomy period, in the name of liberty. Men, women, and children were involved in the massacres which took place at the instigation of the Jacobin chiefs. Hundreds of both sexes were thrown into the Loire, and this was called republican marriage and republican baptism. And it should never be forgotten, that it was not till France as a nation, had denied the existence of a Deity, and the validity of his institutions, that she was visited by such terrible calamities. Let it be "burnt in on the memory" of every generation, that such is the legitimate tendency of infidel opinions. They first destroy the conscience--blunt the moral sense--harden the heart, and wither up all the social and kindly affections, and then their votaries are ripe for any deed of wickedness within the possibility of accomplishment by human agency.

Says an eloquent writer--"When the Sabbath was abolished in France, the Mighty God whose being they had denied, and whose worship they abolished, stood aloof and gave them up,--and a scene of proscription, and assassination, and desolation, ensued, unparalleled in the annals of the civilized world. In the city of Paris, there were in 1803, eight hundred and seven suicides and murders. Among the criminals executed, there were seven fathers who had poisoned their children, ten husbands who had murdered their wives, six wives who had poisoned their husbands, and fifteen children who had destroyed their parents."

It may be profitable here to record the end of several other Jacobin leaders who had been conspicuous during these scenes of atrocity and bloodshed. Public opinion demanded that some of the most obnoxious members should be condemned. After hesitating for some time, at length the convention, pressed by shame on the one side and fear on the other, saw the necessity of some active measure, and appointed a commission to consider and report upon the conduct of the four most obnoxious Jacobin chiefs, Collot d'Herbois, Billaud Varennes, Vadier, and Barrere. The report was of course unfavourable; yet upon the case being considered, the convention were satisfied to condemn them to transportation to Cayenne. Some resistance was offered to this sentence, so mild in proportion to what those who underwent it had been in the habit of inflicting; but it was borne down, and the sentence was carried into execution. Collot d'Herbois, the demolisher and depopulator of Lyons, is said to have died in the common hospital, in consequence of drinking off at once a whole bottle of ardent spirits. Billaud Varennes spent his time in teaching the innocent parrots of Guiana the frightful jargon of the revolutionary committee; and finally perished in misery.

These men both belonged to that class of atheists, who, looking up towards heaven, loudly and literally defied the Deity to make his existence known by launching his thunderbolts. Miracles are not wrought on the challenge of a blasphemer more than on the demand of a sceptic; but both these unhappy men had probably before their death reason to confess, that in abandoning the wicked to their own free will, a greater penalty results even in this life, than if Providence had been pleased to inflict the immediate doom which they had impiously defied.

Encouraged by the success of this decisive measure, the government proceeded against some of the terrorists whom they had hitherto spared, but whose fate was now determined, in order to strike dismay into their party. Six Jacobins, accounted among the most ferocious of the class, were arrested and delivered up to be tried by a military commission. They were all deputies of the mountain gang. Certain of their doom, they adopted a desperate resolution. Among the whole party, they possessed but one knife, but they resolved it should serve them all for the purpose of suicide. The instant their sentence was pronounced, one stabbed himself with this weapon; another snatched the knife from his companion's dying hand, plunged it in his own bosom, and handed it to the third, who imitated the dreadful example. Such was the consternation of the attendants, that no one arrested the fatal progress of the weapon--all fell either dead or desperately wounded--the last were despatched by the guillotine.

After this decisive victory, and last dreadful catastrophe, Jacobinism, considered as a pure and unmixed party, can scarce be said to have again raised its head in France, although its leaven has gone to qualify and characterize, in some degree, more than one of the different parties which have succeeded them. As a political sect, the Jacobins can be compared to none that ever existed, for none but themselves ever thought of an organized, regular, and continued system of murdering and plundering the rich, that they might debauch the poor by the distribution of their spoils. They bear, however, some resemblance to the frantic followers of John of Leyden and Knipperdoling, who occupied Munster in the seventeenth century, and committed, in the name of religion, the same frantic horrors which the French Jacobins did in that of freedom. In both cases, the courses adopted by these parties were most foreign to, and inconsistent with, the alleged motives of their conduct. The Anabaptists practised every species of vice and cruelty, by the dictates, they said, of inspiration--the Jacobins imprisoned three hundred thousand of their countrymen in the name of liberty, and put to death more than half the number, under the sanction of fraternity.

www.bookjungle.com *email: sales@bookjungle.com fax: 630-214-0564 mail: Book Jungle PO Box 2226 Champaign, IL 61825*

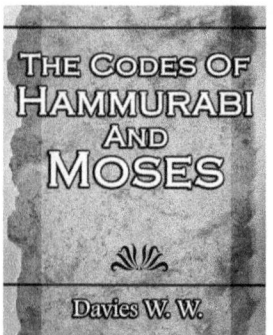

The Codes Of Hammurabi And Moses
W. W. Davies

QTY

The discovery of the Hammurabi Code is one of the greatest achievements of archaeology, and is of paramount interest, not only to the student of the Bible, but also to all those interested in ancient history...

Religion ISBN: *1-59462-338-4* Pages:132
MSRP $12.95

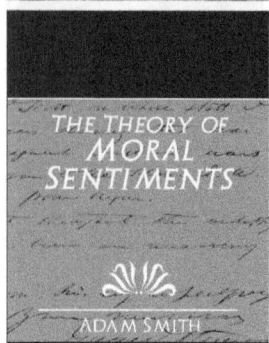

The Theory of Moral Sentiments
Adam Smith

QTY

This work from 1749. contains original theories of conscience amd moral judgment and it is the foundation for systemof morals.

Philosophy ISBN: *1-59462-777-0* Pages:536
MSRP $19.95

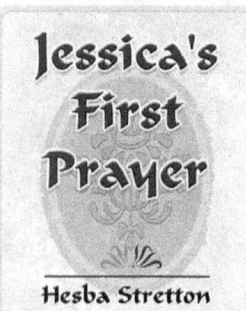

Jessica's First Prayer
Hesba Stretton

QTY

In a screened and secluded corner of one of the many railway-bridges which span the streets of London there could be seen a few years ago, from five o'clock every morning until half past eight, a tidily set-out coffee-stall, consisting of a trestle and board, upon which stood two large tin cans, with a small fire of charcoal burning under each so as to keep the coffee boiling during the early hours of the morning when the work-people were thronging into the city on their way to their daily toil...

Childrens ISBN: *1-59462-373-2* Pages:84
MSRP $9.95

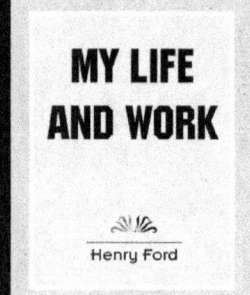

My Life and Work
Henry Ford

QTY

Henry Ford revolutionized the world with his implementation of mass production for the Model T automobile. Gain valuable business insight into his life and work with his own auto-biography... "We have only started on our development of our country we have not as yet, with all our talk of wonderful progress, done more than scratch the surface. The progress has been wonderful enough but..."

Biographies/ ISBN: *1-59462-198-5* Pages:300
MSRP $21.95

www.bookjungle.com email: sales@bookjungle.com fax: 630-214-0564 mail: Book Jungle PO Box 2226 Champaign, IL 61825

The Art of Cross-Examination
Francis Wellman

QTY

I presume it is the experience of every author, after his first book is published upon an important subject, to be almost overwhelmed with a wealth of ideas and illustrations which could readily have been included in his book, and which to his own mind, at least, seem to make a second edition inevitable. Such certainly was the case with me; and when the first edition had reached its sixth impression in five months, I rejoiced to learn that it seemed to my publishers that the book had met with a sufficiently favorable reception to justify a second and considerably enlarged edition. ..

Reference   ISBN: *1-59462-647-2*   Pages:412   MSRP *$19.95*

On the Duty of Civil Disobedience
Henry David Thoreau

QTY

Thoreau wrote his famous essay, On the Duty of Civil Disobedience, as a protest against an unjust but popular war and the immoral but popular institution of slave-owning. He did more than write—he declined to pay his taxes, and was hauled off to gaol in consequence. Who can say how much this refusal of his hastened the end of the war and of slavery ?

Law   ISBN: *1-59462-747-9*   Pages:48   MSRP *$7.45*

Dream Psychology Psychoanalysis for Beginners
Sigmund Freud

QTY

Sigmund Freud, born Sigismund Schlomo Freud (May 6, 1856 - September 23, 1939), was a Jewish-Austrian neurologist and psychiatrist who co-founded the psychoanalytic school of psychology. Freud is best known for his theories of the unconscious mind, especially involving the mechanism of repression; his redefinition of sexual desire as mobile and directed towards a wide variety of objects; and his therapeutic techniques, especially his understanding of transference in the therapeutic relationship and the presumed value of dreams as sources of insight into unconscious desires.

Psychology   ISBN: *1-59462-905-6*   Pages:196   MSRP *$15.45*

The Miracle of Right Thought
Orison Swett Marden

QTY

Believe with all of your heart that you will do what you were made to do. When the mind has once formed the habit of holding cheerful, happy, prosperous pictures, it will not be easy to form the opposite habit. It does not matter how improbable or how far away this realization may see, or how dark the prospects may be, if we visualize them as best we can, as vividly as possible, hold tenaciously to them and vigorously struggle to attain them, they will gradually become actualized, realized in the life. But a desire, a longing without endeavor, a yearning abandoned or held indifferently will vanish without realization.

Self Help   ISBN: *1-59462-644-8*   Pages:360   MSRP *$25.45* www.bookjungle.com email: sales@bookjungle.com fax: 630-214-0564 mail: Book Jungle PO Box 2226 Champaign, IL 61825

QTY

☐ **The Rosicrucian Cosmo-Conception Mystic Christianity** by *Max Heindel* ISBN: *1-59462-188-8* **$38.95**
The Rosicrucian Cosmo-conception is not dogmatic, neither does it appeal to any other authority than the reason of the student. It is: not controversial, but is: sent forth in the, hope that it may help to clear... New Age/Religion Pages 646

☐ **Abandonment To Divine Providence** by *Jean-Pierre de Caussade* ISBN: *1-59462-228-0* **$25.95**
"The Rev. Jean Pierre de Caussade was one of the most remarkable spiritual writers of the Society of Jesus in France in the 18th Century. His death took place at Toulouse in 1751. His works have gone through many editions and have been republished..." Inspirational/Religion Pages 400

☐ **Mental Chemistry** by *Charles Haanel* ISBN: *1-59462-192-6* **$23.95**
Mental Chemistry allows the change of material conditions by combining and appropriately utilizing the power of the mind. Much like applied chemistry creates something new and unique out of careful combinations of chemicals the mastery of mental chemistry... New Age Pages 354

☐ **The Letters of Robert Browning and Elizabeth Barret Barrett 1845-1846 vol II** ISBN: *1-59462-193-4* **$35.95**
by *Robert Browning* and *Elizabeth Barrett*
Biographies Pages 596

☐ **Gleanings In Genesis (volume I)** by *Arthur W. Pink* ISBN: *1-59462-130-6* **$27.45**
Appropriately has Genesis been termed "the seed plot of the Bible" for in it we have, in germ form, almost all of the great doctrines which are afterwards fully developed in the books of Scripture which follow... Religion/Inspirational Pages 420

☐ **The Master Key** by *L. W. de Laurence* ISBN: *1-59462-001-6* **$30.95**
In no branch of human knowledge has there been a more lively increase of the spirit of research during the past few years than in the study of Psychology, Concentration and Mental Discipline. The requests for authentic lessons in Thought Control, Mental Discipline and... New Age/Business Pages 422

☐ **The Lesser Key Of Solomon Goetia** by *L. W. de Laurence* ISBN: *1-59462-092-X* **$9.95**
This translation of the first book of the "Lernegton" which is now for the first time made accessible to students of Talismanic Magic was done, after careful collation and edition, from numerous Ancient Manuscripts in Hebrew, Latin, and French... New Age/Occult Pages 92

☐ **Rubaiyat Of Omar Khayyam** by *Edward Fitzgerald* ISBN:*1-59462-332-5* **$13.95**
Edward Fitzgerald, whom the world has already learned, in spite of his own efforts to remain within the shadow of anonymity, to look upon as one of the rarest poets of the century, was born at Bredfield, in Suffolk, on the 31st of March, 1809. He was the third son of John Purcell... Music Pages 172

☐ **Ancient Law** by *Henry Maine* ISBN: *1-59462-128-4* **$29.95**
The chief object of the following pages is to indicate some of the earliest ideas of mankind, as they are reflected in Ancient Law, and to point out the relation of those ideas to modern thought. Religion/History Pages 452

☐ **Far-Away Stories** by *William J. Locke* ISBN: *1-59462-129-2* **$19.45**
"Good wine needs no bush, but a collection of mixed vintages does. And this book is just such a collection. Some of the stories I do not want to remain buried for ever in the museum files of dead magazine-numbers an author's not unpardonable vanity..." Fiction Pages 272

☐ **Life of David Crockett** by *David Crockett* ISBN: *1-59462-250-7* **$27.45**
"Colonel David Crockett was one of the most remarkable men of the times in which he lived. Born in humble life, but gifted with a strong will, an indomitable courage, and unremitting perseverance... Biographies/New Age Pages 424

☐ **Lip-Reading** by *Edward Nitchie* ISBN: *1-59462-206-X* **$25.95**
Edward B. Nitchie, founder of the New York School for the Hard of Hearing, now the Nitchie School of Lip-Reading, Inc, wrote "LIP-READING Principles and Practice". The development and perfecting of this meritorious work on lip-reading was an undertaking... How-to Pages 400

☐ **A Handbook of Suggestive Therapeutics, Applied Hypnotism, Psychic Science** ISBN: *1-59462-214-0* **$24.95**
by *Henry Munro*
Health/New Age/Health/Self-help Pages 376

☐ **A Doll's House: and Two Other Plays** by *Henrik Ibsen* ISBN: *1-59462-112-8* **$19.95**
Henrik Ibsen created this classic when in revolutionary 1848 Rome. Introducing some striking concepts in playwriting for the realist genre, this play has been studied the world over. Fiction/Classics/Plays 308

☐ **The Light of Asia** by *sir Edwin Arnold* ISBN: *1-59462-204-3* **$13.95**
In this poetic masterpiece, Edwin Arnold describes the life and teachings of Buddha. The man who was to become known as Buddha to the world was born as Prince Gautama of India but he rejected the worldly riches and abandoned the reigns of power when... Religion/History/Biographies Pages 170

☐ **The Complete Works of Guy de Maupassant** by *Guy de Maupassant* ISBN: *1-59462-157-8* **$16.95**
"For days and days, nights and nights, I had dreamed of that first kiss which was to consecrate our engagement, and I knew not on what spot I should put my lips..." Fiction/Classics Pages 240

☐ **The Art of Cross-Examination** by *Francis L. Wellman* ISBN: *1-59462-309-0* **$26.95**
Written by a renowned trial lawyer, Wellman imparts his experience and uses case studies to explain how to use psychology to extract desired information through questioning. How-to/Science/Reference Pages 408

☐ **Answered or Unanswered?** by *Louisa Vaughan* ISBN: *1-59462-248-5* **$10.95**
Miracles of Faith in China
Religion Pages 112

☐ **The Edinburgh Lectures on Mental Science (1909)** by *Thomas* ISBN: *1-59462-008-3* **$11.95**
This book contains the substance of a course of lectures recently given by the writer in the Queen Street Hall, Edinburgh. Its purpose is to indicate the Natural Principles governing the relation between Mental Action and Material Conditions... New Age/Psychology Pages 148

☐ **Ayesha** by *H. Rider Haggard* ISBN: *1-59462-301-5* **$24.95**
Verily and indeed it is the unexpected that happens! Probably if there was one person upon the earth from whom the Editor of this, and of a certain previous history, did not expect to hear again... Classics Pages 380

☐ **Ayala's Angel** by *Anthony Trollope* ISBN: *1-59462-352-X* **$29.95**
The two girls were both pretty, but Lucy who was twenty-one who supposed to be simple and comparatively unattractive, whereas Ayala was credited, as her Bombwhat romantic name might show, with poetic charm and a taste for romance. Ayala when her father died was nineteen... Fiction Pages 484

☐ **The American Commonwealth** by *James Bryce* ISBN: *1-59462-286-8* **$34.45**
An interpretation of American democratic political theory. It examines political mechanics and society from the perspective of Scotsman James Bryce Politics Pages 572

☐ **Stories of the Pilgrims** by *Margaret P. Pumphrey* ISBN: *1-59462-116-0* **$17.95**
This book explores pilgrims religious oppression in England as well as their escape to Holland and eventual crossing to America on the Mayflower, and their early days in New England... History Pages 268

www.bookjungle.com *email:* sales@bookjungle.com *fax:* 630-214-0564 *mail:* Book Jungle PO Box 2226 Champaign, IL 61825

QTY

The Fasting Cure *by Sinclair Upton* ISBN: *1-59462-222-1* **$13.95**
In the Cosmopolitan Magazine for May, 1910, and in the Contemporary Review (London) for April, 1910, I published an article dealing with my experiences in fasting. I have written a great many magazine articles, but never one which attracted so much attention... New Age/Self Help/Health Pages 164

Hebrew Astrology *by Sepharial* ISBN: *1-59462-308-2* **$13.45**
In these days of advanced thinking it is a matter of common observation that we have left many of the old landmarks behind and that we are now pressing forward to greater heights and to a wider horizon than that which represented the mind-content of our progenitors... Astrology Pages 144

Thought Vibration or The Law of Attraction in the Thought World ISBN: *1-59462-127-6* **$12.95**
by William Walker Atkinson *Psychology/Religion Pages 144*

Optimism *by Helen Keller* ISBN: *1-59462-108-X* **$15.95**
Helen Keller was blind, deaf, and mute since 19 months old, yet famously learned how to overcome these handicaps, communicate with the world, and spread her lectures promoting optimism. An inspiring read for everyone... Biographies/Inspirational Pages 84

Sara Crewe *by Frances Burnett* ISBN: *1-59462-360-0* **$9.45**
In the first place, Miss Minchin lived in London. Her home was a large, dull, tall one, in a large, dull square, where all the houses were alike, and all the sparrows were alike, and where all the door-knockers made the same heavy sound... Childrens/Classic Pages 88

The Autobiography of Benjamin Franklin *by Benjamin Franklin* ISBN: *1-59462-135-7* **$24.95**
The Autobiography of Benjamin Franklin has probably been more extensively read than any other American historical work, and no other book of its kind has had such ups and downs of fortune. Franklin lived for many years in England, where he was agent... Biographies/History Pages 332

| Name |
| Email |
| Telephone |
| Address |
| |
| City, State ZIP |

☐ Credit Card   ☐ Check / Money Order

| Credit Card Number |
| Expiration Date |
| Signature |

Please Mail to: Book Jungle
PO Box 2226
Champaign, IL 61825
or Fax to: 630-214-0564

ORDERING INFORMATION

web: *www.bookjungle.com*
email: *sales@bookjungle.com*
fax: *630-214-0564*
mail: *Book Jungle PO Box 2226 Champaign, IL 61825*
or PayPal *to sales@bookjungle.com*

Please contact us for bulk discounts

DIRECT-ORDER TERMS

**20% Discount if You Order
Two or More Books**
Free Domestic Shipping!
Accepted: Master Card, Visa,
Discover, American Express

www.ingramcontent.com/pod-product-compliance
Lightning Source LLC
Chambersburg PA
CBHW080932300426
44115CB00017B/2787